Consumer Behavior

Consumer Behavior

Global Edition

Leon G. Schiffman

J. Donald Kennedy Chair in Marketing
and E-Commerce
Peter J. Tobin College of Business
St. John's University, New York City

Joseph Wisenblit

Professor of Marketing
Stillman School of Business
Seton Hall University, New Jersey

PEARSON

Boston Columbus Indianapolis New York San Francisco Upper Saddle River
Amsterdam Cape Town Dubai London Madrid Milan Munich Paris Montréal Toronto
Delhi Mexico City São Paulo Sydney Hong Kong Seoul Singapore Taipei Tokyo

Editor in Chief: Stephanie Wall
Acquisitions Editor: Mark Gaffney
Senior Acquisitions Editor, Global Editions: Steven Jackson
Assistant Project Editor, Global Editions: Suchismita Ukil
Program Manager Team Lead: Ashley Santora
Program Manager: Jennifer M. Collins
Editorial Assistant: Daniel Petrino
Director of Marketing: Maggie Moylan
Executive Marketing Manager: Anne Fahlgren
Project Management Lead: Judy Leale
Senior Project Manager: Jacqueline A. Martin

Head of Learning Asset Acquisition, Global Editions: Laura Dent
Media Producer, Global Editions: M. Vikram Kumar
Senior Manufacturing Controller, Production, Global Editions: Trudy Kimber
Procurement Specialist: Nancy Maneri
Creative Director: Blair Brown
Senior Art Director: Janet Slowik
Cover Designer: Karen Noferi
Full-Service Project Management: Rammohan Krishnamurthy, S4Carlisle Publishing Services
Cover: © aodaodaodaod/Shutterstock

Credits and acknowledgments borrowed from other sources and reproduced, with permission, in this textbook appear on the appropriate page within text.

Pearson Education Limited
Edinburgh Gate
Harlow
Essex CM20 2JE
England

and Associated Companies throughout the world

Visit us on the World Wide Web at:
www.pearsonglobaleditions.com

© Pearson Education Limited 2015

ISBN 10: 0-273-78713-6
ISBN 13: 978-0-273-78713-6

British Library Cataloguing-in-Publication Data
A catalogue record for this book is available from the British Library

10 9 8 7 6 5 4 3 2 1
14

Typeset in 9.5/11.5 Times LT Std by S4Carlisle Publishing Services

Printed and bound by Courier Kendallville in The United States of America

In Memory of Leslie Lazar Kanuk
Our Coauthor, Colleague, and Friend

Brief Contents

Contents

Preface

New to the Eleventh Edition

Our guiding principle in writing this edition has been the leaping progress towards the inevitable synthesis of media, entertainment content, and marketing. Not long ago, marketers bought advertising space within information and entertainment content produced by print and broadcast media. Today, media and their contents are often "produced" by consumers. In the past, marketers used media's "audience profiles" in deciding where to place "one size fits all" ads. Today, dynamic-ad-servers customize ads based on consumers' Internet browsing behavior, and marketers use behavioral targeting and employ firms that listen to and analyze what consumers are talking about in social media sites. Marketers that once purchased advertising space in only a few magazines or TV sitcoms, today buy ads through multiple ad exchanges and use predictive analytics that assess the effectiveness of their ads.

- New topics: In this edition, we discuss behavioral targeting, customizing products and promotional messages, predictive analytics, reaching "eyeballs" instead of demographic groups, tracking online navigation and analyzing websites' visits, gauging word-of-mouth and opinion leadership online, consumer-generated advertising, and new media platforms, such as mobile and apps advertising.

- New Technologies and Online Practices: In this edition we also address the usage of new technologies and the online practices of all age subcultures. At a time where the loss of privacy is the subject of an intensive public debate, we have charts showing how leading social networks collect data about consumers and a corresponding judgmental analysis in the chapter on ethics.

- We strengthened the book's principal facet, conceived in its first edition in 1978, which is focusing on the strategic applications of understanding consumer behavior. Our cases feature authentic campaigns that advertisers submitted for recognition by Effie Worldwide—a global entity that pays tributes to exceptional marketers. Each chapter opens with a "hands-on" example (some with comments by marketing executives) and exhibits based on recent, empirical data are showcased in all chapters together with guidelines for marketing applications.

- We added sections about sensory audio input, "actual" and "ideal" product-related attitudes, extra measures of cultural values, and empirical data about occupational prestige rankings and social class.

- The presentation about consumers overseas has been updated to include more comprehensive coverage of cross-cultural analysis, charts depicting consumers' spending of disposable income in several countries, brand shares of American products overseas, and profiles of leading global brands.

- Finally, in its first edition, this book was the first one ever to use print ads as illustrations of consumer behavior (a practice that was quickly adopted by all marketing textbooks), and this edition includes over 100 new ads.

Chapter-by-Chapter Updates: In Detail

Part I: Consumers, Marketers, and Technology

Chapter 1 explains consumer behavior as an interdisciplinary framework. It describes the evolution of marketing, prominent marketing strategies, and marketers' social responsibilities. The chapter details the revolutionary impact of technology on strategic marketing, and the interrelationships among customer value, satisfaction, and retention. It concludes with a model of consumer decision-making.

Chapter 2 describes market segmentation, including the demographic, sociocultural, and psychographic bases for segmenting markets. It explores the criteria for selecting target markets, behavioral targeting, and positioning and differentiating products and services.

Chapter 1: Technology-Driven Consumer Behavior

- *Hands-On:* Porsche; Scion
- Technology enriches the marketing exchange
- Behavioral information and targeting
- Interactive communication channels
- Customizing products and ads
- Better pricing and distribution
- Technology and customer satisfaction and retention
- *Showcased:* Ownership of mobile devices, prominent online activities, comparing e-readers, an airline's profitability tiers, and an updated model of consumer decision-making.
- *Ads:* Porsche, Scion, Classico sauce, P*e*TA (People for the Ethical Treatment of Animals), and the U.S. Navy.

Chapter 2: Segmentation, Targeting, and Positioning

- *Hands-On:* Qantas
- Behavioral targeting
- Tracking online navigation
- Geographic location and mobile targeting
- The information "arms race"
- Positioning and repositioning
- *Showcased:* Nielsen's segmentation frameworks, segmenting green consumers, samples of psychographic statements, and Target's behavioral targeting
- *Ads:* Count on Shell, Bertolli pasta, V8 100% Original Vegetable Juice, Mack's Earplugs, Healthy Choice lunch, TOMTOM GPS, and Fage Total yogurt
- *Case:* Porsche

Part II: The Consumer as an Individual

Part II examines the impact of psychological factors on consumer behavior. Chapter 3 discusses the influence of needs, motivation, and personality characteristics. Chapter 4 explores consumer perception, which consists of selecting, organizing, and interpreting marketing stimuli. Chapter 5 describes the learning process and how past shopping experiences affect subsequent buying. Chapter 6 looks at the formation, study, and strategic applications of consumer attitudes.

Chapter 3: Consumer Motivation and Personality

- *Hands-On:* Government of Alberta; Mr. Clean
- *Showcased:* Promotional applications of key psychogenic needs, personality characteristics of opinion leaders and innovators, individuals with a high need for uniqueness, materialistic consumers, compulsive shoppers, and vain persons
- *Ads:* Kaplan Bar Review, Ving hotels, Godiva, Outward Bound Wilderness, Rock Resorts, Yoplait Light, and Reach Listerine.

Chapter 4: Consumer Perception

- *Hands-On:* McCain French Fries; Heinz Tomato Ketchup
- *Showcased:* Sensory audio input and product perception, a price quality relationship "riddle," and brand image updates that create emotional bonds with consumers
- *Ads:* Mitchell Eye Centre, Betty Crocker, Xerox, Crest Whitestrips, Children's Defense Fund, Canadian Dental Association, Gillette Proglide, Saab, Spy Museum, MADD (Mothers Against Drunk Driving), and Sweet' n Low.

Chapter 5: Consumer Learning
- *Hands-On:* Samsung Galaxy Note 3 + Gear; Febreze
- *Ads:* Fresh Step cat litter, V8 soups from Campbell's, Mr. Clean Febreze exotic scents, Clorox Bleach Gel, Ragu pasta sauce, Crest Pro-Health, and American Airlines.

Chapter 6: Consumer Attitude Formation and Change
- *Hands-On:* Snickers Peanut Butter Squared and Snickers Easter Egg
- Primary data-based application of the attitude-toward-object-model
- "Ideal," "concept," and "actual" attitudes in developing a new orange juice
- Alumni donations illustration of self-attribution theory
- *Ads:* Avocado Mexico, Aleve, Phillips' Caplets, Dole Fruit Bowls, Lysol Wipes, Healthy Choice lunch, V8 Fusion vegetable juice, Certified Angus Beef, Method Laundry Detergent, and the American Academy for Orthopedic Surgeons.
- *Case:* Febreze
- *Case:* Superfast Handwash

Part III: Communication and Consumer Behavior

Part III addresses communication and persuasion. Chapter 7 covers the elements of communications and overcoming barriers to effective communications. We outline the differences between the broadcasting communications model (which is rooted in mass and traditional media), and the narrowcasting model (which originates in new media, such as online advertising and social media). The chapter then focuses on the message: its structure, persuasive appeal, and effectiveness. Chapter 8 explores communication channels and the transition from print and broadcast media to social media and mobile advertising. We expore the targeting methods used in old and new communication channels, the role of key entities (such as Google and Facebook), and the electronic evolution of traditional media. Chapter 9 examines the credibility of media and personal sources of information, consumers' reference groups, the role of opinion leaders, and the dynamics of word-of-mouth offline and online.

Chapter 7: Persuading Consumers
- *Hands-On:* Persuasive Appeals—Desley Travel Light, Sojourner Family Peace Center, ALT magazine, and Clorox Bleach
- Narrowcasting versus broadcasting
- Traditional versus new media
- Addressable advertising
- Measures of message effectiveness
- Timely advertising appeals
- *Ads:* British Airways, Mistique Ultra Soft Tissue, "I can't believe its not butter," Sainsbury's, Bucharest's City Police, and Ving hotels.

Chapter 8: From Print and Broadcast Advertising to Social and Mobile Media
- *Hands-On:* Impression-Based Targeting
- Targeting segments versus eyeballs
- Real-time bidding and data aggregators
- Retargeting
- Google's consumer tracking and targeting
- Web-search, display, and mobile ads
- Google's "organic results" and "sponsored space"
- Consumers' permissions for apps' information gathering
- Effective social media campaigns
- Owned, paid, and earned social media channels
- Consumers and mobile media

- Measuring the effectiveness of advertising in new media
- Analyzing website visits
- Gauging influence within social networks
- Google Analytics
- Nielsen's Cross-Platform measures
- Traditional media's electronic evolution
- Webisodes, advergames, and branded entertainment
- *Showcased:* Google's revenues, number of permissions requested from users by the most popular apps, types of permissions requested, M&M's Mr. Red, declining advertising ad pages, and effective tweeting.

Chapter 9: Reference Groups and Word-of-Mouth
- *Hands-On:* Campbell's
- Word-of-mouth in social networks and brand communities
- Klout scores
- Weblogging and twetting
- Buzz agents and viral marketing
- Managing negative rumors online
- Diffusion of Innovations
- *Showcased:* Group membership and comparative versus normative influence, characteristics of conformists, product conspicuousness and reference group influence, motivations of opinion leaders and receivers, characteristics and shopping patterns of fashion opinion leaders, sample items used in the self-designation of opinion leadership, and characteristics of risk-averse consumers
- *Ads:* MADD, the U.S. Navy, ALT magazine, and P*e*TA.
- *Case:* Keystone Light

Part IV: Consumers in Their Social and Cultural Settings

Part IV examines consumers in their social and cultural settings. Chapter 10 examines the family as a consumption unit and its standing within the social class structure. Chapter 11 describes culture and how it is expressed through values, rituals, and customs. It explains how to measure cultural values, and illustrates Americans' core values with ads and consumers' purchases and priorities. Chapter 12 describes how subcultures are derived from ethnicity, religion, geographic location, age, and gender. Chapter 13 explores cross-cultural analysis, how to assess marketing opportunities abroad, and whether or not customize products and promotions in global markets.

Chapter 10: The Family and Its Social Standing
- *Hands-On:* Toyota's Auris, Yaris, Verso, and Avensis
- Parental styles' and children's development
- Empirical measures of family decision-making
- The role of occupational prestige in determining social class
- Current data about the correlation between education and income
- Enriched descriptions of America's social classes
- *Showcased:* Mothers' socialization styles, parental styles and consumer socialization, children's development as consumers, children as three markets, measure of family decision making, occupational prestige rankings, ethics and occupational prestige, seven educational levels and corresponding incomes, descriptions of social classes: "inherited wealth and privilege," "the nouveau rich," "achieving professionals," "faithful followers," "security minded," "the insecure," and "rock bottom."
- *Ads:* Listerine Smart Rinse, Mott's apple juice, MADD, Lever 2000 soap, Ligne Roset furniture, Rock Resorts, Bad Bath & Beyond, and Brain Candy Toys.

Chapter 11: Culture's Influence on Consumer Behavior

- *Hands-On:* Dodge; Dell
- The Rokeach typology and illustrative promotional themes
- Gordon's Survey of Personal and Interpersonal Values
- *Ads:* distraction.gov, Everlast Recovery, 3-in-one oil, Campbell's Chunky, Dove chocolate, Cross pen, HP, Sojourner Family Peace Center, and Campbell's Healthy Request.

Chapter 12: Subcultures and Consumer Behavior

- *Hands-On:* Kohler's Elevance
- *Showcased:* Age and sources of information; online activities and interests of generations Z, Y, X, Baby Boomers, and older Americans; post-retirement segments
- *Ads:* Jeep and MADD.

Chapter 13: Cross-Cultural Consumer Behavior: An International Perspective

- *Hands-On:* Patek Philippe; Frito Lay
- Measures of cross-cultural dimensions
- Linguistic and legal barriers in global marketing
- *Showcased:* Profiles of leading global brands, five charts depicting prominent nations' consumers' disposable income expenditures, and Japan's VALS.
- *Case:* LG Mobile

Part V: Consumer Decision-Making, Marketing Ethics, and Consumer Research

Chapter 14 integrates the psychological, social, and communication elements into a consumer decision-making model, and discuss the adoption of new products. Chapter 15 addresses marketers' social responsibilities and morals with a focus on ethical issues originating from new media, and, particularly, abuses of consumers' privacy. Chapter 16 details the steps of marketing studies and tools of consumer research.

Chapter 14: Consumer Decision-Making and Diffusion of Innovations

- *Hands-On:* GIA; Advil

Chapter 15: Marketing Ethics and Social Responsibility

- *Hands-On:* PeTA
- Stages of consumer socialization and exploitive targeting of children
- Manipulative nutritional labeling
- Encouraging overeating and other undesirable consumption
- Abusing consumers' privacy
- Covert marketing
- Consumer ethics
- *Showcased:* The impact of irresponsible marketing, regulating targeting children online, alternative (award-winning) designs of nutritional labeling, deceptive or false promotional claims, provocative marketing, promoting social causes, and measuring ethical awareness
- *Ads:* Ad Council, NYC Office of Emergency Management, and Utah Transit Authority.

Chapter 16: Consumer Research

- *Hands-On:* Disney's Sophia the First
- *Showcased:* The consumer research process, questions for depth interviews, screener questionnaire, focus group discussion guide, projective techniques, survey methods, wording questions, attitudes' measures, sampling methods, and quantitative versus qualitative research.
- *Case:* Pima Air and Space Museum

Instructor Supplements

Instructor's Manual—This instructor's manual includes sample syllabi, lecture outlines, answers to all end-of-chapter questions, additional activities and assignments for your students. This manual is available for download by visiting www.pearsonglobaleditions.com/Schiffman.

Test Item File—The Test Item File contains more than 1,600 questions, including multiple-choice, true/false, and essay. Each question is followed by the correct answer, the learning objective it ties to, AACSB category, course learning outcome and difficulty rating. It has been thoroughly reviewed by an assessment expert. The Test Item File is available for download by visiting www.pearsonglobaleditions.com/Schiffman.

TestGen—Pearson Education's test-generating software is available from www.pearsonhighered.com/irc. The software is PC/MAC compatible and preloaded with all of the Test Item File questions. You can manually or randomly view test questions and drag and drop to create a test. You can add or modify test-bank questions as needed.

Instructor PowerPoints: This presentation includes basic outlines and key points from each chapter. It includes figures from the text but no forms of rich media, which makes the file size manageable and easier to share online or via email. This set was also designed for the professor who prefers to customize PowerPoints and who wants to be spared from having to strip out animation, embedded files, and other media-rich features.

To Our Families, Colleagues, and Friends

During the intense endeavor of making an already successful textbook even better, we were supported and encouraged by our families and friends. Leon Schiffman wishes to thank his wife, Elaine, for her support and devotion; his children and grandchildren: Janet, David, Nikke and Blake Schiffman; Dana, Brad, Alan, and Noah, Reid, and Allison Sherman; and Melissa and Rob and Jordyn and Emily Slominsky.

Joe Wisenblit thanks Alan Pollack for his counsel and support; Eyal Megged for his expertise on new media strategies; Randi Priluck (Pace University) for her insights and research collaboration; Shira Libhaber for her advice in selecting the ads; and his sister, Ilana and her family: Nir, Daniel, Maya, Eli and Saul Wegrzyn.

We are deeply grateful to Marcy Schneidewind for her tenacity and patience in securing the reprint permissions for the ads and exhibits. Special recognition goes to Stanley Garfunkel for many years of friendship and insights about consumer behavior and Shannon Conlisk for her assistance. Thanks to Jenn Pascoe for the book cover artwork.

At Pearson, we thank Stephanie Wall, our steadfast editor; Jackie Martin, our dedicated project manager, and Shyam Ramasubramony.

We thank our colleagues and friends at the Tobin College of Business at St. John's University, in particular: Dean Victoria Shoaf; A. Noel Doherty and the entire St. John's department of marketing for providing a warm and friendly environment in which to conduct research and write, as well as teach. At Seton Hall University's Stillman School of Business, we thank Dean Joyce Strawser and Department Chair Steve Pirog.

Special thanks to our friends and colleagues: Benny Barak, Barry Berman, Joel Evans, William James, Charles McMellon, Susan Caccavale, and Elaine Sherman of the Zarb School of Business at Hofstra University; Martin Topol and Mary Long of the Lubin School at Pace University; Fredrica Rudell of the Hagan School of Business at Iona College; Steve Gould and other colleagues at Baruch College–CUNY; Mark Kay of Montclair State University; and Deborah J. Cohn at New York Institute of Technology.

We also acknowledge Ken Weinstein, Honeywell International; Hank Edelman and Kelley Smith, Patek Philippe; Ross Copper, Gold n Fish Marketing Group; Lancy Herman, Mediamark Research; Moya Amateau, Ipsos Mendelsohn Research; Bill Carroll, Euromonitor International; Diana Schrage, Kohler Company; Mary Lee Keane and Erica Stoppenbach, Effie Worldwide; Helen Priestley, McCain Foods; and Nir Wegrzyn, BrandOpus, UK.

We are especially grateful to our own consumers, the graduate and undergraduate students of consumer behavior and their professors, who have used the earlier editions of this textbook and provided us with invaluable feedback.

Leon Schiffman

Joe Wisenblit

Pearson would like to thank and acknowledge the following people for their work on the Global Edition:

Contributors

Ali El Hallak, Head of Digital Marketing, Samsung Gulf Electronics, UAE

David Cook, Coventry University, UK

Hamed Shamma, American University in Cairo, Egypt

Jie Liu, Manchester Metropolitan University, UK

Nav Chouhan, Coventry University, UK

Stefania Paladini, Coventry University, UK

Xavier Pierron, Coventry University, UK

Reviewers

Frederick Hong-kit Yim, Hong Kong Baptist University, China

Andrea Rumler, Hochschule für Wirtschaft und Recht Berlin, Germany

Alan Au, The Open University of Hong Kong, China

Marietta Kiss, University of Debrecen, Hungary

Zita Kelemen, Corvinus University of Budapest, Hungary

Osman GÖK, Yasar University, Turkey

Consumer Behavior

Technology-Driven Consumer Behavior

Learning Objectives

1 To understand the evolution of the marketing concept, the most prominent tools used to implement marketing strategies, the relationship between value and customer retention, and the objectives of socially responsible marketing.

2 To understand how the Internet and related technologies improve marketing transactions by adding value that benefits both marketers and customers.

3 To understand the interrelationships among customer value, satisfaction, and retention, and technology's revolutionary role in designing effective retention measures and strategies.

4 To understand consumer behavior as an interdisciplinary area, consumer decision-making, and the structure of this book.

MARKETING is the activity, set of institutions, and processes for creating, communicating, delivering, and exchanging offerings that have value for customers, clients, partners, and society.[1] **Consumer behavior** is the study of consumers' actions during searching for, purchasing, using, evaluating, and disposing of products and services that they expect will satisfy their needs. The core of marketing is identifying unfilled needs and delivering products and services that satisfy these needs. Consumer behavior explains how individuals make decisions to spend their available resources (i.e., time, money, effort) on goods that marketers offer for sale. The study of consumer behavior describes what products and brands consumers buy, why they buy them, when they buy them, where they buy them, how often they buy them, how often they use them, how they evaluate them after the purchase, and whether or not they buy them repeatedly.

People buy cars because they need personal transportation. However, the types of cars people buy are determined not by needs alone, but also by how cars express their owners' characteristics. Therefore, car marketers differentiate their products by how specific car brands and models appeal to buyers' psychology. The tagline in Porsche's Boxster ad in Figure 1.1 states that "unfulfilled dreams cost a lot more,"* and its copy urges buyers to "fulfill their dreams rather than deny them."* Porsche recognized that many people daydream about luxurious items, but, even if they can afford them, they feel guilty about the purchase and often think: "Oh, it costs too much" and "What if I don't like it?" The ad's copy resolves such conflicts with a simple rationale: "It is expensive to fulfill one's dreams, but it is worth the expense." The ad anticipates that some buyers will feel guilty after purchasing the car and assures them that "of all the emotions you can expect while driving a Boxster, regret will never be one of them." It ends with Porsche's classic tagline: "Porsche. There is no substitute."*

Egotism and power are pervasive psychological needs, and marketers often appeal to them in advertisements. The Scion ad in Figure 1.2

*Porsche

FIGURE 1.1 Porsche: "Unfulfilled dreams cost a lot more"

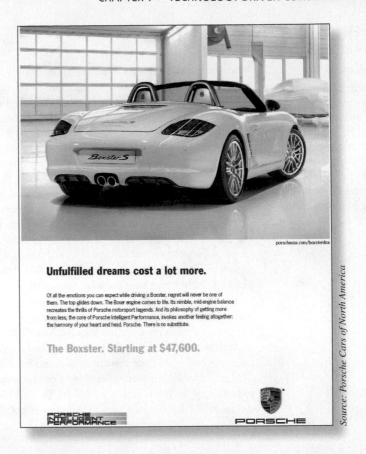

FIGURE 1.2 Scion: "Take On The Machine"

invites potential buyers to "Take On the Machine." Toyota positioned Scion as a car for drivers who like to face challenges, and feel powerful and in control of their environment. Positioning is conveying the product's benefits and image to potential (or existing) customers, so that the product stands out distinctly in their minds and is not viewed as a "me too" item. Positioning is an essential component of marketing and explained fully in Chapters 2 and 4.

In terms of affordability, Porsche and Scion target contrasting groups of people because their prices are very far apart. Nevertheless, the two carmakers share the same objective, which is to persuade drivers to buy their cars. In order to do so, each car must have a distinct image (or perception) in people's minds and appeal to their needs. Porsche's ad tells consumers that although the car is very pricey, it is worth the price because owning it is a dream fulfilled. The Scion, which is a very affordable car, calls upon drivers to take on a personal challenge, presumably because Scion's target market is young people (some of whom might be buying a new car with their own money for the first time) and are likely to respond when "dared."

Although they target entirely different segments, both ads induce (or even provoke) psychological, presumably unfilled needs, and illustrate their marketers' understanding of car buyers' mindsets. Similarly, our objective is to educate our students about the components and intricacies of consumer behavior, and provide them with the skills needed to market products and services.

First, this chapter describes the evolution of the marketing concept, marketing strategies for satisfying consumers' needs, and socially responsible marketing. Secondly, it describes how the Internet and new technologies can improve marketing transactions and benefit marketers and consumers alike. Afterwards, we explain the interrelationships among customer value, satisfaction, and retention, and using technology to design more effective retention strategies. Lastly, we describe consumer behavior as an interdisciplinary subject, how consumers make purchase decisions, and the structure of this book.

The Marketing Concept

Learning Objective

1 To understand the evolution of the marketing concept, the most prominent tools used to implement marketing strategies, the relationship between value and customer retention, and the objectives of socially responsible marketing.

Marketing and consumer behavior stem from the **marketing concept**, which maintains that the essence of marketing consists of satisfying consumers' needs, creating value, and retaining customers. It maintains that companies must produce only those goods that they have already determined that consumers would buy. For example, Classico's pasta sauce contains the same ingredients that consumers use when they make their own sauce. The slogan of the ad in Figure 1.3 is "We made it like you'd make it," which means that the product fulfills consumers' needs and they would buy it. Marketing-oriented companies do not try to persuade consumers to buy what the firm has already produced, but rather to produce only products that they know they can sell, thereby satisfying consumers' needs and turning them into loyal customers. The marketing concept evolved from several prior business orientations focused on production, the product itself, and selling.

The **production concept**, a business approach conceived by Henry Ford, maintains that consumers are mostly interested in product availability at low prices; its implicit marketing objectives are cheap, efficient production and intensive distribution. This approach makes sense when consumers are more interested in obtaining the product than they are in specific features, and will buy what's available rather than wait for what they really want. Before the 20th century, only wealthy consumers could afford automobiles, because cars were assembled individually and it took considerable time and expense to produce each vehicle. Early in the 20th century, Henry Ford became consumed with the idea of producing cars that average Americans could afford. In 1908, Ford began selling the sturdy and reliable Model T for $850—an inexpensive price for that day. Soon he found out that he could not meet the overwhelming consumer demand for his cars, so in 1913 he introduced the assembly line. The new production method enabled Ford to produce good-quality cars more quickly and much less expensively. In 1916, Ford sold Model Ts for $360 and sold more than 100 times as many cars as he did in 1908.[2] In only eight years, Americans got the product that led to our nation's extensive system of highways and the emergence of suburbs and large shopping malls.

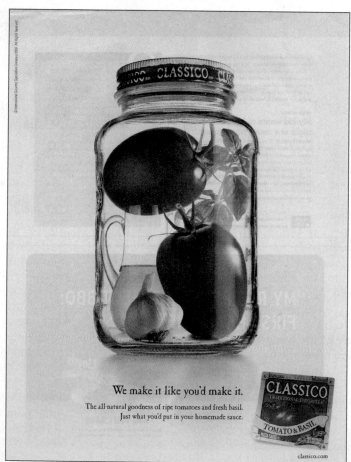

We make it like you'd make it.

The all-natural goodness of ripe tomatoes and fresh basil.
Just what you'd put in your homemade sauce.

classico.com

Source: © *H.J. Heinz Co., L.P., used with permission.*

FIGURE 1.3 An Illustration of the Marketing Concept

Henry Ford's near-monopoly of the car industry did not last. In 1923, as the automobile market was rapidly growing thanks to Ford's mass production, Alfred P. Sloan became president and chairman of General Motors. He inherited a company that was built through takeovers of small car companies that had been producing ill-assorted models unguided by clear business objectives. Sloan reorganized the company and in 1924 articulated the company's product strategy as "a car for every purse and purpose." While Ford continued to produce the Model T until 1927 and stubbornly held onto the production concept, GM offered a variety of affordable mass-produced models, from the aristocratic Cadillac to the proletarian Chevrolet. In addition, Sloan stated: "The best way to serve the customer is the way the customer wants to be served."* About 30 years before the birth of the marketing concept, Alfred Sloan understood the core elements of marketing: all consumers are *not* alike and firms must identify and cater to different customer groups (or segments) and provide solid customer service. Although Ford was the industry's pioneer and considered unsurpassed, within several years GM took over a large portion of Ford's market share and became America's largest car company.[3]

As more and more companies studied customers' needs and offered products that satisfied them well, companies began offering more and more versions, models, and features, often indiscriminately. They were guided by the **product concept**, which assumes that consumers will buy the product that offers them the highest quality, the best performance, and the most features. A product orientation leads the company to strive constantly to improve the quality of its product and to add new features if they are technically feasible, without finding out first whether consumers really want these features. A product orientation often leads to **marketing myopia**, that is, a focus on the product rather than on the needs it presumes to satisfy.

Marketing myopia occurs when companies ignore crucial changes in the marketplace and look "in the mirror rather than through the window." For example, in the 1980s, Apple bundled its software and hardware together and ignored customers who wanted to buy them separately. Apple sold its software, which was better than other operating systems, only when installed on its own, expensive computers. In contrast, Microsoft licensed DOS (disk operating system)—the less efficient and harder-to-operate software—to any manufacturer that wanted to install it on its computers. Most consumers bought the less expensive, DOS-operated computers, and for many years Apple was an insignificant player in the industry. Apple focused on its product and lost sight of the fact that consumers wanted to buy hardware and software separately.

Evolving from the production concept and the product concept, the **selling concept** maintains that marketers' primary focus is selling the products that they have decided to produce. The assumption of the selling concept is that consumers are unlikely to buy the product unless they are aggressively persuaded to do so—mostly through the "hard sell" approach. This approach does not consider customer satisfaction, because consumers who are aggressively induced to buy products they do not want or need, or products of low quality, will not buy them again. Unhappy buyers often communicate their dissatisfactions with the product through negative word-of-mouth that dissuades potential consumers from making similar purchases.

Implementing the marketing concept requires sellers to use consumer research, market segmentation, a combination of the product, price, place, and promotion strategies, provide value and result in long-term customer satisfaction and retention.

Consumer Research

Consumers are complex individuals, subject to a variety of psychological and social needs, and the needs and priorities of different consumer segments differ dramatically. To design products and marketing strategies that fulfill consumer needs, marketers must study consumers' consumption behavior in depth. The term **consumer research** refers to the process and tools used to study consumer behavior (see Chapter 16). Consumer research is a form of **market research**, a process that links the consumer, customer, and public to the marketer through information in order to identify marketing opportunities and problems, evaluate marketing actions, and judge the performance of marketing strategies. The market research process outlines the information required, designs the method for collecting information, manages the data collection process, analyzes the results, and communicates the findings to marketers.

Market Segmentation, Targeting, and Positioning

The focus of the marketing concept is satisfying consumer needs. At the same time, recognizing the high degree of diversity among us, consumer researchers seek to identify the many similarities that exist among the peoples of the world. For example, we all have the same kinds of biological needs, no matter where we are born: the needs for food and nourishment, for water, for air, and for shelter from

---

*Alfred P. Sloan

the environment's elements. We also develop or acquire needs after we are born, which are shaped by the environment and culture in which we live, our education, and our experiences. The interesting thing about acquired needs is that many people share the same ones. This commonality of need or interest constitutes a market segment, which enables the marketer to target consumers with specifically designed products and/or promotional appeals that satisfy the needs of that segment. The marketer must also adapt the image of its product (i.e., "position" it), so that each market segment perceives the product as better fulfilling its specific needs than competitive products. The three elements of this strategic framework are market segmentation, targeting, and positioning.

Market segmentation, targeting, and positioning are the foundation of turning consumers into customers. **Market segmentation** is the process of dividing a market into subsets of consumers with common needs or characteristics. It consists of defining or identifying groups with shared needs that are different from those shared by other groups. **Targeting** means selecting the segments that the company views as prospective customers and pursuing them. **Positioning** is the process by which a company creates a distinct image and identity for its products, services, and brands in consumers' minds. The image must differentiate the company's offering from competing ones and communicate to the target audience that the particular product or service fulfills their needs better than competing offerings do. Successful positioning focuses on communicating the *benefits* that the product provides. Because there are many similar products in almost any marketplace, an effective positioning strategy must communicate the product's *distinct* benefit(s). In fact, most new products (including new forms of existing products, such as new flavors and sizes) fail to capture significant market shares and are discontinued because consumers perceive them as "me-too" products lacking a unique image or benefit.

The Marketing Mix

The **marketing mix (four Ps)** consists of four elements:

1. *Product or service:* The features, designs, brands, and packaging offered, along with post-purchase benefits such as warranties and return policies.
2. *Price:* The list price, including discounts, allowances, and payment methods.
3. *Place:* The distribution of the product or service through stores and other outlets.
4. *Promotion:* The advertising, sales promotion, public relations, and sales efforts designed to build awareness of and demand for the product or service.

Socially Responsible Marketing

The marketing concept—fulfilling the needs of target audiences—is somewhat shortsighted. Some products that satisfy customer needs are harmful to individuals and society and others cause environmental deterioration. Studying consumer behavior results in an understanding of why and how consumers make purchase decisions, so critics are concerned that an in-depth understanding of consumer behavior can enable unethical marketers to exploit human vulnerabilities in the marketplace and engage in other unethical marketing practices to achieve business objectives.

Because all companies prosper when society prospers, marketers would be better off if they integrated social responsibility into their marketing strategies. All marketing must balance the needs of society with the needs of the individual and the organization. The **societal marketing concept** requires marketers to fulfill the needs of the target audience in ways that improve, preserve, and enhance society's well-being while simultaneously meeting their business objectives. Regrettably, some marketers ignore laws and market potentially harmful products. The San Francisco city attorney sued Monster Beverage Corp. in a California court, and accused the company of marketing its caffeinated energy drinks to children despite alleged health risks. The lawsuit represents the latest effort by an increasing number of city, state, and federal authorities to restrict the selling and marketing of energy drinks—which have quickly become an estimated $10 billion industry in the United States. The drinks promise a "kick" and includes caffeine and other stimulants. The lawsuit alleged that Monster was marketing its drinks to children as young as 6 years old, despite warnings from public health authorities that highly caffeinated products can cause brain seizures and cardiac arrest among adolescents. The U.S. Food and Drug Administration (FDA) currently does not set caffeine limits for energy drinks, imposing caffeine limits only on "cola-like" beverages with a regulation that has been in place since the 1950s and caps caffeine at 6 milligrams per ounce. However, the FDA is now reconsidering this regulation.[4]

The societal marketing concept maintains that companies would be better off in a stronger, healthier society and that marketers that incorporate ethical behavior and social responsibility attract and maintain loyal consumer support over the long term. Accordingly, fast-food restaurants should develop foods that contain less fat and starch and more nutrients; marketers should not advertise foods to young people in ways that encourage overeating, or use professional athletes in liquor or tobacco advertisements because celebrities so often serve as role models for the young. An advertising campaign featuring unreasonably slim females with pale faces and withdrawn expressions must be reconsidered because of its potential to increase eating disorders among young women. Of course, eliminating such practices altogether is unreasonable, but curtailing them is not.

Many companies have incorporated social goals into their mission statements and believe that marketing ethics and social responsibility are important components of organizational effectiveness. They recognize that socially responsible activities improve their image among consumers, stockholders, the financial community, and other relevant publics, and that ethical and socially responsible practices are simply good business, resulting not only in a favorable image but ultimately in increased sales. The converse is also true: Perceptions of a company's lack of social responsibility or unethical marketing strategies negatively affect consumer purchase decisions. For instance, McDonald's became the target of television commercials blaming it for heart disease. In the commercial, produced by the nonprofit Physicians Committee for Responsible Medicine, a woman weeps over a dead man lying in a morgue. In his hand is a hamburger. At the end, the golden arches appear over his feet, followed by the words, "I was lovin' it," a twist on McDonald's longtime ad slogan, "I'm lovin' it." A voiceover says, "High cholesterol, high blood pressure, heart attacks. Tonight, make it vegetarian."[5]

A division of Warner Music Group that operates online fan clubs for pop-music stars was forced to pay $1 million to settle charges that it illegally collected personal information from the sites' child users. The Federal Trade Commission charged the company with violating the Children's Online Privacy Protection Act—a law that forbids websites from collecting personal information from users under 13 years of age without parental consent. According to the charges, more than 100,000 users' information was gathered illegally through websites for fans of four pop stars. The four websites "attracted a significant number of children under age 13," according to the lawsuit, and "failed" to meet the requirements established by the children's privacy law.[6] When Google first revealed in 2010 that cars it was using to map streets were also sweeping up sensitive personal information from wireless home networks, it called the data collection a mistake. Subsequently, federal regulators charged that Google had "deliberately impeded and delayed" an investigation into the data collection and ordered a $25,000 fine on the search giant.[7]

There are also many not-for-profit advocacy groups whose mission is to advance causes that are ethically and morally right. Among many others, such causes include animal rights, fighting childhood obesity and overeating, supporting sober and nondistracted driving, fighting drug abuse and deadly diseases, and encouraging environmentally sound practices (see Chapter 15). Figure 1.4 shows an ad by a notorious not-for-profit entity, People for the Ethical Treatment of Animals (PeTA). It features a celebrity and urges us to "share the world" with animals and not mistreat them. By doing so, we will protect and improve the natural environment.

Source: People for the Ethical Treatment of Animals (PeTA)

FIGURE 1.4 PeTA Advocates Socially Responsible Behavior

Technology Enriches the Exchange Between Consumers and Marketers

Learning Objective

2 To understand how the Internet and related technologies improve marketing transactions by adding value that benefits both marketers and customers.

Say you are in a strange city and need a hotel for the night. You pull out your smartphone, search for hotels on Google, and find a nearby one listed at the top of the rankings, with a little phone icon that says, "Call." You tap it, reach the hotel, and ask for a room. And just like that, Google made money. That icon was a so-called "click-to-call ad," and the hotel paid Google for it when you called. Technology has revolutionized the marketing mix, as well as segmentation, targeting, positioning, and customer retention. When consumers use their computers, mobile phones, electronic readers, tablets, and other electronic gadgets, they provide marketers with the kind of information that enables companies to target them immeasurably more effectively than during the pre-Internet days. Thus, online technologies create a "value exchange." Marketers provide value to consumers in the form of information that turns shoppers into sophisticated customers, including opportunities to customize products easily, entertainment content, and much more. While online, consumers provide value to marketers by "revealing themselves," which enables companies to market their products more efficiently and precisely. In other words, consumers "pay" for the Internet's seemingly free content by providing virtually unlimited information about themselves to marketers, who gather, analyze, and use it to target buyers.

Advertisers are offering more and more original content online because viewers are now so accustomed to watching programs on devices like mobile phones and tablets that the lines between traditional television and Internet video have become blurred. Advertisers are also shifting dollars from traditional display advertising to sites like Facebook that can deliver huge audiences. Many advertisers say they worry that with so much new content being thrown at the market on so many different platforms, audiences for individual shows will become even more fragmented and microscopic than they already are.[8]

Surfing online allows consumers to locate the best prices for products or services, bid on various marketing offerings, bypass distribution outlets and middlemen, and shop for goods around the globe and around the clock. They can also compare the features of various product models and engage in social networking with consumers who share the same interests, providing and receiving information about their purchases. Online communications created sophisticated and discerning consumers, who are hard to attract, satisfy, and retain. More than ever before, marketers must customize their products, add value to the physical product or the core of a service, provide the right benefits to the right consumer segments, and position their products effectively. Technology also enables marketers to refine their strategies because they can readily customize their offerings and promotional messages, offer more effective pricing and shorter distribution channels, and build long-term relationships with customers. Marketers that use rapidly advancing technologies to track consumers can identify opportunities for creating new offerings, and improve and extend existing products and services. They can gather comprehensive consumer information by tracking consumers online, requiring prospective buyers to register at their websites, and combining this knowledge with demographic and lifestyle data gathered offline (see Chapter 2).

The following example illustrates a value exchange. At Amazon, buyers can find books instantly, read sample pages and reviews posted by other readers, and begin reading purchased books within minutes after placing their orders (as opposed to going to a physical store, picking up a heavy paper copy, standing in line to pay, and then carrying the book.) Simultaneously, when consumers visit Amazon's website, the company records every aspect of their visits, including the books they looked at, the sample pages and reviews they clicked on, and the time spent on each activity. This enables Amazon to build long-term relationships with customers by developing customized book recommendations that shoppers view upon returning to Amazon's website. Amazon also participates in "information exchange networks" that enable marketers to place ads that "follow" consumers into other websites featuring products that consumers have examined or purchased previously (see Chapter 8).

Consumers Have Embraced Technology

Although many assume that only young consumers visit websites and shop online and "reveal themselves" to marketers, it is not so. As illustrated in Figure 1.5, across age groups, most Americans own technological gadgets. Figure 1.6 details Americans' use of the Internet's most prominent features.[9]

FIGURE 1.5

The Ownership of Technological Gadgets across Age Groups (percentages)

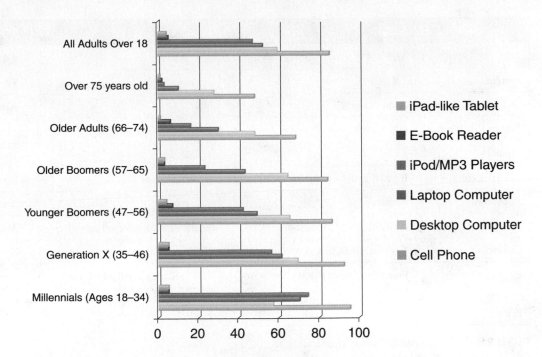

FIGURE 1.6

Americans' Most Prominent Online Activities (percentages)

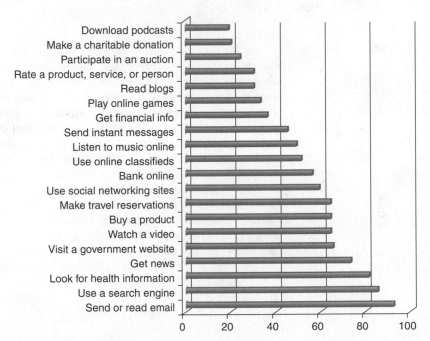

Behavioral Information and Targeting

In the online world, specialized "information exchanges" track who is interested in what through "cookies" (invisible bits of code stored on Web pages). When someone does a search, for example, on cheapair.com for first-class flights to Paris in September, that information is captured by a cookie and cheapair.com can sell that cookie using exchanges such as eXelate or BlueKai. Let's assume that Hilton wishes to target people who visited travel-related sites recently, rather than use banner ads or promotional messages in offline media to attract customers. Hilton logs into the exchange and selects the criteria for the people it wants to reach. Making it simple, let's assume that Hilton's only criterion is people who looked for flights to Paris in September. Upon logging in, the exchange tells Hilton how many cookies that meet its criterion are for sale and then Hilton bids on the price, competing against other advertisers wishing to buy the same cookies.[10] If Hilton wins the auction, it can show its ads to the persons with these cookies embedded in their browsers, and send ads to them whenever they go online, regardless of the sites they visit.

	NOVO	DELONEX	TOME
Size	3.9" × 4.8	3.5" × 4.9	4.0" × 4.1
Weight	7.8 ounces	7.5 ounces	8.6 ounces
Touch Screen	Some models	No	All models
Screen Pixels	600 × 800	758 × 1024	1200 × 1600
Memory	8 GB	16 GB	16 to 64 GB
Battery Life	Up to 8 hours	Up to 11 hours	Up to 12.5 hours
Bookstore	Amazon	Amazon	Amazon and Sony
3G Phone	Available with selected providers	Available with selected providers	Available with all U.S. providers
Overseas Capacity	Yes (roaming charges apply)	No	No
Content Storage	Free *Cloud*Novo storage for Novo content	Free DeLonex*Sky* for DeLonex content	Free storage for content and address book, calendar, and bookmarks
Price	$ 199	$ 279	$ 359

FIGURE 1.7 Comparing E-book Readers

The Internet drastically improved consumers' access to the information they need when they buy products for the first time or replace them. Simultaneously, the Internet enables marketers to gather truly behavioral data about consumers, because they can observe shopping behavior. Before the Internet, marketers gathered behavioral data by relying primarily on buyers' self reports, which often reflected what consumers wanted the marketers to think about them rather than consumers' *actual* buying patterns. For instance, car manufacturers that enable consumers to design their cars online from the "ground up" can quickly determine which colors, features, and accessories are most popular. They can also find out which combinations of features and car attributes are the most desirable and add models with such configurations.

When consumers compare products online, they look at the features and attributes of various models and brands side-by-side. For example, when comparing digital cameras, the most prominent evaluative attributes include the lens, screen, megapixels, light sensor, weight, and photo editing capabilities. Most websites of companies selling comparable brands offer visitors the opportunity to compare models and brands within a single screen, and offer one-click access to more detailed technical information. By observing consumers' comparisons, marketers can identify their direct competitors and the product attributes that consumers consider the most important. Figure 1.7 depicts a comparison of three electronic readers that resemble the options available to customers online for comparing brands of the same products.

Interactive and Novel Communication Channels

Traditional advertising is a one-way process in which the marketer pays large sums of money to reach large numbers of potential buyers via mass media, and can assess whether its promotional messages were effective only after the fact, by looking at sales and post-purchase marketing research studies. In contrast, electronic communications enable a two-way interactive exchange in which consumers instantly react to marketers' messages by, say, clicking on links within websites or leaving them quickly. Thus, marketers can gauge the effectiveness of their promotional messages instantly, instead of relying on delayed feedback (see Chapter 7). In addition, many U.S. homes now have TV cable boxes that enable two-way communications between consumers and broadcasters. Many cable companies are experimenting with technologies that allow consumers to select only the commercials they like to see by using their remote controls. Another example of interactivity is the supermarket scanners that keep track of households' purchases and instantly provide personalized coupons at the checkout counter.

Another facet of interactivity is promotional messages that are designed largely by the customers themselves. For one Super Bowl, rather than relying solely on traditional ad creators, many marketers asked consumers to play a part in creating or choosing that year's big-game commercials. Audi posted three versions of its ad on YouTubeAudi.com and let consumers select which ending should air; Ford Motor's Lincoln brand started a Twitter campaign that asked people to tweet their most memorable road-trip stories. As another example, a Samsung television ad mocking Apple's iPhone incorporated consumer comments from Twitter into its pitch. The spot shows people talking about different features of the new iPhone as they wait in line for an Apple store to open. One of the customers says, "I heard that you have to have an adapter to use the dock on the new one."* Another young man chimes in, "Yeah, yeah, but they make the coolest adapters."* According to Samsung, this ad was based on hundreds of tweets complaining about or poking fun at specific features of the iPhone 5, such as the need for an adapter if a person wants to use the phone with older speakers, chargers, or other accessories.[11]

Technological innovations sometimes force marketers to alter long-established marketing strategies. Consumers can now skip ads using advanced time-shifting and recording devices. Marketers responded by embedding promotional messages directly into TV shows. For example, several department stores, became part of a new reality show entitled Fashion Star. This is only one example of the broadcasters' and marketers' response to digital recording and streaming technology and the eroding value of traditional TV advertising caused by viewers' ability to skip ads easily.[12]

Cross-screen marketing consists of tracking and targeting users across their computers, mobile phones, and tablets. New software enables marketers to try to figure out when a mobile user is the same person as a desktop user. The new technology enables advertisers to "push" ads to mobile phones based on the interests people expressed while surfing the Internet. In one year, mobile ads in the United States grew to $4.1 billion from about $1.5 billion the previous year, though they still represent only 2.4% of total U.S. adverting spending. The new technologies will increase spending on mobile advertising significantly.[13]

Advertising across media platforms is essential. A Nielsen study showed that about 84% of smartphone owners and 86% of tablet owners said they used their mobile device while watching TV at least once during a 30-day period. Nearly half of those tablet owners visited a social networking while watching TV. Therefore, during a broadcast of the MTV Video Music Awards, a well-known rapper appeared in a commercial for Pepsi. At exactly the same time, anyone looking at MTV's website or an MTV mobile application saw interactive ads for the soda maker. Such simultaneous commercial blanketing is aimed at capturing the attention of consumers who watch television while surfing the Web or tweeting.[14]

Customizing Products and Promotional Messages

Oakley is the world's primary seller of high-end sunglasses. For both men and women, the company offers numerous models designed for a variety of lifestyles and sports, and even Asian-fit glasses. Most of Oakley's sunglasses can be customized: Consumers can select frame colors (often in polished or nonpolished forms), choose from among several lens shapes and colors, select different colors for the ear socks and the Oakley icon, and even have their initials elegantly and discreetly etched on the lenses. In addition, they can choose between nonpolarized and polarized (glare-reducing) lenses. Oakley also offers several models of backpacks where consumers can choose the item's primary and contrast colors, as well as the colors of trim, logo, and zipper tape. At Nike's website, buyers can choose among many models of sneakers in different price ranges, customize the selected shoe using several colors and features (e.g., some models even allow buyers to choose the colors of the Nike swoosh and the laces), and put a personal ID on each shoe. Researchers pointed out that customization requires that customers clearly understand their preferences and express them, and also be involved with the product. This indicates that "high involvement" products (i.e., infrequently purchased and pricey items) represent the best prospects for customization.[15]

Companies can also customize promotional messages. For example, an online drugstore may vary the initial display that returning buyers see when they revisit its website. Buyers whose past purchases indicated that they tend to buy national brands will see a display arranged by brand. Past purchasers who bought mostly products that were on sale or generic brands will see a display categorized by price and discounted products.

---

* Suzanne Vranica "Ads Let Viewers Be Mad Men," online.wsj.com, February 2, 2013; Suzanne Vranica, "Tweets Spawn Ad Campaigns," online.wsj.com,

Better Prices and Distribution

The Internet allows consumers to compare prices more effectively than ever before. For example, when consumers browse at department stores, they often use their mobile phones to check out the prices of comparable products in other stores. This has forced stores such as Target and Best Buy to match the online prices of rival retailers.[16] Some stores and brands are creating new personal touches that feature gadgets rather than a doting sales staff. One makeup marketer installed in-store touch-screen televisions to demonstrate the perfect smoky eye, something that was once the exclusive domain of makeup artists. Another store enables shoppers to use a touchpad to personalize the lighting and music in dressing rooms (there is also a button in case they need help).[17] As more books are going electronic, Apple unveiled a new version of its iBooks digital bookstore that would reduce the prices of high school textbooks by almost 90%.[18]

Marketers long ago recognized that consumers research expensive products such as electronics online. However, in trying to find the best deals, more shoppers are now going online to research groceries, personal grooming items, and household maintenance products before buying them in physical stores. In turn, marketers have begun to use advanced technologies, such as smartphone apps, to target shoppers in stores.[19]

In addition to better pricing, distribution strategies are also improving. Combating failed package delivery—a prominent problem of online retailers—Amazon has installed large metal cabinets, named Amazon Lockers, in grocery, convenience stores, and drugstores, that function like virtual doormen, accepting packages for customers for later pickup.[20]

Realizing that, sooner than later, electronic systems will replace cash and credit cards, several retailers have been developing mobile-payments systems to compete with similar products from Google and cell phone companies.[21] A "shopping bible" for women—the magazine *Lucky*—has introduced a service that saves women the cost and time of driving; a shopping site called myLuckymag.com directs readers to buy clothing and accessories directly from more than a dozen retailers.[22] Many online merchants now offer an "automatic recurring shipment" feature, which appeals to shoppers who like to order habitually needed products, like paper goods and personal care products, online.

The Web also enables marketers to improve customer service inexpensively. A waiter at a restaurant in New York City had trouble remembering all the ingredients of the intricate menu's item. He snapped pictures of the dishes, developed a system to categorize information, designed a set of icons specifying everything from potential allergens to temperature choices, and constructed a website available to the restaurant's servers. Soon, other restaurants subscribed to this service in order to train staff, do online scheduling, and provide internal discussion forums.[23]

Grocers like Safeway and Kroger are offering individualized prices based on shoppers' behaviors that could encourage them to spend more. Their pricing encourages a buyer to purchase a bigger box of Tide and bologna if the retailer's data suggests that the shopper has a large family, and expensive bologna if the data indicate that the shopper is not greatly price-conscious. As another example, a 24-pack of Brand X bottled water costs $2.71 for Ms. A but $3.69 for Ms. B. Ms. A's loyalty data indicates that she likes Brand X products, but not its bottled water. The store encourages Ms. A to put another Brand X product into her grocery cart, with the hope that she will keep buying it, whereas Ms. B is unlikely even to try Brand X bottled water. Some stores have a mobile app that allows shoppers to scan products. When they do, the store identifies them through their frequent shopper number or phone number, and knows where in the store they are. Special e-coupons are created on the spot. Thus, if someone is in the baby aisle and they just scanned diapers, the store presents them at that point with a coupon for a baby formula or baby food, based on the presumed age of their baby and what food the baby might be ready for.[24]

Customer Value, Satisfaction, and Retention

Learning Objective

3 To understand the inter-relationships among customer value, satisfaction, and retention, and technology's revolutionary role in designing effective retention measures and strategies.

Customer value is the ratio between customers' perceived benefits (economic, functional, and psychological) and the resources (monetary, time, effort, psychological) they use to obtain those benefits. For example, diners at an exclusive French restaurant in New York City, where a meal with beverages may cost up to $300 per person, expect unique and delicious food, impeccable service, and beautiful decor. When diners receive what they had expected, they leave the restaurant feeling that the experience was worth the money and other resources expended (such as a month-long wait for a reservation). Other diners may go with expectations so high that they leave the restaurant disappointed. In contrast, billions of customers visit thousands of McDonald's restaurants across the globe and purchase standard, inexpensive meals from servers systematically trained by the McDonald's

Corporation to deliver the company's four core standards: *quality, service, cleanliness*, and *value*. Customers flock to McDonald's outlets repeatedly because the restaurants are uniform, customers know what to expect, and customers feel that they are getting value for the resources they expend.

Customer satisfaction refers to customers' perceptions of the performance of the product or service in relation to their expectations. As noted earlier, customers have drastically different expectations of an expensive French restaurant and a McDonald's, although both are part of the restaurant industry. A customer whose experience falls below expectations (e.g., a limited wine list at an expensive restaurant or cold fries served at a McDonald's) will be dissatisfied. Diners whose experiences match expectations will be satisfied. Customers whose expectations are exceeded (e.g., by small samples of delicious food "from the Chef" served between courses at the expensive restaurant, or a well-designed play area for children at a McDonald's outlet) will be very satisfied or even delighted.

Customer Retention

Customer retention involves turning individual consumer transactions into long-term customer relationships by making it in the best interests of customers to stay with the company rather than switch to another firm. It is more expensive to win new customers than to retain existing ones, for several reasons:

1. Loyal customers buy more products and constitute a ready-made market for new models of existing products as well as new ones, and also represent an opportunity for cross-selling. Long-term customers are more likely to purchase ancillary products and high-margin supplemental products.

2. Long-term customers who are thoroughly familiar with the company's products are an important asset when new products and services are developed and tested.

3. Loyal customers are less price-sensitive and pay less attention to competitors' advertising. Thus, they make it harder for competitors to enter markets.

4. Servicing existing customers, who are familiar with the firm's offerings and processes, is cheaper. It is expensive to "train" new customers and get them acquainted with a seller's processes and policies. The cost of acquisition occurs only at the beginning of a relationship, so the longer the relationship, the lower the amortized cost.

5. Loyal customers spread positive word-of-mouth and refer other customers.

6. Marketing efforts aimed at attracting new customers are expensive; indeed, in saturated markets, it may be impossible to find new customers.[25] Low customer turnover is correlated with higher profits.

7. Increased customer retention and loyalty make the employees' jobs easier and more satisfying. In turn, happy employees feed back into higher customer satisfaction by providing good service and customer support systems.

Technology and Customer Relationships

Technologies often enhance customer relationships and retention by engaging consumers with brands. Procter and Gamble is the world's larger manufacturer of beauty and grooming (e.g., fragrances, mouthwash, toothpaste, feminine care) and household care products (e.g., household cleaning, laundry detergents, over-the-counter drugs, and disposable diapers). For every brand, the company's website includes suggestions on how to use the product more effectively. For example, for shampoo, the company provides a "scalp care handbook." For its Gillette shaving blades, the website offers comprehensive advice about facial care and proper shaving. For its detergents, P&G advises consumers how to wash white and colors, which temperature is best for which types of fabrics, and how to handle stains on different materials. Amazon.com sends personalized e-mails to previous buyers announcing newly published books that reflect their interests and are based on past purchases. Nature Valley—the granola bar brand—uses technology inspired by Google Street View. A website called Nature Valley Trail View uses cameras showing hikers, in nearly real time, in the Grand Canyon and other national parks. There is no sales pitch on the site and only a small Nature Valley logo appears on the screen. The marketer's objective is to feature lifestyles that its customers care about, engage them with the brand, and build brand awareness and loyalty.[26]

The opportunities for technology-enabled added value are virtually limitless. Professors can enhance classroom teaching with online networks and tools that enable students to read current and beyond-the-text material and practice and complete assignments from any location and at any time. Online newspapers customized to personal preferences include links to previous articles about consumers' favorite topics and send them e-mails about breaking stories. The most revolutionary example of technology-enabled value added to physical products are Apple's iTunes and its large software selection for editing and posting content online.

Researchers have identified two interrelated forms of customer engagement with marketers: **Emotional bonds** represent a customer's high level of personal commitment and attachment to the company. **Transactional bonds** are the mechanics and structures that facilitate exchanges between consumers and sellers. Savvy marketers always strive to build emotional bonds with customers. Technology, mostly in the form of social media, is the most innovative and versatile tool for engaging customers with companies emotionally and far beyond the selling act.

Social media include means of interaction among people in which they create, share, and exchange information and ideas in virtual communities and networks. Social media use mobile and Web-based technologies to create highly interactive platforms through which individuals and communities share, co-create, discuss, and modify user-generated content. Here are several examples of using social media to engage customers emotionally: Millions of customers take pictures with their cameras and cellphones and post them on shared websites, such as Facebook and Instagram. Because people are spending less and less time looking at magazine ads and TV commercials, marketers came up with "lifestyle advertising," that is, adopting the look and feel of the images consumers find most compelling—the ones they shoot themselves. Some fashion brands created digital ads based on pictures posted by consumers. The Web home pages of several clothing companies now feature real women, rather than professional models, wearing their fashions, and one designer published print magazine ads composed of Instagram photos. When Taco Bell introduced Doritos Locos Tacos, it noticed a lot of Instagram photos of people about to eat their Doritos tacos. The chain then sought and received permission from Instagram to use these photos in a TV spot that looked and felt like Instagram. Many marketers believe that "organic-looking" photos outperform professionally shot images, and some have hired "street-style" photographers who replace professional models with ordinary consumers and photograph them without professional makeup, styling, or lighting for online ads.

In addition to engaging customers with marketers, social media have transformed market research. Many companies can easily collect input about customers' preferences—sometimes without actively questioning consumers. Writers of TV series monitor discussion groups devoted to making critical and humorous observations about broadcasted episodes and rewrite future storylines based on viewers' comments. Similarly, marketers began testing expensive commercials by featuring them in social media first. Before a recent Super Bowl, marketers asked consumers to play a part in creating or choosing the big-game commercials for that year. A car company started a Twitter campaign that asked people to tweet their most memorable road-trip stories.[27]

In the pre-Internet days, Frito-Lay would have used focus groups, surveys, and depth interviews (see Chapter 16) to develop a new potato chip flavor. Instead, the company invited visitors to the new Lay's Facebook app to suggest new flavors and click an "I'd Eat That" button to register their preferences. Some of the results showed that beer-battered onion-ring flavor was popular in California and Ohio, while a churros flavor was a hit in New York. Frito-Lay planned to produce only three of the flavors from its contest, but gave a $1 million prize to the creator of one of those flavors. Frito-Lay has run the contest overseas and discovered chip flavors like hot and spicy crab in Thailand and pickled cucumber in Serbia. When Wal-Mart wanted to know whether to sell lollipop-shaped cake makers, it studied Twitter chatter. Walmart found that cake pops—small bites of cake on lollipop sticks—were becoming popular and people were talking a lot about them. Estée Lauder's MAC Cosmetics brand asked social media users to vote on which discontinued shades to bring back. The stuffed-animal brand Squishable solicited Facebook feedback before settling on the final version of a new toy. Samuel Adams asked users to vote on yeast, color, and other qualities to create a new beer.[28]

Emotional Bonds versus Transaction-Based Relationships

The objective of discerning customers' emotional and transactional motives when buying from a company is to understand the drivers of customer satisfaction, which lead to customer retention and long-term relationships. As consumers buy more and more online, it has become important to understand what makes them satisfied during electronic transactions. Studies have identified the following determinants of customer satisfaction with online websites and merchants:[29]

1. *Adaptation:* The merchant's purchase recommendations match one's needs; one is enabled to order products that are tailor-made; personalized advertisements and promotions; feeling like a unique and valued customer.

2. *Interactivity:* Ability to view merchandise offerings from different perspectives; search tool that enables one to quickly locate products; having tools that make comparisons easy; useful information.

3. *Nurturing:* Receiving reminders about making purchases; providing relevant information for one's purchases; acknowledgment of appreciating one's business; making an effort to increase business with the customer; cultivating a relationship with the customer.

4. *Commitment:* Delivering goods on time; responding to problems encountered; customer-friendly return policies; taking good care of customers.

5. *Network:* Customers sharing experiences about their product purchases on the merchant's website; useful network for sharing experiences; shoppers benefit from the community of prospects and customers sponsored by the merchant.

6. *Assortment:* Merchant provides "one-stop shopping" for most online purchases; site satisfies shopping needs; merchant carries wide assortment and selection of products.

7. *Transaction ease:* Merchant's website can be navigated intuitively; a first-time buyer is able to make a purchase without much help; site is user-friendly and enables quick transactions.

8. *Engagement:* The merchant's site design is attractive; enjoyable shopping at the site; feel that the site is inviting; feel comfortable shopping at the site.

9. *Loyalty:* Seldom consider switching to another merchant; usually click on the merchant's site whenever needing to make a purchase; like to navigate the site; one's favorite merchant to do business with.

10. *Inertia:* Unless becoming very dissatisfied, changing to a new merchant would not be worth the bother; finding it difficult to stop shopping at the site; feeling that the cost in time, money, and effort to change merchants is high.

11. *Trust:* Counting on the merchant to complete purchase transactions successfully; trusting the site's performance; feeling that the merchant is reliable and honest.

Some of these determinants are driven primarily by emotions (e.g., engagement and nurturing), whereas others are factors stemming from the mechanics of the transaction (e.g., assortment and transaction ease). One study developed a four-way categorization of transaction-based and emotional bond-based customers' relationships with marketers.[30] Table 1.1 applies this framework to Amazon's customers.

Emotional bonds with loyal customers may sometimes backfire, especially when social media are involved. Seventh Generation faced plunging reviews from its most loyal customers after introducing a new version of its baby wipes—thicker and moister—and discontinuing the older product. A flood of negative reviews on Amazon lowered the wipes' Amazon star rating from 5 to 2.5 stars in mere weeks. In response, the company then offered both the new and old versions of its Free & Clear baby wipes online. The company also sent out boxes of the old wipes with handwritten notes

TABLE 1.1 Transaction-Based and Emotional Bond-Based Customer Relationships

FANS:	LOYAL CUSTOMERS:
High bonds and high purchase levels. Buyers and sellers cooperate and make adjustments, expecting to share the benefits of future transactions. High level of commitment. If Amazon is out of a product, fans are willing to wait till the product is in stock. Fans recommend the merchant: "I go to Amazon first, always." "They have my business." "Their customer support policies are the best I have encountered." "Their prices are always at least as good as those of other merchants selling the same merchandise." "I use one of my credit cards only for my Amazon purchases."	*Frequent purchasers, but without high bonds.* "Amazon is OK. I shop there frequently, but always check prices elsewhere first." They stay with Amazon because of calculative commitment. They may have an Amazon credit card that gives them purchase points and no annual fees. Thus, switching costs or lack of alternative suppliers lock them in. They stay loyal not because they are emotionally attached, but for purely rational reasons. They are unlikely to recommend a seller on their own. Amazon should induce them to become committed emotionally.
DELIGHTED CUSTOMERS:	**TRANSACTIONAL CUSTOMERS:**
High bonds but modest purchase levels. The expectations of these customers have been exceeded and they are satisfied, but they are not heavy buyers, in general. "I don't buy these products often, but when I do, I go to Amazon first. They are great." Marketers should try to make these customers advocates for the store and send them purchase incentives.	*Low bonds and infrequent purchasers.* They are price-sensitive and prone to deals offered by competitors. They regard the product as a commodity and will buy from the seller offering the lowest price. They switch sellers from transaction to transaction. Amazon must ensure that they are satisfied and contact them to ask if they are. Some may become loyal or delighted customers, and eventually fans.

of apology and refunds to disappointed consumers, and e-mailed customers announcing that the old wipes were becoming available again.[31]

Customer Loyalty and Satisfaction

Customers who are highly satisfied or delighted keep purchasing the same products and brands, provide positive and encouraging word-of-mouth to others, and often become "customers for life." In contrast, those who are less satisfied or feel neutral either switch to a competitor immediately, or wait until another marketer offers them a somewhat lower price and then switch. In addition, highly dissatisfied customers spread negative and often exaggerated word-of-mouth.

A widely quoted study that linked levels of customer satisfaction with customer behavior identified several types of customers:[32]

1. *The Loyalists* are completely satisfied customers who keep purchasing. The *apostles* are loyal customers whose experiences with the company exceeded their expectations and who provide very positive word-of-mouth about the company to others. Companies should strive to create apostles and design strategies to do so.

2. *The Defectors* feel neutral or merely satisfied with the company and are likely to switch to another company that offers them a lower price. Companies must raise defectors' satisfaction levels and turn them into loyalists.

3. *The Terrorists* are customers who have had negative experiences with the company and spread negative word-of-mouth. Companies must take measures to get rid of terrorists.

4. *The Hostages* are unhappy customers who stay with the company because of a monopolistic environment or low prices; they are difficult and costly to deal with because of their frequent complaints. Companies should fire hostages, possibly by denying their frequent complaints.

5. *The Mercenaries* are very satisfied customers who have no real loyalty to the company and may defect because of a lower price elsewhere or on impulse, defying the satisfaction–loyalty rationale. Companies should study these customers and find ways to strengthen the bond between satisfaction and loyalty.

Customer Loyalty and Profitability

Classifying customers according to profitability involves tracking the revenues obtained from individual customers and then categorizing them into tiers. For example, a merchant might use a "customer pyramid" where customers are grouped into four tiers:[33]

1. *The Platinum Tier* includes heavy users who are not price-sensitive and are willing to try new offerings.

2. *The Gold Tier* consists of customers who are heavy users but not as profitable because they are more price-sensitive than those in the higher tier, ask for more discounts, and are likely to buy from several providers.

3. *The Iron Tier* consists of customers whose spending volume and profitability do not merit special treatment from the company.

4. *The Lead Tier* includes customers who actually cost the company money because they claim more attention than is merited by their spending, tie up company resources, and spread negative word-of-mouth.

Marketers must recognize that all customers are not equal. Sophisticated marketers build *selective* relationships with customers, based on where customers *rank* in terms of profitability, rather than merely "striving to retain customers." A customer retention–savvy company closely monitors its customers' consumption volume and patterns, establishes tiers of customers according to their profitability levels, and develops distinct strategies for each group of customers. For example, some stockbrokers program their phones to recognize the phone numbers of high-volume traders to ensure that those calls receive priority. In providing technical support on the phone, customers who have purchased and registered several of a company's products should receive expedited handling. Many New York City restaurants log data on important guests in their computers. One restaurant knows that a well-known food critique prefers his soup served in a cup and enjoys iced tea with cranberry juice in a large glass over lots of ice, a famous rapper likes white Burgundy, and one weekly diner wants only the ends of a loaf in his bread-basket. Restaurant also archive where diners like to sit, when they celebrate special occasions, and whether they prefer their butter soft or hard, Pepsi over Coca-Cola, or sparkling over still water.[34] In contrast, a bank's less profitable customers who, say, make little use of their credit cards or maintain only the minimum balance needed to receive free checking should *not* have penalties waived for bounced checks or late payments. Some companies also identify customer groups that are unlikely to purchase more even if pursued aggressively; such customers are often discouraged from staying with the company, or even "fired" as customers. For example, pay-TV providers became more selective about the customers they want to keep, because of rising programming costs, and focus more on holding onto the subscribers who generate the most revenue and profit, even if that means letting less valuable customers go. Because the pay-TV market is saturated, providers have to rely on raising prices or selling extra services to increase revenue. Thus, lower-end customers who are not taking such services as digital video recorders and broadband became unattractive to retain.[35]

Figure 1.8 depicts a hypothetical classification of an airline's customers along levels of profitability. The figures in the left column show how much money the airline makes per mile in each of its four service classes. The top row represents the number of miles travelled by a given customer. The twelve cells represent the airline's revenue from a given customer based on the amount of miles the customer travelled and the class in which he or she sat. The *diamond* is a customer who travelled at least 250,000 miles in first class in one year, which amounts to $1 million of revenue. The *emeralds* are customers who travel in first class, but not as frequently as the *diamonds,* or customers who travel very frequently in business class. The diamonds and emeralds are the airline's most profitable segments. Airlines provide such travellers with free transportation to the airport, hospitality agents that welcome and check them in, and hosts that usher them into VIP waiting lounges. The diamonds and emeralds receive personal and attentive service during the flight, priority and assistance during luggage collection, and prearranged transportation to their ultimate destinations.

Savvy marketers must also carefully plan customer "demotions." For example, a diamond or an emerald who is some miles short of keeping his or her status at the end of a given year technically must be "demoted" to a lower level, because flight miles are computed annually. However, from a consumer psychology standpoint, people may feel that they did not receive a fair chance to prove themselves as valuable customers within such a limited time frame. Researchers have suggested that minimizing the risk of driving away valuable customers outweighs the additional costs of extending elevated status for another year or two. Companies should enable customers, across all loyalty levels, to maintain their status actively instead of simply having to accept the company's decision. For example, some airlines offer customers who are about to be demoted the opportunity to purchase the revenues (e.g., flight miles) that are "missing" to maintain their elevated status.[36]

The *sapphires* are also a profitable segment, because they fly frequently and in business class. They should receive upgrades to first class as often as possible, but not the extra pampering awarded to the diamonds and emeralds. The *elite* and *select* segments are heavy fliers, mostly in premium economy. The airline should allow them to experience what it is like to fly in business class whenever possible (the beginning of Chapter 2 describes the four in-flight classes at Qantas).

FIGURE 1.8

An Airline's Profitability Tiers

		Miles Travelled Annually and Matching Revenues		
		At least 250,000 miles	At least 150,000 miles	At least 100,000 miles
Airplane's Class and Matching Revenues Per Mile	First Class ($ 4 per mile)	$ 1,000,000 DIAMOND	$ 600,000 EMERALD	$ 400,000 EMERALD
	Business Class ($ 2 per mile)	$ 500,000 EMERALD	$ 300,000 SAPPHIRE	$ 200,000 SAPPHIRE
	Premium Economy ($ 0.6 per mile)	$ 150,000 ELITE	$ 90,000 SELECT	$ 60,000 SELECT
	Economy ($ 0.3 per mile)	$ 75,000 SELECT	$ 45,000	$ 30,000

Measures of Customer Retention

Companies must develop measures to assess their customer retention strategies, and researchers have recommended the following retention measurement methods:

1. *Customer Valuation:* Value customers and categorize them according to their financial and strategic worth so that the company can decide where to invest for deeper relationships and determine which relationships should be served differently or even terminated.

2. *Retention Rates:* The percentage of customers at the beginning of the year who are still customers by the end of the year. According to studies, an increase in retention rate from 80% to 90% is associated with a doubling of the average life of a customer relationship from 5 to 10 years. Companies can use this ratio to make comparisons between products, between market segments, and over time.

3. *Analyzing Defections:* Look for the root causes, not mere symptoms. This involves probing for details when talking to former customers, an analysis of customers' complaints, and benchmarking against competitors' defection rates.

Companies should develop and implement corrective plans stemming from the results of such measurements. Retention strategies could involve actions to improve employee practices, greater top-management endorsement regarding the value of customers and employees, adjustments to the company's reward and recognition systems, and the use of "recovery teams" to eliminate the causes of defections. Companies can also erect barriers to customer switching. They can bundle products by combining several products or services into one package and offering them at a single price. They can also cross-sell (e.g., sell related products to current customers), use cross-promotions (e.g., give discounts or other promotional incentives to purchasers of related products), provide incentives for frequent purchases, and impose termination costs (e.g., penalties for paying off mortgages early).

Internal Marketing

Internal marketing consists of marketing the organization to its personnel. Behavioral and motivational experts agree that employees will "go the extra mile" to try and retain customers only if they are treated like valued "internal customers" by their employers. According to this view, every employee, team, or department in the company is simultaneously a supplier and a customer of services and products. If internal marketing is effective, every employee will both provide to and receive exceptional service from other employees. Internal marketing also helps employees understand the significance of their roles and how their roles relate to those of others. If implemented well, employees will view the service or product delivery from the customers' perspective. Overall, internal marketing is a chain where all employees treat each other as customers. The logistics manager would view the customer services function as his internal customers. The customer service function would see field engineers as their customers. The research and development team would see the manufacturing team as their customers. The relationship works in both directions, up and down the company structure.

The objective of internal marketing is to create personnel who go beyond the call of duty to accommodate customers and create "magic moments" (in Disney's vocabulary) that turn satisfied customers into real fans and truly loyal ones. Disney's "hosts" and "hostesses" (or "cast members," but *never* "employees") are trained to be "aggressively friendly," which is consistent with the company's mission: "To Make People Happy." When a cast member at Disney's Magic Kingdom sees a parent taking a picture of his family, the cast member offers to take the picture instead and with the entire family in it. Disney's objective is to create repeat visitors to its theme parks, where more than 70% of the "guests" (*not* "customers") are repeat visitors. Disney is an expert in consumer behavior because it truly understands how to satisfy and delight customers and create memories that emotionally bond people and Disney.

Customers who experience unexpected and superior treatment are especially likely to become loyal and trusting customers. For example, at the end of a long day at the Magic Kingdom, parents and two tired and cranky children are waiting for the tram to the parking lots. The confused expressions on the couple's faces indicates that they have forgotten the number of the lot where they parked their car (according to Disney, about 30% of guests do so). Supposedly unprompted (but trained to do so), a Disney cast member walks over to the bewildered couple and offers to help. The cast member asks the couple for their approximate time of their arrival, checks which parking lot was closed at about that time, and tells the visitors the likely location of their parked car. Undoubtedly, the grateful visitors will remember this service and also tell the story to others. Of course, the cast member was able to help the guests efficiently because Disney put in place technological information that enables

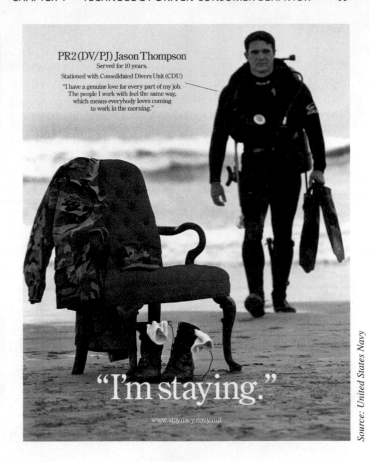

FIGURE 1.9 Internal Marketing at the United States Navy

cast members to go out of their way to help guests, and also implemented an effective internal marketing program that "markets" the company's vision of customer service to its personnel.

The two ads in Figure 1.9 are part of an advertising campaign by the United States Navy aimed at retaining its men and women.

Consumer Behavior Is Interdisciplinary

Consumer behavior stems from four disciplines. **Psychology** is the study of the human mind and the mental factors that affect behavior (i.e., needs, personality traits, perception, learned experiences, and attitudes). **Sociology** is the study of the development, structure, functioning, and problems of human society (the most prominent social groups are family, peers, and social class). **Anthropology** compares human societies' culture and development (e.g., cultural values and subcultures). **Communication** is the process of imparting or exchanging information personally or through media channels and using persuasive strategies.

Consumer Decision-Making

The process of consumer decision-making, featured in Figure 1.10, includes the input, process, and output stages of decision-making.

The *input stage* of consumer decision-making includes two influencing factors: the firm's marketing efforts (i.e., the product, its price and promotion, and where it is sold) and sociocultural influences (i.e., family, friends, neighbors, social class, and cultural and subcultural entities). This stage also includes the methods by which information from firms and sociocultural sources is transmitted to consumers.

The *process stage* focuses on how consumers make decisions. The psychological factors (i.e., motivation, perception, learning, personality, and attitudes) affect how the external inputs from the input stage influence the consumer's recognition of a need, pre-purchase search for information, and evaluation of alternatives. The experience gained through evaluation of alternatives, in turn, becomes a part of the consumer's psychological factors through the process of learning.

The *output stage* consists of two post-decision activities: purchase behavior and post-purchase evaluation.

FIGURE 1.10
A Model of Consumer
Decision-Making

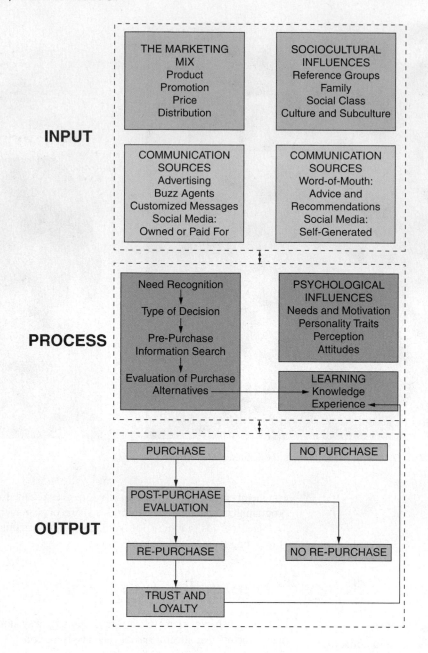

The Structure of This Book

Part I provides an overview of marketing and consumer behavior and the components of strategic marketing. Chapter 1 explains consumer behavior as an interdisciplinary framework centered on people's consumption-related activities. It describes the evolution of marketing, prominent marketing strategies, and marketers' social responsibilities. The chapter also describes the impact of technology and the interrelationships among customer value, satisfaction, and retention. It concludes with a model of consumer decision-making and an overview of this book. Chapter 2 discusses the process of market segmentation, including the demographic, sociocultural, and psychographic bases for segmenting markets. It also explores the criteria for selecting target markets, behavioral targeting, and differentiating offerings among competitors.

Part II describes the consumer as an individual and explains the psychological factors that affect consumer behavior. Chapter 3 discusses how individuals are motivated and the impact of individual personality characteristics on consumer behavior. Chapter 4 explores consumer perception, which is how individuals select, organize, and interpret the stimuli that they are exposed to. In other word, how the way we view the world around us affects our shopping patterns. Chapter 5 explains how we learn, through applying past experiences and behavior to future purchase decisions. Chapter 6 explores how attitudes, which are cognitions and evaluations of objects, influence buying behavior.

Part III addresses the communication and persuasion process along its components: sender, message, media, receiver, and feedback. Feedback alerts the sender as to whether the intended message was, in fact, received. Chapter 7 introduces the elements of the communication process and explains how to overcome the barriers to effective communications. It then discusses the differences between the traditional broadcasting model of communications, which is rooted in mass traditional media, and the narrowcasting model, which originated in new media such as online advertising and social media. Thereafter, the chapter focuses on the message: Its structure, the persuasive appeal used, and measurements of its effectiveness. Chapter 8 explores the communication channels and the transition from print and broadcast media to social media and mobile advertising. The discussion describes targeting consumers by using different media, and the role of prominent online advertising tools such as Google and Facebook. We then address marketing via social media and mobile advertising, and conclude with discussing the electronic evolution of traditional media. Two sources of communications influence people's purchases: Messages from marketers and information from the consumers' peers, family, word-of-mouth, and their social and cultural groups. Chapter 9 begins with an examination of the credibility of information sources and the groups that consumers use as frames of reference. It continues by describing the characteristics of people, known as opinion leaders, who often influence their peers' buying decisions. We conclude by presenting the dynamics and strategic uses of word-of-mouth, with an emphasis on electronic-word-of-mouth.

Part IV examines consumers in their social and cultural settings. Sociology is the study of the development, structure, and functioning of a society (the most prominent social groups are family, peers, and social class). Anthropology compares human societies' culture and development (e.g., cultural values and subcultures). Chapter 10 examines the family as a consumption unit and its standing within the social class structure. It also explores the characteristics and consumption patterns of various social classes. Chapter 11 describes culture and how it is expressed through values, rituals, and customs. It further describes how to measure cultural values and concludes with a presentation of Americans' core values as illustrated by ads and buying priorities. Chapter 12 describes cultural groups, known as subcultures, that share certain beliefs, values, and customs and exist within a larger society. Membership in a subculture can stem from a person's ethnicity, religion, geographic location, age, and/or gender. Chapter 13 explores cross-cultural analysis, which is a key strategic component for companies pursuing markets in countries other than the United States. It also describes how to assess marketing opportunities abroad and whether or not to customize products and promotions in global markets.

Part V consists of three chapters. Chapter 14 discusses the consumer decision-making process and shows how marketers' strategies and the psychological and sociocultural factors covered in Parts II, III, & IV are linked together. The chapter also describes how consumers react to innovative products and the process by which new products are adopted by individuals and societies. Chapter 15 explores marketers' social responsibility and ethically questionable practices such as exploitive targeting, and covert, manipulative and deceptive marketing. The chapter also examines abuses of consumers' privacy and concludes with a discussion on marketing socially desirable causes and behaviors. Chapter 16 describes the methodology of consumer research, including the distinctions between qualitative and quantitative research design.

Summary

Learning Objective 1: To understand the evolution of the marketing concept, the most prominent tools used to implement marketing strategies, the relationship between value and customer retention, and the objectives of socially responsible marketing.

Marketing is the activity, set of institutions, and processes for creating, communicating, delivering, and exchanging offerings that have value for customers, clients, partners, and society. Consumer behavior consists of consumers' actions taken while searching for, purchasing, using, evaluating, and disposing of products and services that they expect will satisfy their needs. Consumer behavior influences how marketers can communicate and deliver products that offer value to customers and society and explains how individuals make decisions to spend their available resources on products and services. Marketing and consumer behavior stem from the marketing concept, which maintains that the essence of marketing consists of satisfying consumers' needs, creating value, and retaining customers. Companies must produce only those goods they have already determined that consumers will buy. Marketing myopia is a focus on the product rather than on the needs that the product presumes to satisfy. The marketing mix (also known as the Four Ps) consists of product, price, place (distribution), and promotion. Market segmentation, targeting, and positioning are the foundation of turning consumers into customers. Market segmentation is the process of dividing a market into subsets of consumers who share common needs or characteristics. Targeting means selecting the segments that the company views as prospective customers and pursuing them. Positioning is the process by which a company creates a distinct image and identity for its products, services, and brands in consumers' minds. The societal marketing concept requires marketers to fulfill the needs of their target markets in ways that improve, preserve, and enhance society's well-being and simultaneously meet their business objectives.

Learning Objective 2: To understand how the Internet and related technologies improve marketing transactions by adding value that benefits both marketers and customers.

Technology has revolutionized the marketing mix, segmentation, targeting, positioning, and customer retention. When consumers use their computers, mobile phones, electronic readers, tablets, and other electronic devices, they provide marketers with the kind of information that enables companies to target them immeasurably more effectively than during the pre-Internet days. Online technologies create a "value exchange": Marketers provide value to consumers in the form of information, opportunities to customize products easily, entertainment content, and much more. While online, consumers provide value to marketers by "revealing themselves," thereby enabling companies to market their products more efficiently and precisely. Surfing online allows consumers to locate the best prices for products or services, bid on various offerings, bypass distribution outlets and middlemen, and shop for goods around the globe and around the clock. Online communication abilities have created sophisticated and discerning consumers, who are hard to attract, satisfy, and retain. More than ever before, marketers must customize their products, add value to the physical product or the core of a service, provide the right benefits to the right consumer segments, and position their products effectively. Technology also enables marketers to refine their strategies because they can readily customize their offerings and promotional messages, offer more effective pricing and shorter distribution channels, and build long-term relationships with customers. By using rapidly advancing technologies to track consumers, marketers can identify opportunities for creating new offerings, as well as improving and extending existing products and services. They can gather comprehensive consumer information by tracking consumers online, requiring prospective buyers to register at their websites, and combining this knowledge with demographic and lifestyle data gathered offline.

Learning Objective 3: To understand the interrelationships among customer value, satisfaction, and retention, and technology's revolutionary role in designing effective retention measures and strategies.

Customer value is the ratio between customers' perceived benefits and the resources they use to obtain those benefits. Customer satisfaction is customers' perceptions of the performance of the product or service in relation to their expectations. Customer retention

involves turning individual consumer transactions into long-term customer relationships by making it in the best interests of customers to stay with the company rather than switch to another firm. It is more expensive to win new customers than to retain existing ones. Technologies allow marketers to retain more customers, and collect highly sophisticated data about shoppers' preferences and post-purchase evaluations. Consumers who are highly satisfied or delighted keep buying the same products and brands, provide positive word-of-mouth to others, and often become "customers for life." Those who are less satisfied or feel neutral either switch to a competitor immediately or wait until another marketer offers them a somewhat lower price and then switch. Dissatisfied customers spread negative and often exaggerated word-of-mouth. Internal marketing is marketing the organization to its personnel.

Learning Objective 4: To understand consumer behavior as an interdisciplinary area, consumer decision-making, and the structure of this book.

Consumer behavior stems from four disciplines: Psychology is the study of the human mind and the mental factors that affect behavior. Sociology is the study of the development, structure, functioning, and problems of human society. Anthropology compares human societies' culture and development. Communication is the process of imparting or exchanging information.

The process of consumer decision-making consists of the input, process, and output stages. The input stage includes two influencing factors: the firm's marketing efforts and sociocultural influences. This stage also includes the methods by which information from firms and sociocultural sources is transmitted to consumers. The process stage focuses on how consumers make decisions. Psychological factors affect how the external inputs influence the consumer's recognition of a need, pre-purchase search for information, and evaluation of alternatives. The output stage consists of two post-decision activities: Purchase behavior and post-purchase evaluation.

This book includes five parts. Part I provides an overview of marketing and consumer behavior and the components of strategic marketing. Part II describes the consumer as an individual and explains the psychological factors that affect consumer behavior. Part III addresses the communication and persuasion process, the revolutionary impact of new media, and the roles of reference groups, opinion leaders, and word-of-mouth. Part IV examines consumers in their social and cultural settings. Part V includes discussions of the consumer decision-making process, consumers' reactions to innovative products, marketers' social responsibility and ethically questionable practices, and the methodology of consumer research.

Review and Discussion Questions

1.1. Describe the interrelationship between consumer behavior and the marketing concept.

1.2. A company is introducing a new E-book reader. Suggest segmentation, targeting and positioning strategies for the new product.

1.3. Define the societal marketing concept and discuss the importance of integrating marketing ethics into a company's philosophy and operations.

1.4. Describe how technology enhances the exchange between marketers and consumers.

1.5. It is often said that consumers receive "free" content online. Is this true? Why or why not?

1.6. Discuss the interrelationships among customer expectations and satisfaction, perceived value, and customer retention. Why is customer retention essential?

1.7. How can marketers use technology to improve customer retention and enhance their bonds with customers?

1.8. Discuss the role of the social and behavioral sciences in developing the consumer decision-making model.

Hands-on Assignments

1.9. Locate two websites that you visit regularly and discuss how they can (and probably do) track your behavior and enable marketers to target you more effectively.

1.10. Locate two examples (one advertisement and one article) depicting practices that are consistent with the societal marketing concept and two examples of business practices that contradict or ignore this concept. Explain your choices.

1.11. Locate two examples of technological innovations designed to enhance customer retention and discuss them.

Key Terms

- anthropology *47*
- communication *47*
- consumer behavior *30*
- consumer research *33*
- cross-screen marketing *39*
- customer retention *41*
- customer satisfaction *41*
- customer value *40*
- emotional bonds *42*

- internal marketing *46*
- market research *33*
- market segmentation *34*
- marketing *30*
- marketing concept *32*
- marketing mix (four Ps) *34*
- marketing myopia *33*
- positioning *34*
- product concept *33*

- production concept *32*
- psychology *47*
- selling concept *33*
- social media *42*
- societal marketing concept *34*
- sociology *47*
- targeting *34*
- transactional bonds *42*

Segmentation, Targeting, and Positioning

Learning Objectives

1. To understand the interrelationship among market segmentation, targeting, and positioning and how to select the best target markets.

2. To understand the bases used to segment consumers, including demographics, psychographics, product benefits sought, and product usage-related factors.

3. To understand behavioral targeting and its key role in today's marketing.

4. To understand how to position, differentiate, and reposition products.

MARKET SEGMENTATION, targeting, and positioning are the foundation of turning consumers into customers. **Market segmentation** is the process of dividing a market into subsets of consumers with common needs or characteristics. Each subset represents a consumer group with shared needs that are different from those shared by other groups. **Targeting** consists of selecting the segments that the company views as prospective customers and pursuing them. **Positioning** is the process by which a company creates a distinct image and identity for its products, services, and brands in consumers' minds. The image differentiates the company's offering from competition by communicating to the target audience that the product, service, or brand fulfills their needs better than alternatives.

Segmentation, targeting, and positioning are interrelated and implemented sequentially. For example, airlines traditionally offered three in-flight service choices: first class, business class, and economy (or coach). Because more and more flyers used their frequent flyer awards to upgrade their seats from coach to business or first class, airlines have steadily lowered the level of service and amenities in first and business classes, and these alternatives lost their appeal over economy class. Rather than pay the high fares for first or business class on commercial airlines, many first and business-class flyers switched to flying on shared, private and corporate jets. When some airlines realized that the traditional in-flight classes—first, business, and economy—no longer attracted three distinct customer segments, they redesigned their services. In order to illustrate such redesigns, the photos in Figure 2.1 show the four classes that Qantas now offers. The redesigned First class offers small, room-size private spaces; seats that turn into flat beds; designer linen and towels; gourmet food and a large selection of wines and alcoholic beverages;

Source: Qantas Marketing

First

Source: Qantas Marketing

Business

Source: Qantas Marketing

Premium Economy

Source: Qantas Marketing

Economy

FIGURE 2.1 Qantas Market Segments

personal attention (one flight attendant for every two or three passengers); and elaborate pre- and post-flight amenities. Business class features generously reclining seats that become nearly flat beds, delicious food and drinks, a personal kit with expensive cosmetics and grooming products, and pre- and post-flight services. Qantas also realized that there is a new segment of flyers: passengers who are willing to pay more for larger seats and more legroom, but not for extras such as fancy meals, free alcohol, and pricey toiletries. To this newly discovered segment, Qantas offers Premium Economy, which features larger and more spaciously placed seats that recline more than those in coach. Qantas also redesigned its Economy class with more comfortable seats and an open buffet of refreshments during the flight.

Qantas targets four distinct segments: coach passengers; premium economy, which costs 50% more than coach; business class, which costs twice as much as premium; and first class, which often costs three or four times as much as business. The four alternatives are clearly differentiated: an almost hotel-like privacy and sleeping accommodations, personal attention, and luxurious amenities in first class; privacy, beds, and extensive amenities in business class; more space, legroom, and generously reclining seats in premium economy; and improved seating and food service in coach.

This chapter describes the criteria and bases for selecting target markets, introduces a new strategy called behavioral targeting, and concludes with a discussion of positioning and repositioning strategies.

Market Segmentation and Effective Targeting

Learning Objective

1 To understand the interrelationship among market segmentation, targeting, and positioning and how to select the best target markets.

All consumers are not alike because they have different needs, wants, and desires, and different backgrounds, education levels, and experiences. Therefore, marketers must offer alternatives that correspond to the needs of different consumer groups or segments. For example, Marriott offers hotel accommodations to travelers, but different travellers have different needs. Thus, JW Marriott offers fine, elegant accommodations with extensive amenities and superior service. The Courtyard by Marriott hotels are conveniently located near cities' business districts and provide quality stays for business travellers. Fairfield Inn & Suites by Marriott offer modestly priced rooms, and Residence Inn by Marriott hotels are designed for long stays of business travellers. Like Marriott, most companies of consumer goods and services provide multiple products for different market segments.

Market segmentation, strategic targeting, and product (or service) positioning are the key elements of marketing consumer goods and services. They enable producers to avoid head-on competition in the marketplace by differentiating their products on the basis of such features as price, styling, packaging, promotional appeal, method of distribution, and level of service. Effectively catering to the distinct needs of consumers by offering them clearly differentiated products is significantly more profitable than mass marketing, in spite of the much higher research, production, advertising, and distribution costs that accompany segmentation and strategic targeting.

Marketers use segmentation research to identify the most appropriate media in which to place advertisements. All media vehicles—from Facebook, Google, and Twitter to TV, radio stations, newspapers, and magazines—use segmentation research to determine the characteristics of their audiences so that they can attract advertisers seeking to reach a given audience. For example, The New York Times and The Wall Street Journal offer separate editions for readers in different areas of the world, as well as online editions that can be customized according to the reader's interests.

Before describing how market segments are identified, we must point out that not every segment is viable or profitable. To be an effective target, a market segment must be identifiable, sizeable, stable and growing, reachable, and congruent with the marketer's objectives and resources.

Identifiable

Marketers divide consumers into separate segments on the basis of common or shared needs by using demographics, lifestyles, and other factors named "bases for segmentation." Some segmentation factors, such as demographics (e.g., age, gender, ethnicity), are easy to identify, and others can be determined through questioning (e.g., education, income, occupation, marital status). Other features, such as the product benefits buyers seek and customers' lifestyles, are difficult to identify and measure.

Sizeable

To be a viable market, a segment must consist of enough consumers to make targeting it profitable. A segment can be identifiable, but not large enough to be profitable. For example, athletic and slim men with wide shoulders and narrow waists often have to buy suits with trousers that are larger than they need (and have them retailored). Other than high-end fashion designers such as Prada and Dolce & Gabbana, most American clothiers make suits only for men who have more generous waists than the relatively small segment of very athletic men.

Stable and Growing

Most marketers prefer to target consumer segments that are relatively stable in terms of lifestyles and consumption patterns (and are also likely to grow larger and more viable in the future) and avoid "fickle" segments that are unpredictable. For example, teenagers are a sizeable and easily identifiable market segment, eager to buy, able to spend, and easily reached. Yet, they are also likely to embrace fads, and by the time marketers produce merchandise for a popular teenage trend, interest in it may have waned.

Reachable

To be targeted, a segment must be accessible, which means that marketers must be able to communicate with its consumers effectively and economically. With the diversification of magazines (and their

TABLE 2.1	Readers' Profiles of Selected Media				
PUBLICATION	AUDIENCE & MEDIAN HOUSEHOLD INCOME	GENDER	MEDIAN AGE	EDUCATION	OCCUPATION
Scientific American	2.8 million $90,000	70% men 30% women	47	62% college + 31% postgraduate 7% unreported	52% managerial 19% decision makers, high tech 13% owner, partner 16% unreported
National Geographic Traveller	7.3 million $72,000	55% men 45% women	42	69% college +	31% professional, managerial
National Geographic	6.7 million worldwide 5.2 million US $68,000	56% men 44% women	45.6	66% college	27% professional, managerial
The Wall Street Journal	911,000 $285,000	63% men 37% women	45	100% college +	Majority are impressive earners and investors

Source: Based on www.scientificamerican.com/mediakit/assets/pdf/audience_demoprofile.pdf wsjmcdiakit.com/downloads/gny_audience_profile.pdf?12060903

online versions), the emergence of TV channels that target narrowly defined interests, and the growth of new media (e.g., sending ads to cell phones), marketers have significantly more avenues for reaching unique segments and can also do so with customized products and promotional messages.

Whether in print or online, magazines and leading newspapers have been one of the best media used to reach narrowly defined market segments. Magazines focus on specific areas of knowledge, interest, or hobbies, such as travel, science, literature, art, home decorating, architecture, occupation, and any leisure activity conceivable. Magazines and newspapers provide extensive profiles of their readers to advertisers wishing to reach groups of consumers with specific characteristics. Table 2.1 describes the readers' profiles of prominent print media.[1] In addition, The Wall Street Journal's readers have an average net worth of $1.6 million; 31% have liquid assets of more than $1 million; 50% spend more than $1,000 with their credit cards per month; 89% visit museums and antique shows regularly; 87% attend the theater, concerts, and the opera. Advertisers use audience profiles in deciding where to place their ads. For example, ads for the opera and the theater often appear in The Wall Street Journal, and ads for educational and pricey cruises are regularly featured in the National Geogtraphic Traveller.

Congruent with the Marketer's Objectives and Resources

Not every company is interested in or has the means to reach every market segment, even if that segment meets the four preceding criteria. For example, in contrast to the four in-flight options that Qantas provides, Southwest Airlines offers only one class of service because its business objective is to provide uniform, inexpensive, no-frills air transportation.

Applying the Criteria

To demonstrate the application of the criteria to selecting a target market, let's assume that Perry & Swift, an investment management firm, is considering adding a hedge fund to its financial services. The company has determined that it has the resources to do so and that adding a hedge fund is congruent with its objectives. Because hedge funds are risky and require sizeable financial investments, their target market is wealthy households with high net worth. Using a P$YCLE Segmentation System, which is part of a database entitled Nielsen NyBestSegments, Perry & Swift identifies a segment entitled *Financial Elite* whose members are the most affluent Americans with the highest amount of income-producing assets. Members of this segment invest in a large variety of financial growth tools, such as stocks, bonds, mutual funds, investment-focused life insurance, and real estate, mostly through financial investment firms. Within this broad group, Nielsen's system features two more precisely defined segments: the *Wealth Market* and *Business Class*. Table 2.2 illustrates how Perry & Swift applied the criteria for effective targeting to the two segments.[2]

TABLE 2.2 An Illustration of Effective Targeting	WEALTH MARKET	BUSINESS CLASS
The segment is identifiable by its demographics	Millions in assets, median household income $137,000, 55+ years old, have graduate and postgraduate education. Kids are grown and have their own families.	Wealthy, median household income $101,000, 45–64 years old, have graduate and postgraduate education. Kids are away from home studying.
Is the segment likely to be profitable?	2.28% of the 2,659,000 U.S. households. Members use many brokers and financial advisers.	1.97% of the U.S. households. Members trade financial instruments frequently.
Is the segment stable?	Members invest regularly in a mix of short- and long-term instruments.	Members are still working and wish to accumulate more wealth before retiring.
How can the segment be reached?	Live in wealthy suburbs or in the wealthiest areas of large cities. Belong to country clubs and read financial magazines.	Live in wealthy suburbs or in the wealthiest areas of large cities. Attend horse races and read financial magazines.
Members' financial aspirations and objectives	Although they hold diversified financial portfolios, are reluctant to invest in risky instruments. Their home(s) are paid for, as is their children's education. Somewhat receptive to making risky investments as part of trust funds they have set up for their grandchildren.	Kids are in expensive schools. Expect to pay for kids' graduate and postgraduate education. Some are looking to buy a second home. Have made successful, risky financial decisions in the past. Feel that they are still young enough to make up for bad investment decisions, if necessary.

Source: Based on selected data from MyBestSegments at claritas.com (May 2012).

As shown in Table 2.2, both segments are likely to be profitable, and Perry & Swift can pursue both or either one. Let's assume that the company decided to focus on the Business Class segment because it has higher growth prospects than the Wealth Market: its members are younger and still accumulating wealth. Therefore, they invest in long-term investments, and their financial aspirations and objectives indicate that they are willing to take greater financial risks, while members of Wealth Market invest in less risky financial instruments. The firm should use Nielsen's ZIP Code geodemographic tool, which is described later in this chapter, to determine which geographic areas of the country include subtantial numbers of the Business Class segment. Then, it should use salespersons and local advertising to recruit customers.

Bases for Segmentation

Learning Objective

2 To understand the bases used to segment consumers, including demographics, psychographics, product benefits sought, and product usage-related factors.

A segmentation strategy begins by dividing the market for a product into groups that are relatively homogeneous and share characteristics that are different from those of other groups. Generally, such characteristics can be classified into two types: behavioral and cognitive.

Behavioral data is evidence-based; it can be determined from direct questioning (or observation), categorized using objective and measurable criteria, such as demographics, and consists of:

1. *Consumer-intrinsic* factors, such as a person's age, gender, marital status, income, and education.
2. *Consumption-based* factors, such as the quantity of product purchased, frequency of leisure activities, or frequency of buying a given product.

Cognitive factors are abstracts that "reside" in the consumer's mind, can be determined only through psychological and attitudinal questioning, and generally have no single, universal definitions, and consist of:

1. *Consumer-intrinsic* factors, such as personality traits, cultural values, and attitudes towards politics and social issues.
2. *Consumption-specific* attitudes and preferences, such as the benefits sought in products and attitudes regarding shopping.

The bases for segmentation are discussed next and separately. However, in reality, marketers use multiple bases. For example, although demographics and lifestyles (or psychographics), which are the most widely used bases, are discussed separately, every psychographic classification of consumers includes their demographics. Whereas demographics *determine* consumers' needs for products (e.g., males and females buy different products) and the ability to buy them (e.g., income), psychographics *explain* buyers' purchase decisions and choices. For example, being a student and having limited financial resources are demographic factors, but how students spend their resources is a function of their lifestyles, values, and interests. Some students buy expensive designer brands, whereas others rummage for clothes in thrift and vintage clothing stores. Some students go to sports events, while others go to the latest nightclubs.

Demographics

Demographic segmentation divides consumers according to age, gender, ethnicity, income and wealth, occupation, marital status, household type and size, and geographical location. These variables are objective, empirical, and can be determined easily through questioning or observation. They enable marketers to classify each consumer into a clearly defined category, such as an age group or income bracket. Similarly, one's social class is defined by computing an index based on three objective and quantifiable variables: income (number of dollars earned), education (number of years studied for the highest degree held), and occupation (prestige scores associated with various occupations). As discussed later, consumers' geographic locations and zip codes can be easily matched with their demographics.

All segmentation plans include demographic data for the following reasons:

1. Demographics are the easiest and most logical way to classify people and can be measured more precisely than the other segmentation bases.

2. Demographics offer the most cost-effective way to locate and reach specific segments, because most of the secondary data compiled about any population consists of demographics (e.g., U.S. Census Bureau, audience profiles of various media).

3. Using demographics, marketers can identify new segments created by shifts in populations' age, income, and location.

4. Demographics determine many consumption behaviors, attitudes, and media exposure patterns. For example, many products are gender-specific, and music preferences are very closely related to one's age. Therefore, local radio stations specializing in various types of music are an efficient and economical way to target different age groups. Leisure activities and interests, as well as the media people read or watch, are functions of their ages, education, and incomes.

Next, we describe the most prominent demographics used in segmenting markets and targeting consumers.

Age

Product needs often vary with consumers' age, and age is a key factor in marketing many products and services. For instance, younger investors—in their mid-20s to mid-40s—are often advised to invest aggressively and in growth stocks, whereas people who are older and closer to retirement should be much more cautious, keep a significant portion of their assets in bonds (which provide stable and safe income), and avoid risky, long-term investments. Age also influences our buying priorities. For example, as a young student, would you say that your opinions regarding what is a "luxury" product are the same as those of your parents or grandparents? The most likely answer is no: your parents, and especially grandparents, would probably criticize your purchases of upscale sneakers, designer shirts and handbags, jeans from Abercrombie & Fitch, and many other things you buy as "ridiculously expensive."

Marketers commonly target age groups. For example, Colgate understands that brushing teeth is not a child's favorite activity, while being proud of one's age is a priority. Therefore, Colgate divides the preteens toothpaste group into four segments and offers each one its own toothpaste. So, while 2-year-olds may feel proud of their first toothpaste, as they become 3 or 4 years old and very involved with growing older, they often demand a different toothpaste than the one they associate with "being babies." Thus, Colgate offers *My First Colgate* to children up to age 2, *Colgate Dora the Explorer* to ages 2 to 5, and *Colgate SpongeBob SquarePants* and *Colgate Pop Stars* to older, preteen children.[3]

Many marketers cater to the needs of 18- to 34-year-old consumers, known as Millennials. For example, as MTV's audience got older, the network developed programs specifically aimed at this segment, and Keds—positioned as "The Original Sneaker"—has started a campaign allowing millennials to express their creativity using Keds sneakers as the canvas for drawing pictures.[4] Every

FIGURE 2.2
Online Activities of Different
Age Groups

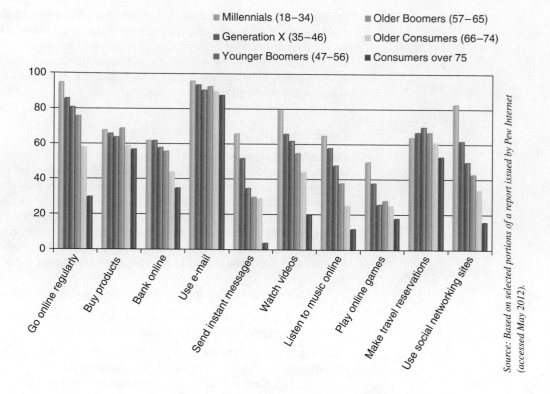

summer, movie studios compete for young adult viewers, because teenagers and people in their very early 20s go to movies frequently and many see the same movies more than once. Therefore, in recent years, Hollywood's summer staples have been sequels and prequels to the movies that have previously been hits among these age groups (e.g., movie series such as Harry Potter, Twilight, and The Hunger Games).[5]

Although the Internet is often described as a "young" medium, consumers of all ages go online regularly. However, people of different ages use online access differently, as featured in Figure 2.2. Not surprisingly, people go online less frequently as they age, but continue using social networking sites and e-mail. Surprisingly, buying online varies only somewhat across age groups.[6]

Gender

Many products and services are inherently designed for either males or females, but sex roles have blurred, and gender is no longer an accurate way to distinguish among consumers in some product categories. Today, more and more magazine ads and TV commercials depict men and women in roles traditionally occupied by the opposite sex. For example, many ads reflect the expanded child-nurturing roles of young fathers in today's society. In contrast, some companies of "men's products" are targeting women specifically. For instance, Van Gogh Blue, a vodka brand, has been targeting 25- to 44-year-old female consumers with a somewhat provocative campaign entitled "You Unbottled."[7] Other companies have introduced gender-specific versions. Frito-Lay overhauled all of its calorie-conscious snacks, making them more appealing to women, and introduced 100-calorie packages of snacks.[8] Recognizing that many advertisers target women 25 to 35, the cable channel VH1 introduced shows to attract them, such as a reality show entitled Mob Wives, which portrays the lives of women who were born, or married, into reputed organized-crime families.[9]

Women have traditionally been the main users of such products as hair coloring and cosmetics, and men have been the main users of shaving tools and preparations. However, men's grooming products are becoming a fast-growing sector as more men use exfoliators, toners, aftershave creams, and cooling and tinted moisturizers. In the past, women bought skin products for men, but today men are buying such products themselves. Recognizing that many men feel embarrassed to be seen looking for cosmetics, many department stores have redesigned the areas where men's grooming products are sold. For example, they now display large signs over the men's grooming products section, so that men will not confuse men's skin care products with women's cosmetics.

SMART CAR CARE

You can help keep your car safe and on the road.

Cars are complex, and it's easy to feel overwhelmed when you look under the hood. But there are plenty of basic things you can do yourself to keep your car safe, economical and dependable. From checking the oil to keeping your tires inflated to the proper pressure, preventive maintenance can extend the life of your car and help save you money. Learn how to keep your vehicle safe and on the road with the new "Smart Car Care" booklet. It's free from Shell. Pick one up at your nearest Shell station, visit countonshell.com or call 1-800-376-0200.

Count on Shell

Source: Shell Oil Company

FIGURE 2.3 Appealing to Women and Changing Gender Roles

Although women's products are generally placed behind counters and with salespeople standing in front and ready to advise, men's products are displayed on open shelves, because many men do not like to speak with salespersons. The store sections where men can buy grooming products feature TVs tuned to sports or financial channels, and semiprivate areas where men can try shaving creams, moisturizers, and other products.[10] Still, studies discovered that nearly half of U.S. men don't use face wash or moisturizer. Dove, a well-established brand of face and body care products, introduced a product line named Dove Men+Care. The products' positioning centers around trying to prove that a man's face needs pampering. The ad, which urges men to "end the face torture," shows the ways a man's face is exposed to harsh elements, such as windburn from a roller coaster, pokes from a child, close shaves, and snowballs.[11]

The ad in Figure 2.3 illustrates targeting women and also shows how stereotypes—such as that women cannot change a car's oil—are no longer true.

Families and Households

Many families pass through similar phases in their formation, growth, and dissolution. At each phase, the family unit needs different products and services. For example, brides are generally happy and spending consumers. Young, single people, for example, need basic furniture for their first apartment, whereas their parents, finally free of child rearing, often refurnish their homes with more elaborate pieces. The **family life cycle** is a classification of the phases that most families go through; each stage represents an important target segment to many marketers (see Chapter 10). A study investigated the impact of major life events on consumption and discovered that occasions such as moving, marriage, a child's birth or adoption, the death of a close family member, significant changes in one's employment, and caring for older relatives are viable segmentation variables when used together with age cohorts.[12]

Traditionally, most marketers have targeted families. They researched the number and kinds of households that buy and own certain products and the media profiles of household decision makers, and then developed appropriate marketing appeals. More recently, marketers began targeting specific marital status groups, such as singles, divorced individuals, single parents, and dual-income married couples without children. For instance, urban, one-person households with incomes greater than $75,000 tend to buy premium alcoholic drinks and beer, books, organic products, and fresh produce, and to shop in green markets and specialized food stores rather than in conventional supermarkets.

Social Class

Income is an important variable for distinguishing between market segments, because it indicates an ability or inability to pay for a product model or brand. Income is often combined with other demographic variables to define target markets more accurately. To illustrate, a combination of high income and age identified the Affluent Elderly segment. Income has also been combined with both age and occupational status to single out the Yuppies, a sought-after subgroup of the baby boomer market (see Chapter 12).

Education, occupation, and income are closely correlated; high-level occupations that produce high incomes usually require advanced education and are more prestigious than occupations requiring less education. Social class is an important base for market segmentation in the form of a weighted index of education, occupation, and income. **Social class** is a hierarchy in which individuals in the same class generally have the same degree of status, whereas members of other classes have either higher or lower status. Studies have shown that consumers in different social classes vary in terms of values, product preferences, and buying habits (see Chapter 10).

Conditions that affect social classes often have a direct effect on marketing. For example, Procter and Gamble (P&G), the world's largest maker of consumer goods and advertiser, has been worried about the financial hardship of America's middle class, which it believes will be long lasting. P&G's definition of "middle class" is households with annual income between $50,000 and $100,000, which amounts to 40% of the country's households. These families are P & G's core customers and, with their net worth declining following the financial crisis and the increased costs of children's education, they have become more price conscious. In response, like many other companies, P & G introduced lower-priced lines of many of its goods, despite the negative impact of this action on the company's earnings.[13] Looking at the other aspect of recessionary times, during the financial crisis very affluent people avoided being seen leaving expensive stores and carrying shopping bags bearing the stores' logos. After the financial markets recovered, the same consumers resumed buying extraordinarily expensive products (e.g., at Neiman Marcus, Chanel coats that cost $9,000 and women's Christian Louboutin shoes that sell for $800) and these goods' prices went up.[14]

Ethnicity

Marketers segment some populations on the basis of cultural heritage and ethnicity because members of the same culture tend to share the same values, beliefs, and customs. In the United States, African Americans, Hispanic Americans, and Asian Americans are important subcultural market segments (see Chapter 12). Culturally distinct segments may be prospects for the same product, but marketers should target them using different promotional appeals. For example, *Cosmopolitan* magazine and other media have started targeting Latin women, a segment that, for a long time, went unnoticed by most media. *Cosmopolitan Latina* targets American-born, bilingual Latinas. *Cosmopolitan* also has editions for women in Argentina, Mexico, and Colombia.[15] Similarly, L'Oreal USA collaborated with Telemundo (an American TV network that broadcasts in Spanish) in building a website for Hispanic consumers.[16]

Geodemographics

Where a person lives determines some aspects of consumption behavior. For example, climates determine the types of clothing most people own, and fashions and styles in large cities are often very different from those in nonurban areas. Local customers, as opposed to visiting tourists, are also a distinct segment. For instance, one study investigated the "local resident gambler" segment in Las Vegas and found that the gaming habits of this group were distinctly different from those of tourists—a segment on which most marketing studies have focused.[17] Sometimes, new market segments emerge because of climatic changes. For example, many travellers are willing to pay unusually high prices to travel to exotic destinations, such as glaciers, coral reefs, ice fields, and tropical rain forests, in order to see them before they become less majestic or disappear altogether because of global warming; in the travel industry, this segment is known as "Tourism of Doom."[18] Another creative example of using geography is Absolut Vodka's introduction of limited editions of flavored vodkas in major cities with the cities' names integrated into the brand (e.g., "Absolut New York" and "Absolut Chicago") and with well-recognized features of the city embedded in the ads (e.g., in an ad for Absolut Chicago, wind is blowing the letters off the bottle).[19] Some marketers have introduced regional products into other markets. For example, Cheerwine—a wine-colored, highly carbonated soda with wild cherry flavor—has been made, for decades, by a family-owned business in North Carolina, where it had a devoted following. Then, the company's management hired an advertising agency and made plans to introduce the product nationally.[20] In the alcoholic beverages industry, as Americans' appetite for flavored spirits has steadily risen, originally local brands introduced flavored versions. Such products include Southern Comfort Fiery Pepper, Jack Daniels Tennessee Honey whiskey, and Red Stag, a black cherry-flavored bourbon made by Jim Beam.[21]

The most popular use of geography in strategic targeting is **geodemographics**, a hybrid segmentation scheme based on the premise that people who live close to one another are likely to have similar financial means, tastes, preferences, lifestyles, and consumption habits (as an old adage states, "Birds of a feather flock together"). The primary application of geodemographics is **PRIZM**,

TABLE 2.3	Nielsen's Segmentation Frameworks
NAME	**DESCRIPTION**
PRIZM	Household segmentation model that groups consumers into 66 PRIZM segments based on socioeconomic ranking, consumer behavior, and media exposure patterns. Each segment is assigned into an SER (socioeconomic rank) based on neighborhood data for income, education, occupation, and home value.
Urbanization Classes	Assigns the 66 segments into 4 types of population density: Urban, Suburban, Second City, and Town & Rural
Social Groups	Each of the 66 segments is classified according to its levels of affluence and urbanization.
Lifestage Classes	Each of the 66 segments is classified into one of the following classes: Younger Years (2 types): 35 years old or younger without kids; middle age without kids at home. Family Life: households with kids living at home. Mature Years (2 types): over 55 years old; ages 45–64 without children living at home.
Lifestage Groups	Each of the 66 segments is classified according to its levels of affluence and Lifestage Classes.
P$YCLE	Every U.S. household is classified into one of 58 consumer segments based on the household's finances and wealth.
Income-Producing Assets (IPA)	Each of the 58 consumer segments is classified into one of seven IPA groups based on retirement accounts, cash, demand deposits, stocks, money market funds, and other assets that can be liquidated easily. Then, each of the 58 segments is classified according to the Lifestage Classes.
ConneXions Groups	Fifty-three segments based on the household's willingness to adopt new technologies early. The segments are: High Tech, Mid Tech, Low Tech, and No Tech. The segments are then classified according to the Lifestage Classes.

offered by Nielsen's MyBestSegments service. Marketers can locate each of PRIZMS's 66 segments according to their postal ZIP Codes. The residents of most ZIP Codes include more than one PRIZM segment, and Nielsen's ZIP Code Look-Up details the relative percentage of each segment within each local population in the United States. If you go to the Look-Up and enter your residence's ZIP Code, you will find out the characteristic of the segments residing in your area and their relative sizes (claritas.com). The sixty-six segments are also classified according to levels of population density (urbanization) and affluence, and placed into one of several Lifestage Classes. These groups are similar to the stages of a typical family's evolution (see Chapter 10). In recent years, Nielsen developed two additional segmentation measures: P$YCLE (based on the household's wealth) and ConneXions (based on the household's receptivity to new technologies). Table 2.3 describes Nielsen's segmentation frameworks.

Green Consumers

Green consumers are attractive prospects for many products and marketers have explored targeting them. One study identified three types of green consumers:

1. *Environmental activists:* "green" enthusiasts and people who adopt lifestyles focused on health and sustainability. They seek foods from farms that not only produce organic products, but also cut down on water use, power use, and trash.

2. *Organic eaters:* concerned about sustaining their own health and not so much about sustaining the planet.

3. *Economizers:* experimenting with buying eco-friendly products in order to save money.[22]

Another study identified four groups of green consumers:[23]

1. *True Greens:* persons who have adopted environmentally friendly behaviors. They try to convince friends to use environmentally friendly products, and avoid buying products that have a negative environmental impact. They switch brands for ecological reasons and are willing to make personal sacrifices to protect the environment. Furthermore, they maintain that the government should do more to protect the environment and educate children regarding future environmental protection, and want companies to be transparent when marketing environmentally friendly products.

2. *Donor Greens:* These individuals feel guilty about their lack of environmentally sound buying behavior, and sometimes consider environmental impacts when purchasing products. They are willing to sacrifice financially to support the environment, but unwilling to change their shopping behaviors.

3. *Learning Greens:* These persons are still learning about environmental issues, but are not actively engaged in ecological causes. They seek easy ways—that do not involve big changes in consumption behavior—to support the environment and sometimes consider environmental impact when purchasing products, but are skeptical about environmentalists' claims.

4. *Non-Greens:* People who do not care about wildlife or environmental issues. They neither engage in environmentally friendly behaviors, nor feel guilty about adversely impacting the environment. Although some of them acknowledge environmental problems, they still buy ecologically unsound products, do not look for green seals when shopping, and believe that it is okay for large companies to act in ways that have negative effects on the environment.

Yet another study divided consumers according to a *spectrum of green,* on which the *darkest greens* are consumers who are willing to pay a premium for eco-friendly products in order to help reduce global warming, and the *lightest greens* are mostly concerned about saving money on their energy bills, rather than saving the planet. Table 2.4 describes five segments of green consumers along the spectrum of green.[24]

TABLE 2.4   Segmenting Green Consumers Along the Spectrum of Green

SEGMENT	ENVIRONMENTAL ATTITUDES	ENVIRONMENTAL BEHAVIORS	MARKETING STRATEGIES
ALPHA-ECOS (darkest green), 43 million U.S. adults	Deeply committed to green causes, saving the planet, and concerned about global warming.	Early adopters of environmentally responsible products (i.e., hybrid autos, organic foods, eco-friendly cleaning products) and willing to buy them at a premium.	In appealing to this group, promote the company's corporate social responsibility in order to gain their trust and reinforce their behaviors.
Eco-Centrics (second most green), 34 million U.S. adults	More concerned about how environmentally responsible products benefit them personally and immediately; view environmental issues abstractly.	Willing to pay more for green products if they believe those products are better for their own health and wellbeing.	Messages that show Eco-Centrics how people's green consumption behaviors benefit the global environment.
Eco-Chics 57 million adults, the largest segment	Not particularly concerned about environmental issues, but undertake efforts to be perceived as green by others.	Buy few green products, if any. Likely to buy green products that are very conspicuous.	Messages that associate environmentally responsible brands with influential public figures and symbols. Encourage the Eco-Chics to use social media as a forum to show their friends and family just how green they are.
Economically Ecos 53 million U.S. adults	Less concerned about saving the planet, but very concerned about saving money. Willing to pay more for green products if convinced it will save them money in the long run.	Hate to waste anything; their behaviors are driven by practicality (i.e., conserving water and energy, recycling).	Promote products by emphasizing their economic, long-lasting, and reusability benefits.
Eco-Moms about 33% of U.S. mothers with children under 18	Interested in cost-effective and socially responsible practices that also play a role in ensuring their families' well-being.	Buy products made in environmentally conscious ways, such as organic foods and green cleaners.	Demonstrate how their green behaviors benefit their families and also help save the earth for future generations to enjoy.

Source: Maryam Banikarim, "Seeing Shades in Green Consumers," ADWEEK, April 19, 2010. Copyrighted 2013. Prometheus Global Media. 103046:913FO

Personality Traits

Many psychographic factors overlap with personality characteristics or traits. Through personality tests—which consist of questions or statements presented to respondents—researchers can study consumers' personality characteristics and apply them in segmenting markets (see Chapter 3). For example, consumers who are open-minded and generally perceive less risk than others in trying new things are likely to be **innovators**—that is, more likely to buy a new product when it is first introduced and before many other consumers buy it. Therefore, marketers of new products must identify these individuals (and also find out their demographics, lifestyles, and values) and target them during introductions of the new products. Furthermore, if personality tests also discover that innovators tend to score high on "exhibition"—a trait where a person wants to be the center of a group—the promotion directed at this group should encourage the innovators to initiate positive word of mouth and tell others about new products. Table 2.5 includes descriptions of three groups of online shoppers segmented on the basis of personality traits and attitudes about buying online.[25]

Psychographics, Values and Lifestyles

In marketing, lifestyles are named **psychographics**, which include consumers' *activities, interests,* and *opinions*. In consumer research, psychographics consists of creating statements and asking respondents to indicate their level of agreement or disagreement with each statement. The dimensions studied include consumers' buying patterns, opinions about consumption and/or social issues, values, hobbies, leisure activities, and many other dimensions. There are no standardized definitions of psychographic dimensions (such as an "active lifestyle" or consumer types like an "impulse buyer" or a "green consumer"), because almost all psychographic terms are defined in the scope of specific studies. Nevertheless, because they are so versatile, psychographics are widely used, and, together with demographics, are included in almost all segmentation frameworks. Table 2.6 shows a sample of psychographic measures Figure 2.4 shows an ad that targets affluent travellers who like to explore new cuisines.

VALS™ (an acronym for "values and lifestyles") is the most popular segmentation system combining lifestyles and values. Drawing on Maslow's need hierarchy and the concept of a person's "social character" (see Chapter 3), researchers at Strategic Business Insights developed a segmentation scheme of the American population known as VALS. It classifies America's adult population into eight distinctive subgroups (segments) based on consumer responses to both attitudinal and

TABLE 2.5   The Personality Traits of Three Segments of Online Shoppers

CHARACTERISTIC	FIRST SEGMENT	SECOND SEGMENT	THIRD SEGMENT
	Consumers who feel that online shopping is risky	Consumers who are open-minded about online shopping	Consumers who feel cautious about online shopping and seek more information about it
Being extraverted and outgoing or reserved	Reserved, keep to themselves	Very extraverted	Reserved, keep to themselves
Trusting or feeling skeptical about online shopping	Skeptical and do not trust online shopping	Trust online shopping fully	Trust online shopping reasonably
Attitude about online shopping	Unfavorable	Favorable, believe that online shopping is pleasant	Favorable but do not find online shopping pleasant
The degree of perceived risk regarding online shopping	High	Low	High
Willingness to shop online	Unwilling	Very willing	Somewhat willing

Source: Based on Stuart J. Barnes, "Segmenting Cyberspace: A Customer Typology for the Internet," European Journal of Marketing, 41, no. 1/2 (2007): 71–93. Copyright © 2007, Emerald Group Publishing Limited.

TABLE 2.6	Samples of Psychographic Measures
PSYCHOGRAPHIC FACTOR	**SAMPLE STATEMENTS**
Values and goals*	• Sense of belonging • Fun and enjoyment in life • Warm relationship with others • Self-fulfillment • Being well respected
Attitudes toward Life**	• Financial security is important to me • My greatest achievements are ahead of me • I am more conventional than experimental • I would rather spend a quiet evening at home than go to a party • My social status is an important part of my life
Apparel and Fashion**	• I buy clothes I like regardless of current fashion • My friends often ask me for advice on fashion • Men do not notice women who do not dress well
Gift Giving**	• I generally give gifts because people expect me to • I try to give gifts that carry personal messages to recipients • Gifts always communicate love and friendship
Control of Life**	• I find it hard to speak in front of a group • When I make friends I always try to make the relationships work • I enjoy making my own decisions • Others usually know what's best for me
Buying Online**	• It requires too much time to set up accounts with online stores • The look of a website is an important factor in my buying decisions • I tell others about my experiences in buying online
Leisure Activities***	• Played adult games (e.g., cards or mahjong) • Visited art gallery or museum • Went hunting or shooting • Went to the movies • Attended a sporting event

* Responses use an "extremely important" to "extremely unimportant" scale
** Responses use a "strongly agree" to "strongly disagree" scale
*** Responses use a "frequently" to "never" scale

demographic questions. Figure 2.5 is a diagram of the VALS segments, and Table 2.7 describes the eight VALS segments.

Examining the diagram from left to right, there are three *primary* motivations: the *ideals motivated* (these consumer segments are guided by knowledge and principles), the *achievement motivated* (these consumer segments are looking for products and services that demonstrate success to their peers), and the *self-expression motivated* (these consumer segments desire social or physical activity, variety, and risk). Furthermore, each of these three major self-motivations represents distinct attitudes, lifestyles, and decision-making styles. Examining Figure 2.5 from top to bottom, the diagram reveals a continuum in terms of resources and innovation—that is, *high resources-high innovation* (on the top) to *low resources-low innovation* (on the bottom). This range of resources/innovation (again, from most to least) includes the range of psychological, physical, demographic, and material means and capacities consumers have to draw upon, including education, income, self-confidence, health, eagerness to buy, and energy level, as well as the consumer's propensity to try new products.

Each of the eight VALS segments contains between 10 and 17% of the U.S. adult population, with Believers, at 17%, being the largest VALS group. In terms of consumer characteristics, the eight VALS segments differ in some important ways. For instance, *Believers* tend to buy American-made products and are slow to alter their consumption-related habits, whereas *Innovators* purchase top-of-the-line and new products, especially innovative technologies. Therefore, for example, it is not surprising that smart marketers of the first intelligent in-vehicle technologies (e.g., global positioning devices) targeted innovators, because they are early adopters of new products. Many business plans have used VALS, and Table 2.8 includes examples of such projects.[26]

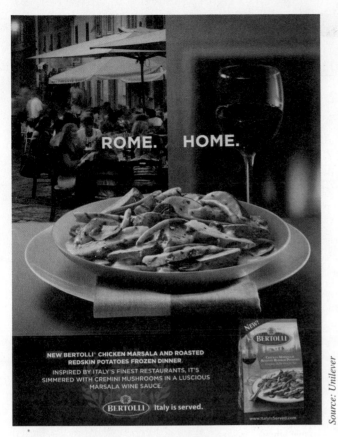

Source: Unilever

FIGURE 2.4 An Appeal to Sophisticated Consumers Who Travel and Explore New Destinations

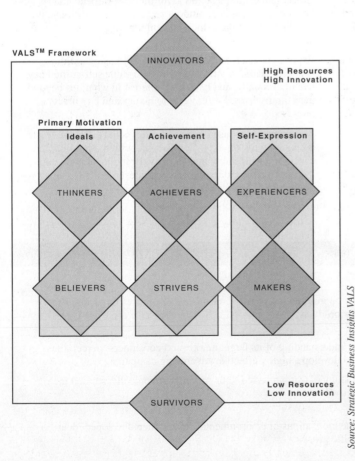

Source: Strategic Business Insights VALS

FIGURE 2.5 Diagram of the VALS™ Segments

Benefit Segmentation

Benefit segmentation is based on the benefits that consumers seek from products and services. The benefits that consumers look for represent unfilled needs, whereas buyers' perceptions that a given brand delivers a unique and prominent benefit result in loyalty to that brand. Marketers of personal care products, such as shampoos, soaps, and toothpastes, create different offerings designed to deliver specific benefits. Colgate is probably the world's most sophisticated marketer of personal care products, and its line of toothpastes is an excellent example for understanding the benefits that consumers seek in regard to care for their teeth and oral hygiene. Colgate's website includes a link entitled "Search by Benefit." Toothpastes are classified into four benefits: (1) long-lasting fresh breath; (2) plaque and gingivitis protection; (3) sensitivity relief; and (4) tooth whitening. For example, *Colgate Total* provides 12 hours of germ fighting, which other toothpastes do not. *Colgate Max Fresh* wipes out bad breath. *Colgate Sensitive Pro-Relief* is for people who have sensitive gums. Other Colgate versions whiten teeth, protect enamel, prevent cavities, fight tartar, combine mouthwash with toothpaste, and provide many other benefits. In addition, the *Colgate Pro-Clinical* line includes three versions—daily cleaning, daily whitening, and daily renewal—and is presumably aimed at encouraging consumers to brush their teeth three times a day.[27] The V8 ad in Figure 2.6 reflects the product's primary benefit, which is consuming vegetables.

A study identified three groups of benefits that consumers commonly seek when visiting each of three service providers: a dentist, a hairdresser, and a travel agent. The study also discovered that consumers' loyalty levels to their service providers correlated positively with the benefits these consumers believed they had received.[28] Service providers can use the findings to improve customer retention. For example, dentists can enhance patients' confidence by post-visit contacts inquiring if patients had experienced any problems following a dental procedure, and also e-mailing patients press clippings featuring the dentist's appearances at conferences or media interviews. Another study explored the relational benefits that banking customers seek from financial firms and identified the same groups of benefits as the study just discussed.[29] Table 2.9 summarizes the benefits identified in the two studies.

Media-Based Segmentation

As more and more forms of media emerge, marketers must study the benefits that consumers seek from adopting these communication tools, so that they can advertise in these media effectively. In one study, consumers singled out *immediacy, accessibility,* and *free cost* as the most relevant features of digital newspapers, while identifying *writing style* and more *depth* and *details* as the key features of traditional newspapers. These findings indicate that publishers of traditional newspapers should position online and paper newspapers as complementing one another and that the two versions represent opportunities for somewhat different types of ads.[30] Another study found that car buyers substituted information searches online for reading print ads in order to reduce the amount of time spent on negotiating prices with car dealers.[31] This means that marketers should approach car buyers who have consulted the Internet differently than those who have not. Another study identified six types of benefits sought by users of mobile electronic devices (see Table 2.10).[32] A Canadian study identified three distinctive segments of online consumers and their characteristics, which are listed in Table 2.11.[33] As

TABLE 2.7 Descriptions of the VALS™ Segments

SEGMENT NAME	MOTIVATION AND RESOURCES	SELECTED DEMOGRAPHICS	VALUES AND CONSUMPTION PATTERNS
Innovators	Abundant resources; motivated by ideals, achievement, self-expression, and self-esteem.	10% of the U.S. population. Median age 45. 65% are married and 72% work full time.	Successful, sophisticated, and curious. Receptive to new ideas and technologies, and buy niche products and services. Concerned about how their purchases express their tastes and personalities. Cultivate tastes for the finer things in life.
Thinkers	Motivated by ideals and have solid resources.	11% of the U.S. population. Median age 56. 75% are married and 55% work full time.	Mature, satisfied, and comfortable; value order and responsibility. Well educated and informed about world, wish to broaden their horizons and open to new ideas. Practical consumers, who look for durability, functionality, and value in products.
Believers	Motivated by ideals and have moderate resources.	16.5% of the U.S. population. Median age 52. 63% are married and 47% work full time.	Conservative, conventional with traditional beliefs, whose priorities are family, religion, and community. Follow routines focused on their homes, families, and social or religious organizations. Predictable consumers who buy established brands, favor U.S. products, and are brand loyal.
Achievers	Motivated by desire for achievement and have solid resources.	14% of the U.S. population. Median age 41. 72% are married and 70% work full time.	Goal-oriented and committed to career and family. Their lives are focused on family, religion, and work. Live conventionally, are politically conservative, and seek predictability and stability. As consumers, they favor products that demonstrate success to their peers.
Strivers	Motivated by achievement and have moderate resources.	11.5% of the U.S. population. Median age 28. 34% are married and 52% work full time.	Trendy, fun loving, and seek approval from others. Don't have enough resources to meet their desires and impulsively buy stylish products that emulate the purchases of people with greater material wealth. Lack the skills they need to move ahead.
Experiencers	Motivated by self-expression and have solid resources.	13% of the U.S. population. Median age 24. 25% are married and 52% work full time.	Young, enthusiastic, and impulsive consumers who seek variety and excitement and savor the new, offbeat, and risky. Favor exercise, sports, outdoor recreation, and social activities. Spend a lot on fashion and entertaining and concerned about appearing "cool."
Makers	Motivated by self-expression and have moderate resources.	12% of the U.S. population. Median age 46. 68% are married and 59% work full time.	Express themselves by building houses, raising children, and fixing cars. Practical people, who value self-sufficiency, live traditionally, and have little interest in what lies beyond their family lives. Prefer value to luxury and buy practical products.
Survivors	No strong primary motivation and low resources.	12% of the U.S. population. Median age 70. 45% are married and 13% work full time.	Live narrowly focused lives and often believe that the world is changing too quickly. Comfortable with the familiar and concerned with safety and security. Brand loyal and seek discounts. As a group, they are a modest market for most products and services.

Source: Reprinted with permission of Strategic Business Insights; www.strategicbusinessinsights.com/VALS

TABLE 2.8 Sample Business Applications of VALS™

TYPE OF APPLICATION	DESCRIPTION
New product development at a manufacturer of wireless devices	Using VALS, the company explored new opportunities to create consumer value and evaluate consumer demand and prospective markets for new products.
Positioning of a Japanese car in the United States	Using VALS, the company enhanced its understanding of its target market and consumers' perceptions of its product and used this knowledge to develop a highly effective advertising campaign.
Communications plan for a company providing pension plans	Using VALS, the company identified customers who preferred to be served electronically, studied their motivations, and developed a more effective website.
Policy development by a non-profit organization	Using VALS, the organization studied the motivations of environmentalists and then developed ideas for environmental campaigns targeting specific groups.

Source: Based on Strategic Business Institute

FIGURE 2.6 V8's Benefit: Consuming Vegetables

Source: Campbell Soup Company

illustrated in this table, marketers should study consumers' demographics and their Internet navigation patterns and segment them accordingly.

Usage Rate Segmentation

Usage rate segmentation is reflects the differences among heavy, medium, and light users, and nonusers of a specific product, service, or brand. Marketers of many products, such as soup, laundry detergent, beer, and dog food, have found that a relatively small group of heavy users accounts for a disproportionately large percentage of the total product usage. For example, about 25% of all those who drink beer account for about 75% of all beer consumed. Therefore, most beer companies direct their advertising campaigns to heavy users rather than spend money trying to attract medium or light users. This also explains the successful targeting of light beer to heavy drinkers under the positioning that it is "less filling" (and thus can be consumed in greater quantities) than regular beer.

Targeting heavy users is a common marketing strategy and is often more profitable than targeting other user categories. However, catering to this segment requires a lot of expensive advertising because all competitors target the same heavy users. Some marketers prefer to target light and medium users with products that are distinct from those preferred by heavy users. For example, every Super Bowl broadcast includes many very expensive commercials for mainstream brands of American beer directed at the product's heavy users. In contrast, the beer section at a Whole Foods supermarket consists of numerous brands from different countries and microbreweries, and with more exotic flavors; these products also cost more than top-selling beer brands and are backed by minimal advertising. Whole Foods targets consumers who drink less beer than those targeted by the Super Bowl ads, but who have more discerning tastes and also greater disposable incomes.

Usage rate segmentation also focuses on the factors that directly affect the usage behavior. For instance, a study of supermarket customers found differences between two segments of buyers in terms of usage frequency, defined as the number of times per week buyers visited the supermarket. The researchers also examined usage frequency in relation to buyers' reasons for purchasing at that

TABLE 2.9	**Clients' Expectations from Their Service Providers (Dentists, Hairdressers, Travel Agents, Financial Firms)**	
SOCIAL BENEFITS	**SPECIAL TREATMENT BENEFITS**	**CONFIDENCE-RELATED BENEFITS**
• Being recognized immediately upon arrival and being known by name to the staff • Having a genuine relationship with the service provider • Being treated in a way that makes them feel important • Being treated as if they were the provider's personal friends	• Having providers go out of their way in searching out the best treatment for each client • Providers paying more attention to client's specific needs • Providers charging reasonable prices; at banks, giving better interest rates • Providers helping clients when something goes wrong • Receiving priority treatment in queues and faster service	• Providers should make clients feel confident that the service will be provided well and correctly • Receiving clear descriptions of services • Being told what to expect • Feeling less anxious during the service process • Providers should convince clients that there is little risk that something will go wrong

TABLE 2.10	Benefits That Consumers Seek When Using Mobile Devices			
LOCATION INFORMATION	**COMMUNICATION**	**SPORTS AND ENTERTAINMENT**	**VALUE-ADDED SHOPPING**	**FINANCIAL SERVICES**
Directions to location; location of the place where they are; weather and news reports	Sending and receiving email, pictures, and texts; chatting with strangers	Receiving sports-related information; accessing adult entertainment; gambling and gaming online; downloading music	Comparing prices; receiving coupons and sales alerts; receiving product information	Banking; trading stocks; filing insurance claims; bidding at auctions; buying tickets; making currency conversions

Source: Based on Gillian Sullivan Mort and Judy Drennan, "Marketing M-Services: Establishing a Usage Benefit Typology Related to Mobile User Characteristics," *Database Marketing & Consumer Strategy Management*, 12 no. 4 (2005): 327–341.

chain, levels of expenditure at the store, travel times to the store and modes of transportation, and whether buyers came in from home, a job, or were simply passing by.[34]

Rate of usage is strongly related to **product awareness status**, which is the degree of a consumer's awareness of the product and its features, and whether or not he or she intends to buy it reasonably soon. The consumer's degree of awareness of the product, along with whether the consumer is unaware and needs to be informed about the product, represent distinct targeting opportunities. A related factor is **product involvement**, which reflects the degree of personal relevance that the product holds for the consumer (see Chapter 5). A study identified three clusters of consumers based on their varied involvement with a wine's "background or history" (i.e., its "appellation of origin") and found significant differences among the clusters in terms of knowledge of wine brands and wine purchases.[35]

Usage Occasion Segmentation

Usage occasion segmentation recognizes that consumers purchase some products for specific occasions, as expressed in the following statements:

- "Whenever our son celebrates a birthday, we take him out to dinner at the Gramercy Tavern"
- "When I'm away on business for a week or more, I try to stay at the Setai"
- "I always buy my wife candy on Valentine's Day"

TABLE 2.11	Segments of Online Consumers		
CHARACTERISTICS	**BASIC COMMUNICATIONS**	**LURKING SHOPPERS**	**SOCIAL STRIVERS**
Percentage of total & gender	39% 75% female	39% 52% female	22% 57% female
Age	41% under 35 41% 35–54 19% over 54	31% under 35 48% 35–54 21% over 54	49% under 35 31% 35–54 20% over 54
Income	39% $49,000 or less 35% $50,000–74,000 26% $75,000 and up	40% $49,000 or less 23% $50,000–74,000 37% $75,000 and up	54% $49,000 or less 27% $50,000–74,000 19% $75,000 and up
Internet use	12.4 hours per week	16.7 hours per week	20.7 hours per week
E-mail	High	Regularly	Regularly
Browsing	Some	High	Some
Shopping	Some	Very high	Some
Blogging	Low	Some	Very high
Chatting	Low	Low	Very high
Video streaming	Low	Some	Very high
Downloading	Low	Some	Very high

Source: Based on Muhammad Alijukhadar and Sylvain Senecal, "Segmenting the online consumer market," *Marketing Intelligence and Planning*, 29 no. 4 (2011): 421–435.

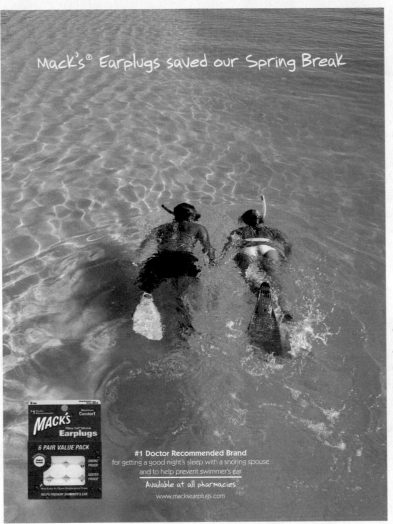

Source: Devin Benner CEO McKeon Products Inc.

FIGURE 2.7 Usage Occasion: Spring Break

Many marketers promote their offerings for holidays or seasons. Kunafa is a classic example. A very common dessert in the Levant, traditionally it is made with nuts and syrup. In Egypt, the country it is rumored to have originated in, the dessert becomes available in all bakeries during Ramadan, the holy month for the followers of Islamic faith. During this period Kunafa is made using chocolates, fruits, and cream, and as red velvet cakes and even cupcakes, in addition to the more conventionally prepared versions. These variations only appear during the month of Ramadan, when the products are actively advertised, but not throughout the rest of the year. As consumers purchase more products online, the marketers of Campbell's Soup, Kraft, Hershey, Kellogg, and other prominent brands have been promoting their products online before the holidays, because consumers spend more money during the weeks before New Year's Eve.[36] The ad for Mack's Earplugs in Figure 2.7 promotes using the product during spring break.

Behavioral Targeting

Behavioral targeting consists of sending consumers personalized and prompt offers and promotional messages designed to reach the right consumers and deliver to them highly relevant messages at the right time and more accurately than when using conventional segmentation techniques. This method is enabled by tracking online navigation, current geographic location, and purchase behavior.

Tracking Online Navigation

Tracking consumers' navigation online includes:

1. Recording the websites that consumers visit.

2. Measuring consumers' levels of engagement with the sites (i.e., which pages they look at, the length of their visits, and how often they return).

3. Recording the visitors' lifestyles and personalities (derived from the contents of consumers' blogs, tweets, and Facebook profiles).

4. Keeping track of consumer' purchases, almost purchases (i.e., abandoned shopping carts), and returns or exchanges.

Long stays and repeat visits to sites indicate a high level of product involvement and purchase intention. Because websites are versatile, marketers can respond quickly to consumers' purchase interests and intentions. For example, customers who visit an online store in search of digital cameras are asked whether they want the cameras displayed by brand or by price. Then, when they visit again, in an attempt to "convert" visitors into buyers, the cameras are immediately displayed in the order the customers preferred during their initial visits.

Geographic Location and Mobile Targeting

Smartphones and GPS devices have created highly effective targeting opportunities. For example, Broadway theaters in New York City can offer unsold seats for the same day's performance at discounted prices by sending messages to the mobile phones of people travelling by cabs through the city's theater district, because a cab's GPS device shows its location on tracking devices.

Customers' mobile devices brought upon problems for brick-and-mortar retailers. Customers frequently engage in **showrooming**, which occurs when consumers use smartphones to scan the bar codes of products displayed in physical stores and then check the items' prices online in order to purchase them at the lowest prices. In order to combat showrooming, some physical stores started **geofencing**, which consists of sending promotional alerts to the smartphones of customers who opted into this service, when the customers near or enter the store.[37]

Purchase Behavior

Many marketers are now using **predictive analytics**, which are measures that forsee consumers' future purchases on the bases of past buying information and other data, and also evaluate the impact of personalized promotions stemming from the predictions. Some of the questions that can be answered by predictive analytics include:

1. When leaving a given page, what content and pages are visitors likely to look at next?
2. Which websites' features (and combinations of features) are likely to persuade people to register with a website?
3. What are the characteristics of visitors who are likely to return to a website and why?
4. What factors make visitors click on specific ads?

Predictive analytics often focuses on *noticing* significant changes in a consumer's buying behavior, because such changes often alert marketers that consumers are going through significant life events, such as the arrival of a new baby, upcoming marriage, and even divorce; during such times, consumers are inclined to spend more money and shop less carefully. For example, Target developed a model that detects changes in women's buying pattern to identify their pregnencies early on. Figure 2.8 describes how this model was used to market baby-related products to Susan, a hypothetical Target shopper. After Susan started buying several products that she had never bought before, Target's predictive analytics signaled that these purchases strongly indicate that Susan is expecting a baby. Using this data and a lot of additional information, Target then started sending Susan applicable promotional offers and also took steps to conceal its spying on her.[38]

The Information "Arms Race"

Collecting and analyzing the right data are the foundations of effective behavioral targeting. Marketers strive to anticipate occurrences and events in consumers' lives that affect the consumers' shopping. Marketers are also eager to discover information about people's interests and the social networks with which they connect online. Because of its strategic importance, the competition for more and more data about consumers has become extraordinarily fierce.

Companies such as Acxiom are virtually unknown to the public, but their databases "know" everything about the majority of American adults, such as a person's age, race, gender, weight, height, marital status, education level, politics, buying habits, household health worries, and vacation dreams. They collect this data from public records, consumer surveys, credit card information, and other sources. Acxiom's servers process more than 50 trillion data "transactions" a year, and its database contains information about 500 million active consumers worldwide, with about 1,500 data points per person. In addition, these firms are rapidly developing increasingly sophisticated methods that "mine" and refine data. They recruited digital experts from Microsoft, Google, Amazon, and Myspace and are using multiplatform databases to predict consumer behavior.[39]

Online marketers customize ads to users based on the users' past activities, which are tracked and collected via "cookies," which are bits of computer code placed on browsers to keep track of online activity. Acxiom integrates what it knows about consumers' offline, online, and even mobile selves, and creates in-depth behavior portraits known as "360-degree view" on consumers. Chapter 15 addresses the ethics of gathering a lot of personal information about consumers without their knowledge.

FIGURE 2.8
Behavioral Targeting

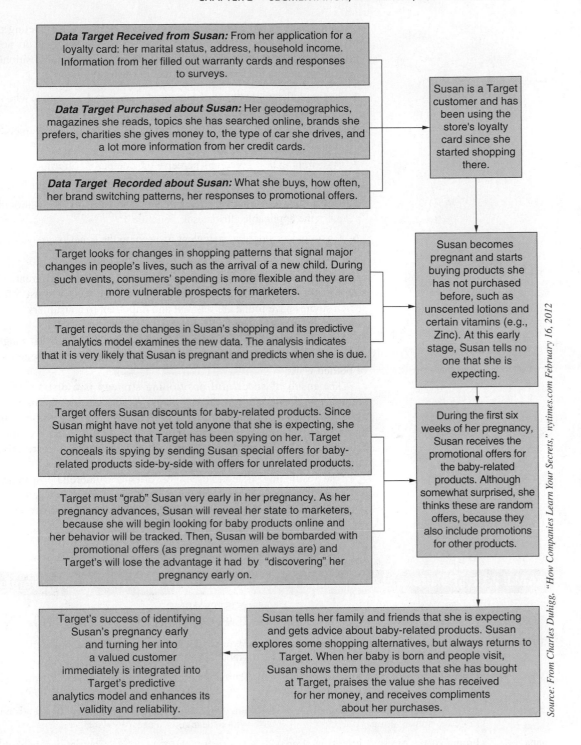

Source: From Charles Duhigg, "How Companies Learn Your Secrets," nytimes.com February 16, 2012

Positioning and Repositioning

Learning Objective

4 To understand how to position, differentiate, and reposition products.

After segmenting the market and selecting targeting prospects, marketers must persuade prospective buyers to buy the products that they offer, rather than competing products. **Positioning** is the process by which a company creates a distinct image and identity for its products, services, or brands in consumers' minds. The image and unique identity are called a "position." The position, which is intangible and exists only in the consumer's mind, represents how marketers want consumers to *perceive* products and brands (see Chapter 4). The result of effective positioning is a unique perception of the product in consumers' minds relative to competing offerings. Most new products fail because consumers perceive them as "me-too" offers that do not provide any advantages or unique benefits over competitive products because they are not positioned effectively.

The positioning process includes the following steps:

1. Defining the market in which the product or brand competes, who the relevant buyers are, and the offering's competition.
2. Identifying the product's key attributes and researching consumers' perception regarding each of the relevant attributes.
3. Researching how conumers perceive the competing offerings on the relevant attributes.
4. Determining the target market's preferred combination of attributes.
5. Developing a distinctive, differentiating, and value-based positioning concept that communicates the applicable attributes as benefits.
6. Creating a positioning statement focused on the benefits and value that the product provides and using it to communicate with the target audiences.

Marketers of different brands in the same category differentiate their labels effectively by stressing the benefits that their brands provide. The benefits must reflect product attributes that research studies have found are relevant and important to consumers. Positioning is especially difficult among commodities, where the physical characteristics of all the brands are identical, such as water. Nevertheless, marketers offer many brands of mineral water that range in price and are positioned differently. Table 2.12 describes the positioning claims, unique benefits, and prices of several brands of bottled water.

The result of successful positioning strategy is a distinctive brand image on which consumers rely in making product choices. A positive brand image also leads to consumer loyalty, promotes consumer interest in future brand promotions, and "inoculates" consumers against competitors' promotions. When new products arrive and the marketplace becomes more crowded, it is increasingly harder to create and maintain a distinctive brand image among many competing ones.

The positioning strategies used most often are: umbrella positioning, premier position, positioning against competition, key attribute, and finding an "un-owned" perceptual position. It must be noted that these strategies are not mutually exclusive and often overlap.

TABLE 2.12 Positioning, Advertised Benefits, and Prices of Bottled Water Brands

BRAND	DESCRIPTION	POSITIONING, UNIQUE BENEFIT	PACKAGING	PRICE*
Tŷ Nant,	From Wales. Award winning. Served at top hotels and restaurants.	Style. Status. Attention-grabbing bottle.	Cobalt or red glass, elegant bottle.	$2.50
Voss	From Norway. From a virgin aquifer that was shielded by ice and rock for centuries.	Purity.	Cylindrical, frosted glass, modern, engraved font.	$3.50
Fiji	From the rain forest. The company is committed to conservation.	Environmental—"drink with a clear conscience."	Conventional glass bottle, printed label.	$2.50
Jana	From Croatia. Artesian water from deep beneath the surface. Pure and balanced.	The perfect pH**.	Conventional tall bottle, printed label.	$2.25
GOTA	From the Guarani Aquifer in Argentina, which is one of the purest reserves of underground water on earth, consists of sandstones deposited 200 million years ago, and is overlaid with igneous basalt of low permeability, which provides a high degree of containment.	Perfectly selected by nature. Provides minerals that help one's body remain young, healthy, and lively.	Clear glass, unconventional clear glass bottle with elegant, dark print.	$3.80

Notes:
* Price of 1 liter bottle
** pH is a measure of a liquid's acidity level.

Source: John Foxx Collection. Imagestate

FIGURE 2.9 An illustration of a mobile user demonstrating the mobile network operator, Mobinil's brand philosophy – "*Dayman maa baad*" or "always together"

Umbrella Positioning

Umbrella positioning is a statement or slogan that describes the universal benefit of the company's offering. At times, this statement does not refer to specific products. McDonald's has used this strategy over the years, with slogans such as: "You deserve a break today" (1971); "Nobody makes your day like McDonald's can" (1981); "Make every time a good time" (2002); and "I'm Lovin' It" (2003).

This strategy works across a spectrum of products, as illustrated by Sila Edible Oils Company and Mobinil in Egypt. Sila focuses on clean, blemish-free oil. In Sila's promo ad, a chef emphasizes healthy living and repeats the phrase "*Monfadlek khodi balek*" ("please take care") while addressing women concerned with their families' health. By doing this, the brand asserts the importance of choosing pure oil for a wholesome diet. So, the brand's tagline promotes its entire offering, and not one specific product.

Mobinil, a mobile network company in Egypt, does the same with its slogan "*Dayman maa baad*" ("always together"). This slogan focuses on the notion of a unified, interconnected community facilitated by a mobile network operator. As a result, Mobinil has become a symbol of union, which greatly contributed to the company's domination of the market for mobile telecommunications services in the country.

Premier Position

This positioning strategy focuses on the brand's exclusivity. For example, the "snobby" positioning of The New York Times is "All the news that's fit to print." Sometimes, the brand centers on the belief that the higher the product's price, the higher its exclusivity. For example, the marketer of Joy (a fragrance brand) positioned it as "the costliest perfume in the world." Although all prestigious fragrances are very expensive, no other perfume marketer has claimed that its product is the *most* expensive. Chapter 4 describes the concept of price-quality relationship.

For years, L'Oreal's hair coloring product presented women with an unstated but obvious question: "Why should I use this product?" and then provided an answer in the form of a positioning statement: "Because I'm Worth It" (coined in 1971). In the age of feminism, this slogan sounds arrogant because it strongly implies that only a woman's physical appearance counts more than her profession and knowledge. Thus, L'Oreal changed its positioning to "Because We're Worth It." In addition to being a more timely tagline, the new slogan can also be readily translated into many languages.[40] Chapter 13 describes the importance of translating brand names and advertising themes to other languages.

Positioning against Competition

Some positioning statements acknowledge competing brands. For example, Avis claims that "We're No. 2. We Try Harder" and indirectly acknowledges the existence of Hertz, the number-one brand in car rentals. The positioning of 7Up as the "Uncola" recognized that Coke dominates the soft drink market. Contrasting one's brand with competitors is very effective in positioning and differentiation,

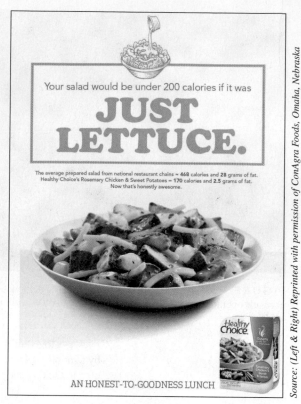

FIGURE 2.10 Differentiation: Healthy Choice versus Italian Subs and Prepared Salads

as illustrated by the Healthy Choice in Figure 2.10. The first ad positions Healthy Choice as a more nutritional lunch than Italian sub sandwiches and the other ad makes the same claim in comparison of prepared salads.

Key Attribute

Positioning based on relevant attributes often expresses the brand's superiority. The marketer of Bounty, a paper towels brand, initially positioned it as "the quicker picker upper" (presumably against Viva, its major competitor), later on as "the quilted picker upper," and then as "the clean picker upper." During an economic downturn, Bounty altered its positioning and appealed to consumers' frugality using the following statements: "With one sheet of Bounty, you'll have confidence in your clean," "One sheet keeps cleaning," and "Thick and absorbent Bounty helps you clean up quickly and easily, so you get more out of each day."[41]

Believing that consumers use brands to express their identities, some marketers have repositioned their products from focusing on functional attributes to focusing on how the products fit into a consumer's lifestyle. However, one study indicated that this approach is undesirable, because consumers' need for "self-expression" can be satiated not only by a brand's direct competitors but also by brands from unrelated product categories.[42]

The ad in Figure 2.11 features a high-definition GPS device that provides the most current traffic information. Thus, the ad's tag line—"Anything Less Is Just GPS"—proclaims the brand's superiority because of its high-definition display.

Un-Owned Position

Linguistically, perception is not a physical object and cannot be "owned." In marketing, the term "un-owned" position loosely means a perception that is not clearly associated with a brand or product. For example, in New York City, the Daily News newspaper specializes in sensationalized stories for readers without much education. In contrast, The New York Times focuses on articles written by famous and credible journalists for educated readers. *Long Island Newsday* positioned itself as "On top of the News and ahead of the Times," and targeted readers who wanted a

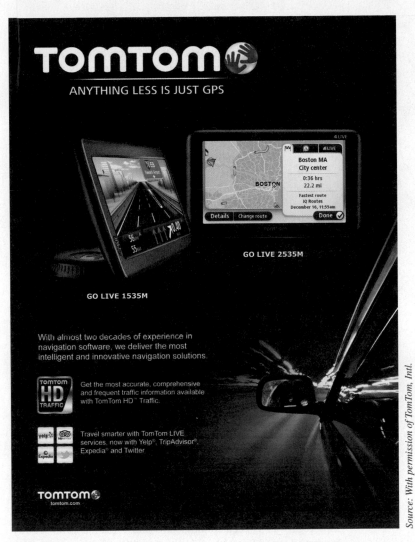

FIGURE 2.11 Positioning Focused on a Key Product Attribute:
A High-Definition GPS

newspaper that was not as "trashy" as The Daily News, but also not as highbrow as The New York Times.

Because unfilled or un-owned perceptual positions present opportunities for competitors, sophisticated marketers create many distinct product versions, often under the same brand, in order to fill as many positions as possible. For example, Visine originally consisted of eye drops to relieve redness. Visine's line now includes items for relief of multi-symptom, allergy, redness, and tired and dry eyes.[43] Crest toothpaste's line includes many categories of toothpaste offering distinct benefits, such as tartar, cavity, and sensitive teeth protection; toothpastes with baking soda and stripes; and Crest Kids. In response to the highly successful *Colgate Total*, Crest introduced a new line named *Crest Pro-Health*. In addition, the *Crest Expressions* line claims to "amaze the mouth," "awaken the senses," and "keep the taste buds tingling."[44] Crest offers each line's toothpaste in pastes, gels, liquid gels, and flavors. The marketers of Crest and Visine studied customers and discovered which attributes represent benefits that consumers seek from their products. By offering product versions that provide distinct benefits and filling as many positions as possible, the makers of Visine and Crest made it virtually impossible for other companies to penetrate their respective markets.

The un-owned position must be in the consumer's mind and not the marketer's. Stated differently, marketers must not look in the mirror (at themselves), but through the window, at consumers. For example, in 1967, a biochemist working for New York's Rheingold Brewery observed (figuratively, he looked in the mirror) that there was no beer catering to diet-conscious drinkers and introduced Gablinger's Diet Beer. The product failed because heavy beer drinkers—who account for more than 80% of all the beer sold—were not diet conscious. Later on, using the same beer formula, Miller introduced Miller Lite as the "less filling" beer, and the product was a great success. Miller discovered (figuratively, by looking at the outside) that heavy beer drinkers wanted a less filling beer so that they could drink more beer without feeling filled. The exact same physical product failed when it was positioned as a diet beer, but succeeded handsomely when it was positioned as a less-filling beer. Beer drinkers perceived the second positioning as beneficial. The Fage yogurt ad in Figure 2.12, for a "Ridiculously thick yogurt," stresses thickness as the product's primary benefit, and also distiguishes Fage from the "much thinner" American yogurts.

Repositioning

Repositioning is the process by which a company strategically changes the distinct image and identity that its product or brand occupies in consumers' minds. Companies do so when consumers get used to the original positioning and it no longer stands out in their minds. Similarly, when consumers begin to view the old positioning as dull, marketers must freshen up their brands' identities. At times, too many competitors stress the same benefit in their positioning, so marketers must uncover other attributes that consumers perceive as important. For instance, at present Fage Greek yogurt is "ridiculously thick" and Chobani (a competing brand of Greek yogurt) is marketed as "authentic, real, and indulgent." Let's assume that a new brand of Greek yogurt is introduced as "thickly authentic." If the new brand begins to gain market share, Fage and Chobani will have to reexamine their positioning claims. Table 2.13 features examples of umbrella repositioning.[45]

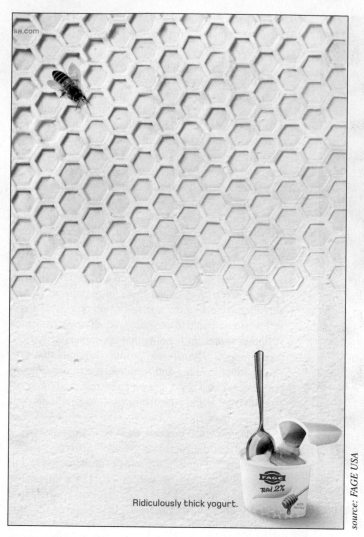

sa.com

Ridiculously thick yogurt.

source: FAGE USA

FIGURE 2.12 Fage Yogurt's Thickness: A Key Attribute and Occupying an "Un-Owned" Position

Another reason to reposition a product or service is to appeal to a new segment. For example, GM tried for years to convince younger consumers that Oldsmobile was not an "old folks" car and tried to reposition it as being "not your father's Oldsmobile." However, this effort failed because the "old folks" image of the brand was strongly set in the minds of car buyers, and GM stopped making this formerly highly successful brand.

A major factor that fueled the financial crisis of fall 2008 was consumers' excessive borrowing in the form of home equity loans. Traditionally, Americans looked forward to paying off their mortgages (the ritual of burning the mortgage note was an American tradition) and associated the term "second mortgage" with desperate borrowing, as a last resort. However, over the years, bank marketers repositioned this negatively perceived loan by luring consumers to get "equity loans" and use the funds for discretionary spending. In reality, an equity loan is a positive expression of the negatively perceived second mortgage. Consumers responded and used equity loans excessively and increasingly unwisely because the banks brilliantly repositioned the dreaded second mortgage. The banks convinced consumers to take advantage of their homes' appreciation and borrow money against the value of those homes. Banks advertised the new credit lines with such statements as "There's got to be at least $25,000 hidden in your house. We can help you find it." Marketers also replaced the term "equity loans" with "equity access," because a "loan" means borrowing, whereas consumers associate "access" with having resources. As the market for these lines of credit grew, the repositioning statements became bluntly aggressive, with slogans such as: "Is your mortgage squeezing your wallet? Squeeze back," "The smartest place to borrow? Your place," "The easiest way to haul money out of your house," and "You've put a lot of work into your home. Isn't it time for your home to return the favor?" The repositioning of the second mortgage was a spectacular success and since the 1980s equity loans ballooned from $1 billion to $1 trillion.[46] Apparently, consumers' needs were fulfilled, but the same strategies that filled these needs destabilized the world's financial structure.

Perceptual Mapping

Perceptual mapping is constructing a map-like diagram representing consumers' perceptions of competing brands along relevant product attributes. Perceptual maps show marketers:

1. How consumers perceive their brands in relation to competition.
2. How to determine the direction for altering undesirable consumer perception of their brands.
3. Gaps, in the form of un-owned perceptual positions, that represent opportunities for developing new brands or products.

The aim of perceptual mapping is to develop repositioning strategies and fine-tune the images (i.e., consumers' perceptions) of products and services. Figure 2.13 features a perceptual map of 10 well-known stores. It represents a hypothetical study in which researchers asked consumers how they perceived 10 stores along two dimensions: (1) "innovative" versus "traditional" and (2) "luxurious" (high-end) versus "thrifty" (low-end). The additional adjectives listed in the four quadrants represent words used to characterize the stores by the study's subjects. For example, consumers viewed Barneys as a very innovative, high-end store, and, additionally, as creative and up-to-date. On the map, Barneys stands by itself and far from Bloomingdale's, its closest competitor. In contrast, consumers perceived Macy's and Old Navy similarly and as rather non-distinct variety stores (note that this is a *hypothetical* example). The management of Macy's should recognize that it has a problem: consumers did not perceive the store accurately, because, in reality, it is neither very thrifty nor traditional. This indicates that the store's promotional messages must focus on "correcting" this image and

TABLE 2.13	Examples of Repositioning	
COMPANY	**PREVIOUS POSITIONING**	**UMBRELLA REPOSITIONING**
Hard Rock Café International	"You know who you are" appealed to the inner rebel in young adults, the company's primary target audiences, by referring to them as "rockers" and making them feel "young at heart."	"See the show" is focused on getting customers to believe that there is always something fun happening at Hard Rock restaurants, hotels, and hotel-casino combinations.
New York Lottery	"You got to be in it to win it." "You never know." "Good things happen in an instant."	"Be Ready" tells players that they are likely to win immediately and experience instant gratification. The "Good things happen in an instant" phrase is used as a tagline.
Yellow Tail, a line of wines imported from Australia	"Open for everything" and "Tails, you win" conveyed that the wine an unpretentious choice for those who do not know much about vintages and pairings.	"The go to" slogan reinforces the previous one and tells consumers that this wine is the default choice for everyday wine and suitable for most occasions.
Condominiums in New York City	High-flying slogans that expressed glamour, such as a condo being "not just an address but also an attitude."	Glitzy pitches and images have been replaced by slogans such as "clean styling and attractive prices." Private roof cabanas were converted into a common roof deck.
Banks	Before the financial crisis in the fall of 2008, banks aggressively promoted home equity loans with such lines "Need Cash? Use Your Home," and "The smartest place to borrow? Your place."	Less than a year after the financial crisis, which many angrily attributed to the banks' aggressive promotion of irresponsible spending (among other factors), the common theme in the banks' ads became "Can't we just move on?," illustrated by such semi-apologetic slogans as "We make money with you, not off you."
Chili's restaurant chain	Focused on the food itself and showed close-ups of food being prepared in slow motion.	Focused on the restaurant's personality and value and engaging the customer. For example: "Get out of the office more often, with Chili's $6 Lunch Break combos."

Sources: Stuart Elliott, "Choosing Between a Hard Rock and a Place," 11.22.10 nytimes.com; Stuart Elliott, "It Only Takes an Instant, Lottery Ads Declare," 5.9.11 nytimes.com; Stuart Elliott, "A Wine Brand Creates a New Theme to Help Spur Growth," 8.29.11 nytimes.com; Vivian S. Toy, "Goodbye, Glitzy Condo Pitches," 8.20.10 nytimes.com; Louise Story, "In Ads, Banks Try the Warm, Cozy Approach," 6.9.09 nytimes.com; Andrew Newman, "Bold Commercials and Flavors Aim to Spice Up Chili's Brand," nytimes.com, September 29, 2011.

convincing consumers that Macy's is more high-end than Old Navy. The study's respondents viewed Modell's and H & M as close competitors, and the Gap and Banana Republic as close competitors and middle-of-the-road in terms of pricing and innovativeness. To management, this indicates that the two stores must be positioned more clearly in consumers' minds. Bergdorf Goodman and Saks 5th Avenue were perceived as high-end competitors, and with Saks as a more traditional store.

FIGURE 2.13 A Perceptual Map of Well-Known Stores

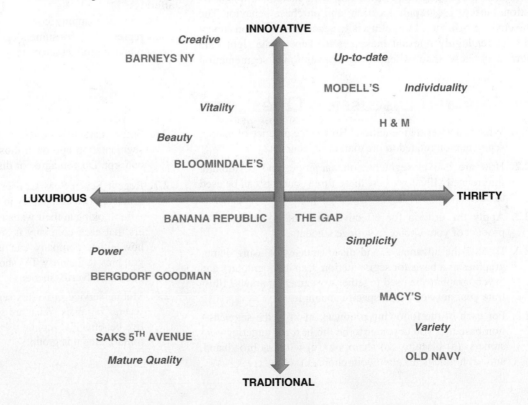

Summary

Learning Objective 1: To understand the interrelationship among market segmentation, targeting, and positioning and how to select the best target markets.

Market segmentation consists of dividing a potential market into distinct subsets of consumers. Each subset represents a consumer group with common needs and characteristic. Targeting means selecting one or more segments and approaching each one with a specially designed marketing mix. Besides aiding in the development of new products, segmentation studies assist in the redesign and repositioning of existing products, in the creation of promotional appeals, and in the selection of advertising media. To be a viable target market, a segment must be identifiable, sizeable, stable or growing, accessible, and congruent with the marketer's objectives and resources.

Learning Objective 2: To understand the bases used to segment consumers, including demographics, psychographics, product benefits sought, and product usage-related factors.

A segmentation strategy begins by dividing the market for a product into groups that are relatively homogeneous and share characteristics that are different from those of other groups. Broadly speaking, the shared characteristics include consumers' behaviors (e.g., how often do they buy the product) as well as their cognitions (e.g., attitudes towards new products). The bases for segmentation include demographics, personality and psychographics, geodemographics, product benefits, media exposure, usage rate, and usage occasion.

Learning Objective 3: To understand behavioral targeting and its key role in today's marketing.

Behavioral targeting consists of sending consumers personalized and prompt offers and promotional messages based on marketers' tracking of one or more of the following factors: online navigation, current geographic location, and purchase behavior. The objective of behavioral targeting is to reach the right consumers and deliver highly relevant messages to them at the right time more accurately than when using conventional segmentation

techniques. Many marketers use predictive analytics, which consists of methods predicting consumers' future purchases on the bases of past buying information and other data, and evaluating the impact of personalized promotions stemming from the predictions. Collecting the right data and analyzing it strategically are essential to effective behavioral targeting. Marketers collect and use information about consumers' interests, personal lives, and the social networks with which they connect online for targeting them with customized products and promotional messages.

Learning Objective 4: To understand how to position, differentiate, and reposition products.

After segmenting the market and selecting targeting prospects, marketers must persuade prospective buyers to buy the products that they offer, rather than competing products. Positioning is the process by which a company creates a distinct image and identity for its products, services, or brands in consumers' minds. The image and unique identity are called a "position." The "position," which is intangible and exists only in the consumer's mind, represents how consumers perceive the product. Positioning is more important to the ultimate success of a product than are its actual characteristics, although products that are poorly made will not succeed on the basis of image alone. The result of effective positioning is a unique perception of the product in the mind of the consumer. Most new products fail because consumers perceive them as "me too" offers that do not provide any advantages or unique benefits over competitive products.

Repositioning is the process by which a company intentionally changes the distinct image and identity that its products, services, and brands occupy in consumers' minds. Several reasons may force marketers to reposition products, such as many competitors focusing on the same product attribute in positioning their offerings.

Perceptual mapping consists of constructing a map-like diagram representing consumers' perceptions of competing brands along relevant product attributes.

Review and Discussion Questions

2.1. What is market segmentation? How is the practice of market segmentation related to the marketing concept?

2.2. How are market segmentation, targeting, and positioning interrelated? Illustrate how these three concepts can be used to develop a marketing strategy for a product of your choice.

2.3. Apply the criteria for effective targeting to marketing a product of your choice to college students.

2.4. Discuss the advantages and disadvantages of using demographics as a basis for segmentation. Can demographics and psychographics be used together to segment markets? Illustrate your answer with a specific example.

2.5. For each of the following products, identify the segmentation base that you consider to be the best for targeting consumers: (a) biscuits, (b) shampoo, (c) wireless broadband, and (d) holidays. Explain your choices.

2.6. Some marketers consider benefit segmentation to be the segmentation approach most consistent with the marketing concept. Do you agree or disagree with this view? Why?

2.7. Regent Seven Seas Cruises and Royal Caribbean International are two companies in the vacation and travel industry. After looking at their websites, describe the kind of consumers that each company is seeking to attract. Also, describe how either company can use demographics and psychographics to identify TV shows and magazines in which to place its advertisements.

2.8. Mobile service providers segment their customers based on several variables. What are some of these variables? Identify five benefits that mobile users might seek that could be used for targeting this group.

2.9. Using one of the frameworks described in Table 2.3, find at least two suitable segments for one of the following products: (1) SUVs; (2) financial retirement plans; or (3) LED TVs. Using Nielsen's online Zip Code Look-Up, identify the closest location of consumer clusters belonging to these segments to your home. Describe the segments you chose and why, and the locations you looked up.

2.10. Explain how marketers can use each of the following pieces of data in predictive analytics:

a. The websites consumers visit.

b. Consumers' levels of engagement with visited websites (i.e., the pages viewed, length of visits, frequency of return to the site).

c. Visitors' and consumers' interests, lifestyles, and personalities (e.g., from the contents of their blogs, tweets, and Facebook profiles).

d. Visitors' purchases, almost purchases, abandoned carts, and product returns and exchanges.

2.11. How would you segment the market of consumers who would like to order Oakley sunglasses online? Explain your answer.

2.12. What is umbrella positioning? Illustrate its pros and cons with the help of an example.

2.13. How is the understanding of consumers' perceptions of a product's attributes used to position a brand within that product category?

2.14. What is the relationship between benefit segmentation and positioning?

2.15. Why do marketers have to reposition their brands? Illustrate with examples.

2.16. How might retailers reevaluate the segmentation base of social class during a recession? What kinds of tactics might they use, and how might this help the customer and the retailer?

2.17. Describe the relationship between behavioral targeting and predictive analytics.

Hands-on Assignments

2.18. Select a product and brand that you use frequently and list the benefits you receive from using it. Without disclosing your list, ask a fellow student who uses a different brand in this product category (preferably a friend of the opposite sex) to make a similar list for his or her brand. Compare the two lists and discuss the differences and similarities among the benefits that you and your friend seek from the same product category.

2.19. Does your lifestyle differ significantly from your parents' lifestyle? If so, how are the two lifestyles different? What factors cause these differences?

2.20. Have a look at one of your social media accounts. How many "Likes" do you have? How many comments do you have? How quickly do people post comments in response

to your content? How many people are you following? What are the things that people are interested in, and what topics do they engage in the most? Explain how this information could prove valuable to marketers.

2.21. Imagine you are the brand director of a successful, but mature antiseptic cream gradually heading toward the decline stage of product life cycle. How might you go about repositioning your product? How will this affect the life of the antiseptic cream?

2.22. Find three print advertisements directed at three different clusters, each one belonging to one of the three frameworks listed in Table 2.3: PRIZM, P$YCLE, and ConneXions. Explain your choices.

Key Terms

- behavioral data *56*
- behavioral targeting *69*
- benefit segmentation *65*
- cognitive factors *56*
- innovators *63*
- demographic segmentation *57*
- family life cycle *59*
- geodemographics *60*
- geofencing *70*
- market segmentation *52*
- perceptual mapping *76*
- positioning *71*
- predictive analytics *70*
- PRIZM *60*
- product awareness status *68*
- product involvement *68*
- psychographics *63*
- repositioning *75*
- showrooming *70*
- social class *60*
- targeting *52*
- umbrella positioning *73*
- usage occasion (situation) segmentation *68*
- usage rate segmentation *67*
- VALS *63*

Case One:

Porsche

"How Porsche Created New Relevance for a Revered Icon"

Lead Agency: **Cramer-Krasselt**
Contributing Agencies: **Struck Axiom/OmnicomMediaGroup**

Strategic Challenges

Was America's luxury sports car category on the ropes? With the uncertain economic times, it seemed no one needed a sports car and it was no longer publicly acceptable to share a longing for one—let alone the sports car of all sports cars, a Porsche.

This was the problem weighing on the minds of the Porsche team in 2010. In the larger sports car category, which was down 56%, Porsche was experiencing precipitous declines. Since 2007, sales of the 911—Porsche's revered icon, and the heart and soul of the brand—were down 54%. Not only were 911 sales down dramatically, sales of *all* two-door Porsche sports cars (including the 911, Boxster, and Cayman) had fallen an unprecedented 58%. Thus, the loss of relevance and diminished road presence of the 911, Porsche's flagship model, had wide reverberations that strongly affected the very identity of Porsche.

The key challenge: Figuring out how to sell a product that's synonymous with success and status during a time when affluent consumers were examining, reexamining, and justifying each and every purchase.

The challenge was exacerbated by several factors. Porsche had no new product to generate buzz. In fact, the 911 was in the last year of its current model cycle, and the new 911 model, the Type 991, had already been publicly announced and was eagerly anticipated by Porsche enthusiasts. Those who were interested in buying a new 911 were on the sidelines, waiting for the new model, and some dealers were taking orders. To meet its aggressive sales goals, Porsche knew it had to reach beyond its core enthusiasts, and establish brand relevance with a larger audience, many of whom had never owned or considered a Porsche before. Porsche intended to sell its current $80,000-plus vehicle without any major promotional or pricing programs, and with a communications budget that was half that of its closest competitor.

Objectives

1. Change Brand Perceptions: Within the challenging economic environment, the company had to make the Porsche 911 and mid-engine models (Boxster and Cayman) relevant and worth their price.
2. Dealer Lead Generation: With the 911 sales down 54%, people weren't even putting Porsche sports cars on their shopping lists, and dealers were running low on leads. Porsche had to significantly increase purchase consideration and "find a dealer" requests on its website.
3. Sales: With the new 911 model going into production, the company needed to increase existing 911 sales and ultimately sell the remaining models. To do this, it had to broaden its audience and create new brand relevance—reaching both men and women, many of whom had never even considered a Porsche.

Insights

Porsche assumed that for those who could afford it, the economic downturn had made owning a Porsche socially unacceptable. People didn't want to pull up to their driveway in a shiny new sports car, for fear of looking insensitive to all that was going on around them, including neighbors and friends who might be struggling financially.

This assumption was wrong. Potential customers weren't afraid to spend the money, but the economic times were dictating *how* they spent it. *"I respect and like the 911. I even test-drove one about five years ago before I bought my Mercedes. It's definitely a great sports car, but it didn't have the luxury touches I was looking for. It felt too impractical to drive every day.—It's a great third car, but not a daily driver"* (quote from a customer).

Buying a Porsche wasn't socially unacceptable; it was personally unjustifiable. *"If I bought a Porsche, when would I actually drive it?"* *"Now isn't the time to buy a weekend toy* (quotes from customers). Customers perceived Porsche as an *epic* sports car.

This perceived epic sports car status of the 911 Porsche kept people away from showrooms and resulted in dated brand images. The timeless shape of the 911 had slowly evolved over the years, but with no radical exterior changes to cue reconsideration, many prospects assumed that the car was more for racing than daily driving. They thought the interior of the cars had nothing more than three pedals and a gear shift, resulting in a rough and uncomfortable ride they wouldn't want to drive daily, making it hard to justify spending more than $80,000. Even though they wanted a sports car, what they needed was one car that could comfortably fill multiple roles—and because they didn't see Porsche as this type of car, they compromised. They settled for luxury cars with less magic but more versatility, even calling them their "compromise cars."

Porsche's research studies discovered that few people realized that the 911s are built to be driven every day, year round. They are not precious, but solid and substantial. The company needed to expand the Porsche 911 and mid-engine driving occasions and let people know that Porsches are comfortable, functional, and intended to be driven every day.

The Big Idea

Porsches are amazing sports cars designed to be driven hard every day, making everyday driving more magical.

Questions

1. Before you read this case, did you believe that Porsche cars were meant to be driven everyday or only for special occasions? Explain your answer.

2. Since it was founded, in 1931, the core of the Porsche brand was "outstanding engineering, tradition, and versatility." How does the "everyday magic" campaign fit within the core's three elements?

3. Was the campaign designed to reposition the Porsche 911? Explain your answer.

4. Although not stated overtly, the campaign targeted *two* segments. Which ones? Explain your choices.

5. Find three print ads for the "everyday magic" campaign (available online) and evaluate their persuasive effectiveness. Do you find any of these ads "unrealistic?" Explain.

6. How would Porsche determine whether the campaign's objectives were achieved?

Source: Effie Worldwide, Effie Showcase Winners. Reprinted by permission. Porsche is a 2012 Silver Effie Winner. For information on Effie's programs for students, visit the Collegiate Effies at www.effie.org

Consumer Motivation and Personality

Learning Objectives

1 To understand the dynamics of motives, needs, and goals and how they shape consumer behavior.

2 To understand motivation theories and their applications to consumer behavior.

3 To understand how to identify and measure motives.

4 To understand the scope of personality and theories of its development.

5 To understand how innovativeness and other personality traits influence consumer behavior.

6 To understand the personification of products and brands and its strategic applications.

7 To understand self-image and its impact on consumer behavior.

MOTIVATION is the driving force that impels people to act. It represents the reasons one has for acting or behaving in a particular way. **Needs** are circumstances or things that that are wanted or required, and they direct the motivational forces.

Human beings' most basic needs are biological and fulfilling them sustains physical existence and safety. For example, when parents send their kids to school they expect a physically safe environment. The ad in Figure 3.1 targets drivers by showing parents' concerns for their children's safety when the youngsters get off a school bus. The slogan "It shouldn't be this dangerous" urges drivers to stop when they see flashing lights and ensure that kids get home safely.

Personality consists of the inner psychological characteristics that both determine and reflect how we think and act, which together form an individual's distinctive character. Consumers often purchase products and brands because advertisers have given them "personalities" that differentiate them from competing offerings. **Brand personification** occurs when consumers attribute human traits or characteristics to a brand. A "brand personality" provides an emotional identity for a brand, which produces sentiments and feelings toward it among consumers. For example, consumers often view certain brands as "exciting," sophisticated," or "warm."

Brand personification is a form of **anthropomorphism**, which refers to attributing human characteristics to something that is not human. For example, Figure 3.2 features Mr. Clean, who is one of America's most beloved and instantly recognized "persons." The brand and mascot are owned by Procter and Gamble and used for positioning and marketing cleaning solutions and related items. The mascot was introduced in the 1950s, quickly became a best seller, and "his" product line now includes bathroom cleaners, a magic eraser, multisurfaces liquids and sprays, cleaning tools, and "Pro" items for heavy and outdoor cleaning. Procter and Gamble continues to add items to the brand and consumers buy them because they personify Mr. Clean: He is strong, tenacious, competent, dependable, and friendly.

This chapter begins with a discussion of consumers' needs and motivation and then describes how consumers' personalities influence their buying behavior.

FIGURE 3.1 An Appeal Directed at Safety Needs

FIGURE 3.2 Brand Personification

The Dynamics of Motivation

Learning Objective

1 To understand the dynamics of motives, needs, and goals and how they shape consumer behavior.

Motivation drives consumers to buy and is triggered by psychological tension caused by unfulfilled needs. Individuals strive both consciously and subconsciously to reduce this tension through selecting goals and subsequent behavior that they anticipate will fulfill their needs and thus relieve them of the tension they feel. Whether gratification is actually achieved depends on the course of action pursued. Personality characteristics guide the goals that people set and the courses of action they take to attain these goals.

The foundation of marketing is identifying and satisfying needs. Marketers do not create needs, although in many instances they strive to make consumers more keenly aware of unfelt or dormant needs. Savvy companies define their business in terms of the consumer needs they satisfy rather than the products they produce and sell. Because consumers' basic needs do not change, but the products that satisfy them do, a corporate focus on developing products that will satisfy consumers' needs ensures that the company stays in the forefront of the search for new and effective solutions. By doing so, such companies are likely to survive and grow despite strong competition or adverse economic conditions. In contrast, companies that define themselves in terms of the products they make may suffer or even go out of business when their products are replaced by competitive offerings that better satisfy consumers' needs.

For example, Procter and Gamble defines its business as "providing branded products and services of quality and value that improve the lives of the world's consumers"*—a need-focused definition— rather than stating that the company sells products such as detergents, shampoos, diapers, household cleaners, and dozens of other items (i.e., a product-oriented approach). Similarly, the mission of the Ritz Carlton Hotels and Resorts is not to provide rooms for overnight stays, but "the genuine care and comfort of guests," through providing customers an experience that "enlivens the senses, instills well-being, and fulfills even the unexpressed needs and wishes"** of guests. The diagram in Figure 3.3 illustrates the process of motivation.

Needs

There are two types of human needs: **Physiological needs** are innate (biogenic, primary) and fulfilling them sustains biological existence. They include the need for food, water, air, protection of the body from the outside environment (i.e., clothing and shelter), and sex.

Psychological needs are learned from our parents, social environment, and interactions with others. Among many others, they include the needs for self-esteem, prestige, affection, power, and achievement.

Both types of needs affect our buying decisions. For example, all individuals need shelter from the elements and therefore buy homes. However, the kind of homes they buy is the result of psychological, learned needs. A young, professional couple working in New York City's financial district is likely to buy a loft downtown, because they have no children and want to live in a somewhat unusual space, which they can decorate modernly and impress their friends. However, a couple in their 60s, whose kids have left their suburban home, may buy a home in a managed community that has a pool, clubhouse, and other communal amenities, where they are likely to meet new friends with whom they can socialize and travel.

Goals

Goals are the sought-after results of motivated behavior, and all human behavior is goal oriented. There are two types of goals: **Generic goals** are outcomes that consumers seek in order to satisfy physiological and psychological needs. **Product-specific goals** are outcomes that consumers seek by using a given product or service. For example, when a student tells his parents that he wants to become an entrepreneur, he expresses a generic goal. If he says he wants to earn an MBA from Stanford, he expresses a product-specific goal. The ad for the Kaplan Bar Review course in Figure 3.4

FIGURE 3.3
The Motivation Process

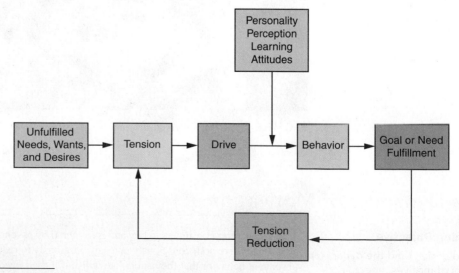

* Proctor & Gamble
** Ritz Carlton

tells prospective students that they can "conquer the bar." That is, they can achieve a generic goal (i.e., passing the bar exam) by completing the Kaplan course (i.e., a product-specific goal).

As consumption became technology-driven, marketers have become keenly interested in the motivations of bloggers and individuals who post comments online. Such individuals influence other consumers, because people perceive both positive and negative reviews from other consumers as more credible information than advertisements. In fact, many bloggers shape the views of thousands of consumers, and many have documented their influence by following the number of responses that they get to their postings and tweets (see Chapter 9). Marketers would be delighted to have any—even the smallest—degree of influence over online writers whose essays and comments focus on products and consumption, because understanding the motivations of the writers often enables marketers to influence what is being written. One study identified three motivations for blogging: (1) self-expression; (2) documenting one's life (i.e., keeping a diary); and (3) identifying other influential bloggers.[1] Table 3.1 summarizes the motivations of consumers who share information on Facebook.[2]

Need Arousal

Most of an individual's needs are dormant much of the time. The arousal of any need at a specific moment in time may be caused by biological stimuli, emotional or cognitive processes, or stimuli in the outside environment. A drop in blood sugar level or stomach contractions will trigger awareness of a hunger need. A decrease in body temperature will induce shivering, which makes the individual aware of the need for warmth. Most of these physiological cues are involuntary, but they arouse needs that cause uncomfortable tensions until they are satisfied. For example, a person who is cold may turn up the heat in his bedroom and make a mental note to buy a warm sweater to wear around the house.

In cognitive arousal, random thoughts can lead to a cognitive awareness of a need to act. For instance, a greeting card company's ad might remind a viewer that her grandchild's birthday is next week, and that it is time to run out and purchase a gift and a birthday card, and be ready for the

TABLE 3.1	Motivations of Facebook Users

INFORMATION SHARING

To provide information
To share information that might be useful to others
To share news

CONVENIENCE AND ENTERTAINMENT

Because it's enjoyable
Because it's an easy way to stay in touch with people
Because I just like to use it

PASSING TIME

Because I'm bored
Because I have nothing better to do
Because everyone else is doing it

INTERPERSONAL UTILITY

To meet people with similar backgrounds
To meet people with same interests as mine

CONTROL

Because I want someone to do something for me
To tell others what to do

PROMOTING WORK

To promote the organization I work for
To promote my personal work

birthday party. Many promotional messages are cues designed to arouse consumer needs. Without these cues, consumers' needs may remain dormant. Thus, creative marketing messages arouse needs by stimulating a psychological desire or imbalance in consumers' minds. The goal then becomes to act on the desire, and reduce the felt imbalance by buying products.

Selecting Goals

Usually, consumers set purchase-related goals that satisfy more than one need. We buy clothing for protection and for a certain degree of modesty; in addition, our clothing fulfills a wide range of personal and social needs, such as acceptance by others. People with different needs may seek fulfillment by selecting the same goal, and people with the same needs may seek fulfillment via different goals. For example, two people driven by the need for achievement might seek fulfillment in different ways. One may seek advancement and recognition through a professional career, whereas the other may choose to run marathons.

For any given need, there are many different and appropriate goals. The goals that individuals select depend on those individuals' personal experiences and knowledge, physical capacity, prevailing cultural norms and values, and the goal's accessibility in the individuals' physical and social environments. For example, a young woman may wish to get a deep, even tan and may envision spending time in the sun as a way to achieve her goal. However, if her dermatologist advises her to avoid direct exposure to the sun, she may settle for a self-tanning cosmetics instead. The goal object has to be both socially acceptable and physically accessible. If cosmetic companies did not offer effective alternatives to tanning in the sun, our young woman would either have to ignore the advice of her dermatologist or select a substitute goal, such as fair (but undamaged) youthful-looking skin.

The motivation to select goals can be either positive or negative. We may feel a driving force *toward* some object or condition or a driving force *away* from some object or condition. For example, a person may be encouraged to start exercising in order to avoid health problems (i.e., a negative outcome) or in order to look more attractive and dynamic (i.e., a positive outcome). Positive outcomes that we seek are called **approach objects**; negative outcomes that we want to prevent are called **avoidance objects**. For instance, a college is an approach object to a high school graduate who is motivated by the desire for higher education. Another person knows that his parents would criticize him if he does not go to college, so he goes to college to avoid being criticized. Both individuals have the same goal—college education—but are motivated to adopt that goal in opposite ways.

Needs and Goals Are Interdependent

Needs and goals are interdependent; neither exists without the other. However, people are often not as aware of their needs as they are of their goals. For example, a teenager may not consciously be aware of his social needs, but may join a number of chat groups online to meet new friends. Similarly, people are aware that they need to buy certain items, but may have different goals when they go shopping. One study contrasted the shopping motivations of pairs of mothers and daughters and discovered that daughters go to malls for recreational or social shopping, whereas their mothers tend to be more purposeful in their shopping.[3] Another study identified several factors that motivate people to go shopping:[4]

1. Seeking out specific goods, such as going to to supermarket to buy foods or a hardware store to purchase needed tools or materials.

2. Recreational shopping occurs when consumers do not have an urgent product need in mind, but go shopping for the personal enjoyment of shopping.

3. Activity-specific shopping, which includes such motivations as sensory stimulation, gift shopping, and bargain hunting.

4. Demand-specific shopping, in which consumers are motivated by such factors as service convenience, store atmosphere, assortment innovations, and assortment uniqueness.

Needs Are Never Fully Satisfied

Human needs are never fully or permanently satisfied. As individuals attain their goals, they develop new ones. If they do not attain their goals, they continue to strive for old goals or they develop substitute goals. For example, a person may partially satisfy a need for power by working as an administrative assistant to a local politician, but this vicarious taste of power may not sufficiently satisfy her need; thus, she may strive to work for a state legislator or even to run for political office herself. In this instance, temporary goal achievement does not adequately satisfy the need for power, and the individual strives ever harder to satisfy that need more fully.

New Needs Emerge as Old Ones Are Satisfied

Some motivational theorists believe that a hierarchy of needs exists and that new, higher-order needs emerge as lower-order needs are fulfilled.[5] For example, a man whose basic physiological needs (e.g., food, housing, etc.) are fairly well satisfied may turn his efforts toward achieving acceptance among his neighbors by joining their political clubs. Once he is confident that he has achieved acceptance, he then may seek recognition by giving lavish parties or building a larger house.

Success and Failure Influence Goals

Individuals who achieve their goals usually set new and higher goals for themselves. They raise their aspirations because success in reaching lower, earlier goals makes them more confident of their ability to reach higher goals. Conversely, those who do not reach their goals sometimes lower their aspirations. For example, a college senior who is not accepted into medical school may try instead to become a dentist.

The effects of success and failure on goal selection have strategic implications for marketers. Goals should be reasonably attainable and advertisements should not promise more than can be delivered; instead, they should only promise what the product is able to live up to. Furthermore, products and services are often evaluated by the size and direction of the gap between consumer expectations and objective performance. Thus, even a good product will not be repurchased if it fails to live up to unrealistic expectations created by ads that overpromise. Similarly, consumers often regard mediocre products with greater satisfaction than is really warranted if the products' performance exceeds their expectations.

When people cannot attain their primary goals, they often set "substitute goals." Although the substitute goal may not be as satisfactory as the primary goal, it may be sufficient to dispel uncomfortable tension. Continued deprivation of a primary goal may result in the substitute goal assuming primary-goal status. For example, a woman who has stopped drinking whole milk because she is dieting may actually begin to prefer skim milk. A man who cannot afford a BMW may convince himself that a new, sporty, and less expensive Japanese car has an image he prefers.

Frustration and Defense Mechanisms

Frustration is the feeling that results from failure to achieve a goal, and **defense mechanisms** are cognitive and behavioral ways to handle frustration. At one time or another, everyone has experienced the frustration that comes from the inability to attain a goal. The barrier that prevents attainment of a goal may be personal (e.g., limited physical or financial resources) or an obstacle in the physical or social environment (e.g., a storm that causes the postponement of a long-awaited vacation). Regardless of the cause, individuals react differently to frustrating situations. Some people manage to cope by finding their way around the obstacle or, if that fails, by selecting a substitute goal. Others are less adaptive and may regard their inability to achieve a goal as a personal failure. Such people are likely to adopt a defense mechanism to protect their egos from feelings of inadequacy.

People cope with frustrations differently. For example, two young women yearn for European vacations that they cannot afford. The coping woman may select a less expensive vacation trip to Disneyland or a national park. The other woman, who cannot readily cope with frustration, may react with anger toward her boss for not paying her enough money to afford the vacation she desires, or she may persuade herself that Europe is unseasonably and uncomfortably warm this year. These latter two possibilities are examples, respectively, of **aggression** and **rationalization**, defense mechanisms that people sometimes adopt to protect their egos from feelings of failure when they do not attain their goals. Other defense mechanisms include **regression**, **withdrawal**, **projection**, **daydreaming**, **identification**, and **repression**. These defense mechanisms are described in Table 3.2. This list of defense mechanisms is far from exhaustive, because individuals tend to develop their own ways of redefining frustrating situations to protect their self-esteem from the anxieties that result from experiencing failure. Marketers often consider this fact in their selection of advertising appeals and construct advertisements that portray a person resolving a particular frustration through use of the advertised product. The

TABLE 3.2	Defense Mechanisms
DEFENSE MECHANISM	**DESCRIPTION AND ILLUSTRATIONS**
Aggression	In response to frustration, individuals may resort to aggressive behavior in attempting to protect their self-esteem. The tennis pro who slams his tennis racket to the ground when disappointed with his game or the baseball player who physically intimidates an umpire for his call are examples of such conduct. So are consumer boycotts of companies or stores.
Rationalization	People sometimes resolve frustration by inventing plausible reasons for being unable to attain their goals (e.g., not having enough time to practice) or deciding that the goal is not really worth pursuing (e.g., how important is it to achieve a high bowling score?).
Regression	An individual may react to a frustrating situation with childish or immature behavior. A shopper attending a bargain sale, for example, may fight over merchandise and even rip a garment that another shopper will not relinquish rather than allow the other person to have it.
Withdrawal	Frustration may be resolved by simply withdrawing from the situation. For instance, a person who has difficulty achieving officer status in an organization may decide he can use his time more constructively in other activities and simply quit that organization.
Projection	An individual may redefine a frustrating situation by projecting blame for his or her own failures and inabilities on other objects or persons. Thus, the golfer who misses a stroke may blame his golf clubs or his caddy.
Daydreaming	Daydreaming, or fantasizing, enables the individual to attain imaginary gratification of unfulfilled needs. A person who is shy and lonely, for example, may daydream about a romantic love affair.
Identification	People resolve feelings of frustration by subconsciously identifying with other persons or situations that they consider relevant. For example, slice-of-life commercials often portray a stereotypical situation in which an individual experiences a frustration and then overcomes the problem by using the advertised product. If the viewer can identify with the frustrating situation, he or she may very likely adopt the proposed solution and buy the product advertised.
Repression	Another way that individuals avoid the tension arising from frustration is by repressing the unsatisfied need. Thus, individuals may "force" the need out of their conscious awareness. Sometimes repressed needs manifest themselves indirectly. The wife who is unable to bear children may teach school or work in a library; her husband may do volunteer work in a boys' club. The manifestation of repressed needs in a socially acceptable form is called *sublimation*, another type of defense mechanism.

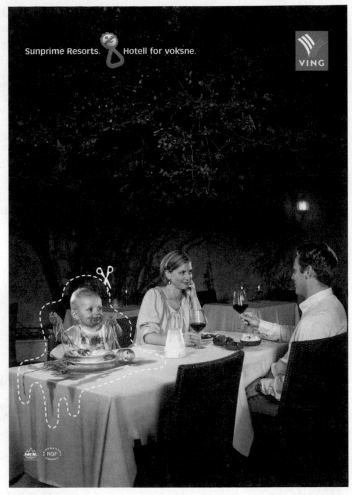

Source: Ving Norgeas

FIGURE 3.5 An Appeal to Daydreaming

ad in Figure 3.5 playfully suggests that parents who are frustrated because their vacations are not relaxing sometimes daydream (or fantasize) about their kids "disappearing." The ad's tagline and the funny visual "cut outs" tell parents that Ving Resorts is a place where their daydreams come true.

Systems of Needs

Learning Objective

2 To understand motivation theories and their applications to consumer behavior.

Over the years, several psychologists have developed lists of human needs, but there is no single, comprehensive, and commonly accepted list. Although there is little disagreement about physiological needs, there are distinct differences of opinion about defining and categorizing needs with nonphysical origins, that is, psychological (or psychogenic) needs.

Murray's List of Psychogenic Needs

In 1938, the pioneering psychologist Henry Murray prepared an extensive list of psychogenic needs, which represented the first systematic approach to the understanding of nonbiological human needs. Murray believed that although each need is important in and of itself, needs can be interrelated, can support other needs, and can conflict with other needs. For example, the need for dominance may conflict with the need for affiliation when overly controlling behavior drives away friends, family, and spouses. Murray also believed that environmental circumstances strongly influence how psychogenic needs are displayed in behavior. For example, studies have indicated that people with a high need for achievement tend to select more challenging tasks. Also, people with high needs for affiliation are part of large social groups, spend more time in social interaction, and feel lonely when faced with little social contact.

Murray organized his needs into five groups: *ambition, materialistic, power, affection,* and *information* needs. Later on, the psychologist Allen Edwards developed a self-administered *personality*

TABLE 3.3	Psychogenic Needs Applicable to Consumer Behavior	
NEED	ILLUSTRATIVE CHARACTERISTICS	PROMOTIONAL APPLICATIONS
Achievement: accomplish tasks, succeed, and overcome obstacles.	Do the best and work hard in any undertaking. Be able to do things better than others.	Messages that encourage and illustrate success (e.g., advertising education).
Exhibition: shock or thrill others and be the center of attention.	Tell amusing jokes at parties. Say things that others regard as witty and clever.	Messages showing attention from others when they notice one's possessions (e.g., expensive cars).
Affiliation: spend time, form strong friendships and attachments with others.	Be loyal to and share things with friends. Help friends in trouble. Be confided in by others and told about their troubles.	Messages showing people enjoying themselves in large groups (e.g., vacations, shopping situations).
Power/Dominance: control, influence, and lead others.	Seek leadership in groups. Supervise and direct the actions of others.	Messages showing actual or symbolic dominance (e.g., being a chief executive; owning a powerful car).
Change: seek new experiences and avoid routine.	Doing new and differ like eating in new restaurants, going on trips, and avoiding conventional situations.	Messages stressing novelty, uniqueness, and breaking with routines (e.g., adventure travel and active vacations).
Order: keeping things neat and organized.	Planning and organizing the details in any undertaking. Setting definite times for activities.	Promoting devices that save space and keep things firmly in place (e.g., dividers and organizers for closets, drawers, and garages).

inventory that became one of the most widely used tools in the study of personality traits. Table 3.3 lists the definition and illustrative characteristics of several needs researched by Murray and Edwards that are most relevant to consumer behavior.

Maslow's Hierarchy of Needs

Psychologist Abraham Maslow formulated a theory of human motivation based on the notion that there is a hierarchy of human needs.[6] **Maslow's hierarchy of needs** consists of five levels of human needs, which rank in order of importance from lower-level (biogenic) needs to higher-level (psychogenic) needs. The theory states that individuals seek to satisfy lower-level needs before higher-level needs. The lowest level of unsatisfied needs motivates a person's behavior. When that need is fairly well satisfied, the individual is motivated to fulfill a need in the next level of the hierarchy. When that need is satisfied, the need in the next level is one's primary motivator, and so on. However, if a person experiences renewed deprivation regarding a formerly met lower-level need, that need becomes the dominant factor in the person's motivation, even if only temporarily. For example, if a person who is well off and trying to satisfy his ego needs loses his job, he reverts or "goes back" to trying to satisfy his security needs; if he gets a new job that pays well, thus satisfying security needs, he will once again "move" to a higher level in the hierarchy.

Figure 3.6 presents a diagram of Maslow's hierarchy of needs. For clarity, the levels appear as mutually exclusive. According to the theory, however, there is some overlap among the levels, as no need is ever completely satisfied. Thus, to some extent, all levels of need below the level that is currently dominant continue to motivate behavior. Nevertheless, the prime motivator—the major driving force within the individual—is the lowest level of need that remains largely unsatisfied.

Physiological Needs

Maslow maintained that **physiological needs** are the first and most basic level of human needs. These primary needs, which are required to sustain biological life, include food, water, air, shelter, clothing,

FIGURE 3.6

Maslow's Hierarchy of Needs

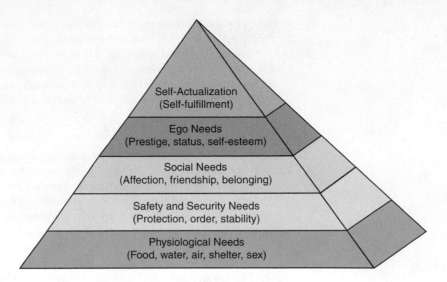

and sex—all biogenic needs. According to Maslow, physiological needs are dominant when they are chronically unsatisfied: "For the man who is extremely hungry, no other interest exists but food. He dreams food, he remembers food, he thinks about food, he emotes only about food, he perceives only food, and he wants only food."[7]

Safety Needs

After physiological needs have been satisfied, **safety and security needs** become the driving force behind an individual's behavior. These needs are concerned not only with physical safety, but also with order, stability, routine, familiarity, and control over one's life and environment. For example, health and the availability of health care are important safety concerns. Savings accounts, insurance policies, education, and vocational training are all means by which individuals satisfy the need for security.

Social Needs

The third level of Maslow's hierarchy consists of **social needs**, such as love, affection, belonging, and acceptance.

Egoistic Needs

When social needs are more or less satisfied, the fourth level of Maslow's hierarchy becomes operative. This level includes **egoistic needs**, which can take either an inward or an outward orientation:

1. *Inwardly directed ego needs* reflect an individual's need for self-acceptance, self-esteem, success, independence, and personal satisfaction.

2. *Outwardly directed ego needs* include the needs for prestige, reputation, status, and recognition from others.

Need for Self-Actualization

According to Maslow, once people sufficiently satisfy their ego needs, they move to the fifth level. The **self-actualization need** refers to an individual's desire to fulfill his or her potential—to become everything that he or she is capable of becoming. For example, an artist may need to express herself on canvas; a research scientist may strive to find a new drug that eradicates cancer. Advertising an organization as one that "lets you do great things," or enables you to "be all you can be," appeals to the need for self-actualization.

Evaluation of Maslow's Theory

Maslow's theory states that higher-order needs become the driving force behind human behavior as lower-level needs are satisfied. The theory says, in effect, that dissatisfaction, not satisfaction, motivates behavior. The need hierarchy has received wide acceptance in many social disciplines because it appears to reflect the assumed or inferred motivations of many people in American society. The five levels of needs are sufficiently generic to encompass most individual needs. The major problem with the theory is that it cannot be tested empirically; there is no way to measure precisely how satisfied one level of need must be before the next higher need becomes operative. The need hierarchy is very closely bound to the American culture (i.e., it appears to be both culture- and time-bound). In non-Western countries, the needs specified by Maslow are ranked differently. Indeed, research indicated that in some countries, safety, love, and belonging are at the apex of the needs pyramid.[8]

Marketing Applications of Maslow's Theory

Despite its limitations, Maslow's hierarchy has been a highly useful framework for marketers. Maslow's needs hierarchy is readily adaptable to market segmentation and the development of advertising and other marketing communications appeals, because there are consumer goods designed to satisfy each of the need levels, and because most needs are shared by large segments of consumers. For example, individuals buy health foods, medicines, and low-fat products to satisfy physiological needs. They buy insurance, preventive medical services, and home security systems to satisfy safety and security needs. Consumers buy personal care and grooming products (e.g., cosmetics, mouthwash, shaving cream), as well as most clothes, in order to satisfy social needs. They purchase high-tech and luxury products, such as elaborate sound systems, high-end wristwatches, sports cars, and expensive furniture, to fulfill ego and esteem needs. Postgraduate college education, hobby-related products, and exotic and physically challenging adventure trips are often sold as ways of achieving self-actualization.

Advertisers and other forms of marketing messages can also use the need hierarchy to position products; that is, to develop a strategy that will make consumers perceive a product or brand as its marketer intends. The need hierarchy is a versatile tool for developing positioning strategies because different appeals for the same product can be based on different needs. For example, a study that tested the appeal of different military recruitment slogans found that the two slogans that resonated well with potential recruits were "Be All You Can Be" and "The Few, the Proud, the Marines." The slogans that most respondents disliked were "I Want You" and "Join the People Who've Joined the Army."[9] Clearly, egoistic and self-actualization needs are the prime motivators behind joining the armed forces.

A Trio of Needs

Another framework for organizing human needs is known as the trio of needs: the needs for power, affiliation, and achievement (these needs are reflected in Table 3.3 and also in Maslow's needs hierarchy). Individually, each of the three needs can affect consumer motivation.

Power

The **power need** is an individual's desire to control his or her environment. It includes the need to control other persons and various objects. This need appears to be closely related to the ego need, in that many individuals experience increased self-esteem when they exercise power over objects or people.

Affiliation

Affiliation is a well-researched social motive that significantly influences consumer behavior. The **affiliation need** is very similar to Maslow's social need and suggests that behavior is strongly influenced by the desire for friendship, acceptance, and belonging. People with high affiliation needs tend to be socially dependent on others and often buy goods that they feel will meet with the approval of friends. Teenagers who hang out at malls or techies who congregate at computer shows often do so more for the satisfaction of being with others than for the purpose of making a purchase.

Achievement

Individuals with a strong **achievement need** often regard personal accomplishment as an end in itself. They are self-confident, enjoy taking calculated risks, actively research their environments, and value feedback, often in the form of monetary rewards. People with high achievement prefer situations in which they can take personal responsibility for finding solutions.[10] Because of this, portraying achievement is a useful promotional strategy for many products and services, especially those targeting educated and affluent consumers. (Figure 3.4 represents an appeal based on the need for achievement, as does Figure 11.4.)

The Measurement of Motives

Learning Objective

3 To understand how to identify and measure motives.

How are motives identified? How are they measured? How do researchers know which motives are responsible for certain kinds of behavior? These are difficult questions to answer because motives are hypothetical constructs; that is, they cannot be seen or touched, handled, smelled, or otherwise tangibly observed. For this reason, no single measurement method can be considered a reliable index of motivation. Instead, researchers usually rely on a combination of research techniques when trying to establish the presence and/or the strength of various motives. By combining several research methods—including responses to questionnaires or survey data (i.e., self-reports of opinions and behaviors) and insights from focus group sessions and depth interviews (i.e., to discover underlying motives)—consumer researchers achieve more valid insights into consumer motivations than they would by using any single technique.

Self-Reporting

Self-reported measures of motives consist of written statements which ask respondents to indicate how relevant each statement is to them. The researchers administering these measures politely ask respondents not to think too much before providing their answers, because, if they do so, they might figure out what the statements measure and not answer honestly. If so, the subjects' responses are likely to reflect not who they *are*, but how they *wish* to be perceived. For example, a respondent who figures out (correctly) that the statement "one does one's best work when the assignment is difficult" measures a person's need for achievement, may "strongly agree" with the statement even if she does not really find it applicable because she wants to be perceived as an achiever. If used correctly, self-reported measures assess people's motives fairly accurately.

Qualitative Research

Frequently, respondents may be unaware of their motives, or may be unwilling to reveal them when asked directly. In such situations, researchers use **qualitative research** to delve into the consumer's unconscious or hidden motivations. Many qualitative methods also termed **projective techniques** because they require respondents to interpret stimuli that do not have clear meanings, based on the assumption that the subjects will "reveal" or "project" their subconscious, hidden motives onto the ambiguous stimuli. The findings of qualitative research methods are highly dependent on the training and experience of the analyst; the findings represent not only the data themselves but also what the analyst thinks they imply. Though some marketers are concerned that qualitative research does not produce hard numbers that objectively "prove" the point under investigation, others are convinced that qualitative studies are sometimes more revealing than quantitative studies (see Chapter 16). The major types of qualitative methods used to study motivation are featured in Table 3.4, together with applicable examples.[11]

Motivational Research

The term **motivational research**, which should logically include all types of research into human motives, has become a "term of art." It refers to qualitative studies conducted by Dr. Ernest Dichter in the 1950s and 1960, which were designed to uncover consumers' subconscious or hidden motivations. Based on the premise that consumers are not always aware of the reasons for their actions, motivational research attempted to discover underlying feelings, attitudes, and emotions concerning product, service, or brand use. This premise reflects Sigmund Freud's psychoanalytic theory of personality, which maintains that unconscious needs or drives—especially biological and sexual drives—are at the heart of human motivation and personality.

When Dr. Dichter, trained as a clinical psychoanalyst in Vienna, arrived in the United States in the late 1930s, he joined a major New York advertising agency rather than establish a clinical

TABLE 3.4	Qualitative Measures of Motives
RESEARCH METHOD	**DESCRIPTION AND EXAMPLES**
Storytelling	Storytelling consists of having customers tell real-life stories regarding their use of the product under study. By using this method to study parents' perceptions of diapers, Kimberly-Clark discovered that parents viewed diapers as clothing related to a particular stage in the child's development. Thus, if their children wore diapers too long, parents became distressed and embarrassed because it was an overt sign of their failure to toilet-train their children. The company introduced its highly successful Huggies Pull-Ups training pants—a product that established a new category in the U.S. diaper industry.
Word Association	In the **word association method**, respondents are presented with words, one at a time, and asked to say the first word that comes to mind. This method is highly useful in determining consumers' associations with existing brand names and those under development. In sentence completion, respondents are asked to complete a sentence upon hearing the opening phrase (e.g., "People who drive convertibles . . .").
Thematic Apperception Test	Developed by Henry A. Murray, the **Thematic Apperception Test** consists of showing pictures to individual respondents and asking them to tell a story about each picture. For example, Clearasil employed an image of a female looking into a mirror under the caption "Here is a teenager looking into the mirror and seeing pimples." The researchers discovered that teenagers view their lives as fast-paced and socially active and that the discovery of a pimple abruptly disturbs the swiftness of their lives. The resulting advertising depicted a teenage male walking briskly down the street and spotting a pimple on his face in a store window. All motion around him stops. He applies Clearasil, the pimple disappears, and life resumes its pace.
Drawing Pictures	Visual images are often used to study consumers' perceptions of various brands and to develop new advertising strategies. For example, when respondents were asked to draw pictures of the typical Pillsbury cake-mix user, their drawings depicted old-fashioned, chubby females wearing frilly aprons. When asked to draw pictures of the Duncan Hines cake-mix user, their drawings showed slim, "with it" women wearing heels and miniskirts. These findings provided important input to Pillsbury concerning the need to reposition its product.
Photo Sorts	In a study using photo sorts conducted by the advertising agency for Playtex (a manufacturer of bras), respondents received stacks of photos depicting different types of women and asked to select pictures portraying their own self-images. Although many of the respondents were overweight, full-breasted, and old-fashioned in appearance, they selected photos showing physically fit, well-dressed, and independent women. The advertising agency advised Playtex to stop stressing the comfort of its bras in its ads and designed a new campaign showing sexy, thin, and big-bosomed women under the slogan: "The fit that makes the fashion."

Sources: Emily Eakin, "Penetrating the Mind by Metaphor," New York Times, February 23, 2002, B9, Bl 1; Ronald B. Leiber, "Storytelling: A New Way to Get Close to Your Customer," Fortune, February 3, 1997; and Bernice Kramer, "Mind Games," New York, May 8, 1989, 33–40.

practice. Dr. Dichter applied Freud's psychoanalytical techniques to the study of consumer buying habits and used qualitative research to figure out *why* consumers did what they did. Marketers became fascinated by the glib, entertaining, and sometimes surprising explanations offered for consumer behavior, especially since many of these explanations were grounded in sex. For example, Dichter told marketers that consumers bought cigarettes and Life Saver candies because of their sexual symbolism, that men regarded convertible cars as surrogate mistresses, and that women baked cakes to fulfill their reproductive yearnings. Before long, almost every major advertising agency in the country had a psychologist on staff to conduct motivational research studies. Table 3.5 includes a sample of product profiles created by Dichter and his colleagues.

Modern motivational research includes many qualitative methods and procedures and is well established in consumer research.[12] It includes research methods not only from psychology, but also from sociology and anthropology. Qualitative consumer research methods, consisting of focus group sessions and depth interviews, are routinely used by businesses seeking to gain deeper insights into the *whys* of consumer behavior. Motivational research often reveals unsuspected consumer

TABLE 3.5	Examples of Dichter's Subconcious Interpretations
PRODUCT	**SUBCONSCIOUS INTERPRETATION**
Baking	Baking expresses femininity and motherhood by evoking nostalgic memories of delicious odors pervading the house when the mother was baking. When baking a cake, a woman is subconsciously and symbolically going through the act of giving birth, represented by the baked product being pulled from the oven. Thus, when a woman bakes a cake for a man, she is offering him a symbol of fertility.
Automobiles	A car allows consumers to convert their subconscious urges to destroy and their fear of death—two key forces in the human psyche—into reality. For example, the expression "step on it" stems from the desire to feel power, and the phrase "I just missed that car by inches" reflects the desire to play with danger. Based on this view, Dichter advised Esso (now Exxon) to tap into consumers' aggressive motives for driving cars in promoting the superiority of its gasoline product. The slogan "Put a tiger in your tank" was developed as a result of his advice. Dichter also maintained that cars have personalities, and that people become attached to their cars and view them as companions rather than objects. This notion stands behind his views that a man views a convertible as a mistress and a sedan as his wife.
Dolls	Dolls play an important part in the socialization of children and are universally accepted as an essential toy for girls. Parents choose dolls that have the kind of characteristics they want their children to have, and the doll is an object for both the parents and the children to enjoy. When Mattel introduced Barbie in 1959, the company hired Dichter as a consultant. His research indicated that although girls liked the doll, their mothers detested the doll's perfect bodily proportions and Teutonic appearance. Dichter advised Mattel to market the doll as a teenage fashion model, reflecting the mother's desire for a daughter's proper and fashionable appearance.
Ice cream	Ice cream is an effortless food that does not have to be chewed and that melts in your mouth, a sign of abundance, an almost orgiastic kind of food that people eat as if they want it to run down their chins. Accordingly, Dichter recommended that ice cream packaging should be round, with illustrations that run around the box panel, suggesting unlimited quantity.

motivations concerning product or brand usage and is often used to develop ideas for promotional campaigns. Qualitative research also enables marketers to explore consumer reactions to product ideas and advertising copy at an early stage, and avoid the costly errors resulting from using ineffective and untested ads. Furthermore, motivational research findings provide consumer researchers with insights that serve as the foundations of structured, quantitative marketing research studies, which employ larger and more representative consumer samples than qualitative studies.

Building on the studies of Dr. Dichter and other motivational researchers, the Qualitative Research Consultants Association (QRCA) was established with the objective of applying an interdisciplinary orientation to consumer motivation research. The membership of QRCA consists of qualitative researchers who regularly conduct focus groups and one-on-one, in-depth interviews for client marketing companies that seek to identify the underlying needs and motives of their customers. Through its publications and conferences, the QRCA has brought about an expansion of the methodologies used in consumer research.

The Nature and Theories of Personality

Learning Objective

4 To understand the scope of personality and theories of its development.

Personality consists of the inner psychological characteristics that both determine and reflect how we think and act. The emphasis in this definition is on *inner characteristics*—those specific qualities, attributes, traits, factors, and mannerisms that distinguish one individual from other individuals. As discussed later in this chapter, the deeply ingrained characteristics that we call personality influence the individual's product choices: They affect the way consumers respond to marketers' promotional efforts, and when, where, and how they consume many products or services. Therefore, the identification of specific personality characteristics associated with consumer behavior has been highly effective in the development of market segmentation and promotional strategies.

The Facets of Personality

Psychologists' research into human personality has not been uniform. Some have emphasized the influence of heredity and early childhood experiences on personality development. Others have stressed broader social and environmental influences. Some theorists view personality as a unified whole, whereas others focus on specific traits. Overall, researchers agree on the following: (1) personality reflects individual differences; (2) personality is generally consistent and enduring; and (3) although it is enduring, personality can change.

Personality Reflects Individual Differences

Because the inner characteristics that constitute an individual's personality are a unique combination of factors, no two individuals are exactly alike. Nevertheless, many individuals may possess a single or even a few personality characteristics, but not others. For instance, some people can be described as "high" in consumer ethnocentrism (i.e., unwillingness to accept foreign-made products), whereas others can be described as "low" in ethnocentrism (i.e., not reluctant to buy foreign-made products). Personality enables marketers to categorize consumers into different groups on the basis of one or several traits, because consumers who belong to a given segment are often "high" on a particular personality characteristic, whereas consumers from another segment score "low" on that same characteristic.

Personality Is Consistent and Enduring

Generally, an individual's personality tends to be both consistent and *generally* enduring. Indeed, the sibling who comments that her sister "has always cared a great deal about her clothes from the time she was a toddler" is supporting the contention that personality has both consistency and endurance. Both qualities are essential if marketers are to explain or predict consumer behavior in terms of personality. Marketers cannot change consumers' personalities to conform to their products. However, if they know which personality characteristics influence specific consumers' responses, they can appeal to the relevant traits inherent in their target consumers. For instance, if a marketer knows that one of the firm's products attracts consumer innovators, it can create marketing messages that appeal to innovative consumers.

Personality May Change

Although personality is generally enduring, under certain circumstances, personalities change. For instance, major life events, such as marriage, the birth of a child, the death of a parent, or a change of job and/or profession strongly affect personality. One's personality changes not only in response to abrupt events, but also as part of a gradual maturing process: "He's more mature, and now he's willing to listen to points of view that differ from his own," says an aunt after not seeing her nephew for several years.

Theories of Personality

There are three major theories of personality: (1) Freudian theory, (2) neo-Freudian theory, and (3) trait theory. We have chosen them over other theories because each has played a role in the study of the relationship between consumer behavior and personality.

Freudian Theory

The premise of **Freudian theory** is that *unconscious* needs or drives, especially sexual and other biological drives, are at the heart of human motivation and personality. Freud constructed his theory on the basis of patients' recollections of early childhood experiences, analysis of their dreams, and the specific nature of their mental and physical adjustment problems. Freud proposed that the human personality consists of three interacting systems: the id, the superego, and the ego. Figure 3.7 shows the interrelationships among Freud's three interacting systems.

The **id** is the "warehouse" of primitive and impulsive drives—basic physiological needs such as thirst, hunger, and sex—for which the individual seeks immediate satisfaction without concern for the specific means of satisfaction. The Godiva ad in Figure 3.8 captures the mystery and excitement aroused by these "primal forces."

In contrast to the impulsive (and selfish) id, the **superego** is the individual's internal expression of society's moral and ethical codes of "proper" or "correct" conduct. The superego's role is to see that individuals satisfy their needs in a socially acceptable fashion. Thus, the superego is a kind of "brake" that restrains or inhibits the impulsive forces of the id. Finally, the **ego** is the individual's conscious control. It functions as an internal monitor that attempts to balance the impulsive demands of the id and the sociocultural constraints of the superego.

CHAPTER 3 • CONSUMER MOTIVATION AND PERSONALITY **97**

FIGURE 3.7
Freud's Theory

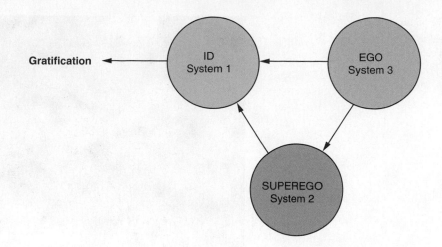

Freud emphasized that an individual's personality is formed as he or she passes through a number of distinct stages of infant and childhood development: the *oral*, *anal*, *phallic*, *latent*, and *genital* stages. According to Freudian theory, an adult's personality is determined by how well he or she deals with the crises that are experienced while passing through each of these stages (particularly the first three). For instance, if a child's need for food is not adequately satisfied at the first stage of development, he may become "fixated" at this stage, and, as an adult, his personality will reflect dependence on others. As another example, an individual who is treated impatiently during toilet training may become an adult obsessed with cleanliness and neatness.

Neo-Freudian Personality Theory

Neo-Freudian theory maintains that, in addition to Freud's concepts, social relationships play a crucial role in the development of personality. Several of Freud's colleagues disagreed with his contention that personality is primarily instinctual and sexual in nature. These neo-Freudians believed that social relationships are fundamental to the formation and development of personality. For instance, Alfred Adler viewed human beings as seeking to attain various rational goals, which he called *style of life*. He also placed much emphasis on the individual's efforts to overcome *feelings of inferiority* (i.e., by striving for superiority). Harry Stack Sullivan, another neo-Freudian, stressed that people continuously attempt to establish significant and rewarding relationships with others. He focused on the individual's efforts to reduce tensions such as anxiety.

Karen Horney was also interested in anxiety and studied the impact of child–parent relationships on the individual's desire to reduce feelings of anxiety. Horney proposed that individuals be classified into three personality groups:[13]

1. **Compliant individuals** are those who move *toward* others and wish to be loved, wanted, and appreciated.
2. **Aggressive individuals** are those who move *against* others and desire to excel and win admiration.
3. **Detached individuals** are those who move *away* from others and seek independence, self-reliance, self-sufficiency, and freedom from obligations.

Researchers developed a personality test based on Horney's theory (the CAD test) and used it to study consumer behavior.[14] The initial CAD research uncovered a number of tentative relationships between college students' scores and their product and brand usage patterns. For example, highly compliant students liked name-brand products such as Bayer aspirin, whereas aggressive subjects preferred Old Spice deodorant over other brands (seemingly because of its masculine appeal); and highly detached students were heavy tea drinkers (possibly reflecting their desire not to conform).

Many marketers use aspects of neo-Freudian theories intuitively. For example, marketers who position their products or services as providing an opportunity to belong or to be appreciated by others in a group or social setting are following Horney's characterization of the compliant individual. To illustrate, an ad for a digital camera featuring others complimenting the photographer's pictures appeals to compliant persons. An ad featuring a rider on a black mountain bike riding alone down steep hills appeals to aggressive persons.

FIGURE 3.8
An Appeal to Id-Like Primitive
Drives: Feeling Like a Diva

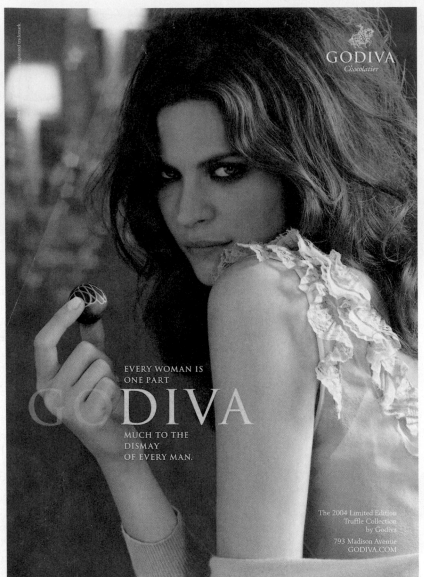

source: Godiva Chocolates

Trait Theory

Trait theory represents a departure from the qualitative, nonempirical approaches of the Freudian
and neo-Freudian movements. **Trait theory** focuses on empirical measures of personality in terms
of specific psychological characteristics, called "traits." Traits are personal characteristics or features
that set one person apart from another person. Trait theorists use personality tests (or inventories) that
pinpoint individual differences in terms of "high" versus "low" scores on specific traits. Researchers
developed tailor-made, single-trait personality tests for consumer behavior studies. These personality tests measure such traits as **innovativeness** (how receptive a person is to new consumer-related
experiences or the early consideration and purchase of new products and services), **materialism** (the
degree of the consumer's attachment to worldly possessions), and **ethnocentrism** (the consumer's
likelihood to accept or reject foreign-made products).

Researchers have discovered that personality traits are linked to consumers' consumption of
broad product categories rather than specific brands. For example, a statistical correlation between
a given personality trait and whether or not an individual regularly eats peanut butter is more likely
to occur than a correlation between that trait and the brand of peanut butter purchased. Furthermore, marketers study the influence of personality on consumption behavior because such knowledge enables them to segment consumers effectively, and develop advertisements that target specific
segments. In the next section, we discuss several personality traits that provide particularly useful
insights about consumer behavior.

Personality Traits and Consumer Behavior

Learning Objective

5 To understand how innovativeness and other personality traits influence consumer behavior.

We now explore the relationship between personality traits and consumer behavior. We begin with a discussion of the personality traits related to one's receptivity to new products. Afterwards, we examine the personality traits that are closely related to this dimension, which are dogmatism, social character, and the need for uniqueness. We note that these traits apply to the behavior of all consumers, whether or not they are among the first to purchase newly introduced products. Lastly, we describe other consumption-related personality traits, including optimum stimulation level (OSL), sensation seeking, variety or novelty seeking, need for cognition, visualizers versus verbalizers, materialism, fixated consumption, compulsive consumption, and consumer ethnocentrism.

Consumer Innovators and Innovativeness

Innovators are the first to try new products, product line extensions, and services because they are open to new ideas and practices. Their response to newly introduced products is critical to the success or failure of new products. Consumer innovators are enthusiastic about innovative products and can speed up the market acceptance of innovations, because they tell others about their purchases and often show them the new products. Furthermore, as more consumer innovators discuss the new products online, their domains of innovative behavior expand.[15] Table 3.6 presents illustrative opinions of an innovator of high-tech products.

Innovativeness is the degree of a consumer's willingness to adopt new products and services shortly after the products are introduced. One study discovered four motivational factors that inspire consumer innovativeness:

1. *Functional factors* reflect interest in the performance of an innovation.
2. *Hedonic factors* relate to feeling gratified by using the innovation.
3. *Social factors* reflect the desire to be recognized by others because of one's pursuit of innovations.
4. *Cognitive factors* express the mental stimulation experienced by using an innovation.[16]

Whereas most researchers view innovativeness as a single personality trait, one study identified three levels of innovativeness:[17]

1. *Global innovativeness*—a trait that exists independent of any product-related context and represents the "very nature" of consumers' innovativeness
2. *Domain-specific innovativeness*—a narrowly defined activity within a specific domain or product category
3. *Innovative behavior*—actions or responses that indicate early acceptance of change and adoption of innovations (e.g., being among the first to purchase new and different products or services).

TABLE 3.6	Illustrative Opinions of an Innovator of High-Tech Products

- I'm not brand loyal; I'm always looking for the "best" and "latest" in consumer technology.
- When I go into a technology store, I tend to tell the staff about the products, rather than them telling me.
- My friends often ask me questions before they purchase things dealing with new consumer technologies.
- I enjoy buying and trying very new consumer technology.
- When I see something new in the technology stores that I regularly visit, I "play" with it.
- I often get bored with rather new technological products and give them to my friends.
- I often look at technological websites and blogs, or social network sites, for more information about new technologies.
- I always read the technology section in the newspaper and then go online to check out the new products described.
- Every year, I look up the annual "holiday gift buying guides" because they always feature many technological products.

As expected, there is a positive relationship between innovativeness and using the Internet and new technologies. One study reported that heavy Internet shoppers saw themselves as being able to control their own future, used the Internet to seek out information, enjoyed change, and were not afraid of uncertainty.[18] Another study found that while online banking was positively associated with Internet-related innovativeness (i.e., domain-specific innovativeness), global consumer innovativeness was negatively related to embracing online banking; these results highlight the importance of researching domain-specific innovativeness.[19] Researchers have also discovered that consumer innovativeness strongly affects consumers' likelihood to purchase brand extensions, and therefore firms introducing such products must target innovative consumers.[20] Several studies showed that consumer innovativeness shaped buying decisions to a greater degree than such factors as price consciousness, value consciousness, and perceived price variation.[21]

Dogmatism

Dogmatism is one's degree of rigidity—the opposite of being open-minded—toward information and opinion contradictory to one's beliefs and views (i.e., closed-mindedness).[22] A person who is highly dogmatic approaches the unfamiliar defensively and with uncertainty and discomfort. In contrast, a person who is less or not dogmatic readily considers unfamiliar or opposing beliefs. Generally, consumers who are not dogmatic prefer innovative products rather than traditional ones.

Highly dogmatic consumers tend to be more receptive to ads that contain appeals from authoritative figures, such as celebrities and experts. In contrast, low-dogmatic consumers are more receptive to messages that stress factual differences, product benefits, and other product-usage information. Researchers found that consumers scoring high on the traits of "openness to experiences" (similar to low dogmatism) and "extraversion" (which is related to personal energy, ambition, venturesomeness, and being outgoing) responded favorably to emotional messages, and were likely to purchase and become loyal to the brand advertised.[23]

Social Character: Inner- versus Other-Directedness

Inner-directed consumers rely on their own inner values or standards in evaluating new products and are likely to be consumer innovators. Conversely, **other-directed** consumers look to others for guidance as to what is appropriate or inappropriate and are unlikely to be consumer innovators. Inner- and other-directed consumers are receptive to different types of promotional messages. Inner-directed people prefer ads that stress product features and personal benefits, whereas other-directed people prefer ads that feature social acceptance and respond favorably to appeals portraying social or group interactions. The ad in Figure 3.9 features an inner-directed person experiencing adventure and wildness by himself. The ad's secondary tagline—"This is Outward Bound. This challenge belongs to you"—focuses on a person's inner-directedness.

Need for Uniqueness

Many consumers acquire and display material possessions because they want to be differentiated from other people. Consumers' **need for uniqueness** is defined as an individual's pursuit of differentness relative to others that is achieved through the acquisition of consumer goods in order to enhance one's personal and social identity. Individuals with a high need for uniqueness adopt new products and brands quicker than others. They prefer creative products that counter conformity and are outside group norms, and avoid the similarity reflected in buying mainstream products.

Understanding this personality trait is highly pertinent to the fashion industry, because clothing trends and styles are ever changing. Many marketers target people with a high need for uniqueness with marketing stimuli designed to enhance self-perceptions of uniqueness. Illustrative opinions of a consumer with a high need for uniqueness appear in Table 3.7.

Optimum Stimulation Level

Optimum stimulation level (OSL) is the degree to which people like novel, complex, and unusual experiences (i.e., high OSL) or prefer a simple, uncluttered, and calm existence (i.e., low OSL). Research has found that consumers seeking high levels of optimum stimulation are more willing to take risks, more likely to try new products and be innovative, and seek to maintain high optimum stimulation levels while shopping.[24] A study of college students' tendency to purchase "mass customized" clothes (e.g., a pair of jeans that is specially measured, cut, and sewn so they offer a better fit or appearance) discovered that people with high OSL wanted to: 1. "experiment with personal

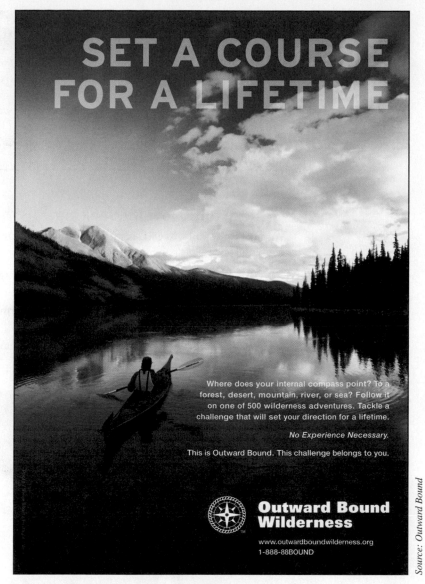

FIGURE 3.9 An Appeal to Inner-Directed Consumers

appearance" (e.g., "I try on some of the newest clothes each season to see how I look in the styles"), and 2. "enhance their individuality" (e.g., "I try to buy clothes that are very unusual").[25]

OSL scores also reflect a person's desired level of lifestyle stimulation. For instance, consumers whose actual lifestyles are equivalent to their OSL scores said that they are "quite satisfied" with their lives, whereas those whose lifestyles are understimulated (i.e., their OSL scores are greater than their lifestyle) felt "bored." This suggests that the relationship between consumers' lifestyles and their OSLs probably influences their choices of products or services and how they manage and spend their time. For instance, a person who feels bored (an understimulated consumer) is likely to be attracted to a vacation that offers a great deal of activity and excitement. In contrast, a person who feels overwhelmed (an overstimulated consumer) is likely to seek a quiet, isolated, relaxing, and rejuvenating vacation.

Sensation Seeking

Closely related to the OSL concept is **sensation seeking**: one's need for varied, novel, and complex sensations and experiences, and the willingness to take risks for the sake of such experiences. For example, many teenage males with high sensation-seeking scores engage in "extreme sports" forms of biking, skateboarding, and rollerblading. One study discovered that consumers who scored high on sensation seeking and innovativeness were more likely to incorporate volunteerism into their vacations.[26] The ad for Rock Resorts in Figure 3.10 displays the tagline "BE" as a cue for a sensual experience, and the ad's copy invites guests to "embrace the true spirit" and "sectrets" of a special destination.

TABLE 3.7	Illustrative Opinions of a Young Executive with a High Need for Uniqueness

- When I travel, I'm always seeking out unusual gifts for myself.
- I'm happy when other people tell me that my taste is "different" and "uncommon."
- I work at maintaining my own unique persona.
- Some of my acquaintances think I'm somewhat of a weirdo in my seeking to be different.
- Standing out and being different is important to me.
- I stop buying brands when everyone starts to buy them.
- Being different is my own personal trademark.

Variety and Novelty Seeking

Another trait similar to OSL is variety or novelty seeking. In consumer behavior, **variety and novelty seeking** consists of:[27]

1. *Exploratory purchase behavior* includes switching brands to experience new, different, and possibly better alternatives.

2. *Vicarious exploration* consists of gathering information about new and different product alternatives and contemplating buying them.

3. *Use innovativeness* means using an already adopted product in a new or novel way.

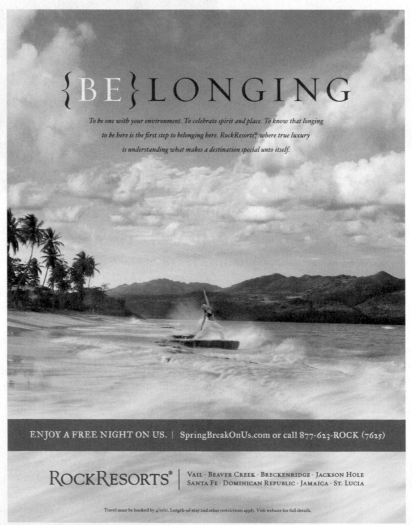

Source: RockResorts

FIGURE 3.10 An Appeal to Sensation-Seeking Consumers

Seeking variety is particularly relevant to technological products (e.g., smartphones), where many models offer an abundance of functions while other provide only basic features. For example, high variety-seeking consumers are likely to purchase the latest smartphones, whereas consumers with low variety-seeking are likely to stick with their existing phones.

Need for Cognition

A **need for cognition (NFC)** measures a person's craving for or enjoyment of thinking. Consumers who are high in NFC respond to ads that contain a lot of product-related information and descriptions, whereas consumers who are relatively low in NFC are attracted to the background or peripheral aspects of an ad, such as an attractive model or well-known celebrity. A study showed that including diagnostic product information in advertising (e.g., information that allows consumers to evaluate product quality and distinguish between brands) increased ad persuasion for high NFC consumers, but not for low NFC consumers.[28] Along the same lines, another study found that individuals low in NFC accepted a marketer's recommended alternatives more readily than high NFC consumers did.[29]

Need for cognition also plays a role in consumers' use of the Internet. Studies showed that high NFC persons were more likely than others to seek product information, current events, and educational resources online.[30] Other studies discovered that people high in NFC concentrated on the objectives of their planned online activities, whereas low-NFC persons were distracted by the vast amount of data on the Web and unable to focus on their intended online activities.[31]

Visualizers versus Verbalizers

Researchers found out that some people prefer the written word as a way of securing information, whereas others are influenced by images. **Verbalizers** prefer promotional messages containing a lot of written, textual, and verbal information. **Visualizers** are more receptive to pictorial images, and include:

1. *Object visualizers*, who encode and process images as a single perceptual unit.
2. *Spatial visualizers*, who process images piece by piece.

Individuals scoring high on object visualization tend to score low in spatial visualization, and vice versa. Furthermore, whereas visual artists generally excel in object imagery, scientists and engineers do best with spatial imagery.[32]

Although most ads consist of both verbal and pictorial information, some ads are significantly more visual than others. The Yoplait ad in Figure 3.11 appeals mostly to visualizers; it conveys the yogurt's palatal "richness" with a picture and almost no text. The Listerine ad in Figure 3.12 appeals to both visualizers and verbalizers; it includes a picture that clearly stands out, as well as a lot of verbal information about the product.

Consumer Materialism

Materialism gauges the extent to which an individual is preoccupied with purchasing and showing off physical possessions that are mostly nonessential and often conspicuous luxury goods. A study that compared the extent of consumer materialism among young adults (aged 18 to 35) from China and their American counterparts discovered that the Chinese were more materialistic than the Americans.[33] The study concluded that as the economic conditions in China improved, Chinese society accepted materialism readily. In contrast, as the U.S. economy became uncertain and volatile, young American consumers became more reserved and frugal.

Highly materialistic consumers define themselves by acquiring possessions. They value buying and showing off their belongings, are often self-centered and selfish, live cluttered lives, and often do not experience personal satisfaction or happiness from their possessions alone.[34] In contrast, consumers who are less materialistic do not define themselves by what they possess and are more interested in seeking fulfilling experiences and enjoying them, often with others. They are not particularly impressed by what they and others have, but rather how they enjoy life. One study discovered that "tightwads" spend less than they had intended, because they felt discomfort about paying for their purchases. In contrast, "spendthrifts" felt no discomfort about paying and

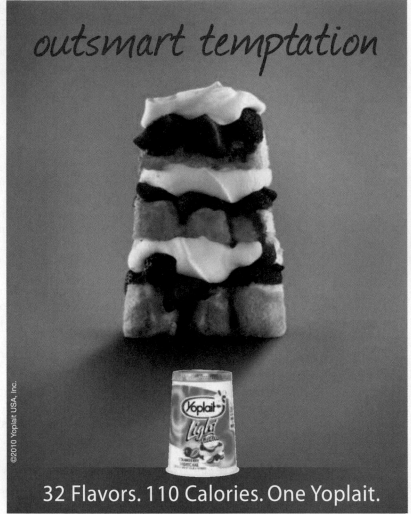

outsmart temptation

32 Flavors. 110 Calories. One Yoplait.

©2010 Yoplait USA, Inc.

Source: Used with permission of General Mills

FIGURE 3.11 An Appeal to Visualizers

typically spend more than they intended to.[35] A Canadian study discovered that 25% of people who remembered dreams recalled dreams about buying things. In reality, many of the respondents thought about the products they dreamed about (and sometimes even sought more information about them), told others about their dreams, and even considered purchasing the products dreamt about.[36] Table 3.8 profiles materialistic consumers.

Fixated Consumption

In the context of consumer behavior, **fixated consumption** refers to collectors' and hobbyists' tendency to accumulate items that are related to their interests and show them off to friends and others with similar interests. People collect anything: from free items, such as matchbooks from hotels and restaurants they have visited around the world, to glass paperweights that cost thousands of dollars, vintage motorcycles and cars, art, and century-old wines. Fixated consumers share the following characteristics:

1. A passion for and interest in the category of what they collect.
2. Willingness to invest a lot of effort in adding to their collections.
3. Spending a lot of time and discretionary income searching and buying more items for their collections.
4. Aggressively competing in auctions.

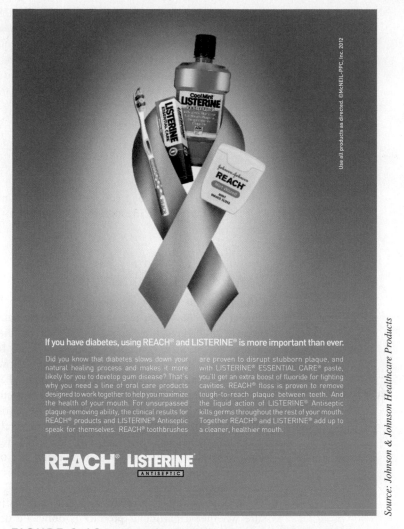

Source: Johnson & Johnson Healthcare Products

FIGURE 3.12 An Appeal to Both Visualizers and Verbalizers

TABLE 3.8	Selected Characteristics of Materialistic Consumers

- Consider purchasing "things" to be very important.
- Enjoy seeking out things that give them pleasure.
- Believe in the saying: "He (she) who dies with the most toys wins."
- Define themselves by what they wear and possess.
- Believe that they feel better off than those who have fewer possessions.
- Enjoy treating themselves to new possessions.
- Feel more important when they go shopping for new things.

Compulsive Consumption

Compulsive consumption is addictive and out-of-control buying that often has damaging consequences for both the compulsive shopper and those around him or her. Examples of compulsive consumption problems are uncontrollable shopping, gambling, drug addiction, alcoholism, and even eating disorders. Furthermore, the ease of online buying has made compulsive shopping more widespread. Research discovered that at least 75% of compulsive buyers are females.[37] Compulsive shoppers purchase items that they do not need and often do not end up using, and many require psychological intervention in order to eliminate or even control severe compulsive shopping. Research suggests that easy availability of credit cards contributes to compulsive consumption

TABLE 3.9 Illustrative Characteristics of Compulsive Consumers
• Have an irresistible urge to shop as soon as they enter a shopping mall. • Often buy products they do not need despite having little money left. • They feel compelled to spend the money they have left at the end a period. • Feel others would be horrified if they knew about their shopping habits. • Buy things although they cannot afford them. • Buy things to make themselves feel better. • Knowingly write checks that will bounce.

behavior, especially among college students.[38] Marketers must ensure that their promotional messages do not encourage irresponsible consumption. Table 3.9 lists several characteristics of compulsive consumers.

Consumer Ethnocentrism

Ethnocentrism is the consumer's willingness to buy or not buy foreign-made products. Highly ethnocentric consumers feel that it is inappropriate or wrong to purchase foreign-made products, because of the resulting economic impact on the domestic economy, whereas nonethnocentric or less ethnocentric consumers tend to evaluate foreign-made products—ostensibly more objectively—for their extrinsic characteristics (e.g., "How good are they?"). A post-9/11 study found that Americans' ethnocentrism increased in the United States as a result of the 9/11 terrorist attacks and natural disasters.[39] Research has also found that ethnocentrism varies by country and product. For example, Mexican consumers are more ethnocentric than their French and American counterparts; and Malaysian consumers, while preferring to purchase slacks, shirts, undergarments, and belts that are locally manufactured, want to buy imported sunglasses and watches.[40] Other evidence shows that some older American consumers, in remembrance of World War II, still refuse to purchase German- and/or Japanese-made products, whereas some German and Japanese consumers feel similarly about American-made products.[41]

Presently, due to globalization and multinational marketing, consumers may not know for sure whether a particular product is domestic or imported. For example, some of the models Toyota sells in the United States are manufactured in Japan, some in the United States, and others are in both countries. Several studies tried to classify products by their "degree of globalization," or "degree of cultural uniqueness." One study showed that, for some consumers, the "country of assembly" and the "country of design" played a role in deciding whether or not to purchase products.[42] A study of business school students in New York City examined eight different products, from green tea to jazz music, to determine if they differ in terms of "degree of globalization," that is, the product's degree of cultural uniqueness.[43]

Marketers successfully target ethnocentric consumers by stressing nationalistic themes in their promotional appeals (e.g., "Made in America" or "Made in France"), because these consumers are more likely to buy products made in their native lands. To illustrate the strategy of ethnocentric appeal, Honda, the Japanese automaker, in an indirect appeal to ethnocentric Americans, advertised that its Accord wagon is "Exported from America" (reinforcing the fact that some of its automobiles are made in the United States). However, a study examining the preferences of UK consumers across eight product categories found that domestic country bias (i.e., a preference for products manufactured in the consumer's country of residence) varied among product categories. This means that domestic manufacturers cannot always expect that local consumers will automatically prefer their offerings over imported ones.[44] Furthermore, one research study found that low-knowledge consumers' product attitudes (i.e., the consumer has little knowledge about the product) have been more strongly influenced by country-of-origin perceptions than high-knowledge consumers' product attitudes.[45] One study showed that highly ethnocentric Chinese consumers did not favor bilingual signs and messages (in Chinese and English) and were thus less likely to buy the advertised products.[46]

Personality and Color

Consumers not only ascribe personality traits to products and services, but some also associate personality characteristics with specific colors. For instance, consumers associate Coca-Cola with red, which connotes excitement. Blue bottles are sometimes used to sell wine because the color blue appeals particularly to female consumers. Yellow connotes novelty and black sophistication. Brands can create a sophisticated, upscale, or premium image (e.g., Miller Beer's Miller Reserve) by using primarily black labeling or packaging. A combination of black and white communicates that a product is carefully engineered, high tech, and sophisticatedly designed. For instance, Nike produced shoes in black, white, and a touch of red for selected models of its sports shoes because this color combination connotes high performance. Many fast-food restaurants use combinations of bright colors, like red, yellow, and blue, for their roadside signs and interior designs because research discovered that consumers associate these colors with fast service and inexpensive food. In contrast, most fine restaurants use sophisticated colors like gray, white, shades of tan, or other soft, pale, and muted tones to underscore their classy environments and good service. Table 3.10 lists various colors, their personality-like meanings, and associated marketing insights.

TABLE 3.10	Personality Traits Associated with Colors	
COLOR	**PERSONALITY LINK**	**MARKETING INSIGHTS**
Blue	Commands respect, authority	• America's favored color • IBM holds the title to blue • Associated with club soda • Men seek products packaged in blue • Houses painted blue are avoided • Low-calorie, skim milk • Coffee in a blue can perceived as "mild"
Yellow	Caution, novelty, temporary, warmth	• Eyes register it fastest • Coffee in yellow can tastes "weak" • Stops traffic • Sells a house
Green	Secure, natural, relaxed or easygoing, living things	• Good work environment • Associated with vegetables and chewing gum • Canada Dry ginger ale sales increased when it changed its sugar-free package from red to green and white
Red	Human, exciting, hot, passionate, strong	• Makes food "smell" better • Coffee in a red can perceived as "rich" • Women have a preference for bluish red • Men have a preference for yellowish red • Coca-Cola "owns" red
Orange	Powerful, affordable, informal	• Draws attention quickly
Brown	Informal and relaxed, masculine, nature	• Coffee in a dark-brown can was "too strong" • Men seek products packaged in brown
White	Goodness, purity, chastity, cleanliness, delicacy, refinement, formality	• Suggests reduced calories • Pure and wholesome food • Clean, bath products, feminine
Black	Sophistication, power, authority, mystery	• Powerful clothing • High-tech electronics
Silver, Gold, Platinum	Regal, wealthy, stately	• Suggests premium price

Source: From "Color Schemes" by Bernice Kanner in *New York Magazine* 4/3/1989. Reprinted by permission of Bernice Kanner/New York Magazine.

Product and Brand Personification

Learning Objective

6 To understand the personification of products and brands and its strategic applications.

Earlier in this chapter, we introduced the notion of "product personality." **Brand personification** occurs when consumers attribute human traits or characteristics to a brand. A "brand personality" provides an emotional identity for a brand, which produces sentiments and feelings toward the brand among consumers. For instance, consumers perceive Perdue chickens as very fresh, Nike as the athlete in all of us, and BMW as being performance driven. A brand's personality can either be functional ("dependable and rugged") or symbolic ("the athlete in all of us"). A distinct brand personality differentiates the brand from similar offerings, and creates favorable attitudes toward the brand, higher purchase intentions, and brand loyalty.

Research shows that of all the elements of the marketing mix, promotional messages have the greatest influence in creating a brand personality. One study explored dimensions of brand personality for products marketed by 64 American multinational corporations. It analyzed 270 websites of these corporations, in the United States, UK, France, Germany, and Spain, and discovered five underlying dimensions of brand personality: *excitement*, *sophistication*, *affection*, *popularity*, and *competence*.[47]

Product and brand personifications are forms of **anthropomorphism**, which refers to attributing human characteristics to something that is not human. For example, a study focusing on anthropomorphized products found that the ease with which consumers could anthropomorphize a product was a function of how the product was advertised and the inclusion or absence of references to or depictions of human-like product features. Consumers perceived products presented as having human features more favorably than products without human attributes.[48] One study investigated the relationship between brand personality and two human characteristics:

1. *Attachment anxiety*—the degree to which people are concerned about whether they are worthy of love.
2. *Avoidance anxiety*—one's view of others in the context of attachment.

The study discovered that people who were preoccupied with their self-worth and had a negative view of people (i.e., high anxiety and high avoidance) preferred an *exciting* brand personality, whereas those with high anxiety and a favorable view of people (i.e., low avoidance) preferred a *sincere* brand personality. Many researchers have advised marketers to study the personality traits of their consumers before personifying their brands in promotional messages.[49]

Consumers personify brands because marketers have given their offerings human characteristics through repetitive and effective advertising. For example, the M&M "person" (see Figure 8.4) originated from asking consumers: "If an M&M (a chocolate-coated peanut variety) were a person, what kind of person would it be?" For decades, the M&M "person" has been one of America's best-loved and most widely recognized characters. The manufacturer of Mr. Coffee—an automatic-drip coffee maker—unexpectedly found that, in focus groups, consumers referred to Mr. Coffee as if it were a person, with such expressions as "he makes good coffee" and "he's got a lot of different models and prices." The brand's marketer then personified the machine and, in subsequent studies, discovered that consumers perceived Mr. Coffee as "dependable," "friendly," "efficient," "intelligent," and "smart." In several focus groups, participants described several well-known brands of dishwashing liquid as "demanding taskmasters" and "high-energy people." In another study, French young adults (aged 18 to 23) perceived Coca-Cola as friendly, creative, charming, and elegant (among other characteristics), and that such perceptions led to trust, attachment, and commitment to the brand.[50]

Some consumers become "brand zealots" and develop a relationship with brands beyond the functions of these products. An example of this behavior is VW Beetle owners who give their cars names, and who have been seen talking to their vehicles and affectionately stroking them. Another example is the Harley-Davidson motorcycle owners who go so far as to get Harley tattoos. One friend of the authors refers to his garbage disposal as "Garby," and calls his expensive cappuccino machine "Princessa," whom he usually praises for making a lot of froth and seldom rebukes for making too little.

The framework in Figure 3.13, which has been applied to personifying many brands of consumer goods, depicts 5 underlying dimensions of a brand's personality—sincerity, excitement, competence, sophistication, and ruggedness—and 15 more narrowly defined characteristics, such as down-to-earth, daring, reliable, upper class, and outdoors.

FIGURE 3.13

A Brand Personality Framework

Source: Journal of Marketing Research, 1997. American Marketing Association.

Product Personality and Gender

A product's personality frequently endows products and brands with gender. For instance, Celestial Seasonings' Tracy Jones was given a feminine persona, whereas Mr. Coffee was given a masculine personality. Products' assigned genders vary by culture: In certain cultures, consumers may perceive coffee and toothpaste to be masculine products, whereas bath soap and shampoo are viewed as feminine. Another study examined the personality characteristics that Hispanic shoppers associate with well-known U.S. retailers. In focus groups conducted in Spanish in several American cities, researchers discovered that Hispanic consumers ascribed personality characteristics to retailers. For example, Walmart was frequently characterized as a detail-oriented, successful businesswoman; Old Navy was described as "a woman who is friendly and gardens"; and Sears as "an elegant man driving an expensive car."[51]

Product Personality and Geography

Consumers associate some brands with geographic locations (e.g., Buxton Natural Mineral Water, a brand owned by Nestlé Waters, and sourced from the ancient and picturesque town of Buxton in the heart of England), and such associations often enhance the memory and the likeability of these brands. Interestingly, geographic brand names can be either real or fictitious. For instance, Philadelphia Cream Cheese is actually made in Illinois, but many consumers associate it with a city known for its historical role in the founding of the United States. Whether the brand's association with a location is real or fictitious, the perceived location's image enhances the brand's equity. Many customers immediately associate the name Aurora Zone with healthful winter activities in the Nordic countries. The carefully chosen brand name indicates that it provides holiday packages and organizes tours solely for the viewing of the Aurora Borealis, even though the company originated in the more prosaic Northumberland in the UK.

Website Personality

As consumers navigate the Internet, many of them become emotionally attached to certain websites. A recent study identified four personality characteristics of websites: (1) *intelligent* (i.e., searchable, comprehensive, fast, and concise); (2) *fun* (i.e., colorful, attractive, interactive, and dynamic); (3) *organized*; and (4) *sincere* (i.e., straightforward and down-to-earth).[52] These finding suggest that incorporating personality traits into the design of websites can generate more favorable attitudes among visitors and more clicks on the site's pages.

The Self and Self-Image

Learning Objective

7 To understand self-image and its impact on consumer behavior.

Self-image represents the way a person views herself or himself. Perceptions of self are often related to the purchases of products and services, because consumers often select products that are consistent with their self-images and enhance them. In fact, consumers have multiple "selves," because people act differently in different situations. For instance, a person is likely to behave in different ways with parents, at school, at work, at a museum opening, or with friends at a nightclub.

Each individual has an image of himself or herself as a certain kind of person, with certain traits, skills, habits, possessions, relationships, and behaviors. One's self-image originates in a person's background and experience. Many products and brands have symbolic value for individuals because their images are consistent with the ways these people perceive themselves, and consumers buy offerings that are congruent with their self-image and avoid products and brands that are not. A recent study uncovered an interesting correlation between food consumption and self-image. Apparently, as Americans are becoming larger, because of consuming increasingly larger portions and too much food, many people who are overweight see themselves as being of normal or average weight.[53]

Consumer behavior researchers identified four components of self-image:

1. **Actual self-image** is the way consumers see themselves;
2. **Ideal self-image** is how consumers would like to see themselves;
3. **Social self-image** is how consumers feel others see them; and
4. **Ideal social self-image** is how consumers would like others to see them.

Consumers select the type of self-image that guides them in the context of buying situations. For instance, with everyday household products, consumers might be guided by their actual self-images, whereas for some socially enhancing or socially conspicuous products, they might be guided by their social self-images. When it comes to an important and strong personal goal or wish, like losing weight and feeling better about oneself and one's appearance, people are often guided by either their ideal self-images or ideal social self-images.

The concept of self-image has strategic implications for marketers. For example, companies can segment their markets on the basis of relevant self-images and then position their products or services as symbols of such. These strategies reflect the marketing concept: Marketers study the needs of a consumer segment (with respect to both the product category and as the product's or brand's reflection of self-image) and then develop and market an offering that meets both criteria. Jockey—a marketer of undergarments—recognizes the importance of self-image.

The Extended Self

Consumers' possessions can confirm or extend their self-images. For instance, acquiring a sought-after pair of "vintage" Levi jeans might enrich a teenager's self-image, because she might see herself as being more desirable, fashionable, and successful when she wears those pants. Researchers suggested that possessions are extensions of self in the following ways:[54]

1. *Actually*, by allowing the person to do things that otherwise would be very difficult or impossible to accomplish (e.g., problem solving by using a computer).
2. *Symbolically*, by making the person feel better (e.g., being considered the "best dressed" at work).
3. *Conferring status or rank*, for example, being an art collector and owning a rare and well-known masterpiece.
4. *Feelings of immortality* by leaving valuable bequests after death.

Altering the Self

Sometimes consumers wish to change or improve their selves. Clothing, grooming aids or cosmetics, accessories (such as sunglasses, jewelry, tattoos, or even colored contact lenses), and makeovers offer consumers opportunities to enhance their appearance and thereby alter their selves. In using self-altering products, consumers frequently attempt to express their new selves or take on the appearances of particular types of people (e.g., a military person, physician, business executive, or college professor).

Personal vanity is closely related to both self-image and alteration of the self. Vanity is often associated with acting self-important, self-interested, or admiring one's own appearance or achievements. Researchers discovered two types of vanity: (1) *physical vanity*, which is excessive concern with or inflated view of one's physical appearance; and (2) *achievement vanity*, which is excessive concern with or inflated view of one's personal achievements. They found that both vanity types correlated with a high level of materialism, high use of cosmetics, concern with clothing,

TABLE 3.11 Illustrative Characteristics of Vain Persons
• Always want to look their best.
• Always concerned with their appearance.
• Believe that others notice and envy their looks.
• Believe that others find them sexually appealing.
• Obsessed with personal achievements.
• Want their achievements to be highly regarded by others.
• Believe that they are a good example of success.
• Believe that others wish they were as successful as them.

and importance of belonging to prestigious country clubs.[55] Table 3.11 lists several characteristics of vain people. From a marketing viewpoint, these features indicate that vain consumers: (1) are a lucrative market for personal care and beauty products; (2) welcome promotional messages showing that they attract others' attention; and (3) are receptive to promotional messages featuring personal achievement.

Summary

Learning Objective 1: To understand the dynamics of motives, needs, and goals and how they shape consumer behavior.

Motivation drives consumers to take action by producing a psychological tension caused by unfulfilled needs. Individuals strive to reduce this tension through selecting goals and subsequent behavior that they anticipate will fulfill their needs and thus relieve them of the tension they feel. There are two types of human needs: Physiological needs are innate and fulfilling them sustains life. They include the need for food, water, air, protection of the body from the outside environment (i.e., clothing and shelter), and sex. Psychological needs are learned from our parents, social environment, and interactions with others. Among many others, they include the needs for self-esteem, prestige, affection, power, learning, and achievement. Goals are the sought-after results of motivated behavior; all human behavior is goal oriented and focused on satisfying physiological and psychological needs. Need-driven human activity never ceases because: (1) Needs are never fully satisfied; they continually cause actions designed to attain or maintain satisfaction. (2) As needs are satisfied, new and higher-order needs emerge, cause tension, and induce activity. (3) People who achieve their goals set new and higher goals for themselves.

Learning Objective 2: To understand motivation theories and their applications to consumer behavior.

Human beings share the same biogenic and similar psychological needs. However, different people assign different priorities to psychological needs. Maslow's hierarchy-of-needs theory proposes five levels of human needs: physiological needs, safety needs, social needs, egoistic needs, and self-actualization needs. Other needs widely integrated into consumer advertising include the needs for power, affiliation, and achievement.

Learning Objective 3: To understand how to identify and measure motives.

There are self-reported and qualitative methods for identifying and measuring human motives, and researchers use these techniques in tandem to assess the presence or strength of consumer motives. Motivational research and its current extended form (commonly referred to as qualitative research) seek to delve below the consumer's level of conscious awareness, and identify underlying needs and motives. Quantitative research has proved to be of value to marketers in developing new ideas and advertising copy appeals. Self-reported measures of motives consist of presenting written statements to respondents and asking respondents to indicate how relevant each statement is to them.

Learning Objective 4: To understand the scope of personality and theories of its development.

Personality consists of the psychological characteristics that both determine and reflect how a person responds to his or her environment. Although personality tends to be consistent and enduring, it may change abruptly in response to major life events, as well as gradually over time. Three theories of personality are prominent in the study of consumer behavior: psychoanalytic theory, neo-Freudian theory, and trait theory. Freud's psychoanalytic theory provides the foundation for the study of motivational research, which operates on the premise that human drives are largely unconscious in nature and motivate many consumer actions. Neo-Freudian theory tends to emphasize the fundamental role of social relationships in the formation and development of personality. Trait theory focuses on empirical measures of personality in terms of specific psychological characteristics, called traits, that set one person apart from another.

Learning Objective 5: To understand how innovativeness and other personality traits influence consumer behavior.

Trait theory postulates that individuals possess innate psychological traits (e.g., innovativeness, novelty seeking, need for cognition, materialism) to a greater or lesser degree, and that these traits can be measured by specially designed scales or inventories. Several personality traits are solidly related to innovativeness: dogmatism, social character (i.e., inner- versus other-directedness), and the need for uniqueness. These personality traits, as well as others (such as optimum stimulation level, sensation seeking, variety or novelty seeking, need for cognition, visualizer or verbalizer status, consumer materialism, fixated consumption, compulsive consumption, and consumer ethnocentrism) strongly affect consumption behavior and understanding them enables marketers to develop effective persuasive strategies.

Learning Objective 6: To understand the personification of products and brands and its strategic applications.

Some consumers attribute human-like qualities to products and brands. Marketers who study and understand the meaning of such product and brand personalities can use them to shape consumers' responses to promotional messages and enhance their emotional connections to products and brands. A product's personality frequently endows products and brands with gender. Consumers associate some brands with geographic locations, and such associations often enhance their memory and likeability of brands. Many

consumers who are heavy Internet users become emotionally attached to certain websites, and several researchers have studied the ascribing of personality traits to websites.

Learning Objective 7: To understand self-image and its impact on consumer behavior.

Each individual has a perceived self-image (or multiple self-images) that is an expression of his or her traits, habits, possessions, and relationships. Consumers frequently attempt to preserve, enhance, alter, or extend their self-images by purchasing brands that appeal to their self-image(s), and also by shopping at stores that they perceive as consistent with their relevant self-image(s). Consumer behavior researchers identified four components of self-image: (1) actual self-image, (2) ideal self-image, (3) social self-image, and (4) ideal social self-image. Understanding the dimensions of self-image enables marketers to design effective promotional messages targeting various segments.

Review and Discussion Questions

3.1. Discuss the statement "Marketers don't create needs; needs preexist marketers." Can marketing efforts *change* consumers' needs? Why or why not? Can they *arouse* consumer needs? If yes, how?

3.2. Consumers have both innate and acquired needs. Give examples of each kind of need and show how the same purchase can serve to fulfill either or both kinds of needs.

3.3. Think of a product or service of your choice. Now enumerate ways in which it could be marketed to target consumers as both an approach object and an avoidance object. Cite appropriate examples.

3.4. Maslow's hierarchy of needs begins with the primacy of physiological needs and puts self-actualization at the top of the pyramid. Some academics have claimed that this theory is flawed. Discuss why this might be true.

3.5. How can marketers use consumers' failures at achieving goals in developing promotional appeals for specific products and services? Give examples.

3.6. For each of the following products, select one level from Maslow's hierarchy of human needs. Describe how you would use the need you selected in promoting the product to a market segment of your choice. The products are: e-readers, expensive shoes, and vacation homes.

3.7. What are the features of qualitative research, and what are the techniques used to undertake this type of research?

3.8. a. How do researchers identify and measure human motives? Give examples.

b. Does motivational research differ from quantitative research? Discuss.

c. What are the strengths and weaknesses of motivational research?

3.9. How would you explain the fact that, although no two individuals have identical personalities, personality is sometimes used in consumer research to identify distinct and sizable market segments?

3.10. Contrast the major characteristics of the following personality theories: (a) Freudian theory, (b) neo-Freudian theory, and (c) trait theory. In your answer, illustrate how each theory is applied to the understanding of consumer behavior.

3.11. Describe personality trait theory. Give five examples of how personality traits can be used in consumer research.

3.12. Research has found that the target market selected by the maker of a digital camera consists primarily of individuals who are other-directed and also have a high need for cognition. How can the camera's marketer use this information in promoting its product?

3.13. Describe the type of promotional message that would be most suitable for each of the following personality market segments, and give an example of each: (a) highly dogmatic consumers, (b) inner-directed consumers, (c) consumers with high optimum stimulation levels, (d) consumers with a high need for recognition, and (e) consumers who are visualizers versus consumers who are verbalizers.

3.14. Is there likely to be a difference in personality traits between individuals who readily purchase foreign-made products and those who prefer American-made products? How can marketers use the consumer ethnocentrism scale to segment consumers?

3.15. A marketer of health foods would like to segment its market on the basis of self-image. Describe how the marketer can use actual self-image and ideal self-image to do so.

Hands-on Assignments

3.16. Find two advertisements that depict two different defense mechanisms (Table 3.2) and discuss their effectiveness.

3.17. Find three advertisements that illustrate the needs for power, affiliation, and achievement and discuss their effectiveness. (Each advertisement should depict one of the three needs.)

3.18. Find two examples of ads that are designed to arouse consumer needs and discuss their effectiveness.

3.19. Have a look at a magazine and pick out two to three full-page ads. Which stages of Maslow's hierarchy of needs do they apply to? Do any of the ads cover more than one of the stages?

3.20. Look around the room and select a product in view. How could you use brand personification to promote this product to consumers?

Key Terms

- Achievement need *92*
- Actual self-image *110*
- Affiliation need *92*
- Aggression *88*
- Aggressive individuals *97*
- Anthropomorphism *82*
- Approach objects *86*
- Avoidance objects *86*
- Brand personification *82*
- Compliant individuals *97*
- Compulsive consumption *105*
- Daydreaming *88*
- Defense mechanisms *87*
- Detached individuals *97*
- Dogmatism *100*
- Ego *96*
- Egoistic needs *91*
- Ethnocentrism *98*
- Fixated consumption *104*
- Freudian theory *96*
- Frustration *87*
- Goals *84*

- Generic goals *84*
- Id *96*
- Ideal self-image *110*
- Ideal social self-image *110*
- Identification *88*
- Inner-directed *100*
- Innovativeness *99*
- Innovators *99*
- Maslow's hierarchy of needs *90*
- Materialism *98*
- Motivation *82*
- Motivational research *93*
- Need for cognition (NFC) *103*
- Need for uniqueness *100*
- Needs *82*
- Neo-Freudian theory *97*
- Optimum stimulation level (OSL) *100*
- Other-directed *100*
- Personality *82*
- Physiological needs *84*
- Power need *92*
- Product-specific goals *84*

- Projection *88*
- Projective techniques *93*
- Psychological needs *84*
- Qualitative research *93*
- Rationalization *88*
- Regression *88*
- Repression *88*
- Safety and security needs *91*
- Self-actualization need *91*
- Self-image *109*
- Self-reported measures of motives *93*
- Sensation seeking *101*
- Social needs *91*
- Social self-image *110*
- Superego *96*
- Thematic Apperception Test *94*
- Trait theory *98*
- Variety and novelty seeking *102*
- Verbalizers *103*
- Visualizers *103*
- Withdrawal *88*
- Word association method *94*

Consumer Perception

PERCEPTION is the process by which individuals select, organize, and interpret stimuli into a meaningful and coherent picture of the world. It can be described as "how we see the world around us." Two individuals may be exposed to the same stimuli, but how each person recognizes, selects, organizes, and interprets these stimuli is a highly individual process based on each person's own needs, values, and expectations.

Consumers act and react on the basis of their perceptions, not on the basis of objective reality. For each individual, "reality" is a totally personal phenomenon, based on that person's needs, wants, values, and personal experiences. Thus, to the marketer, consumers' perceptions are much more important than their knowledge of objective reality. For if one thinks about it, it's not what actually *is* so, but what consumers *think* is so, that affects their actions and their buying habits. And, because individuals make decisions and take actions based on what they perceive to be reality, it is important that marketers understand the notion of perception and its related concepts to determine more readily what factors influence consumers to buy.

Since the 1970s, the identity of McCain, the UK's largest seller of frozen chips was a signature in a rectangular black box, which conveyed the brand's expertise in freezing technology. Like the microwave and vacuum cleaner, symbols of modern convenience, the brand represented the advances made in domestic innovation. However, a renewed interest in where food comes from and how it is made, meant that McCain had to start communicating about "the produce behind the process," reassuring consumers that McCain chips are just potatoes cut up and cooked in sunflower oil. This communication started with a successful advertising campaign "It's all good," but it needed to go further. McCain hired BrandOpus—a strategic design firm—to develop a new visual identity. Nir Wegrzyn, CEO, BrandOpus, stated: "We were challenged by McCain to imbue their brand identity with new meaning. The new identity shifts the McCain brand from the cold freezer aisle, into the world of being a provider of real, natural, wholesome food." Helen Priestley, McCain Marketing Director, commented: "The new visual identity establishes the sunshine as the

Source: McCain Foods Limited

FIGURE 4.1 A McCain Chips Visual Identity

Source: McCain Foods Limited

FIGURE 4.1 B McCain's Packages

new symbol for the brand and reflects the warmth and positivity of the natural world that McCain products originate from."[1] Figure 4.1 A shows consumers' perceptions of the new and old brand identities and Figure 4.1 B features the old package on the left side and the new one on the right.

Periodically, companies update their visual identities. When doing so, they must be careful, because changes that deviate "too much" from the old and familiar designs confuse consumers. Figure 4.2 shows an update of the package of Heinz Tomato Ketchup. Because today's consumers want healthier foods, Heinz substituted the little green pickle, which has appeared on the ketchup label for decades, with a tomato on a vine. It also enlarged the word TOMATO, while leaving the size of the word KETCHUP unchanged. In addition, Heinz redesigned the small packets of ketchup commonly available at fast-food outlets: The new packet is in the shape of a bottle of ketchup and the product's visual identity is much more prominent. Heinz modernized its packages without diluting its identity and in a manner that maintained and even enhanced consumers' instant recognition of Heinz Tomato Ketchup. In Figure 4.2, the old package appears on

Source: H.J. Heinz Company

FIGURE 4.2 Heinz's Old and New Packages

the left side and new one on the right. Note that the phrase "Fridge Door Fit" does not appear on the new package. Years ago, there were many designs of refrigerators and not all brands came in "door friendly" packages. Today, fitting in the fridge's door is no longer a unique attribute.

Later on, we explain the concept of the **just noticeable difference (JND),** which maintains that any changes in logos and packages must be within certain "limits" in order to ensure that consumers still recognize the items instantly after the changes. Heinz's new label was well within the JND. In contrast, one year, for the holidays, Coca-Cola packaged regular Coke in snow-white cans. Many consumers complained that the holiday can was confusingly similar to Diet Coke's silver cans, and the company brought back the familiar, red can immediately. While Heinz's new package was well within the range of the JND, Coca-Cola's white can was above the JND, which resulted in consumer confusion and complaints.

The Elements of Perception

Learning Objective

1 To understand the elements of perception and their role in consumer behavior.

Perception is all about consumers' *subjective* understandings and not *objective* realities. Altering subjective "wisdom" is difficult, or even impossible. For instance, for decades, Science Diet—sold mostly in specialty stores and priced quite high—has been the premier dog and cat food because it was based on the claims that, following scientific laboratory research, the food included vitamins, grains, and other special ingredients. However, in recent years, consumers' preferences changed and pet owners became fond of pet foods that mimicked their own diets, such as natural and organic foods. At this point, Science Diet's claim of engineered nutrition became a liability and its sales sharply declined. The brand's marketer responded with Science Diet Nature's Best, the ingredients of which included lamb, brown rice, soybean meal, and apples. Still, the new offering did poorly because consumers continued to perceive Science Diet as an artificial and unnatural product.[2]

Nevertheless, changing a brand image, or **repositioning,** is necessary. For example, for decades, Chevrolet was positioned as an American icon, with such slogans as "See the USA in Your Chevrolet," Heartbeat of America," and "Baseball, Hot Dogs, Apple Pie and Chevrolet." As GM started to sell the brand globally, it needed a new slogan that would create a united, global perception of the brand. The first new slogan it tried was "Chevy Runs Deep," but this tagline proved to be mundane and unexciting. Subsequently, GM began to advertise Chevrolet under the slogan "Find New Roads," which the company believes to be exciting, flexible, and also easily translated into other languages.[3] Interestingly, the Chevrolet brand name is not included in the new tagline.

Raw sensory input by itself does not produce or explain the coherent picture of the world that most adults possess. Indeed, the study of perception is largely the study of what we subconsciously add to or subtract from raw sensory inputs to produce our own private picture of the world. Human beings are constantly bombarded with stimuli during every minute and every hour of every day. The sensory world is made up of an almost infinite number of discrete sensations that are constantly and subtly changing. According to the principles of sensation, intensive stimulation "bounces off" most individuals, who subconsciously block (i.e., adapt to) a heavy bombardment of stimuli. Otherwise, the billions of different stimuli to which we are constantly exposed might confuse us and keep us perpetually disoriented in a constantly changing environment. However, neither of these consequences tends to occur, because perception is not a function of sensory input alone. Rather, perception is the result of two different kinds of inputs that interact to form the personal pictures—the perceptions—that each individual experiences. One type of input is physical stimuli from the outside environment; the other consists of people's expectations, motives, and what they have learned from previous experiences. The combination of these two very different kinds of input produces for each of us a very private, very personal picture of the world. Because each person is a unique individual, with unique experiences, needs, wants, desires, and expectations, it follows that each individual's perceptions are unique. This explains why no two people see the world in precisely the same way.

Individuals are very selective as to which stimuli they "recognize"; they subconsciously organize the stimuli that they do recognize according to widely held psychological principles, and they interpret such stimuli (give meaning to the stimuli) subjectively in accordance with their personal needs, expectations, and experiences. The following sections examine each of these three aspects of perception: the selection, organization, and interpretation of stimuli.

Sensory Input

Sensation is the immediate and direct response of the sensory organs to stimuli. A **stimulus** is any unit of input to any of the senses. Examples of stimuli (i.e., sensory inputs) include products, packages, brand names, advertisements, and commercials. **Sensory receptors** are the human organs

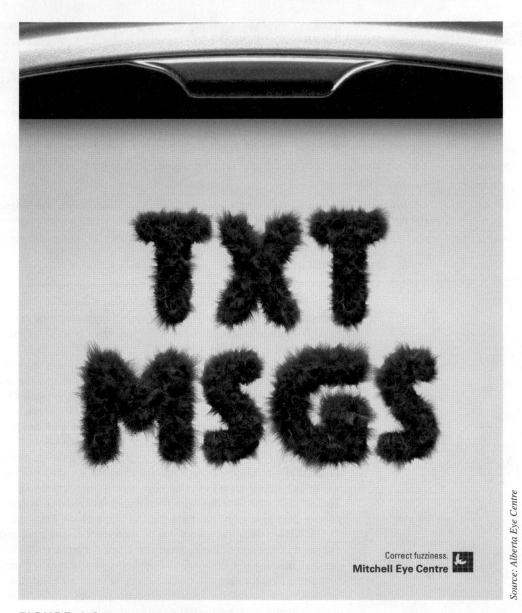

FIGURE 4.3 Sensory Input: Mitchell Eye Centre

(the eyes, ears, nose, mouth, and skin) that receive sensory inputs. Their sensory functions are to see, hear, smell, taste, and touch. All of these functions are called into play, either singly or in combination, in the purchase, use, and evaluation of consumer products. Human sensory sensitivity refers to the experience of sensation. Sensitivity to stimuli varies with the quality of an individual's sensory receptors (e.g., eyesight or hearing) and the amount (or intensity) of the stimuli to which he or she is exposed. For example, a blind person may have a more highly developed sense of hearing than the average sighted person and may be able to hear sounds that the average person cannot. Figure 4.3 shows an ad for the Mitchell Eye Centre that humorously depicts the consequences of fuzzy vision.

Sensation itself depends on energy change within the environment where the perception occurs (i.e., on differentiation of input). A perfectly bland or unchanging environment, regardless of the strength of the sensory input, provides little or no sensation at all. Thus, a person who lives on a busy street in midtown Manhattan would probably receive little or no sensation from the inputs of such noisy stimuli as horns honking, tires screeching, and fire engines clanging, because such sounds are so commonplace in New York City. In situations in which there is a great deal of sensory input, the senses do not detect small changes or differences in input. Thus, one honking horn more or less would never be noticed on a street with heavy traffic.

As sensory input *decreases*, however, our ability to detect changes in input or intensity *increases*, to the point that we attain maximum sensitivity under conditions of minimal stimulation. This accounts

TABLE 4.1	Sensory Audio Input and Product Perception
PRODUCT	SOUND AND ITS CONSUMER MEANING
Snapple	Consumers perceive the sound of the "pop" as an indicator of product safety. When the company came up with the right snap sound, it was able to eliminate the plastic seal around the bottle's cap.
VW Jetta	The car door's "thump" is an indication of quality. The company played and mentioned the door thump in ads for a new model.
Mascara	Consumers perceive the sound and duration of the "click" heard when taking the cover off as indicators of quality.
Eye shadow	A more pronounced "click" heard when opening the compact case symbolizes higher quality.
Tip markers	Consumers like the "screech" because it represents "boldness."
Tampons	Realizing that women dislike opening tampon packages that omit sound, P & G redesigned the product's packaging. The plastic's "crinkle" was carefully balanced and the new adhesive strip makes no sound when opened.
Spray bottle	Method made the nozzle of its spray bottle almost indistinguishable because consumers perceive a quiet nozzle as an indicator of quality.

for the statement, "It was so quiet I could hear a pin drop." The ability of the human organism to accommodate itself to varying levels of sensitivity as external conditions vary not only provides more sensitivity when it is needed, but also protects us from damaging, disruptive, or irrelevant bombardment when the input level is high.

Most marketing communications appeal to sight and sound. However, smell and touch also represent considerable opportunities for targeting consumers. The importance of smell in communication was strongly supported by two Americans who developed a scientific explanation of how people associate memories with smells (and won the 2004 Nobel Prize in Physiology for this work), as well as other studies demonstrating the impact of fragrance on product and store choices.[4] Scented strips have been part of perfume ads for years, but have also been used by other marketers: for example, scented stickers with coffee aromas were placed on the front page of a daily newspapers, and the scent of chocolate cookies was emitted from ads for milk placed in bus stops. Recognizing that the use of an ambient scent in a retail environment enhances the shopping experience for many consumers and makes the time they spend examining merchandise, waiting in line, and waiting for help seem shorter than it actually is, stores like Abercrombie & Fitch use strong fragrances throughout their facilities. One study discovered that product scent enhanced memory of the product more than ambient scent (i.e., scent in the environment when the product is sold). In addition, when a product was scented, memory of the nonscent-related attributes of the product also increased.[5]

Regarding the sense of touch, several studies indicated that touching a product influences persuasion and that touching could be used as a persuasive tool.[6] Another example of increasing sensory input is to add more merchandise and create more clutter in existing spaces. For example, during periods where consumers feel reluctant to spend money, Dollar General raised the height of its standard shelves and Best Buy tested carrying bigger items, such as bicycles and Segways, to fill in the space created by thinner TVs and smaller speakers.[7]

A sound, like a picture, may be "worth a thousand words." As shown in Table 4.1, many companies have invested large amounts of resources in designing products and packages that emit just the right audio sensory input, after studying how consumers perceive the volumes and pitches of sounds.[8]

The Absolute Threshold

The lowest level at which an individual can experience a sensation is called the **absolute threshold**. The point at which a person can detect a difference between "something" and "nothing" is that person's absolute threshold for that stimulus. To illustrate, the distance at which a driver can note a specific billboard on a highway is that individual's absolute threshold. Two people riding together may first spot the billboard at different times (i.e., at different distances); thus, they appear to have different absolute thresholds. Under conditions of constant stimulation, such as driving through a "corridor" of billboards, the absolute threshold increases (i.e., the senses tend to become increasingly dulled). After an hour of driving through billboards, it is doubtful that any one billboard will make an impression. Hence, we often speak of "getting used to" a hot bath, a cold shower, or the bright sun. As our exposure to the stimulus increases, we notice it less. **Sensory adaptation** is "getting used to" certain sensations; that is, becoming accommodated to a certain level of stimulation and becoming less able to notice a particular stimulus.

Sensory adaptation is a problem that concerns many national advertisers, which is why they try to change their advertising campaigns regularly. They are concerned that consumers will get so used to their current print ads and TV commercials that they will no longer "see" them; that is, the ads will no longer provide sufficient sensory input to be noted. In an effort to cut through the advertising clutter and ensure that consumers perceive their ads, some marketers try to increase sensory input—and sometimes, marketers' efforts backfire. For example, the FCC approved rules that require cable operators and TV stations to quiet louder-than-normal TV commercials.[9]

As another example, following consumers' complaints, most department stores have eliminated the roaming spritzers of perfume who, for decades, have been spraying fragrances in stores' aisles assuming that consumers would buy a fragrance after getting a whiff.[10]

Many of the promotional methods aimed at increasing sensory input take the form of ambush marketing or experiential marketing.

Ambush Marketing

Ambush marketing consists of placing ads in places where consumers do not expect to see them and cannot readily avoid them.[11] Examples include brand names stamped on eggs in a supermarket, featured on video screens in taxis, placed in subway tunnels between stations, or featured on doctors' examination tables. Other examples are placing giant, fake pieces of advertised sushi on an airport's baggage carousel; featuring brands on the bottom of the trays where consumers place small personal items during security checks at airports; ads on dry cleaners' shirt boxes; and projecting ads on the sides of large buildings at night in large cities. Additional locations where ads are not expected but have been featured include inside urinals in men's restrooms, on muffin displays, and on the hoods of cars as attendants filled them with gas. Vanilla paired with jasmine aromas were placed in apartments for sale in a Las Vegas condo and scents were added to the handles of men's shaving razors.

Experiential Marketing

Experiential marketing allows customers to engage and interact with brands, products, and services in sensory ways in order to create emotional bonds between consumers and marketing offerings. Examples of this method include consumers' opportunities to closely examine NASCAR's race cars in Times Square, New York City, and Ford asking car owners to hold house parties where guests could see, sit in, and even drive the cars. In an innovative promotion of its Stove Top stuffing brand, during one winter month, Kraft Foods heated several Chicago bus stops featuring ads for the brand. The objective was to convey the product's "warmth" to waiting passengers.

The Differential Threshold

The minimal difference that can be detected between two similar stimuli is called the **differential threshold** or the **just noticeable difference (JND)**. A nineteenth-century German scientist named Ernst Weber discovered that the JND between two stimuli was not an absolute amount, but an amount relative to the intensity of the first stimulus. **Weber's law**, as it has come to be known, states that the stronger the initial stimulus, the greater the additional intensity needed for the second stimulus to be perceived as different. For example, during economic downturn, consumers become very price sensitive and are likely to note even small changes in price. However, during such times, companies feel a squeeze on their profit margins because people are doing more with less. For example, if a marketer of a 16-ounce bag of whole-wheat pasta raises the price from $3.99 to $4.25, most consumers will notice. Therefore, instead of raising the price, the marketer leaves the price unchanged, but lowers the quantity to 13.25 ounces per bag. Because this change is relatively small—that is, below the JND—most consumers will not notice it, unless they look at the package carefully. Other examples of below-the-JND decreases, which are very common during economic downturns, are: boxes of baby wipes went to 72 from 80 count; 16-ounce cans of corn went to 15.5 ounces and then to 14.5 ounces; the amount of chips in a Doritos bag declined by 20% over a period of 2 years. Sometimes, marketers promote the smaller packages as premium versions. For example, Kraft introduced "Fresh Stacks" of premium saltines: Each box has 15% fewer crackers than a standard box, but the price of both boxes was identical.[12]

The JND's Implications for Product Pricing and Improvement

Weber's law has important applications in marketing. Manufacturers and marketers endeavor to determine the relevant JNDs for their products for two reasons. First, they want to prevent changes (e.g., reductions in product size or quality, or increases in product price) from becoming readily discernible to the public

1936	1955	1965	1969

Source: Marcy Schneidewind/General Mills Marketing Inc.

1972	1980	1986	1996

FIGURE 4.4 Changes in the Betty Crocker Symbol

(i.e., remain below the JND). Second, they want to ensure that product improvements (e.g., improved or updated packaging, larger size, or lower price) are very apparent to consumers, but without being wastefully extravagant (i.e., they are at or just above the JND).

When it comes to product improvements, marketers very much want to meet or exceed the consumer's differential threshold; that is, they want consumers to readily perceive any improvements made in the original product. Marketers use the JND to determine the amount of improvement they should make in their products. Improvements below the JND will not be perceived and will hurt the credibility of a marketer promoting the product as "new and improved." For example, when Apple came up with some new products for which it claimed sharper displays, many consumers were disappointed because, apparently, the improvements were below the JND and therefore unperceived. However, when Apple introduced Retina Displays, they were hailed as a breakthrough technology because the improvements were far above the JND and easily noticeable.

The JND'S Implications for Logos and Packaging

Marketers often want to update their existing package designs without losing the recognition of loyal consumers. They usually make a number of small changes, each carefully designed to fall below the JND so that consumers will perceive only minimal difference between succeeding versions. For example, Figure 4.4 shows how Betty Crocker, the General Mills symbol, has been updated seven times from 1936 to 1996, but the basic elements of the symbol changed only minimally from one update to the next, in order to maintain continuous consumer recognition.

Figure 4.5 illustrates how Xerox, during its more than 100-year history, updated the company's logo many times. However, the logo was always updated carefully, with the JND in mind and without moving too drastically away from the previous logo that consumers readily recognized.

Marketers who do not consider the impact of the JND when introducing new logos may anger their loyal customers. For example:

1. Within a few days after introducing its new logo in several stores, The Gap received negative comments expressing resentment from customers. The firm immediately brought back its well-known and liked logo. Apparently, the new logo was too far beyond the JND of many consumers and too great of a change in The Gap's visual identity.

2. On its fortieth anniversary, the Starbucks name was removed from its logo, leaving only a more stylish illustration of the green mermaid. The company also revealed two future evolutions of its logo to be introduced, successively, on its fiftieth and sixtieth anniversaries. In spite of initial

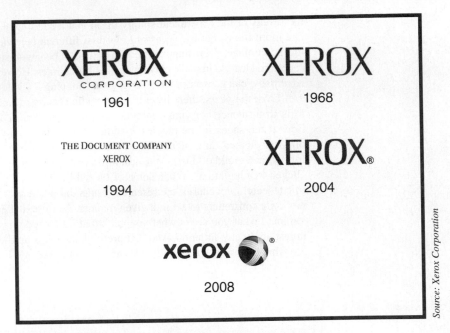

Source: Xerox Corporation

FIGURE 4.5 Changes in the Logo of the Xerox Company

complaints from consumers, the company did not bring the old logo back. Apparently, although the change is clearly above the JND, Starbucks' management believes that, as time passes, consumers will accept it.

3. For decades, Tropicana's brand symbol for its premium juice packaging has been an orange with a straw in it. Then, a new logo was introduced, depicting a large glass of orange juice. Apparently, the change was above the JND. Consumers complained, saying that they could no longer find their beloved premium orange juice in supermarkets and that the new package was similar to inexpensive store brands.

Subliminal Perception

Chapter 3 described how motivation sometimes occurs below one's level of conscious awareness. People can be "stimulated" below their level of conscious awareness as well. That is, they can perceive stimuli without being consciously aware that they are doing so. Stimuli that are too weak or too brief to be consciously seen or heard may nevertheless be strong enough to be perceived by one or more receptor cells. This process is called **subliminal perception**, because the stimulus is beneath the threshold, or "limen," of conscious awareness, though obviously not beneath the absolute threshold of the receptors involved.

The effectiveness of so-called subliminal advertising was reportedly first tested at a drive-in movie theater in New Jersey in 1957, where the words "Eat popcorn" and "Drink Coca-Cola" were flashed on the screen during the movie. Exposure times were so short that viewers were unaware of seeing any message. It was reported that during the six-week test period, popcorn sales increased 58% and Coca-Cola sales increased 18%, but these findings were later reported to be false. Years later, it was discovered that although the simple subliminal stimulus "COKE" served to arouse thirst in subjects, the subliminal command "DRINK COKE" did not have a greater effect, nor did it have any behavioral consequences.

Despite the many studies of subliminal persuasion, there is no evidence that subliminal advertising persuades people to buy goods or services. A review of the research indicates that subliminal perception has no effect on attitudes toward products and consumption behavior, and that most of its effects were "researched" in highly artificial situations.[13] A study from done in a laboratory setting, supports this conclusion. Subjects were asked to keep a running total of numbers flashed on a screen, where they were also exposed to images of either IBM or Apple logos, shown at a speed faster than could be consciously seen. The subjects then performed a creativity exercise. The subjects subliminally exposed to the Apple logo scored higher on the creativity test than those exposed to the IBM logo or to no logo at all.[14] Some interpret these results to mean that a brand can make you perform better. For example, if you wear a swimsuit worn and endorsed by a champion swimmer, you will swim faster. Others argue that the results of the experiment simply mean that a subliminal stimulus may trigger certain associations and motivations, but not necessarily lead to different behavior. However, there is tangential indication that subliminal advertising may reduce antisocial behavior, such as that subliminal antishoplifting messages broadcasted in malls may lower shoplifting rates. However, there is no credible evidence that such advertising can get consumers to engage in shopping—a voluntary and pleasant behavior.

Over the years, there have been sporadic reports of marketers using subliminal messages in efforts to influence consumption behavior. For example, in 1995, Disney was accused of using subliminal messages in the movies Aladdin (where the hero allegedly whispers "good teenagers, take off your clothes" in a subaudible voice) and The Lion King (where the letters "S-E-X" are allegedly formed in a cloud of dust). At times, it has been difficult to separate truth from fiction regarding such alleged manipulations. When some of the subliminal methods were tested methodically using scientific research procedures, the research results did not support the notion that subliminal messages can persuade consumers to act in a given manner. As to sexual embeds, most researchers are of the opinion that "what you see is what you get"; that is, a vivid imagination can see whatever it wants to see in just about any situation. And that pretty much sums up the whole notion of perception: Individuals see what they want to see and what they expect to see.

Perceptual Selection

Learning Objective

2 To understand why consumers process only a small amount of the information they receive.

Subconsciously, consumers are very selective when exposed to stimuli. An individual may look at some things, ignore others, and turn away from still others. In actuality, people receive (i.e., perceive) only a small fraction of the stimuli to which they are exposed. Consider, for example, a woman at a Whole Foods Market. She may be exposed to more than 30,000 products of different colors, sizes, and shapes; to perhaps 300 people (looking, walking, searching, talking); to smells and tastes (from fruit, meat, and sample displays); to sounds within the store (audio announcements, music, cooking demonstrations); and many other stimuli. Yet she manages on a regular basis to visit the store, select the items she needs, pay for them, and leave, all within a relatively brief period of time, without losing her sanity or her personal orientation to the world around her. This is because she exercises *selectivity* in perception.

Which stimuli get selected depends on two major factors, in addition to the nature of the stimulus itself: (1) consumers' previous experience as it affects their expectations (what they are prepared, or "set," to see), and (2) their motives at the time (their needs, desires, interests, and so on). Each of these factors can increase or decrease the probability that a stimulus will be perceived.

The Stimulus

Physical stimuli that affect consumers' perceptions of products and evoke attention include the product itself, its attributes, package design, brand name, advertisements, and commercials (including copy claims, choice and sex of model, positioning of model, size of ad, and typography), and placement of promotional messages within the advertising space. Ads that contrast with their environments are very likely to be noticed. The use of a dramatic image of the product against a white background with little copy in a print advertisement, the absence of sound in a commercial's opening scene, an ad appearing where consumers do not expect it—all offer sufficient contrast from their environments to achieve differentiation and merit the consumer's attention.

Contrast is one of the most attention-compelling attributes of a stimulus. Advertisers often use extreme attention-getting devices to achieve maximum contrast and, thus, penetrate the consumer's perceptual "screen." The Crest ads in Figure 4.6 illustrate a good use of contrast. They evoke contrast because they show two objects—cherries and coffee—colored in white, which is an inaccurate. Crest's benefit comes through clearly: Eating cherries or drinking coffee stains teeth and Crest can remove such stains. Other forms of contrast are unexpected and unrealistic images.

Shocking and unrealistic images provoke attention. The ads in Figure 4.7 are from a campaign created by the Children's Defense Fund, an advocacy group. It depicts the potential tragic, long-term costs of cutting government-financed initiatives for children. One ad depicts a pregnant woman whose head is that of an infant girl and explains that cutting just $4,000 of Medicaid and food stamps from a girl in a low-income home is likely to get her to drop out of school. Then, the teenager might become pregnant, which will cost taxpayers a lot of money because the government pays huge sums for teen pregnancies. A second ad shows a tattooed man in a prison cell, whose head is that of an infant boy. The ad warns that eliminating early education investments now increases the infant's chances of going to prison later by up to 39%, and paying for that imprisonment will cost taxpayers nearly three times

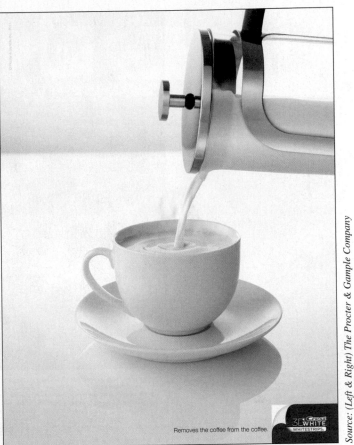

Removes the cherry from the cherries.

Removes the coffee from the coffee.

Source: (Left & Right) The Procter & Gample Company

FIGURE 4.6 Contrasts Provoke Attention: Crest Removes Stains from Teeth

more per year than the cost of the child's education. The images of combining infant faces with adult bodies are shocking and make the ads highly noticeable.[15]

Expectations

People usually see what they expect to see, and what they expect to see is usually based on familiarity, previous experience, or a set of expectations. In a marketing context, a person tends to perceive products and product attributes according to his or her own expectations. A student who has been told by his friends that a particular professor is interesting and dynamic will probably perceive the professor in that manner when the class begins; a teenager who attends a horror movie that has been billed as terrifying will probably find it so. Sometimes, stimuli that conflict sharply with expectations receive more attention than those that conform to expectations. One study found that people who believed that they had prepared the dishes they tasted rated the food almost twice as high as others who tasted the same food but did not prepare it.[16] These results have implications for many "I made it myself" products. Marketers should stress the self-preparation aspects in all the promotions for those products, because such statements are likely to enhance their customers' satisfaction.

For years, some marketers have used blatant sexuality in advertisements for products to which sex is not relevant, in the belief that such advertisements would attract a high degree of attention. However, ads with irrelevant sexuality often defeat the marketer's objectives, because readers tend to remember the sexual aspects of the ad (e.g., the innuendo or the model), but not the product or brand advertised. Nevertheless, some advertisers continue to use erotic appeals in promoting a wide variety of products, (see Chapter 7).

Motives

People tend to perceive the things they need or want: The stronger the need, the greater the tendency to ignore unrelated stimuli in the environment. A student who is looking for a new cell phone provider is more likely to notice and read carefully ads for deals and special offers regarding such services

FIGURE 4.7 Shocking Images Induce Attention: Children's Defense Fund

than his roommate who is satisfied with his present cellular service. In general, there is a heightened awareness of stimuli that are relevant to one's needs and interests and a decreased awareness of stimuli that are irrelevant. An individual's perceptual process simply attunes itself more closely to those elements in the environment that are important to him or her. Someone who is overweight is more likely to notice ads for diet foods; a sexually repressed person may perceive sexual symbolism where none exists.

Marketing managers recognize the efficiency of targeting their products to the perceived needs of consumers. For example, a marketer can determine through marketing research what different segments of consumers view as the ideal attributes of the products they need and wish to purchase. The marketer can then segment the market on the basis of those needs, and vary the product advertising, so that consumers in each segment will perceive the product as meeting their own special needs, wants, or interests.

Selective Perception

As the preceding discussion illustrates, the consumer's selection of stimuli from the environment is based on the interaction of expectations and motives with the stimulus itself. **Selective exposure** occurs when consumers *tune into* messages that they find pleasant or with which they are sympathetic, and they *actively avoid* painful or threatening ones. They also selectively expose themselves to advertisements that reassure them of the wisdom of their purchase decisions.

Consumers exercise a great deal of selectivity in terms of the attention they give to commercial stimuli. **Selective attention** is consumers' *heightened* awareness of stimuli that meet their needs or interests and *minimal* awareness of stimuli irrelevant to their needs. Thus, consumers are likely to note ads for products that would satisfy their needs and disregard those in which they have no interest. People also vary in terms of the kinds of information in which they are interested and the form of message and type of medium they prefer. Some people are more interested in price, some in appearance, and some in social acceptability. Some people like complex, sophisticated messages; others like simple ones.

Perceptual defense takes place when consumers subconsciously *screen out* stimuli that they find psychologically threatening, even though exposure has already taken place. Thus, threatening or otherwise damaging stimuli are less likely to be consciously perceived than are neutral stimuli at the same level of exposure. Furthermore, individuals sometimes unconsciously distort information that is not consistent with their needs, values, and beliefs. One way to combat perceptual defense is to vary and increase the amount of sensory input. For example, because surveys showed that most smokers no longer pay attention to the written warning labels on cigarette packs, some laws now require tobacco firms to feature graphic health warnings on cigarette packs and vary the text of these messages.

Consumers often protect themselves from being bombarded with stimuli by "blocking" some stimuli from conscious awareness. They do so out of self-protection, because of the visually overwhelming nature of the world in which we live. The popularity of such devices as TiVo and DVRs, which enable viewers to skip over TV commercials with great ease, is, in part, an outcome of individuals' quest for avoiding exposure to unwanted stimuli, such as commercials.

Perceptual Organization

Learning Objective

3 To understand how consumers organize consumption-related information.

People do not experience the numerous stimuli they select from the environment as separate and discrete sensations; rather, they tend to organize them into groups and perceive them as unified wholes. Thus, the perceived characteristics of even the simplest stimulus are viewed as a function of the whole to which the stimulus appears to belong. This method of perceptual organization simplifies life considerably for the individual. The principles underlying perceptual organization are often called **Gestalt psychology** (in German, "Gestalt" means "pattern or configuration"). Three of the basic principles of perceptual organization are figure and ground, grouping, and closure.

Figure and Ground

The term **figure and ground** refers to the interrelationship between the stimulus itself (i.e., figure) and the environment or context within which it appears (i.e., ground). As noted earlier, stimuli that contrast with their environment are more likely to be noticed. A sound must be louder or softer, a color brighter or paler. The simplest visual illustration consists of a figure on a ground (i.e., background). The figure is perceived more clearly because, in contrast to its ground, it appears to be well defined, solid, and in the forefront. The ground is usually perceived as indefinite, hazy, and continuous. The common line that separates the figure and the ground is generally attributed to the figure rather than to the ground, which helps give the figure greater definition. Consider the stimulus of music. People can either "bathe" in music or listen to music. In the first case, music is simply background to other activities; in the second, it is the figure. Figure is more clearly perceived because it appears to be dominant; in contrast, ground appears to be subordinate and, therefore, less important.

Prior experiences affect how figure and ground pattern are perceived. For example, a short time following the destruction of the World Trade Center on September 11, 2001, by hijacked airplanes, one of the authors came across an ad for Lufthansa (Germany's national airline) that featured a flying jet, photographed from the ground up, between two glass high-rise buildings. Rather than focusing on the brand and the jet (i.e., the figure), all the viewer could think about was the two tall glass towers in the background (i.e., the ground), and the possibility of the jet crashing into them. When the author presented the ad to his students, many expressed the same thoughts. Clearly, this figure–ground reversal was the outcome of the painful events that occurred in September 2001.

Advertisers have to put advertisements together carefully to make sure that the stimulus they want noted is seen as figure and not as ground. The musical background must not overwhelm the jingle; the background of an advertisement must not detract from the product. Print advertisers often silhouette their products against a nondistinct background to make sure that the features they want noted are clearly perceived. The Canadian Dental Association ad in Figure 4.8 illustrates how people cannot notice gum disease, but dentists can. The gums are the "ground" that surrounds a "figure." The "figure" is gum disease, which cannot be seen easily, because, unless you are a dentist, the figure and ground are not easily distinguishable when gum disease occurs. In some cases, the blurring of figure and ground is deliberate. A well-known Absolut Vodka campaign ran print ads in which the figure (the shape of the Absolut bottle) was poorly delineated against its ground, challenging readers to search for the bottle; the resulting audience "participation" produced more intense ads and greater consumer attention.

NOT EVERYBODY CAN SEE IT, BUT YOUR DENTIST CAN.
BOOK AN EXAM TODAY.

CANADIAN DENTAL ASSOCIATION

Source: Canadian Dental Association

FIGURE 4.8 Figure and Ground Reversal

The picture of the woman in Figure 4.9 is another example of figure–ground reversal. How old would you say she is? Look again very carefully. Depending on how you perceive figure and how you perceive ground, she can be either in her early 20s or her late 70s. Marketers must test their advertisements in order to ensure that they do not confuse consumers because there is no clear indication of which is figure and which is ground.

Obscuring the Distinction Between Figure and Ground

A marketing technique based on the principle of figure-and-ground consists of inserting advertisements into entertainment content. **Product placement** takes place when the advertised product (i.e., the figure) is deliberately integrated into the TV show or film (i.e., the ground) in one or more of the following ways:[17]

1. The product is used by the cast (e.g., in such shows as Survivor and American Idol).
2. The product is integrated into the plot (e.g., a Sex and the City episode centered around Absolut vodka was entitled "Absolut Hunk").
3. The product is associated with a character (e.g., the character is also the product's advertising spokesperson).

One study found that a brand integrated and prominently featured in a TV program may produce *negative* feelings toward the brand among viewers who liked the program *a lot*, but those who liked the program *less* were more likely to develop *positive* attitudes toward the brand.[18] Thus, advertisers must be extremely careful in using product placement.

Source: E.G. Boring, "A New Ambiguous Figure," American Journal of Psychology, Vol. 42 (3), (July 1930): 444

FIGURE 4.9 Depending on One's Perception of Figure and Ground, the Women Is Either Old or Young

Increasingly and deliberately, consumers avoid watching TV commercials by using time-shifting devices such as DVRs programmed to delay a live broadcast by, say, fifteen minutes, sophisticated remote controls, or the "skip ad" option online. In response, advertisers have been trying to outsmart consumers by creating their own shows (i.e., content). Budweiser created a reality show entitled The Big Time, featuring Budweiser logos on the contestants' clothing. Kmart founded an online show for teenage girls entitled First Day, in which all the cast members wear Kmart clothes. Three large stores—Saks Fifth Avenue, Macy's, and H&M—created a national reality TV show entitled Fashion Star, which features their store buyers (i.e., those who decide on the clothes the store sells) as the judges of aspiring fashion designers, who appear as the contestants.[19] These practices show how clever marketers can blur the distinction between figures (i.e., promotional message or symbol) and ground (i.e., the program's content) and expose consumers to advertisements even if the consumers try to avoid them.

Grouping

Grouping refers to people's instinctive tendency to group stimuli together so that they become a unified picture or impression. The perception of stimuli as groups or chunks of information, rather than as discrete bits of information, facilitates memory and recall. Marketers use grouping to imply certain desired meanings in connection with their products. For example, an advertisement for tea may show a young man and woman sipping tea in a beautifully appointed room before a blazing hearth. The overall mood implied by the grouping of stimuli leads the consumer to associate the drinking of tea with romance, fine living, and winter warmth.

We remember and repeat our social security numbers, because we automatically group them into three "chunks," rather than trying to remember nine separate numbers. Similarly, we recall and repeat phone numbers in three segments: the area code, first three digits, and the last four digits. Also, for decades, Americans had five-digit Zip Codes grouped as a single chunk; when four additional digits were added to Zip Codes, the U.S. Postal Service has faced a challenge in its quest to get Americans to recall the extra digits, because it was trying to add a new chunk of information to a strongly established grouping pattern.

Grouping has implications for placing products in supermarkets. For example, as part of a new in-store marketing campaign, Vlasic's pickle jars were moved from the aisles where they had traditionally been placed to locations next to the products with which pickles are eaten, such as hamburgers and buns.[20] The placement of Coca-Cola products in supermarkets is a brilliant example of grouping. The company creates "interaction points" by placing different-size Coca-Cola bottles and its bottled water next to foods with which they are "connected." For example, bottled water is placed near salad bars and family-size bottles of Coke next to takeout counters containing large portions of prepared foods.

Closure

Closure is people's instinct to organize pieces of sensory input into a complete image or feeling. Individuals need closure, which means that if they perceive a stimulus as incomplete, they are compelled to figure out its complete meaning. If a message they receive is incomplete, they consciously or subconsciously fill in the missing pieces. If the full understanding of a promotional message requires completion and some mental effort, consumers are likely to take the time to figure out its meaning in order to feel closure. For example, the Gillette ads in Figure 4.10, are better remembered than completed ones, because a person facing partial content feels compelled to finalize it so as to achieve closure. Some examples of ads that induce closure include: (1) asking consumers to un-scramble words (e.g., a Clorox ads listing unexpected uses of the product, such as, when unscrambled, read "dog bowl" and a baby's "teething ring"); (2) showing pictures and asking consumers to name the activities or items shown (e.g., Figure 15.3); (3) including words with missing letters and asking consumers to fill in the blanks; and (4) asking consumers to match, say, occupations with people shown wearing different styles of clothes.

The need for closure has interesting implications for marketers. Promotional messages in which viewers are required to "fill in" information beg for completion by consumers, and the very act of completion serves to involve consumers more deeply in the message. In a related vein, advertisers have discovered that they can achieve excellent results by using the soundtrack of a frequently viewed television commercial on radio. Consumers who are familiar with the TV commercial perceive the audio track alone as incomplete; in their need for completion, they mentally play back the ad's visual content from memory.

Source: (Top & Bottom) The Gillette Company

FIGURE 4.10 Consumers Will "Fill In" The "Missing" Parts of the Gillette Ads

Perceptual Interpretation: Stereotyping

Learning Objective

4 To understand why and how consumers "add" biases to stimuli and the implications of this tendency for marketing.

The preceding discussion has emphasized that perception is a personal phenomenon. People exercise selectivity as to which stimuli they perceive, and they organize these stimuli on the basis of certain psychological principles. The interpretation of stimuli is also uniquely individual, because it is based on what individuals expect to see in light of their previous experiences, the number of plausible explanations they can envision, and their motives and interests at the time of perception.

Stimuli are often highly ambiguous. Some stimuli are weak because of such factors as poor visibility, brief exposure, high noise level, or constant fluctuation. When stimuli are highly ambiguous, an individual will usually interpret them in such a way that they serve to fulfill personal needs, wishes, interests, and so on. This is the principle that provides the rationale for the projective tests discussed in Chapter 3. Such tests provide ambiguous stimuli (such as incomplete sentences, unclear pictures, or untitled cartoons) to respondents who are asked to interpret them. How a person describes a vague illustration is a reflection not of the stimulus itself, but of the subject's own needs, wants, and desires. Through the interpretation of ambiguous stimuli, respondents reveal a great deal about themselves.

Individuals carry biased pictures in their minds of the meanings of various stimuli, which are termed **stereotypes**. Sometimes, when presented with sensory stimuli, people "add" these biases to what they see or hear and thus form distorted impressions. Several years ago, an ad for Benetton featuring two men—one black and one white—handcuffed together, which was part of the "United Colors of Benetton" campaign promoting racial harmony, produced a public outcry because people perceived it as depicting a white man arresting a black man. Clearly, this perception was the result of stereotypes, as there was nothing in the ad to indicate that the white person was arresting the black person rather than the other way around. Marketers must be aware of possible stereotypes, because these images reflect people's expectations and influence how stimuli are subsequently perceived.

The Saab ad in Figure 4.11 is a prime example of trying to dispel a stereotype. Apparently, Saab discovered that many consumers (possibly, many Swedes) perceived its cars as similar to luxury cars made in Germany (presumably because some Saab and BMW models look similar). The ad's tagline is "Nicht German," which means "Not German," and its copy reads as follows: "We mean no disrespect to our Bavarian neighbors. After all, German luxury cars are some of the finest in the world. But here, in Sweden, Saabs are designed for a different kind of driver."* The ad then details the specific features of the car model advertised.

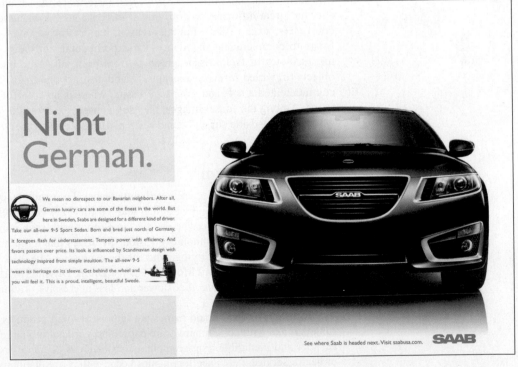

FIGURE 4.11 Dispelling a Stereotype: Saab Is Not German

Source: Saab Cars North America

---

* Saab ad copy

There are many reasons behind stereotyping. Generally, people stereotype because it makes the processing of sensory input quicker and easier. For example, many children have been educated to offer their seats on a bus to older persons, because, presumably, older persons are physically weak. On occasion, however, an athletic older person may refuse the offer, or even be insulted by it, because he or she feels that stereotyping all older persons as weak is an insult. Similarly, we often typecast movie stars as, say, "action heroes" and may be reluctant to see a romantic comedy in which they play a leading role. We must note that stereotyping consists of oversimplifying an image either positively or negatively. Therefore, when we pass an H&M store that just opened, we immediately know that it offers fashionable clothing at reasonable prices. In this case, the stereotype is positive and the result of previous shopping and H&M's positive image.

The triggers of stereotyping are physical appearance, descriptive terms, first impressions, and the halo effect.

Physical Appearance

People tend to attribute the qualities they associate with certain types of people to others who resemble them, whether or not they consciously recognize the similarity. For this reason, the selection of models for print advertisements and for television commercials can be a key element in their persuasiveness. Culturally, attractive models are likely to be more persuasive and have a more positive influence on consumer attitudes and behavior than average-looking models; attractive men are perceived as more successful businessmen than average-looking men. However, using attractive models without any other considerations does not increase ads' effectiveness. Thus, advertisers must ensure that there is a rational match between the product advertised and the physical attributes of the model used to promote it. For example, highly attractive models are likely to be perceived as having more expertise regarding *enhancement* products (e.g., jewelry, lipstick, perfume), but not *problem-solving* products (e.g., products that correct beauty flaws such as acne or dandruff). The SPYMUSEUM.ORG ads shown in Figure 4.12 poke fun at physical stereotyping with the headline "nothing is what it seems" and a portrayal of people who presumably are spies, although they "do not look like spies." That is, they defy most people's mental images of spies.

Products' physical appearance often influences consumers' judgments. A study indicated that the perceived taste of orange juice and consumers' ability to distinguish between three levels of sweetness were influenced by subtle color variations of the juice and also, somewhat unexpectedly, that such variations influenced perceived taste more than brand and price.[21] The shape of packages has great influence on consumers' impressions (as discussed later in this chapter) and affects consumers' expectations. For this reason, ice cream packages are round because this shape was found to communicate abundance. An experimental study investigated how consumers construed the attributes of facial tissue products from print ads, each including one of the following three objects (in varied forms): cats, sunsets, and abstract paintings. The study found that a "fluffy cat" communicated a soft and *expensive* tissue, whereas a "colorful cat" conveyed a soft and *colorful* tissue. Among the sunset images, the "soft sunset" expressed a soft, expensive, and colorful tissue, whereas a "roadside sunset" conveyed a neither soft nor colorful but an inexpensive product.[22]

Descriptive Terms

Stereotypes are often reflected in verbal messages. For example, consumers who eat foods with elaborate names such as "succulent Italian seafood filet" are very likely to rate those foods as tastier and more appealing than those who eat the same foods with such mundane names as "seafood filet." As another example, the common expression "he drives like a real man" connotes fast, aggressive, and even somewhat reckless driving, whereas the expression "he drives like a woman" portrays the driver as effeminate. The ad from Mothers Against Drunk Driving (MADD) in Figure 4.13 dispels the "effeminate" image by stating that slower and less aggressive driving represents more responsible driving for *both* genders.

Although distinct brand names are important to all products or services, associations that consumers make with certain names are particularly crucial in marketing services, because services are abstract and intangible. For example, names such as "Federal Express" and "Humana" (a provider of health services) are excellent names because they are distinctive, memorable, and relevant to the services that they offer. In contrast, "Allegis"—a short-lived brand name aimed at creating a business travel concept by combining United Airlines, Hertz, and Hilton and Westin Hotels under one umbrella—failed because it conveyed nothing to consumers about the type of services it offered.[23]

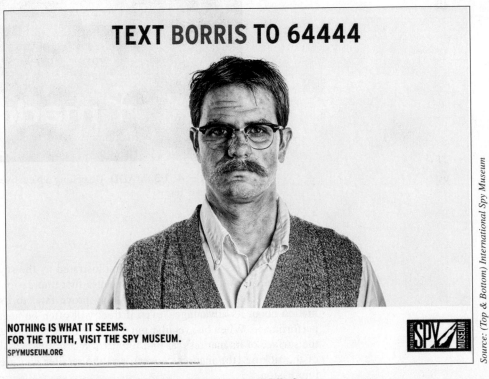

FIGURE 4.12 Stereotypes: What Do Spies Look Like?

Advertisers must be careful about using canned stereotypes and "common wisdom" in their persuasive messages. For example, gender-role stereotypes view young boys as having "instrumental" orientation focused on problem solving and young girls as having "communal" orientation focused on relationships and group harmony. A study examined young children's attitudes toward ads that included "instrumental" scripts (e.g., eating a cracker will make you strong) and "communal" scripts (e.g., a cracker is a great snack to have with your friends). The study found that preadolescent children did not necessarily respond more favorably to messages that included stereotypical gender-role attributes.[24]

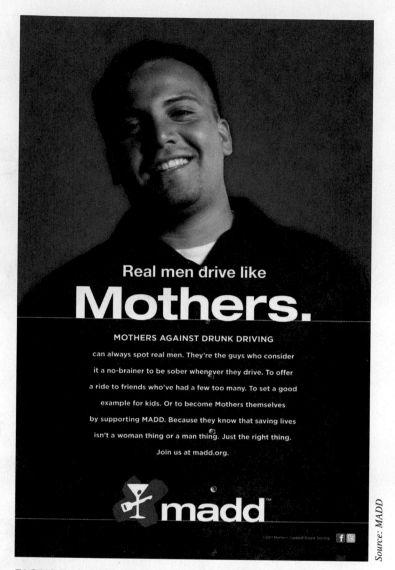

Source: MADD

FIGURE 4.13 MADD: Dispelling a Negative Stereotype Caused by Descriptive Terms

First Impressions

First impressions tend to be lasting, as illustrated by the saying that "You'll never have a second chance to make a first impression." Because first impressions are often lasting, introducing a new product before it has been perfected may prove fatal to its ultimate success; subsequent information about its advantages, even if true, will often be negated by the memory of its early poor performance. When one retailer put a picture of an aloe vera leaf and the wording "Aloe Vera" on the surface of its mattress, at first impression consumers assumed that aloe vera was a component of the ticking (the mattress cover), and the retailer had great difficulty in dispelling this initial impression.[25]

Halo Effect

The **Halo effect** refers to the overall evaluation of an object that is based on the evaluation of just one or a few dimensions. The linguistic definition of "halo" signifies light, honor, and glory. Thus, in marketing, the term refers to a prestigious image of a product "rubbing off on" other products marketed under the same brand name. For example, consumers who admire Porsche cars will be willing to spend a lot of money on sunglasses and other accessories sold under the same brand name. Historically, the term refers to situations in which the evaluation of a single object or person on a multitude of dimensions is based on the evaluation of just one or a few dimensions (e.g., a man is trustworthy, fine, and noble because he looks you in the eye when he speaks). Consumer behaviorists broadened the notion of the halo effect to include the evaluation of multiple objects (e.g., a product line) on the basis of the evaluation of just one dimension (a brand name or a spokesperson). Using this broader definition, marketers can take advantage of the halo effect when they extend a brand name associated with one line of products to another line. The lucrative field of **licensing** is based on the halo effect. Manufacturers and retailers hope to acquire instant recognition and status for their products by associating them with well-known names.

Tampering with the perceived halo effect of a product or brand can be disastrous. For example, in an attempt to enhance the image of JW Marriott, the Marriott hotel chain's upscale brand, Marriott took over the Righa Royal Hotel, an upscale hotel in New York City, and renamed it the JW Marriott New York. When the new name signs went up, scores of regular, upscale customers, who always stayed at the Righa when visiting New York City, canceled their reservations because they did not want to tell colleagues to contact them at the Marriott. The company restored the Righa Royal Hotel name, with the JW Marriott name included in smaller print.[26]

Consumer Imagery

Learning Objective

5 To understand the elements of consumers' imagery.

Consumer imagery refers to consumers' perceptions of all the components of products, services, and brands, and to how consumers evaluate the quality of marketers' offerings. Products and brands have images and symbolic values for consumers based on the unique benefits that these products claim they provide. The following section examines consumers' perceived images of products, brands, services, prices, product quality, retail stores, and manufacturers.

Brand Image

The desired outcome of effective **positioning** is a distinct "position" (or image) that a brand occupies in consumers' minds. This mental "position" must be unique and represent the core benefit the brand provides. Most new products fail because they are perceived as "me too" offerings that do not offer consumers any advantages or unique benefits over competitive products. The essence of the marketing concept is to create products that fulfill consumer needs. However, as more and more brands within a given product category fulfill consumers' needs effectively, consumers often rely primarily on the brand's image and claimed benefits in their purchase decisions. Furthermore, in today's highly competitive marketplace, a distinctive brand image is very difficult to create and maintain. For example, the BlackBerry has been a highly successful product and dominated the market, and was probably the first smartphone introduced. However, consumers perceive many newer smartphones as being more fun and exciting than the BlackBerry, which they perceive as mainly suitable for business and not for personal use and multitasking. Clearly, if it is to remain a viable competitor in the smartphone market, BlackBerry must broaden its appeal.[27]

Take, for example, the chore of washing clothes, where the consumer's need is straightforward: To end up with clean clothes. However, the manner in which this need is fulfilled and the clothes are cleaned differs among brands' competitive claims. The *manner* of bringing about the clean clothes (i.e., fulfilling a need) is the brand's claimed benefit. The more unique the benefit and the way it is communicated to consumers, the more likely it is that the perceived image will differentiate the brand from its competitors. A unique perceived image leads to brand loyalty, where consumers buy the brand consistently and neither try nor switch to other brands. Table 4.2 lists the benefit claims and intended perceived images of several detergent brands.[28]

Occasionally, a brand's image must be updated. Consumers often view products that have been around for a long time as boring, especially when newer alternatives are introduced. Sweet'N Low pioneered the artificial sweeteners category, but in recent years had to compete with newer products. The ads in Figure 4.14 show how Sweet'N Low uses pink—the color by which it is widely recognized—to convey a more playful and artistic image. Other examples of brand image updates, focused on creating emotional bonds between the products and consumers, are described in Table 4.3.[29]

Package Image

In addition to the product's name, appearance, and features, packaging also conveys the brand's image. For example, the Tide detergent version that predominantly promises stain removal comes in

TABLE 4.2		Benefit Claims of Detergent Brands
BRAND	**BENEFIT**	**BENEFIT CLAIM**
Ecos	Environmentally friendly	Made by Earth Friendly Products and provides power-packed clean without toxins, petrochemicals, bleach, ammonia, phosphates or other harmful ingredients.
Caldrea	Sweet Pea Detergent	Mild but highly effective in removing stains and especially formulated for washing the clothes of babies and children. Tested by dermatologists and includes oils and surfactants derived from plants.
Cheer	Protects against wear and tear	One of the numerous detergent brands made by P&G. Protects against fading, color transfer, and fabric wear. Comes in powder or liquid and with or without bleach.
Ivory Snow	Mild and pure	Also a P&G brand. Provides mild cleansing and purity for a simple clean.
Tide	"Fabric cleaning and care at its best"	The best-selling detergent in the United States and also a P&G brand. The benefit offered is an "umbrella position" (see Chapter 2) within which P&G developed more than 30 versions of Tide, each with a unique benefit. For example, Ultra Tide with Bleach (an alternative to chlorine bleach), Tide Downy (with a touch of softness and freshness), and Tide Free ("No dyes. No perfumes. No worries").

Source: (Left & Right) Cumberland Packing Corporation

FIGURE 4.14 Sweet'N Low's More "Playful" Package Conveys More Fun and a Livelier Image

an orange plastic container with a large handle on its side and conveys the "heaviness" of the product, because consumers associate heaviness with the power to remove stains. In contrast, the New Tide Total Care products, which promise scents of fresh morning, rain, and spring days, come in slimmer, slicker packages in brighter shades of orange than the regular Tide, and the handle is angled and congruent with the more sophisticated benefit claim of this version of Tide. The container of the Ivory Snow detergent is white, round, and without a handle; this implies that the detergent should be squeezed into the washer, thus supporting the "gentle cleanliness" claim of this brand.

The perception of scent and the associations made with different aromas vary greatly among individuals. For this reason, it is extremely difficult to convey an "image" of a fragrance. To buyers of perfumes, the only tangible evidence of the product's nature and quality is the packaging, the cost of which often accounts for up to 50% of the total cost of the perfume. A study identified several holistic (or Gestalt) designs of packages, each conveying a distinct, prominent brand impression.

TABLE 4.3	Brand Image Updates Designed to Create Emotional Bonds between Brands and Consumers	
BRAND	**THEME**	**ADVERTISING CAMPAIGN**
Dell Computer	"More You"	Focused on personalizing technology and getting consumers to think about how they can use the products' features rather than focusing on the products' technical specifications.
StarKist Tuna	"Sorry, Charlie" (reworked)	Reworks the brand's vintage "Sorry, Charlie" slogan. Some refer to ads based on nostalgia as "comfort marketing"—an approach whose objective is to evoke fond memories of mascots and songs.
Quaker Oats	"Go humans, go"	Reflects Americans' optimism and determination to explore new frontiers. It hails the pursuit of dreams and aims at lifting consumers' spirits, and is also articulated in Quaker Oats commercials where the announcer proclaims: "The power of Quaker is in everything we make."
Lay's Potato Chips	"Happiness is simple"	Features actual farmers who grow potatoes used to make the chips. They appear genuine, simple, and plain-spoken. The idea is to get consumers to think of Lay's as a food rather than a snack. The campaign's theme is "Happiness is simple," and the website features a "Happiness Exhibit."
Google	Nostalgia, engaging consumers in technology	Employs classic TV commercials from the 1960s and 70s. It demonstrates how Web ads can be engaging and stir the soul rather than being strictly transactional and informative. For example, a classic 1972 "Hilltop" spot for Coke featured a chorus singing "buy the world a Coke and keep it company." The Google ad asks consumers to send free Cokes around the world to people they have never met through mobile applications and customized vending machines.
Mott's Apple Juice	"Words to grow by"	Aimed at mothers of children aged 6 and younger and focused on joining them together. The mothers are invited to share their thoughts on raising a family in a dedicated Web site.
Colonial Williamsburg	"Be part of the story"	The campaign is for an attraction that recreates life in 18th-century Virginia; it is focused on "engagement interaction" and seeks to establish an active role for visitors.

Sources: Mark Hachman, "Dell's 'More You' Ads Mean a Renewed Consumer Push," 7.5.11 online.wsj.com; Stuart Elliott, "Google Remixes Old Campaigns, Adding a Dash of Digital Tools," 3.8.12 nytimes.com; Stuart Elliott, "In New Ads, Stirring Memories of Commercials Past," 1.12.12 nytimes.com; Stuart Elliott, "Sit Under the Apple Tree With Me, Juice Brand Asks," 6.7.10 nytimes.com Stuart Elliott, "Promoting a Potato Chip Using Many Farmers, and Less Salt," May 25, 2010, nytimes.com; Stuart Elliott, "So, Virginia, What's the Story," nytimes.com February 1, 2010.

For each package type, the study also identified the brand personality features that consumers associate with it. Generic images of the package types and the corresponding perceptions appear in Figure 4.15.[30]

Service Image

Compared with manufacturing firms, service marketers face several unique problems in positioning and promoting their offerings. Because services are intangible, image becomes a key factor in differentiating a service from its competition. Thus, the marketing objective is to enable the consumer to link a specific image with a specific brand name. Many service marketers have developed strategies to provide customers with visual images and tangible reminders of their service offerings. These include delivery vehicles painted in distinct colors, restaurant matchbooks, packaged hotel soaps and shampoos, and a variety of other specialty items. Many service companies feature real service employees in their ads (as tangible cues) and use people-focused themes to differentiate themselves.

The design of the service environment is an important aspect of service positioning strategy, and sharply influences consumer impressions. For example, targeting the dynamic and technologically oriented Generation Y, many stores significantly increased the sensory stimuli provided within the store, including live DJs, dim lighting, scented environments, loud ultramodern music, flat-screen TVs, and live models. Some Apple stores are open 24 hours and are designed to keep Apple users there even if they are not buying products. Thus, the stores include long tables and chairs with electrical outlets and wireless online access so that Apple users can work on their own projects and also interact with other users. One study indicated that the arousal level within the store environment must match the expectations of the shoppers in order to avoid perceived over- or understimulation.[31]

PACKAGE	MASSIVE	CONTRASTING	NATURAL	DELICATE	NONDESCRIPT
Shape	a	b	c	d	e
Perceived as	Robust and unelaborative	Nonharmonious and irregular	Harmonious and archetypical	Muted, sleek, delicate, elaborate, and attention-getting	Simple, clean, discreet, undifferentiable from others
Characteristics	Unexciting, un-sophisticated but rugged (i.e., strong, robust)	Exciting and rugged but lacking in the necessary ability (i.e., competence)	Sincere and sophisticated	Competent and sophisti-cated but not rugged	Low sincerity, unexcit-ing and not robust

Source: U.R. Orth and K. Malkewitz, "Holistic Package Designs..." *Journal of Marketing* 72 (May 2008): 64–81.

FIGURE 4.15 Perceptions of Perfume Bottles

Perceived Price

Perceived price is the customer's view of the value that he or she receives from the purchase. For example, consumers generally perceive a low price for a meal at a fast-food outlet, as well as a high price for a meal at a gourmet restaurant, as consistent with the value that they receive in both instances and therefore as fair. However, many reasonable consumers may argue that paying about $500 per person for a meal (there are several restaurants in New York City that charge these prices, and the meals do not include wine or alcohol) is unreasonable, because they cannot see how *any* meal can be equivalent to the value of $500.

How a consumer perceives a price—as high, low, or fair—strongly influences both purchase intentions and post-purchase satisfaction. Consider the perception of price fairness, for example. Customers often pay attention to the prices paid by other customers (such as senior citizens, frequent flyers, affinity club members), and sometimes perceive such differential pricing as unfair. No one is happy knowing he or she paid more (sometimes much more) for an airline ticket or a movie ticket than the person in the next seat. Perceptions of price unfairness affect consumers' perceptions of product value and, ultimately, their willingness to patronize a store or a service. Researchers also discovered that perceived price fairness affects customer satisfaction; this indicates that marketers using differential prices must anticipate customers' potential feelings of being exploited.[32]

Products advertised as "on sale" tend to create enhanced customer perceptions of savings and value. Different formats used in sales advertisements have differing impacts, based on consumers' reference prices. A **reference price** is any price that a consumer uses as a basis for comparison in judging another price. Reference prices can be external or internal. An advertiser generally uses a higher *external* reference price ("sold elsewhere at . . .") in an ad offering a lower sales price, to persuade the consumer that the product advertised is a really good buy. *Internal* reference prices are those prices (or price ranges) retrieved by the consumer from memory. Internal reference prices play a major role in consumers' evaluations and perceptions of value of an advertised price deal, as well as in the believability of any advertised reference price. However, consumers' internal reference prices change. For example, as the prices of flat-screen TVs declined sharply due to competition and manufacturers' abilities to produce them more cheaply, consumers' reference prices for this product have declined as well, and they no longer perceive flat-screen TVs as a luxury product that only a few can afford.

The issue of reference prices is complex and the focus of many studies. For example, one study discovered that fair price, rather than expected price, determined consumers' reference price for a new product category, whereas expected price had more impact than fair price on reference prices for existing product categories.[33] Another study showed that reference pricing coupled with

TABLE 4.4 Consumer Reactions to Unexpected Prices

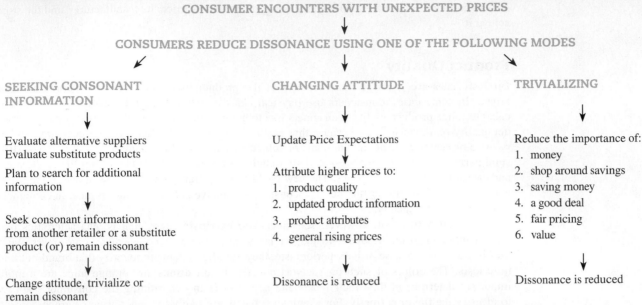

CONSUMER ENCOUNTERS WITH UNEXPECTED PRICES
↓
CONSUMERS REDUCE DISSONANCE USING ONE OF THE FOLLOWING MODES

SEEKING CONSONANT INFORMATION	CHANGING ATTITUDE	TRIVIALIZING
Evaluate alternative suppliers Evaluate substitute products	Update Price Expectations	Reduce the importance of:
Plan to search for additional information	Attribute higher prices to: 1. product quality 2. updated product information 3. product attributes 4. general rising prices	1. money 2. shop around savings 3. saving money 4. a good deal 5. fair pricing 6. value
Seek consonant information from another retailer or a substitute product (or) remain dissonant		
Change attitude, trivialize or remain dissonant	Dissonance is reduced	Dissonance is reduced

Source: J. Lindsey-Mulliken "Beyond Reference Price..." *Journal of Product and Brand Management* 12 nos. 2/3 (2003): 141. Emerald Publishing Group

limited-time availability (e.g., regularly $599, now $359 and on sale, 3 days only) produced more favorable price and store perceptions than each technique used alone.[34] Still another study illustrated the "right side effect" in relation to consumers' perceptions of discounts. When consumers saw regular and sale prices with the same left digits (e.g., 23 and 22), they perceived larger discounts when the right digits were smaller than 5 than when the right digits were higher than 5. Thus, consumers may perceive a discount from $23 to $22 as providing more value than a discount from $19 to $18.[35] Another study demonstrated that price discounts immediately increased buying intentions and lowered consumers' future reference prices.[36] Generally, a discount of $10 is more appealing on a product whose regular price is $20 than on a product whose regular price is $60. One study discovered that when consumers thought of their reference prices, a $10 discount sometimes seemed less appealing when the price was $20 than when it was $60.[37] These studies illustrate that marketers must be cautious when raising prices and always consider consumers' reference points when they do so.

Naturally, consumers tend to believe that the selling prices of market offerings are considerably higher than their perceived fair prices. When an advertised reference price is within a given consumer's acceptable price range, it is considered plausible and credible. If the advertised reference point is outside the range of acceptable prices (i.e., implausible), it contrasts with existing attitudes and will not be perceived as a valid reference point, thus adversely affecting both consumer evaluations and the advertiser's credibility. When consumers encounter prices that are significantly different from their expectations, they feel inharmonious (i.e., dissonant) and engage in "dissonance reduction" (see Chapter 6). They seek additional information, form cognitions that justify the high price, then consider buying other brands or trivialize some aspects of the buying situation. Table 4.4 explains how consumers handle dissonant situations caused by unexpectedly high prices.[38]

Perceived Quality

Learning Objective

6 To understand how consumers determine the quality of products and services.

Products and services can deliver high quality factually, as determined, say, by experts' judgments of scientific tests. However, if consumers do not perceive offerings as superior products that satisfy their needs and provide value, they will not purchase them, regardless of objective evidence. The perceived quality of products and services is based on a variety of informational cues that consumers associate with the offerings. Some of these cues are intrinsic to the product or service; others are extrinsic. Either singly or together, such cues provide the basis for perceptions of product and service quality. In this section, we first discuss the issues that make evaluating the quality of services more difficult than evaluating the quality of products. We then examine other cues that consumers consider in evaluating quality, including the product's price, its manufacturer, and the store selling it.

Product Quality

Intrinsic cues are physical characteristics of the product itself, such as size, color, flavor, or aroma. In some cases, consumers use physical characteristics (e.g., the flavor of ice cream or cake) to judge product quality. Consumers like to believe that they base their evaluations of product quality on intrinsic cues, because that enables them to justify their product decisions (either positive or negative) as being "rational" or "objective" choices. For example, the package of Hillshire Farm sliced meat was redesigned after studies showed that consumers want to see the meat and care a lot about how it looks. The new package has a transparent window showing the product. It also has a shallower tub, because consumers perceive neatly fanned-out meat in containers as being of higher quality.[39]

More often than not, however, consumers use **extrinsic cues**—that is, characteristics that are not inherent in the product—to judge quality. For example, though many consumers claim they buy a brand because of its superior taste, they are often unable to identify that brand in blind taste tests. The colors of such products as powdered fruit drinks and orange juice are a more important determinant than their labels and actual taste in determining the consumer's ability to identify the flavor correctly. For example, subjects are likely to view purple or grape-colored drinks as "tart" in flavor, and the orange-colored version as "flavorful, sweet, and refreshing." Many studies have shown that the packaging influences consumers' perceptions of products. For example, a study reported that both consumers who rated popcorn's taste as unfavorable and those who rated the same taste as favorable consumed more of the product when the container size was increased.[40] A study that compared how consumers perceive store brands and national brands discovered that consumers used extrinsic cues as indicators of quality.[41] An experimental study of how people judge the quality of two foods—shrimp and cheese—at two price levels and

Source: Journal of Brand Management, published F. Vigneron and LW Johnson "Measuring Perceptions of Brand Luxury," Journal of Brand Management 11, No. 6 (July 2004): 484. Reproduced with permission of Palgrave Macmillan

FIGURE 4.16 Measuring Perceptions of Brand Luxury

two consumption situations (i.e., elegant and less elegant surroundings) found out that perceived price had a positive impact on perceived quality among highly involved consumers. In addition, elegant surroundings positively affected the subjects' perceived quality of the foods and the pleasure felt when eating them.[42]

In the absence of actual experience with a product, consumers often evaluate quality on the basis of cues that are external to the product itself, such as price, brand image, manufacturer's image, retail store image, or even the perceived country of origin. For example, Häagen-Dazs, an American-made ice cream, has been incredibly successful with its made-up (and meaningless) Scandinavian-sounding name. The success of Smirnoff vodka, made in Connecticut, can be related to its apparent Russian derivation. One study found that the wine region was the most important determinant of consumers' perceived quality of wines and that Napa Valley and Sonoma had the strongest regional images among American vineyards.[43]

There are many ways to measure perceptions of quality. A scale that measures perceptions of brand luxury—a construct that is often related to perceived quality—is shown in Figure 4.16. This instrument measures perceptions of the brands' utilitarian, as well as personal, hedonic elements.[44]

Service Quality

It is more difficult for consumers to evaluate the quality of services than the quality of products. This is true because of certain distinctive characteristics of services: They are *intangible*, they are *variable*, they are *perishable*, and they are *simultaneously produced and consumed*. To overcome the fact that consumers are unable to compare competing services side-by-side as they do with competing products, consumers rely on surrogate cues (i.e., extrinsic cues) to evaluate service quality. In evaluating a doctor's services, for example, they note the quality of the office and examining room furnishings, the number (and source) of framed degrees on the wall, the pleasantness of the receptionist, and the professionalism of the nurse; all contribute to the consumer's overall evaluation of the quality of a doctor's services. One study found that online dating services generally fail to meet users' expectations because potential daters want to screen prospective partners by "experiential" attributes (e.g., rapport) whereas online dating providers only enable users to screen by "searchable" attributes (e.g., income). The study also found that using "virtual dates" (thus providing a tangible cue about the service) increased users' satisfaction with the online dating service.[45]

Because the actual quality of services can vary from day to day, from service employee to service employee, and from customer to customer (e.g., in food, in waitperson service, in haircuts, even in classes taught by the same professor), marketers try to standardize their services in order to provide consistency of quality. The downside of service standardization is the loss of customized services, which many consumers value.

Unlike products, which are first produced, secondly sold, and subsequently consumed, most services are first sold and then produced and consumed simultaneously. Whereas a defective product is likely to be detected by factory quality control inspectors before it ever reaches the consumer, an inferior service is consumed as it is being produced; thus, there is little opportunity to correct it. For example, a defective haircut is difficult to correct, just as is the negative impression caused by an abrupt or careless waiter.

During peak demand hours, the interactive quality of services often declines, because both the customer and the service provider are hurried and under stress. Without special effort by the service provider to ensure consistency of services during peak hours, service image is likely to decline. Many marketers try to change demand patterns in order to distribute the service more equally over time. For example, some restaurants offer significantly less expensive "early bird" dinners for consumers who come in before 7:00 p.m.

The most widely accepted framework for researching service quality stems from the premise that a consumer's evaluation of service quality is a function of the magnitude and direction of the gap between the customer's *expectations of service* and the customer's *assessment (perception) of the service* actually delivered.[46] For example, a brand-new graduate student enrolled in an introductory marketing course at a highly reputable university has certain expectations about the intellectual abilities of her classmates, the richness of classroom discussions, and the professor's knowledge and communication skills. At the end of the term, her assessment of the course's quality will be based on the differences between her expectations at the start of the term and her perceptions of the course at the end of the semester. If the course falls below her expectations, she will view it as a service of poor quality. If her expectations are exceeded, she will view the course as a high-quality educational experience.

The expectations of a given service vary widely among different consumers of the same service. These expectations stem from word-of-mouth consumers have heard about the service, consumers' past experiences, the promises made about the service in its ads and by its salespersons, the purchase alternatives available, and other situational factors. If the level of service received significantly exceeds these expectations, the service is perceived as of high quality and generates more customer satisfaction, increased probability of repeat patronage, and favorable word of mouth.[47] Also, marketers should never make promises that they cannot realistically deliver, because such claims raise customers' expectations and significantly increase the likelihood of lower perceived service quality when the service delivered is good, but not outstanding.

The **SERVQUAL scale** measures the "gaps" between customers' *expectations* of the services that they had purchased and their *perceptions* of the services that they had actually *received*. Measuring these discrepancies (or "gaps") includes two factors:

1. **Outcomes**, which focus on whether or not the services purchased were delivered *reliably*. For example, did a flight you took deliver you to your destination?

2. **Processes**, which focus on *how* the core services were delivered. That is employees' responsiveness, assurance, and empathy in handling customers. For example, how polite and understanding were the airlines' people if, say, your flight was delayed and you came close to missing a connection?

The processes enable service companies to exceed, not merely meet, customers' expectations. For instance, Amazon's core service (its "outcome dimension") is selling many types of products and brands. However, Amazon's advantage over competition is exceeding customers' expectations through superior "processes," which consists of its E-book readers and instant and reliable delivery of e-books, advanced database that generates recommendations for customers, shipment tracking system, the ability to preorder books yet to be published months in advance, subscriptions that include unlimited deliveries without shipping fees, and many other options.

Price/Quality Relationship

Look at the six polo shirts in Figure 4.17. Which two are the most expensive? Write their numbers down. Next, look at endnote 48 for this chapter (the chapter endnotes begin at the end of the text) and write down the names of the stores and designers of the shirts you selected, but do not look at the information for the other shirts.[48] Now, look at the two shirts again and decide whether you still believe they are the most expensive. Then, pick two other shirts and repeat this exercise.

FIGURE 4.17 Which Shirt Is the Most Expensive?

Let's assume that you picked shirts 2 and 3 as the most expensive. After looking at the end-note, you discovered that shirt 2 sells at Macy's and was designed by Polonimo, and shirt 3 sells at Camicia—a fashionable store in New York City's Soho area—and was designed by Bertoliani. You now have three pieces of information (i.e., sensory input): The shirts' photos, the stores that carry them, and their designers' names. Thinking of Camicia, you are likely to mentally "group" (associate) it with other fashionable stores in Soho, and the name Bertoliani probably evokes images of fashion-ably dressed, perfectly groomed, and athletic Italian men drinking espresso in Rome—the ones you saw featured in countless ads. You now decide that shirt 3 is the most expensive and also the most fashionable. However, your fellow classmate—who also picked shirts 2 and 3 initially—believes that the Polonimo shirt sold at Macy's is the most expensive.

You first saw only the photos of the shirts (sensory input), without any additional information. Then, the information about the stores and designers (more sensory input) determined how you "saw" the shirts in your mind. Your mental image of the shirts you had selected—was your subjective inter-pretation of the three pieces of visual and written sensory input. Unsurprisingly, your classmate's in-terpretation of the same information was different. After you study this chapter, you will realize why and how what you just experienced happened, and the key role of perception in consumer behavior. The answer to the question "which shirt is the most expensive?" is listed in endnote 49.[49]

Perceived product value has been described as a trade-off between the product's perceived ben-efits (or quality) and the perceived sacrifice— monetary and nonmonetary—necessary to acquire it. A **price/quality relationship** forms when consumers rely on price as an indicator of product quality; in short, they believe more expensive products are better. Some consumers who decide according to a price/quality relationship are actually relying on a well-known (and, hence, more expensive) brand name as an indicator of quality without actually relying directly on price per se. Because price is so often an indicator of quality, some product advertisements deliberately emphasize a high price to underscore the marketers' claims of quality. Marketers understand that, at times, products with lower prices may be interpreted as lesser quality. At the same time, consumers rely on the price and brand name when evaluating the product's prestige and symbolic value and use more concrete attributes of a product, such as performance and durability, to judge its overall performance. For these reasons, mar-keters must understand all the attributes that customers use to evaluate a given product and include all applicable information to counter any perceptions of negative quality associated with a lower price. In one study, subjects rated the pain in their wrist, artificially caused by an electric shock, after taking a pain reliever, which was actually a dummy, placebo pill. Half the subjects were told that the medica-tion they took costs $2.50 per dose, and the others learned that it costs 10 cents; in reality, all subjects received identical pills. Eighty-five percent of those who received the more expensive pill reported significant pain reduction, whereas only 61% of those who took the cheaper pill reported such relief. Clearly, consumers tend to believe that more expensive medications are more effective; this finding is consistent with previous research showing that consumers perceive generic drugs to be less effective than brand name medications, even though, chemically, the two medications are identical.[50]

In addition to price, consumers also use such cues as the brand and the store in which the product is bought to evaluate its quality. They view price as an indicator of quality if they have little infor-mation to go on, or if they have little confidence in their own ability to make the product or service choice on other grounds. When the consumer is familiar with a brand name, or has experience with a product (or service), or the store where it is purchased, price declines as a determining factor in prod-uct evaluation and purchase.

Many products and services are sold as "bundles" (e.g., sets of different pens, tickets to a se-ries of ballet performances), and price discounts lead to more sales of bundled products. A study showed that bundle discounts may have unforeseen results in the form of perceptions of lower qual-ity of all the items in the bundle, which will negatively affect future sales when these items are sold individually.[51]

Some price/quality perceptions are related to personal happiness. In one study, the researcher asked readers of a blog to list the 10 most expensive things they had ever bought, and then list the 10 purchases that had brought them the most happiness. Some products—such as boats and expensive weddings—did not deliver happiness per dollar. Still, there was considerable overlap between the most-expensive list and the most-happy list. Many people included their homes, college educations, vacations, and high-priced electronics in both lists.[52]

Store Image and Perceived Quality

Retail stores have images of their own that influence the perceived quality of the products they carry and consumers' decisions about where to shop. These images stem from the merchandise they carry, the brands sold and their prices, the level of service, the store's physical environment and ambiance, and its typical clientele (this can often be determined from the cars parked in the store's parking lot). One study demonstrated that consumers who have a strong positive image of a store did not find negative word-of-mouth about that store credible.[53]

The width and type of product assortment affect retail store image. Grocery retailers, for example, are often reluctant to reduce the number of products they carry out of concern that perceptions of a smaller assortment will reduce the likelihood that consumers will shop in their stores; they carry primarily widely advertised, best-selling brands. In contrast, Whole Foods Markets—a relatively small supermarket chain—has carved itself a profitable niche by carrying a smaller but highly selective range of products in comparison to conventional supermarkets. Whole Foods stores carry organic (perceived as healthier) products, many of which were bought from mom-and-pop producers; all food products carried are screened for artificial ingredients; and the chain no longer sells products with hydrogenated fats. The chain has been much more profitable than conventional supermarkets in spite of its limited product assortment. Clearly, the unique benefit that a store provides is more important than the number of items it carries in forming a favorable store image in consumers' minds. However, because Whole Food's prices are significantly higher than those of other supermarkets, the chain's nickname has become "Whole Paycheck" and made it rough for the company to attract new consumer segments. The company has been planning to open smaller stores carrying less expensive products, but it must first rid itself of its top-dollar reputation, which, unfortunately, has coined a catchy slogan.[54]

Customers often use brand, store image, and price together as a product quality indicators. When brand and retailer images become associated, the less favorable image becomes enhanced at the expense of the more favorable image. Thus, when a low-priced store carries a brand with a high-priced image, the image of the store will improve, whereas the image of the brand will be adversely affected. For that reason, marketers of prestigious designer goods often attempt to control the outlets where their products are sold. When upscale stores sell leftover expensive items to discount stores, they remove the designer labels from these goods as part of the agreements they have with the manufacturers.

Pricing discounts also affect store image. Stores that offer frequent, small discounts on large numbers of items are more likely to be perceived as "discount stores" and less prestigious than stores offering larger discounts on a smaller number of products. This has important implications for retailers' positioning strategies. In times of heavy competition, when it is tempting to hold frequent large sales covering many items, such strategies may result in an unwanted change in store image. For example, Lord and Taylor in New York City, formerly positioned as an upscale, high-class department store, advertises sales so frequently and so often fills its aisles with racks proclaiming bargain prices, that its upscale image has been tarnished, and its customer mix has changed. Marketers must also consider how price reductions of specific products affect consumers' perceptions. Poorly chosen price promotions cause confusion and may detract from consumers' perceptions of the store.

Manufacturer's Image and Perceived Quality

Consumer imagery extends beyond perceived price and store image. Manufacturers who enjoy a favorable image generally find that their new products are accepted more readily than those of manufacturers who have a less favorable or even a "neutral" image. Consumers also associate certain attributes with manufacturers. For example, Apple is perceived as "different" from other computers and smartphones. A Swatch is perceived as commonplace and inexpensive, whereas watches made by Rolex and Patek Philippe are perceived as expensive status symbols.

Institutional advertising is promotion that is designed to promote a company's overall image without overtly referring to specific products. For example, an ad for Siemens—a global conglomerate—used the slogan "The world of tomorrow needs answers that last" and featured energy-producing windmills placed in the open seas. The ad positioned the company as innovative, forward looking, and socially responsible, a corporate image that is likely to be strategically beneficial. For example, if residents of American communities located directly on the ocean perceive Siemens favorably, they would not mind seeing Siemens windmills from their homes, and would not object to them , whereas persons with neutral or unfavorable attitudes towards companies that "invade" their communities might object to and even prevent the placing of the windmills.

Although some marketers argue that product and service advertising do more to boost the corporate image than institutional advertising does, others see both types of advertising—product and institutional—as integral and complementary components of a total corporate communications program. When the reputation of Walmart was tarnished by allegations of unfair labor practices, sexual discrimination, and the publication of data indicating that the company caused most of America's trade imbalance with China, the company published ads stating that "Walmart Is Working for Everyone." In addition, the company's executives appeared on TV talk shows and met with community groups and government officials to dispel the negative associations.[55] Wal-Mart's troubles continued when a consumer advocacy group initiated an ad campaign that posed the question "Where would Jesus shop?" and argued that people of faith should not shop at the store during the holiday season because of the store's bad wages, benefits, and overseas child labor policies. This negative advertising also illustrates using Jesus' "halo effect"—a term discussed earlier.[56]

In Chapter 2 and within the discussion of repositioning, we discussed how banks' advertising triggered irresponsible consumer spending, which contributed to the financial calamity of 2008. Since then, many banks have been running ads that portray them as "warm" and "cozy" corporations. Examples of advertising slogans designed to convey this image include "where bankin's (*sic*) funner (*sic*)," "a better kind of bank," and "we make money with you, not off you."[57] Also, viral messages online can severely, negatively, and almost instantly affect a company's image. For example, Progressive Corporation—an auto-insurance company—sided with a driver who killed another driver whom they had insured, when the deceased driver's family sued the other driver for negligence. Progressive did so to avoid paying $75,000 to the family of the dead driver. One family member then described, in a blog, how Progressive sided with the killer of a person insured by them. The message "went viral" all over the Internet and generated a lot of angry comments against Progressive, as well as threats by many of its customers to cancel their insurance.[58]

Perceived Risk

Learning Objective

7 To understand consumers' perceived risks and how they handle and reduce those risks.

Consumers must constantly make decisions regarding what products or services to buy and where to buy them. **Perceived risk** is the uncertainty that consumers face when they cannot foresee the consequences of their purchase decisions. This definition highlights two relevant dimensions of perceived risk: uncertainty and consequences.

The degree of risk that consumers perceive and their own tolerance for risk taking are factors that influence their purchase strategies. It should be stressed that consumers are influenced by risks that they perceive, whether or not such risks actually exist. Risk that is not perceived—no matter how real or how dangerous—will not influence consumer behavior. The perception of risk is also a function of how the information is presented. For instance, one study discovered that, in evaluating prescription drugs, consumers greatly overestimated the actual likelihood of adverse events when these were described with words such as "common" or "rare." However, when the commercials induced positive moods, consumers engaged in more nuanced evaluation of product risk information and used it in judging the efficacy and other attributes of the products.[59]

In most situations, consumers' perceived risk is a function of multiple factors. The elements of perceived risk are functional risk, physical risk, financial risk, social risk, psychological risk, and time risk, which are listed and explained in Table 4.5.

Perceived Risk Varies

Consumer perception of risk varies, depending on the person, the product, the situation, and the culture. The amount of risk perceived depends on the specific consumer. Some consumers tend to perceive high degrees of risk in various consumption situations; others tend to perceive little risk. For example, adolescents who engage in high-risk activities, such as fast, complicated, and daring rollerblading or bicycling maneuvers, obviously perceived lower risk than those who do not engage in such high-risk activities. High-risk perceivers are often described as **narrow categorizers** because they limit their choices (e.g., product choices) to a few safe alternatives. They would rather exclude some perfectly good alternatives than chance a poor selection. Low-risk perceivers have been described as **broad categorizers** because they tend to make their choices from a much wider range of alternatives. They would rather risk a poor selection than limit the number of alternatives from which they can choose.

An individual's perception of risk varies with product categories. For example, consumers are likely to perceive a high degree of risk (e.g., functional risk, financial risk, time risk) in the purchase of a LED TV set because it is a very new and, so far, "unproven" product in terms of its superiority over HD TVs.

The degree of risk a consumer perceives is also affected by the shopping situation. At first, many consumers felt uncertain about buying products online. The market dominance that online

TABLE 4.5	The Elements of Perceived Risk	
TYPE OF PERCEIVED RISK	**DEFINITION**	**EXAMPLE**
Functional risk	Product will not perform as expected.	Can the E-book reader operate a whole day without having to be recharged?
Physical risk	Product can harm self and others; risk to self and others.	Is organic unpasteurized milk safe to drink? (Many states do not permit unpasteurized milk, but many greenmarkets carry it because it is organic.)
Financial risk	Product will not be worth its cost.	Will a new and cheaper model of an LED TV monitor become available six months from now?
Psychological risk	Poor product choice will bruise the consumer's ego.	Will I be embarrassed when my friends see me with a mobile phone that is not a smartphone?
Time risk	Time spent in product search may be wasted if the product does not perform as expected.	Will I be forced to compare all the different carriers' calling plans again if I experience a lot of "dropped calls" with the one I selected?

merchants gained over the years indicates that, because of positive shopping experiences and word-of-mouth, consumers now perceive little risk in online shopping. Obviously, this lower level of perceived risk is due to better technologies that enable buyers to examine the product online in greater detail and even "use" some products virtually. One study of online banking demonstrated that most consumers want to use online payments (mostly to meet deadlines and avoid past-due late penalties), but their willingness or unwillingness to do so is a function of their perceived risk of the security of online payment systems.[60] Studies also found that higher levels of consumer trust reduced perceived risk regarding shopping online.[61] Two studies discovered that the amount of product information posted on websites affects consumer risk perception and satisfaction, as well as the relationships among perceived risk, satisfaction, intention to revisit, purchase intent, and the process of the decision making itself.[62]

Consumers handle perceived risk differently, and the prominent ways to reduce purchase-related risk are summarized in Table 4.6.

The concept of perceived risk has major implications for the introduction of new products. Because high-risk perceivers are less likely than low-risk perceivers to purchase new or innovative products, it is important for marketers to provide such consumers with persuasive risk-reduction strategies, such as a well-known brand name (sometimes through licensing), distribution through reputable retail outlets, informative advertising, publicity, impartial test results, free samples, and money-back guarantees. Also, consumers can reduce perceived risk by using online resources that enable them to generate side-by-side comparisons depicting detailed charts of the features, prices, and ratings of all the available models within a given product category.

TABLE 4.6	Consumers Can Reduce Perceived Risk
METHOD	**DESCRIPTION**
Seek information	Consumers seek information about the product and product category through word-of-mouth communication (from friends and family and from other people whose opinions they value), from salespeople, and from the general media. They spend more time thinking about their choice and search for more information about the product alternatives when they associate a high degree of risk with the purchase.
Remain brand loyal	Consumers avoid risk by remaining loyal to a brand with which they have been satisfied instead of purchasing new or untried brands. High-risk perceivers are more likely to be loyal to their old brands and less likely to purchase newly introduced products.
Rely on brand image	When consumers have had no experience with a product, they tend to "trust" a favored or well-known brand name. They often think well-known brands are better and are worth buying for the implied assurance of quality, dependability, performance, and service.
Rely on store image	If consumers have no other information about a product, they often trust the judgment of the merchandise buyers of a reputable store and depend on them to have made careful decisions in selecting products for sale. Store image also provides assurance of return privileges and adjustment in case of dissatisfaction.
Buy the most expensive model or brand	As indicated in the discussion of price/quality relationship, consumers often feel that the most expensive model is probably the best in terms of quality.

Summary

Learning Objective 1: To understand the elements of perception and their role in consumer behavior.

Perception is the process by which individuals select, organize, and interpret stimuli into a meaningful and coherent picture of the world. Perception has strategy implications for marketers because consumers make decisions based on what they perceive rather than on the basis of objective reality. The lowest level at which an individual can perceive a specific stimulus is that person's absolute threshold. The minimal difference that can be perceived between two stimuli is called the differential threshold or just noticeable difference (JND). Consumers perceive most sensory stimuli above the level of their conscious awareness; however, weak stimuli can be perceived below the level of conscious awareness (i.e., subliminally). Research refutes the notion that subliminal stimuli influence consumers' buying decisions.

Learning Objective 2: To understand why consumers process only a small amount of the information they receive.

Consumers' selections of stimuli from the environment are based on the interaction of their expectations and motives with the stimulus itself. People usually perceive things they need or want, and block the perception of unnecessary, unfavorable, or painful stimuli. The principles of selective perception include the concepts of selective exposure, selective attention, and perceptual defense. Which stimuli get selected depends on two major factors, in addition to the nature of the stimulus itself: (1) consumers' previous experience as it affects their expectations (what they are prepared, or "set," to see), and (2) their motives at the time (their needs, desires, interests, and so on). Each of these factors can increase or decrease the probability that a stimulus will be perceived.

Learning Objective 3: To understand how consumers organize consumption-related information.

Consumers organize their perceptions into unified wholes according to the principles of Gestalt psychology: Figure and ground, grouping, and closure. Each of these concepts has important implications for understanding consumer behavior. The term "figure" refers to the promotional message and "ground" represents the environment or context within which the figure appears. Because consumers are bombarded with stimuli, they often actively seek to avoid promotional messages. Marketers try to obscure the difference between figure and ground so that their ads do not "stand out" from the contents of entertainment, such as movies and TV shows. They often use product placements, which occur when an advertised product (i.e., the figure) is deliberately integrated into a TV show or film (i.e., the ground). The perception of stimuli as groups or chunks of information, rather than as discrete bits of information, facilitates memory and recall. People instinctively try to organize pieces of sensory input into a complete image or feeling (i.e., they seek closure). Thus, if they perceive that a stimulus is incomplete, they feel compelled to figure out its complete meaning.

Learning Objective 4: To understand why and how consumers "add" biases to stimuli and the implications of this tendency for marketing.

The interpretation of stimuli is highly subjective and is based on what the consumer expects to see in light of previous experience, on motives and interests at the time of perception, and on the clarity of the stimulus itself. Individuals carry biased pictures in their minds of the meanings of various stimuli, which are termed stereotypes. Sometimes, when presented with sensory stimuli, people "add" these biases to what they see or hear and form distorted impressions. Stereotypes that distort objective interpretation stem from physical appearances, descriptive terms, first impressions, and the halo effect.

Learning Objective 5: To understand the elements of consumers' imagery.

Consumers perceive images of products and brands. The perceived image of a product or service (how it is positioned) is more important to its ultimate success than are its actual physical characteristics. Products and services that are perceived distinctly and favorably have a much better chance of being purchased than products or services with unclear or unfavorable images. The main elements of consumer imagery are consumers' perceptions of brands, packages, services, and prices.

Learning Objective 6: To understand how consumers determine the quality of products and services.

Consumers' perceived quality of products and services is based on a variety of informational cues that they associate with the offerings. Some of these cues are intrinsic to the product or service; others are extrinsic. Either singly or together, such cues provide the basis for perceptions of product and service quality. In the absence of direct experience or other information, consumers often rely on price as an indicator of quality. How a consumer perceives a price—as high, low, or fair—has a strong influence on purchase intentions and satisfaction. Consumers rely on both internal and external reference prices when assessing the fairness of a price. Products and services can deliver high quality factually, as determined, say, by experts' judgments of scientific tests. However, if consumers do not perceive offerings as superior products that satisfy their needs and provide value, they will not purchase them, regardless of objective evidence.

Learning Objective 7: To understand consumers' perceived risks and how they handle and reduce those risks.

Consumers often perceive risk in making product selections because of uncertainty as to the consequences of their decisions. In most situations, consumers' perceived risk is a function of multiple factors. The elements of perceived risk are functional risk, physical risk, financial risk, psychological risk, and time risk. Consumer strategies for reducing perceived risk include increased information search, brand loyalty, buying a well-known brand, buying from a reputable retailer, buying the most expensive brand, and seeking reassurance in the form of money-back guarantees, warranties, and pre-purchase trials. The concept of perceived risk has important implications for marketers, who can facilitate the acceptance of new products by incorporating risk-reduction strategies into their new-product promotional campaigns.

Review and Discussion Questions

4.1. How does sensory adaptation affect advertising effectiveness? How can marketers overcome sensory adaptation?

4.2. Discuss the differences between the absolute threshold and the differential threshold. Which one is more important to marketers? Explain your answer.

4.3. For each of these products—chocolate bars and cereals—describe how marketers can apply their knowledge of the differential threshold to packaging, pricing, and promotional claims during periods of (a) rising ingredient and materials costs and (b) increasing competition.

4.4. Does subliminal advertising work? Support your view.

4.5. How do advertisers use contrast to make sure that their ads are noticed? Would the lack of contrast between the ad and the medium in which it appears help or hinder the effectiveness of the ad?

4.6. What are the implications of figure-and-ground relationships for print ads and for online ads? How can the figure-and-ground construct help or interfere with the communication of advertising messages?

4.7. Why do marketers sometimes reposition their products or services? Illustrate your answer with examples.

4.8. Why is it more difficult for consumers to evaluate the effective quality of services than the quality of products?

4.9. Discuss the roles of extrinsic and intrinsic cues in the perceived quality of: (a) wines, (b) restaurants, (c) smartphones, and (d) graduate education.

Hands-on Assignments

4.10. Find three print examples of the kind of promotional methods that constitute ambush or experiential marketing. Evaluate each example in terms of the effectiveness of the sensory input provided.

4.11. Define selective perception, and relate one or two elements of this concept to your own attention patterns in viewing print advertisements and online commercials.

4.12. Select a company that produces several versions of the same product under the same brand name (do not use one of the examples discussed in this chapter). Visit the firm's website and prepare a list of the product items and the benefits that each item offers to consumers. Are all these benefits believable, and will they persuade consumers to buy the different versions of the product? Explain your answers.

4.13. Apply the concepts that address consumers' perceptions of service quality to evaluate this course at this point.

Key Terms

- absolute threshold *118*
- ambush marketing *119*
- broad categorizers *143*
- closure *128*
- consumer imagery *133*
- differential threshold (just noticeable difference, JND) *119*
- experiential marketing *119*
- extrinsic cues *138*
- figure and ground *125*
- Gestalt psychology *125*
- grouping *127*
- halo effect *132*

- institutional advertising *142*
- intrinsic cues *138*
- just noticeable difference (JND) *116*
- licensing *133*
- narrow categorizers *143*
- perceived price *136*
- perceived risk *143*
- perception *114*
- perceptual defense *125*
- Positioning *133*
- price/quality relationship *141*
- product placement *126*
- reference price *136*

- repositioning *116*
- selective attention *124*
- selective exposure *124*
- sensation *116*
- sensory adaptation *118*
- sensory receptors *116*
- SERVQUAL scale *140*
- stereotypes *129*
- stimulus *116*
- subliminal perception *121*
- Weber's law *119*

Consumer Learning

EARNING IS applying your knowledge and past experience to present circumstances. Samsung, the manufacturing company for Galaxy Note, a global leader in the smartphone market, uses its experiences to cater to its audience base even while tapping newer markets. The ads in Figure 5.1, introducing the two new Galaxy products together—Galaxy Note 3 + Galaxy Gear—are aimed at an audience with a higher standard of living in the Gulf region, with the implicit message that the new competitively priced smartphone, with high-end technology in an attractive shell, is quite the bargain. Samsung cleverly uses the message "Design Your Life" in the ads to tell its customers that the smartphone along with the one-of-a-kind Gear will help them organize and micro-manage almost every aspect of their lives. The Gear, a strap-on wearable device akin to a wristwatch, allows you to stay connected even while you are away from the phone. The brand wants its products to be seen as a stylish status symbol allowing consumers to only be their best, thereby making Samsung Galaxy Note 3 + Gear an integral part of their customers' existence.

What makes teaching and learning effective? First, students are more likely to be responsive to a knowledgeable teacher – in this case, the teaching-learning process is geared toward consumers who are already familiar with the smartphone and the company, and are willing to try a bolder device! Samsung is able to deliver an effective learning experience because it is a highly dependable multinational, leading worldwide in the smartphone category. Second, consumers are more likely to learn from messages that are fun and attract attention, just as they respond better to a knowledgeable teacher. Consumers will notice and believe Samsung's advertisements – learning and relating to the attractive message that Samsung displays.

Samsung also utilizes repetition, the third element of learning, which, in advertising, means restating the campaign's key message in many forms across different media. Following this principle, Samsung strategically placed its ads highlighting the Galaxy Note 3 + Gear and repeated the message on various advertising media using diverse visuals and targeting

Source: Samsung Gulf Electronics

FIGURE 5.1 Samsung Ads Featuring Consumer Learning

different market segments; but, like the ads shown here, they all bear the same missive.

Reinforcement, which is the final element of learning, involves rewarding those who try the new product. Today's consumers are tech-savvy and appreciate gadgets that can make life better at the simplest touch; Samsung promises consumers a medium that will enable them to redesign their lives in an *easier* and *bolder* fashion, and the ad campaigns are used to reinforce this message.

While the S Pen (stylus) and the Galaxy Gear are just accessories to the phone itself, they reward consumers with increased functionality, exclusivity, and a technologically superior experience.

Next, we discuss the elements of learning and apply them to developing marketing strategies aimed at getting consumers to try and continue buying new products. The chapter concludes with a discussion of the methods used to measure the results of learning experiences.

The Elements of Consumer Learning

Learning Objective

1 To understand the elements of learning in the context of consumer behavior.

Learning is the process by which individuals acquire the purchase and consumption knowledge and experience they apply to future, related behavior. **Consumer learning** is a process that evolves and changes as consumers acquire knowledge from experience, observation, and interactions with others and newly acquired knowledge affects future behavior. It ranges from simple and often reflexive responses to marketing stimuli (such as packaging, product colors, and promotional messages), to learning abstract concepts and making decisions about purchasing complex and expensive products.

Not all learning is deliberately sought. Though much learning is *intentional* (i.e., it is acquired as the result of a search for information), a great deal of learning is *incidental*, acquired by accident or without much effort. For example, some ads may induce learning—like the new products under a familiar brand name featured in the two ads in Figure 5.1—without learning being deliberately sought, whereas other ads are sought out and carefully read by consumers contemplating major purchases. Learning consists of four elements: motives, cues, responses, and reinforcement.

Motives

Uncovering consumer motives is the primary objective of marketers, who seek to teach consumers how they can fill their needs by buying certain products and brands. Unfilled needs lead to **motivation**, which spurs learning. For example, men and women who want to take up bicycle riding for fitness and recreation are motivated to learn all they can about bike riding and practice often. They may seek information concerning the prices, quality, and characteristics of bicycles and learn which bicycles are the best for the kind of riding that they do. They will also read any articles in their local newspapers about bicycle trails and seek online information about "active vacations" that involve biking or hiking. Conversely, individuals who are not interested in bike riding are likely to ignore all information related to that activity. The degree of relevance, or "involvement," determines the consumer's level of motivation to search for information about a product or service and, potentially, engage in learning.

Cues

Cues are stimuli that direct motivated behavior. An advertisement for an exotic trip that includes bike riding may serve as a cue for bike riders, who may suddenly "recognize" that they "need" a vacation. The ad is the cue (or stimulus) that suggests a specific way to satisfy a salient motive. In marketing, price, styling, packaging, advertising, and store displays are cues designed to persuade consumers to fulfill their needs by buying specific products.

Only cues that are consistent with consumer expectations can drive motivation. Thus, marketers must provide cues that match those expectations. For example, consumers expect designer clothes to be expensive and to be sold in upscale retail stores. Thus, high-fashion designers should sell their clothes only through exclusive stores and advertise only in upscale fashion magazines. Each aspect of the marketing mix must reinforce the others if cues are to become stimuli that guide consumer actions in the direction the marketer desires.

Responses

In the context of learning, **response** is an individual's reaction to a drive or cue. Learning can occur even when responses are not overt. The automobile manufacturer that provides consistent cues to a consumer may not always succeed in stimulating a purchase. However, if the manufacturer succeeds in forming a favorable image of a particular automobile model in the consumer's mind, it is likely that the consumer will consider that make or model when he or she is ready to buy a car.

A response is not tied to a need in a one-to-one fashion. Indeed, as noted in Chapter 3, a need or motive may evoke a whole variety of responses. For example, there are many ways to respond to the need for physical exercise besides riding bicycles. Cues provide some direction, but there are many cues competing for the consumer's attention. Which response the consumer makes depends heavily on previous learning; that, in turn, depends on how previous, related responses have been reinforced.

Reinforcement

Reinforcement is the reward—the pleasure, enjoyment, and benefits—that the consumer receives after buying and using a product or service. For the marketer, the challenge is to continue to provide consumers with an ongoing positive product or service, thus reinforcing future purchases. To illustrate, if a person visits a restaurant for the first time, likes the food, service, and ambience, and also feels he or she received value for the money paid, that customer was reinforced and is likely to dine at the restaurant again. If that person becomes a regular customer, the restaurant's owner should further reinforce the customer's continued patronage by, for example, giving the customer a free drink and recognizing the person by name upon arrival. Of course, the quality of the food and service must be maintained, as they are the key elements reinforcing the customer's continued visits. In contrast, if a patron leaves a restaurant disappointed with the quality of the food or the service or feels "ripped off," reinforcement has not occurred. Because of the absence of reinforcement, it is unlikely that the customer will visit the restaurant again.

Figure 5.2 applies the four elements of learning to Procter & Gamble's introduction of Febreze, a spray that eliminates bad smells. The chart illustrates the effects of Febreze's initial positioning, which did not follow the principles of learning; the product did poorly. When the product was repositioned in a manner consistent with the principles of learning, it sold much better.[1]

There is no single, universal theory of how people learn. Broadly, there are two models of learning: behavioral and cognitive. Next, we describe these theories and their applications to consumer behavior. Afterwards, we explain how consumers store, retain, and retrieve information, cognitive learning, and how learning is measured.

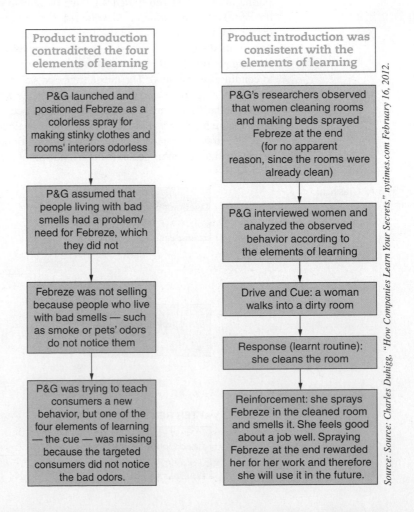

FIGURE 5.2 Procter & Gamble's Febreze

Product introduction contradicted the four elements of learning

P&G launched and positioned Febreze as a colorless spray for making stinky clothes and rooms' interiors odorless

P&G assumed that people living with bad smells had a problem/need for Febreze, which they did not

Febreze was not selling because people who live with bad smells — such as smoke or pets' odors do not notice them

P&G was trying to teach consumers a new behavior, but one of the four elements of learning — the cue — was missing because the targeted consumers did not notice the bad odors.

Product introduction was consistent with the elements of learning

P&G's researchers observed that women cleaning rooms and making beds sprayed Febreze at the end (for no apparent reason, since the rooms were already clean)

P&G interviewed women and analyzed the observed behavior according to the elements of learning

Drive and Cue: a woman walks into a dirty room

Response (learnt routine): she cleans the room

Reinforcement: she sprays Febreze in the cleaned room and smells it. She feels good about a job well. Spraying Febreze at the end rewarded her for her work and therefore she will use it in the future.

Source: Charles Duhigg, "How Companies Learn Your Secrets," nytimes.com February 16, 2012.

Learning Objective

2 To understand behavioral learning, classical conditioning, and the roles of stimulus generalization and discrimination in developing and branding new products.

Classical Conditioning

Behavioral learning is sometimes referred to as **stimulus-response learning** because it is based on the premise that observable responses to specific external stimuli signal that learning has taken place. Behavioral learning is not concerned with the *process* of learning, but rather with the *inputs* and *outcomes* of learning; that is, in the stimuli that consumers select from the environment and the observable behaviors that result. Three forms of behavioral learning with great relevance to marketing are classical conditioning, instrumental (or operant) conditioning, and observational (or modeling) learning.

Classical conditioning is viewed as a "knee-jerk" (or automatic) response that builds up through repeated exposure and reinforcement. For instance, if Tyler's friends compliment him on his expensive Prada boots, he is likely to save money to buy a pair of Prada sneakers. If he sees a Prada ad in a magazine, Tyler will immediately recall his friends' compliments and feel good about himself and his prior purchase. Ivan Pavlov, a Russian physiologist, developed the concept of classical conditioning. Pavlov maintained that conditioned learning results when a stimulus that is paired with another stimulus that elicits a known response produces the same response when used alone. Pavlov demonstrated what he meant by "conditioned learning" in his studies with dogs. Genetically, dogs are always hungry and highly motivated to eat. In his experiments, Pavlov sounded a bell and then immediately applied a meat paste to the dogs' tongues, which caused them to salivate. After a number of such pairings, the dogs responded the same way—that is, they salivated—to the bell alone as they did to the meat paste.

Applying Pavlov's theory to human behavior, consider the following situation: For several years during high school, you always watched your favorite TV sitcom—which begins with the show's musical theme—with your best friend and every night at 7:00 p.m. Then you and your best friend went to different colleges. After you settled down in your new dorm, at 7:00 p.m. you turned on the TV to watch your favorite sitcom and the show's musical theme came on. You immediately thought about your friend and felt sad about watching the show alone. Feeling sad when you think about a best friend from whom you are now separated is a natural, human response and is therefore an **unconditioned stimulus** (i.e., a stimulus that occurs naturally in response to given circumstances). Furthermore, before you started watching the sitcom with your friend every night, the show's musical theme was a neutral stimulus that elicited neither behavior nor any feelings. Later on, while watching the sitcom alone, the same music triggered a particular response—feeling sad—so it has become a **conditioned stimulus** (i.e., a stimulus that became associated with a particular event or feeling as a result of repetition). Feeling sad whenever you hear the music is a **conditioned response** (i.e., a response to conditioned stimulus). The music triggered sadness because of the role of repetition in the process of conditioning. You heard the same musical theme while watching TV with your friend for years, and always at the same time; if you had done so only occasionally, the music would not have triggered sadness. Figure 5.3 depicts Pavlov's model and an analogous example of classical conditioning.

The strategic applications of classical conditioning to consumer behavior are associative learning, repetition, stimulus generalization, and stimulus discrimination.

FIGURE 5.3A Classical Conditioning

FIGURE 5.3B

Associative Learning

Contemporary behavioral scientists view classical conditioning as learning of associations among events that enable consumers to expect and anticipate events. Rather than being a reflexive action, this is seen as **cognitive associative learning**—not the acquisition of new reflexes, but the acquisition of new knowledge about the world. From this viewpoint, the consumer is an information seeker who uses logical and perceptual relations among events, along with his or her own preconceptions, to form a sophisticated representation of the world.

The Role of Repetition

In advertising, **repetition** is the key to forming associations between brands and fulfillment of needs. For example, having a healthy mouth and good oral hygiene are a human need (i.e., unconditioned stimulus), which many consumers associate with the word "Crest." Why? Because after more than 50 years of *repetitive advertising* and uncountable ads, upon hearing or seeing the name "Crest" consumers think of a premium product for keeping their mouth and teeth healthy and protected from bacteria, diseases, and deterioration. Crest is a *conditioned stimulus* and the consumers' associations are *conditioned responses*. Furthermore, consumers associate Crest with scores of versions of toothpaste, toothbrushes, teeth whitening, flossing, and mouth-rinsing products, all marketed under the Crest brand name. Both the conditioned stimulus and the response are results of hearing or seeing Crest's advertisements again and again—in other words, repetitively.

Repetition increases the strength of the association between two stimuli and slows down forgetting this connection. However, the amount of repetition that aids retention is limited. Although repetition beyond what is necessary for the initial learning aids retention, at some point an individual becomes satiated with numerous exposures, and both attention and retention decline. This effect is called **advertising wear-out**, and marketers reduce it by using different ads expressing the same message or advertising themes, as illustrated by the two Fresh Step ads in Figure 5.4 (although the furniture indicate that the ads target different socioeconomic groups). As another example, HSBC positions itself as "the world's local bank." An advertising campaign, entitled "Different Values," consisted of about 20 ads centered on the theme that "different values make the world a richer place." The ads illustrated that one's point of view is subjective and reflects one's values and, therefore, the same object can have different meanings depending on one's culture and viewpoint. The featured objects varied, although the central theme remained the same. For example, a container of pills (the object pictured in one of the ads) may represent "prevention" (e.g., vitamins), "cure" (e.g., antibiotics), or "escape" (e.g., illegal substances).

Although all advertisers use repetition in trying to teach consumers, not everyone agrees on *how much* repetition is enough. Some marketing scholars believe that just three exposures to an advertisement are needed: One to make consumers *aware* of the product, a second to show consumers the *relevance* of the product, and a third to *remind* them of its benefits. This exposure pattern is called the **three-hit theory**. Other researchers suggest that as many as 11 to 12 repetitions are needed to achieve the three objectives. One study indicated that email advertisements that consumers found relevant influenced their learning and attitudes much more than the number of exposures.[2]

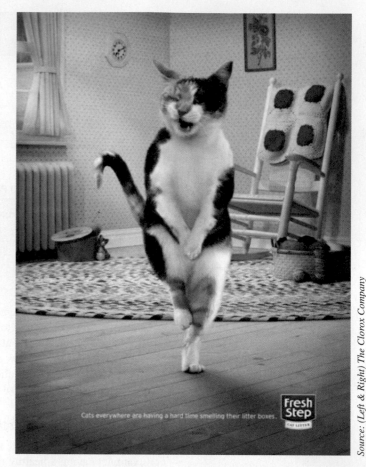

Source: (Left & Right) The Clorox Company

FIGURE 5.4 The Same Advertising Message Expressed Differently

Stimulus Generalization

According to classical conditioning theorists, learning depends not only on repetition but also on individuals' ability to "generalize." Pavlov found, for example, that a dog could learn to salivate not only to the sound of a bell, but also to similar sounds such as jangling keys or coins. Responding the same way to slightly different stimuli is called **stimulus generalization**.

Stimulus generalization explains why some imitative me-too products succeed in the marketplace: Consumers confuse them with the original product they have seen advertised. It also explains why manufacturers of private-label brands try to make their packaging closely resemble that of the national brand leaders. They are hoping that consumers will confuse their packages with the leading brand and buy their product rather than the leading brand.

There are four strategic applications of stimulus generalization to branding and managing product lines: product line extensions, product form extensions, family branding, and licensing.[3]

Product Line Extensions

Product line extensions are additions of related items to an established brand; these are likely to be adopted because they come under a known and trusted brand name.[4] For example, what comes to one's mind upon seeing the V8 symbol? The most likely answer is a small can of vegetable juice sold via vending machines and convenience stores and larger bottles of the brand sold in supermarkets. Most consumers associate drinking vegetable juice and eating vegetables with consuming vitamins, antioxidants, and agents boosting the immune system.

While most consumers associate V8 with vegetables, originally, they did not associate soups with V8. Why did Campbell's (which owns V8), "interfere" with consumers' long-established cognitions by introducing the soups featured in Figure 5.5? Each time consumers bought V8 vegetable juice, they were "rewarded" because the juice tasted good and they were consuming a healthy product. When new products carrying the V8 brand name are advertised, consumers are likely to associate them with the many, prior rewarding experiences of consuming V8 vegetable juice, including

FIGURE 5.5 A Product Line Extension: V8 Soups

the perceived health benefits that are the core of this brand. In learning terms, consumers will apply what they already know about V8 to its new product and probably try the new item. The extension of the V8 line to other products is also a form of family branding, which consists of marketing different products under the same brand name.

The two Mr. Clean products shown in Figure 5.6 are examples of line extensions under a brand name that has been a best seller since the 1950s and represented by a mascot that consumers view as a strong, tenacious, competent, dependable, and friendly "person" (see Figure 3.2).

Product Form Extensions

Offering the same product in a different form but under the same brand is a **product form extension**. For example, Listerine, a mouthwash in the form of liquid and a leading brand, introduced Listerine PocketPacks—a solid form of its product (see Figure 5.7). Clorox Bleach—one of the most recognized brand names among clothing care products—has been sold only as a liquid since its introduction many decades; building upon the brand's universal recognition as a quality product, the company introduced Bleach Gel.

Family Branding

Another strategy stemming from stimulus generalization is **family branding**, which consists of marketing different products under the same brand name. For example, Campbell's, originally a marketer of soups, continues to add new food products to its product line under the Campbell's brand name, such as chunky, condensed, kids, and lower sodium soups; frozen meals named Campbell's Super Bakes; and tomato juice.

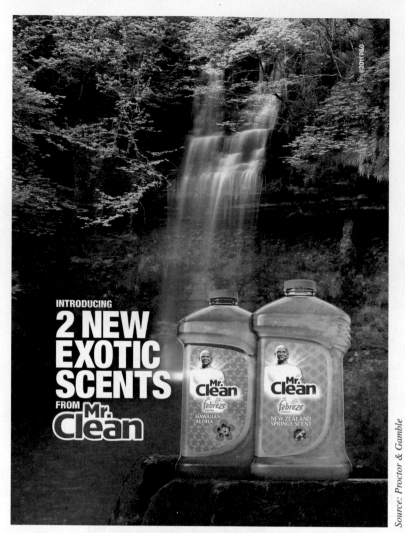

FIGURE 5.6 Mr. Clean's Product Line Extensions

Source: Proctor & Gamble

Licensing

Licensing is contractually allowing a well-known brand name to be affixed to the products of another manufacturer. The names of designers, manufacturers, celebrities, corporations, and even cartoon characters are attached, for a fee (i.e., "rented out") to a variety of products, enabling the licensees to achieve instant recognition and implied quality for the licensed products. Some successful licensors include Liz Claiborne, Tommy Hilfiger, Calvin Klein, and Christian Dior, whose names appear on an exceptionally wide variety of products, from sheets to shoes and luggage to perfume.[5]

Corporations also license their names and trademarks to marketers of related products. For example, Godiva chocolates licensed its name for Godiva liqueur. Corporations also license their names and logos for purely promotional purposes: For example, the phrase "Always Coca-Cola" is printed on clothing, toys, coffee mugs, and the like, none of which are made by Coca-Cola.

The number of different products affiliated with a given brand—originating in line and form extensions, family branding, and licensing—will strengthen the brand name, as long as the brand's owner ensures that the additions are of high quality and consistent with the brand's image and positioning. Failure to do so will negatively affect consumer confidence and evaluations of all the brand's products. One study showed that brands that include diverse products are likely to offer more successful brand extensions than brands that include similar products. The study also confirmed that consumers' reactions to the brand's extensions are strongly related to the distinct benefits these items provide.[6]

Stimulus Discrimination and Product Differentiation

Stimulus discrimination, the opposite of stimulus generalization, is the selection of a specific stimulus from among similar stimuli. The core objective of positioning (see Chapter 2) is to "teach" consumers to discriminate (or distinguish) among similar products (i.e., similar stimuli) and form a unique image for a brand in their minds. Therefore, the objective of marketers' persuasive messages is to convey a brand's unique benefits effectively and differentiate it from competition. Unlike the marketers of brands known as "imitators"—which are often obscure or store brands—who hope that consumers will "generalize" by confusing their brands with well-positioned ones, market leaders' objective is to convince and enable consumers to clearly distinguish (or discriminate) between their products and the imitators.

Most product differentiation strategies are designed to distinguish a product or brand from that of competitors on the basis of an attribute that is relevant, meaningful, and valuable to consumers. It is always difficult to unseat a brand leader once stimulus discrimination has occurred. One explanation is that the leader is usually first in the market and has had a longer period to "teach" consumers (through advertising and selling) to view the brand as the best alternative within a given product category. Apple is a prominent example of differentiating a product. Its early ads explicitly stated that Apple's innovative products represent a distinctive and extraordinary way of thinking. These ads' tag line was "Think Different" and they brilliantly conveyed this notion by featuring famous geniuses, such as Albert Einstein and Jim Henson, who thought "outside the box" and came up with ideas that changed the world.

Classical conditioning theory underpins many ways of influencing consumer behavior through repetition, stimulus generalization, and stimulus discrimination. However, although a great deal of consumer behavior is shaped by repeated advertising messages stressing the unique attributes of various brands, consumers also buy the same brands repeatedly because they are continuously rewarded. The role of reinforcements (or rewards) in shaping learning is discussed next.

Source: The Clorox Company

FIGURE 5.7 A Product Form Extension: Clorox Bleach Gel

Instrumental Conditioning

Learning Objective

3 To understand instrumental conditioning and the objectives and methods of reinforcement.

Instrumental conditioning (or **operant conditioning**) is based on the notion that learning occurs through a trial-and-error process, with habits formed as a result of rewards received for certain responses or behaviors. Like classical conditioning, instrumental conditioning requires a link between a stimulus and a response. However, in instrumental conditioning, the stimulus that results in the most rewarded response is the one that is learned. For example, after visiting stores, consumers know which stores carry the type of clothing they prefer at prices they can afford to pay. Once they find a store that carries clothing that meets their needs, they are likely to patronize it to the exclusion of other stores. Every time they purchase a shirt or a sweater there that they really like, their store loyalty is rewarded (reinforced), and they are likely to become repeat customers.

The American psychologist B. F. Skinner constructed the model of instrumental conditioning. According to Skinner, most learning occurs in environments where individuals are "rewarded" for choosing an appropriate behavior. In consumer behavior terms, instrumental conditioning suggests that consumers learn by means of a trial-and-error process in which some purchase behaviors result in more favorable outcomes (i.e., rewards) than others. A favorable experience is the *instrument* of teaching the individual to repeat a specific behavior.

Like Pavlov, Skinner developed his model of learning by working with animals. Small animals, such as rats and pigeons, were placed in his "Skinner box." If they behaved as Skinner desired—such as pressing a particular lever or pecking keys—he rewarded them with food pellets. Skinner and his many adherents have done amazing things with this learning model, including teaching pigeons to play ping-pong and even to dance. In a marketing context, the consumer who tries several brands and

FIGURE 5.8 A Model of
Instrumental Conditioning

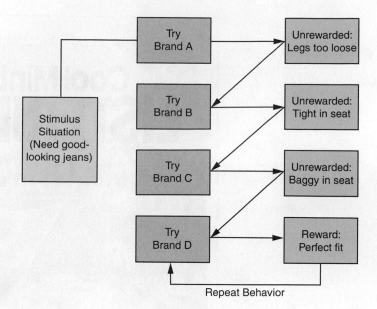

styles of jeans before finding a style that fits her figure (i.e., reinforcement) has engaged in instrumental learning. Presumably, the brand that fits best is the one she will continue to buy. This model of instrumental conditioning is presented in Figure 5.8.

Reinforcing Behavior

Skinner distinguished between two types of reinforcement that influence the likelihood that a response will be repeated. The first type, **positive reinforcement**, rewards a particular behavior and thus strengthens the likelihood of a specific response during the same or similar situation. For example, a child receives ice cream when passing an ice cream stand and receives pleasure from eating it. Then, whenever he passes by the stand he asks for ice cream. **Negative reinforcement** is the removal of an unpleasant stimulus and it strengthens the likelihood of a given response during the same or similar circumstances. For example, a child has a cold and also hates swallowing pills. Her mother convinces her to take Advil and her cold symptoms go away (i.e., the unpleasant stimulus is removed). Next time she has a cold, most likely the girl will readily agree to swallow a pill, and might even ask specifically for an Advil. Therefore, marketers of headache remedies use negative reinforcement when they illustrate the unpleasant symptoms of an unrelieved headache, as do marketers of mouthwash when they show the loneliness suffered by someone with bad breath. In each of these cases, the consumer is encouraged to avoid the negative consequences and remove the unpleasant stimulus by buying the advertised product.

Either positive or negative reinforcement can be used to elicit a desired response. However, negative reinforcement should not be confused with *punishment*, which is designed to *discourage* behavior. For example, receiving a speeding ticket and having to pay a fine is not negative reinforcement; it is a form of punishment designed to discourage future speeding. But what constitutes "punishment" is tricky. For example, a driver can perceive the fine as "paying" for a bad behavior and continue speeding; this individual apparently believes that each time he speeds he will merely have to pay for his bad behavior. Therefore, in addition to paying fines, speeding drivers receive "points" on their licenses and can lose their driving rights (and the opportunities to speed) if they speed too many times. In a frequently cited study, researchers discovered that when a day care center started "punishing" parents who picked up their kids late by charging them about $3, late pickups actually *increased*, because parents viewed the fine as the price for being tardy.[7] The "punishment" actually legitimized being late and *encouraged* the behavior it was designed to lessen.

Extinction and Forgetting

Extinction occurs when a learned response is no longer reinforced and the link between the stimulus and the expected reward breaks down. When consumers become unsatisfied with a service (e.g., at a restaurant), the link between the stimulus (i.e., the restaurant) and expected satisfaction is no longer reinforced and the consumers won't come back. Behavior that is not reinforced becomes "unlearned."

Note that there is a difference between extinction and forgetting. Diners who have not visited a once-favorite restaurant for a long time simply forget how much they used to enjoy eating there and their behavior is "unlearned" because of lack of use rather than lack of reinforcement. **Forgetting** is often related to the passage of time, and thus is also called "decay. " Marketers overcome forgetting by contacting customers who stopped buying their products and giving them incentives aimed at persuading the customers to start buying their products again.

Customer Satisfaction and Retention

Savvy marketers reinforce customer satisfaction by consistently providing high quality. Marketers must provide the best value for the money and simultaneously avoid raising consumers' expectations beyond what the products can deliver. Companies must not assume that more attractive prices and broader product lines will make customers more satisfied. Instead, companies that create personal connections with customers, and offer diverse product lines and competitive prices, because these are the most effective reinforcements, which bring about repeat patronage. Most frequent shopper programs are based on the notion that the more a consumer uses the service, the greater the rewards. Another form of reinforcement is rewarding customers who refer other customers. One study discovered that although rewards increased referrals, there was no difference in referral likelihood between smaller and larger rewards. In addition, for existing customers with strong ties to the marketer providing the reward, these incentives did not increase referral likelihood.[8] However, several studies discovered that satisfied customers are often fickle and disloyal when a lot of competition exists.[9]

Reinforcement Schedules

Product quality must be consistently high and satisfy customers every time they buy the product—but additional rewards do not have to be offered during every transaction, because *occasional* rewards often effectively reinforce consumers' patronage. For example, airlines occasionally upgrade a passenger at the gate; here, the *possibility* of receiving a reward is the reinforcement and incentive for continued patronage.

Psychologists have identified three reinforcement schedules: Continuous, fixed ratio, and variable ratio. With **continuous reinforcement**, a reward is provided after each transaction, such as a free after-dinner drink or fruit plate always served to regular patrons of a restaurant. A **fixed ratio reinforcement** schedule provides reinforcement every nth time the product or service is purchased (say, every third time). For example, a retailer may send a credit voucher to account holders every three months, based on a percentage of the customer's purchases during the prior quarter. A **variable ratio reinforcement** schedule rewards consumers on a random basis. Gambling casinos operate on the basis of variable ratios. People pour money into slot machines (which are programmed to pay off on a variable ratio), hoping for the big win. Variable ratios tend to engender high rates of desired behavior and are somewhat resistant to extinction; apparently, for many consumers, hope springs eternal. Other examples of variable ratio schedules include lotteries, sweepstakes, door prizes, and contests that require certain consumer behaviors for eligibility.

Shaping

Reinforcement performed *before* the desired consumer behavior actually takes place is called **shaping**. Shaping increases the probability that certain desired consumer behavior will occur. For example, retailers recognize that they must first attract customers to their stores before they can expect those customers to do the bulk of their shopping there. Many retailers provide some form of preliminary reinforcement (shaping) to encourage consumers to visit their stores. For example, some retailers offer loss leaders—popular products at severely discounted prices—to the first hundred or so customers to arrive, because those customers are likely to buy more products at the store rather than only the discounted items. By reinforcing the behavior that is needed to enable the desired consumer behavior, marketers increase the probability that the desired behavior will occur. Car dealers recognize that to sell new-model cars, they must first encourage people to visit the showrooms and test-drive the cars. They hope that the test drive will result in a sale. Using shaping principles, many car dealers encourage showroom visits by providing small monetary or other gifts to those who test-drive the cars, and a rebate check upon placement of an order. They use a multistep shaping process to achieve the desired consumer learning.[10]

Massed versus Distributed Learning

As illustrated previously, timing has an important influence on consumer learning. Should a learning schedule be spread out over a period of time, which is termed **distributed learning**, or should it be "bunched up" all at once, which is called **massed learning**? The question is an important one for advertisers planning a media schedule, because massed advertising produces more initial learning, whereas a distributed schedule usually results in learning that persists longer. When advertisers want an immediate impact (e.g., to introduce a new product or to counter a competitor's blitz campaign), they generally use a massed schedule to hasten consumer learning. However, when the goal is long-term repeat buying on a regular basis, a distributed schedule is preferable. A distributed schedule, with ads repeated on a regular basis usually results in long-term learning that is relatively immune to extinction.

Observational Learning

Learning Objective

4 To understand the role of observational learning in consumer behavior.

Observational learning (or **modeling**) is the process through which individuals learn behavior by observing the behavior of others and the consequences of such behavior. For this type of learning to occur, reinforcement must take place. For example, Joe—a commuter—notices that more and more train riders are using e-readers, so he buys one to try it out, knowing that he has 30 days to return it. Then, a conductor whom Joe knows and sees daily compliments him on the purchase and also

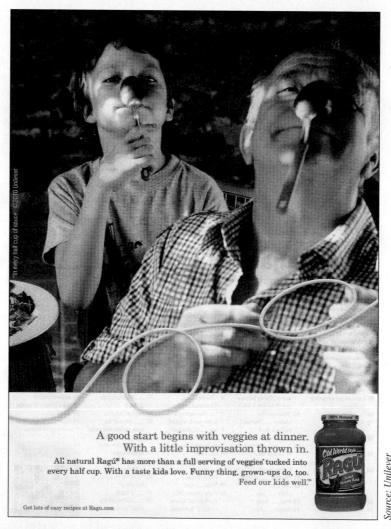

FIGURE 5.9 Eating Ragu Is Fun: Observational Learning from Grandfather to Grandson

asks questions about the device. Joe's purchase was the result of observational learning. Because the conductor's compliments reinforced his purchase (and also because he likes the device and it works well), Joe decides to keep the device.

Advertisers recognize the importance of observational learning in selecting the models they feature in advertisements, whether celebrities or unknowns. If a teenager sees an ad that depicts social success as the outcome of using a certain brand of shampoo, she will want to buy it. If her brother sees a commercial that shows a muscular young athlete eating Wheaties—"the breakfast of champions"—he will want to eat it, too. Indeed, a lot of advertising is based on observational learning. Many ads feature likeable models achieving positive outcomes to common problem situations through use of the advertised product. Children learn much of their social and consumer behavior by observing their older siblings and parents. They imitate the behavior of those they see rewarded, expecting to be rewarded similarly if they adopt the same behavior. The Ragu ad in Figure 5.9 illustrates a child's observational learning from his grandfather.

Information Processing

Learning Objective

5 To understand the elements of information processing, including receiving, storing, and retrieving consumption-related information.

A lot of learning occurs through consumer thinking and problem solving. Sometimes we resolve purchase-related dilemmas instantly. In other situations, we search for information and carefully evaluate what we learned. This kind of learning, called **cognitive learning**, consists of mental processing of data rather than instinctive responses to stimuli. Therefore, we examine the structure and components of information processing, which are diagrammed in Figure 5.10, before explaining cognitive learning.

The human mind processes the information it receives. Consumers process product information by attributes, brands, comparisons between brands, or a combination of these factors. The number and complexity of the relevant attributes and available alternatives influence the intensity or degree of information processing. Consumers with higher cognitive abilities acquire more product information and consider more product attributes and alternatives than consumers with lesser ability.

The more experience a consumer has with a product category, the greater is his or her ability to make use of product information. Greater familiarity with the product category also increases learning during new purchase decisions for items within the same category. The components of information processing are storing, retaining, and retrieving information.

Storing Information

The human memory is the center of information processing. Information processing occurs in stages and in three sequential "storehouses" where information is kept: The sensory, short-term, and long-term stores.

Sensory Store

The **sensory store** is the mental "space" in the human mind where sensory input lasts for just a second or two. If it is not processed immediately, it is lost. All data come to us through our senses, but the senses do not carry whole images, like a camera. Each sense receives a piece of information (such as the smell, color, shape, or feel of a flower) and transmits it to the brain in parallel, where the perceptions of a single instant are synchronized and perceived as a single image for only a brief moment. Because consumers are constantly bombarded with stimuli from the environment, they subconsciously block out a great deal of information that they do not need or cannot use. For marketers, this means that although it is relatively easy to get information into the consumer's sensory store, it is difficult to make a lasting impression. Furthermore, the brain automatically and subconsciously

FIGURE 5.10 Information Processing

"tags" all perceptions with a value, either positive or negative; this evaluation, added to the initial perception in the first microsecond of cognition, tends to remain unless further information is processed. This explains why first impressions tend to last and why it is hazardous for a marketer to introduce a product prematurely into the marketplace.

Short-Term Store

The **short-term store** is where information is processed and held for just a brief period. Anyone who has ever looked up a number in a telephone book, only to forget it just before dialing, knows how briefly information lasts in short-term storage. If information in the short-term store undergoes the process known as **rehearsal**, which is the silent, mental repetition of information, it is then transferred to the long-term store. The transfer process takes from 2 to 10 seconds. If information is not rehearsed and transferred, it is lost in about 30 seconds or less. The amount of information that can be held in short-term storage is limited to about four or five items.

An interesting experiment illustrated how the short-term store operates. A researcher walked over to a pedestrian and asked for directions. While the pedestrian was responding, two workmen carrying a large door walked between the researcher and the respondent; while hidden by the door being moved, the researcher switched places with another person. Only about half the pedestrians noticed that they were talking to someone else afterward.[11]

Long-Term Store

The **long-term store** is the mental "space" where information is retained for extended periods of time, in contrast to the short-term store, where information lasts only a few seconds. Although it is possible to forget something within a few minutes after the information reaches long-term storage, it is more common for data in long-term storage to last for days, weeks, or even years. A study of three generations of automobile consumers discovered that people's earliest memories and experiences regarding cars defined what car brands meant to them and affected their brand preferences later in life.[12]

Information Rehearsal and Encoding

The amount of information available for delivery from short-term storage to long-term storage depends on the amount of rehearsal it receives. Failure to rehearse an input, either by repeating it or by relating it to other data, can result in fading and eventual loss of the information. Information can also be lost because of competition for attention. For example, if the short-term store receives a great number of inputs simultaneously from the sensory store, its capacity may be reduced to only two or three pieces of information.

The purpose of rehearsal is to hold information in short-term storage long enough for encoding to take place. **Encoding** is the process by which we select a word or visual image to represent a perceived object. Marketers help consumers encode brands by using brand symbols. Kellogg's uses Tony the Tiger on its Frosted Flakes; the Green Giant Company has its Jolly Green Giant. Dell Computer turns the *e* in its logo on its side for quick name recognition, and Apple uses its stylish and distinctive insignia.

Processing and remembering a picture takes less time than learning verbal information, but both types of information are important in forming an overall mental image. A print ad with both an illustration and body copy is more likely to be encoded and stored than an illustration without verbal information. High-imagery copy produces greater recall than low-imagery copy, and marketers realize that almost every ad should include some form of an illustration. In one study, consumers were given goals and then asked to memorize ads. The study found that an ad-memorization goal enhanced attention to the body text, pictures, and brand design. A brand-learning goal produced attention to the body text, but also inhibited attention to the pictorial design. One may conclude that text-dominant ads activate brand learning and pictorial-dominant ads activate ad appreciation.[13]

Encoding of commercials is related to the context in which they are featured. For example, while watching TV, some parts of a program may require viewers to commit a larger portion of their cognitive resources to processing (e.g., when a dramatic event takes place versus a casual conversation). When viewers commit more cognitive resources to the program than the ads, they encode and store less of the information conveyed by a commercial. This suggests that commercials requiring relatively little cognitive processing may be more effective within or adjacent to a dramatic program setting than commercials requiring more elaborate processing. Viewers who are very involved with a television show respond more positively to commercials adjacent to that show and have more positive purchase intentions. Recent exposure to related information also facilitates encoding. A study found that publicity about advertising campaigns before they were started facilitated better recall of brands featured in subsequent advertising.[14]

When consumers receive too much information and then have difficulty encoding and storing it, **information overload** occurs. For example, in product categories where several strong brands are heavily promoted, consumers do not remember product information featured in ads that promote new brands. Consumers can also become cognitively overloaded when they receive a lot of information in a limited time. Such overload leads to consumer frustration, confusion, and poor purchase decisions.

Information Retention and Retrieval

Information does not merely remain in long-term storage waiting to be retrieved. It is constantly organized and reorganized, as new chunks of information are received and new links among those chunks are created. For example, a memory of a product's name may be activated by relating it to the spokesperson appearing in its advertising.

Product information stored in memory is brand based, and consumers interpret new information consistently with the way in which it has already been organized. One study demonstrated that "brand imprinting"—messages that merely establish the brand's identity—if conducted before presentation of the brand's benefits, facilitated consumer learning and retention of information about the brand.[15] Studies also showed that a brand's "sound symbolism" (a theory suggesting that the sounds of words convey meanings) and the brand's "linguistic characteristics" (e.g., unusual spelling) affected the encoding and retention of the brand name.[16]

A key component of retention is called **chunking**, defined as the process during which consumers recode what they have already encoded; this process often results in recalling additional relevant information. Marketers have studied the kinds and numbers of groupings (or "chunks") of information that consumers can handle. They discovered that that consumers' recall declined when the chunks featured in advertisements did not match the ones stored in the consumers' minds. Also, consumers who are more knowledgeable about a product category can absorb more complex chunks of information than less knowledgeable consumers.

Retrieval is the process by which people recover information from the long-term store; it is frequently triggered by external cues. For example, when we see a product in the store or on TV, we automatically retrieve the applicable information our brains have stored. If the brand is distinctive and heavily advertised, or if we had a memorable experience using it, the retrieval will be quicker than that for less sought-after brands. Some scientists used brain-imaging technologies, normally used in medicine, to examine information retrieval. For example, when men looked at racy sports cars, their reward centers were activated. In an experiment involving soft drinks, two different brain regions were at play. When some loyal drinkers of Coke and others of Pepsi tasted two soft drinks with the brands unidentified, their brains' reward system was activated. The respondents were then asked which of the two they liked better. Afterward, they were told the brand of the drink they liked better in the blind taste test. At that point, their brains' memory region (where information regarding brand loyalty is stored) was activated and overrode the preferences the participants indicated after tasting the soft drink, but before knowing which brand they had tasted. That is, if the brand they said they liked better was *not* their regular brand, they changed their minds regarding which drink they liked better during the blind taste test.[17]

Unexpected elements improve consumers' ad retention only when those elements are relevant to the advertising message. For example, an ad for a brand of stain-resistant, easy-to-clean carpet shows an elegantly dressed couple in a beautiful dining room setting where the man inadvertently knocks the food, the flowers, and the china to the floor. The elegance of the actors and the upscale setting make the accident totally unexpected, whereas the message remains highly relevant: The mess can be cleaned up easily without leaving a stain on the carpet. Because this ad is very dramatic, it is likely to be remembered (or retrieved) when the consumer is exposed to any of the elements of the ad thereafter. However, unexpected cues are not the same as incongruent ones. Although consumers notice ads containing cues that are incongruent with the products advertised, they are unlikely to remember them. For instance, a print ad showing a nude woman sitting on a piece of office furniture would very likely attract readers' attention, but would probably not increase the likelihood that the ad purveyor would be remembered or subsequently retrieved. In one experiment, where subjects were manipulated into making choices among four desserts based on memory or on the actual stimuli (the desserts themselves), researchers discovered that memory-based product choices were guided more by feelings (e.g., an urge for tasty food), whereas stimulus-based choices were guided more by deliberative considerations (e.g., the need to follow a sensible diet).[18]

A greater number of competitive ads in a product category leads to lower recall of all brands' advertising claims, because consumers are confused by many competing ads and they find it hard to retrieve information. Under such conditions, ads can activate the retrieval of cues for competing brands. For example, consumers may believe that the long-running and attention-getting television campaign featuring the Eveready Energizer Bunny is an ad for Duracell batteries.

Cognitive Learning

Learning Objective

6   To understand cognitive learning as a framework for consumer decision-making.

Cognitive learning is the systematic evaluation of information and alternatives needed to solve a recognized but unfilled need or unsolved problem. Unlike behavioral learning, which consists of instinctive responses to stimuli, cognitive learning involves deliberate mental processing of information. Cognitive psychologists focus on the roles of motivation and mental processes in producing a desired response, rather than the immediate response to a given stimulus.

Cognitive learning occurs when a person has a goal and must search for and process data in order to make a decision or solve a problem. For a long time, consumer researchers believed that all consumers passed through a complex series of mental and behavioral stages in arriving at a purchase decision. These stages ranged from awareness of the purchase options (exposure to information), to evaluation and preferences regarding the alternatives available, to possibly trying one or more versions of the product, and then buying or not buying it (behavior expressed as adoption or rejection). For example, a consumer looking to purchase a super-slim, point-and-shoot digital camera (the goal) must choose among many brands and models (problem solving). The consumer will first get to know the features of different models (exposure to information resulting in knowledge), then develop preferences and evaluations regarding the different alternatives, and then decide which model to buy and which ones not to purchase (rejection).

The ad for Crest Pro-Health toothpaste in Figure 5.11 is based on cognitive learning. Let's assume that Betty has had her teeth cleaned every six months—as recommended by dentists—and the tartar and plaque on her teeth has been removed regularly. But, as she grew older, her gums became sensitive and occasionally painful. During her regular cleaning, her dentist tells her that she has occasional gingivitis, which is an inflammation of the gums, and advises her to

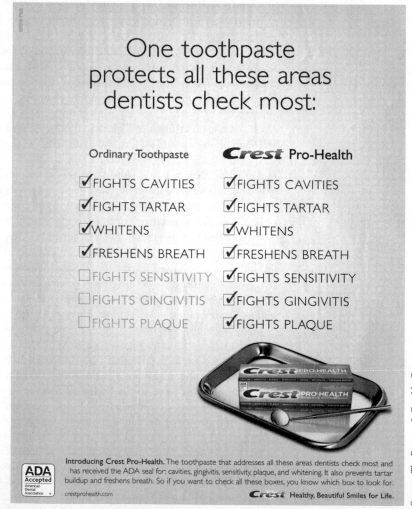

FIGURE 5.11 Cognitive Learning: Crest Pro-Health

Source: The Proctor & Gamble Company

| TABLE 5.1 | Representations of Cognitive Learning | | | |
GENERIC STAGES OF COGNITIVE LEARNING	TRI-COMPONENT ATTITUDE MODEL	AIDA	INNOVATION ADOPTION	INNOVATION DECISION-MAKING
Knowledge	Cognitive	Attention	Awareness	Knowledge
Evaluation	Affective	Interest and Desire	Interest and Evaluation	Persuasion
Behavior	Conative	Action	Trial and Adoption	Decision and Confirmation

use toothpaste specifically designed to battle this condition. Previously, Betty regarded toothpaste as a "commodity," considered all brands to be similar, and bought whichever brands were on sale. But, following her dentist's advice, she now faces a new problem and unfilled need: Finding a toothpaste specifically designed to fight gingivitis. She then sees the Crest ad, and, although Crest Pro-Health is more expensive, she starts using it. Subsequently, her gums no longer hurt and her dentist compliments her on her excellent oral hygiene. Betty engaged in cognitive learning: She faced a problem, looked for a solution, read about the benefits of Crest Pro-Health in the ad, and started using the product consistently, which resulted in relief from pain and thus reinforced what she had learned.

Researchers developed several models depicting sequential information processing and cognitive learning, which are featured in Table 5.1. Although the models use different terms to designate the sequences they depict, in essence they all follow the three-stage generic sequence listed in the table's leftmost column.

Consumer Involvement and Hemispheric Lateralization

Learning Objective

7 To understand consumer involvement and passive learning, and their impact on purchase decisions and the retention and recall of promotional communications.

Initially, marketing scholars believed that complex processing of information applied to all purchases, expensive and cheaper alike. Later on, theorists realized that many purchases, especially routine ones, do not involve extensive information processing and evaluation. Such purchases are of minimal personal relevance, as opposed to highly relevant, search-oriented purchases. This understanding led to the conceptualization and study of consumer involvement.

Consumer involvement is the degree of personal relevance that the product or purchase holds for the consumer. **High-involvement purchases** are very important to the consumer (e.g., in terms of perceived risk) and thus provoke extensive problem solving and information processing. Under this scenario, both automobiles and dandruff shampoo can represent high-involvement purchases: The automobile because of its high perceived financial risk (to most people), and the shampoo because of high perceived social risk (to some people). **Low-involvement purchases** are not very important, hold little relevance, have little perceived risk, and provoke limited information processing.

Measurements of Consumer Involvement

There is great variation in the conceptualization and measurement of consumer involvement. Throughout the marketing research literature, "involvement" has been defined in numerous ways, including product involvement, brand involvement, and advertising involvement. Because there is no universal definition of involvement, there is no single way to measure it. Some measures gauge cognitive factors, such as the importance of a purchase to a buyer and the risk perceived with the purchase; other measures focus on the behavioral aspects of involvement and appraise such factors as the search for and evaluation of product information. The most popular measurement tool is self-administered surveys that assess the consumer's cognitions or behaviors regarding a particular product or product category, and measure involvement on a continuum (not as a dichotomy). For example, a scale measuring involvement with, say, e-books might require respondents to express their attitudes on five-point, bi-polar **semantic differential scales** on ranges between paired adjectives, such as important—unimportant, relevant—irrelevant, exciting—unexciting, priceless—worthless, and interesting—boring.

Strategic Applications of Consumer Involvement

Marketers aspire to create customers who are involved with the purchase and view the brand they buy as unique. Many studies have shown that high involvement with the product category, and also perception of a given brand as superior, leads to brand loyalty.[19] Although there is no generalized profile of a highly involved consumer, many studies have investigated the personal characteristics related to involvement level. For example, researchers found a relationship between ethnicity and involvement; appeals portraying Hispanic identities were effective in advertising low-involvement items, but not high-involvement products.[20]

Research indicates that the context in which the promotional message appears has an impact on involvement. One study discovered that consumers who were highly involved in the sports program they watched recalled commercials significantly better than those who were less involved with the program.[21] Another study found that involvement with video games affected brand memory. Players who were initially unfamiliar with the game, but became highly involved with it while learning how to play, recalled many of the brands embedded in the game. When they became experienced players, they became less involved with the game and recalled fewer of the brands it featured.[22] Many marketers now show avatars—animated, virtual-reality, people-like figures—in websites. Avatars have been effective, and studies have found that this is because they often engage consumers in learning about and becoming involved with products and services. One study discovered that *attractive* avatar sales agents were effective in selling to consumers with moderate product involvement, whereas *expert* avatars were more effective sales agent for products with high involvement levels.[23] In addition to increasing product and brand involvement, marketers must also expand customer involvement with their ads; they can use sensory appeals, unusual stimuli, celebrity endorsers, and scores of innovative techniques online to increase the persuasiveness of their promotions.

Highly involved consumers engage in long-term relationships with products and brands, and increasing involvement levels enhances these bonds. The best strategy for increasing the personal relevance of products to consumers is the same as the core of modern marketing: Providing benefits that are important to customers, differentiating the offering from its competition, improving the product and adding relevant benefits (especially as competition intensifies).

Hemispheric Lateralization

Hemispheric lateralization (split-brain theory) stems from medical research done in the 1960s; its premise is that the human brain is divided into two distinct cerebral hemispheres that operate together, but "specialize" in processing different types of cognitions. The left hemisphere is the center of human language; it is the linear side of the brain and primarily responsible for reading, speaking, and reasoning. The right hemisphere of the brain is the home of spatial perception and nonverbal concepts; it is nonlinear and the source of imagination and pleasure. Put another way, the left side of the brain is rational, active, and realistic; the right side is emotional, metaphoric, impulsive, and intuitive. Some argue that computers emulate many of the sequential functions of the left side of the brain and that we should employ the imaginative, right brain to a greater degree in making business decisions.[24] Figure 5.12 shows an American Airlines ad literally depicting the split-brain theory.

Passive Learning

A pioneer consumer researcher applied hemispheric lateralization to watching TV. He theorized that when consumers watch advertising on TV, they "passively" process right brain, pictorial information.[25] The researcher considered TV a primarily pictorial medium, and TV viewing as a right-brain activity, consisting of passive and holistic processing of images viewed on the screen. He also maintained that TV is a low-involvement medium. The core of cognitive learning is that consumers deliberate about purchases, seek and evaluate applicable information, form attitudes toward the purchase alternatives available, and then make purchase decisions. According to these models, behavior *follows* the cognitive processing of information. In contrast, advocates of **passive learning** maintain that repeated exposure to TV commercials, which is low-involvement information processing, induces purchases *prior* to consumers' information processing and the formation of attitudes.

As opposed to TV, printed, verbal and static information in newspapers is processed by the brain's left side. Therefore, print media are considered high involvement. Accordingly, the processing of printed advertising takes place in the left brain, and along the cognitive learning sequences featured in Table 5.1. In contrast, advertising that consists mostly of moving images and pictorial information is processed holistically by the right side of the viewer's brain, with minimum involvement.

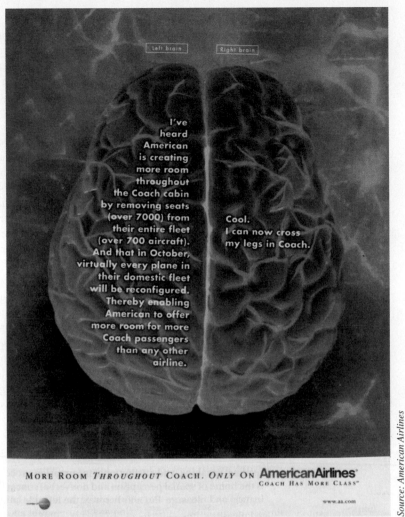

Source: American Airlines

FIGURE 5.12 Hemispheric Lateralization

The right brain's passive processing of information is consistent with classical conditioning. Through repetition, the product is paired with a visual image (e.g., a distinctive package) to produce the purchase of the advertised brand. Accordingly, during passive learning and exposure to low-involvement media, continuous repetition of advertisements is the key factor in producing purchase behavior. This line of thinking also suggests that television commercials are most effective when they are of short (15 or 20 seconds) and repeated frequently. Right-brain information processing underscores the importance of the visual components of advertising. Strong visuals in TV commercials and in-store displays generate familiarity with the brand and induce purchase behavior. Pictorial cues are more effective at generating recall and familiarity with the product, whereas verbal cues (which trigger left-brain processing) generate cognitive activity that encourages consumers to evaluate the advantages and disadvantages of the product.

Outcomes and Measures of Consumer Learning

Learning Objective

8 To understand how to measure the results of consumer learning.

For marketers, the goals of consumer learning are increased market share and brand-loyal consumers. These goals are interdependent: Brand-loyal customers are the core of a stable and growing market share, and brands with larger market shares have disproportionately large numbers of loyal buyers. Marketers' promotions are designed to teach consumers for whom the brands promoted provide the best solutions for satisfying unfilled needs. Thus, marketers must measure to what extent consumers have learned the information contained in promotional messages. The most popular measures of consumer learning are recognition and recall of messages and attitudinal and behavioral evaluations of brand loyalty.

Recognition and Recall Measures

The purpose of recognition and recall tests is to determine whether consumers remember seeing an ad and the extent to which they have read it and can recall its content. Recognition tests are based on **aided recall**, whereas recall tests use **unaided recall**. In a **recognition test**, the consumer is shown an ad and asked whether he or she remembers seeing it and can remember any of its salient points. In a **recall test**, the consumer is asked whether he or she has read a specific magazine or watched a specific television show, and, if so, whether he or she can recall any ads or commercials seen, the product and brand advertised, and any notable points about the offerings promoted.

For example, the **Starch Readership Ad Study** evaluates the effectiveness of magazine advertisements according to three criteria: Noticing the ad, associating the ad with the brand advertised, and involvement with the ad (defined as having read most of the ad text). At the start of a Starch survey, respondents are presented with a magazine issue and asked whether they have read it. Those who respond positively are then shown each ad that had appeared in that issue—with the brand name concealed—and asked questions that measure recall and recognition of the ad. The study output consists of tagged advertisements, with the tags showing the percentage of readers who have "noticed" each ad, were able to "associate" the ad with the brand advertised, and "read most" of the ad's copy. Advertisers can then gauge the effectiveness of each ad by comparing its scores on the Starch measures to similar-sized ads, competitors' ads, and their own prior ads. Starch also appraises consumers' intentions to buy and likelihood to engaging in word-of-mouth about the product after reading the ad. A study using Starch readership scores demonstrated that consumers received more information from advertisements for *shopping products* (e.g., high-priced clothing and accessories) than from ads for *convenience goods* (e.g., low-priced items purchased routinely). Surprisingly, they also received less information from ads for *search products*, that is, very expensive, durable items purchased infrequently and following an extensive information search. These findings show that marketers may not be including enough information when advertising search products.[26]

Brand Loyalty

Brand loyalty is a measure of how often consumers buy a given brand; whether or not they switch brands and, if they do, how often; and the extent of their commitment to buying the brand regularly. To marketers, a high degree of brand loyalty is the most desired outcome of consumer learning and an indication that they have effectively "taught" consumers a given behavior (i.e., buying the marketer's brands consistently). Marketers agree that brand loyalty has two components—behaviors and attitudes—and that both must be measured. Attitudinal measures gauge consumers' overall feelings about the brand, including their future purchase intentions. Behavioral measures focus on observable, factual behaviors, such as the quantity purchased, purchase frequency, and repeated buying. Table 5.2 lists the key characteristics of brand-loyal consumers.[27]

Behavioral learning scientists who favor the theory of instrumental conditioning believe that brand loyalty results from an initial product trial that was reinforced through satisfaction, which led to repeat and continuous patronage. In contrast, researchers of cognitive learning believe that consumers engage in extensive problem solving, information search, and evaluation of alternatives that eventually lead to a strong brand preference and ongoing purchase behavior. Nevertheless, consumer behavior researchers agree that if a consumer finds many brands in a particular category to be "acceptable," he or she is unlikely to be brand loyal. Therefore, marketers must differentiate their products from competition so that they stand out and consumers become reluctant to view other brands as "acceptable."

TABLE 5.2 Characteristics of Brand-Loyal Consumers

1. They tend to stick with brands that they know and trust and with the best-known brands.
2. They believe that staying with the brands they like simplifies their lives.
3. They let friends try other products and switch only if a product is really outstanding.
4. They avoid buying something different just for the sake of being different.
5. They view liked brands as "friends," with whom they want to maintain relationships.
6. They believe that they save money by not buying new brands.
7. They view themselves as "brand-loyal shoppers."

The degree of brand loyalty depends on three factors: (1) the consumer's risk aversion or variety seeking; (2) the brand's reputation and availability of substitute brands; and (3) social group influences and peers' recommendations. There are three types of brand loyalty:

1. **Covetous brand loyalty** includes no consistent purchase of a given brand, in spite of strong attachment to it.
2. **Inertia brand loyalty** is purchasing the brand because of habit and convenience, but without any emotional attachment to it.
3. **Premium brand loyalty** means high attachment to the brand and repeat purchase.[28]

Low involvement with a given product category results in habitual buying without emotional attachment to any brand (i.e., inertia loyalty). Consumers perceive minor or no differences among brands and buy a brand repeatedly only because of familiarity and convenience. Premium loyalty represents truly brand-loyal consumers. They are committed to the brand, unlikely to switch to other brands, and likely to go out of their way to buy the same brand (e.g., if a supermarket ran out of their brand, they would drive to another store).

Brand Equity

High brand loyalty greatly increases a brand's monetary value. The term **brand equity** represents the intrinsic value of a brand name. This value stems from the foundations of brand loyalty: The consumer's perception of the brand's superiority, the social esteem that using it provides, and the customer's trust and identification with the brand.

Brands that are heavily promoted for extended periods attain ample name recognition and consumer loyalty, which result is high brand equity. Because of the escalating costs of developing new products and their high failure rates, many companies capitalize on their brands' equity in the forms of family branding and product line extensions rather than launching new brands. Brand equity facilitates the acceptance of new products, allocation of preferred space by distributors, and charging premium prices. Brand equity is most important for low-involvement purchases, such as inexpensive consumer goods that are bought routinely and with little processing of cognitive information. In such circumstances, the most important strategy is continuous advertising designed to prevent extinction and forgetting.

Brand names are the most valuable assets of marketers of consumer goods and services. Among the best-known brands are Apple, Coca-Cola, Campbell's, Disney, Google, Hallmark, and Sony. These names are global, "cultural icons" and enjoy powerful advantages over the competition. According to studies, some the highest equity brands are: Among airlines—Alaska/Horizon, Hawaiian, Delta, and United; among luxury cars—Mercedes-Benz, BMW, Lexus, Acura, Infiniti, Porsche, and Audi; among sports apparel—UnderArmour, Nike and Columbia; and among household cleaners—Lysol All Purpose, Clorox, and Mr. Clean Multi-Purpose.[29]

Summary

Learning Objective 1: To understand the elements of learning in the context of consumer behavior.

Learning is the process by which individuals acquire the purchase and consumption knowledge and experience they apply to future, related behavior. Consumer learning is a process that evolves and changes as consumers acquire knowledge from experience, observation, and interactions with others and newly acquired knowledge affects future behavior. It ranges from simple and often reflexive responses to marketing stimuli (such as packaging, product colors, and promotional messages), to learning abstract concepts and making decisions about purchasing complex and expensive products. The elements of learning are motives (drives), cues, responses, and reinforcement.

Learning Objective 2: To understand behavioral learning, classical conditioning, and the roles of stimulus generalization and discrimination in developing and branding new products.

Behavioral learning (also referred to as stimulus-response learning) maintains that observable responses to external stimuli signal that learning has taken place. Behavioral learning focuses on the inputs and outcomes of learning; that is, on the stimuli that consumers select from the environment and the behaviors that result. There are three forms of behavioral learning: classical conditioning, instrumental (or operant) conditioning, and observational (or modeling) learning.

Classical conditioning (also known as Pavlovian conditioning) is learning where repetion causes the conditioned stimulus to signal the occurrence of the unconditioned stimulus. The strategic applications of classical conditioning to consumer behavior are associative learning, repetition, stimulus generalization, and stimulus discrimination.

Learning Objective 3: To understand instrumental conditioning and the objectives and methods of reinforcement.

Instrumental learning theorists believe that learning occurs through a trial-and-error process in which positive outcomes (i.e., rewards) result in repeat behavior. Both positive and negative reinforcement can be used to encourage the desired behavior. Reinforcement schedules can be total (consistent) or partial (fixed ratio or random). The timing of repetitions influences how long the learned material is retained. Massed repetitions produce more initial learning than distributed repetitions; however, learning usually persists longer with distributed (i.e., spread out) reinforcement schedules.

Learning Objective 4: To understand the role of observational learning in consumer behavior.

Observational learning (or modeling) is the process through which individuals learn behavior by observing the behavior of others and the consequences of such behavior. Advertisers recognize the importance of observational learning in their selection of models, whether celebrities or unknowns. Many ads feature likeable models achieving positive outcomes to common problem situations through the use of the advertised product.

Learning Objective 5: To understand the elements of information processing, including receiving, storing, and retrieving consumption-related information.

The human mind processes the information it receives. Consumers process product information by attributes, brands, comparisons between brands, or a combination of these factors. The number and complexity of the relevant attributes and available alternatives influence the intensity or degree of information processing. Consumers with higher cognitive abilities acquire more product information and consider more product attributes and alternatives than consumers with lesser ability. The elements of memory are the sensory store, the short-term store (or working memory), and the long-term store. The processes of memory include rehearsal, encoding, storage, and retrieval.

Learning Objective 6: To understand cognitive learning as a framework for consumer decision-making.

Cognitive learning is the systematic evaluation of information and alternatives needed to meet a recognized unfilled need or solve a problem. Unlike behavioral learning, which focuses on largely instinctive responses to stimuli, cognitive learning consists of deliberate mental processing of information. Instead of focusing on repetition or the association of a reward with a specific response, cognitive theorists emphasize the role of motivation and mental processes in producing a desired response. Several models of cognitive learning are discussed throughout this book.

Learning Objective 7: To understand consumer involvement and passive learning, and their impact on purchase decisions and the retention and recall of promotional communications.

The consumer involvement model proposes that people engage in limited information processing in situations of low importance or relevance to them, and in extensive information processing in situations of high relevance. Hemispheric lateralization (split-brain) theory gave rise to the notion that television is a low-involvement medium that results in passive learning and that print and interactive media encourage more cognitive information processing.

Learning Objective 8: To understand how to measure the results of consumer learning.

Measures of consumer learning include recall and recognition tests, and attitudinal and behavioral measures of brand loyalty. Brand loyalty consists of both attitudes and actual behaviors toward a brand, and both must be measured. For marketers, the major reasons for understanding how consumers learn are to teach consumers that the marketers' brand is best and to develop brand loyalty. Brand equity represents the intrinsic value of a brand name. This value stems from the foundations of brand loyalty: The consumer's perception of the brand's superiority, the social esteem that using it provides, and the customer's trust and identification with the brand.

Review and Discussion Questions

5.1. How can the principles of: (a) classical conditioning and (b) instrumental conditioning be applied to the development of marketing strategies?

5.2. Describe in learning terms the conditions under which family branding is a good policy and those under which it is not.

5.3. Neutrogena, a company known for its "dermatologist recommended" skin care products, introduced a line of shaving products for men. How can the company use stimulus generalization to market these products? Is instrumental conditioning applicable to this marketing situation? If so, how?

5.4. Which form of learning—classical conditioning, instrumental conditioning, observational learning, or cognitive learning—best explains the following consumption behaviors: (a) buying a six-pack of Gatorade, (b) preferring to purchase jeans at a Diesel Store, (c) buying an e-reader for the first time, (d) buying a new car, and (e) switching from one cell phone service to another? Explain your choices.

5.5. Define the following memory structures: Sensory store, short-term store (working memory), and long-term store. Discuss how each of these concepts can be used in the development of an advertising strategy.

5.6. How does information overload affect the consumer's ability to comprehend an ad and store it in his or her memory?

5.7. Discuss the differences between low- and high-involvement media. How would you apply the knowledge of hemispheric lateralization to the design of TV commercials and print advertisements?

5.8. Why are both attitudinal and behavioral measures important in measuring brand loyalty?

5.9. What is the relationship between brand loyalty and brand equity? What role do both concepts play in the development of marketing strategies?

5.10. How can marketers use measures of recognition and recall to study the extent of consumer learning?

Hands-on Assignments

5.11. Imagine that you are the instructor of this course and that you are trying to increase student participation in class discussions. How would you use reinforcement to achieve your objective?

5.12. Visit a supermarket. Can you identify any packages where you think the marketer's knowledge of stimulus generalization or stimulus discrimination was incorporated into the package design? Note these examples and present them in class.

5.13. Find two ads: one targeting the left side of the brain and another targeting the right side. Explain your choices.

Key Terms

- advertising wear-out *153*
- AIDA *165*
- aided recall *168*
- behavioral learning (stimulus-response learning) 152
- brand equity *169*
- brand loyalty *168*
- chunking *163*
- classical conditioning *152*
- cognitive associative learning *153*
- cognitive learning *161*
- conditioned response *152*
- conditioned stimulus *152*
- consumer involvement *165*
- consumer learning *150*
- continuous reinforcement *159*
- covetous brand loyalty *169*
- cues *150*
- distributed learning *160*
- encoding *162*
- extinction *158*
- family branding *155*

- fixed ratio reinforcement *159*
- forgetting *159*
- hemispheric lateralization (split-brain theory) *166*
- high-involvement purchases *165*
- inertia brand loyalty *169*
- information overload *163*
- innovation adoption *165*
- innovation decision making *165*
- instrumental conditioning (operant conditioning) *157*
- learning *148*
- licensing *156*
- long-term store *162*
- low-involvement purchases *165*
- massed learning *160*
- motivation *150*
- negative reinforcement *158*
- observational learning (modeling) *160*
- passive learning *166*
- positive reinforcement *158*
- premium brand loyalty *169*

- product form extensions *155*
- product line extensions *154*
- recall test *168*
- recognition test *168*
- rehearsal *162*
- reinforcement *151*
- repetition *153*
- response *150*
- retrieval *163*
- semantic differential scale *165*
- sensory store *161*
- shaping *159*
- short-term store (working memory) *162*
- Starch Readership Ad Study *168*
- stimulus discrimination *156*
- stimulus generalization *154*
- three-hit theory *153*
- tri-component attitude model *165*
- unaided recall *168*
- unconditioned stimulus *152*
- variable ratio reinforcement *159*

6

Consumer Attitude Formation and Change

Learning Objectives

1   To understand what attitudes are, how they are formed, and their role in consumer behavior.

2   To understand the tri-component attitude model and its applications.

3   To understand the structures of multi-attribute models and their use in altering consumers' attitudes.

4   To understand how to alter consumers' attitudes by making particular needs prominent.

5   To understand the role of cognitive elaboration in altering attitudes.

6   To understand how attitudes can precede behavior in the form of cognitive dissonance and the resolution of conflicting attitudes.

7   To understand the ways people assign causality to events and apply this knowledge to consumer behavior.

AN ATTITUDE is a learned predisposition to behave in a consistently favorable or unfavorable way toward a given object. In the context of consumer behavior, an "object" can be a product, brand, service, price, package, advertisement, promotional medium, or the retailer selling the product, among many other aspects of consumption.

Attitudes are learned from direct experience with the product, **word-of-mouth**, exposure to mass media, and other information sources that consumers are exposed to. Attitudes reflect either favorable or unfavorable evaluations of the attitude object and motivate consumers to either buy or not buy particular products or brands. Consumers buy products toward which they have positive and favorable feelings; therefore, marketers must ensure that consumers maintain these attitudes following the purchase so that they keep buying same products repeatedly.

Marketers who introduce new items strive to form favorable consumer attitudes toward the new products in order to get consumers try them, like them, and continue buying them. Doing so is difficult because people are often unreceptive to the unfamiliar, at least initially. One way to establish positive consumer attitudes toward new products is to capitalize on products that consumers already like and buy regularly. For example, SNICKERS® Peanut Butter Squared—a new product featured in Figure 6.1—is targeted primarily at peanut butter lovers. The ad tells consumers who "like" peanut butter cups that they will be even fonder—that is, "love"—squares of peanut butter covered with SNICKERS® chocolate.

Another way of influencing attitudes is to relate them to social or cultural events. For example, the ad for SNICKERS® Egg in Figure 6.1 features the product together with an Easter egg. Playfully, the ad states that SNICKERS® "ripped off" the egg shape from Easter and ends with the tagline "It's Easter. Only more satisfying," which tells consumers that the SNICKERS® Egg enhances the Easter celebration. This ad is part of a campaign with the theme "SNICKERS® Satisfies."

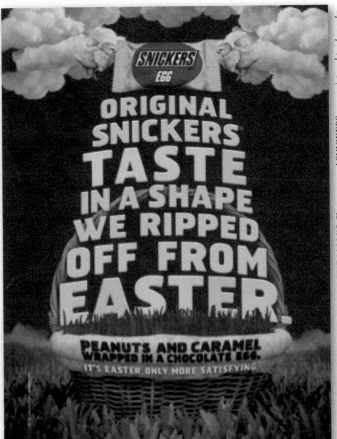

Source: (Left & Right) DOVE, M&M'S, THE M&M'S Character and SNICKERS are registered trademarks of Mars, Incorporated. These trademarks and advertisements are used with permission. Mars, Incorporated is not associated with Pearson Education, Inc.

FIGURE 6.1 SNICKERS® Ads Designed to Influence Attitudes

Attitudes and Their Formation

Learning Objective

1   To understand what attitudes are, how they are formed, and their role in consumer behavior.

As consumers, all of us have many attitudes toward products, services, advertisements, the Internet, and retail stores, among many others. Whenever we are asked whether we like or dislike a product (e.g., Black and White cookies), a service (e.g., American Airlines), a particular retailer (e.g., J. Crew), a specific direct-online marketer (e.g., Amazon.com), or an advertising theme (e.g., "Snickers Satisfies"), we are being asked to express our attitudes. By studying consumers' attitudes, marketers try to determine whether consumers will accept new products the company is considering, gauge why market segments were not persuaded by promotional themes, or learn how target customers are likely to react to new products, packages and the like. To illustrate, Nike or Reebok frequently study consumers' attitudes towards the functional and aesthetic design of athletic footwear. They regularly gauge reactions to their latest advertising and other marketing messages designed to form and change consumer attitudes. Attitudes are cognitions and not easily observable, but researchers can assess them by asking questions or making inferences from behavior. For example, if a researcher questions a student and discovers that he purchases Lady Gaga recordings from iTunes often and listens to them a lot, the researcher will *infer* that the student likes Lady Gaga and has a positive attitude towards her (and also towards iTunes).

Attitudes are directed at objects, such as products, product categories, brands, services, promotional messages, websites, media, retailers, and many other entities. We must note that although attitudes generally lead to behavior, they are not synonymous with behavior. Sometimes, attitudes reflect either a favorable or an unfavorable evaluation of the attitude object, which might or might not lead to behavior. Attitudes might propel consumers *toward* a particular behavior or repel them *away* from such.

Consumers Learn Attitudes

Consumers form new attitudes and also change existing attitudes. They often form positive attitudes towards new items under the same brand that they have been buying repeatedly and have been satisfied with. Nevertheless, consumers often try new products, product models, and different brands. If such trial purchases meet or exceed their expectations, then they develop favorable attitudes toward those objects. Generally, the more information consumers have about a product or service, the more likely they are to form attitudes about it, either positive or negative. However, if the product is irrelevant to them, the consumers will not cognitively process any of the available and applicable information. Furthermore, consumers often use only a limited amount of the information available to them. Typically, only two or three prominent beliefs about a product play a role in the formation of attitudes, and less important beliefs carry little weight. Therefore, advertisements should be focused on the key points that differentiate products from competitors, and not detail too many of the products' features.

How do consumers form their initial attitudes toward "things"? For example how do young adults form attitudes toward Hanes or Calvin Klein underwear, or J. Crew or Gap casual wear, or Anne Klein or Brooks Brothers business clothing? Would they buy their underwear, casual wear, and business clothing at Walmart, Sears, Saks Fifth Avenue, or Nordstrom? How do family members and friends, admired celebrities, mass-media advertisements, and even cultural memberships, influence the youngsters' attitudes about buying apparel? Why do some attitudes persist for a long time while others change often? Marketers must know the answers to such questions in order to influence the applicable attitudes. Next, we discuss the sources and factors that play a role in determining consumers' attitudes towards marketing objects.

Sources of Attitude Formation

Personal experience, family and friends, media, the Internet, and (increasingly) social media strongly affect attitudes. A primary source of attitudes toward products is the consumers' direct experiences in trying and evaluating them. Recognizing the importance of direct experience, marketers attempt to get consumers to try new products by offering cents-off coupons, free samples, and other inducements. If consumers try and like the new products, they will form positive attitudes and buy them again. In addition to personal experience, the family strongly impacts people's initial shopping-related attitudes (see Chapter 10). For instance, young children who were rewarded for good behavior with sweet foods and candy often retain a taste for (and positive attitude toward) sweets as adults.

Marketers increasingly use online advertising to shape the attitudes of small and specialized consumer niches, because new technologies enable them to customize advertising messages and also some products. Online, marketers can target consumers on the basis of their demographic, psychographic, or geo-demographic profiles with personalized product offerings (e.g., watches or sets of golf clubs for left-handed people), and messages demonstrating that they understand consumers' special needs and desires. Targeted online marketing can shape attitudes more effectively than other media because the promotional messages address the needs and concerns of precise micro-segments, whereas messages carried by traditional media generally reach diverse and large segments, as well as many consumers who have neither need for nor interest in the product advertised. Research has also shown that attitudes stemming from direct experience (e.g., product usage) are more enduring and resistant to competitors' messages than attitudes originating from promotional messages only (i.e., those developed without trying the product).

The Role of Personality Factors

Personality traits significantly influence the formation of attitudes. For example, individuals with a high **need for cognition** (i.e., those who crave information and enjoy thinking) are likely to form positive attitudes in response to promotions that include a lot of detailed, product-related information. In contrast, consumers who are relatively low in this need are more likely to form positive attitudes in response to ads that feature attractive models or celebrities, or other peripheral cues about the products advertised. Attitudes toward new products are particularly influenced by personality characteristics related to one's innovativeness (see Chapter 3).

Attitudes Are Consistent with Behaviors

Similar attitudes consistently lead to the same behaviors. However, despite their consistency, attitudes are not permanent and can change either seldom or frequently. Normally, we expect consumers'

TABLE 6.1	Examples of Situations That Influence Attitudes	
PRODUCT/SERVICE	**SITUATION**	**ATTITUDE**
Energizer Batteries	Hurricane is coming	"I know that the hurricane is going to knock out my electricity, so I'd better be prepared."
Mini Cooper	Buying a new car	"With gas prices so high, I've got to trade in my SUV and buy a car that gets 30 mpg!"
Cheerios	High cholesterol	"They've been advertising how Cheerios can lower cholesterol for so long that it must be true."
The Wall Street Journal	Extra cash on hand	"I have to decide whether to invest in stocks or just put my money in a money market fund."
Delta Airlines	Friend's bachelor party	"My friend's bachelor party is in Las Vegas, and I want to be there."
Maxwell House Coffee	Need to stay awake	"I had a late date last night, but I've got a lot of work to do this morning at the office."
Stouffer's Easy Express Meals	Want dinner at home	"I'm tired of eating out night after night."

behavior to correspond with their attitudes. For example, if a study showed that Mexican consumers prefer Japanese cars over Korean automobiles, we would expect that a Mexican consumer will buy a Japanese car when he replaces his current vehicle. However, circumstances often disrupt the consistency between attitudes and behavior. For example, the Mexican consumer might be unable to afford the car he prefers and buy the Korean car instead. In this case, affordability is a "situational" factor.

Attitudes Occur within Situations

Attitudes occur within and are affected by situations. In this context, "situations" are events and circumstances that influence the relationships between attitudes and behaviors at particular times. Situations can cause consumers to behave in ways seemingly inconsistent with their attitudes. For instance, if Margaret purchases a different brand of sun protection lotion each time she runs low, her brand switching may reflect a negative attitude toward towards the brands she has tried. In reality, she may have purchased different brands because she wanted to save money and bought only the ones on-sale. The opposite may also be true. If Edward stays at a Hampton Inn each time he goes out of town for business, we may erroneously infer that he has a particularly favorable attitude toward Hampton Inn. In fact, Edward may find Hampton Inn to be merely "acceptable" and prefer to stay at the Hilton or Marriott. However, because he owns his own business and travels at his own expense, he may feel that Hampton Inn is "good enough."

Consumers may have different attitudes toward a particular object, each corresponding to particular circumstances. For instance, when Scott replaces his old station wagon, he considers buying a new SUV, so that he can drive his children and their friends to after-school and weekend activities comfortably. However, when he realizes how expensive driving the SUV to work—30 miles each day—would be, he reconsiders his intention. Then, he speaks with a co-worker who owns a Ford Escape Hybrid SUV and finds out that his colleague is very satisfied with the car's gas mileage. The gas mileage is better than Scott's old car and he finds the car affordable. He then purchases a Ford Escape so that he can save money on gas and drive his children and their friends to their after-school and weekend activities.

When studying attitudes, researchers can easily misinterpret the relationship between attitudes and behavior, unless they consider the context of the situation. Table 6.1 lists situations that might influence consumer attitudes.

The Tri-Component Attitude Model

Learning Objective

2   To understand the tri-component attitude model and its applications.

Researchers constructed several models that explain how attitudes affect behavior. First, we examine the tri-component model, and then describe multi-attribute frameworks. The **tri-component attitude model** maintains that attitudes consist of three components: Cognitive, affective, and conative, as shown in Figure 6.2.

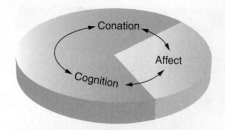

FIGURE 6.2 Tri-Component Attitude Model

The Cognitive Component

The **cognitive component** consists of a person's *cognitions*, that is, the knowledge and perceptions of the features of an attitude object that the person acquired from direct experience with the attitude object and information from various sources. This knowledge and perceptions commonly are expressed as *beliefs*; that is, the consumer believes that the attitude object possesses or does not possess specific attributes. Table 6.2 illustrates the beliefs of a hypothetical consumer about two TV technologies.

The Affective Component

The **affective component** represents the consumer's *emotions* and *feelings* regarding the attitude object, which are considered *evaluations*, because they capture his or her global assessment of the attitude object (i.e., the extent to which the individual rates the attitude object as "favorable" or "unfavorable," "good" or "bad").

Affect-laden experiences also manifest themselves as "emotionally charged states" (e.g., happiness, sadness, shame, disgust, anger, distress, guilt, or surprise). These and other emotional states may enhance or amplify the experience itself, as well as subsequent recollections. For instance, if a person visiting a shopping center feels particularly joyous during shopping there, he will spend more time doing so and recall with great pleasure the time spent at the shopping center. In addition, he may encourage his friends to visit the center. Table 6.3 illustrates the measurement of consumers' feelings and emotions toward a product.

Another measure of a person's emotions toward an object, shown in Table 6.4, is a **semantic differential scale**, which is a type of rating scale consisting of a series of bi-polar adjectives (e.g., good/bad, pleasant/unpleasant) anchored on a continuum. Many researchers believe that a person's attitude can be derived directly from this measure because, presuamably, the scales reflect beliefs cognitions, as well as emotions toward the attitude object.

The Conative Component

The **conative component** reflects the likelihood that an individual will undertake a specific action or behave in a particular way with regard to the attitude object. In consumer research, the conative component is treated as an expression of the consumer's *intention to buy*. Buying intention scales are used to assess the likelihood of a consumer purchasing a product or behaving in a certain way. Table 6.5 shows examples of intention to buy measures. Interestingly, consumers who are asked to respond to an intention to buy question appear to be more likely to actually make a brand purchase for positively evaluated brands (e.g., "I will buy it"), as contrasted with consumers who are not asked to respond to an intention question. This suggests that a positive brand commitment in the form of a positive answer to an attitude intention question positively affects the actual brand purchase.

Altering Consumers' Attitudes

Altering consumer attitudes is an important marketing strategy. The goal of leading brands is to strengthen and maintain the existing positive attitudes of customers, so that they will not

TABLE 6.2	Beliefs about Two TV Technologies	
PRODUCT ATTRIBUTE	**LED TV**	**3D TV**
Off-angle viewing	Image fades slightly from the right.	Excellent image from all angles.
Screen reflectivity	Small	Medium.
Motion blur	Negligible	Negligible.
Color saturation	Excellent	Good.
Remote control ease of use	His friend had used it easily when they watched TV together.	His friend has had the TV for 3 months, but could not use it without consulting the manual.
Compatibility with cable company's DVR.	His friend said it took him 15 minutes to connect the TV and DVR.	His friend had to call the cable company and have them come to his house to connect the TV and DVR.

TABLE 6.3	Measuring Consumers' Feeling and Emotions about Aramis Aftershave

For the past 30 days you have had a chance to try Aramis Aftershave. We would appreciate it if you would identify how your face felt after using the product during this 30-day trial period. For each of the words below, please mark an "X" in the box corresponding to how your face felt after using Aramis Aftershave.

	VERY				NOT AT ALL
Relaxed	[ ]	[ ]	[ ]	[ ]	[ ]
Attractive looking	[ ]	[ ]	[ ]	[ ]	[ ]
Tight	[ ]	[ ]	[ ]	[ ]	[ ]
Smooth	[ ]	[ ]	[ ]	[ ]	[ ]
Supple	[ ]	[ ]	[ ]	[ ]	[ ]
Clean	[ ]	[ ]	[ ]	[ ]	[ ]
Refreshed	[ ]	[ ]	[ ]	[ ]	[ ]
Younger	[ ]	[ ]	[ ]	[ ]	[ ]
Revived	[ ]	[ ]	[ ]	[ ]	[ ]
Renewed	[ ]	[ ]	[ ]	[ ]	[ ]

TABLE 6.4	Semantic Differential Scales Measuring Consumers' Attitudes Toward Aramis Aftershave

Compared to other aftershaves, Aramis aftershave is:

Refreshing	[1]	[2]	[3]	[4]	[5]	[6]	[7]	Not refreshing
Fragrant	[1]	[2]	[3]	[4]	[5]	[6]	[7]	Not fragrant
Pleasant	[1]	[2]	[3]	[4]	[5]	[6]	[7]	Unpleasant
Appealing to others	[1]	[2]	[3]	[4]	[5]	[6]	[7]	Unappealing to others

TABLE 6.5	Intention-to-Buy Measures

Which of the following statements best describes the chance that you will buy Aramis Aftershave the next time you purchase an aftershave?

_____I definitely will buy it.

_____I probably will buy it.

_____I am uncertain whether I will buy it or not.

_____I probably will not buy it.

_____I definitely will not buy it.

How likely are you to buy Aramis Aftershave during the next three months?

_____Very likely

_____Likely

_____Uncertain

_____Unlikely

_____Very unlikely

succumb to competitors' special offers and other inducements designed to win them over. In contrast, in product categories, such as detergents—where Tide is the primary brand—or athletic shoes—where Nike dominates the market—competitors often try to change the strong and positive attitudes consumers have toward the market leaders in an attempt to get consumers to switch brands.

Changing attitudes about products and brands is difficult because consumers frequently resist evidence that challenges strongly held attitudes or beliefs and tend to interpret any ambiguous information in ways that reinforce their preexisting attitudes.[1] There are two primary strategies for changing consumers' attitudes: Changing an offering's overall image, or referring to specific product attributes. Next, we discuss the first strategy. In the following section, which explains multi-attribute models of attitudes, we address the second approach.

Changing Beliefs about Products

The strategy of changing beliefs in order to change attitudes concentrates on changing beliefs or perceptions about the brand itself. This is by far the most common form of advertising appeal. Advertisers constantly are reminding us that their products have "more" or are "better" or "best" in terms of some important product attribute. For example, an ad for Kraft's Miracle Whip claims that using this product makes a tastier turkey sandwich than mayonnaise does. To support this claim, the ad points out that Miracle Whip has "more flavor and half the fat" of mayonnaise.

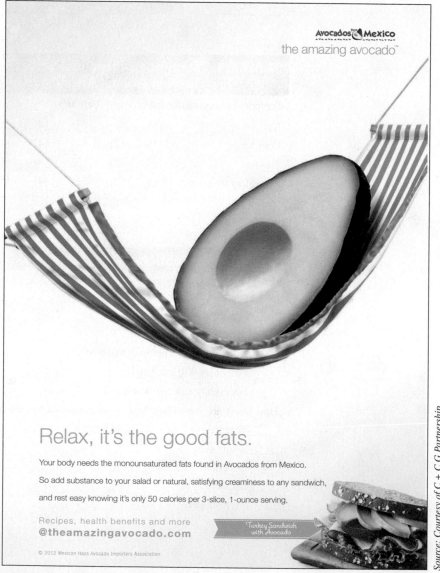

Source: Courtesy of C + C G Partnership

FIGURE 6.3 Changing Beliefs about Avocados

Information aimed at changing an attitude must be compelling and repeated many times if it is to overcome people's natural resistance to abandoning established attitudes. For example, people believe that avocados contain too much fat. The ad shown in Figure 6.3 focuses on changing these beliefs, stating: "Relax. It's the good fats."

Changing Brand Image

The strategy of changing brand image consists of attempting to alter consumers' *overall* assessment of the brand; marketers employ this approach by using inclusive promotional statements designed to set their brands apart from the competition. Examples of such statements include "this is the largest-selling brand" or "the one others try to imitate." An AT&T campaign was designed to enhance the brand's image without any references to products or services offered under the brand name. AT&T's slogan "Rethink 'possible'" was developed to change the attitudes of many who felt overwhelmed by technology in its favor and to increase consumers' confidence in technology, with taglines such as "It's what you do with what we do."[2] As another example, many ads have used the well-recognized phrase "A New Beginning" to bolster a brand's overall image and revive consumer interest.

Changing Beliefs about Competing Brands

Another attitude-change strategy involves changing consumer beliefs about *competitors'* brands or product categories. For instance, an advertisement for Eclipse chewing gum makes a dramatic assertion of the brand's superiority over other gums by stating: "Most other gums just mask bad breath. We kill the germs that cause it." The ad for Aleve in Figure 6.4 refutes the notion that more pills relieve pain more effectively than fewer pills, and is designed to establish unfavorable attitudes toward Tylenol. Similarly, the ad for Lysol Sanitizing Wipes in Figure 6.8 establishes negative attitudes toward an entire category of competing products. The ad states that Lysol's competitors—paper towels—spread germs, whereas Lysol wipes kill them. The Aleve ad is an example of **comparative advertising** and the Lysol one depicts a **two-sided message** (see Chapter 7).

FIGURE 6.4

Changing a Belief: "More Pills Doesn't Mean More Pain Relief"

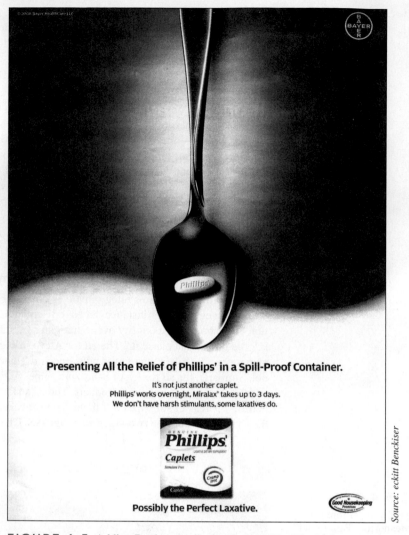

FIGURE 6.5 Adding Product Attributes: Caplets (Not Liquids) and Also Cramp Free

Multi-Attribute Attitude Models

Learning Objective

3 To understand the structures of multi-attribute models and their use in altering consumers' attitudes.

Multi-attribute attitude models portray consumers' attitudes as functions of their assessments of the objects' prominent attributes. First, we discuss the attitude-toward-object model and the use of product attribute in changing consumers' attitudes and developing new products. Next, we discuss the attitude-toward-behavior model, the theory of reasoned action, the theory of trying to consume, and the attitude-toward-ad model.

Attitude-Toward-Object Model

The **attitude-toward-object model** maintains that a consumer's evaluation of a product is a function of:

1. The extent to which the product has (or lacks) each of a given set of attributes.
2. The importance of each of these attributes to the consumer.

In other words, consumers generally have favorable attitudes toward those brands that they believe have better performance on the attributes that they view as important than other brands, and unfavorable attitudes toward those brands that they feel do not meet these criteria.[3]

In a study done to illustrate this model, 96 marketing students rated three brands of smartphones—iPhone, Blackberry, and Android—along the 11 attributes listed in Table 6.6. These ratings represent the students' beliefs regarding the extent to which each brand possesses a specific attribute. Students then indicated the level of importance attached to each attribute. Subsequently, the researchers

| TABLE 6.6 | Application of the Attitude-Toward-Object Model |

ATTRIBUTE	ATTRIBUTE'S IMPORTANCE	IPHONE		BLACKBERRY	
		PRESENCE OF ATTRIBUTE	PRESENCE × IMPORTANCE	PRESENCE OF ATTRIBUTE	PRESENCE × IMPORTANCE
Long battery life	3.77	2.64	9.9528	2.34	8.8218
High-resolution screen	3.1	3.62	11.222	2.15	6.665
Voice-activated commands	1.8	3.49	6.282	2.25	4.05
Carrier provides unlimited data transmission	3.52	3	10.56	2.62	9.2224
Carrier does not require long-term contract	2.43	1.79	4.3497	1.66	4.0338
High-quality camera	3.12	3.51	10.9512	2.07	6.4584
Camera has a flash	2.98	3.44	10.2512	2.62	7.8076
High-resolution video recording	2.52	3.3	8.316	1.93	4.8636
Carrier provides external unlimited data storage	2.72	2.82	7.6704	2.36	6.4192
Physical keyboard	1.9	1.16	2.204	3.34	6.346
Smartphone allows multitasking	3.36	3.38	11.3568	2.57	8.6352
TOTALS			93.1161		73.323

ATTRIBUTE	ATTRIBUTE'S IMPORTANCE	ANDROID	
		PRESENCE OF ATTRIBUTE	PRESENCE × IMPORTANCE
Long battery life	3.77	2.31	8.7087
High-resolution screen	3.1	2.97	9.207
Voice-activated commands	1.8	2.61	4.698
Carrier provides unlimited data transmission	3.52	2.48	8.7296
Carrier does not require long-term contract	2.43	1.95	4.7385
High-quality camera	3.12	2.84	8.8608
Camera has a flash	2.98	2.83	8.4334
High-resolution video recording	2.52	2.67	6.7284
Carrier provides external unlimited data storage	2.72	2.52	6.8544
Physical keyboard	1.9	2.18	4.142
Smartphone allows multitasking	3.36	2.72	9.1392
TOTALS			80.24

multiplied the importance "weights" by the ratings for each phone. For example, "long battery life" emerged as the most important attribute in a cell phone (3.77 out of a total of 5 possible points), and the iPhone scored higher on this attribute than the other two phones (2.64), which contributed to its high overall rating. Among the three brands, Blackberry was the only one with a physical keyboard, and therefore scored the highest on this feature (3.34), but this feature has the second-lowest importance rating (1.9), which lowered Blackberry's overall rating.

The totals show that respondents believed that the iPhone is far better than the other two models—but we must note that such perceptions do not necessarily represent the *actual* facts. For example, let's assume that, in reality, the Blackberry's screen resolution is much better than the iPhone's, although consumers *believe* that the iPhone has a better screen. As we already established in our discussion of positioning (Chapter 2), what matters most is how consumers *perceive* the product. Therefore, considering the (hypothetical) results of this study, Blackberry's marketer should promote the brand's screen resolution in its ads in order to "correct" consumers' misperceptions of its product.

Marketers use the attitude-toward-object model in developing promotions designed to change consumers' attitudes in favor of the brands advertised. They do so by adding new product attributes, changing consumers' perceptions of attributes, and also developing new products after researching consumer preferences.

Adding an Attribute

Adding a product or brand attribute means either adding an attribute that previously was ignored or adding one that represents an improvement or innovation. For example, to add a previously ignored or unknown attribute or benefit, an ad might point out that yogurt has more potassium than a banana (a fruit associated with a high quantity of potassium). The comparison of yogurt and bananas can enhance attitudes toward yogurt among consumers who wish to take in more potassium.

Another form of adding an attribute is innovation. To illustrate, a bottle of Wish-Bone® Salad Spritzer™ includes a pump that enables consumers to spray a mist of dressing on a salad, thus allowing them to control how much dressing they put on salads more precisely. Figure 6.5 shows an ad for Phillips' Caplets, which are a new form of laxative, because laxatives previously were available only as liquids. The new caplets are also "cramp free," which is a newly added attribute. In addition to portraying an innovative attribute, the ad is also aimed at changing beliefs about a competitor: Within the small print, the ad states that the Phillips' laxative works overnight, whereas its competitor—Miralax—takes up to three days to have an effect. Sometimes, *eliminating* a product feature may change attitudes favorably. For example, after conducting consumer studies, many marketers of personal care products now offer unscented or alcohol-free items.

Changing the Perceived Importance of Attributes

In the discussion of benefit segmentation (Chapter 2), we illustrated how different brands provide consumers with different benefits and how they are positioned accordingly. For example, in headache remedies, there is the division between aspirin (e.g., Bayer), acetaminophen (e.g., Tylenol), and naproxen sodium (e.g., Aleve). Marketers of personal care items sell multiple versions of the same product that provide somewhat different, narrowly defined benefits, in order to maintain or gain market share. For instance, Colgate Total provides 12 hours of germ fighting, Colgate Max Fresh wipes out bad breath, and Colgate Sensitive Pro-Relief is for people who have sensitive gums.

Some companies discover product attributes that most consumers pay little or no attention to and feature them in ads. Apparently, Dole discovered that some buyers of prepackaged fruit are unaware that other brands do not immerse the fruit in 100% fruit juice. The objective of the ad in Figure 6.6 is to use consumers' unawareness to differentiate Dole's product.

Developing New Products

Marketers often use the attitude-toward-object model during the development of new products. Consider the following hypothetical example: The Tropicana company is planning to add a new item to its product line. The company's market researchers identified four attributes as the key determinants in consumers' attitudes toward orange juice: Amount of pulp, degree of sweetness, strength of flavor, and color. Then, Tropicana conducted a three-stage study:

1. Using the scales shown in Figure 6.7A, the researchers asked consumers who drank orange juice regularly to describe their "ideal" juice, along the four attributes.

Source: Reckitt Benckiser

FIGURE 6.6 Changing the Importance of an Attribute: Real Fruit Must Be Packaged in Real Fruit Juice

	1	2	3	4	5	6	
No pulp	☐	☐	☐	☐	☐	☐	Lots of pulp
Not sweet	☐	☐	☐	☐	☐	☐	Very sweet
Weak flavor	☐	☐	☐	☐	☐	☐	Strong flavor
Dim orange	☐	☐	☐	☐	☐	☐	Bright orange

FIGURE 6.7A Semantic Differential Scales

2. Realistically, Tropicana could not produce the "ideal" juice, because it could not offer it at a competitive price. Instead, the respondents rated a "concept" juice representing a product that Tropicana *could* sell. The "concept" juice was similar to the "ideal" one, but not identical.

3. Tropicana *made* an "actual" new orange juice, which consumers tasted and rated.

As Figure 6.7B shows, compared with the "ideal," the "actual" product had too little pulp and was far too sweet, but the flavor of both products was nearly the same. Regarding color, it appears that although Tropicana did not match the ideal or the product concept, the company improved the color in the actual product by making it closer to the ideal. These findings indicate that Tropicana must change the "actual" product so that it matches consumers' preferences, by making it less sweet and adding pulp.

Attitude-Toward-Behavior Model

The **attitude-toward-behavior model** captures theindividual's attitude toward *behaving* or *acting* with respect to an object, rather than merely the person's attitude toward the object itself. Using the

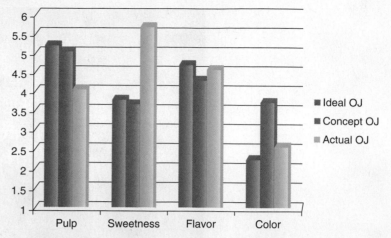

FIGURE 6.7B The "Ideal," "Concept," and "Actual" Compared

attitude-toward-behavior model to understand consumers may sometimes be more useful than using the attitude-toward-object model. For instance, a consumer looking for a new car might like Lexus cars (i.e., *positive* attitude towards the *object*), but not be ready or willing to buy an expensive Lexus (i.e., a *negative* attitude towards the *behavior* associated with the object).

A Taiwanese study examined consumers' attitudes toward the *act* (or behavior) of shopping online and revealed that these attitudes reflected nine desired benefits: (1) effectiveness and modern, (2) purchase convenience, (3) information abundance, (4) multiform and safety, (5) service quality, (6) delivery speed, (7) homepage design, (8) selection freedom, and (9) name familiarity.[4]

Theory of Reasoned Action

Like the tri-component model, the **theory of reasoned action (TRA)** incorporates the cognitive, affective, and conative components. Additionally, it holds that researchers must measure the *subjective norms* that influence a person's intention to act before gauging the level of intention. Subjective norms are the person's feelings as to what relevant others (e.g., family, friends, roommates, co-workers) think of the action the person contemplates. That is, would they support the anticipated action or not. For example, if a student wanted to get a tattoo but first considered whether her parents or boyfriend would approve or disapprove of her contemplated behavior, her consideration of others' opinions is her subjective norm.

Two factors underlie subjective norms: *normative beliefs* that the individual attributes to relevant others, and the individual's *motivation to comply* with the preferences of the relevant others.[5] In order to understand subjective norms correctly, researchers must measure both factors. For instance, the subjective norms of a student contemplating getting a tattoo (i.e., the "purchase") consist of answers to the following questions: (1) Who are her relevant others (e.g., parents and boyfriend)? (2) What are her beliefs about how each relevant other would respond to her tattoo (e.g., "Mom would consider the tattoo an object often associated with gangs, but my boyfriend would love it")? (3) To what extent complying with the preferences of the relevant others plays a role in her decision? In other words, is she sufficiently motivated to defer to the relevant others or not?

Theory of Trying-To-Consume

The **theory of trying-to-consume** represents cases where the outcome of a contemplated action (e.g., a purchase), stemming from a positive attitude, is uncertain, but is still being pursued by the consumer. A person trying to consume faces two types of obstacles that may prevent the desired outcome (see examples in Table 6.7):

1. *Personal impediments,* such as a consumer who is trying to find "just the right tie" to go with a suit, for less than $50, or a person trying to lose weight, but loves cookies.

2. *Environmental impediments,* such as the reality that "just the right tie" costs more than $50, or realizing that one cannot continue eating cookies and lose weight, and that there are no low-calorie cookies that taste good.[6]

TABLE 6.7	Potential Impediments to Trying to Consume

PERSONAL IMPEDIMENTS

"I wonder whether my nails will be long enough by the time of my wedding."

"I want to try to lose 2 inches off my waist by my birthday."

"I'm going to try to get us tickets for the Jimmy Buffet concert for our anniversary."

"I'm going to attempt to be able to run 5 miles by my birthday."

"I am going to increase how often I exercise from three to five times a week."

"Tonight I'm not going to have dessert at the restaurant."

ENVIRONMENTAL IMPEDIMENTS

"Only the first 500 people at the football game will receive a team cap."

"Sorry, the Jaguar you ordered didn't come in from England on the ship that docked yesterday."

"There are only two cases of Merlot in our stockroom. You better come in sometime today."

"I am sorry. We cannot help you. We are closing the gas station because of an electrical outage."

Researchers have also studied situations where consumers *fail to try to consume*, and identified two reasons why they do so. First, such consumers do not recognize all the consumption options available. Secondly, they prefer to self-sacrifice or delay gratification.[7]

Attitude-Toward-the-Ad Model

The **attitude-toward-the-ad model** proposes that the feelings consumers form when they see and hear ads significantly impact their attitudes towards the brands advertised.

Research among Asian Indian U.S. immigrants has explored attitudes toward 12 advertisements and purchase intention of six different products that the ads featured. The study found a positive relationship between attitude toward the advertisement and purchase intention for each of the advertised products; that is, if consumers liked the ad, they were more likely to purchase the product.[8] Other consumer research that examined general attitudes toward advertising in Bulgaria and Romania (recent members of the European Union) found that consumers in those nations were more positive about the institution of advertising (i.e., as a marketing tool) than they were about the actual advertisements used to promote products and services. Furthermore, while the main personal use of advertising in Bulgaria was information acquisition, the entertainment value of advertising was the strongest personal use in Romania.[9]

Changing the Motivational Functions of Attitudes

Learning Objective

4 To understand how to alter consumers' attitudes by making particular needs prominent.

Sometimes marketers must try to change negative consumer attitudes about their products, companies, or marketing practices. Frequently, the negative attitudes are not the result of bad products or promotion, but stem from uncontrollable circumstances. For example, several years ago, the U.S. Food and Drug Administration advised pregnant or nursing women and also young children to eat less canned tuna, due to concerns about the bioconcentration of mercury, a neurotoxin, in the fish. Subsequently, consumption of the three main brands of canned tuna—Bumble Bee, Chicken of the Sea, and StarKist—declined substantially. The three competing brands commissioned an advertising campaign to reverse consumers' negative feelings toward canned tuna. The theme of the campaign was "Tuna the Wonderfish," and through TV and online commercials, print ads, digital screens, posters, and materials placed in gyms and health clubs, it humorously portrayed that eating tuna is fun. Online, "tunathewonderfish.com" featured recipes and wacky characters called "the tuna lovers," and sang the praises of tuna with slogans such as "tuna is good for your heart," "part of a healthy diet," and "great on the go." These messages were designed to restore consumers' confidence in tuna by telling them that eating tuna is not only healthy, but also fun. The product's marketers knew that consumers liked canned tuna but were hesitant to eat it because of information that, although directed at a relatively small segment (i.e., pregnant women), negatively affected the perceptions of many consumers.[10]

The resons (or motivations) behind people's attitudes are known as "functions." Changing attitudes by appealing to consumers' motivations is known as the **functional approach**.[11] Accordingly, attitudes are classified into four functions: The utilitarian function, ego-defensive function, value-expressive function, and knowledge function.

The Utilitarian Function

The **utilitarian function** stems from the belief that consumers' attitudes reflect the utilities that brands provide. When a product has been useful or enabled us to perform certain tasks in the past, our attitude toward it tends to be favorable. One strategy for changing attitudes in favor of a product is by demonstrating to consumers that the product possesses a utilitarian purpose(s) that they may not have considered. The ad in Figure 6.8 illustrates how Lysol Wipes are more utilitarian than paper towels.

The Ego-Defensive Function

The **ego-defensive function** maintains that people form attitudes in order to protect themselves from sensing doubt and to replace uncertainty with feelings of security and confidence. For example, many consumers believe that salads from restaurants or salad bars—commonly eaten during lunch—are healthy and not fattening. The Healthy Choice ad in Figure 6.9 refutes this belief by

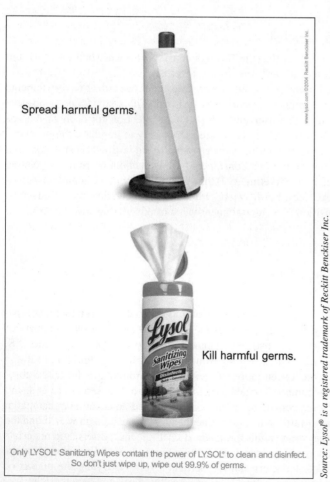

Source: Lysol® is a registered trademark of Reckitt Benckiser Inc.

FIGURE 6.8 An Appeal Based on the Utilitarian Function: Paper Towels Spread Germs but Lysol Wipes Kill Them

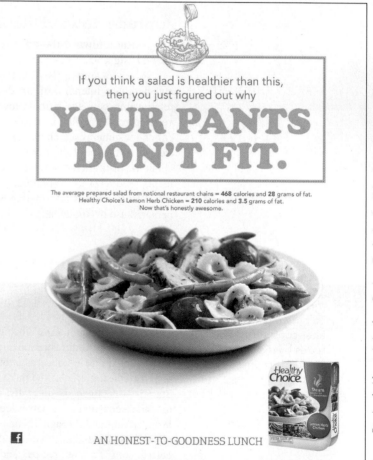

Source: Reprinted with permission from ConAgra Foods, Omaha, Nebraska

FIGURE 6.9 Appealing to the Ego-Defensive and Value-Expressive Functions: If You Discover That Your Pants No Longer Fit, Would You Still Believe That Prepared Salads Contain Few Calories?

Source: Campbell Soup Company

FIGURE 6.10 An Appeal Based on the Knowledge Function: Americans Do Not Eat Enough Vegetables, but You Can

humorously stating that such salads are fattening, unlike Healthy Choice, which is positioned as an "honestly labeled healthy lunch." The reference to honesty implies that the other offerings are not labeled correctly.

The Value-Expressive Function

The **value-expressive function** maintains that attitudes reflect consumers' values and beliefs, and that marketers can create ads that either support or refute these notions. For example, many nutrition-conscious consumers probably believe that prepared salads are healthy and low in calories. In addition to appealing to the ego-defensive function, the ad in Figure 6.9 also challenges the false belief that prepared salads are healthy and nutritious.

The Knowledge Function

The **knowledge function** holds that people form attitudes because they have a strong need to understand the characters of the people, events, and objects they encounter. Therefore, many firms use ads centered upon the consumer's "need to know." Accordingly, marketers often try to alter consumers' attitudes in favor of their brands by providing them with facts of which they were unaware. For instance, a message for a new allergy medication might include a bar graph demonstrating the product's superiority by contrasting its allergy symptom relief abilities with those of other allergy medications. The V8 Fusion ad in Figure 6.10 appeals to the knowledge function because it provides consumers with a fact that they may have not known: Namely, most Americans do not eat enough vegetables. Similarly, the Angus Beef ad in Figure 6.11 makes consumers more knowledgeable by illustrating the names of various beef cuts with pictures.

Associating Brands with Worthy Objects or Causes

Another way to influence attitudes is to relate them to social or cultural events. For example, the ad in Figure 6.1 associates SNICKERS® with nostalgic memories of Easter "egg hunt." The ad for Method detergent in Figure 6.12 associates the product with a worthy cause—ecological concern—by mocking mainstream detergents that come in huge and environmentally harmful jugs.

Research into brand-cause alliances has investigated the relationship between the "cause" and the "sponsor." One study found that although both the brand and the cause benefited from such alliances, less familiar causes benefited more from association with a positive brand than did highly familiar causes.[12] The results of another study indicated that if corporate sponsors do not explicitly reveal their motives for a company-cause or a product-cause association, consumers will form their own beliefs about the connection between the company or brand and the cause.[13] This indicates that sponsors should tell consumers the reasoning behind their sponsorships, rather than allowing consumers to guess, possibly incorrectly, why the sponsorship was formed.

Source: Certified Angus Beef® brand

FIGURE 6.11 An Appeal Based on the Knowledge Function: The Names and Pictures of Beef Cuts

Source: © Method Products, Inc: advertising agency: Droga5

FIGURE 6.12 Associating Method Detergent with Ecological Concerns

The Elaboration Likelihood Model

Learning Objective

5 To understand the role of cognitive elaboration in altering attitudes.

The **elaboration likelihood model (ELM)** proposes that attitudes can sometimes be changed by either one of two different routes to persuasion—a central route or a peripheral route—and that the cognitive elaboration related to the processing of information received via each route is different. The central and peripheral routes to persuasion reflect **extensive** and **limited problem solving** (see Chapter 14), and also correspond with **high-** and **low-involvement purchases** (see Chapter 5). The premise of this model is that consumers carefully evaluate the merits and weaknesses of a given product when they consider the purchase to be very relevant. Conversely, consumers engage in very limited information search and evaluation (or little cognitive elaboration) when the purchase holds little relevance or importance for them. Thus, for high-involvement purchases, the **central route to persuasion**—which requires considered thought and cognitive processing—is likely to be the most effective marketing strategy. For low-involvement purchases, the **peripheral route to persuasion**—which requires relatively little thought and information processing—is likely to be effective. In this instance, because the consumer is less motivated to exert cognitive effort, learning occurs through repetition, the passive processing of visual cues, and holistic perception. Highly involved consumers use attribute-based information to evaluate brands, whereas less-involved consumers apply simpler decision rules. In marketing to highly involved consumers, the quality of the argument presented in the persuasive message, rather than the imagery of the promotional message, has the greater impact on the consumption decision.

The route to persuasion has important implications for promotion. For example, comparative ads (see Chapter 7) are more likely to be processed centrally (purposeful processing of message arguments), whereas noncomparative ads are commonly processed peripherally (with little message elaboration and a response derived from other elements in the ad). A study demonstrated that the correlation between a consumer's product involvement and objective product knowledge was higher for *utilitarian* products than for products designed to bring about pleasure (termed *hedonic* products); for hedonic products, the correlation between subjective knowledge and product involvement was higher than for utilitarian products.[14] Assuming that *subjective* knowledge is the result of interpreting the imagery presented in the ad (i.e., the peripheral route) and that *objective* knowledge is the outcome of the factual information the ad provides (i.e., the central route), marketers should consider the product's degree of utilitarianism in selecting either the central or peripheral route in promoting that product.[15]

The central route applies to attitude change when a consumer's motivation or ability to assess the attitude object is high; that is, attitude change occurs because the consumer actively seeks out information relevant to the attitude object itself. When consumers exert the effort to comprehend, learn, or evaluate the available information about the attitude object, learning and attitude change occur via the central route.[16]

In contrast, when a consumer's motivation or assessment skills are low (i.e., low involvement), learning and attitude change occur via the peripheral route and without consumer processing of information that is relevant to the attitude object itself. In such cases, attitude change often is an outcome of secondary inducements such as cents-off coupons, free samples, beautiful background scenery, great packaging, or the encouragement of a celebrity endorsement. Research indicated that, in some low-involvement situations, both central and secondary inducements initially played equal roles in evoking attitudes. However, the central inducement had the greater "staying power"; that is, over time it was more persistent than the secondary one. Additionally, among subjects low in product knowledge, advertisements with terminology and factual data—that is, the central route—produced more favorable attitudes toward brands and ads than secondary cues.[17]

Cognitive Dissonance and Resolving Conflicting Attitudes

Learning Objective

6 To understand how attitudes can precede behavior in the form of cognitive dissonance and the resolution of conflicting attitudes.

So far, our discussion has maintained the traditional (and rational) view that consumers develop their attitudes *before* taking action (e.g., "Know what you are doing before you do it"). However, there are theories that refute the "attitude precedes behavior" perspective. Specifically, cognitiv dissonance theory and attribution theory provide different explanations as to why and how behavior sometimes *precedes* attitude formation.

Cognitive dissonance occurs when a consumer holds conflicting thoughts about a belief or an attitude object.[18] For instance, after consumers have made a commitment to buy an important and pricy object—for example, made a down payment on a new house or an expensive car—they often begin to feel cognitive dissonance when they think of the unique, positive qualities of the alternatives not selected ("left behind"). When cognitive dissonance occurs after a purchase, it is called **post-purchase dissonance**. Because expensive and important purchases require compromise and choice among similar alternatives (e.g., similar homes in the same community), post-purchase dissonance in such instances commonly occurs, and leaves consumers with an uneasy feeling about their behavior (the purchase decision). Thus, marketers must ensure that these consumers resolve conflicting cognitions by changing their attitudes to conform to their behaviors.[19]

In the case of post-purchase dissonance, attitude change is an *outcome* of an action or behavior already undertaken. The conflicting thoughts and dissonant information that follow a purchase induce most consumers to change their attitudes so that the attitudes become consonant with their purchase behaviors. What makes post-purchase dissonance relevant to marketing strategists is the premise that marketers must help consumers reduce the unpleasant feelings created by the thoughts about alternatives that were "given up." Consumers can reduce their post-purchase dissonance in several ways:

1. Rationalize their decisions.
2. Seek advertisements that support their choices (while avoiding dissonance-creating competitive ads).
3. Try to "sell" friends on the positive features of the purchase made (i.e., "the consumer as a sales agent").
4. Look to satisfied owners for reassurance (e.g., meet homeowners in the community where the newly purchased house is located).

For example, consider a young man who has just purchased an engagement ring for his girlfriend and then sees the following magazine ad: "How can you make two months' salary last forever?" Because the purchase was expensive and the groom-to-be is likely to be experiencing dissonance, the ad might relieve his conflicts because it says that although the engagement ring did cost a great deal, the future bride will cherish it for the rest of her life.

Researchers have discovered different types and levels of dissonance. A study of durable consumer goods identified three segments of dissonant consumers: High-dissonance segment, low-dissonance segment, and "concerned about needing the purchase" segment.[20] As described earlier, consumers can try to reduce cognitive dissonance on their own. In addition, marketers can help consumers do so through ads specifically aimed at reinforcing consumers' decisions. For example, complimenting consumers on their wise decisions, offering them stronger guarantees or warranties, increasing the number and effectiveness of purchase-related contacts (e.g., post-purchase contacts by real estate agents to new home buyers who are waiting to close on the property), or providing more detailed information about the product while it is on order. In reducing dissonance, personal contacts may be more effective than advertisements; several studies indicated that most buyers believe that advertisers stretch the truth about their products in their promotions.[21] A study suggested that overly aggressive salespeople actually induce dissonance because consumers feel that they were "pushed" to make the purchases. Conversely, skilled salespeople can reduce dissonance by providing information and reassurance, and even turn consumers into loyal customers.[22]

Resolving Conflicting Attitudes

Attitude-change strategies are designed to resolve actual or potential cognitive conflicts between two attitudes. For example, George is conservative on social issues, a devoted Episcopalian, and also an active Republican. During one presidential elections, the Republican nominee for president was significantly less conservative than George and also a member of another religion. Therefore, George's attitudes conflicted: He wanted to vote for his party, but disliked the party's nominee. George faced a dilemma and had three options: (1) Not vote at all, although he has never missed voting; (2) Vote for the Democratic candidate, which was utterly unacceptable; or (3) Develop more positive attitudes about the Republican candidate and vote for him. After attending the Republican convention as a delegate, speaking to other delegates, listening to the speeches, and even briefly meeting the nominee for president, George decided that the candidate's positions on social issues were, after all, close to his own and also became less concerned regarding the nominee's religion. Thus, George resolved his conflicting attitudes by altering them in favor of the only voting option that was consistent with his past behavior.

In fact, the party's officials recognized that many other Republicans felt the same way that George did before the convention, and they hired marketing consultants whose task was to take measures to change such attitudes. The consultants taught delegates how to address the doubts of their peers during seemingly spontaneous, casual conversations. Also, the speeches and films about the candidate, shown during the convention, included subtle appeals and cues designed to resolve conflicting attitudes. In essence, these measures resembled the strategies that savvy marketers use in similar situations. Of course, George and many others with similar, initial conflicting attitudes were unaware that these strategic communications were taking place during the convention.

Assigning Causality and Attribution Theory

Learning Objective

7   To understand the ways people assign causality to events and apply this knowledge to consumer behavior.

As a group of loosely interrelated social psychological principles, **attribution theory** attempts to explain how people "assign causality" (e.g., blame or credit) to events, on the basis of either their own behavior or the behavior of others.[23] In other words, a person might say, "I contributed to the American Red Cross because it really helps people in need," or "He tried to persuade me to buy an LED, rather than a 3D TV, because he'd make a bigger commission." In attribution theory, the underlying question is *why*: "Why did I do this?" "Why did he try to get me to switch brands?" Making inferences about one's own or another's behavior is an important factor in understanding attitude formation and change.

Many companies sponsor socially beneficial events and causes because they hope that consumers would attribute their efforts to "genuine concern." Research indicates that better "matches" between sponsors and events or causes result in more favorable consumer attributions. Evidence also suggests that consumers are willing to reward high-effort firms (i.e., they will pay more for and/or evaluate the product higher) if they feel that the company has made an extra effort to make better products or provide better consumer services.[24]

Self-Perception Attributions

Self-perception attribution reflects the way people see themselves in the causalities they form about prior behaviors and the attitudes they develop thereafter. It is useful to distinguish between *internal* and *external* attributions. Let us assume that Bradley has just used video-editing software for the first time and his video of his South American vacation was well liked by the members of his photography club. After receiving the compliments, if he had thought: "I'm really a natural at editing my digital videos," his statement would reflect an *internal attribution*, because he had given himself credit for the outcome (e.g., his ability, his skill, or his effort). In contrast, if Bradley concluded that his work was due to a user-friendly video-editing program, the assistance of another club member, or just "luck," he would be making an

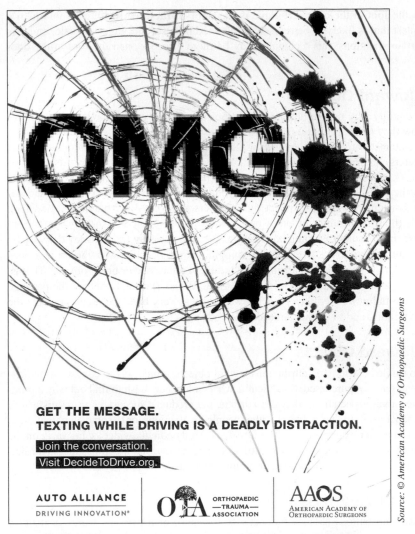

GET THE MESSAGE.
TEXTING WHILE DRIVING IS A DEADLY DISTRACTION.

Join the conversation.
Visit DecideToDrive.org.

AUTO ALLIANCE
DRIVING INNOVATION®

ORTHOPAEDIC —TRAUMA— ASSOCIATION

AAOS
AMERICAN ACADEMY OF ORTHOPAEDIC SURGEONS

Source: © American Academy of Orthopaedic Surgeons

FIGURE 6.13 Internal Attribution for Texting and Driving Accidents

external attribution. In the external attribution Bradley might think, "my great video is beginner's luck," whereas in the internal attribution he thought that "the video is good because of me."

Marketers can feature either internal or external attributions in promotions. For instance, ads for video-editing software should persuade users to *internalize* their successful use of the software. If they attribute their photos' quality to their skills rather than the software's capabilities, they would probably buy its new versions. Alternatively, if users *externalize* their success, they would attribute it to "beginner's luck," which is unrelated to the software itself and unlikely to get them to buy updates and advanced editions. Research indicated that appealing to internal attributions persuaded consumers to consider buying the products advertised.[25]

According to the principle of **defensive attribution**, people generally accept (or take) credit for success (internal attribution), but assign failure to others or outside events (external attribution). Thus, promotional messages should encourage consumers to perceive themselves as the reasons for their success and reassure them that the advertised products will always make them feel this way. Similarly, persuasive messages aimed at getting people to abandon and refrain from socially undesirable behavior should appeal to internal attributions. The OMG ad in Figure 6.13, whose tagline is: "GET THE MESSAGE," bluntly tells drivers who text and drive to attribute the calamities they cause to their own (internal) behavior and not to external causes (e.g., traffic, road conditions).

Foot-in-the-Door Technique

The **foot-in-the-door technique** consists of getting people to agree to large requests after convincing them to agree to a small and modest request first. The rationale behind this method is that agreeing to a small request creates a bond between the requester and the requestee. After fulfilling a modest request, the rquestee is likely to fulfill a larger request because of several reasons. First, the requestee does not want to disappoint the requestor, with whom he feels he has bonded. Secondly, the requestee actually becomes interested in the objective of the request. As discussed earlier, cognitive dissonance theory indicates that people tend to develop attitudes to justify prior actions. People's compliance with minor requests and subsequent compliance with more substantial requests is based on the premise that individuals look at their prior behavior (e.g., compliance with minor requests) and conclude that they are the kind of persons who generally agree to requests from others (i.e., an internal attributions). For example, someone who has donated $25 to the Michael J. Fox Foundation for Parkinson's Research is more likely to make a subsequent $100 donation than a person who was asked to donate $100 to begin with. The initial request of $25 was a "foot in the door," and "paved the way" towards a more substantial request.

Some research into the foot-in-the-door technique focused on understanding how specific incentives (e.g., cents-off coupons of varying amounts) influence consumer attitudes and subsequent purchase behavior. It discovered that different-size incentives created different degrees of internal attribution, which, in turn, led to different amounts of attitude change. For instance, individuals who tried brands without any inducements, or bought brands repeatedly, formed increasingly positive attitudes toward the brands (e.g., "I buy this brand because I like it"). In contrast, individuals who received samples were less likely to form positive attitudes about the brands they had tried (e.g., "I tried this brand because it was free").

Contrary to expectations, bigger incentives do not always lead to positive attitude changes. If an incentive is too big, marketers run the risk that consumers will externalize the cause of their behavior to the incentive (i.e., "I did it because I got a large incentive, but I didn't really like the product") and be *less* likely to change their attitudes and purchase the brand again. Instead, what seems most effective are *moderate* incentives, which are significant enough to stimulate initial purchase of the brand, but still small enough to encourage consumers to internalize their positive usage experiences and create positive attitude changes.[26]

In contrast with the foot-in-the-door technique is the **door-in-the-face technique**, in which a large, costly first request that is likely to be refused is followed by a second, more realistic, and less costly request. In certain situations, this technique may be more effective than the foot-in-the-door technique.[27]

Attributions Toward Others

In addition to understanding why people develop causalities about their own behaviors, it is important to understand how they make attributions towards others. As already stated, every time a person asks "why?" about a statement or action of another or other persons (whether family members, peers, salespeople, or marketers), attribution theory applies. To illustrate, in evaluating the words or deeds of, say, a salesperson, a consumer tries to determine whether the salesperson's motives are in his best interests. If he views the salesperson's motives favorably, the consumer is likely to respond accordingly. Otherwise, the consumer is likely to reject the salesperson's words and purchase elsewhere. Suppose, for example, that a consumer orders a new Canon digital point-and-shoot camera from Amazon.com. Because the consumer is going on vacation, she agrees to pay for next-day delivery by FedEx, instead of relying on Amazon's free five-day shipping. If the package with the camera does not arrive when it should, the consumer can attribute the failure to either one or both "others." That is, she can blame Amazon (failing to get the product out on time), FedEx (failing to deliver the package on time), or both (a dual failure). Alternatively, if the weather was very bad, she might attribute the delivery failure to the weather and to neither Amazon nor FedEx.

Attributions Toward Objects

Researchers have also studied consumers' attributions toward objects, which, in the context of marketing, are the products and services purchased. Specifically, when consumers wish to find out why a product met or failed to meet their expectations, they can attribute the product's successful or unsatisfactory performance to the product itself, to themselves, to other people or situations, or to some combination of these factors. To recap an earlier example, when Bradley successfully edited a video of his vacation, he could attribute that success to the software (product attribution), to his own skill (self or internal attribution), to a fellow member in his photo club who helped him (external attribution), or to all three.

Analyzing Self-Attributions

After people have made attributions about a product's performance or a person's words or actions, they often attempt to figure out whether the inferences they have made were correct. To illustrate, let's consider two scenarios: (1) an alumnus who is considers donating a large sum to the university where he earned his MBA; and (2) an amateur photographer who is contemplating buying a new and expensive photo printer. Both situations require a substantial outlay of funds, and the fact that they are considered demonstrates that the two persons have made initial attributions of causality: The alumnus believes that the donation will improve the MBA program's reputation and growth, and the photographer believes that the printer will enhance the quality of her work. Both persons are likely to seek reinforcement for their initial attributions, and researchers have identified three factors that they are likely to consider when doing so: Distinctiveness, consistency, and consensus. Table 6.8 explains these factors and describes the photographer and alumnus's hypothetical deliberations.[28]

TABLE 6.8	Reviewing Self Attributions		
SCENARIO	DISTINCTIVENESS	CONSISTENCY OVER TIME AND VARIED SITUATIONS	CONSENSUS
An alumnus considering donating money to his MBA program	How distinctive will my contribution be? Do many others make larger donations? Will I become part of a select group if I donate?	Can I afford to donate regularly? Will I be able to contribute money if the university asks for a special donation (e.g., for building a new student center)?	If I ask my friends, would most of them agree that I should make a donation, or will their opinions vary?
An amateur photographer who sees that, when printed on the latest HP printer, her photos look much better	Am I the only one who sees this marked difference, or do other notice the same?	Will I see the same superiority of the HP printer when I take other photos? Or is the advantage I see mostly a function of what this particular photo shows?	If I ask my friends, would most of them agree that my pictures look better when printed on the HP printer, or would some notice the difference and others not?

Summary

Learning Objective 1: To understand what attitudes are, how they are formed, and their role in consumer behavior.

An attitude is a learned predisposition to behave in a consistently favorable or unfavorable way toward a given object. In the context of consumer behavior, object is interpreted broadly to include the product, brand, service, price, package, advertisement, promotional medium, retailer selling the product, and many other aspects. Attitudes are learned from direct experience with the product, word-of-mouth, exposure to mass media, and other information sources. Attitudes reflect either favorable or unfavorable evaluations of the attitude object and they motivate consumers to either buy or not buy particular products or brands. Consumers buy products toward which they have favorable inclinations, so marketers must ensure that consumers maintain positive attitudes following purchases and remain loyal customers.

Attitudes are relatively consistent with the behavior they reflect. However, despite their consistency, attitudes are not necessarily permanent; they do change, and sometimes even frequently. Attitudes occur within and are affected by situations, events or circumstances that influence the relationship between attitudes and behavior. Personality traits significantly influence attitudes.

Learning Objective 2: To understand the tri-component attitude model and its applications.

The tri-component attitude model proposes that attitudes consist of three components: Cognitive, affective, and conative. The cognitive component represents the knowledge and perceptions of the features of an attitude object. The affective component reflects emotions and feelings, which are considered evaluations, because they capture the person's global assessment of the attitude object. The conative component is the likelihood that an individual will undertake a specific action or behave in a particular way with regard to the attitude object (i.e., consumer's intention to buy).

Learning Objective 3: To understand the structures of multi-attribute models and their use in altering consumers' attitudes.

Multi-attribute attitude models portray consumers' attitudes as functions of their assessments of the objects' prominent features. Multi-attribute models include the attitude-toward-object model, the attitude-toward-behavior model, the theory of reasoned action, the theory of trying-to-consume, and the attitude-toward-ad model. Multi-attribute models can be used when adding product attributes, changing consumers' perceptions of attributes, and developing new products.

Learning Objective 4: To understand how to alter consumers' attitudes by making particular needs prominent.

Altering attitudes according to consumer motivations is termed the functional approach, which classifies attitudes into four functions: The utilitarian, ego-defensive, value-expressive, and knowledge functions. Associating a brand with a well-liked object can also alter attitudes.

Learning Objective 5: To understand the role of cognitive elaboration in altering attitudes.

Attitudes can sometimes be changed by either one of two different routes to persuasion, depending on the degree of cognitive elaboration used when consumers process information. One route requires extensive thought and cognitive processing, and is typically employed in situations where consumers are highly involved and perceive a lot of risk regarding the purchase considered. The second route, which requires relatively little thought and information processing, occurs during less important purchases.

Learning Objective 6: To understand how attitudes can precede behavior in the form of cognitive dissonance and the resolution of conflicting attitudes.

In most cases, attitudes precede and guide behavior. Sometimes, consumers act first and only afterward develop attitudes about actions already undertaken, which creates conflicting thoughts about the attitude object. Because important purchase decisions (i.e., buying a new home) require compromise and choices among similar alternatives, post-purchase conflicts are common. Marketers must ensure that customers resolve cognitive conflicts by changing their customers' attitudes to conform to their behavior.

Learning Objective 7: To understand the ways people assign causality to events and apply this knowledge to consumer behavior.

People assign causality (i.e., blame or credit) to events, their own behaviors, and the behaviors of others. The way people see themselves is reflected in the causalities they form about prior behaviors and the attitudes they develop thereafter. In trying to change consumption-related attitudes, especially with regard to products that require self-participation, marketers must understand how people make attributions, toward others and objects, and also how they analyze their own attributions.

Review and Discussion Questions

6.1. Explain how situational factors influence the degree of consistency between attitudes and behavior.

6.2. Because attitudes are learned predispositions to respond in particular ways, why don't marketers measure only purchase behavior and ignore attitudes?

6.3. Explain a person's attitude toward visiting Disney World in terms of the tri-component attitude model.

6.4. How can the marketer of a "nicotine patch" (a device that assists individuals to quit smoking) use the theory of trying-to-consume? Using this theory, identify two segments of smokers that the marketer should target and explain how to do so.

6.5. Explain how can the product manager of a breakfast cereal change consumer attitudes toward the company's brand by: (a) Changing beliefs about the brand, (b) Changing beliefs about competing brands, (c) Changing the relative evaluation of attributes, and (d) Adding an attribute.

6.6. The department of transportation of a large city is launching an advertising campaign that encourages people to switch from private cars to mass transit. How can the department use the following strategies to change commuters' attitudes: (a) Changing the basic motivational function, (b) Changing beliefs about public transportation, (c) Using self-perception theory, and (d) Using cognitive dissonance.

6.7. Should the marketer of a popular computer graphics program prefer consumers to make internal or external attributions? Explain your answer.

6.8. A college student has just purchased a new Apple iPad. What factors might cause the student to experience post-purchase dissonance? How might the student try to overcome it? How can the retailer who sold the computer help reduce the student's dissonance? How can the computer's manufacturer help?

Hands-on Assignments

6.9. Find two print ads, one illustrating the affective component and the other illustrating the cognitive component. Discuss each ad in the context of the tri-component model. Why has each marketer taken the approach it did?

6.10. What sources influenced your attitude about this course before it started? Has your initial attitude changed since the course started? If so, how?

6.11. Describe a situation in which you acquired an attitude toward a new product through exposure to an advertisement.

Describe a situation in which you formed an attitude toward a product or brand on the basis of personal influence.

6.12. Find advertisements that illustrate each of the four motivational functions of attitudes. Describe how each ad either reinforces an existing attitude or is aimed at changing an attitude.

6.13. Think back to the time when you were selecting a college. Did you experience dissonance after you had made a decision? Why or why not? If you did experience dissonance, how did you resolve it?

Key Terms

- affective component *176*
- attitude *172*
- attitude-toward-behavior model *183*
- attitude-toward-object model *180*
- attitude-toward-the-ad model *185*
- attribution theory *190*
- central route to persuasion *188*
- cognitive component *176*
- cognitive dissonance *189*
- comparative advertising *179*
- conative component *176*
- defensive attribution *191*
- door-in-the-face technique *192*

- ego-defensive function *186*
- elaboration likelihood model (ELM) *188*
- extensive problem solving *188*
- foot-in-the-door technique *191*
- functional approach *186*
- high-involvement purchases *188*
- knowledge function *187*
- limited problem solving *188*
- low-involvement purchases *188*
- multi-attribute attitude models *180*
- need for cognition *174*
- peripheral route to persuasion *188*

- post-purchase dissonance *189*
- self-perception attribution *190*
- semantic differential scale *176*
- theory of reasoned action *184*
- theory of trying-to-consume *184*
- tri-component attribute model *175*
- two-sided message *179*
- utilitarian function *186*
- value-expressive function *187*
- word-of-mouth *172*

Case Two: *Procter & Gamble*

Febreze "Breathe Happy Campaign Launch"

Lead Agency: **GREY**

Strategic Challenges

Febreze was once a breath of fresh air in the category, but the competition caught up.

In 1998, Febreze entered the air care category with a revolutionary product. Rather than simply perfuming the air, its unique formula actually eliminated odors on fabrics and replaced them with a fresh scent. Febreze became known as THE odor-eliminating brand and enjoyed great success. Recognizing a good thing when they saw one, the competition responded by launching similar products that provided the same benefit. "Brand Health" data indicated that P&G had lost its distinct positioning. The company once "owned" odor elimination, but now shared this equity with competitors Glade (category leader by dollar share) and Airwick (third in the category by dollar share).

Air care brands became indistinguishable.

As competitors expanded to offer products similar to Febreze, the category became nebulous. Innovation from any camp was replicated and marketing efforts were immediately countered. Products became increasingly similar with indistinguishable claims. Almost all advertising featured generic imagery, presenting freshness fantasies in idealized worlds. Toxic levels of advertising diluted P&G's marketing efforts and made people unable to tell the brands apart.

Cynical consumers ceased to believe brand claims and Febreze growth declined.

Research revealed that the company's audience (25- to 65-year-old moms who want constant assurance that their homes are clean and fresh) had grown cynical about the category's advertising. Because many cheaper, less advanced brands were making similar claims but did not live up to their promises, people struggled to know whom to believe, and became skeptical about all air care products. Consumers concluded that all brands' claims were overinflated and bought lower-priced products. With Febreze costing up to three times more than its competitors, P&G struggled to sustain sales.

Objectives

1. Restore faith in Febreze's odor-eliminating capabilities in a way consumers will remember.
2. Generate buzz for the Febreze brand and its advertising.
3. Restore the distinctiveness of the Febreze brand.

Insights

People's reactions to bad smells are stronger than their reactions to nice ones.

Focus groups reaffirmed that P&G's audience wanted to create a "welcoming home" by keeping it clean, tidy, and fresh, and that they were concerned about bad smells destroying this atmosphere. The threat of malodors did not only made them uncomfortable, but triggered passionate descriptions of unpleasant smells, reflecting their disgust of uncleanliness. P&G realized that focusing on the problem rather than the solution could help Febreze stand out among the other brands.

What we smell can be more important than what we see.

In-home interviews helped P&G understand Febreze's role in creating a "welcoming home" in greater depth, uncovering the most influential insight: When judging if a home is "welcoming," a messy-looking home can still be clean, but a smelly home can *never* be clean. This was best encapsulated by one respondent's comment on the issue: "When you walk into an unappealing room, you can close your eyes, but you can't turn off your nose."

Smelling is believing.

Observations of shoppers in stores revealed that consumers were spraying the product in the aisle after picking it off the shelf. This indicated that firsthand experience of the product is vitally important in influencing the consumer's choice of a brand.

The Big Idea

Involve real people in visceral experiences to prove that Febreze makes even the filthiest places smell nice, no matter what they look like.

Questions

1. Apply the principles of perception to the three insights listed in the case.

2. Are the three objectives aimed at repositioning Febreze? Explain your answer.

3. How would P&G determine whether the campaign's objectives have been achieved?

4. On You Tube, you can find several commercials that "brought to life" the "big idea." Describe three of them and discuss their persuasive effectiveness.

5. Several versions of Febreze are now on the market (febreze.com). Apply the concept of benefit segmentation to three of them.

Source: Effie Worldwide, Effie Showcase Winners. Reprinted by permission. Febreze is a 2012 Bronze Effie Winner. For information on Effie's programs for students, visit the Collegiate Effies at www.effie.org

Case Three:

Lifebuoy/Unilever Asia Private Limited
"Superfast Handwash"

Lead Agency: **Lowe Lintas and Partners**

Target Markets

The three markets chosen—India, Saudi Arabia, and Pakistan—were the most significant to Unilever because of their sizes and growth opportunities. If it did not "fire" in these markets, Unilever would not be a viable player in the global liquid handwash market.

India: The largest and most valuable among all of Unilever's markets. Lifebuoy was an established brand in India in bar soaps, but the brand's closest competitor owned more than half the market in the liquid handwash category.

Saudi Arabia: The largest market in the Middle East, where Unilever faced a dominant competitor that was growing even larger.

Pakistan: The second largest market in the Indian subcontinent, with two strong Unilever competitors.

Strategic Challenges

In the three countries, antibacterial handwash was widely used, but there were established antibacterial liquids that have been household names for years.

To illustrate the importance of consumers' need for the product and knowledge of its effectiveness, let's consider Argentina. Because of a swine flu outbreak, public messaging exhorted people to wash with soap but did not specify antibacterial soap. Hence, consumers questioned the necessity of an antibacterial soap.

Because Lifebuoy Handwash was high-priced, it was expected to appeal to higher-income groups. This was a difficult issue because, in India, the brand's bar soaps were popular among lower-income groups.

In each of the three markets, competitors offered "all powerful" antibacterial solutions. Consumers perceived these products as "germ killers" that offered long-lasting, all seasons protection.

In Pakistan, India, and Saudi Arabia, Lifebuoy had to create a unique image. It was a new, high-priced entrant to the liquid handwash category, and could not easily take on dominant competitors.

Across the three countries, Unilever wanted to target higher-income mothers who were potential handwash users and convince them to use Lifebuoy Handwash for their families. These mothers had kids aged between 4 and 12 years and were using competitive brands. When it came to protection, the target mothers believed that their families deserved the best and were not willing to compromise. This gave Unilever a foot in the door opportunity. If the company could convince these mothers that Lifebuoy offered the *best* protection, it had a chance to capture meaningful market shares.

Objectives

1. Increase preference for Lifebuoy among higher-income segments (defined by a socioeconomic classification index).

    This would be tracked by a consumer household panel that Unilever commissioned through a retail audit agency.

2. Establish the Lifebuoy proposition as unique and differentiate it from the competition.

    This would be tracked by using quantitative research among consumers after the communication had run for at least a month to measure recall of messaging.

Insights

Through lab research, Unilever could claim that Lifebuoy were better than competitors' products on germ kill: it could kill *even more* germs.

During consumer research studies, when the results of the lab research were shown to them, consumers said this was unbelievable. Proof or no proof, they were unwilling to budge. That's when Unilever realized that beating competitors by going head to head against them would not work.

During the same lab tests that showed that Unilever's product killed *more* germs than the competitors' products, the R&D scientists also discovered that Lifebuoy could kill germs *faster* than the competing products. In fact, Unilever's handwash could protect hands from germs in 10 seconds, whereas all other handwashes took one full minute to do so!

This was exciting, but Unilever did not want to make the same mistake as before of just using facts and figures to position its product. Rather than going in with just the *claim* (what good is a faster handwash anyway?), the company looked extensively for a consumer angle to frame the "faster kill" claim. It was while observing children's habits that the company hit a gold mine!

Universally, children are always in a rush or lazy while doing things they don't particularly enjoy (e.g., eating vegetables, doing their homework, etc.). *When it comes to hand-washing, it is no different.* For kids, it is an unnecessary chore that they do as quickly as possible, as they just want to be finished with it.

So, regardless of how many germs anyone claimed that their product would kill, it would all be rendered useless by the habits of children, who always wash in a hurry.

The campaign titled "Superfast Handwash" used the underlying insight on children's behavior not only to make germ protection in just 10 seconds new and relevant for Lifebuoy, but also to render the competition's perceived high ground on germ protection vulnerable. The double blow of a new parameter of time, combined with the lens of children's habits, managed to dislodge the company's competitors as the last word in germ protection in consumers' minds.

The Big Idea

Lifebuoy Superfast Handwash: 99.9% germ protection in just 10 seconds—because children are always in a hurry, especially when it comes to hand-washing.

Questions

1. Design one TV commercial (a story board) and one print ad that "bring to life" the "big idea."

2. Why didn't Unilever use factual-information (e.g., results of lab tests) about the "faster kill" to differentiate Lifebuoy from competition?

3. How did Unilever use qualitative and quantitative research (see Chapter 16) to develop the positioning claim for Lifebuoy?

4. Does the name "Lifebuoy" convey the product's core benefit effectively? Why or why not?

5. Over time, should Unilever combine the "more germs" and "faster kill" claims into positioning Lifebuoy?

6. It is unlikely that competitors would let Unilever take market shares away from them in the liquid antibacterial handwash category. How can they fight Unilever?

Source: Effie Worldwide, Effie Showcase Winners. Reprinted by permission. Superfast Handwash is a 2012 Bronze Effie Winner. For information on Effie's programs for students, visit the Collegiate Effies at www.effie.org

Persuading Consumers

Learning Objectives

1   To understand the elements and persuasive capabilities of communication, as well as the barriers to effective communication.

2   To understand the distinctions between broadcasting and narrowcasting.

3   To understand how to design persuasive messages effectively.

4   To understand the effectiveness and limitations of prominent advertising appeals.

5   To understand how to measure the effectiveness of advertising messages.

COMMUNICATION IS the transmission of a message from a sender to a receiver via a medium of transmission (also named "channel"). In addition to these four components—sender, receiver, medium, and message—the fifth essential component of communication is **communication feedback**, which alerts the sender as to whether the intended message was, in fact, received. Senders *encode* their messages by using words, pictures, symbols, spokespersons, and persuasive appeals, and then the receivers *decode* them. If the messages are to be persuasive, the receivers must decode the messages as the senders intended (see Figure 7.5).

Marketers (the message senders) can choose among numerous persuasive appeals when they design and send advertising messages to consumers (the receivers). The advertising appeal used is the **encoding** of the message. The following ads represent four prominent persuasive appeals. Figure 7.1 uses a humorous appeal to show that Delsey luggage is very light. Humor is the most widely used advertising appeal. The ad in Figure 7.2 depicts fear and is from a campaign urging victims of domestic violence to seek help before their conditions becomes deadly (the explosives represent abusive fists). Fear is effective in discouraging negative behaviors such as drug abuse and distracted driving. The ad in Figure 7.3 shows a (rather mild) sex appeal. Sex appeals have "stopping power," but must be used carefully, as they may distract consumers from the product advertised if used unwisely. The ad in Figure 7.4 compares washing clothes with added Clorox Bleach to using detergent only. The ad actually "admits" that clothes can be laundered *without* Clorox. Later on, we explore the advantages and risks of acknowledging alternatives, such as not using the product at all (i.e., a two-sided message), or even mentioning competing brands by name (i.e., comparative advertising) in promotional messages.

We begin with a discussion of the elements of communication and overcoming barriers to effective communication. Next, we present two models of media communications: Broadcasting and narrowcasting.

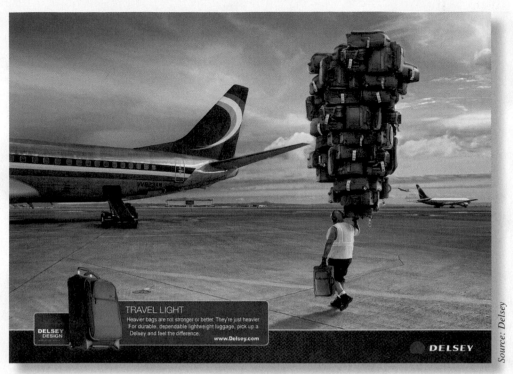

FIGURE 7.1 A Humorous Appeal: Delsey Luggage

FIGURE 7.2 A Fear Appeal: Family Peace Center

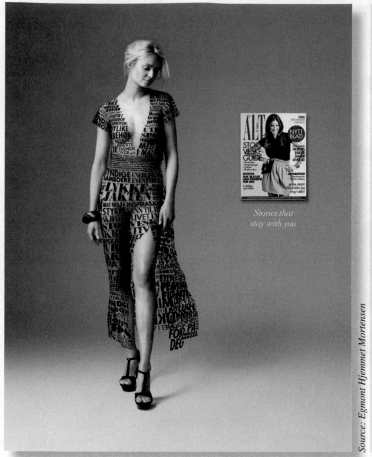

Source: Egmont Hjemmet Mortensen

FIGURE 7.3 A Sexual Appeal: ALT Magazine

Source: The Clorox Company

FIGURE 7.4 A Two-Sided Message

Thereafter, we explain the correct structure of persuasive messages and discuss the advantages and limitations of the most popular advertising appeals. After transmitting their ads, marketer must measure the effectiveness of their messages, and they do so by employing the methods discussed in the last section of this chapter.

The Communication Process

Learning Objective

1 To understand the elements and persuasive capabilities of communication, as well as the barriers to effective communication.

Communications can be either impersonal or interpersonal. In marketing, the sources of **impersonal communications** are messages that companies transmit through their marketing departments, advertising or public relations agencies, and spokespersons. The targets, or receivers, of such messages are usually a specific audience or several audiences that the organization is trying to inform, influence, or persuade. The senders of **interpersonal communications** may be either **formal sources** (e.g., a salesperson in a physical or virtual retail location) or **informal sources** (e.g., peers with whom the consumer communicates face-to-face or via electronic means). The key factor underlying the persuasive impact of a personal or interpersonal message received from either a formal or informal source is the source's credibility; that is, the extent to which the receiver trusts and believes the source sending

FIGURE 7.5 Communication Model

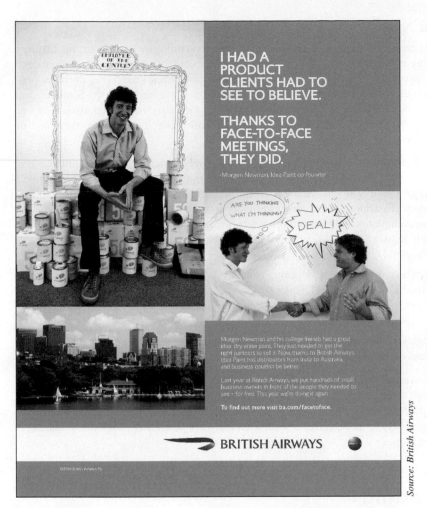

Source: British Airways

FIGURE 7.6 The Importance of Interpersonal Communication

the message. The influence of interpersonal sources can have a great effect on consumers' shopping patterns, and the perceived honesty and objectivity of the sender of the communication can have an enormous impact on how the communication is accepted by the receivers (see Chapter 9).

Compared with impersonal communications in mass media, a key advantage of interpersonal communications is their ability to obtain *immediate* feedback through verbal as well as nonverbal cues. Experienced speakers are very attentive to feedback and constantly modify their messages based on what they see and hear from the audience. Immediate feedback is the factor that makes personal selling so effective, because it enables the salesperson to tailor the sales pitch to the expressed needs and observed reactions of each prospect. Similarly, immediate feedback in the form of inattention serves to alert the college professor to jolt students who text during class. The professor can abruptly and dramatically stop the lecture, firmly ask the "texters" to leave the classroom, and state that the material covered at that point would appear on the next exam. The British Airways ad in Figure 7.6 focuses on the importance of interpersonal communications.

In consumer behavior terms, the sender of the message can be a marketer transmitting an advertisement to consumers or a person telling another consumer about a product. This chapter focuses on the marketer as the source, whereas Chapter 9 discusses consumers as the sources of messages that are transmitted via **word-of-mouth**. **Media** are the channels for transmitting communications. **Traditional media** are the original communications channels that advertisers have used and are generally classified as print (newspapers, magazines, billboards) and broadcast (radio, television); these media are impersonal because all receivers get the same message, and the communications are one-way because the receivers cannot interact with the senders. **New media** are online channels, social networks, and mobile electronic devices. These media are drastically more advanced than traditional media because they allow marketers to send personalized messages to individual consumers who can respond to the messages immediately. These responses indicate to marketers whether or not their persuasive efforts have been effective. Chapter 8 explores both forms of media.

Several "barriers" affect the accuracy with which consumers interpret messages. The most prominent ones are selective exposure and psychological noise.

Selective Exposure

Selective exposure refers to consumers' selectivity in paying attention to advertising messages. They read ads carefully for products they are interested in and tend to ignore advertisements that have no interest or relevance to them. Furthermore, technology provides consumers with increasingly sophisticated means to control their exposure to media. Consumers can now control their exposure to mass media and avoid commercials while watching TV by using the pause function when a string of commercials starts and then quickly returning to the broadcast once the ads are over. Viewers can also **time shift** by recording TV shows and viewing them at their leisure while skipping over commercials. Readers of newspapers and magazines online can create personalized editions of these publications and avoid many ads, and satellite radio allows consumers to avoid hearing radio ads altogether. Caller ID, phone answering machines, the government's "do not call" list, and other devices allow consumers to screen out telemarketing and other unsolicited contacts from marketers.

Psychological Noise

Just as telephone static can impair a phone conversation, **psychological noise** in the form of competing advertising messages or distracting thoughts can affect the reception of a promotional message. A viewer faced with the clutter of nine successive commercial messages during a program break may actually receive and retain almost nothing of what he has seen. Similarly, an executive planning a department meeting while driving to work may be too engrossed in her thoughts to "hear" a radio commercial. Marketers use the following strategies to overcome or limit psychological noise:

1. Repeated exposure to an advertising message surmounts psychological noise and facilitates message reception. Thus, repeating an ad several times is a must (see Chapter 5). The principle of redundancy is also seen in advertisements that use both illustrations and text copy to emphasize the same points. To achieve even more advertising redundancy, many marketers now place their messages in such places as video games, movie theaters, elevators, supermarket floors, baggage carousels, subway turnstiles, and even public restrooms (see discussion of **ambush marketing** in Chapter 4).

2. Copywriters often use *contrast* to break through the psychological noise and advertising clutter and attract consumers' attention (see Chapter 4). Contrast includes featuring an unexpected outcome; increasing the amount of *sensory input* (such as color, scent, or sound); and identifying, through testing, message appeals that attract more attention.

3. Digital technologies allow marketers to monitor the consumer's visits to websites, infer the person's interests, and design and send customized promotional messages to that person.

Of course, effective **positioning** and providing value are the most effective ways to ensure that a promotional message stands out and is received and decoded appropriately by the target audience. Advertisements for products that are perceived to be unique and provide better value than competitive products are more likely to be received in their intended ways than other promotional messages within the advertising clutter.

Broadcasting versus Narrowcasting

Learning Objective

2 To understand the distinctions between broadcasting and narrowcasting.

The term **traditional media** is synonymous with broadcast media (or mass media) and consists of channels where all receivers receive the same one-way messages from marketers (i.e., they cannot send direct responses to the messages' sources). In sharp contrast, **new media** are channels of **narrowcasting**, defined as means that permit marketers to send messages that are:

1. *Addressable* and directed to specific persons or small audiences rather than groups of consumers.

2. *Customized* and based on data gathered from tracing consumers' surfing and clicks online, in combination with other information, to either small groups or individual consumers. The additional data includes the receiver's location (which can be determined from an IP address or a GPS integrated into a mobile device) and information from "cookies" installed on the hard drive of a digital device.

3. *Interactive* because, in most narrowcasts, an action by the consumer—in the form of a click on a link or banner—triggers the transmission of a message.

4. More *response-measurable* than traditional broadcasted ads because communication feedback is more accurate and received sooner.

Traditional media and communications models that have been used for decades are presently undergoing fundamental changes. Advertisers are unhappy with the current broadcast media because they are reaching increasingly smaller and more fragmented audiences and getting fewer "eyeballs" for the money spend for TV ads. Consumers can avoid commercials with increasing ease, and a large number of broadcasted advertising messages reach many people who are not interested in (and unlikely to purchase) the products advertised. Advertisers complain that the Nielsen ratings do not accurately reflect the ethnic composition of the U.S. population and do not adequately monitor "time shifted" TV viewing. Cable operators realize that they have the means to monitor media viewing more accurately, but are also deeply aware of the privacy concerns of their subscribers. The TV networks, which have lost vast audiences to cable channels, realize that continuing to provide free programming underwritten by advertising revenues generated from reaching massive audiences of prime-time shows—a model in place since the early 1950s—may no longer be feasible. The networks, cable companies, and advertisers agree that the new communications model calls for targeting smaller groups of consumers who are already interested in the products advertised, and to whom they must provide more interactive and enticing ways of viewing promotional messages. In short, driven by technology, communications is going through the greatest changes since the development of spoken and written language, and traditional media are being integrated into or replaced by new media.

Addressable Advertising

Probably, most of the readers have purchased products at Amazon.com, rented a movie at Netflix. com, or traded an item on eBay.com. These premier online merchants analyze the purchase behaviors of their users (including consumers' ratings of the products rented or bought) and utilize this data to make customized, or addressable, recommendations to individual users about future offerings. Thus, **addressable advertising** consists of customized messages sent to particular consumers. These messages are based mostly on the consumers' prior shopping behavior, which marketers have observed and analyzed.

Data aggregators (see Chapter 8) use data from users' browsers, Google, Yahoo!, and Facebook to build models that marketers use to design the different ads customers see, which are also a function of the viewers' demographics and past advertising exposure.[1] A study demonstrated that consumers favor interactive websites where they feel that they receive personalized messages and can easily contact the seller after the purchase, via, for example, chats with the sellers' representatives.[2]

For example, advertising on cell phones is gaining popularity because mobile phones are an ideal forum for personalized advertising. A TV network has teamed up with an online social network to recruit participants for an experiment in addressable and location-based advertising.[3] A publishing company started delivering educational content via cell phones.[4] Several providers of wireless services teamed up with companies by rewarding subscribers who agreed to receive ads on their cell phones with reduced rates and other incentives.[5] As the number of cell phones and other wireless communications devices continues to grow, mobile advertising is likely to become a component of most advertisers' media plans.

Twitter—the most popular short-messaging service—enabled advertisers to send messages to users based on indications of what the users like. For instance, a company that sells soft drinks can elect to show paid ads to Twitter users who are fans of professional football. Twitter can identify a football fan, say, by analyzing whether the Twitter user "follows" football players or commentators, or recirculates Twitter messages from those sources.[6] TV advertisers are now able to vary their spots based on audience demographics, changes in weather, sales goals, or the campaigns of competitors. For example, Wendy's designed ads that were customized according to the weather. TV viewers in certain locations saw either a chili spot or a Frosty ad. When it was more than 60 degrees, Wendy's showed the Frosty ads; when it was colder, the chili ad ran.[7] Almost all online newspapers now allow readers to pick and choose only the stories that interest them.

Cable TV operators have a tremendous amount of data about their viewers and are moving away from advertising based mostly on subscribers' geographic locations and the one-message-fits-all approach. For instance, ads for dog food will only go to households that have dogs. One company is experimenting with using data from remote controls to follow what a person is watching, and then matching that information and programs' contents to infer that person's gender and age. It can also use census and syndicated data for further refinement. Then the cable TV company sends targeted ads to individual households.[8]

Designing Persuasive Messages

Learning Objective

3 To understand how to design persuasive messages effectively.

A **message** is the thought, idea, attitude, image, or other information that the sender wishes to convey to the intended audience, and it can be *verbal* (spoken or written), *nonverbal* (a photograph, an illustration, or a symbol), or a combination of the two. The sponsor, who may be an individual or an organization, must first establish the objectives of the message, select an appropriate medium for sending it, and design (encode) the message in a manner that is appropriate to each medium and to each audience. The objectives of a persuasive message include creating awareness of a service, promoting sales of a product, encouraging (or discouraging) certain practices, attracting retail patronage, reducing post-purchase dissonance, creating goodwill or a favorable image, or any combination of these and other communications objectives.

The source of the message (the sender) must *encode* the message in such a way that its meaning is interpreted by the targeted audience in precisely the intended way. Marketers encode messages by using words, pictures, symbols, spokespersons, and special channels. The message receivers *decode* the messages they receive on the basis of their personal experiences, characteristics, and motives. To encode a message in a form that the audience will understand and thus receive its intended meaning (i.e., decode it successfully), the sender must know exactly what he or she is trying to say and why (i.e., message objectives) and understand the target audience's personal characteristics. According to **cognitive learning** models, (see Chapter 5) exposure to a message leads to interest and desire for the product and, ultimately, to buying behavior. In addition, personality traits affect a person's reactions to various promotional appeals (see Chapter 3).

The decisions that marketers must make in designing a message include selecting images, creating advertising copy, using positive or negative message framing, choosing between one-sided or two-sided messages, and deciding on the order of presentation.

Images and Text

Messages that depict images are often more effective than those with text only, as reflected in the famous saying "One picture is worth a thousand words." The ad for Mistique tissues in Figure 7.7 conveys the product's purpose and effectiveness mostly visually rather than verbally.

Many studies have investigated the interaction between visual and verbal cues and their ability to attract and capture consumers' attention in likable ways. One study showed that ads' *visual complexity* plays a central role in this regard. Advertisements are visually complex when they contain dense perceptual features and/or when they have elaborate creative designs. The study found that *feature complexity* hurts attention to the brand and attitude toward the ad, whereas *design complexity* enhances paying attention to the ad, raises its comprehensibility, and improves attitude toward the ad. The study demonstrated that marketers must assess the visual complexity of advertisements and use their findings to enhance their ads' "stopping power."[9]

Sometimes, marketers are influenced by the same economic, social, and cultural conditions and thus use similar phrases reflecting these conditions in their advertising copy. For example, given our increasingly busy lives, the growing complexity of technology, and the uncertain economic picture, many marketers have been using the words "simply," "simple," "easy," "honest," and "clear" in their ads. A new brand of orange juice was named "Simply Orange." McDonald's offered "the simple joy of a wholesome breakfast." Ads for one bank declared: "Saving is simple when no one charges you for it"; and ads for Ivory soap urged: "Keep it pure, clean and simple."[10]

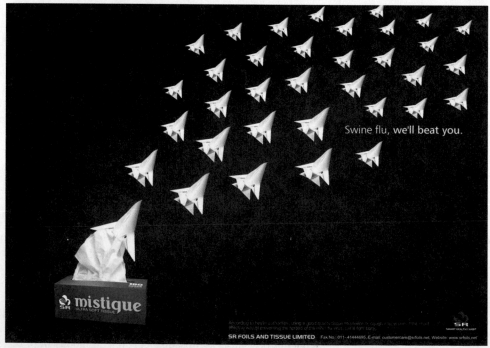

Source: SR Foils and Tissue Limited

FIGURE 7.7 Nonverbal Communication

Message Framing

Should a marketer stress the benefits to be gained by using a specific product, that is, **positive message framing**; or the benefits to be lost by not using the product, that is, **negative message framing**? Research suggests that the appropriate message framing decision depends on the consumer's attitudes and characteristics as well as the product itself. For example, one study found that persons with a low need for cognition were more likely to be persuaded by negatively framed messages.[11] Another study found that individuals with an *independent self-image* (i.e., who view themselves as defined by unique characteristics) were more persuaded by messages stressing an approach goal (positive framing); those with an *interdependent self-view* (i.e., who view themselves as defined by others) found messages that stress avoidance goals more convincing (negative framing).[12] A study of advertised products that enabled the early detection of disease indicated that positively framed anecdotal messages were less persuasive than negatively framed anecdotal messages.[13] Another study discovered that negative message framing was more effective than positive framing when respondents had less opportunity to process the information in the ad, but less effective when respondents had more opportunity to process the ad content.[14]

One-Sided versus Two-Sided Messages

Should a marketer pretend that its products are the only ones of their kind, that is, use a **one-sided message**; or should the company acknowledge competing products, that is, use a **two-sided message**? Some marketers stress only positive factors about their products and pretend that competition does not exist. However, when competition does exist and when it is likely to be vocal or obvious, such advertisers tend to lose credibility with the consumer. Figure 7.4 features a two-sided message. Another example is an ad for Ultra Dawn—a dishwashing liquid—proclaiming that the product is twice as strong as "the other guy." It acknowledges competition, but not by name. "I Can't Believe It's Not Butter!" is a butter substitute. Advertisements featuring the product often end with the question, "I Can't Believe It's Not Butter, can you?" The ad in Figure 7.8 is a two-sided message because it acknowledges the product's competitors (that is, butter and butter-substitue brands) without mentioning any.

The credibility of an advertised claim can often be enhanced by disclaiming the superiority of some product features or by not claiming that the product is a universal solution. For example, an ad for a men's hair regrowth product may state that, after clinical testing, whereas almost half the men using the product experienced modest to dense hair regrowth, about a third experienced minimal hair regrowth, and about one-sixth had no regrowth whatsoever. The admission that the product did not always work enhances the credibility of the ad.

The decision of whether to use a one- or two-sided message also depends on the nature of the audience and competition. If the audience is friendly (e.g., if it uses the advertiser's products), if it initially favors the communicator's position, or if it is not likely to hear an opposing argument, then a one-sided (supportive) message that stresses only favorable information is most effective. However, if the audience is critical or unfriendly (e.g., if it uses competitive products), if it is well educated, or if it is likely to hear opposing claims, then a two-sided message is likely to be more effective. Two-sided messages can also be very effective when consumers are likely to see competitors' negative counterclaims or when their predispositions toward the brand are negative.

Order Effects

Is it best to present your commercial first or last? Communications researchers have found that the *order* in which a message is presented affects audience receptivity. For example, on TV, the commercials shown first are recalled the best, whereas those in the middle are recalled the least. When just two competing messages are presented, one after the other, the evidence as to which position is more effective is somewhat conflicting. Some researchers have found that the material presented first produces a greater effect, that is, a **primacy effect**. Others have found that the material presented last is more effective, that is, a **recency effect**. Magazine publishers recognize the impact of order effects by charging more for ads on the front, back, and inside covers of magazines than for the inside magazine pages, because of their greater visibility and recall.

Order is also important in listing product benefits within an ad. If audience interest is low, the most important point should be made first to attract attention. However, if interest is high, it is not necessary to pique curiosity, so product benefits can be arranged in ascending order, with the most important point mentioned last. When both favorable information and unfavorable information are to be presented (as in an annual stockholders' report), placing the favorable material first often

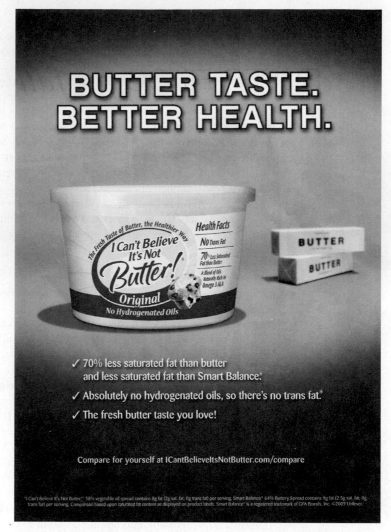

FIGURE 7.8 A Two-Sided Message: I Can't Believe It's Not Butter—
a Butter Substitute—versus "Real" Butter

produces greater tolerance for the unfavorable news. A study found that revealing the brand name
at the onset of a message enhances brand recall and message persuasiveness.[15]

Persuasive Advertising Appeals

Learning Objective

4 To understand the effectiveness and limitations of prominent advertising appeals.

Many researchers have studied the promotional appeals that marketers can use and the factors that
influence ad persuasiveness. For example, one study showed that informational appeals were particularly effective in high-involvement situations, whereas positive emotional appeals did better in
low-involvement situations. The study also found that different promotional appeals should be used in
extensions of existing brands as opposed to new brands. Differences in the impact of various promotional appeals, in both low- and high-**consumer involvement** conditions, were greater for new brands
than for brand extensions (see Chapter 5).[16] Another study discovered that, in addition to characteristics of the endorser or the appeal used, people's **need for cognition (NFC)** (see Chapter 3), played a
role in responses to ads. The higher a person's NFC, the less he or she is likely to consider peripheral
cues, such as endorser likeability, in processing the ad and become persuaded (or not) by ads on the
basis of their actual promotional appeals.[17]

The most widely used advertising appeals are comparative, fear, humor, sex, and timeliness.

Comparative Advertising

Comparative advertising is a widely used marketing strategy in which a marketer claims product superiority for its brand over one or more explicitly named or implicitly identified competitors, either on an overall basis or on selected product attributes. Some critics of the technique maintain that comparative ads often assist recall of the competitor's brand at the expense of the advertised brand. However, the wide use of comparative advertising indicates that marketers are confident that comparative ads exert positive effects on brand attitudes, purchase intentions, and actual purchases. Among more sophisticated consumers, comparative ads elicit higher levels of cognitive processing and better recall, and are likely to be perceived as more relevant than noncomparative ads.

Research studies have investigated many aspects of comparative promotions. A study that tested the degree of negativity in comparative messages (by using positive, negative, and mildly negative comparative messages) for several products reported that negative elements in an ad contributed to its effectiveness as long as they were believable or were offset by some elements that made the ad appear neutral.[18] Another study uncovered gender differences in response to comparative ads; comparative ads generated greater levels of brand-evaluation involvement among men but not among women. Among women, attention-getting comparative appeals produced inferences regarding the ads' manipulative intentions and reduced purchase likelihood.[19] Yet another study found that "promotion-focused" consumers (i.e., those focused on the aspirational aspects and the likely positive consequences of a purchase) reacted to comparative messages differently than "prevention-focused" consumers (i.e., those focused on the presence or absence of negative outcomes such as safety). In comparative ads, negative framing led prevention-focused consumers to evaluate the advertised brand positively and the other brand negatively. Among promotion-focused consumers, positive framing led to positive evaluation of the advertised brand but did not affect evaluations of the comparison brand.[20]

There has been considerable concern regarding the potential for comparative advertising to mislead consumers, including several legal actions against companies by the Federal Trade Commission. Consumer advocates have pursued the development of specific measures designed to gauge a comparative ad's ability to mislead consumers. In addition, comparative ads may result in legal disputes. Although the law requires companies to produce "reasonable factual evidence" in support of comparative claims, deciding what constitutes such evidence is difficult.

In the UK, fierce rivalry between major supermarket chains has resulted in several court cases focusing on their actions. German supermarket chain Aldi received damages from Tesco as a result of the latter's use of erroneous and unfair price comparisons as part of an in-store marketing campaign.[21] Tesco had not compared like-for-like products, had used incorrect prices for Aldi products, and had failed to compare equivalent quantities. Aldi cited an example of an ad featuring a bag of mint humbugs claiming that Tesco had compared prices between the two stores, stating that the weight of both bags was 250 g when in fact the weight of the Tesco bag was 200 g.

Sainsbury's complained to the Advertising Standards Authority (ASA) regarding Tesco's "Brand Promise" scheme, which compares the cost of a typical basket of Tesco's own-brand goods with the equivalents of rivals.[22] Sainsbury's argued that it was unethical to compare own-brand items on price alone without taking into account other product factors such as provenance, ingredients, and CSR. The ASA did not uphold the challenge – Sainsbury's response was an ad campaign that promised to protect consumers' rights to a fair comparison.[23] One example of such a comparison is shown in Figure 7.9.

In the ad campaign, Sainsbury's claimed that in spite of no apparent difference between most big supermarkets claiming to match prices, its products are Fair Trade, gauranteeing a fair deal for the producers irrespective of market forces.

Fear Appeals

Fear is an effective appeal and is often used in marketing communications. Some researchers have found a negative relationship between the intensity of fear appeals and their ability to persuade, so strong fear appeals tend to be less effective than mild fear appeals. A number of explanations have been offered for this phenomenon. Strong fear appeals concerning a highly relevant topic (such as cigarette smoking) cause the individual to experience cognitive dissonance, which is resolved either by rejecting the practice or by rejecting the unwelcome information. Because giving up a comfortable habit is difficult, consumers more readily reject the threat. This they do by a variety

Source: Bayer HealthCare LLC

FIGURE 7.9 An Illustration of Comparative Advertising

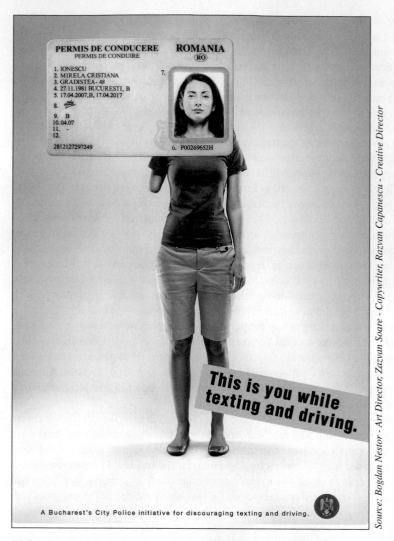

A Bucharest's City Police initiative for discouraging texting and driving.

This is you while texting and driving.

Source: Bogdan Nestor - Art Director, Zazvan Soare - Copywriter, Razvan Capanescu - Creative Director

FIGURE 7.10 A Fear Appeal: Discouraging Distracted Driving

of techniques, including denial of its validity ("There still is no real proof that smoking causes cancer"), the belief that they are immuned to personal disaster ("It can't happen to me"), and a diffusing process that robs the claim of its true significance ("I play it safe by smoking only filter cigarettes"). Therefore, marketers should use reasonable but not extreme fear appeals and recognize that fear appeals are not always appropriate. For example, information labels affixed to full-fat, reduced-fat, and nonfat products are likely to be more effective than warning labels. Congruent with the "it can't happen to me" mentality, fear appeals are often used in targeting young people, who often feel overly confident.

Strong fear appeals are often employed to discourage distracted driving caused by using mobile phones and texting, as well as drunk driving. In one study, more females than males said that fear appeals will change distracted driving and suggested using interviews with people who had been affected by distracted driving accidents in advertisements against this behavior. Also, more males than females said that using legal action would discourage distracted driving.[24] The ad featured in Figure 7.10 employs a very graphic image in its fear appeal. One study discovered that a strong graphic threat message had a greater effect for an unfamiliar issue than for a familiar issue. For an issue with which the subjects were very familiar, adding information to a weak-threat fear appeal increased the perceived severity of the undesired behavior. The perceived severity of threat and perceived probability of occurrence significantly influenced people's intentions to adopt the recommended behavior.[25]

Fear appeals are commonly used in antidrug campaigns. Such ads are more likely to be effective if they portray both the negative social consequences of drug use and the physical damage that drugs inflict on one's body. Fear appeals are unlikely to be effective among persons who score high on the personality variable termed **sensation seeking** (see Chapter 3). A high sensation seeker is more likely to use drugs and react negatively to fear-focused antidrug messages, feeling that he or she is immortal. Male and females appear to react differently to fear appeals. A five-month study of high school students discovered that short-term cosmetic fear appeals (such as yellow teeth or bad breath) used in ads to stop or reduce smoking were more persuasive for males, whereas long-term health fear appeals (such as getting cancer later in life) were more persuasive for females.[26]

Many ads arouse fear with images that provoke revulsion: Examples include mutilated bodies from drunk driving accidents, close-ups of lungs destroyed by smoking, and teeth and brains ruined by drug use. Several studies showed that adding disgust to a fear appeal enhanced message persuasion and compliance beyond that of appeals that elicited only fear.[27] However, portraying disgust might backfire. For example, in a campaign to discourage heavy consumption of soft drinks, New York City's health department featured an ad that depicted a "man drinking fat" and claimed that drinking a can of soda a day makes a person 10 pounds fatter a year. The ad was withdrawn because many complained that it was too revolting, and others claimed that the link between sugar and fat has not been fully scientifically proven.

Based on scores of studies about using fear in advertising, marketers should follow several guidelines:

1. Understand the target audience's reaction to a fear appeal, as well as its previous experiences. For example, those who are already following the behavior recommended but are not yet fully "converted" are likely to react differently than those who are fully "converted." Similarly, different age groups probably react differently to fear appeals, as do persons in different subcultures. Also, people who tried to change their behavior and failed will react differently than those trying to do so for the first time.

2. Beware the boomerang effect. When some persons are exposed to a fear appeal that encourages them to eliminate a strong habit, such as smoking, they may feel angry and resentful and immediately reach for a cigarette in defiance.

3. Realize that changing behavior is a long and complex process. Therefore, persons in different stages of this task react differently to fear appeals.

4. Study the extent to which the fear appeal encourages people to take action but without arousing too much anxiety, because high levels of anxiety may cause people to reject the message or avoid it altogether.

5. Determine whether to use a rational or emotional fear appeal.

6. Plan, over the long term, to repeat advertising using fear appeals. Recognize, though, that repeating these messages too often may reduce their credibility.

7. Accept that some addicts may not respond to fear appeals. For example, many heavy smokers or drinkers do not respond to explicit, clearly visible, and graphic warning labels.

8. Consider alternatives to fear appeals. For example, reward-focused appeals or even portraying humor and happiness when trying to discourage certain conduct may sometimes work better than using fear.

Humorous Appeals

Many marketers use humorous appeals in the belief that humor will increase the acceptance and persuasiveness of their advertising communications. Humor is the most widely used of all advertising appeals; by some estimates, it is used in 80 percent of all ads. Therefore, humor is the most studied advertising appeal. The findings of scores of studies on using humor in advertising indicated that:

1. Humor attracts attention and enhances liking of the product advertised.

2. Humor does not harm the comprehension of ads, and, in some cases, it actually aids comprehension.

3. Humor does not always increase an ad's persuasive impact or a source's credibility. For example, one study showed that humor might actually *distract* from cognitive processing of the central benefits of the brand.[28]

4. Humor that is relevant to the product is more effective than humor unrelated to the product.

5. Humor is more effective in ads for existing products than in ads for new products, and more effective in targeting consumers who already have a positive attitude toward the product.

6. Using humor is more appropriate for advertising low-involvement than high-involvement products.

7. The effects of humorous ads vary by the audience demographics.

8. The impact of humor is related to the receiver's personality. For example, higher sensation seekers were found to be more receptive to humorous appeals than lower sensation seekers.[29]

A study developed a measure of a personality trait, named **need for humor** that is focused on a person's tendency to enjoy, engage, or seek out amusement and suggested that these cognitive factors can better explain how consumers respond to humorous advertisements.[30] Another study discovered that ad recall was damaged when the humor was expected, and this adverse effect was more pronounced in individuals with low need for humor.[31] Humorous ads were found to be more memorable when humor was strong and related to the message.[32] Placing product in humorous movie scenes evoked positive emotions.[33]

Humor enables marketers to come up with highly creative ads that can sometimes backfire. For example, Ragu pasta came up with a campaign—designed to form emotional attachment to the product—focused not on the utility of the food, but on its ability to soothe embarrassing childhood memories. One ad showed a young boy entering his parents' bedroom as the accompanying jingle said: "Parents in bed, but it's just 8 o'clock. That's why they taught you that you should always knock." The ad then cut to the boy eating a bowl of pasta with sauce and the song concluded, "You need Ragu, 'cause growin' up is tough. Give him Ragu, he's been through enough." While most consumers found the ad to be creative and funny, some criticized it because of the insinuation of sex.[34] The Ving resorts ad in Figure 7.11 uses humor by showing how parents sometimes wish to "cut off" their noisy children from supposedly restful vacations.

Wordplay

Punning (or wordplay) means a humorous "double meaning." For example, an ad campaign for Moore Paint carried the theme "For those who know more"—with the play on the words "more" and "Moore." The ads appeared mostly in social media, particularly Facebook, rather than

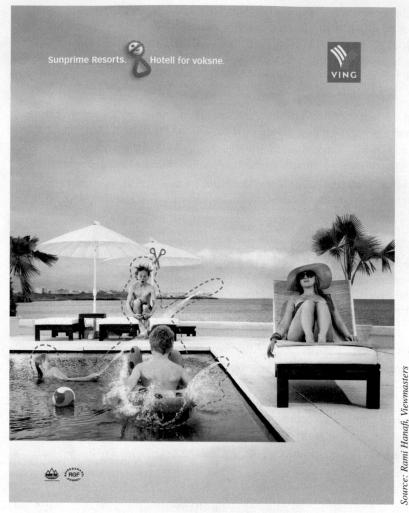

Sunprime Resorts. Hotell for voksne.

VING

FIGURE 7.11 A Humorous Appeal: Parents Daydream about Their Children "Disappearing" while Vacationing at Ving Resorts

Source: Rami Hanafi, Viewmasters

traditional media.[35] Data from **Starch Ad Readership Studies** (see Chapter 5) showed that consumers are more likely to read ads that employ puns than those that do not.[36]

Punning can also be used in imagery. For instance, Chuck Norris, a martial arts fighter and actor, lent his name to advertising Era detergent, a value brand priced lower than the premium Tide. The product is advertised as "Chuck Norris approved" with the tagline "a lot of fight for a little dough."[37]

Sexual Appeals

There is a lot of sensual advertising in the print media, the airwaves, and online. Advertisers have been provoking attention with nudity and sex, and promotional messages often include a lot of explicit and daring sexual imagery, extending far beyond the traditional product categories of fashion and fragrance into such categories as shampoo, beer, cars, and travel services, among many others.

Online, marketers have used sexual appeals that are highly innovative and much more daring than those in magazines and network TV. For example, Air New Zealand's safety video on YouTube featured a flight crew that was nude except for body paint applied to mimic uniforms, including neckties on men and scarves on women. Zappos, an online retailer, used a combination of nudity and technology in its campaign. The ads featured naked models in New York City and one ad featured a naked woman riding a Vespa. Other ads showed naked models doing everyday things like jogging, hailing a cab, and playing Frisbee in public. On the Zappos website, viewers were asked to "dress" the naked models with Zappos clothes. Zappos print ads included quick-response codes that, when scanned into smartphones, took users to a website with fictional videos allowing viewers to dress the models.[38]

There is little doubt that sexual themes have attention-getting value, but studies show that they rarely encourage actual buying. Often, sexual advertising appeals detract consumers from the message content and tend to interfere with message comprehension, particularly when there is substantial information to be processed. Because the visual sexual elements in an ad are more likely to be processed than the ad's verbal content, the cognitive processing of the product information may be incomplete. In addition, nudity may negatively affect the product message.

Receptivity to sexual appeals varies among consumers. For example, one study identified two psychological constructs that have an impact on consumers' responses to ads that depict nudity. The first is "sexual self-schema," which is one's cognitive view of the self with regard to sexuality. Sexual schemas originate in persons' past experiences and influence their reactions to sex-related promotional themes. The second is **sensation seeking**, which is the pursuit of novel and exciting sensations and experiences (see Chapter 3). The study discovered that sensation-seeking persons responded favorably to nudity in advertising and that one's sexual schema played only a modest role.[39] Another study indicated that more extroverted people were receptive to sexual appeals and that such appeals should not be used in targeting consumers who are quiet, shy, and reserved.[40] Clearly, marketers must exercise caution in using nudity because not all consumers will react favorably, and some may even feel alienated or offended.

The type of interest that sexual advertising evokes often stops exactly where it starts—with sex. If a sexually suggestive or explicit illustration is not relevant to the product advertised, it has little effect on consumers' buying intentions. This highlights the potential risk of sexually oriented advertising: The advertiser may be giving up persuasiveness to achieve "stopping power." When using sex to promote a product, the advertiser must be sure that the product, the ad, the target audience, and the use of sexual themes and elements all work together. Nevertheless, when sex is relevant to the product, it can be an extremely potent theme. For example, the advertisers of fragrances for either men or women often use highly romantic or suggestive visuals in their ads, implying that use of the fragrance will result in a meaningful or sultry romance.

Timeliness Appeal

During and following the financial crisis of September 2008, many marketers came up with advertising appeals designed specifically for tough economic times. For example, an ad for a health club urged consumers to make "a renewed commitment to lead a healthy life during these challenging times." An ad for a chain restaurant promoting an inexpensive meal used humor by stating: "It's one thing to bail out Wall Street. But who's gonna bail you out?"[41] Other marketers came up with appeals promoting products as affordable and sensible rather than indulgent and fabulous.[42] An ad campaign for a shopping district consisted of ads that did not suggest products to buy but instead listed fun and upbeat things to do, such as catching snowflakes on one's tongue.[43] Finally, some Halloween ads reflected the tough economic times with such appeals as "Incredible savings that are almost scary."[44] Table 7.1 describes advertising themes used during America's down economy.[45]

TABLE 7.1 Advertising Appeals During Economic Downturn	
OBJECTIVE	**CAMPAIGN THEME**
Restore confidence in banks	Humor: "We love Chase and not just because they have a million dollars."
Make people feel good during down economic times	Happiness: Bank of America: "Bank of opportunity"; Coca Cola: "Open happiness"; Western Union: "Yes"; Ads for a Broadway show promise "a happy moment" during "challenging times" and predict better times ahead.
Attract consumers who became more sensible	Advertising products as affordable and sensible rather than indulgent and fabulous. Not appealing to conspicuousness or status. Avoiding aspirational advertising.
Attract buyers who felt uncomfortable about buying real estate	Initially, an ad for an NYC condo proclaimed it to be "not just an address, it's an attitude," and showed beautiful young people dining out or shooting pool. During the economic downturn, new marketing materials promised "clean styling and attractive pricing," and featured a child reaching for a juice box at a local market and an older gentleman leaving the building with his dog.
"Comfort marketing": Appeal to nostalgia	Bringing back vintage characters, themes, and jingles to evoke past fond memories that make shoppers feel better about buying products. Reassuring consumers who demand value for their money that they are buying products that have stood the test of time.
Encourage consumers who are short on cash to paint and renovate their homes themselves	Selling paint: The marketers chose not to show people painting walls or interiors, because such ads remind people that painting is a mundane chore. Instead, they attempted to position paint as the mind-space of the consumers and appeal to their imaginations and emotions. For example, one ad stated that: "To others, a wall is a canvas, an invitation, a blank slate"; the voiceover continued, to a lush soundtrack: "The right color can turn any wall into so much more."

Sources: Stuart Elliott, "Ads That Soothe When Banks Are Failing," nytimes.com, October 7, 2008; Stuart Elliott, "Down Economic Times Elicit Upbeat Consumers," nytimes.com, March 10, 2009; Vivian Toy, "Goodbye, Glitzy Condo Pitches," nytimes.com, August 20, 2010; Patricia Cohen, "Marketing Broadway: Selling Hope for a Song," nytimes.com, December 10, 2008; Andrew Newman, "Using Appeals to Emotions to Sell Paint," nytimes.com, June 7, 2010; Stuart Elliott, "In New Ads, Stirring Memories of Commercials Past," nytimes.com, January 12, 2012.

Measures of Message Effectiveness

Learning Objective

5 To understand how to measure the effectiveness of advertising messages.

Because marketing communications are usually designed to persuade a target audience to act in a desired way (e.g., to purchase a specific brand or product, to vote for a specific candidate), their ultimate test is the receiver's response. Therefore, the sender must obtain feedback as promptly and as accurately as possible. Only through feedback can the sender determine whether and how well the message has been received. **Communication feedback** is an essential component of both interpersonal and impersonal communications because it enables the sender to reinforce or change the message to ensure that it is understood in the intended way.

Compared with impersonal communications in mass media, a key advantage of interpersonal communications is the ability to obtain *immediate* feedback through verbal as well as nonverbal cues. Immediate feedback is the factor that makes personal selling so effective, because it enables the salesperson to tailor the sales pitch to the expressed needs and observed reactions of each prospect. Experienced speakers are very attentive to feedback and constantly modify their presentations based on what they see and hear from the audience. Similarly, immediate feedback in the form of inattention alerts a teacher to jolt a dozing class awake with a deliberately provocative statement such as: "This material will probably be on the next exam."

It has always been very important for sponsors of impersonal communications to obtain feedback as promptly as possible, so that they can revise a message if its meaning is not being received as intended or if the message did not reach (at least in large part) the intended audience. Unlike interpersonal communications feedback, mass communications feedback is rarely direct; instead, it is usually inferred. Senders infer how persuasive their messages are from the resulting action (or inaction) of the targeted audience. Receivers buy (or do not buy) the advertised product; they renew (or do not renew) their magazine subscriptions; they vote (or do not vote) for the political candidate. Another type of feedback that companies seek from mass audiences is the degree of **customer satisfaction** (or dissatisfaction) with a product purchase. They try to discover—and correct as swiftly as possible—any problems with the product in order to retain their brand's image of reliability (e.g., through hotlines and online contacts).

Marketers measure their communications' **persuasion effects**, that is, whether the message was received, understood, and interpreted correctly; and their **sales effects**, that is, whether the messages of a given campaign have generated the sales level defined in the campaign's objectives. In addition, advertisers gauge the **media exposure effects** of their messages by buying data from firms that monitor media audiences (e.g., Nielsen) and conduct audience research to find out which media are read and which television programs are viewed more extensively than others. (see Chapter 8).

The sales effects of mass communications are difficult to assess (although retailers usually can assess the effectiveness of their morning newspaper ads by midday on the basis of sales activity for the advertised product). A widely used method of measuring the sales effects of food and other packaged goods advertising is based on the Universal Product Code (UPC), which is tied to computerized cash registers. Supermarket scanner data can be combined with data from other sources (e.g., media and promotional information) to measure the correlation between advertisements, special promotions, and sales.

Physiological measures track bodily responses to stimuli. For example, *eye tracking* is a method where a camera tracks the movement of the eye across store shelves and gauges the labels or brands to which respondents paid more attention. Another method, *brain wave analysis*, tracks the degree of attention paid to the components of viewed advertisements through monitoring electrical impulses produced by the viewer's brain. *Facial electromyography* (facial EMG) is a technique that tracks the electrical activity and subtle movements of facial muscles so as to gauge the emotions generated by different types of TV commercials.

Attitudinal measures gauge consumers' cognitive responses to messages, including their levels of engagement and involvement with the messages tested. For example, TV programs or commercials are shown in a theater setting and viewers use dials (located in their armrests) to indicate their levels of interest or disinterest in the clips viewed. In self-administered studies, marketers use **semantic differential scales** and **Likert scales** (see Chapter 16) to test ads and find out whether consumers liked the messages and understood them correctly.

Marketers must measure which advertisements are remembered by their target audience(s). In addition to the **recall** and **recognition tests** discussed in Chapter 5 (i.e., the **Starch Ad Readership Study**), researchers use **day-after recall tests** in which viewers of TV shows or listeners to radio broadcasts are interviewed a day after watching or listening to a given program. Participants are asked to describe the commercials they recall. The recall of a commercial and its central theme is evidence of its attention-getting and persuasive power.

Summary

Learning Objective 1: To understand the elements and persuasive capabilities of communication, as well as the barriers to effective communication.

Communication is the transmission of a message from a sender to a receiver via a medium (or channel) of transmission. In addition to four basic components—sender, receiver, medium, and message—the fifth essential component of communication is feedback, which alerts the sender as to whether the intended message was, in fact, received. Senders encode their messages by using words, pictures, symbols, spokespersons, and persuasive appeals, and then the receivers decode them. If the messages are to be persuasive, the receivers must decode them as the senders intended. Communications can be either impersonal or interpersonal. Impersonal communications consist of messages that companies transmit through their marketing departments, advertising or public relations agencies, and spokespersons. The senders of interpersonal communications can be either formal sources (e.g., a salesperson in a physical or virtual retail location) or informal sources (e.g., peers with whom the consumer communicates face-to-face or via electronic means). The key factor underlying the persuasive impact of a personal or interpersonal message received from either a formal or informal source is the extent to which the receiver trusts and believes the source sending the message.

Media are the channels for transmitting communications. Traditional media are the original communications channels that advertisers have used, and are generally classified as print (newspapers, magazines, billboards) and broadcast (radio, television). New media are online channels, social networks, and mobile electronic devices. These media are drastically more advanced than traditional media because they allow marketers to send personalized messages to individual consumers who can respond to the messages immediately.

The two most important barriers that affect the accuracy with which consumers interpret messages are selective exposure and psychological noise. Selective exposure refers to consumers' selectivity in paying attention to advertising messages. Psychological noise, in the form of competing advertising messages or distracting thoughts, can affect the reception of a promotional message.

Learning Objective 2: To understand the distinctions between broadcasting and narrowcasting.

The term traditional media is synonymous with broadcast media (or mass media) and consists of channels where all receivers get the same one-way messages from marketers (i.e., they cannot send direct responses to the source of the messages). New media are channels of narrowcasting, defined as channels that permit marketers to send addressable, customized messages, based on data gathered from tracing consumers' surfing and clicks online, in combination with other information, to either small groups or individual consumers. Addressable advertising consists of customized messages sent to particular consumers. These messages are based mostly on the consumers' prior shopping behavior, which marketers have observed and analyzed.

Learning Objective 3: To understand how to design persuasive messages effectively.

Some of the decisions that marketers must make in designing a message include selecting images, creating advertising copy, using positive or negative message framing, choosing between one-sided or two-sided messages, and determining the order of presentation. Messages that depict images are often more effective that those with text only. Positive message framing stresses the benefits to be gained by using a specific product. Negative message framing stresses the benefits to be lost by not using the product. A one-sided message pretends that the product advertised is the only one in existence. Two-sided messages acknowledge competing products. The primacy effect indicates that material presented first is more noticeable and persuasive than subsequent materials. The recency effect holds that the material presented last is more noticeable and persuasive than preceding materials.

Learning Objective 4: To understand the effectiveness and limitations of prominent advertising appeals.

Marketers have many options to choose from when selecting promotional appeals, but the ones most widely used are comparative advertising, humor, fear or sexual appeals, and well-timed ads. Comparative advertising is a very common marketing strategy in which a marketer claims product superiority for its brand over one or more explicitly named or implicitly identified competitors, either on an overall basis or on selected product attributes. Though some critics of the technique maintain that comparative ads often assist recall of the competitor's brand at the expense of the advertised brand, the wide use of comparative advertising indicates that marketers are confident that comparative ads exert positive effects on brand attitudes, purchase intentions, and actual purchases. Fear is an effective appeal often used in marketing communications. Some researchers have found a negative relationship between the intensity of fear appeals and their ability to persuade, in that strong fear appeals tend to be less effective than mild fear appeals.

Humor is the most widely used approach because many marketers believe that humor will increase the persuasiveness of their communications. Humor attracts attention, enhances liking of the product advertised, and also enhances consumer comprehension of the ads. Humor that is relevant to the product is more effective than humor unrelated to the product. Humor is more effective in ads of existing products than in ads of new products, and more effective in targeting consumers who already have a positive attitude toward the product. Punning is wordplay, often consisting of a humorous double meaning.

Sexual appeals have attention-getting value, but studies show that they rarely encourage actual consumption behavior. Often, sexual advertising appeals detract from the message content and tend to interfere with message comprehension, particularly when there is substantial information to be processed. When using sex to promote a product, the advertiser must be sure that the product, the ad, the target audience, and the use of sexual themes and elements all work together. Timely appeals are exemplified by the many ads that appeared during and following the financial crisis of September 2008, which contained messages designed specifically for tough economic times.

Learning Objective 5: To understand how to measure the effectiveness of advertising messages.

Marketers measure their communications' persuasion effects (whether the message was received, understood, and interpreted correctly) and their sales effects (whether the messages of a given campaign have generated the sales level defined in the campaign objectives). Advertisers also gauge the exposure and persuasion effects of their messages by buying data from firms that monitor media audiences and conduct audience research to find out which media are read, which television programs are viewed, and which advertisements are remembered by their target audience(s).

Physiological measures track bodily responses to stimuli. Attitudinal measures gauge consumers' cognitive responses to messages, including their levels of engagement and involvement with the messages tested. Semantic differential and Likert scales are used in testing ad copy to assess whether respondents like the message, understand it correctly, and regard it as effective and persuasive. Researchers also use day-after recall tests, in which viewers of TV shows or listeners to radio broadcasts are interviewed a day after watching or listening to a given program and asked to describe the commercials they recall.

Review and Discussion Questions

7.1. Explain the differences between feedback from interpersonal communications and feedback from impersonal communications. How can the marketer obtain and use each kind of feedback?

7.2. List and discuss the effects of psychological noise on the communications process. What strategies can a marketer use to overcome psychological noise?

7.3. Discuss the strategic differences between traditional media channels and new media.

7.4. Compare broadcasting and narrowcasting and explain why are marketers moving away from using broadcasting and into narrowcasting and addressable marketing.

7.5. How can marketers construct and transmit addressable ads? Illustrate with a promotion of a product or service of your choice.

7.6. Should marketers use more verbal copy than artwork in print ads? Explain your answer.

7.7. For what kinds of audiences would you consider using comparative advertising? Why?

7.8. What are the advantages and disadvantages of using humor in advertising?

7.9. Why must marketers use fear appeals in advertising cautiously? How can they do so?

7.10. Do sexual appeals work better than other appeals? Explain your answer and illustrate with examples.

7.11. How is communications feedback related to the measurement of persuasion and sales effects?

7.12. A marketer of a new car model launched through commercials during the Super Bowl intends to use attitudinal measures, as well as day-after recall tests, to estimate the commercials' effectiveness. How should the company do so?

Hands-on Assignments

7.13. Find two print advertisements: One illustrating a one-sided message and the other a two-sided message. Which of the measures discussed in this chapter would you use to evaluate the effectiveness of each ad? Explain your answers.

7.14. Find print ads using each of the following advertising appeals: Fear, sex, and humor. Discuss their effectiveness and persuasive value in class.

7.15. Watch an hour-long TV program and its commercials, without writing any notes. A day later, list all the commercials you can recall seeing. For each commercial, identify: (a) The message framing approach used, and (b) Whether the message was one-sided or two-sided. Discuss what you had remembered in the context of selective exposure and psychological noise.

Key Terms

- addressable advertising *203*
- ambush marketing *202*
- attitudinal measures *212*
- cognitive learning *204*
- communication *198*
- communication feedback *198, 212*
- comparative advertising *206*
- consumer involvement *206*
- customer satisfaction *212*
- data aggregators *203*
- day-after recall test *212*
- encoding *198*
- formal source *200*
- impersonal communications *200*
- informal source *200*
- interpersonal communications *200*
- Likert scale *212*
- media *201*
- media exposure effects *212*
- message *203*
- narrowcasting *202*

From Print and Broadcast Advertising to Social and Mobile Media

Learning Objectives

1 To understand the strategic superiority of impression-based (eyeballs) targeting over segment-based targeting.

2 To understand Google's targeting and advertising capabilities and its value to both consumers and marketers.

3 To understand the dynamics of social media and its strategic and promotional advantages over other media.

4 To understand how consumers use mobile media and their reactions to mobile advertising.

5 To understand how to measure the effectiveness of advertising in traditional and social media.

6 To understand the advancement of print and broadcast media into electronic communications.

Targeting Segments versus Eyeballs

The most important strategic impact of technology on marketing has been the ability to target consumers more precisely and effectively. Technology enables **impression-based targeting**—illustrated in Figure 8.1—through which advertisers specify the criteria describing the persons they wish to reach online and then bid in real time for the opportunities to reach them. A person reached is termed an "eyeball" or "impression." Impression-based targeting is implemented through **real-time bidding**, which is a technique that allows advertisers to reach the right user, in the right place, at the right time, and also sets the price that advertisers pay for each "eyeball" or "impression" (i.e., for each person reached). Specialized companies—generally known as "data aggregators"—enable advertisers to place bids on the opportunities to reach specific users, who meet a given criteria, on an impression-by-impression basis.

Before the arrival of the new targeting technologies, since the emergence of traditional advertising media (i.e., newspapers, magazines, radio, and television), TV networks, magazines, and newspapers have sold advertising space by offering marketers the opportunity to reach audiences (or segments) whose demographics and psychographics (lifestyles) matched those of the marketers' target markets. **Segment-based targeting** occurs when advertisers *prenegotiate* prices for advertising space in media (e.g., magazines or TV shows) whose audiences largely (but never completely) match the profiles of the consumers the advertisers wish to target. However, the audiences marketers reach via these media are larger and more diverse than their target markets and nearly always include many people who have no interest in the products advertised. For decades, after paying prenegotiated prices, marketers of competing (and often similar) products have been placing their ads within the same TV shows and magazines. Under this model, advertisers viewed the *creativity* of the ads, rather than the media where they *appeared*, as the key to the ads' persuasive effectiveness.

In contrast, **data aggregators** construct consumer profiles—based on cookies documenting people's online surfing (and other applicable information about them)—and identify prospective customers for specific products. Advertisers then

FIGURE 8.1

Impression-Based Targeting

THE MARKETER	THE CONSUMER
BlueKai — a "data aggregator" — monitors the cookies on Adam's browser and also matches his IP and ZIP Code, which enables it to estimate Adam's income and other demographics. Adam's estimated annual income is between $85,000 and $125,000 and he is 40 to 55 years old. BlueKai "packages" Adam and classifies him into "urban adventurers."**(a)**	For his winter vacation, Adam booked a trekking vacation on the Inca Trail in Peru and was looking for a handheld GPS. He visited several websites that included advice about selecting a GPS and also those of the largest GPS marketers: Garmin, TomTom, and Magellen. Every time Adam was online, a "cookie," indicating the day, time, websites, and exact pages he visited was saved on his browser.
The three GPS marketers are aware that many people go on active vacations in December and that these travellers are often looking for GPS devices. The three companies use the same criteria for selecting target consumers: (1) "urban adventurers"; (2) people who have visited at least three websites that are related to active travel in the past month.**(b)**	Adam visits The New York Times online and many advertisers engage in real-time bidding for the right to display their ads to him
The New York Times alerts advertisers and BlueKai that Adam is visiting its site. The three GPS makers engage in real-time bidding for displaying ads to Adam and Garmin wins. This bidding occurs within milliseconds, as The New York Times' page loads on Adam's computer.**(c)**	A banner advertising Garmin's GPS appears on The New York Times page next to the text. Every time Adam goes online, the bidding process happens. If Garmin continues to win the biddings, its ad will "follow" Adam online and, possibly, on every website he visits.**(d)**

Notes:
a. BlueKai has thousands of profiles, and sells many different services and delivery methods. There are scores of data aggregators, and the services they offer to advertisers and their data models vary greatly. BlueKai does not provide advertisers with *named* customers, but with the *browsers* of *anonymous* individuals who meet certain criteria at a given time.
b. It is unlikely that all three companies will set the exact same profiles. The profiles set are often broader and allow thousands of advertisers to bid on the impressions.
c. In reality, thousands of advertisers bid for the impression (i.e., Adam's "eyeballs"), not just GPS marketers. The bids are in small amounts of cents and typically are quoted in CPM—cost per thousand impressions.
d. The "following" may occur for a long or short time after the initial ad is displayed, depending on the degree of competition among advertisers to reach consumers like Adam.

Learning Objective

1   To understand the strategic superiority of impression-based (eyeballs) targeting over segment-based targeting.

compete for reaching the right "eyeballs" online by placing monetary bids. Because cookies are embedded in users' browsers, the data aggregators do not know the *names* of the consumers they "offer for sale," but recognize them as represented by their *browsers*. Thus, they offer advertisers browsers, and each browser represents an "impression." As illustrated in Figure 8.2, Facebook leads the way in the number of impressions created on the Internet.[1]

The Advantages of Impression-Based Targeting

Impression-based targeting offers several advantages over segment-based marketing:

1. Advertisers employing segment-based promotion invariably pay for reaching people who are neither inclined to buy their products when they see the ads nor likely to become future customers. Additionally, these persons also tune out advertisements for products they are not interested in. Recognizing this shortcoming early on, John Wanamaker (1838–1922)—one of the pioneers of buying advertising space—stated: "Half the money I spend on advertising is wasted; the trouble is I don't know which half." Impression-based targeting enables marketers to identify which "halves" of their advertising expenditures are wasted and design messages that reach primarily those who are likely to become customers.

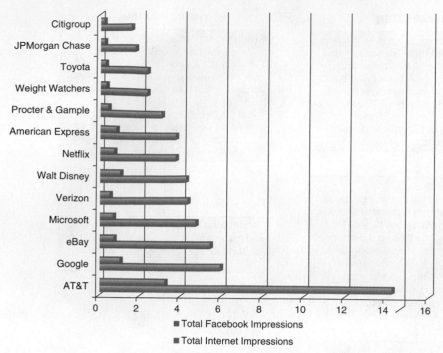

FIGURE 8.2 Internet and Facebook Impressions

2. In addition to being mostly "one-size-fits-all," messages sent via traditional media are one-way communications, and the consumers who receive them cannot interact with their contents. In contrast, receivers of impression-based ads can view and rotate images, click on links for detailed information about the products, compare brands, and much more.

3. According to the communications model, consumers' responses to ads represent feedback or measures of the ads' effectiveness. Feedback from ads placed in traditional media is delayed and often of limited use. For example, it is impossible to determine the impact of a very expensive Pepsi ad shown during the Super Bowl. The advertiser has no way of knowing how many consumers have reached for a Pepsi upon seeing the ad or purchased a Pepsi shortly after seeing it. In contrast, receivers' interest in impression-based ads can be determined immediately by observing the elements they click on within the ads, how long they stay at the website, and how often they return, among other measures (discussed later in this chapter).

4. Consumers can easily escape TV ads by **time shifting**, which involves starting to watch a show about fifteen minutes after it begins and using devices that allow them to skip commercials easily. In fact, advertisers have been fighting advanced ad-skipping features, and some TV channels rejected ads promoting electronics with such devices.[2] Researchers have also discovered "binge viewers," people who record an entire season of a TV series and then watch all the episodes consecutively and without the commercials.[3]

Impression-based ads often "follow" consumers online and keep reminding them about the products they were interested in. **Retargeting** occurs when ads for specific products that consumers have already pursued online "follow" them and show up repeatedly whenever they go online using the same computer. For example, when a consumer looks at, say, hiking boots at Amazon.com, a cookie is placed into that person's browser, linking it with the boots. When that consumer (or another person using the same computer) visits other sites, he or she still sees an ad for the boots on the screen.[4]

Google's Consumer Tracking and Targeting

Learning Objective

2 To understand Google's targeting and advertising capabilities and its value to both consumers and marketers.

Google is the most widely used search engine online and a prominent advertising medium. Across browsers, most online surfers use Google to find answers to questions, locate websites and sources for products and services, track down information, and much more. Google is the largest provider of the data and targeting tools that advertisers need for impression-based targeting, as well as the major supplier of real-time bidding to advertisers seeking impressions among consumers who fit certain criteria.

Google reaches consumers by using:

1. **Web-search ads**, which are ads generated by consumers' searches.

2. **Online display ads**, which are fixed banners that do not vary according to users' profiles or search patterns, posted on websites.

3. **Mobile advertising**, which are ads that appear on mobile devices in Google search results, on content websites, and in apps.

Google's most prominent use is as a search engine. After online users type in queries, two areas appear on the screen. The "organic results" are the links directing users to sites and resources that are applicable to their Google searches. The "sponsored space"—typically appearing on the right side or the top—consists of advertising banners that Google has sold to advertisers or "sponsors." For

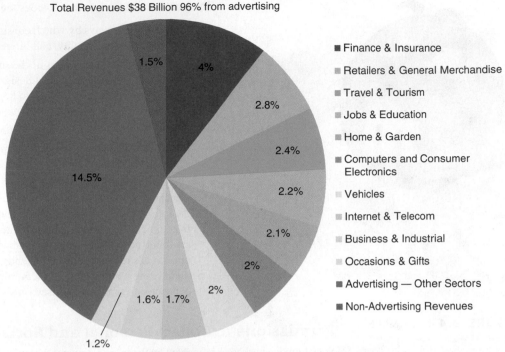

FIGURE 8.3 Google's Advertising Revenues

example, customers looking to buy flowers for Mother's Day and typing the word "flowers" into the search line will be directed to places where they can buy flowers (these links appear below the search line). Most likely, links to flower outlets close by will appear on the first search page, because Google identifies searchers' Zip Codes via their IP addresses. But, on the right side or top of the screen, consumers will see the banners of flower outlets that bid on these advertising spaces and won. Because Mother's Day generates more flower sales than any other occasion, it is likely that these banners will advertise major flower distributors, such as 1-800-FLOWERS. That is because only major outlets in the flower industry would have placed highly competitive bids on advertising space that is particularly expensive on Mother's Day.

Each time a potential customer clicks on a sponsored banner ad, the advertiser pays Google a fee. The fees can range from a few cents for terms that very few (if any) users are likely to enter in the search engine, to several dollars (and up) for words that many users are likely to type in; the latter are what bring up ads sponsored by large marketers. The advertisers' costs-per-click also vary according to whether or not the same user has clicked on the ad previously (measuring the effectiveness of online ads is discussed later in this chapter).

Another source of revenue for Google is graphical and video ads posted on YouTube, which is owned by Google, and on thousands of non-Google sites. Google also runs a shopping site where retailers pay for being displayed in Google's product-search engine.[5] Figure 8.3 depicts the sources of Google's advertising revenues; as shown, most of the revenues come from the marketers of consumer goods.

Consumers and Social Media

Learning Objective

3 To understand the dynamics of social media and its strategic and promotional advantages over other media.

Social media refers to means of interactions among people in which they create, share, and exchange information and ideas in virtual communities and networks. Social media depend on mobile and Web-based technologies to create highly interactive platforms through which individuals and communities share, co-create, discuss, and modify user-generated content.[6] However, even in the "new" and "non-traditional" social media, marketing symbols that have been around for decades are used. For instance, marketers are increasingly featuring their "mascots" online, because they feel that customers will bond with mascots featured in social media just like they did when the mascots appeared in other media. Figure 8.4 features the M&M'S® "person"—a beloved American icon, who has appeared in social media in recent years, as well as in print and broadcast media for decades.

Source: DOVE, M&M'S, the M&M'S Character and SNICKERS are registered trademarks of Mars, Incorporated. These trademarks and advertisements are used with permission. Mars, Incorporated is not associated with Pearson Education, Inc.

FIGURE 8.4 Red M&M'S®

The structure of social media includes the following elements:

1. Profiles are the ways by which consumers tell others about themselves (i.e., their age, personality, and interests).

2. Friends are trusted members of the social network used. They are allowed to post comments that designated members of the network can read. The networks allow users to keep tabs on what their friends are doing online (e.g., posting new pictures or updating their profiles).

3. Groups within social networks help users find people with similar interests.

4. Social networks create interactions among group members via "discussion boards" and by allowing members to post pictures, music, video clips, and other tidbits for the groups' members to view.

5. Consumers must have opt-ins and opt-outs that allow them to control the information they share with friends and the information they receive from others. A Nielsen study indicated that about one-third of consumers found ads on social networks annoying. However, 26% were more open to ads recommended by friends, another 26% said that they did not mind being identified based on their social media profiles, and 17% felt connected to brands advertised on social networking platforms.[7]

Permissions to Collect Personal and Social Information

Social media marketing is enabled by the information consumers provide about themselves and their social contacts, mostly via "apps" that they buy cheaply or receive for free. **Apps** (short for "applications") are chunks of software—installed on one's computer, tablet, or smartphone—that are gateways to games, online resources, and social networking. Apps also collect users' personal information and provide them to the apps' developers. Using apps illustrates the importance of the "free" content-for-information model discussed in Chapter 1. For example, Facebook provides a "free" service, but users "pay" for it, indirectly, by providing Facebook with data about their interests, hobbies, activities, opinions, shopping, friendships, and social contacts. Facebook uses this data to attract advertisers who, in turn, use this information to develop highly targeted and sophisticated promotional messages.[8]

Like all entities on the Internet, Facebook is required to ask users for permission to use the data they provide. A survey conducted by The Wall Street Journal identified the most widely used apps on Facebook and the number of permissions for information each app asks from users (see Figure 8.5). Then, the study identified the number and type of permissions sought by the most popular apps. As illustrated in Figure 8.6, users are asked to provide four kinds of information:

1. *Basic permissions* include name, identification, gender, photo, personal demographics, and list of friends.

2. *User permissions* are requests to allow the installation of the applications on the users' computers.

3. *Friends permissions* include requests to share information the users have about friends using the same app.

4. *Sensitive information requests* include questions about users' highly personal lives and opinions, such as political or religious affiliation and even sexual orientation. For instance, an app entitled "Between You and Me" asked questions about users' and their friends' sexual orientations; other quiz-type apps often pose provocative questions, such as "Is your friend's butt cute?"[9] (The ethics of the mechanics used to secure permissions are discussed in Chapter 15.)

Social Advertising's Best Practices

Marketers listen to the interactions, or social conversations, and use the information gathered to generate more buzz for their products within social networks. For instance, the BMW brand is almost a century old; however, it is using 21st-century techniques to connect with consumers. It was quick to understand the power of social media in educating its potential clients, especially by shunning away from corporate speak, and has since learned how to reach and appeal to the sensibilities of its target audience on social networks. The success is undeniable—with 13.4 million fans on Facebook, 2.4 million on Google+, and more than 200,000 followers on Twitter, BMW is generating more buzz than Mercedes, Ferrari, or Toyota. A recent survey comparing Mercedes' and BMW's efforts on social media awarded the palm unequivocally to BMW, based on the number of mentions,

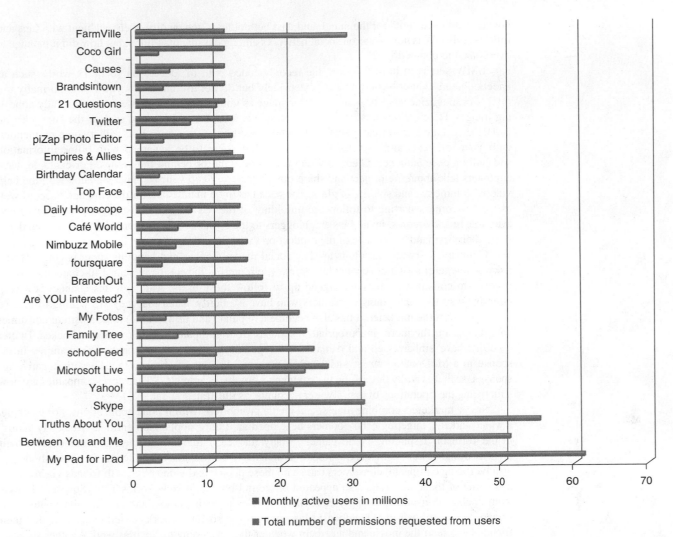

FIGURE 8.5 Numbers of Permissions Sought by Prominent Apps

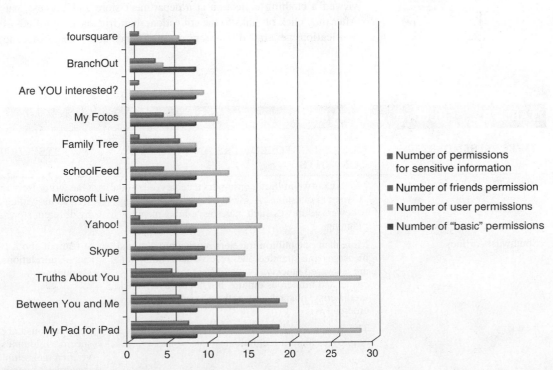

FIGURE 8.6 Types of Permissions Sought

how the audience "felt" for the brand, and, last but not least, the quality of engagement with fans and followers. BMW is now a star on social networks among car manufacturers, but how did it manage to overcome the competition?

BMW seems to have followed the recommended path to success on social networks such as Facebook and Twitter—communicate extensively but do not use the words you would normally use for TV or magazine ads, speak the same language as your audience, and use a lot of visually appealing images. Here are few tips on how to successfully launch new products, such as the latest electric BMW i3: Create a teaser campaign on Facebook well before the launch to gather some momentum with your followers and generate interest. You want them to be rewarded with prime information and build a core audience. Create a video that is personal or behind the scenes. For example, have engineers talk about the project and share tips or secrets. Keep your audience updated with the help videos, comments, and sharing of ideas. The pace has to be maintained for the core audience, as well as for newcomers starting to follow the unfolding of the release. When the new car is released and available in showrooms, invite fans and bloggers to the event so they can spread the word around and share their firsthand experience of the product on their networks.

Companies' Twitter accounts are key social media devices and handling them is complex and risky. A marketer's Twitter account lets users, who represent the company, send 140-character texts— tweets—to consumers who have signed up to follow these users. Although this channel is a very effective way to reach young consumers who have explicitly stated that they are willing to receive messages from the marketer, it has also become a popular (and unwelcome) mechanism of consumer complaints. Furthermore, inappropriate responses from companies' employees and hacked Twitter accounts have embarrassed and damaged the reputations of numerous brands. For example, in response to a McDonald's tweet under "#McDStories," legions of critics joined in with negative responses, such as vividly describing the company's cruelty to animals.[10] Therefore, companies are now structuring the operations of their Twitter accounts, as illustrated in Table 8.1.[11]

Savvy marketers combine their social media promotions with iPhone applications. For example, a wine marketer targeting echo boomers developed an iPhone application entitled "Rock My Whirl" in the form of a spinning-bottle game.[12] Many marketers allow consumers to interact with their brands' designs. For example, Cosmopolitan magazine allows consumers to star in photo shoots for an advertising campaign; consumers can share these photos and video clips with friends via YouTube and some of these materials also appeared on digital boards in New York's Time Square.[13] InStyle .com enables consumers to apply celebrity hairstyles to their photos, and another site invites consumers to design their own handbags. Many movies use social networks to tell consumers that their friends have seen the movie and ask them whether they are going to see it as well. Another successful practice is encouraging buzz. For example, some websites notify consumers that their friends viewed a clothing collection at a department store and suggest that they should check it out also. After they click on links to the collection, their friends are notified. Most likely, these back-and-forth notifications generate discussions among friends about the clothes they saw.

TABLE 8.1	Effective Tweeting Illustrations	
TWEETS' SENDERS	**NUMBER OF FOLLOWERS AND TWEETS' CONTENTS**	**TWEETS' WRITERS**
Whole Foods Supermarkets	More than two million consumers receive recipes and answers to questions. A weekly Twitter chat among followers addresses such issues as holiday menu planning.	One writer from the company's main account, as well as individual accounts created and handled by different stores.
Southwest Airlines	More than one million travelers receive promotional messages and stranded ones receive help. Complaints are answered quickly. Tweets reflect the company's casual and humorous culture, but not always; a social media crisis plan takes over the account during emergencies.	A team of about 10 people from the company's customer relations department handles the account.
Best Buy	The account has about 40,000 followers. Qualified employees answer technological questions.	Several thousand employees, who have studied specific guidelines and enrolled via a site that verified their employment status, respond to customers' questions.

Numerous sites ask consumers to take polls. For example, an airline's website asked consumers to vote on their favorite in-flight technological feature (e.g., Wi-Fi) and then informed them how many consumers, in total, voted and how many of their friends had done so. Several upper-end watchmakers teamed up and created a very expensive, experimental watch that was designed primarily to create buzz about very pricy watches. The only promotion for the product was getting watch enthusiasts to write about this unusual watch in their blogs.[14] However, aggressive advertising on social media can backfire. For example, when Walmart purchased 50 million ads on Facebook, which were placed on users' Facebook pages, many consumers who resent Walmart's labor practices demanded the removal of these ads.[15]

Most companies selling consumer goods have integrated social media into their advertising campaigns. Established brands—such as Coca-Cola, Volkswagen, AT&T, Ritz Crackers, and Men's Fitness magazine—are directing viewers of their ads to their Twitter messages or Facebook pages, sometimes with sophisticated, cloud-based ad platforms. For example, an ad for a cleaning product read: "Clean should smell better" and instructed users to "Hover to expand." When users hovered, they reached the company's Facebook page.[16] Small and unknown brands, which do not have the resources to advertise nationally, have been using social media aggressively to widen their exposure.[17] The growth of social media has also changed long-standing practices. To generate advanced excitement about Super Bowl ads—which are always eagerly anticipated—many advertisers released limited versions of the ads and other "teasers" during Christmas, two months before the game.[18] In the not-for-profit sector, during one of the most destructive hurricanes in history, transit agencies used social media extensively to calm irate riders and keep them informed.[19]

One of the myths regarding social media has been that it reaches only young consumers. However, the age gap on social networks has been narrowing rapidly. In one year, only 9% of Internet users 55 to 64 years old used social networking, but 43% of this age group reported doing so two years later.[20]

The characteristics of effective social media campaigns are:

1. Social media campaigns must be planned together with advertising in traditional media.

2. Marketers must consider the fact that social media simultaneously reaches several audiences (i.e., consumers, retailers, and other parties with whom the company does business), which justifies larger advertising budgets.

3. Executives should closely examine consumers' clicks on the "like" buttons and "mine" and use data from their Facebook pages to develop new niches for their products (sometimes with partners in other product categories).

4. Bosses who tweet personally strengthen the connections between their brands and customers.

5. Employees should be encouraged to tweet, but guidelines for such communications must be set and monitored for compliance.[21] However, research suggests than many CEOs resent (and even fear) using Twitter.[22]

Social Media Communication Channels

There are several types of social media channels:[23]

1. **Owned social media**, which consist of messages sent by marketers to consumers via channels that the marketers control.

2. **Paid social media**, which consist of messages sent via channels that are not owned by the marketers, who pay for using the channels.

3. **Earned social media**, which are channels where consumers pass along messages about brands to one another.

Commonly, when using paid social media, an advertiser (e.g., Walmart) pays the social network (e.g., Facebook) only after users click on its ads. However, more and more advertisers prepay for large blocks of ads placed on social media users' pages or sent to them via live news feeds.

The most widely used platforms to transmit social message are:

1. Branded blogs and micro-blogging platforms (e.g., Twitter) that encourage interactions among consumers; these messages resemble conversations.

2. Social networks such as Facebook and Myspace.

3. Widgets, gaming, and other applications that users can download.

4. Mobile phones (discussed in the following section).

Most companies use several platforms simultaneously.[24]

Consumers and Mobile Advertising

Learning Objective

4 To understand how consumers use mobile media and their reactions to mobile advertising.

Mobile advertising consists of sending promotional messages to consumers' cell phones, iPads, electronic readers, and other devices that people carry while on the go. Initially, the extent of mobile advertising in other countries, especially in Europe and even more so in Southeast Asia, was far greater than in the United States. However, one report indicated that U.S. companies have spent more on mobile advertising than any other country, including Japan, which had been the leader in mobile advertising. During a recent year, advertisers spent more than $6.43 billion globally on mobile media, with the United States contributing $2.3 billion and Japan following with $1.7 billion. Nevertheless, mobile advertising still accounts for just 1% of the total advertising spending in the United States and worldwide. The primary reason for the growth of mobile advertising is that more and more people are using smartphones and other mobile Internet devices such as tablets and e-readers.[25] Mobile advertising should be distinguished from mobile-advertising campaigns on social networks, which consist of ads that pop up on, for example, Facebook mobile news feeds to its users after marketers have purchased this advertising space from Facebook.[26]

Consumer Response to Mobile Advertising

Because mobile advertising is a new medium, it is important to understand how and why consumers use mobile devices and their reactions to such ads. One study discovered that mobile devices provide four types of value to users:

1. *Monetary value:* The device provides good value for the money that also exceeds the value consumers receive from using nonmobile communication devices.

2. *Convenience value:* Saving time and money, improving efficiency, and making life easier.

3. *Emotional value:* Feeling good and relaxed when using the device.

4. *Social value:* Being accepted by others and impressing them.

The results indicated that the higher the values consumers receive from mobile devices, the more likely they are to use the devices to purchase products and engage in word-of-mouth about what they bought.[27]

Studies have identified cross-cultural differences among consumers' responses to mobile ads. A study of Japanese men showed that mobile ads generated effective word-of-mouth. A study of European consumers showed that cross-cultural differences impact the effectiveness of mobile advertising. Research on Korean shoppers indicated that their attitudes toward mobile advertising depended mainly on the convenience of the interface and their ability to control content. Research of Chinese consumers showed that ease of use, perceived usefulness, and trust were the key factors in receptivity to mobile advertising. Researchers also found that the adoption of mobile "broadcasting" in Japan, Germany, and Korea was positively related to the extent of access to mobile devices and the entertainment and social interaction they provide.[28]

One study investigated the influence of the language and source of text advertisements on attitudes toward and purchase intentions regarding products advertised on mobile devices. The researchers found that reputable companies with highly perceived credibility can use *entertaining* language, but companies with less credibility and poorer reputations should create *serious*, clear, and concise mobile ads.[29]

The Advantages and Shortcomings of Mobile Advertising

An analysis of a large sample of mobile ads indicated that:

1. Mobile marketers are still spending most of their money on search ads. **Search advertising** is placing online advertisements on Web pages that show results from search engine queries.

2. Marketers have been creating mobile ads that are fun, pay rewards, and help customers find useful information (e.g., referrals).

3. As smartphone screens became larger, marketers began using mobile ads that take over the entire screen.

4. Some mobile marketers have been experimenting with inserting ads in places where consumers do not expect to see any, in an effort to overcome consumers' tuning-out of promotional messages. For example, Facebook and Twitter have slipped ads into the flow of

digital conversations. Some models of the Kindle e-reader display messages for local services, regardless of whether users use the device or let it "go to sleep."

5. Many advertisers use banner ads on mobile devices' screens because such ads are cheap, although most recognize that consumers find banners annoying.[30]

Another practice that is becoming increasingly popular is developing technologies that enable advertisers to link what consumers do on their computers with their cell phones. For example, Google can send consumers cell phone ads that are congruent with their searches on home computers.[31] At the same time, mobile advertising has its limitations: First, smartphones' screens are rather small. Secondly, it is technically impossible to use cookies with apps the way it is with browsers. Thus, marketers cannot track actions and optimize their ads the way they do in response to customers' computer surfing.[32] Marketers also recognize that most consumers are reluctant to receive ads when using their cell phones.

In spite of its limitations, mobile advertising has one outstanding capability: It can identify users' geographic locations and deliver contextually relevant offers. For example, consider a consumer driving with a GPS navigation device (on a smartphone) who receives an ad for a sale in a store located near a highway exit several miles away. The consumer reacts to the message, stops by the store, purchases the item, and pays by credit card. The data about the purchase are immediately entered into a database that includes demographic information about the consumer, as well as the person's usage of mobile devices. Later on, the consumer receives an email thanking her for the purchase and asking her to subscribe to "alerts" about future sales. Probably immediately, the data about the entire shopping encounter are integrated with the data of thousands of persons who responded to such mobile ads, allowing marketers to create profiles of the types of buyers who respond to mobile ads. Another example is a recent joint venture between iPhone and Amazon.com. iPhone or iPad users can now use special software that enables them to browse through products offered by Amazon.com (and other large retailers) and purchase the products. Furthermore, users of the iPhone can use the device to take photos of any products they see in stores or outside and transmit them to Amazon.com. Amazon then matches these photos with available products and sends its recommendations to the customers.[33] Yet another example of the selling power of online and mobile media—stemming largely from buyers' ability to customize their purchases—is a large music label that reported selling more than half of its total U.S. music via paid digital downloads, where buyers purchased individual songs (e.g., via iTunes) instead of CD albums.[34] Taxis in New York City are now equipped with TV screens that display commercials for the stores that they pass, which the vehicles' GPS devices pinpoint.[35] As yet another example, one company distributed mobile phones to college students and offered them discounted calling rates in exchange for agreeing to receive ads.[36]

There are several mobile advertising platforms. For example, Google and Apple provide advertising space on applications supported by their mobile devices.[37] Some TV ads feature bar codes that consumers can scan using their cell phones and obtain immediate information about products.[38] Because searching for items, as well as entering credit card numbers, can be cumbersome given most cell phones' small screens, many retailers are now simplifying the search engines on their mobile sites.[39] Google even offers an application (named "Google Goggles") that enables consumers to take pictures of an object, say a movie poster, and find out more about the movie without typing anything into a search engine.[40] Other retailers are experimenting with applications that allow consumers to find products in the store and even scan them for payment. In some subway stations in London and South Korea, consumers can scan bar codes of products displayed on posters, buy them, and have the products delivered to their homes shortly afterwards.[41] One marketer of tennis wear enables attendees of a tennis event to order customized shirts from their mobile phones and pick them up at the stadium immediately after the match.[42] Another example of creative mobile promotion is a restaurant that enables "culinary voyeurism" via a live video feed from its kitchen to the mobile phones of diners or customers with reservations.[43]

What's in Store for Consumers?

Predicting the future is tricky and often inaccurate. However, it is obvious that social media is increasingly integrating with mobile devices and that more and more of our interactions with people, products, and information occur digitally and not physically. For example, "near field communications" is a new technology that allows smartphones to communicate with each other wirelessly and without Wi-Fi. Clearly, this will make exchanges of content among friends and marketers and consumers faster and more prominent. Some even predict the emergence of a "Smobile (social + mobile) Web." Because online search results are increasingly driving purchase decisions, companies will compete increasingly and aggressively in transmitting relevant, timely, and creative content daily to consumers' stationary and mobile communication devices. Gadgets that provide us with timely promotions, such as glasses embedded with maps featuring commercial outlets that we are passing on the street, will become progressively cheaper and popular (a prototype of such "Google Glasses" already exists).[44] In summary, we will be receiving constant access to our social lives, information, and buying opportunities, at any time, via our mobile devices.

Measuring Media's Advertising Effectiveness

Learning Objective

5 To understand how to measure the effectiveness of advertising in traditional and social media.

Effective advertising is the result of careful and systematic planning. Therefore, advertisers should use the following steps in designing social media campaigns:[45]

1. Define the campaign's objectives and strategic approaches.
2. Examine the platforms available and determine which ones to use so as to achieve the objectives.
3. Produce the campaign's content using internal or external resources.
4. Examine the pricing models for securing access to social media, which, unlike pricing for advertising space on traditional print and broadcast communication channels, vary greatly. Then, set the expenditures needed to achieve the campaign objectives.
5. Measure the campaign's effectiveness.

The measures discussed in Chapter 7 assess the extent to which consumers noticed, paid attention to, liked, and remembered promotional messages, but not whether exposure to a given ad induced an *actual* purchase. For the most part, marketers *infer* the purchase behaviors triggered by ads from broad sets of sales data, as it is rarely possible to identify a cause-and-effect relationship between a given message and the resulting purchase behavior. In contrast, promotions placed in social media employ "electronic cookies," which are digital tracking devices that enable senders to monitor the receivers' responses precisely and often immediately. However, even with electronic tracking, some advertisers have removed their Facebook ads because they had trouble measuring whether the ads led to sales.[46]

The most widely used measures of the effectiveness of online promotions are analyses of website visits, users' influence within social networks, and the audiences' demographics.[47] More sophisticated measures include Google Analytics and Nielsen's cross-platform measurement.

Analyzing Website Visits

Marketers who analyze website visits usually track the following metrics:

1. *Unique visitors.* The number of visitors to the website that have accessed its content. User profiles (based on their Web addresses) are also monitored.
2. *Cost per unique visitor.* The total cost of placing the application or ad divided by the number of unique visitors.
3. *Return visits.* The average number of times a user returns to the site within a specific period.
4. *Time spent.* The average amount of time from the start of the visit until the end of the last activity on the page.
5. *Page views.* The average number of pages that users have clicked through.
6. *Interaction rate.* The proportion of viewers who interact with an ad or application.
7. *Actions.* The actions taken during visits, such as entering contests, responding to poll questions, redeeming coupons, playing games, posting comments, sending messages, inviting friends, and downloading or uploading materials and applications.
8. *Conversation-related measures.* Data including the number of unique visitors participating, the number of related links that participants reach during the conversation and the duration between the first and last posts, and the average time between posts.
9. *Visitor demographics.* (a) Examining how the target audience navigates around the site and which demographic profiles have the most engagement; (b) Evaluating whether the content created is a good match with the users and whether it converts many into buyers; and (c) Determining how to improve the sell rate and reduce the cost per impression.[48]

Gauging Influence within Social Network

As an example, one's degree of influence on Twitter is measured as follows: The person's number of followers, the number of people following the followers, the frequency of updating tweets, and the extent to which his or her tweets are referenced or cited.

Twitter also identified several types of users: *Celebrities* have many followers but follow very few, if any, users. *Conversationalists* follow about the same number of users as follow them. *Spammers* "collect" users with the intent to push content to as many people as possible.

Google Analytics

Google Analytics is a service offered by Google that evaluates the effectiveness of websites and profiles their users by collecting and analyzing the following data:

1. Tracking where visitors come from: Referrals, search engines, display advertising, pay-per-click networks, email campaigns, and other digital links (e.g., clicks within PDF documents).

2. Customers' actions after they "land" at the initial page: Viewing other pages, downloading files, registering with the site, and other actions.

3. Website visitors' geographic location and their visits' lengths. This method also assigns websites' users into profiles and segments them.

Google Analytics enables marketers to measure the effectiveness of their websites and promotional efforts and, to an extent, predict the impact of planned advertising campaigns on customers' behavior. In addition, Google Analytics' e-commerce service tracks sales activity and performance and provides marketers with their sites' transactions, revenue, and many other commerce-related metrics. Marketers can also identify pages, links, and promotional efforts that perform poorly and do not achieve the sites' objectives (e.g., "converting" visitors to users, generating repeat visits, and getting users to register).

Media Exposure Measures

Since advertising in mass media started (initially in newspapers and magazines) approximately in the middle of the nineteenth century, advertisers have recognized that many messages were reaching consumers who had no interest in the products advertised and that accurately gauging the persuasive effectiveness of ads placed in mass media was impossible. **Media exposure effects** measure how many consumers were exposed to the message and their characteristics. Consumer research companies assess *how many* consumers received the message and construct a profile of the receivers. The largest syndicated company that collects such data and sells it to advertisers is Nielsen. Originally, Nielsen monitored TV viewing, but it now maintains many panels of consumers who have consented to the monitoring of certain aspects of their media exposure and consumption.

There are many other companies that monitor consumers' media and advertising exposure. For example, comScore monitors online traffic and Web visits and also tracks mobile advertising on cell phones. Mediamark Research Inc. (MRI) provides magazines with data on their *circulations* as well as a descriptive *audience profiles* (breakdowns of readers by gender, median age, and household income). Arbitron measures the audiences of radio broadcasts.

Broadcasters, publishers, and owners of websites use media exposure measures to determine the size of their audiences and set the rates that they charge advertisers for placing promotional messages in their media. However, disputes regarding the results of audience measurements are common. For example, for years advertisers argued that Nielsen's panels did not adequately represent minorities, and media companies claimed that the company failed to properly measure viewers who use time-shifting devices. More recently, one website's estimate of its monthly number of visitors was 1.8 million, whereas comScore's estimate of the same audience was only 421,000. The major sources of such discrepancies are uncertainties about how to measure Internet use in the workplace and consumers who delete the cookies (small identifying files placed on a computer's hard drive) that are essential in counting website visits. Many believe that a better tracking system is crucial for the growth of online advertising.[49]

Nielsen's Cross-Platform Measurement

Media exposure measures assess *how many* consumers received the message, and also profiles them. The largest syndicated companies that collect such data and sell it to marketers are Nielsen and Arbitron. Nielsen now has many consumer panels who provide continuous data about media exposure and consumption. Arbitron is known primarily for monitoring radio broadcast audiences and, more recently, for developing **portable people meters**, which are small devices, equipped with GPS, that the consumers clip onto their belts and wear all day (in exchange for monetary incentives). The devices monitor codes embedded in the audio streams of media that consumers receive (e.g., TV and radio programs and in-store announcements) and also have the capacity to capture visual images of the screens and written materials that consumers are exposed to (e.g., billboards and other out-of-home media, magazines and newspapers, and online surfing). At night, the devices are plugged into cradles and transmit the data collected to Arbitron. Recently, Nielsen bought Arbitron and integrated the PPM technologies into cross-platform effectiveness measures that compete with newer companies that have been developing similar techniques (e.g., comScore).[50]

Traditional Media's Electronic Evolution

Learning Objective

6 To understand the advancement of print and broadcast media into electronic communications.

Print and broadcast media are one-way communications where all the members of a given audience receive the same one-way messages from marketers. Newspapers, magazines, TV, and radio use segment-based targeting. Because each individual has his or her own traits, characteristics, interests, needs, experience, and knowledge, senders of advertising messages segment their audiences into groups that are homogeneous in terms of relevant characteristics, including media exposure patterns. Segmentation enables senders to create specific messages for each target group and to run them in specific media that are seen, heard, or read by the relevant target group. It is unlikely that a marketer could develop a single message that would appeal simultaneously to its total audience. A cost-effective media choice has been closely matching the *advertiser's consumer profile* to a *medium's audience profile*. Rather than selecting one media category to the exclusion of others, most advertisers use a multimedia campaign strategy, with one primary media category carrying the major burden of the campaign and other categories providing supplemental support.

Newspapers and Magazines

Newspapers provide access to large audiences and are effective for reaching large audiences. However, they are generally inadequate when it comes to reaching consumers with specific demographics. Newspaper ads can be designed and published quickly, but they have a short life. There is considerable clutter because many messages, particularly for local services and research outlets, compete for attention. Nevertheless, because of redemptions of specific promotions and timely measurement of sales volume after the ads are published, feedback can be collected quickly. Advertising costs are determined by size of ad and the medium's circulation. Newspaper ads are affordable for local businesses and enable joint advertising by national manufacturers and local sellers. However, online advertising enables mom-and-pop firms, which have never had the funds for traditional advertising, to promote their businesses, and major players in the digital adverting business, such as Facebook and Groupon, are competing for small businesses.[51] By some estimates, in 2014, local business will spend about 10% of their total advertising expenditures on online promotions (i.e., $3.1 billion out of $35 billion).[52]

Magazines reach specific geographic, demographic, and interest-focused groups and enable more precise targeting than newspapers, with visually high-quality ads. Special-interest magazines are highly credible. Magazines offer long message life and increased exposure to ads because of pass-along readership. At the same time, ads require longer lead time for production, and numerous magazines do not guarantee ad placement in a particular position within the magazine. Feedback from magazine ads is often delayed and is measured via Starch scores (see Chapter 5). Advertising rates are determined by cost of page, which is a function of the magazines' circulation, and top magazines charge very high rates. In recent years, magazine advertising has declined rapidly. As shown in Figure 8.7, magazine ad pages during a recent year have declined considerably, as they did in prior years.[53] Figure 8.8 depicts the decline in advertising in popular magazines.[54]

Although most magazines and newspapers are still printed on paper, almost all now offer online editions and many are planning to phase out their paper editions. Online, both magazines and newspapers can flourish by offering readers customized editions that are based on the readers' interests. For example, readers of The New York Times or The Wall Street Journal no longer have to flip pages to find the stories that they wish to read. They can subscribe to online versions where the stories that they are interested in appear immediately and include links to previous articles about the topics covered and other relevant information. For example, a Sports Illustrated story about soccer might include electronically linked references to past matches. In addition, advertisers can customize the messages sent to readers.

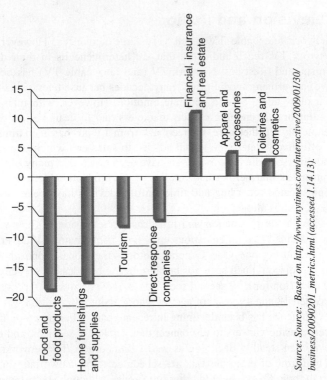

FIGURE 8.7 The Decline (and Some Growth) in the Number of Magazine Ad Pages for Major Industries during 2011 (percentages)

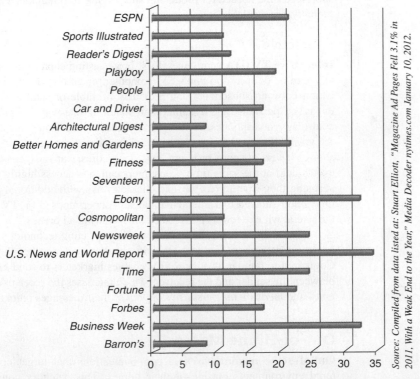

FIGURE 8.8 The Decline in Ad Pages in Popular Magazines over Three Years (percentages)

The prices of magazines' online editions are nearly always bundled with subscriptions to the print editions, but their costs have been going up. For example, Condé Nast, publisher of high-end titles like Vogue and The New Yorker, raised prices on its bundled print and electronic subscriptions, effectively making print subscribers pay more for online versions that they previously received for free. However, it appears that consumers are willing to pay the higher prices: Condé Nast subscribers who chose to sign up for digital subscriptions renewed at a 25% higher rate than those who did not.[55]

Television and Radio

Network and cable TV reach very large audiences. However, many programs, particularly on network TV, reach audiences that are heterogeneous in their demographics, spending power, interests, and lifestyles. Network TV (and later cable TV) has been the most desirable (and expensive) advertising medium for many decades because television enables marketers to send messages that draw attention and generate emotion. However, with many TV ads for competing and often similar brands creating clutter, marketers had to design short-duration messages and repeat them frequently. Furthermore, the feedback from TV ads has been imprecise and did not enable marketers to effectively determine which ads led to sales and which ones did not. Because TV reaches large and diverse audiences, marketers have been aware that many of their TV commercials reached many consumers that neither had interest in the products advertised nor became customers. Also, more sophisticated recording and time-shifting devices have been allowing viewers to avoid seeing TV commercials altogether.

Both the production and broadcast of television ads are very expensive and, with more and more forms of communications emerging, some major TV advertisers are changing course. For example, during one year, General Motors—traditionally one of the largest advertisers at the Super Bowl—discontinued such ads because of the broadcast's very high costs, which have reached about $3.8 million for a 30-second spot.[56] Also, most network TV programs were designed to reach people between 18 and 49 years of age, of whom about 25.1 million watched TV daily in the U.S.—but this key audience has been declining in recent years.[57] Furthermore, the lure of YouTube and Netflix has been causing viewers to disconnect their cable-TV services, and the numbers of pay-TV subscribers have been steadily declining as well.[58] In addition, TV networks must now allow online streaming in real time of programs that are scheduled to be shown later on, during prime viewing time, such as Olympic Games held in other time zones, although such streaming can cannibalize the scheduled broadcast and reduce exposure to paid commercials.[59]

Radio's advantages are its high geographic and demographic audience selectivity, as well as the short lead time needed for producing and placing commercials. Presently, almost all radio broadcasts, globally, are available online.

Interactive TV

Interactive TV (iTV) combines TVs' broadcasting capabilities and the interactivity of the Internet. iTV can be delivered to one's TV, computer, or mobile device in the form of a *two-way* communication between subscribers and providers of cable or satellite TV. Viewing on iTV is much more engaging, personal, and dynamic than watching one-way TV programs. For example, using remote controls or smartphones, viewers of Top Chef can vote on contestants, immediately see the results of the votes, download recipes, see behind-the-scenes segments, and even buy products featured on the show. Viewers of sports programs can view scores, statistics, and alerts of the results of other sporting events held at the same time. Consumers can also access highly targeted content, customize the advertising they wish to receive, and click on links with additional information during a commercial.[60] One study showed that interactive banners superimposed on TV commercials significantly reduced the rate at which viewers changed channels during ad breaks.[61]

Several cable companies are now using targeting technology to route ads to specific households based on data about income, ethnicity, gender, and whether the homeowner has children or pets. Compared to regular television, iTV enables marketers to send *addressable ads*, deploy *interactivity* between the sender and the receiver (which increases the receiver's level of engagement with the content), and *measure the persuasive impact* of their messages quickly and effectively.

Out-of-Home Media

Out-of-home media consist of communications that target consumers in captive and less cluttered environments outside of their homes. This category consists of new promotional tools as well as some older means that were significantly updated with new technology. For instance, **captive advertising screens** are placed in locations where consumers spend time, such as elevators, cinemas, retail stores, restaurants, bars, fitness clubs, college campuses, and transit. Digital billboards and displays, with interactive capabilities, are placed in transit locations, events, and stores. A billboard promoting a show on citizen surveillance used a built-in camera to take pictures of passersby with the notification "Person of Interest Identified." Those individuals then received access to their "classified files" to send to their friends or post online.[62]

Ambient advertising (experiential advertising) consists of constructing sensory environments that simulate an actual experience with the product. For example, during the cold holiday season, Kraft Foods built and maintained heated bus shelters (in Chicago and other northern cities), designed to convey to consumers the warm feeling they would get if they ate Kraft stuffing.[63] By some estimates, spending on digital out-of-home media during a recent year was $2 billion and expected to rise 12.5% during the next one.[64]

Branded Entertainment

Branded entertainment (product placement) consists of featuring products within the contents of entertainment, such as TV, movies, video games, among others. When TV emerged as an advertising medium (in the early 1950s), companies sponsored the most popular TV shows and featured their products prominently within the broadcasts. Over the years, paid-for *embeds* of products and brands have appeared in most films and TV shows. Due to consumers' ability to avoid viewing commercials, advertisers' expenditures on branded entertainment have increased significantly. Apparently, marketers believe that they can build and increase product awareness by integrating brands into the content of entertainment programs, where consumers cannot avoid them (the forms of such integration were discussed in Chapter 4).

Many programs that are billed as "entertainment" are, in fact, showcases for prominently featuring products and forming emotional connections between brands and consumers (e.g., The Apprentice, Top Chef, Survivor, and various "makeover" programs). Products have also appeared on the sets on news broadcasts and within the dialogues of programs. Legislators have increasingly criticized overly aggressive product placements (the ethical aspects of product placement are discussed in Chapter 15).[65] By some estimates, globally, companies have been spending between $25 and $30 billion annually on branded entertainment, with American companies spending the most.

In addition to embedding brands in films and TV programs, many marketers have developed **webisodes** (i.e., short videos shown online featuring entertainment centered around a brand) and **advergames**, which are video games with embedded brands. A study showed that, overall, advergames enhanced brand recall. However, repeatedly playing the same game had no effect on brand recall, but did have a negative impact on brand attitude, indicating viewer wear-out.[66]

Summary

Learning Objective 1: To understand the strategic superiority of impression-based (eyeballs) targeting over segment-based targeting.

Since the emergence of traditional advertising media (newspapers, magazines, radio, and television), TV networks, magazines, and newspapers have sold advertising space by offering marketers the opportunity to reach audiences whose demographics and psychographics (lifestyles) match those of the marketers' target markets. However, the audiences marketers reached via these media were larger and more diverse than their target markets and almost always included many people who had no interest in the products advertised. In contrast, today's sophisticated tracking of consumers enables data aggregators to construct consumer profiles—based on cookies documenting people's online surfing (and other applicable information about them)—and identify prospective customers for specific products. Advertisers then compete to reach the right "eyeballs" online by placing monetary bids.

Segment-based targeting occurs when advertisers prenegotiate prices for advertising space in media (e.g., magazines or TV shows) whose audiences largely (but never completely) match the profiles of the consumers the advertisers wish to target. Impression-based targeting occurs when advertisers specify the criteria describing the persons they wish to reach online and then bid in real time for the opportunities to reach such people. A person reached is termed an "eyeball" or "impression." Impression-based ads often "follow" consumers online and thus keep reminding them about the products they were interested in. Retargeting occurs when ads for specific products that consumers have pursued online "follow" them and show up repeatedly whenever they go online using the same computer.

Learning Objective 2: To understand Google's targeting and advertising capabilities and its value to both consumers and marketers.

Google is the most widely used search engine online and a prominent advertising medium. Consumers using Google are reached by three types of ads: (1) Web-search ads (generated by consumers' searches); (2) Online display ads (fixed banners that do not vary according to users' profiles or search patterns, posted on websites); and (3) Mobile ads (ads that appear on mobile devices in Google search results, on content websites, and in apps).

Google's most prominent use is as a search engine. After an online user types a query, two areas appear on the screen. The "organic results" are the links directing users to sites and resources that are applicable to their Google searches. The "sponsored space"—typically appearing on the right side or the top—consists of advertising banners that Google has sold to advertisers or "sponsors." Each time a potential customer clicks on a sponsored banner ad, the advertiser pays Google a fee. The fees can range from a few cents for terms that very few users are likely to enter in the search engine, to several dollars (and up) for words that many users are likely to type in.

Learning Objective 3: To understand the dynamics of social media and its strategic and promotional advantages over other media.

Social media refers to means of interactions among people in which they create, share, and exchange information and ideas in virtual communities and networks. Social media depend on mobile and Web-based technologies to create highly interactive platforms through which individuals and communities share, co-create, discuss, and modify user-generated content. The structure of social media includes consumers' profiles, friends and groups within social networks, interactions among group members, and opt-ins and opt-outs that people use to control the information they post or receive online.

Social media marketing is enabled by the information consumers provide about themselves and their social contacts, mostly via apps that they buy cheaply or receive for free. Apps (short for "applications") are chunks of software—installed on one's computer, tablet, or smartphone—that are gateways to games, online resources, and social networking. Apps also collect users' personal information and provide them to the apps' developers. There are several types of media channels: Owned social media, paid social media, and earned social media.

Social media campaigns must be planned together with advertising in traditional media. Marketers must consider the fact that social media simultaneously reaches several audiences (i.e., consumers, retailers, and other parties with whom the company does business), which justifies larger advertising budgets. Executives should closely examine consumers' clicks on the "like" buttons and mine data from their Facebook pages to develop new niches for their products.

Learning Objective 4: To understand how consumers use mobile media and their reactions to mobile advertising.

Mobile advertising refers to sending promotional messages to consumers' cell phones, iPads, electronic readers, and other devices that people carry while on the go. Mobile advertising can identify users' geographic locations and deliver contextually relevant offers. As smartphone screens become larger, marketers are increasingly using mobile ads that take over the entire screen. Some mobile marketers have been experimenting with inserting ads in places where consumers do not expect to see any, in an effort to overcome consumers' tuning-out of promotional messages. Social media is increasingly integrating with mobile devices as more and more of our interactions with people, products, and information occur digitally rather than physically.

Learning Objective 5: To understand how to measure the effectiveness of advertising in traditional and social media.

A widely used measure of effectiveness is analysis of websites' visits, including the number of unique visitors, cost per unique visitor, return visits, visit length, pages viewed and links clicked, actions taken during visits, and visitors' demographics. There are also measures of users' influence within social networks.

Google Analytics is a service offered by Google that evaluates the effectiveness of websites and profiles their users. It enables marketers to measure the effectiveness of their websites and promotional efforts and, to an extent, predict the impact of planned advertising campaigns on customers' behavior. Marketers can also identify pages, links, and promotional efforts that perform poorly and do not achieve the sites' objectives.

Media exposure effects measure how many consumers were exposed to the message, as well as their characteristics. Broadcasters, publishers, and owners of websites use media exposure measures to determine the size of their audiences and set the rates they charge advertisers for placing promotional messages in their media. Services that sell media exposure data to marketers have developed portable people meters (PPMs), which are small devices, equipped with GPS, that consumers clip onto their belts and wear all day (in exchange for monetary incentives). The devices monitor codes embedded into the audio streams of media that consumers receive, and also have the capacity to capture visual images of the screens and written materials that consumers are exposed to.

Learning Objective 6: To understand the advancement of print and broadcast media into electronic communications.

Traditional print and broadcast media have been evolving into more sophisticated forms. Newspapers provide access to large audiences and are effective for reaching large audiences. However, they are generally inadequate when it comes to reaching consumers with specific demographics. Newspaper ads can be designed and published quickly, but they have a short life. Newspaper ads are affordable for local businesses and enable joint advertising by national manufacturers and local sellers. Magazines reach specific geographic, demographic, and interest-focused groups and enable more precise targeting than newspapers, with ads of high visual quality. Special-interest magazines are highly credible. Magazines offer long message life and increased exposure to ads because of pass-along readership. Although most magazines and newspapers are still printed on paper, almost all now offer online editions, and many are planning to phase out their paper editions. Online, both magazines and newspapers offer readers customized editions that are based on the readers' interests. In addition, advertisers can customize the messages sent to readers.

Network and cable TV reach very large audiences. However, many programs, particularly on network TV, reach audiences that are heterogeneous in their demographics, spending power, interests, and lifestyles. In addition, more sophisticated recording and time-shifting devices have been allowing viewers to avoid seeing TV commercials. Interactive TV (iTV) combines TV broadcasts and the interactivity of the Internet. iTV can be delivered to a TV, computer, or mobile device in the form of a two-way communication between the subscriber and providers of cable or satellite TV.

Other forms of media are not genuinely new technologically, but are innovative and growing. Out-of-home media consist of communications vehicles that target consumers in captive and less cluttered environments outside of their homes. This category consists of new promotional tools as well as some older means that were significantly updated with new technology. Ambient advertising (also known as experiential advertising) consists of promotions designed to simulate an actual consumer experience with the product. Branded entertainment (product placement) is created by featuring products within the contents of entertainment, such as TV, movies, video games, and online sites, among others. Marketers have developed webisodes (short videos, shown online, that feature entertainment centered around brands) and advergaming (video games played at homes, arcades, or online with brand or brands embedded).

Review and Discussion Questions

8.1. Strategically speaking, why is impression-based targeting better than segment-based targeting?

8.2. Describe Google's role in advertising online.

8.3. List and describe four advantages of social media over traditional media.

8.4. Compare the advantages and disadvantages of the following measurement techniques: Google Analytics, media exposure effects, and Nielsen's cross-platform measures.

8.5. List and describe two advantages and two disadvantages of mobile advertising.

8.6. Why has advertising on network TV and in magazines been steadily declining?

Hands-on Assignments

8.7. Take pictures of two illustrations of out-of-home media, present them in class, and describe why are they effective or not.

8.8. List and describe five product placements that you have seen in TV shows and movies.

8.9. Join one of the apps in Figure 8.4 and categorize the permission you have been asked for according to the four permissions categories discussed in this chapter.

Key Terms

- advergames *231*
- ambient advertising (experiential advertising) *231*
- apps *220*
- branded entertainment (product placement) *231*
- captive advertising screens *230*
- data aggregators *216*
- earned social media *223*
- Google Analytics *227*
- impression-based targeting *216*
- interactive TV (iTV) *230*
- media exposure effects *227*
- mobile advertising *218*
- online display ads *218*
- out-of-home media *230*
- owned social media *223*
- paid social media *223*
- portable people meters *228*
- real-time bidding *216*
- retargeting *218*
- search advertising *224*
- segment-based targeting *216*
- social media *219*
- time shifting *218*
- webisodes *231*
- Web-search ads *218*

Reference Groups and Word-of-Mouth

Learning Objectives

1 To understand the credibility of reference groups and their influence on consumer behavior.

2 To understand the persuasive power and credibility of spokespersons, endorsers, celebrities, salespersons, vendors, and media.

3 To understand the dynamics and measurement of opinion leadership and word-of-mouth.

4 To understand the strategic applications, advantages, and potential perils of word-of-mouth.

5 To understand the process for diffusion of innovations, and adopter categories as distinct market segments.

REFERENCE GROUPS are groups that serve as sources of comparison, influence, and norms for peoples' opinions, values, and behaviors. Within any setting, including consumer behavior, people are strongly influenced by what others think and how they behave. The most important reference group is the **family** because it provides children with the skills, knowledge, attitudes, and experiences necessary to function as consumers, a process called **consumer socialization** (see Chapter 10). Other important reference groups are a person's **social class**, (see Chapter 10), **culture** (see Chapter 11), and **subculture** (see Chapter 12). The Campbell's ad in Figure 9.1 illustrates the how families influence young children's brand preferences.

Word-of-mouth consists of communications where satisfied customers tell other people how much they like a business, product, service, or event (although the information transmitted can also be negative). Word-of-mouth is one of the most credible forms of buying-related information because consumers view others who don't stand to gain personally by promoting something as highly credible. It can take place face to face or via electronic communications, and the exchangers of the information may know each other personally or only online. Word-of-mouth occurs often when neighbors talk across their lawns or over a cup of coffee; when friends and neighbors share stories about shops and products that they like (or dislike); and in texting, emailing, chat rooms, and online social communities, among other forms of communication. It has been said that "word-of-mouth is the best advertising" because reference groups, such as friends, neighbors, relatives, and other consumers a person meets online in social networks, chat rooms, and through Twitter, strongly influence one's consumption behavior. This influence is strong because people perceive others like themselves as having nothing to gain from their purchase recommendations. Consumers view reference groups with which they have personal contacts as more credible than advertisements and other promotions sent by marketers. The ad featured in Figure 9.2 encourages mothers to engage in word-of-mouth and rave about Campbell's soup.

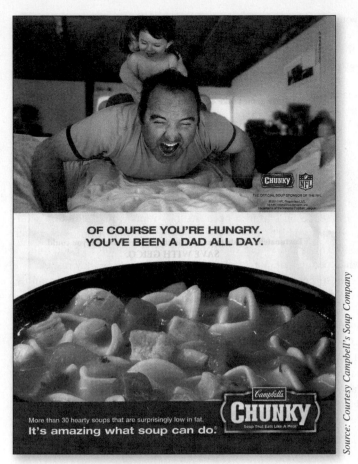

Source: Courtesy Campbell's Soup Company

FIGURE 9.1 The Family Is a Reference Group: Campbell's Chunky Soup

Source: Campbell's

FIGURE 9.2 Stirring Up Word-of-Mouth Among Mothers: Campbell's Chicken Stars

We begin this chapter with a discussion of source credibility and the influences of selected reference groups. We then review several sources of information that are sponsored by marketers, such as spokespersons and endorsers. Next, we discuss the process of opinion leadership and conclude with an overview of the strategic applications of word-of-mouth.

Source Credibility and Reference Groups

Learning Objective

1 To understand the credibility of reference groups and their influence on consumer behavior.

Reference groups have a high degree of **source credibility**, defined as a source's persuasive impact, stemming from its perceived expertise, trustworthiness, and believability. When the source of communications about a product is well respected and highly thought of by the intended audience, the message is much more likely to be believed. Conversely, a message from a source considered unreliable or untrustworthy is likely to be received with skepticism and probably rejected. In discussing credibility, we must distinguish between formal and informal sources of information. A **formal source** is either a person or medium providing consumption-related information and hired and paid by an organization. An **informal source** is a person whom the message receiver knows personally, such as a parent or friend who gives product information or advice, or an individual met and respected online.

Reference Group Influence

Many hotel bathrooms feature "standardized" signs urging guests to reuse their towels in order to help save the environment. One hotel used a message stating that: "Most of your fellow guests reused their towels. Please help us save the environment and reuse yours." This "social norm" message persuaded about 25% more people to reuse towels. Subsequently, a more detailed social norm message stated that: "Most of the guests who have stayed in this room reused their towels. Please help us save the environment and reuse yours." Responding to this message, even more guests reused their towels.[1] From a communication perspective, the "social norm" messages were more persuasive than the "standard" message because they were credible and believable, whereas most guests perceived the standard messages, at least partially, as efforts by hotels to cut down on expenses. In contrast, messages stating that *others* have acted responsibly were convincing because most people adhere to social norms. People can be persuaded by various sources, such as consumers like themselves, the media, and salespeople, only if they trust these sources. People readily reject messages from sources that they do not trust and perceive as biased and not credible.

Reference groups serve as comparative and normative frames of reference for a person's values and behaviors. **Normative influence** consists of learning and adopting a group's norms, values, and behaviors. The most pertinent normative influence comes from groups to which people naturally belong, such as family, peers, and members of one's community. Generally, normative influence occurs among members of the same socioeconomic group. For example, families have a large normative influence on children because they mold young children's initial consumption-related values. Such as which foods to select for good nutrition, appropriate ways to dress for specific occasions, how and where to shop, or what constitutes "good value". **Comparative influence** arises when people compare themselves to others whom they respect and admire, and then adopt some of those people's values or imitate their behaviors. For example, when a recently-graduated student who holds a "start of the ladder" position in a corporation admires her boss and aspires to live like the boss and have similar possessions, the boss exerts comparative influence on the lower-level employee.

The concept of reference group can be also used metaphorically. Ads for the Art of Shaving—a line of upscale shaving products—have appeared under the tagline "Welcome to the brotherhood of shaving." The idea behind this theme is to make men feel that they belong to a select group of metrosexuals who care greatly about personal grooming and shaving and are trusted experts to each other. The campaign's ads have appeared only in magazines, unlike ads for other shaving products that appear on TV and in print, because a TV campaign may "dilute" the "insider mystique of the brand."[2]

Types of Reference Groups

A group to which a person belongs to, or realistically can join, is called a **membership group**. For example, the group of men with whom a young executive plays poker weekly would be considered his membership group. A **symbolic group** is a group to which an individual is unlikely to belong, but whose values and behaviors that person adopts. For instance, professional tennis players may constitute a symbolic group for an amateur tennis player, who identifies with certain players and imitates their behavior (e.g., by purchasing a specific brand of tennis racquet or tennis shoe). However, the amateur tennis player does not (and probably never will) qualify for membership as a professional tennis player because she has neither the skills nor the opportunity to compete professionally. Table 9.1 illustrates the relationship between group membership and the type of group influence.

Consumption-Related Reference Group

The consumption-related groups that influence consumers' attitudes and behavior include friendship groups, shopping groups, virtual communities, and advocacy groups.

TABLE 9.1 Group Membership and Type of Influence	NORMATIVE INFLUENCE	COMPARATIVE INFLUENCE
Membership Group	High level of conformity to the standards of immediate membership groups, such as family and peers. The influencer and influenced belong to same socioeconomic group and are both aware of the influence.	Conformity to the standards of groups that the influenced aspires to join, and probably will. The two parties are one or two socioeconomic groups apart. The influenced and influencer probably know each other and are aware of the influence.
Symbolic Group	No significant influence. The influencer is outside the influenced reference group. The influenced are unaware of the unlikely influencers' norms.	High degree of influence, although the influenced know that they will never join the influencers. Socially, the parties are far apart, but the influencers recognize the degree of their influence.

Friendship Groups

Seeking and maintaining friendships is a basic drive for most people. Friends fulfill a wide range of needs: They provide companionship, security, and opportunities to discuss problems that an individual may be reluctant to discuss with family members. Friendships are also a sign of maturity and independence, for they represent a breaking away from the family and the forming of social ties with the outside world. Often, friendships are formed at work. People who work together often get to know, respect, and become credible sources of information for one another regarding purchases.

Shopping Groups

People may shop together just to enjoy shopping or to reduce their perceived risk; that is, they may bring someone along whose expertise regarding a particular product category will reduce their chances of making incorrect purchases. In instances where none of the members of the shopping group knows much about the product under consideration (such as an expensive home entertainment center), members may feel more confident with a collective decision. Referral programs are an important element of shopping groups. For example, a warehouse membership club (e.g., Costco or Sam's Club) might offer rewards to current members who convince others to join. Such programs may reward only the current customer (member) for finding a new customer, may reward only the new customer, or may reward both parties (either equally or unequally). A study found that although both current and potential members preferred getting entire rewards (100 percent each), current members found a 50/50 distribution to be more appropriate if the member they recruited had to make a financial investment to join (e.g., pay a membership fee).[3]

Another example of a shopping group is the shared experience of waiting in line. Retail experts say that by standing in a crowd, shoppers see themselves as making the right buying decision—a concept known as "social proof." Retailers also recognize the value of keeping shoppers waiting, because waiting crowds create attention and generate sales even after the initial frenzy has died down.[4]

Virtual Communities

Many websites encourage consumers to leave comments and have others respond to them. Most young adults have extensive "buddy lists" and regularly communicate with people whom they have met online but never in person. Online, it does not matter if you are tall or short, thin or fat, handsome or average looking, and many feel free to express their thoughts and even be intimate with those they have never met face to face. The anonymity of the online environment allows people the freedom to express their views and benefit from others' views. One study investigated "foodies," an online group dedicated to the preparation and consumption of food and drinks, whether at home or in restaurants. The groups' members post recommendations for restaurants and foods across the world. The findings showed that the "foodies" paid great attention to the accuracy of their postings and took great care in not posting potentially misleading information.[5]

The fact that people can share their interests, hobbies, and opinions with thousands of peers online has benefited marketers. For example, for more than 60 years, American TV producers have broadcasted entertainment programs supported by advertising fees. Much like a book or a movie, the contents of these programs were designed without significant input from the audiences. Generally, Nielsen ratings have been used to gauge the success of TV programs and determine the advertising rates on various broadcasts. After watching them, many viewers frequently discussed TV programs at their offices' water coolers, and some may have even talked back to their televisions while watching. However, the writers and producers of these programs had no reliable way to listen to what viewers were saying. Several years ago, avid TV viewers set up a website named televisionwithoutpity.com, which provides TV viewers with a forum to discuss, complain about, or compliment popular TV shows. Visitors to the website share their opinions about programs' plotlines—often with a humorous touch—and make guesses about future developments; some even make suggestions regarding the content of future episodes. Because viewers who post their comments are very involved with the programs they watch, the producers of the shows can read their postings and get a sense of audiences' reactions to plotlines and dialogues. Then, the writers can incorporate such feedback into future episodes. Because TV shows are filmed several weeks prior to a broadcast, writers can also change future episodes in ways that reflect the viewers' postings. For example, if viewers indicate that they are bored with or irritated by a particular story line, it can be revised or even concluded sooner than planned.

Advocacy Groups

The objective of consumption-focused advocacy groups is to assist consumers in making decisions and support consumers' rights. There are two types of advocacy groups: Entities organized to correct a specific consumer abuse and then disband, and groups whose purpose is to address broader, more pervasive problem areas and operate over an extended period of time. A group of irate parents who join together to protest the opening of an adult X-rated video rental store in their neighborhood, or a group of neighbors who attend a meeting of the local highway department to demand that additional stop signs be placed on specific corners, are examples of temporary, cause-specific consumer-action groups. An example of an enduring consumer-action group is Mothers Against Drunk Driving (MADD), a group founded in 1980 and operating today throughout the United States in the form of local chapters in all major cities and all state capitals. MADD representatives serve on numerous public advisory boards and help establish local task forces to reduce drunk driving. Additionally, the organization supports laws that restrict alcoholic beverage advertising and is opposed to any advertising that may have a negative impact on young people.

Factors Affecting Reference Group Influence

The degree of influence that a reference group exerts on an individual's behavior depends on the individual, product, and social factors. These factors include conformity, the group's power and expertise, the individual's experience and personality, and the conspicuousness of the product.

Conformity

The objective of some marketers, especially market leaders, is to enhance consumer conformity. They often do so by portraying reference group influences in their promotions. In contrast, marketers of new brands or brands that are not market leaders often try to convince consumers to be different and not follow the crowd. To influence its members, a reference group must:

1. Inform or make members aware that the brand or product exists.

2. Provide the individual with the opportunity to compare his or her own thinking with the attitudes and behavior of the group.

3. Influence the individual to adopt attitudes and behavior that are consistent with the group's norms.

4. Legitimize the member's decision to use the same products as other members.

The MADD ad in Figure 9.3 discourages a reckless conduct—drunk driving—that young people (especially males) often engage in because they want to be liked by their "buddies" and, especially when intoxicated, participate in risky and often tragic behaviors encouraged in party-like "macho" settings. The ad implies that driving with drunken buddies legitimizes one's drunk driving, because peers are an important reference group. Young adults will respond to this message because it is credible. The ad portrays reference group influence that ended up tragically and is likely to persuade young men not to make the same mistake that the dead driver did. Table 9.2 lists several characteristics of individuals who are likely to conform to groups' behaviors and established practices.

Groups' Power and Expertise

Different reference groups may influence the beliefs, attitudes, and behaviors of individuals at different times or under different circumstances. For example, the dress habits of a young staff member working for a conservative law firm may vary, depending on her place and role. She conforms to the dress code of her office by wearing conservative clothing and skirts or dresses that end below the knee by day, but may wear more trendy, flamboyant, revealing styles when she goes out with her friends.

LAST ROUND WITH MY BUDDIES

Source: MADD Canada

FIGURE 9.3 Discouraging Conformity to Group Influence

TABLE 9.2   Characteristics of Conformists

1. They feel that if someone is behaving in a certain way in a group, that is the right way to behave.
2. They prefer wearing stylish clothing and pay attention to what others are wearing.
3. They try to fit in during social gatherings so as not to be out of place.
4. They are guided by others' behavior if they feel unsure how to behave in a situation.
5. They often behave in a manner they feel others want them to behave.
6. They change their mannerisms and approaches if they feel that someone they are interacting with disapproves of them.
7. They often pick up slang expressions from others and start using them.
8. They always pay close attention to others' reactions to their behaviors.

Consumers who are primarily concerned with approval from others usually adopt the same products and brands as those group members who have status. When consumers are preoccupied with the power that a person or group can exert over them, they often purchase products that conform to the norms of that person or group in order to be complimented on their choices. However, unlike reference groups that are not power based, "power groups" may bring about behaviors, but not changes in attitudes. Individuals may conform to the behavior of powerful persons or groups, but probably will neither change their attitudes nor internalize their choices.

Relevant Information and Experience

Individuals who have firsthand experience with a product or service, or can easily obtain detailed information about it, are less likely to be influenced by the advice or example of others. In contrast, persons who have little or no experience with an item, and do not trust advertising messages, are more likely to seek out the advice or example of others. For instance, when a young corporate sales rep wants to impress his client, he may take her to a restaurant that he has visited before and liked or to one that has been highly recommended by a restaurant guide. If he has neither personal experience nor information, he may seek the advice of a friend, or imitate the behavior of others by taking the client to a restaurant that is frequented by executives whom he views as role models. One study examined how product and consumer characteristics moderate the influence of online consumer reviews on product sales using data from the video game industry. The findings indicated that online reviews were more influential for less popular games and games whose players had greater Internet experience.[6]

The ad for the U.S. Navy in Figure 9.4 shows a sailor, who, to young civilians, is a member of a symbolic reference group that, unlike most symbolic groups, they can potentially join. The ad's objective is to encourage young men and women become members of a select group—the Navy. The ad shows a sailor who has the information and experience to advocate joining the Navy. Potential recruits are likely to find him a credible role model and believe his statement that in addition to moving ships (by using propellers), the Navy has given him a promising career and "advanced" (or propelled) his future.

Product Conspicuousness

The degree of reference group influence on purchase decisions varies according to product conspicuousness. A conspicuous product is one that stands out and is noticed by

FIGURE 9.4   A Credible Role Model

others, such as an expensive watch or a newly released digital camera. Products that are especially conspicuous and status revealing (e.g., a large diamond ring) are most likely to be purchased with an eye to the reactions of relevant others. The ALT magazine ad in Figure 9.5 features a conspicuous product. Privately consumed products that are less conspicuous (shaving cream or bath soap) are less likely to be purchased with a reference group in mind. Table 9.3 depicts a framework illustrating that more-conspicuous products are subject to greater reference group influence, both in terms of owning the product to begin with and the brand or type owned. The opposite is true for less-conspicuous products. For example, a person's reference group will have strong influence on whether or not to have a tattoo or piercing, as well as on the type of piercing one gets or the design of a tattoo, because both are highly visible. Because some people wear jewelry and others do not, reference groups are likely to influence only the type of jewelry a person chooses to wear, but not whether or not to wear jewelry. In contrast, a reference group will influence neither one's decision to use or not use toothpaste (because everyone uses this product) nor the brand chosen (because the brand of toothpaste one uses is invisible to others).

Walk down any street in America and you will see someone wearing a hat, T-shirt, or jacket emblazoned with the logo of a famous sports team. Similarly, while driving, look at the license plates of passing cars. Very quickly, you will see license plates containing variations of the names and logos of universities, favorite sports teams, environmental groups, and many other institutions and causes. Research has found that among those attending a sporting event, the more an individual identifies with a particular team, the more likely he is to purchase the products of the companies that sponsor that team.[7] Interestingly, technology has affected conspicuousness. Before e-readers, many women avoid reading printed erotica in public, because they were concerned that the books' titles, which were visible on the covers for others to see, would reflect badly on them and reinforce the "dumb blonde"

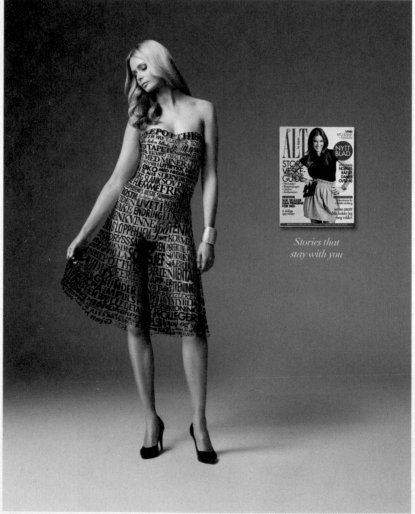

Source: Egmont Hjemmet Mortensen

FIGURE 9.5 A Conspicuous Product

TABLE 9.3 Product Conspicuousness, and Reference Group Influence[a]

	PRODUCTS	REFERENCE GROUP INFLUENCE ON BUYING OR NOT BUYING	REFERENCE GROUP INFLUENCE ON BRAND
Very Conspicuous	Piercing	+	+
	Tattoo	+	+
	Jewelry	=	+
	Baseball cap	=	+
	Smartphone and apps	=	+
	Magazine read online	=	+
	Dance clubs	=	+
	Hairspray	−	−
	Contact lenses	−	−
	Undergarments	−	−
Not Conspicuous At All	Toothpaste	−	−

[a] + considerable influence; = neutral; − no influence

stereotype. However, with e-readers, what one reads publicly is invisible and scores of erotica books have been written and rapidly sold; several even became best sellers.[8]

Personality Characteristics

Several personality traits affect the degree of a reference group's influence on its members. People who are compliant, have a tendency to conform need to be affiliated and liked by others, and are other-directed are more receptive to group influences. Competitive people who desire to control other people and events and are inner-directed are less likely to look for guidance from reference groups.

Credibility of Spokespersons, Endorsers, and Other Formal Sources

Learning Objective

2 To understand the persuasive power and credibility of spokespersons, endorsers, celebrities, salespersons, vendors, and media.

Source credibility is the believability of the endorser, spokesperson, or individual in an advertisement. The spokesperson can be an actual customer, a company employee, a celebrity, or a model. Researchers have identified the following dimensions in measuring the credibility of a person or organization: Expertise, trustworthiness, attractiveness, and likability. Consumers recognize that the intentions of commercial entities (e.g., manufacturers, service companies, financial institutions, retailers) are to generate profits and therefore view marketers as less credible than informal reference groups. Companies can convey credibility through solid past performance, good reputation, product quality, and good service. Their perceived credibility is also a function of the image and attractiveness of their spokespersons, the reputation of the retailers that carry their offerings, and the media where they advertise. One study of sponsorships of sporting teams showed that a clearly perceived fit between the sponsor and the entity being supported strongly enhanced the sponsor's credibility.[9]

Firms with well-established reputations have an easier time selling their products than firms with lesser reputations. Consumers perceive well-established and liked brands as credible and, therefore, these brands often introduce new items under the same brand name. Marketers also use **institutional advertising**, which consists of promoting a company's image without referring to any of its specific offerings.

Not-for-profit sources generally have more credibility than for-profit (commercial) sources. Formal sources that are perceived to be "neutral"—such as Consumer Reports (an American magazine published monthly since 1936), a consumption-related report, or an exposé in reputable media—have greater credibility than commercial sources, because they are viewed as more objective in their product assessments. That is why *publicity* is so valuable to a manufacturer: Consumers believe citations of products in editorial contexts more than they do paid advertisements.

Endorsers and Spokespersons

Many studies have investigated the relationship between the effectiveness of the messages and the spokespersons or endorsers they feature. The key findings of this research are as follows:

1. The synergy between the endorser and the type of product or service advertised is very important. The greater the fit between the celebrity and the product endorsed, the higher the persuasiveness of the message. Therefore, for example, for personal grooming products, a physically attractive celebrity spokesperson is likely to enhance message credibility and generate a favorable and enduring attitude toward the brand. For products unrelated to physical appearance (e.g., detergents), an attractive endorser is unlikely to have an effect. A glamorous celebrity endorser is more likely to be perceived as a credible source, and positively affect attitudes toward the brand, if featured in an ad for a *hedonistic* product (e.g., a very expensive watch) than for a *utilitarian* one (e.g., an inexpensive, everyday watch).

2. Endorsers whose demographic characteristics (e.g., age and ethnicity) are similar to those of the target audiences are viewed as more credible and persuasive than those whose characteristics are not. For instance, consumers with strong ethnic identifications are more likely to be persuaded by endorsers of similar ethnicities than individuals with weaker ethnic identifications. A person's ethnic identification is the degree to which she identifies herself as a member of her ethnic group.

3. Although consumers may like an ad featuring a famous endorser, they will buy the product advertised only if they trust the marketer as well. Thus, when marketers measure the persuasiveness of advertising messages that feature famous endorsers, they must also measure consumers' attitudes toward the brands advertised, as well as consumers', purchase intentions.

4. Marketers who use celebrities in testimonials or endorsements must ensure that the message contents are congruent with spokespersons' qualifications. A tennis star can believably endorse a brand of an analgesic and comment about how it relieves sore muscle pain. However, a recitation of medical evidence supporting the brand's superiority over other brands is beyond his or her expected knowledge and expertise, and thus may reduce (rather than enhance) message credibility. One study indicated that both perceived expertise and trustworthiness might change consumers' attitudes favorably toward products, and that trustworthy sources did not alter attitudes without being perceived as experts.[10]

Thus, in selecting endorsers, marketers must ensure that there is a synergy among the celebrity's trustworthiness, expertise, physical attractiveness, and the product or brand endorsed. They must also take into account the celebrity's number of prior endorsements, because consumers perceive celebrities who appear in commercials too often as less credible than celebs with lesser commercial exposure.

Celebrities

Celebrities, particularly movie stars, TV personalities, popular entertainers, and sports icons, are a symbolic reference group because they are liked, admired, and often have a high degree of perceived credibility. Therefore, many marketers use them to promote their products and services; by some estimates, 25% of U.S. commercials include celebrity endorsers.[11] To their fans and much of the public, celebrities represent an idealization of a life that most people imagine that they would love to live. Advertisers spend enormous sums of money to have celebrities promote their products, with the expectation that the reading or viewing audience will react positively to the celebrity's association with their products.

The "pitchman" (or woman) who appears in a promotional message has enormous influence on the credibility of the message. Of all the benefits that a celebrity might contribute to a firm's advertising program—fame, talent, credibility, or charisma—credibility is the most important. By celebrity credibility, we mean the audience's perception of both the celebrity's *expertise* (how much the celebrity knows about the product area) and *trustworthiness* (how honest the celebrity is about what he or she says about the product).[12] To illustrate, when a celebrity endorses only one product, consumers are likely to perceive the product in a highly favorable light and purchase it. In contrast, when a celebrity endorses a variety of products, his or her perceived credibility is reduced because then the economic motivation underlying the celebrity's endorsements becomes too pronounced.[13] A study that examined the impact of celebrity athlete endorsers on teens found that such endorsers generated favorable word-of-mouth and increased consumers' brand loyalties. This study also found that female teens provided more favorable word-of-mouth about products endorsed by their favorite celebrity athletes than did male teens.[14] Today's sophisticated consumers are seeking greater authenticity in marketing from the brands they like. Thus, PepsiCo had a hybrid project with Beyoncé that included her appearances in commercials, as well as a multimillion-dollar fund to support some of her creative projects. Pepsi's goal was to enhance its reputation with consumers by acting as an artistic patron instead of simply paying for celebrity endorsements.[15]

Marketers employ celebrities in promotion in the following ways:

1. **Celebrity testimonial**—Based on personal usage, the celebrity attests to the product's quality. A campaign for golf equipment featured Justin Timberlake—adored by millions of teens and young adults—in an attempt to make the game of golf more appealing and "sexy."[16] A TV ad for an advanced model of the iPhone featured Martin Scorsese—a legendary movie director—using the phone's Siri feature to schedule appointments and check traffic conditions.

2. **Celebrity endorsement**—Celebrities appear on behalf of products, with which they may or may not have direct experience or familiarity. For example, Chuck Norris—the martial art star—has been featured in social media ads for Era detergent. The campaign's theme is that Era is as tough on stains as Chuck Norris is on the "bad guys" (in movies). Figure 9.6 features "K.J." Noons—a kickboxing and martial arts champion—as a spokesperson for a not-for-profit organization named People for the Ethical Treatment of Animals (PETA). "K.J." is a tough fighter and he states that while he and his opponents in the ring are equally matched, animals often need protection from violence and abuse by bigger and stronger humans. The depiction of a strong, tough person protecting helpless animals makes the message credible.

3. **Celebrity actor**—The celebrity plays a part in a commercial for the product.

4. **Celebrity spokesperson**—The celebrity represents the brand or company over an extended period. For example, James Bond—one of the world's iconic superheroes—has become a spokesperson for the Omega watch and the exclusive Aston Martin luxury car.

Not all companies feel that using celebrity endorsers is the best way to advertise. Some companies avoid celebrities because they fear that if the celebrity gets involved in some undesirable act or event (e.g., an ugly matrimonial problem, a scandal, or an arrest and criminal charges), the resulting press coverage will negatively affect sales of the endorsed brand. For example, after Rush Limbaugh—a conservative and often combative radio talk show host—called a young female student a "slut" and "prostitute" because she supported contraception, a lot of marketers stopped advertising on his show.[17] Similarly, after stories about John Travolta's gay sexual escapades appeared in the media, he was immediately replaced in ads for a very expensive watch, although he had appeared in those ads for years. Tiger Woods also lost many of his commercial endorsement gigs after it was revealed that he had cheated on his wife with strippers and was addicted to sex. Aflac Insurance fired a famous comedian, who supplied the voice of the company's duck mascot for more than a decade, after he posted jokes about the earthquake and tsunami in Japan.[18] Oscar Pistorius, a double amputee who races on carbon-fiber blades and competed in the Olympics, has been featured in many Nike campaigns; one ad showed him starting to sprint with the CAP: "I am the bullet in the chamber."* However, Nike dropped Pistorius from its ad campaigns after the South African sports star was charged with murder in the shooting death of his girlfriend.[19]

Source: Creative Agency: 358 Helsinki. Photo: Rami Hanafi, Viewmasters

FIGURE 9.6 A Celebrity Endorsement

* Associated Press, "Nike Makes No Plans for Pistorius in Future Ads," online.wsj.com, February 18, 2013.

Many ads show everyday consumers endorsing products. For instance, TV commercials for Broadway shows often feature people raving about a musical as they are coming out of the theater. One study discovered that "slice-of-life commercials"—promotional messages showing typical consumers in everyday situations—were more effective than commercials featuring either a fantasy or emotional appeals. The ethnicity and gender of the model affected the customers' perceptions of credibility.[20]

Salesperson Credibility

Salespeople who engender confidence and who give the impression of honesty and integrity are most persuasive. A salesperson who "looks you in the eye" often is perceived as more honest than one who evades direct eye contact. For many products, a sales representative who dresses well and drives an expensive, late-model car may have more credibility than one without such outward signs of success. For other products, a salesperson may achieve more credibility by dressing in the role of an expert. For example, a person selling home improvement products is likely to be perceived as more credible if he looks like someone who has just climbed off a roof or out of a basement, rather than like a banker.

Vendor Credibility

The reputation of the retailer who sells the product has a major influence on message credibility. Products sold by well-known, quality stores carry the added endorsement (and implicit guarantee) of the store itself (e.g., "If Amazon.com recommends it, it must be a good book"). The aura of credibility generated by a reputable vendor reinforces the manufacturer's message as well. That is why so many ads for national brands often list the stores carrying the product.

The consumer's previous experience with the product or vendor has a major impact on the credibility of the message. Fulfilled product expectations increase the credibility accorded to future messages by the same advertiser; unfulfilled product claims or disappointing product experiences reduce the credibility of future messages. Thus, the key basis for message credibility is the ability of the product, service, or brand to deliver consistent quality, value, and satisfaction to consumers.

Medium Credibility

The reputation of the medium that carries the advertisement also enhances the credibility of the message. For example, the image of Vogue confers an added status on the products advertised in that magazine. Most consumers believe that a respectable medium would only advertise products that it "knows" to be of good quality. Because specialization implies knowledge and expertise, consumers regard advertising they see in special-interest magazines and websites as more credible than ads in general-interest sources.

A source's credibility may rapidly decline. For decades, Oprah Winfrey has been one of the most credible sources in America. However, her credibility declined sharply after her show hosted a writer who made up the supposedly personal accounts of hardships and other dramatic experiences that he published in a book about his life. Similarly, Dan Rather, a very famous journalist, was fired from his position on 60 Minutes—a highly respected TV news magazine created in 1968—after he cited erroneous facts in a broadcasted segment. Clearly, such negative events are likely to adversely affect the reputations of products advertised during these TV shows; although the effects are mostly temporary, marketers must be prepared for these repercussions.

Effects of Time on Source Credibility

When information is transferred from the short-term memory to the cerebral cortex (where long-term memory is located), over time, it is separated from the context in which it was learned. For example, although you know that the nation's capital is Washington, D.C., you probably do not remember how you learned this piece of information. One's disassociation of the message from its source over time, and remembering only the message content but not its source, is called the **sleeper effect**. Thus, though a high-credibility source is initially more influential than a low-credibility source, studies show that both positive and negative credibility effects tend to disappear after six weeks or so. Furthermore, the theory of **differential decay** suggests that the memory of a negative cue (e.g., a low-credibility source) simply decays faster than the message itself, leaving behind the primary message content. However, reintroduction of the same or similar message by the source serves to jog the audience's memory, and the original effect remanifests itself; that is, the high-credibility source remains more persuasive than the low-credibility source. For marketers, the implication of the sleeper effect and differential decay is that messages featuring high-credibility spokespersons must be repeated regularly if they are to maintain high levels of persuasiveness.

Word-of-Mouth and Opinion Leadership

Learning Objective

3 To understand the dynamics and measurement of opinion leadership and word-of-mouth.

Originally, sociologists who studied the communications process among peers named it **opinion leadership**, defined as the process by which one person—the opinion leader—informally influences others, who might be either opinion seekers or recipients. This influence occurs between two or more people, neither of whom is or represents a commercial seller or would gain directly from providing advice or information. Opinion receivers view the intentions of opinion leaders as being in their best interests, because the opinion leaders receive no material gain for the advice they provide. Because opinion leaders often base their product comments on firsthand experience, their advice reduces the opinion receivers' perceived risk and anxiety in the course of buying new products. Furthermore, opinion leaders view any feedback they get about their prior recommendations from opinion receivers as credible and are likely to include it in the advice they provide to others in the future.

Opinion leaders provide both information and advice. They talk about their experiences with products and advise others whether or not to buy products or brands. The information that opinion leaders transmit includes advice on selecting the best brands, using the products correctly, where to buy the products, and other aspects. Opinion leaders are particularly important when it comes to recommending service providers with whom they have had personal relationships, such as doctors, lawyers, hairdressers, garage mechanics, restaurants, or travel companies, because small service businesses have very limited advertising resources, and the main way they can get new customers is via recommendations by existing clients.

Generally speaking, opinion leadership is *category specific*; that is, opinion leaders often specialize in certain product categories about which they offer information and advice. When other product categories are discussed, however, they are just as likely to reverse their roles and become opinion receivers. A person may be very knowledgeable about cars and a lot of people may ask for his advice when contemplating buying a new automobile. But, when he considers buying, say, a new iMac, he may seek advice from someone else whom he considers an opinion leader regarding technology; this might even be the same person who asked the iMac buyer for advice when buying a new car.

Getting the attention of trendsetters is crucial for most companies because a tweet or a Facebook post can generate great interest. New York's Comic Con—an annual gathering of comic-book and science-fiction fans—included representatives from Mattel, Disney, and Nintendo, among others. Marketers realize that attendees at such events are people who are setting trends. They are the early adopters of science-fiction-related items and the people who make them "hot" and immensely popular.[21]

Opinion leadership is a two-way street. A word-of-mouth encounter may start by one party offering advice or information about a product to another party. However, this opinion leader may become an opinion receiver later on. For example, a student going on her first job interview may seek information from other students who have already gone on several job interviews (i.e., opinion leaders). She might ask them about the questions posed, how they dressed, and which aspects of the interviews they found unexpected and stressful. However, after her own interview, she is likely to share her experiences with those who had advised her. At that point, those who previously advised her become opinion receivers and will probably share her insights about interviewing with others seeking their advice in the future. Indeed, the input from opinion receivers to opinion leaders becomes part of the opinion leaders' expertise. The motivations of opinion leaders and receivers are featured in Table 9.4.

Characteristics of Opinion Leaders

Just who are opinion leaders? Can they be recognized by any distinctive characteristics? Can they be reached through specific media? Marketers have long sought answers to these questions, for if they are able to identify the relevant opinion leaders for their products, they can design marketing messages that will inspire opinion leaders to communicate with and influence the consumption behavior of others. For this reason, consumer researchers have attempted to develop a profile of the opinion leader. This has not been easy to do, because opinion leaders often specialize in certain product categories about which they offer information and advice. When other product categories are at issue, they become opinion receivers. A person who is considered particularly knowledgeable about home

TABLE 9.4 The Motivations of Opinion Leaders and Receivers	
OPINION LEADERS	**OPINION RECEIVERS**
Self-Involvement	
• Reduce post-purchase dissonance	• Reduce perceived risk
• Gain attention from others	• Reduce search and shopping time
• Show off expertise	
• Experience "converting" others	
Product Involvement	
• Express satisfaction or complain about a product or service	• Learn additional and more efficient ways to use products
	• Learn about newly introduced products
Social Involvement	
• Express friendship by providing others with consumption-related information	• Buy products that have the approval of others

electronics may be an opinion leader in terms of this subject, yet when it comes to purchasing a new washing machine, the same person may seek advice from someone else—perhaps even from someone who has sought his advice on home electronics.

Although it is difficult to construct a profile of the opinion leader without focusing on a particular product category, studies indicate that, in the context of consumer behavior, opinion leaders share the following characteristics, which are also

1. Opinion leaders are highly knowledgeable regarding a particular product category, follow new products that come into the markets, and are often consumer innovators in their area of expertise.

2. Opinion leaders are self-confident, outgoing, and sociable. They readily discuss products and consumption behaviors with others.

3. Opinion leaders read special-interest publications and regularly visit websites devoted to the specific topic or product category in which they specialize. They have specialized knowledge that enables them to make effective recommendations to relatives, friends, and neighbors.

4. Usually, opinion leaders and receivers belong to the same socioeconomic and age groups.

Word-of-mouth is highly important in the fashion industry where styles change frequently and "social approval" is a key factor in one's decision to adopt a particular fashion or not. Table 9.5 lists the most noted characteristics of fashion opinion leaders.

Measuring Opinion Leadership

Consumer researchers can measure the degree of opinion leadership and its impact on consumption behavior by using one of the following methods: (1) The self-designating method, (2) The sociometric method, and the (3) The key informant method. Additionally, Klout scores measure people's degree of influence online.

TABLE 9.5 Characteristics of Fashion Opinion Leaders
1. Their opinions on fashions count with others.
2. When it comes to fashionable clothing, people turn to them for advice.
3. People know that they know how to pick fashionable clothing.
4. They often persuade people to buy the fashions they like.
5. They influence people's opinions about clothing.
6. They find shopping stimulating and an adventure.
7. They enjoy shopping with friends and family.
8. They enjoy shopping when they try to find just the perfect gifts.
9. They often go shopping when they want to treat themselves to something special.
10. They shop to keep up with the new trends and fashions.

TABLE 9.6	Sample Items Used in the Self-Designation of Opinion Leaders (responses on a "Strongly Agree" to "Strongly Disagree" scale)

1. I am usually the first one in my circle of friends to know about new technologies.
2. I know more about technologies than most people.
3. My opinions about technologies count with other people.
4. When considering buying a new technological product, people turn to me for advice.
5. I often influence others' opinions about technologies.
6. People know that I use the same products that I recommend.
7. I often influence people to buy the same technological products that I like.

Self-Designating Method

The **self-designating method** employs a self-administered questionnaire that requires respondents to evaluate the extent to which they have provided others with information about a product category or specific brand or have otherwise influenced the purchase decisions of others. Table 9.6 lists sample questions that can be used in a study of technological opinion leaders. Marketers use the self-designating technique more often than other methods because it is self-administered and can be easily incorporated into marketing research questionnaires. However, this method relies on consumers' self-evaluations, and respondents often overestimate their roles as opinion leaders.

Sociometric Method

The **sociometric method** measures the person-to-person communications about a product or brand among members of a community where most people know each other by name (e.g., a college dormitory or sorority). Respondents are asked to identify:

1. The specific individuals (if any) to whom they provided advice or information about the product or brand under study.
2. The specific individuals (if any) who provided them with advice or information about the same product or brand.

If respondents identify one or more individuals to whom they have provided some form of product information and those individuals confirm the respondents receive "opinion leadership points." Then, the people from whom the respondents received advice are interviewed and asked to confirm the respondents' reports. On the basis of these interviews, respondents receive "opinion receivership points." One's designation as an opinion leader or receiver is based on comparing the two sets of scores.

Sociometric questioning provides the most valid results for designating opinion leaders and receivers. However, the questioning is expensive and analyzing the results is complex. In addition, this method can be used only within populations where most members know each other by name and regularly interact; it is inapplicable for studies that use large samples.

Key Informant Method

Researchers can also study opinion leadership by using a **key informant**, that is, a person who is keenly knowledgeable about the nature of social communications among members of a specific group. Researchers ask the key informant to identify those individuals in the group who are opinion leaders. However, the key informant does not have to be a member of the group under study. For example, a professor can be a key informant and identify those among his students who are most likely to be opinion leaders about a particular product. This research method is relatively inexpensive because it involves collecting data from one person only, whereas the self-designating and sociometric methods require questioning many respondents. Marketers seldom employ the key informant method, though, because it is very difficult to find a single individual who can objectively identify opinion leaders within a given consumer group.

Klout Scores

The **Klout score** measures people's influence online based on their abilities to generate engagement and feedback to what they post. For example, if a person posts a picture of a new restaurant online and others respond, possibly by also visiting the restaurant and posting reviews, the person accumulates Klout points. Klout measures influence on a scale of 1 to 100 (the average Klout score is 40); the greater one's ability to drive conversations and inspire social actions such as likes, shares, and re-tweets, the higher one's score will be. The Klout score focuses on the amount of conversation and interactions that people generate, rather than the volume of their posts; that is, the score is designed to determine one's degree of influence and not merely activity. Klout sells the information it "mines" to customers like airlines and banks. Those companies then offer "secret" rewards or more responsive customer service to the people with high scores. For example, one airline began allowing people with Klout scores over 40 to visit its first-class airport lounge. Some hotels examine people's Klout scores as they check in and provide perks to guests with higher scores.[22]

As Klout scores became increasingly popular among businesses trying to identify and reach opinion leaders online, Klout broadened the sources from which it "mines" information. To measure real-world influence more accurately, Klout added Wikipedia to the mix. If a person has been featured on a Wikipedia page and that page has a high Google PageRank (a value indicating the importance of a particular page), the person's score will rise; if others link to that Wikipedia page, the score will climb even higher. Klout also added a feature called "moments," which are posts that generated action from the people in one's social networks, such as tweets that received a lot of re-tweets and replies, or a Facebook post that started a discussion among one's friends.

Strategic Applications of Word-of-Mouth

Learning Objective

4 To understand the strategic applications, advantages, and potential perils of word-of-mouth.

In marketing, word-of-mouth consists of transmitting advice and other types of information about products, brands, and shopping experiences. Until about 15 years ago, any consumption-related information transmitted by a consumer could reach relatively few people (e.g., the person's friends, family, work groups, and members of other organizations to which the person belonged). Today, one's review of a movie, book, product, university, professor, and even employer can be easily and quickly posted online and reach thousands of people. Furthermore, constantly emerging new technologies allow people to compile and post increasingly sophisticated and attention-getting materials online and vividly share their consumption experience with others, both visually and verbally.

Word-of-mouth taking place online is called **e-wom** and occurs in social networks, brand communities, blogs, chat rooms, and tweets.

Social Networks

Online, **social networks** are virtual communities where people share information about themselves with others, generally with similar interests, with whom they have established relationships that, for the most part, exist only in cyberspace. Because consumption and the products people buy are integral parts of their lives, their online profiles and discussions with others include a tremendous amount of purchase information and advice. The major social networks are Facebook, YouTube, Twitter, and Myspace.

One study identified three dimensions underlying consumers' engagement in e-wom:

1. *Tie strength*—the degree of intimacy and frequency of contacts between the information seeker and the source.
2. *Similarity* among the group's members in terms of demographics and lifestyles.
3. *Source credibility*—the information seeker's perceptions of the source's expertise.[23]

Another study investigated how consumers react to negative e-wom and found out that readers of negative reviews of *hedonic* products (i.e., products used mainly for pleasure) attributed the comments to the reviewers' internal and non-product-related reasons and did not consider them useful. However, readers of negative reviews for *utilitarian* products attributed the reviews to product-related reasons and found them more useful than positive reviews.[24] One study researched the impact of the type of e-wom on consumers' likelihood to transmit the information further. It discovered that highly involved consumers received and transmitted more *rational* product information (e.g., the tablet that has the highest-definition screen and fastest processor) than information appealing to *emotions* (e.g., "When I got it, I just 'bonded' with this tablet and other students looked at me when I used it in class").[25] One study investigated the impact of "social connectedness" on word-of-mouth. The results showed that *moderately* connected people (i.e., the majority of the sample) were as willing as *highly* connected persons to engage in word-of-mouth. The researchers attributed these findings to people's need to give advice and the enjoyment of sharing information with others.[26]

Brand Communities

A **brand community** is a specialized, nongeographically bound community formed on the basis of attachment to a product or brand. Generally, admirers of a particular item, often with nostalgic emotions and in possession of versions that are no longer made, find others with similar interests and form a community fostering a feeling of belonging across geographic, linguistic, and cultural barriers. Brands around which such networks have emerged include Harley-Davidson motorcycles, Barbie dolls, and PEZ candy. Although marketers may attempt to join communities centered on their brands, such efforts may be unwise, because the brand community's members join the forum to interact with other consumers and may view the marketer as an unwelcome outsider.

Weblogs

Scores of websites enable anyone post information on anything and everything quickly, for free, and from any location and at any time. Many sites also offer continuous access to chat rooms where discussions among many participants take place in real time. On these sites, consumers are free to express opinions, describe experiences with products and services, solicit purchase advice, and read others' testimonials about products and brands. Another medium for disseminating word-of-mouth is the blog (short for "Weblog"). A **blog** is a discussion or informational site published on the Internet and consisting of discrete entries ("posts"). At first, blogs were the works of single individuals or small groups, and most covered only a single topic. Today, most blogs have multiple authors and are often managed by media outlets, companies, and other interest groups. A **microblog** has less content than the traditional blog and allow users to exchange small elements of content, such as short sentences, individual images, and video links, mostly via Twitter. **Twitter** is an online social networking service and microblogging service that enables its users to send and read text-based messages of up to 140 characters, known as "tweets."

With millions of blogs online, and their readers' frequent tweets, blogs have become the most powerful platform for exchanging consumption-related information. For example, after a dissatisfied consumer posted information on a group discussion site that U-shaped Kryptonite bicycle locks could be picked with a Bic ballpoint pen, within a few days, a number of blogs posted videos demonstrating how this could be done. Four days after the original posting, Kryptonite issued a statement promising that their new line of bicycle locks would be tougher. However, bloggers kept up the pressure and shortly thereafter The New York Times and the Associated Press published articles about the problem. Over the following 10 days, about 1.8 million people read postings about Kryptonite, and the company announced that it would offer free exchange for unsecured locks.[27]

There is an interesting paradox in the dynamics of e-word-of-mouth: Although marketers have virtually no control over the information exchanged, online platforms are probably their most important sources of consumer information. The fact that the phrase "I Googled" a particular topic, person, or product is now part of America's language demonstrates the nearly universal use of the Web as a primary source of information. Additionally, digital platforms provide consumers with more comprehensive product information than advertising messages, and this information is often perceived as more credible than data provided in ads. Furthermore, all major sales' websites enable consumers to compare prices, outlets, and versions of products. Lastly, consumers can find scores of suggestions online regarding a variety of ways to use a product.

Monitoring word-of-mouth online has become very beneficial. The number of comments posted on Twitter and other social media websites about television shows has exploded, to the point where those comments now affecting the shows' plotlines. For example, writers of USA Network's drama Covert Affairs framed the final episode of the show's second season to respond to constant questions on Twitter about whether a lead character, Auggie Anderson, would regain his lost eyesight.[28]

Stimulating Word-of-Mouth

Marketers long ago realized the power of word-of-mouth communications between consumers, which it is almost always more effective than promotional messages paid for by advertisers, and they often encourage it in ads (see Figure 9.2). Long before the emergence of the Web, marketers portrayed word-of-mouth in advertisements, stimulated word-of-mouth among consumers through advertising slogans such as "tell your friends how much you like our product,"* and instituted referral programs through which customers were rewarded for bringing in new clients. For example, a campaign for Vaseline Clinical Therapy asked female consumers who received free samples of the product to "freely prescribe it to anyone they thought might need it."* The venue selected for the campaign was Kodiak Island—a remote location in Alaska known for its harsh weather.[29] One study seeded ads for mobile phones with prominent bloggers and followed them for several months. The study discovered that these bloggers, in an effort to build their individual reputations within social networks, enhanced the advertisers' promotional messages. The bloggers not only communicated the marketing messages, but also converted them—through language, substance, or tone—to conform to the norms and expectations of potential buyers.[30]

Commercials for Broadway shows often portray people exiting the theater, raving about the show they have just seen and telling others to come and see the performance. It is also widely recognized that the amount of word-of-mouth is positively related to movies' box office revenues, especially during the first week or so after the movies open. While stimulating interpersonal communications is not new, the emergence of e-wom resulted in a surge in the amount of money and creativity devoted to online campaigns and strategic initiatives centered on viral marketing and the use of buzz agents.

Viral Marketing

Viral marketing (viral advertising) is a marketing technique that uses pre-existing social networks and other technologies to produce increases in brand awareness or to achieve other marketing objectives through encouraging individuals to pass along email messages or other contents online. It uses self-replicating viral processes, analogous to the spread of computer viruses. Viral marketing may take the form of video clips, interactive Flash games, **advergames**, e-books, brandable software, images, text messages, and email messages. For example, a company marketing hair gel posted humorous audiovisual clips on the Web as part of a continued spoof and satire of hair products and encouraged viewers to pass along the clips' Web location to others.[31] In another example, Facebook "mined" members' postings about movies and then sent marketing messages to the members' friends with invitations to rent the same movies from Netflix.[32] A study discovered that consumers who found out about a new cell phone service through friends' posted recommendations were 24% more likely to view the cell phone service provider positively than people who found out about the service elsewhere.[33]

Email is the key tool of viral marketing because so many people routinely forward emails to others, and many have preset email groups for sharing different types of information (e.g., a "Joke list"). A study that investigated the motivations for passing along emails found that:[34]

1. People were receptive only to emails from people they knew. The kind of emails they received included jokes, virus alerts, inspirational stories, requests to vote on certain issues, video clips, and links to other websites.

2. The main reasons for not forwarding emails were outdated, dull, and inappropriate contents. About one-third of the forwarded emails included personalized notes from the forwarders, and most of the senders did not alter the emails' original subject lines.

3. The key reasons for forwarding emails were enjoyment (e.g., fun, entertaining, exciting) and helping others (i.e., let others know that the senders care about them). The forwarders also reported that they only passed along contents that they believed the receivers would find interesting and appropriate.

The findings of research studies indicate that marketers using viral campaigns must create relevant messages that the initial recipients will enjoy and find fun. Because forwarded emails are often sent with the original subject lines, these must be worded carefully. However, viral marketing campaigns viewed as too aggressive generated negative postings in blogs and chat forums, including accusations of invasion of privacy and spam generation.[35] A study of Chinese college students indicated that they were more likely to pass along emails and text messages if their friend did so as well and if they believed the recipients would find the messages fun and interesting.[36]

Sometimes, though, viral marketing becomes problematic. For instance, a viral drinking game known as "icing" became highly popular among college students. The game consisted of fast and hazardous "competitive" consumption of Smirnoff's Ice malt beverage among friends. Thousands of videos depicting people "icing" each other, including during occasions such as weddings and graduations, rapidly appeared on scores of websites and focused on the "brothers icing each other" theme. Smirnoff was rumored to have started this viral campaign, but the company denied the accusation.

---

* Stephanie Clifford, "Spreading the Word (and the Lotion) in Small-Town Alaska," nytimes.com, October 9, 2008.

Marketers reward customers for "e-referrals." For example, eBay and Amazon always remind users to send notices of their purchases or auction winnings to their friends. It must be noted that referral programs existed long before the Internet and online commerce. For decades, marketers have been utilizing such promotions as "bring a friend and get one extra month when you renew your membership at the gym," and dentists have been giving reduced prices for teeth cleaning to patients who recommended them to their friends. Nevertheless, the Internet and social networks have enabled marketers to develop faster, broader-reaching, and more effective referral programs.

Buzz Agents

Many firms enlist typical consumers to serve as their **buzz agents**—consumers who promote products clandestinely and generally receive free product samples but not monetary payments. For example, buzz agents may bring a brand of barbeque sauce to a Fourth of July party, read books promoted by publishers on mass transit with the titles clearly visible, suggest to store owners who do not carry a given product that they should do so, and talk other consumers into trying certain products during shopping trips. Buzz agents are motivated by being called upon to serve as opinion leaders and get an ego boost by appearing knowledgeable to their peers and having access to new products before others do.[37]

Many technology start-ups with limited promotional budgets employ buzz agents by initiating "ambassador programs" on college campuses. For example, Foursquare, an app that allows friends to keep in touch constantly, used an ambassador to promote the use of the program among her fellow students, and even got the college newspaper to carry a story about the app. Another student became an ambassador for Stylitics, a new fashion-focused social networking site. She put up posters, distributed flyers, and featured the website on her Facebook page. In addition to their increased recognition on campus, the ambassadors gain internship-like work experience and some even receive "ambassador points" which they can redeem at retail outlets.[38] Another example is Samsung Nation, an online loyalty program, offers rewards to consumers who talk up Samsung. Participants play games on the website (where they learn more about Samsung's products), win virtual points, and get others to join. Those who are most active in posting online comments about Samsung earn "Twitterati" badges. The company carefully studies the profiles and behaviors of the most active members, because they are the ones most likely to become innovators when Samsung introduces new products.[39]

Several companies offer buzz-related services to marketers. For example, bzzagent.com recruits people to spread word-of-mouth and assists its clients in creating marketing buzz campaigns. Similarly, Procter and Gamble created a company known as Tremor specializing in targeting teens and their families. Tremor screens applicants for buzz agent positions and selects only those who are likely to be effective word-of-mouth communicators. Some marketers hire actors or fashion models to go out and simulate demand for their products. For instance, a campaign for a new brand of flavored vodka hired actors and models to visit bars and nightclubs and order martinis made with the new brand. The actors pretended that they were ordering a well-established cocktail, but the real objective of this effort was to *create* a *new* drink. Similarly, in a recent campaign for an online gambling site in London, cab drivers were asked to steer passengers to a discussion about poker, direct them to the gambling site, and even provide "free hand" coupons to passengers who expressed considerable interest.[40]

Managing Negative Rumors

Long ago, marketers realized that it is impossible to control word-of-mouth communications. Negative comments or untrue rumors can sweep through the marketplace and undermine products. Such rumors may suggest that a product was produced under unsanitary conditions or contains unwholesome or culturally unacceptable ingredients. Rumors may also suggest that the product has harmful effects, such as a medication being depressant or stimulant, or including ingredients that cause cancer. Another example of a harmful rumor is information suggesting that a firm is owned or influenced by an unfriendly or misguided foreign country, governmental agency, or religious cult.

The Internet is a prolific ground for spreading negative rumors. Digital technologies now enable disgruntled consumers to reach millions of people easily and describe their often-exaggerated negative experiences with products and services. Consider a disgruntled airline passenger, an unhappy retail customer, or even a student unhappy with a professor—all of whom can post their stories and opinions online for all to see and respond to. When two brothers in New York City found that Apple was charging $200 to replace a failed battery, they set up ipodsdirtysecret.com. Consumers critical of Starbucks can vent their anger at ihatestarbucks.com; in fact, there are hundreds of ihate.com websites.

Compared with positive or even neutral comments, negative comments are relatively uncommon. For this reason, consumers are especially likely to notice negative information and avoid the products or brands subjected to such criticism. In the entertainment sector, many films, musicals, and plays have quickly floundered because of negative buzz, as have quite a few newly introduced food products. Consumers, it turns out, share negative experiences with others much more readily than positive ones.

Marketers refer to persistent spreaders of negative word-of-mouth online as "determined detractors." Perhaps the best known determined detractor is the person who ate nothing but McDonald's food for 30 days and produced an extremely critical documentary about the experience, entitled Super Size Me. Furthermore, disgruntled buyers can reach very large audiences by posting exaggerated and overly dramatic clips featuring negative product and service encounters on YouTube. One study discovered that some consumers who posted unfavorable information wanted to vent negative feelings or warn others. Others sought exposure, self-enhancement, social benefits, and even economic rewards.[41]

Diffusion of Innovations: Segmenting by Adopter Categories

Learning Objective

5   To understand the process for diffusion of innovations, and adopter categories as distinct market segments.

Over time, positive word-of-mouth leads to the widespread adoption of products that fulfill needs, work well, are clearly differentiated, and provide value. However, not all consumers adopt new products or new versions of existing products simultaneously. The concept of **adopter categories** is a classification that depicts where consumers stand in relation to other consumers in terms of the first time they purchase an innovation (e.g., a new product or model). This classification, which was developed by sociologists who conceived a theory entitled the Diffusion of Innovations, consists of five categories of adopters: Innovators, early adopters, early majority, late majority, and laggards. In marketing terms, each category represents a distinct market segment, so marketers must study each group in order to target it effectively.

Because the adopter categories model was developed by sociologists, applying it to consumer behavior is not straightforward. Sociologically, the model assumes that *all* members of a given society would, eventually, adopt the innovation. Thus, the number of people belonging to each category was calculated in a manner resembling a statistical normal distribution: Innovators—the first 2.5% to adopt; Early adopters—the next 13.5%; Early majority—the next 34%; Late majority—the following 34%; and the Laggards—the last 15%.

However, marketers cannot assume that, for example, every consumer will eventually buy an e-book reader. Therefore, they define "society" as everyone assumed to be in the market for the product shortly, or at some future time, after the introduction of an innovation. Marketers generally define innovators as approximately the first 10% of the total potential adopters of a particular product. This figure stems from historical data collected from various industries where product innovations are common. Then, marketers estimate the percentages of consumers belonging to the remaining adopter categories. Figure 9.7 uses e-book readers to demonstrate the original diffusion of innovations model. The characteristics of each adopter category are described next.

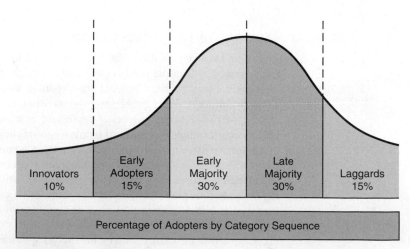

FIGURE 9.7 Hypothetical Adopter Categories of e-Book Readers

Innovators

The **innovators** are the earliest consumers to buy new products. They are prepared to take the risk that the product will not work well, become unavailable, or be quickly replaced by an improved model (i.e., they are broad categorizers). They are often willing to pay somewhat higher prices for newly introduced products, because they enjoy being the first to own gadgets and show them off. When targeting innovators, ads should show them using new products conspicuously and being noticed and even asked questions by others (e.g., "Where did you get that?" "Do you like it?" "I have an older model, do you think I should switch to the one you are using?"). Many innovators like to shop with others; Table 9.7 details typical shopping patterns of fashion innovators.

Early Adopters

The **early adopters** are consumers who buy new products within a relatively short period following introduction, but not as early as the innovators. They are venturesome, likely to engage in word-of-mouth, and also likely to assist others who are considering adopting the new products. Ads targeting members of this segment should show them praising the new products.

Early Majority

The **early majority** consists of consumers who buy innovations after the early adopters have done so. This segment is larger than the preceding two groups combined. For example, when a new model of an e-reader was introduced, they waited for prices to decline and, after quite a few people purchased it (and its price declined), they decided to buy the new model. The ads targeting members of this group should assure them that the product has been successful and provide them with purchase incentives.

Risk aversion is defined as the reluctance to take risks and low tolerance of ambiguous situations, as illustrated by the consumption-related characteristics of risk-averse consumers in Table 9.8. Members of the early majority are somewhat risk averse, whereas the late majority and laggards are highly risk-averse consumers.

TABLE 9.7	Shopping Activities of Fashion Innovators

1. They are the first in their circles to know who are the latest "hot" designers and emerging fashion trends.
2. They shop much more for new fashions than their friends.
3. They are among the first in their circles to buy new outfits and fashions.
4. They know more about fashion than most people.
5. If they find out that new clothing is available in stores, they check them out.
6. They like to touch clothing and other products in stores for fun, even if they do not intend to buy them.
7. They are reluctant to buy clothes that they cannot touch.
8. They feel more confident about buying clothing and other products after touching them and examining them physically.

TABLE 9.8	Characteristics of Risk-Averse Consumers

1. They always read and follow the manufacturers' warnings about removing products' tags and back plates and use products exactly as instructed by manufacturers.
2. When it comes to medications (including over-the-counter products), they always obey the instructions on how to take the medicines and carefully read the restrictions and potential side effects.
3. They feel reluctant to buy products that they have never used before.
4. If products come in assembled or unassembled forms, they buy the assembled versions even if these are a bit more expensive.
5. They do not improvise when they cook and follow recipes fully.

Late Majority

Members of the **late majority** are risk averse and slow to adopt innovation. They wait until most other consumers have adopted the new product before buying it. When they finally buy their first e-readers, they are likely to buy older models, which marketers sell at lower prices, and alway look for extensive guarantees. If these consumers are happy with their initial purchases, they are likely to become members of the early majority and likely to buy newly introduced e-readers.

Laggards

The **laggards** are the very last consumers to adopt innovations. By the time they get around to purchasing their first e-readers, the innovators and early adopters have already switched to the most advanced models. Laggards are high-risk perceivers and the last ones to recognize the value of innovative products.

Non-Adopters

Marketers often "write off" non-adopters, but not all non-adopters are the same, and understanding nonusers is important. For instance, one study found two distinct segments among non-adopters of Internet banking:

1. *Prospective adopters,* who could potentially become customers.
2. *Persistent non-adopters,* who are very unlikely to become customers.

The study suggested that online banks should identify prospective customers among nonusers rather than lump all nonusers into a single category.[42]

Summary

Learning Objective 1: To understand the credibility of reference groups and their influence on consumer behavior.

Within any setting, including consumer behavior, people are strongly influenced by how others think and behave. Reference groups are groups that serve as sources of comparison, influence, and norms for people's opinions, values, and behaviors. Word-of-mouth consists of communications where satisfied customers tell other people how much they like a business, product, service, or event, although word-of-mouth can also be negative.

The perceived honesty, objectivity, expertise, and trustworthiness of reference groups make them highly credible sources. Consumers perceive people whom they know personally as more credible than paid-for promotional messages. People learn norms and values mostly from families and peers. They also imitate and adopt the values and habits of persons whom they respect or admire. The groups to which people belong, as well as groups that they aspire to join, influence their norms and behaviors. Consumption-related groups also influence consumers' attitudes and behavior. Sociocultural groups that determine people's behavior, norms, morals, and consumption patterns include family, social class, culture, subculture, and (for global consumers) cross-culture.

Learning Objective 2: To understand the persuasive power and credibility of spokespersons, endorsers, celebrities, salespersons, vendors, and media.

The perceived credibility of spokespersons, endorsers, and other sources that companies use in their advertising is the key to the ads' effectiveness. The spokesperson can be an actual customer, a company employee, a celebrity, or a model. Companies also convey their credibility through solid past performance, good reputation, high product quality, and good service. Their perceived credibility is also a function of the image and reputation of the retailers that carry their offerings and the media where they advertise. Marketers employ celebrities for product testimonials and endorsements, as well as spokespersons and actors in commercials.

Over time, consumers disassociate messages from their sources; they tend to remember only the messages' contents, but not their sources. Therefore, marketers must regularly repeat messages that feature high-credibility spokespersons in order to maintain the messages' persuasiveness.

Learning Objective 3: To understand the dynamics and measurement of opinion leadership and word-of-mouth.

Opinion leadership is the process by which one person—the opinion leader—informally influences others, who might be either opinion seekers or recipients. This influence occurs between two or more people, neither of whom represents a commercial seller nor would gain directly from providing advice or information. Opinion leaders who have expertise in a given product category provide advice and influence the consumption of others within the same category. They also follow any new items introduced closely, and are the first to buy new items. They tend to be self-confident, outgoing, and sociable. Several research methods are aimed at identifying opinion leaders.

Learning Objective 4: To understand the strategic applications, advantages, and potential perils of word-of-mouth.

Electronic word-of-mouth takes place online and occurs in social networks, brand communities, blogs, chat rooms, and tweets. Marketers hire buzz agents and initiate viral marketing to stimulate word-of-mouth in cyberspace. Buzz agents are consumers who promote products clandestinely and generally receive free product samples but not monetary payments. Viral marketing is a marketing technique that uses pre-existing social networks and other technologies to produce increases in brand awareness or to achieve other marketing objectives through encouraging individuals to pass along email messages or other contents online.

It is impossible to control word-of-mouth communications. Negative comments, frequently in the form of untrue rumors, can sweep through the marketplace and undermine a product. The Internet is a prolific ground for spreading negative rumors because disgruntled consumers can reach millions of people easily and exaggerate (or even lie about) their negative experiences with products and services.

Learning Objective 5: To understand the process for diffusion of innovations, and adopter categories as distinct market segments.

Over time, positive word-of-mouth leads to the widespread adoption of products. However, not all consumers adopt new products or new versions of existing products simultaneously. Sociologists who studied how innovations are adopted within societies identified five categories of adopters: Innovators, early adopters, early majority, late majority, and laggards. The concept of adopter categories is a classification scheme that depicts where consumers stand in relation to other consumers in terms of the first time they purchase an innovation (e.g., a new product). Each category represents a distinct market segment, so marketers must study each group in order to target it effectively.

Review and Discussion Questions

9.1. Why is an opinion leader a more credible source of product information than an advertisement for the product? Are there any circumstances in which information from advertisements is likely to be more influential than word-of-mouth?

9.2. What are reference groups? List and discuss at least four groups that influence your purchases. For each group, indicate whether its influence is comparative or normative (or, possibly, both) and explain your answers.

9.3. What is the difference between membership groups and symbolic groups? List one membership group and one symbolic group that influence your purchases. Explain which group influences you more and why.

9.4. How can companies strategically use buzz agents and viral marketing? Illustrate with examples.

9.5. Compare the advantages and disadvantages of the methods of measuring opinion leadership.

9.6. How can marketers use social networks, brand communities, and weblogs to locate new customers and target them?

9.7. List and discuss the factors that affect the credibility of formal communications sources of product information. What factors influence the perceived credibility of informal communications sources?

9.8. You are the marketing vice president of a large soft-drink company. Your company's advertising agency is in the process of negotiating a contract to employ a superstar female singer to promote its product. Discuss the reference group factors that you would consider before the celebrity is hired.

9.9. What are the implications of the sleeper effect for the selection of spokespersons and the scheduling of advertising messages?

9.10. Amazon has introduced a new e-book reader that is more expensive than previous models but has many more features. How can the company use the adopter categories in marketing this product?

Hands-on Assignments

9.11. With a paper and pencil, spend one hour watching a network television channel during prime time. Record the total number of commercials that aired. For each commercial that used a celebrity endorser, record the celebrity's name, the product or service advertised, and whether the celebrity was used in a testimonial, as an endorser, as an actor, or as a spokesperson.

9.12. Describe two situations in which you served as an opinion leader and two situations in which you sought consumption-related advice or information from an opinion leader. Indicate your relationship to the persons with whom you interacted. Are the circumstances during which you engaged

in word-of-mouth communications consistent with those described in the text? Explain.

9.13. Find ads that encourage consumers to engage in word-of-mouth communications.

9.14. Prepare a list of negative rumors that you (or your friends) have heard recently about a company or a product.

9.15. Locate an online company that recruits buzz agents and register as one. Keep a diary of all your contacts with the organization for about one month. Summarize the diary and discuss whether the company was right to make you a buzz agent and explain why or why not.

Key Terms

- adopter categories *252*
- advergames *250*
- blog *249*
- brand community *249*
- buzz agent *251*
- celebrity actor *243*
- celebrity endorsement *243*
- celebrity spokesperson *243*
- celebrity testimonial *243*
- comparative influence *236*
- consumer socialization *234*
- culture *234*

Case Four:

Keystone Light/MillerCoors
"Canhole"

Lead Agency: **Leo Burnett/Arc Worldwide**

Strategic Challenges

Summer is the season for beer: Billions of dollars are up for grabs; the competition for floor space, incremental displays, and "customer activation" is intense and hotly contested.

The big dogs rule: Miller Lite, Coors Light, Bud Light, Budweiser, and Corona rule the summer months, which makes it difficult for smaller, below-premium brands such as Keystone Light to get any attention from distributors or retailers. Typically, Keystone Light can only place statics stickers on in-store coolers to plead its case to shoppers.

Pricing challenges made it more difficult: Beer companies, including MillerCoors, have raised the price of the below-premium segment (closing the price gap) in an effort to get drinkers to trade up to the pricier premium brands—which is the companies' priority and vital to overall performance. However, this pricing strategy couldn't have happened at a worse time for Keystone Light. Its target consumers were being hit hard by the sagging economy and were looking for even more value while still trying to get out and have some summer fun with their buddies.

The overall challenge: In the sea of big-name brands during the summer, how does the company give a smaller, below-premium beer a reason to be featured at retail?

Objectives

1. **Stave off decline of the Keystone Light business in the convenience store channel** by stealing share, volume, and display opportunities from the company's key competitor: Anheuser-Busch's below-premium powerhouse, Natural Light.
2. **Increase overall Keystone Light brand engagement** to help establish a purpose and personality for Keystone Light's new brand character (Keith Stone), in order to increase interaction, acceptance, and sharing by consumers.

Insights

The company's target was a simple guy with simple needs, which was named "The Cruiser." He doesn't have a lot of money, so he's learned to be resourceful and inventive with things he has on hand in order to have a good time.

For him, a great meal is a frozen burrito, a bag of Doritos, and a warm hot dog right off the roller. He enjoys the occasional fart joke and ribbing his buddy because his sister can kick his butt at Halo (with one hand tied behind her back). He's comfortable with who he is and values friendship over all else. He has also built a fair number of beer pyramids in his day.

Once the company understood the Cruiser and how he behaves, it needed to know what he does during the summer. Using a combination of quantitative and qualitative research, the company discovered that the Cruiser's summer is all about "Bro-ments." He gets together with more friends, more often, during the summer. The Cruiser values impromptu, memorable experiences that are the outcome of ingenuity and inventive social occasions. In other words, he likes spending time with his buddies, telling jokes, and not acting his age—all while drinking beer. This is basic male bonding stuff termed "Bro-ments."

The Big Idea

Bro-ments in a Box

Questions

1. In order to give the Cruiser an incentive that appealed to his fun-loving ingenuity and inventiveness, every time he bought a pack of Keystone Light, he got a completely self-contained Cornhole game. The Cruiser had to punch out the perforated hole designed into the box and use his crushed empty cans of Keystone Light as "bags" during hours of summer party and sport Bro-ments with his buddies. The company named this fun activity "CANHOLE." How would this promotion help achieve any of the company's objectives?

2. How can Cruisers use Canhole to connect with others on the Internet and social networks? How can the company encourage the Cruisers to do so? How does Maslow's Hierarchy of needs applicable to this situation?

3. Apply the concept of product involvement to the Canhole promotion and the second objective.

4. Suggest "cross merchandising" opportunities for Canhole. That is, getting marketers of products that Cruisers might consume during Canhole games to participate in the promotion. Explain your choices.

5. List and discuss three likely personality traits of the Cruiser.

6. Develop a psychographic profile of the Cruiser.

7. Looking at the PRIZM groups' descriptions online, select three segments that are likely to include a large number of Cruisers. Explain your choices.

Source: Effie Worldwide, Effie Showcase Winners. Reprinted by permission. Keystone Light is a 2012 Silver Effie Winner. For information on Effie's programs for students, visit the Collegiate Effies at www.effie.org

The Family and Its Social Standing

Learning Objectives

1   To understand the family as a consumer socialization agent.

2   To understand family decision-making and its members' consumption-related roles.

3   To understand the role of the family life cycle in market segmentation and targeting.

4   To understand the consumption patterns of nontraditional families and non-family households.

5   To understand the impact of social stratification on consumer behavior.

6   To understand how to measure social class and segment consumers accordingly.

7   To understand the demographics, lifestyles, and consumption patterns of America's social classes.

8   To understand how to employ geo-demographics to locate target markets.

THIS CHAPTER describes two **reference groups** that have a powerful impact on consumer behavior: Family and social class. A **family** is defined as two or more persons related by blood, marriage, or adoption residing together. In Western societies, there are three types of families: Married couples, nuclear families, and extended families. A married couple and one or more children constitute a **nuclear family**. The nuclear family, together with at least one grandparent or other relation living within the household, is called an **extended family**.

The **family life cycle** is a composite variable that combines marital status, size of family, age of family members (focusing on the age of the oldest or youngest child), and employment status of the head of household, and then classifies the family into a "typical" stage. The four ads in Figure 10.1 feature Toyota models catering to different types of families. The Toyota Auris hatchback model is a sporty car. It features a "diffuser," with reflectors on each side, which gives it a stylish look. The Yaris subcompact is promoted as a car on which one can get a "great deal." The Verso is a seven-seater family car featuring elegant style and comfort. The Avensis is available as a sedan or wagon and features a refined design and touch-screen multimedia.

Each car model appeals to a different stage of the family life cycle. The sporty Auris is for bachelors or newly married couples who have no children and want to enjoy their new life together. As evident in the ad for the Yaris, a child is on the way. The young couple probably feels anxious about their finances (maybe because the mother has quit her job) and are therefore seeking a car at a reasonable price. Next, the couple

Source: Andreas Ackerup, Saarti Sweden

(a) Bachelors or Honeymooners: Toyota Auris

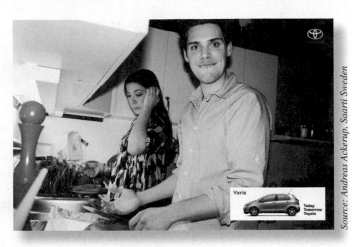

Source: Andreas Ackerup, Saarti Sweden

(b) Newlyweds: Toyota Yaris

Source: Andreas Ackerup, Saarti Sweden

(c) Married with Small Children: Toyota Verso

Source: Andreas Ackerup, Saarti Sweden

(d) Large Family: Toyota Avensis

FIGURE 10.1 Toyota's Models Target Different Stages of the Family Life Cycle

has two young kids and, presumably, more financial re-sources (e.g., the father had advanced in his career and the mother might have gone back to work) and are likely to purchase the Verso—a stylish family car. Moving forward, the kids are growing up and thus (as with all young kids) must be in front of a screen at all times. Assuming that the couple's disposable income went up (e.g., dual income), it's time for the Avensis, with its stylish design and built-in multimedia gear.

The first part of this chapter describes the influence of the family on its members' development as consumers, as well as how the family functions as a consumption unit and the dynamics of family decision-making. We explore households that fit into the family life cycle, as well as atypical and non-family living situations.

Each household, whether family or non-family, belongs to a social class. **Social class** is the division of members of a society into a hierarchy of distinct status classes, in which members of a class have relatively the same status and members of the other classes have either more or less status. The second part of this chapter examines the demographics and consumption patterns of America's social classes. It describes how to measure social class and segment and target consumers according to social standing. The chapter concludes with examples of how social-class membership affects consumption habits, tastes, and values.

The Family as a Socialization Agent

Socialization refers to the process of teaching people behave in a way that is acceptable to their society. In the context of marketing, the most important role of the family is the socialization of family members, ranging from young children to adults. This process includes imparting to children the basic values and modes of behavior consistent with their culture, including moral principles, interpersonal skills, dress and grooming standards, appropriate manners and speech, and the selection of suitable educational and occupational or career goals.

Parental socialization responsibilities have been expanding because it has become increasingly harder for young adults to find good jobs. Parents thus feel that their children must be ahead of others from a very young age—a competitive pressure that often results in demanding daily schedules for many children (e.g., daily preschool classes, after-school classes, play dates, weekend enrichment, and sports and arts programs). Some have argued that the barrage of structured activities and constant exposure to mass media and online social networks provide children with very little time to explore their own creativity.[1] Nevertheless, the socialization of young children provides marketers with opportunities to establish relationships between children and brands very early in the children's lives. Very often, such connections extend into a person's adolescence, teenage years, and adulthood. The ad for Listerine Smart Rinse in Figure 10.2 is an example of a marketer's initiative to establish a bond between a brand and very young children.

The aspect of childhood socialization that is particularly relevant to the study of consumer behavior is **consumer socialization**, which is defined as the process by which children acquire the skills, knowledge, attitudes, and experiences necessary to function as consumers. Numerous studies have researched how children develop consumption skills. Many preadolescent children acquire their consumer behavior norms by observing their parents and older siblings, who function as role models and provide cues for learning consumption skills. Studies indicate that young children perceive their families as more reliable sources of information about consumption than advertising; however, peers have the most influence on teenagers' and adolescents' consumption.[2] Research has also shown that younger children react positively to advertisements employing spokespersons featured in parental roles, whereas teens often like products specifically because their parents disapprove of their purchases.[3] Figure 10.3 illustrates the sources that influence children's socialization over time and indicates that socialization is a two-way process. The two-directional arrows indicate that a young person is both socialized and influences those who are doing the socializing.

The **socialization agent** is the person or organization involved in the socialization process because of frequency of contact with the individual and control over the rewards and punishments given to the individual.[4] Mothers are stronger consumer socialization agents than fathers because mothers are usually more involved with their children and often control their children's exposure to commercial messages. Additionally, mothers most often provide instruction in the skills needed to become consumers and regulate the amount of money children can spend and how they spend it.

The ad for Mott's juice in Figure 10.4 depicts a mother as a socialization agent who is teaching her children that juices with less sugar are healthier. Researchers identified distinct socialization styles among mothers, based on mothers' attitudes toward marketing, which are described in Table 10.1.[5]

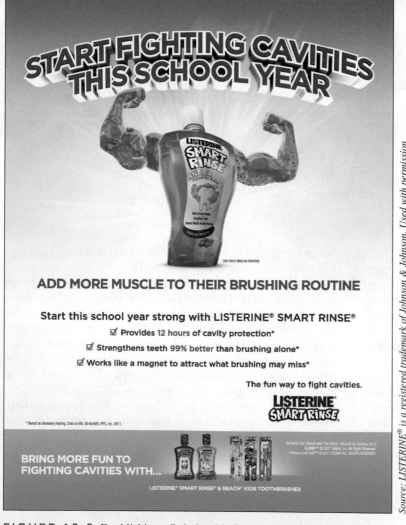

Source: LISTERINE® is a registered trademark of Johnson & Johnson. Used with permission

FIGURE 10.2 Establishing a Relationship Between Children and a Brand

FIGURE 10.3
Socialization Sources

FIGURE 10.4
Socialization Agent

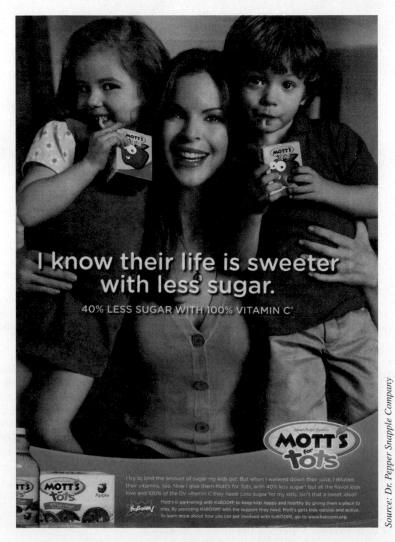

TABLE 10.1 Mothers' Socialization-Related Attitudes	
MARKETING RECEPTIVE	**MARKETING RESISTANT**
The Balancer: Married and has a career. Multitasks and teaches her children how to become good consumers. Lets children learn from experience and make buying mistakes.	The Protector: Highest income and education among all the segments. Rational and teaches her children to shop and spend responsibly. Resents the influence of the media on her children.
The Nurturer: Focused on her family and often sacrifices her own desires to meet the wants of her children. Trusts well-known companies and brands.	The Struggler: Does not have the money to indulge her children's requests. Very price- and value-conscious shopper. Views her life negatively.
The Diva: Self-focused and seeks acceptance and attention from others; is a conspicuous consumer. Views her children as a part of her image, and often gives in to children's requests to make her life easier.	The Stoic: Culturally and socially isolated. Views herself as a caretaker and homemaker. Loves her children but feels emotionally distanced from them. Deliberates regarding purchases.

There is no universal model of how children develop their consumption skills; learn to understand the role of advertising in the formation of buying preferences; and master the relationship between monetary resources, value, and limits on buying. Next, we describe three aspects of consumer socialization.

Parental Styles and Consumer Socialization

Several decades ago, sociologists began to study the impact of parental styles on children's development, and later on marketers applied those findings to consumer socialization. Figure 10.5 features a classification of parental stules along two dimensions: *permissive* versus *restrictive* and *very nurturing* versus *non-nurturing*. The table identifies four parental styles and lists their respective attitudes toward advertising, consumption, and yielding to children's buying requests. The four parental styles include: **indulgent parents**, who are very nurturing and highly permissive during consumer socialization; **neglecting parents**, who are very permissive, but provide their children with little or no nurturing during consumer socialization; **authoritative parents**, who are very nurturing and also very restrictive with respect to consumer socialization; and lastly, **authoritarian parents**, who are very restrictive and not nurturing during consumer socialization.

FIGURE 10.5 Parental Styles and Consumer Socialization

Consumer Socialization Is Learning

Children learn the importance of possessions at an early age, as demonstrated by a child seeing a commercial for a doll or action figure on television, pointing to the screen, and shouting "I want that!" A study conducted with school-aged children in Minnesota found that materialism increases from middle childhood (ages 8–9) to early adolescence (ages 12–13), and then declines from early to late adolescence (ages 16–18). The research also found an inverse relationship between self-esteem and materialism in children and adolescents (i.e., children with high self-esteem are more likely to express lower levels of materialism, and vice versa).[6] Furthermore, the study noted that rather than blaming the media for the materialism exhibited by children and adolescents, finding ways to increase their self-esteem is a more positive approach. Another study found that adolescents use ridicule as a mechanism to exchange information about what should and should not be consumed and valued; ridicule is also a form of ostracizing peers who shop unlike most do.[7] A Canadian study of college students (with the majority being full-time students, and 85% living at home with parents) indicated that older college students were influenced by their parents, and less influenced by their peers and media.[8] The study also found that older college students were more competent consumers than their younger counterparts.

The model in Table 10.2 details stages that children go through in learning to function as consumers, and identifies their sources of information at each stage.

Adult and Intergenerational Consumer Socialization

The socialization process is ongoing, beginning in early childhood and extending throughout a person's life. After childhood, as teenagers and adolescents, young consumers continue learning about consumption and many become skeptical about some aspects of marketing. One study found that more socially affluent adolescents were less skeptical of advertising than their less affluent peers. Lower socioeconomic status adolescents, having less money than their wealthier peers, were more critical of advertising claims. Additionally, the study found that Internet usage was negatively related to skepticism, possibly because Internet surfers can skip ads and only visit websites that interest them.[9]

When newly married people establish their own households, adjusting to consuming as a couple is the continuation of socialization. Similarly, the adjustment of a soon-to-be-retired couple, perhaps moving to a warmer climate, is also part of ongoing socialization. Even a family that is welcoming a pet into its home faces the challenge of socializing the pet so that it fits into the family environment. Research found that pet owners treat their pets as full-fledged family members. For instance, 58% of those surveyed indicated that they have sent or received a holiday card from their dogs or cats, and 78% regularly talked in different voices ("I wuv you") to their pets and referred to them as family members.[10]

TABLE 10.2	Children's Development as Consumers	
STAGE	MEDIAN AGE	DESCRIPTION
Shopping with parents and observing	12 to 15 months	Children notice all the items that are fun to eat and play with and begin to recall specific ones. They learn how shopping satisfies needs. Parents may buy some items to reward children for good behavior.
Making requests while shopping with parents	2 years	By age 2, children begin to connect advertising with items in the stores and delight parents with their cognitive development. They request items–mostly foods and toys–by pointing. Children also begin to pay more attention to advertising and some insist on watching more TV.
Selecting with permission while shopping with parents	3 1/2 years	Children are climbing off shopping carts and walking besides parents. They recognize most brands of cereal, snacks, ice cream and frozen deserts and know their locations. Many have favorite brands and even stores, and parents begin to select brands and items that their children prefer.
Independent purchases while shopping with parent	5 1/2 years	A child's first independent purchase is likely to be in a supermarket, convenience or department store. Children begin to understand the limits of monetary resources and some may feel frustrated when denied items because they are too expensive or do not represent good value.
Shopping independently	8 years	Parents gradually, and often reluctantly, begin to allow children to go to stores alone. The first independent trip is likely to be to a convenience store. Children discover the wonders of shopping and having to decide among many choices.

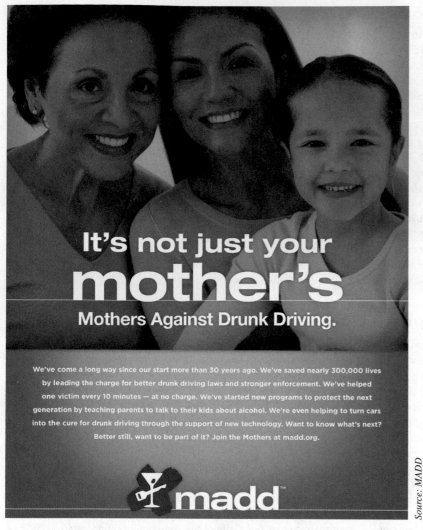

Source: MADD

FIGURE 10.6 Intergenerational Socialization

Many product preferences and brand loyalties are transferred from one generation to another, sometimes across three or four generations.[11] For instance, in the U.S. brand preferences for products such as peanut butter, mayonnaise, ketchup, coffee, and canned soup are frequently passed on from one generation to another. In some families—like Asian households—grandparents not only play an important role in teaching younger members consumption-related skills, but also participate in all major consumption decisions. Very often, Asian grandparents live with their children and grandchildren. The ad in Figure 10.6 illustrates an "intergenerational transfer" of values regarding safe driving.

The Family's Supportive Roles

The family has several supportive functions that are part of the socialization process and consumer behavior. These include economic well-being, emotional support, and suitable family lifestyles.

Economic Well-Being

The most important economic function of the family is to provide financial resources to its members and allocate its income in a way that supports all members adequately. The data in Table 10.3 show how an "average" U.S. family spent its money over one year. The largest expenditures were on housing, transportation, food at home, pension and social security, health care, food away from home, and entertainment.[12]

TABLE 10.3	How the "Average" Family Spends Its Money	
EXPENDITURE CATEGORY	DOLLARS	PERCENT
Food at home	3,753	8.1
Food away from home	2,619	5.6
Alcoholic beverages	435	0.1
Housing	16,895	36.3
Apparel and services	1,725	3.7
Transportation	7,658	16.5
Health care	3,126	6.7
Entertainment	2,693	5.8
Reading	110	0.2
Tobacco products	380	0.7
Life and other personal insurance	309	0.8
Pensions and social security	5,471	11.7
Miscellaneous	1,320	2.8
Total of above	46,494	

Source: U.S. Census Bureau, "Average Annual Expenditures of All Consumer Units by Selected Major Types of Expenditures: 1990 to 2009,"Statistical Abstract of the United States: 2012, Table 684. http://www.census.gov/comendia/statab/2012/1250684.pdt. Accessed 6/20/2012

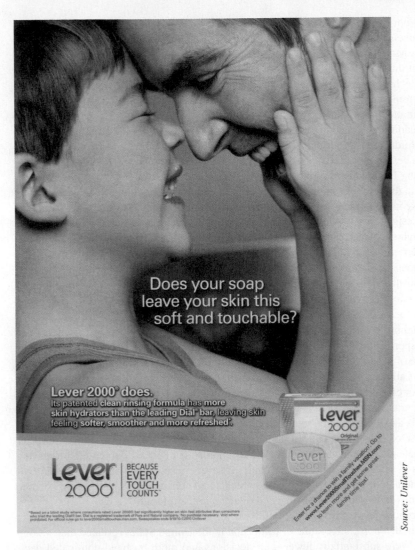

Source: Unilever

FIGURE 10.7 The Family Provides Emotional Support

Emotional Support

A core function of the family is providing its members with love, affection, and intimacy. When most women had no jobs outside the home, children received most of their emotional support from their mothers. However, as more and more women joined the labor force—with some pursuing more demanding and lucrative careers than their husbands—men have played an increasingly important role in rearing children. If the family cannot provide adequate assistance when it is needed, it may turn to a counselor, psychologist, or other professionals. In most communities, there are educational and psychological centers designed to assist parents who want to help their children improve their learning and communication skills or better adjust to their environments. The Lever soap ad in Figure 10.7 shows how the family provides emotional support.

Suitable Family Lifestyles

What people view as a "suitable" lifestyle reflects their experiences while growing up. Their parents' priorities regarding learning and education, recreational activities, hobbies, setting of career goals, media exposure, and shopping habits are all part of the lifestyle that children imitate, at least to some degree, when they set up their own households. Changing family lifestyles are greatly influencing consumption patterns. For example, the growth of the demand for convenience foods and rising popularity of fast and takeout foods are the result of career moms having little if any time for household chores. With both spouses working, many parents are increasingly aware of the importance of spending quality time with their children.

Family Decision-Making and Consumption-Related Roles

Learning Objective

2 To understand family decision-making and its members' consumption-related roles.

Marketers recognize that families operate as units in terms of consumption behavior, and many researchers have studied the dynamics of family decision-making. Specifically, marketers focus on husband–wife decision-making, the relative influence each family member has regarding consumption, children's role in family decision-making, and the multiple roles that family members may assume regarding the purchase, use, and maintenance of their homes, products and services.

Husband–Wife Decision-Making

Marketers have studied each spouse's relative influence in consumption and identified four patterns of husband–wife decision-making:

1. **Husband-dominated decisions** are those where the husband's influence is greater than the wife's.

2. **Wife-dominated decisions** are those where the wife's influence is greater than the husband's.

3. **Joint decisions** are those where the husband's and wife's influences are equal.

4. **Autonomic decisions** are those where either the husband or the wife is the primary or only decision maker.

The relative influence of a husband and wife on a particular consumer decision depends mainly on the product or service category. For instance, during the 1950s, the purchase of a new automobile was strongly husband-dominated, whereas food and financial banking decisions were often wife-dominated, but these patterns are no longer the case. Some studies indicate that women influenced 85% of all decisions regarding car purchases and bought about 45% of all vehicles sold in the U.S. independently. More than half of female car buyers sought advice from expert sources before buying a new car, spent more time in the purchasing process than men (17 weeks versus 15), and, on average, visited three dealerships, seeking both the best price and polite treatment.[13]

Carmakers and automobile dealers have studied the specific needs of women drivers. For example, GM pays particular attention to details in trim, fabric, colors, compartments, and shapes and positioning of controls. In addition, storage is a big deal to women buyers, whether it's room for groceries, handbags, kids' toys, foldable seats, or car booster seats. Many car manufacturers have considered women's heights in the design of seating and steering columns, as well as designing door handles that women drivers with long fingernails can grab easily. Apparently, both men and women like "aggressive and elegant" lines in the form of "smoothness from one end to the other with no rough edges and a tight, flush design." Like men, women want performance and design, but they also want more features. Examples of features designed with women in mind include inside door handles that are individually illuminated with dim lights, concave consoles with attractive buttons and digital information displays, and entertainment system screens that can be raised and lowered by the push of a button.[14]

Traditionally, women have controlled their families' day-to-day household spending, but men were in charge of major decisions on banking and financial planning. However, one study indicated that British women are now more likely than their husbands to choose banks and make provisions for future savings and spending. The study showed that 91% of households where women were in charge of financial planning had significant savings, but only 82% of households had such savings when men had that responsibility. This was especially true among younger couples; in households with males over the age of 45, men tended to be in charge of money matters. The study predicted that a majority of women of all ages would be in charge of most households' financial decision by 2020. Furthermore, among couples under the age of 45, women were more likely than men to choose the family's bank (52% of households), take control of making detailed future plans for savings (52%), and pay day-to-day bills and keep track of spending (54%). Apparently, women are better savers; the results showed that 37% of single men had no savings, compared to 30% of single women. Greater control of families' finances by women will increase households' savings, as women tend to have a longer-term orientation to saving and also be more cautious savers in selecting where to hold and invest savings. This might also mean that mortgage repayments and consumer spending could become less vulnerable to turmoils in employment or financial markets in the future.[15]

Husband–wife decision-making is related to cultural influence. Research comparing husband–wife decision-making in the People's Republic of China and in the United States revealed that, among Chinese couples, there were substantially fewer joint decisions and more husband-dominated decisions for many household purchases than among American spouses.[16] However, when comparing urban and rural Chinese households, the research showed that in large cities, such as Beijing, married couples were more likely than rural couples to share equally in purchase decisions. Another study compared family decision-making among American and Singaporean families; that study discovered that joint decision-making was characteristic of American families, whereas Singaporean families' decisions were often husband dominant.[17]

Children's Influence on Family Decision-Making

Over the past several decades, children have played a more active role in what the family buys, as well as in the family decision-making process. Children's growing influence is the result of families having fewer children (which increases the influence of each child), the existence of more dual-income couples who can afford to permit their children to make a greater number of the choices, and encouragement by the media to allow children to "express themselves." In addition, single-parent households often push their children toward household participation and self-reliance. For example, kids in supermarkets make an average of 15 requests, of which about half are typically granted.[18]

One study, which included interviews with both parents and their children, focused on the influence of children during family decisions regarding vacations. The researchers pointed out that although children believed that they had a large degree of influence on vacation-related decisions, their parents viewed the children's influence as merely moderate.[19] Another notable study investigated the tactics that children use when they want their parents to buy them something or to "get their way" during family decisions. The study identified the following tactics that children typically use:

1. *Pressure:* The child demands, threatens, and tries to intimidate the parents.
2. *Exchange:* The child promises something (e.g., to "be good" or clean his room) in exchange.

3. *Rational:* The child uses a logical arguments and factual evidence.

4. *Consultation:* The child seeks parents' involvement in the decision.

5. *Ingratiation:* The child tries to get the parent in a good mood first and then make the request.[20]

One study identified a group termed "teen Internet mavens"—teenagers who spend considerable time on the Internet and are very proficient in searching for information and responding to requests from others. The study showed that the mavens believed that they were more influential in researching and evaluating family purchases than their parents, which the parents confirmed.[21]

Children Are Three Markets

An expert on marketing to children pointed out that children should be divided into three separate markets, as described in Table 10.4. Many marketers can apply this framework to targeting different segments of the children's market. For example, when viewing children as influencers, marketers of food products and vacations should depict kids' involvement in these decisions, but must do so in a subtle way and not feature children pressuring their parents to buy products. In addition, recognizing that children form brand preferences early, marketers should show how thankful kids are when their parents buy certain brands.

Measuring Family Decision-Making

Measuring family decision-making is complex, because family members may not agree with each other's perspective about their relative influence during purchase decisions, which also precludes interviewing them together. Nevertheless, Table 10.5 features an instrument designed to measure family decision-making.

Family Members' Roles

Table 10.6 shows another perspective on family decision-making which consists of identifying the roles that members play in buying decisions. For example, many parents are *gatekeepers*, who control the information that reaches the family's children by using the parental control features available on TVs, computers, and other communication devices. As described earlier, *indulgent* and *authoritative* parents are attentive gatekeepers. When targeting these parents, electronics makers should emphasize their products' sophisticated information-control features. Companies selling SUVs should recognize that children might be *influencers* in the family's purchase of a new model, although they are neither the *deciders* nor *buyers* of family cars. Children from dual-income households are often the *deciders*, *buyers*, and *preparers* of foods, so marketers of cuisine goods must study the roles of children in this area of the family's consumption. For example, children should be able to open packaging safely and easily, and understand measurement units and preparation instructions. Because children—in the role of *maintainers*—often perform housekeeping chores by themselves, makers of, say, vacuum cleaners should observe how children use their products and make sure that kids can do so safely.

TABLE 10.4	Children as Three Markets	
ROLE	DESCRIPTION	EXAMPLES
Children as influencers	Children make requests when accompanying parents on shopping trips and also at home.	Items for themselves (toys, electronics, clothing). Items for homes (furniture, food and beverage preferences). Services for the entire family (vacations, restaurants).
Children as a primary market	Children who shop independently while shopping with their parents or buy things with their own money.	The most commonly purchased products are snacks/sweets, toys, games, clothes, movies, sport events, concerts and video games.
Children as future consumers	Children start contemplating future purchases: "When I grow up I will buy myself . . ."	The future consumers are fully aware of brands, and marketers should focus on building relationships with them.

TABLE 10.5 Measure of Family Decision-Making Regarding Vacations

1. About your family and household:

   Two spouses _____

   One spouse or parent _____ Mother _____ Father

   Number of children 12 years old or younger _____

   Do any other adults live in your household? Please specify _____

2. How does your family make vacation-related decisions? The questionnaire below lists the typical decisions that must be made and we ask you to indicate how much influence each member(s) of your family has regarding each one. For example, if the wife is the most influential party in deciding on how to travel to the vacation's destination (e.g., fly or drive), please put a checkmark in the column entitled "wife" and the row entitled "most influential" next to "how to get to the destination" (listed in the first column on the left). Leave any boxes that are not applicable blank (e.g., the household includes no teenagers).

DECISIONS	DEGREE OF INFLUENCE	HUSBAND	WIFE	CHILDREN 12 YEARS OLD OR YOUNGER	TEENAGERS
Whether to go on vacation or not	Most influential				
	Very influential				
	Somewhat influential				
	Least influential				
	No influence at all				
How much to spend on the vacation	Most influential				
	Very influential				
	Somewhat influential				
	Least influential				
	No influence at all				
When to go on vacation	Most influential				
	Very influential				
	Somewhat influential				
	Least influential				
	No influence at all				
Type of vacation (e.g., Disney, national parks, biking, camping)	Most influential				
	Very influential				
	Somewhat influential				
	Least influential				
	No influence at all				
Destination(s)	Most influential				
	Very influential				
	Somewhat influential				
	Least influential				
	No influence at all				
How to get to the destination (e.g., drive or fly)	Most influential				
	Very influential				
	Somewhat influential				
	Least influential				
	No influence at all				

TABLE 10.6	Family Members' Consumption-Related Roles
ROLE	DESCRIPTION
Influencers	Family member(s) who provide information to other members about a product or service.
Gatekeepers	Family member(s) who control the flow of information about products and services into the family.
Deciders	Family member(s) with the power to decide which product to buy and where.
Buyers	Family member(s) who make the actual purchase of a particular product or service
Preparers	Family member(s) who transform the product into a form suitable for consumption by other family members.
Users	Family member(s) who use the service or consume the product.
Maintainers	Family member(s) who service or repair the product so that it continues to function well.
Disposers	Family member(s) who initiate or carry out the disposition of a product or the discontinuation of the service.

The Family Life Cycle

Learning Objective

3 To understand the role of the family life cycle in market segmentation and targeting.

The **family life cycle** represents the life stages of a typical family. It is a composite variable that combines marital status, size of family, age of family members (focusing on the age of the oldest or youngest child), and employment status of the head of household, and then classifies the family into a "typical" stage. The ages of the parents and the relative amount of disposable income are inferred from the family's stage in the cycle. As illustrated in this chapter's opening, Toyota's car models were designed with the family life cycle in mind. Although it is no longer typical of American families, because of the emergence of non-family households and families that cannot be placed into a "typical" phase, the family life cycle remains a widely used form of segmentation, and is also used to analyze the consumption of households that do not fit neatly into it.

The family life cycle starts with bachelorhood and then moves on to marriage (and the creation of the family unit). Marriage usually leads to the growth of the family when children arrive, and later on to family contraction, as grown children leave the household. The cycle ends with the dissolution of the family unit due to the death of one spouse. The stages of the family life cycle are featured in the following sections.

Bachelorhood

The **bachelorhood** stage refers to young single men and women, mostly college educated, who have incomes that allow them to leave home and establish their own households. Increasingly, though, even employed college graduates continue to live at home and save toward setting up their own homes. Single persons spend considerable amounts on clothing, cars, and travel and entertainment. Marketers should differentiate between singles who live at home (with their parents) and those who have left it. The ads in Figures 10.8 and 10.9 target single and affluent women, who can afford expensive furniture and vacations.

Honeymooners

The **honeymooners** stage refers to young and newly married couples. Educated, engaged couples have a combined discretionary income. If both establish career paths, their incomes grow steadily. A spouse going back to graduate school usually calls for curtailing spending and a more moderate lifestyle. People with considerable discretionary incomes are prime targeting prospects. Most couples overspend on their weddings (see the ad in Figure 10.10). Afterward, they are in the market for home furnishings, travel, and financial planning services. Because many young husbands and wives both work, these couples often have a combined income that permits them to purchase more indulgent possessions, as well as save and invest money.

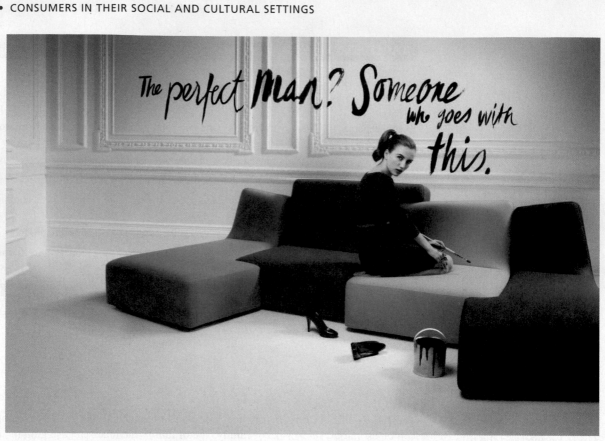

Source: Ligne Roset

FIGURE 10.8 Targeting Women in the Bachelorhood Stage: High-Priced Furniture

FIGURE 10.9

Targeting Women in the Bachelorhood Stage: Exclusive Vacations

Source: RockResorts, LLC.

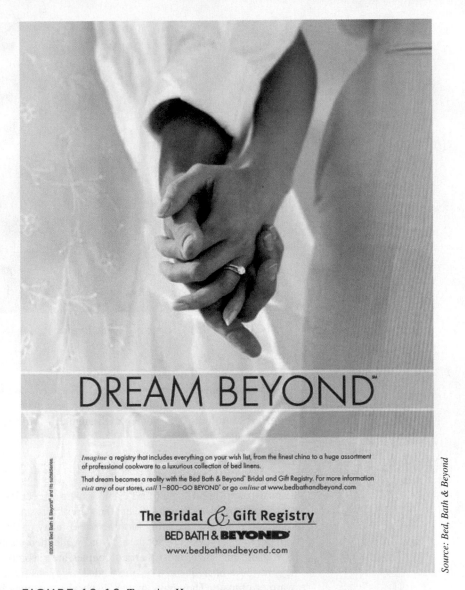

FIGURE 10.10 Targeting Honeymooners

Honeymooners have considerable start-up expenses when establishing a new home. They must find a place to live, buy furniture, and decorate and set up their households. They are the prime targets of marketers in many sectors, and of advisory magazines (e.g., Homes and Gardens), as well as decorators, designers, architects, and financial planners.

Parenthood

The **parenthood** stage designates married couples with at least one child living at home. This is the longest stage of the family life cycle. The ad for toys that help children's cognitive development in Figure 10.11 targets young parents (the ads in Figures 10.4 and 10.7 do the same).

Parenthood (also known as the "full-nest" stage) usually extends over more than a twenty-year period. Because of its long duration, this stage can be divided into shorter phases. The *preschool phase*, *elementary school phase*, *high school phase*, and *college phase*. Throughout these parenthood phases, the interrelationships of family members and the structure of the family gradually change. Furthermore, the financial resources of the family change significantly, as one (or both) parents progress in their careers and as child rearing and educational responsibilities gradually increase and then decrease as children become self-supporting.

Many magazines target parents and children of different ages, either together or separately. For example, there are many special-interest publications, such as Humpty Dumpty, designed for the young child who is just learning to read; Scholastic Magazine, for the elementary school pupil; Boy's

FIGURE 10.11 Targeting Young Parents

Life, for young boys; and American Girl, Seventeen, and Glamour for teen and young adult girls interested in fashion. In addition, a relatively new magazine, Cookie, is targeting the parents in the more than 22 million U.S. homes with annual incomes in excess of $75,000 and children under 10 years of age.[22]

Post-Parenthood

The **post-parenthood** stage refers to older married couples with no children living at home. Because parenthood extends over many years, the start of this stage (also known as "empty nest") is traumatic for some parents and liberating for others. For many parents, this stage represents the opportunity to do all the things they could not do or afford while their children lived home or went to college.

During this stage, most married couples are financially secure and have a lot of leisure time. They travel more frequently, take extended vacations, and are likely to purchase a second home in a warmer climate. They have higher disposable incomes because of savings and investments, and they have fewer expenses (no mortgage or college tuition bills). They look forward to being involved grandparents. Therefore, families in the post-parenthood stage are an important market for luxury goods, new automobiles, expensive furniture, and vacations to faraway places. Chapter 12 discusses postretirement consumer behavior.

Dissolution

The **dissolution** stage refers to the family with one surviving spouse. If the surviving spouse is in good health, is working or has adequate savings, and has supportive family and friends, the adjustment is easier. The surviving spouse (women live longer than men) often tends to follow a more economical lifestyle. Many surviving spouses seek each other out for companionship; others enter into second (or third and even fourth) marriages (Chapter 12 describes the characteristics of older consumers).

Summary of the Family Life Cycle

The traditional family life cycle concept details the types of products and services that a household or family might be most interested in at each stage. In addition, it is also possible to trace how the family life cycle concept affects a single product or service over time. As an example, a qualitative study conducted in Denmark indicates that family life cycle stage influences the experiences that consumers seek during their vacations. For example, less "traditional" vacations when single, such as backpacking through Europe, and more "traditional" vacations when married with a young child, such as a week at a Caribbean island hotel.[23]

Nontraditional Families and Non-Family Households

Learning Objective

4 To understand the consumption patterns of nontraditional families and non-family households.

When targeting segments that do not represent "typical" families or households, marketers must distinguish between two groups:

1. **Nontraditional families**, defined as families that do not readily fit into the family life cycle.
2. **Non-family households**, defined as living situations that are not legally defined as families (e.g., couples who live together but are not married).

The most common nontraditional family forms and non-family households are also described in Table 10.7. At one time, these forms of families and households were relatively rare and marketers ignored them. However, what is considered a "typical" family or household has changed considerably over time. For instance, traditional families represented 81% of all U.S. households in 1970, but only 66% percent in 2010. The number of households consisting of married couples with children under 18 decreased from 40% in 1970 to about 20% in 2010, and the number of "not married, no children" households (i.e., non-family households) rose from almost 19% in 1970 to 34% in 2010.[24] During this same time frame, the percentage of family households without a spouse present rose from 11% to almost 18%, and the number of people living alone grew from 17% in 1970 to almost 27% in 2010. Also, whereas in 1970, 65% of men and 60% of women age 18 and older were married, by 2010 these figures had declined to 53% of men and 50% of women.[25]

Figure 10.12 illustrates the significance of non-family household in the United States. As people get older, many more non-family households emerge, and, because of increased life expectancy, this segment has been growing and marketers must not ignore it. Figure 10.13 shows that, across age groups, there are significantly more women than men living in non-family households, and this ratio becomes even more pronounced as people age.[26]

Consumer Behavior of Nontraditional Families and Households

Several studies have focused on nontraditional families and non-family households. One study discovered that married couples make more purchase decisions separately, whereas cohabitating couples make their decisions together.[27] When households undergo status changes (such as divorce, temporary retirement or job loss, a new person joining the household, or the death of a family

TABLE 10.7   Descriptions of Nontraditional Households

NONTRADITIONAL FAMILIES

Childless couples	Many couples, especially those who delayed marrying in order to advance their careers at a young age, choose not to have children.
Couples who marry in their late 30s and later	Many career-oriented men and women may live together for years and, even if they get married eventually, are likely to have no more than one child.
Divorced single parents	More single-parent families because of high divorce rates.
"Nesters"—Children returning to their parents' homes	Young single-adult children who return home to avoid the expenses of living alone while establishing their careers. Divorced daughters or sons, sometimes with their children, return home to their parents. Frail elderly parents who move in with children. Newlyweds living with in-laws in order to save money before setting up their own households

NON-FAMILY HOUSEHOLDS

Unmarried couples	People who choose to live together with or without children.
Single parents	Women (mostly) or man who choose to adopt children or have their own and raise them without the other biological parent.
Gay couples (married or not)	Several states allow gay marriages and many other recognize domestic partnerships. Many gay couples adopt or have their own children with heterosexuals, who may or may not be involved in rearing the children.

Source: Compiled from data at: U.S. Census Bureau, Census 2010 Summary File 1 counts shown in American Fact Finder. http://www.comsus.gov/prod/cen2010/briefs/c2010 br-14/ Accessed 6/21/12.

member), their consumption patterns and preferences change. Sometimes, these households represent lucrative target markets. For example, divorce often requires that one (or both) of the former spouses find a new residence, buy new furniture, and perhaps find a job. Thus, divorced people are likely to contact real estate agents, visit furniture stores, and, sometimes, contact headhunters or seek professional career guidance. In addition, the residences and consumption patterns of newly divorced parents must accommodate the needs of visiting children, whose influence regarding buying may change following a divorce. One study pointed out that children in newly formed single-parent households have greater influence in the choice of the large items and holiday vacations than children from intact families.[28]

Advertising to Nontraditional Households

Targeting consumers like the ones featured in Table 10.7 represents a marketing dilemma. On the one hand, marketers of many products must now acknowledge the existence of segments that consist of nontraditional households. On the other hand, some members of traditional families might react negatively to portrayals of nontraditional households, because of religion and beliefs as to what is or is not "right." Marketers must come up with ads that appeal to both types of households without offending either one. For example, if advertisements for baby food portray only children being reared by young parents, unmarried, single, and older parents might not find them persuasive. However, some young parents rearing children might find ads showing single or divorced parents offensive. Therefore, ads for baby food should focus on the children's happiness, health, and warm relationship with those rearing them and leave the "definition" of the households shown up to the viewers.

An ad that shows two young professional women talking over a beer with the tagline "he likes my kid and he drinks brand X," implies, of course, that the woman speaking is either divorced or has had a child out of wedlock. Although many young and "with it" people are likely to find this ad clever, it might offend more traditional individuals. Over the years, more and more ads have shown

FIGURE 10.12

Number of Family and Non-Family Households by Age (in millions)

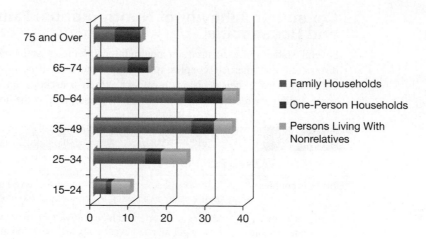

FIGURE 10.13

Number of Non-Family Households: No Spouse Present by Gender, Age, and Household Size (in millions)

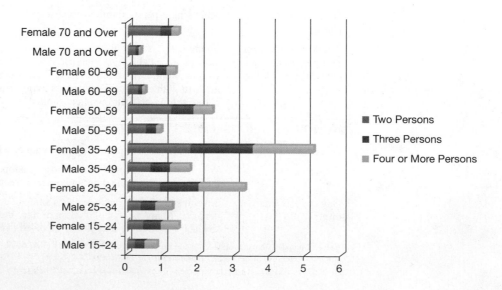

divorced people, single parents, and unmarried and gay couples. On several occasions, conservative groups have publicly criticized such ads and even boycotted the products advertised. Although marketers can no longer ignore lucrative market segments that some might find objectionable, they must design ads that are persuasive but unlikely to be controversial.

Dual Spousal Work Involvement Household Classification System

Figure 10.14 shows a classification system named "dual spousal work involvement," which consists of eight types of households based on combinations of occupations and "career-related motivations." The eight groups shown differ in consumption patterns. For example, dual low-occupation and non-working wife and low-occupation husband households consumed a lot of fast and convenience foods but very few healthy and nutritious items. In contrast, dual, very high-occupation career couples consumed many healthful items and few convenience foods.[29]

FIGURE 10.14

Dual Spousal Work Involvement

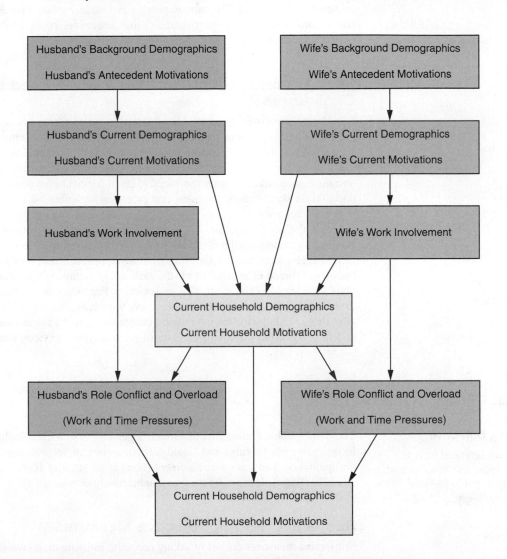

Social Standing and Consumer Behavior

Learning Objective

5 To understand the impact of social stratification on consumer behavior.

Social class is the division of members of a society into a hierarchy of distinct status classes, so that members of each class have relatively the same status and members of all other classes have either more or less status. Some form of class structure (or social stratification) has existed in all societies throughout history. In contemporary societies, people who are better educated or have prestigious occupations have more status relative to other members of the same society. Belonging to a given social class also reflects the differences in the values, attitudes, and behaviors (including consumer behavior) among members of the different social classes. Social class is a continuum along which society's members—usually as households—are placed into one stratum; that is, "assigned" to a social class according to their relative prestige within that society.

Social Class and Social Status

Social class stems from **social status**, which is the degree of prestige the members of one social class have in comparison with members of other social classes. Status is composed of several factors, including *wealth* (amount of economic assets), *power* (the degree of influence over others), and the amount of *esteem* one receives from others.

According to social comparison theory, individuals compare their own material possessions with those owned by others in order to determine their relative social standing. This is especially apparent in a materialistic society, where status is often associated with consumers' purchasing power. Thus, people with more purchasing power (and more possessions) have more status and those with less money have less status. The more expensive and exclusive one's possessions are, the more status one has. In addition, two other demographics that determine social standing are occupational status and educational attainment.

Social Class Is Hierarchical and Often Used to Segment Consumers

Social-class categories are ranked in a hierarchy, ranging from low to high status. Members of a specific social class perceive members of other social classes as having either more or less status than they do. When it comes to consumption, people look for cues indicating that others are either equal to them (about the same social class), superior to them (higher social class), or inferior to them (lower social class). Marketers often use social class to segment consumers, because members of the same social class share values, attitudes, and priorities regarding all the aspects of their lives, including consumer behavior.

Social-class hierarchies are reflected in consumption patterns. Consumers purchase certain products because these products are favored by members of either their own or a higher social class (e.g., a high-priced Swiss wristwatch), but avoid products that they perceive as "lower-class" (e.g., a "no-name" brand of sneaker or off-the-rack suits). Relationships between product usage and social-class membership exist in all Western societies. For example, Germans perceive instant coffee as an upscale product, whereas French consumers view it as a downscale product.[30] Many studies discovered that social class often determined consumer attitudes toward adopting certain products or not, and strongly influenced their purchases of product types, services, and brands.

Measuring Social Class

Learning Objective

6   To understand how to measure social class and segment consumers accordingly.

The demographic factors that determine a person's social class include income (usually household income), wealth (savings and liquid assets), source of income or wealth (inherited or self-made), occupation, and educational attainment (number of years of formal education or the highest degree attained). Social class can be measured subjectively or objectively.

Subjective versus Objective Measures

Subjective measures consist of asking people to estimate their own social class. A typical subjective measure consists of the following question:

"Which of the following four categories best describes your social class: Lower class, lower-middle class, upper-middle class, or upper class?"

Lower class	[ ]
Lower-middle class	[ ]
Upper-middle class	[ ]
Upper class	[ ]
Do not know/no answer	[ ]

When researchers use subjective measures of social class, many people identify themselves, often incorrectly, as belonging to the middle class. In fact, most people, both in the United States and other countries and cultures, tend to classify themselves in the middle strata. For example, every year in Japan, a "Life of the Nation" survey asks citizens to place themselves into one of five social-class categories: upper, upper-middle, middle-middle, lower-middle, and lower class. Whereas in the late 1950s more than 70% of respondents placed themselves in one of the three middle-class categories, this percentage has increased, and in more recent surveys about 90% categorized themselves as middle class.[31]

Many researchers maintain that responses to subjective measures represent the participants' *self-perceptions* and sense of belonging or *identification* with others, rather than comparisons with others belonging to different social groups. Thus, subjective measures actually reflect one's **social-class consciousness**, defined as a person's level of identification with a given social class.

Objective measures consist of demographic variables and asking respondents factual questions about themselves, their families, or their places of residence. Objective measures of social class include one or more of the following variables: Occupation, amount of income, education, and other related factors (e.g., source of income). These data are often incorporated into geo-demographic clustering, where Zip Code and residence/neighborhood information are employed to locate consumers with certain incomes, levels of education, and other socio-demographic items (see Chapter 2).

Marketers and providers of geo-demographic data rely heavily on socioeconomic data from the U.S. Census Bureau. Social class consists of a person's education, occupation, and income, which are closely correlated variables in almost all households. In measuring a household's social standing, the occupation and education measured are those of the "head of household," as designated by the household's members. After we examine each of the three demographics separately, we discuss several social class indices that combine them.

Occupation

People's occupations reflect their social standing relative to other members of the same society. It is often considered to be the best gauge of social class and status, as is illustrated by the often-asked question "What do you do for a living?" We use the responses to this question to "size up" people upon meeting them for the first time and form our initial impressions. Occupational prestige reflects a society's priorities and morals. For example, within the Judeo-Christian tradition, human life is paramount; hence, in the Western world, medicine and nursing are prestigious occupations. In contrast, the communist system held collectivism in high regard; individualism was considered weak and undesirable. As a result, in the Soviet Union (which finally collapsed in 1992), the medical profession was not a prestigious occupation, and medical standards and facilities were far inferior to Western ones. Under communism, very large, uniform, unattractive, blocky, and mostly gray structures were expressions of the "collective will," and their engineers and builders were highly respected. Hence, under communism, it was easy to become a physician, but only a select few were admitted to engineering schools. In the Western world, it is very difficult to be admitted to medical school and become a physician, because we have great respect for life and health and want to ensure that those who treat us medically are truly skilled and thoroughly educated.

Unlike income or educational attainment, occupational prestige cannot be determined objectively (or numerically). Instead, occupational rankings are based on public opinion as measured by administering surveys to large national samples (sized between 1,000 and 3,000 people). One method of calculating job prestige—named the *ladder of social ranking*—consists of giving respondents index cards with about 100 or so jobs listed on them and asking them to arrange the cards from the most to the least prestigious. Another method consists of questioning respondents directly. For example, the results of the Harris Poll (featured in Figure 10.13) are based on responses to the following question: "*I am going to read off a number of different occupations. For each, would you tell me if you feel it is an occupation of very great prestige, considerable prestige, some prestige, or hardly any prestige at all?*"*

An **occupational prestige ranking** represents society's collective beliefs regarding the occupation's social worth and desirability, as stemming from the knowledge required to attain it (i.e., educational level) and the material rewards that occupants receive (i.e., income). Interestingly, prestige rankings reflect society's historical events and changing economics, as illustrated by the Harris Poll surveys of occupational prestige (2007 is the latest survey available), which are featured in Figure 10.15. As shown, the prestige of firefighters and police and military officers has increased steadily after the 9/11 terrorist attacks and the subsequent engagement of the American military in operations overseas. The prestige of business-related executives has been low, probably because of the insider-trading and accounting scandals of the past decade. Many surveys have

---

* The Harris Poll #86, August 4, 2009 By Regina A. Corso, Director, The Harris Poll, Harris Interactive

FIGURE 10.15

Occuptional Prestige Ranking: Percentage Responding that Occupation Has "Very Great Prestige"

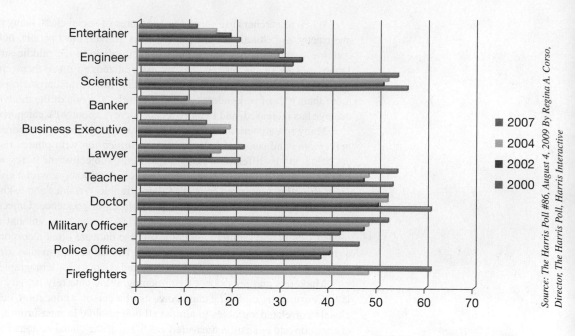

Source: The Harris Poll #86, August 4, 2009 By Regina A. Corso, Director, The Harris Poll, Harris Interactive

shown that the occupational prestige of bankers and stockbrokers continued to plummet following the financial blowup of 2008 and the stagnant economy that followed. The prestige of doctors has steadily increased, despite the continuing debate over medical costs and the emergence of health insurance coverage as the most prominent social problem in the United States. In the Harris Poll study, occupations that more than one-quarter of respondents indicated had "hardly any prestige at all" included stockbrokers, union leaders, real estate brokers, and entertainers.

Another way to gauge an occupational prestige is the degree of ethics and honesty associated with it. As principles for our behavior, ethics and honesty are the most important behavioral guidelines within our culture. The Golden Rule, originating in biblical times and mandating that you "treat others as you would like others to treat you,"; George Washington's statement that "I cannot tell a lie"; and President Lincoln's fame as "Honest Abe" have been part of every child's education in the U.S., and personal honesty is regarded as a virtue. The Gallup Poll has continuously measured Americans' perceptions of the honesty and ethics associated with popular occupations by using the following question: *"Please tell me how you would rate the honesty and ethical standards of people in these fields—very high, high, average, low, or very low?"** The professions perceived as *most* honest and ethical (by more than 50% of respondents) are featured in Figure 10.16A, and the ones viewed as the *least* honest and ethical (by 40% or more of respondents) are listed in Figure 10.16B.

Education

The more education people have, the more likely it is that they are well paid, have prestigious occupations, and therefore belong to higher social classes than the less educated. According to the latest estimates from the U.S. Census Bureau, there are now 114 million households in the United States, with an average of 2.59 persons per household. Figure 10.17 illustrates the correlation between educational attainment and the amount of household income.[32] The "pies" represent different educational attainment levels and the incomes associated with them. As education increases, so does income. For example, the size of the "slice" representing incomes between $25,000 and $34,999 is significantly larger among high school graduates (Figure 10.17D), as compared with those who went to high school but did not graduate (Figure 10.17C). The "slice" representing the $100,000 and over income group occupies about 45% in the "pie" of the "bachelor's degree and higher" group (Figure 10.17G), which illustrates that college education makes people more affluent.

Social-class membership is often mirrored in one's education. For example, students at the most selective universities in the country are often the sons and daughters of alumni and upper-class Americans, whereas lower-class children are often encouraged to "get a good job." In a series of articles on social class, a 50-year-old man, whose father was a factory worker, was quoted: "The whole concept of life was that you should get a good job in the factory . . . if I'd said I wanted to go to college, it would have been like saying I wanted to grow gills and breathe underwater."[33] Almost

---

* Gallup, Honest and Ethics Poll

FIGURE 10.16A

High Ethics and Honesty: Percentage Responding "High" or "Very High" Honesty

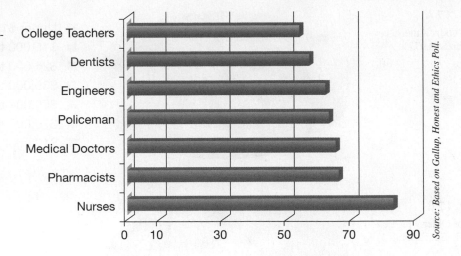

FIGURE 10.16B

Low Ethics and Honesty: Percentage Responding "Low" or "Very Low" Honesty

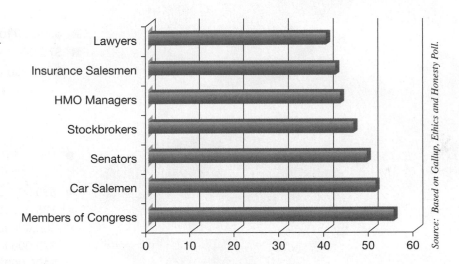

one in three Americans in their mid-twenties today is a college dropout (compared to one in five in the late 1960s), and most of those are members of poor and working-class families. In contrast, the children of the middle and upper classes generally graduate from college "because they can hardly imagine doing otherwise."[34]

Income

Individual or family income is frequently used to measure social standing. When using income as a measure, it is important to study the *source* of income, as well as its amount. It is also important to distinguish between *income* and *wealth*. Wealth is based on savings, may include inheritance, and is often the outcome of having network and alliances, some of which expand over generations. Income often represents only the ability to spend more, whereas net worth (i.e., wealth) can be used to create more financial resources. The distribution of net worth in the United States has become markedly unbalanced over the past few decades. In the year 2001, the richest 1% of households possessed almost 34% of all net worth; the bottom 90% of all households accounted for only 28.5% of all net worth. Since then, the rich have gotten richer, and the poor have gotten poorer.[35]

Although income is a commonly used estimate of social-class standing, many consumer researchers maintain that it is not a good measure. Some point out that a blue-collar electrician and a white-collar administrative assistant may both earn $87,000 a year, but will spend their incomes differently because of the difference between their educations and occupations. The same is true in the case of a prominent physician and a successful plumbing contractor, each earning $200,000. The amount of income represents the *ability* to spend money, but *how* the money is spent is determined by peoples' priorities, which are reflections of their education, occupation, and social contacts.

FIGURE 10.17A

Twenty-Five or Older Americans' Incomes (Median $50,971)

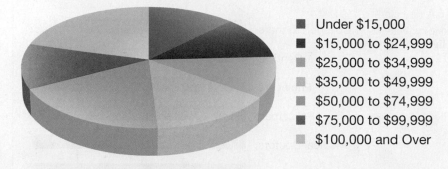

- Under $15,000
- $15,000 to $24,999
- $25,000 to $34,999
- $35,000 to $49,999
- $50,000 to $74,999
- $75,000 to $99,999
- $100,000 and Over

FIGURE 10.17B

Incomes of 25 or Older with Less than Ninth-Grade Education (Median $21,635)

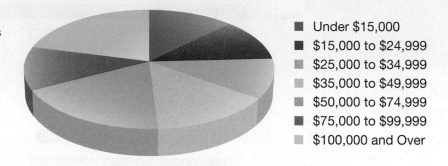

- Under $15,000
- $15,000 to $24,999
- $25,000 to $34,999
- $35,000 to $49,999
- $50,000 to $74,999
- $75,000 to $99,999
- $100,000 and Over

FIGURE 10.17C

Incomes of 25 or Older with Some High School Education (Median $25,604)

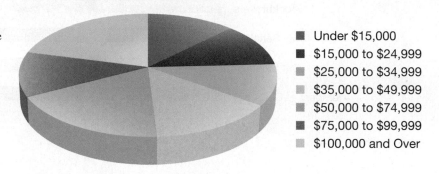

- Under $15,000
- $15,000 to $24,999
- $25,000 to $34,999
- $35,000 to $49,999
- $50,000 to $74,999
- $75,000 to $99,999
- $100,000 and Over

FIGURE 10.17D

Incomes of 25 or Older High School Graduates (Median $39,647)

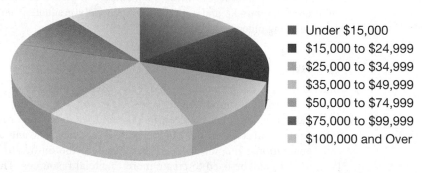

- Under $15,000
- $15,000 to $24,999
- $25,000 to $34,999
- $35,000 to $49,999
- $50,000 to $74,999
- $75,000 to $99,999
- $100,000 and Over

FIGURE 10.17E

Incomes of 25 or Older with Some College But without Degree Education (Median $44,301)

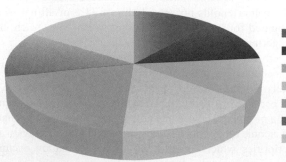

- Under $15,000
- $15,000 to $24,999
- $25,000 to $34,999
- $35,000 to $49,999
- $50,000 to $74,999
- $75,000 to $99,999
- $100,000 and Over

Source: (Figure 10.17A-E) U.S. Census Bureau, Statistical Abstract of the United States, 2012; census.gov/prod/2011pubs/12statab/income Accessed 6/21/2012.

FIGURE 10.17F

Incomes of 25 or Older with
Associate College Degree (Median
$67,728)

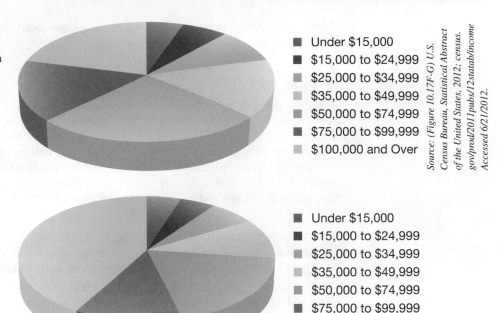

- ■ Under $15,000
- ■ $15,000 to $24,999
- ■ $25,000 to $34,999
- ■ $35,000 to $49,999
- ■ $50,000 to $74,999
- ■ $75,000 to $99,999
- ■ $100,000 and Over

Source: (Figure 10.17F-G) U.S. Census Bureau, Statistical Abstract of the United States, 2012; census. gov/prod2011pubs/12statabincome Accessed 6/21/2012.

FIGURE 10.17G

Incomes of 25 or Older with
Bachelor's Degree or Higher
(Median $82,722)

- ■ Under $15,000
- ■ $15,000 to $24,999
- ■ $25,000 to $34,999
- ■ $35,000 to $49,999
- ■ $50,000 to $74,999
- ■ $75,000 to $99,999
- ■ $100,000 and Over

Magazines are an excellent medium because they reach selective consumer segments in terms of income, education, and occupation. For example, marketers who target upper-middle-class consumers should consider placing ads in Wine and Food magazine because most of its readers are young, educated, and hold managerial positions.[36]

Multivariable Measures

A **multivariable index** consists of more than one demographic variable and combines several socioeconomic factors to determine social-class standing. Many believe that these indices reflect the complexity of social class better than single-variable indexes. For instance, a research study that explored consumers' perceptions of mail and phone order shopping—using a composite of income, occupational status, and education—discovered that the consumers with higher social standing preferred buying by phone or mail over in-store shopping.[37] The same research also found that downscale consumers preferred in-store shopping to buying from catalogues or by phone. Thus, retailers such as Kmart and Walmart that target working-class consumers should use direct-marketing and catalogs cautiously. In contrast, retailers catering to upscale consumers, such as Neiman Marcus and Saks Fifth Avenue, have been very successful in using catalogs to sell even extraordinarily expensive goods to affluent consumers.

The most widely used multivariable measures are:

1. **Index of Status Characteristics (Warner's ISC)** is a weighted measure of the following socioeconomic variables: Occupation, source of income (not amount of income), house type, and dwelling area (quality of neighborhood).[38]
2. **Socioeconomic Status Score (SES)** was developed by the U.S. Bureau of the Census, and combines three socioeconomic variables: Occupation, family income, and educational attainment.[39]

Social Classes' Characteristics and Consumer Behavior

Learning Objective

7 To understand the demographics, lifestyles, and consumption patterns of America's social classes.

There is no uniform definition as to how many distinct classes depict the class structure of the U.S. population. Most early studies divided Americans into five or six social-class groups. Other researchers have found nine-, four-, three-, and even two-class schemas suitable. The choice of how many separate classes to use depends on the amount of detail that the researcher believes is necessary to adequately explain the attitudes or behavior under study.

Lifestyles, consumption patterns, leisure activities, hobbies, media exposure, and many other factors are homogeneous within and heterogeneous among social classes. Table 10.8 presents an overview of the American population as divided into seven social classes, and Figure 10.18 shows the distribution of America's population by social class.

Upward Mobility

Social-class membership in the United States is not as fixed as it is in many other countries and cultures (e.g., the UK and India). Americans have traditionally believed in **upward mobility**, defined as the opportunity to move from a lower social class to a higher one, because of the wide availability of educational resources (e.g., expensive top schools, but also inexpensive state and city universities providing high-quality education) and the opportunities produced by the free enterprise, capitalistic economy. Indeed, the classic Horatio Alger tale of a penniless young orphan who manages to achieve great success in business and in life is the central theme in many American novels and movies.

TABLE 10.8	Social-Class Profiles of the United States

THE UPPER-UPPER CLASS—INHERITED WEALTH AND PRIVILEGE
- Also known as "upper crust," "WASPS," or "blue bloods"
- Less than 1% of the population together with the Nouveau Rich
- Inherited privilege, wealth, and trust funds
- Status and wealth are passed on from generation to generation (homes, trust funds)
- Multigenerational wealth and leadership positions (e.g., presidents, senators, judges)
- Serve as trustees and on boards of directors for universities, hospitals, charities
- Control and own significant portions of corporate America
- Heads of major financial institutions; owners of long-established firms
- Attended exclusive boarding schools and Ivy League universities
- Belong to exclusive clubs, "summer" together, marry people "like themselves"
- Accustomed to wealth, so do not spend money conspicuously
- Consider "toys" bought to display wealth publicly (e.g., yachts) to be vulgar
- Hobbies: Shooting, sailing, parasailing, golf, horseback riding

THE NOUVEAU RICH—MONEY IS KING
- Also known as the "lower-uppers," "super rich," or "capitalist class"
- Less than 1% of the population together with the Upper-Upper
- Have millions and often billions of dollars but seldom inherited wealth
- Some have little or no college education (e.g., celebrities)
- Some are entrepreneurs (often in the technology sector) who attended top universities
- Often isolated from others because of bodyguards and large entourages
- Often featured in tabloids, gossip columns, and public scandals
- Strive to join the Upper-Uppers (e.g., by marriage), mostly unsuccessfully
- Highly conspicuous consumption—the more vulgar, the better
- Prime target for "hot" (and mostly short-lived) fashion and interior design trends
- Employ large staffs—chefs, nutritionists, maids, nannies, personal assistants

THE UPPER-MIDDLE CLASS—ACHIEVING PROFESSIONALS
- Key features are high educational attainment and professional achievement
- Approximately 15% of the population
- Career-oriented, highly educated professionals whose work is largely self-directed
- Corporate managers, business owners, doctors, lawyers, professors
- College graduates, many with advanced degrees
- Active in professional networks, community, and social activities
- Trendsetters in health, fitness, and environmental causes
- Have a keen interest in obtaining the "better things in life"
- Homes, cars, and travel symbolize their achievements
- Consumption is often conspicuous, but not vulgar
- Some are very child oriented

(Continued)

TABLE 10.8   Social-Class Profiles of the United States (continued)

THE LOWER-MIDDLE CLASS—FAITHFUL FOLLOWERS

- Semi-professionals and craftspeople with an average standard of living
- About 30% of the population
- Primarily nonmanagerial white-collar workers and highly paid blue-collar workers
- Most have some college education and are white-collar
- Strive to achieve respectability and be good citizens
- Raise their children to be good and honest adults
- Value religion and are involved in its social activities
- Value and price conscious and avoid fads and "hot" styles

THE UPPER-LOWER CLASS—SECURITY-MINDED

- Also known as the "working class," solidly blue collar, no college education
- About 30% of the population
- High school education
- Clerical and mostly blue-collar workers whose work is highly routinized
- Adequate standard of living dependent on the number of income earners
- Strive for security (often gained from union membership)
- View work as a means to "buy" enjoyment
- Want children to behave properly
- High wage earners in this group may spend impulsively
- Interested in items that enhance their leisure time (e.g., TV sets, hunting equipment)
- Males typically have a strongly "macho" self-image
- Males are sports fans, heavy smokers, beer drinkers

THE WORKING POOR—THE INSECURE

- Also known as the "lower class"
- About 13% of the population
- Service, clerical, and some blue-collar workers
- Low on the social ladder
- High economic insecurity and risk of poverty
- Some high school education

THE UNDERCLASS—ROCK BOTTOM

- Also known as the "lower-lower class"
- About 12% of the population
- Limited or no participation in the labor force; uneducated, unskilled laborers
- No political or social power and unable to improve their communities
- Reliant on the government, often unemployed and without health insurance
- Children are often treated poorly
- Live a day-to-day existence

Source: Based on MRI Spring 2012, www.fwmedia.com, accessed July 16, 2012

FIGURE 10.18

The Distribution of Social Classes in the United States

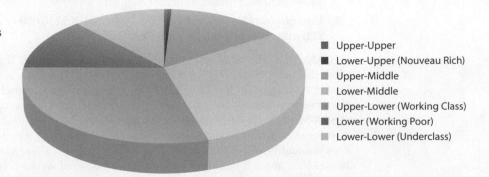

- Upper-Upper
- Lower-Upper (Nouveau Rich)
- Upper-Middle
- Lower-Middle
- Upper-Lower (Working Class)
- Lower (Working Poor)
- Lower-Lower (Underclass)

Because upward mobility has been attainable in American society, the higher social classes have been reference groups for ambitious men and women of lower social status. Examples are the new management trainee who strives to dress like the boss, the middle manager who aspires to belong to an exclusive country club, or the graduate of a community college who gives up necessities in order to save money to send her son to Yale.

Marketers recognize that many people aspire to have the same lifestyles and possessions as the members of higher social classes. Therefore, they frequently depict products and symbols associated with higher classes when advertising to the middle or even lower class. For example, Ralph Lauren's flagship store in New York City, on Madison Avenue, is located in the Rhinelander Mansion—built in the French Renaissance style more than a century ago—and is decorated with dark, fine antique furnishing and dark carpets, resembling generations-old wealth. The Polo logo also references the upper class, because many members of this select group own polo ponies and belong to clubs that sponsor polo matches. Many of Lauren's clothing items carry crests resembling insignia designating European nobility.

About a century ago, a sociologist conceptualized the **trickle-down effect**. Originally applied to fashion, the concept stated that members of lower classes adopt the fashions of the upper class and maintain them even after the upper class has abandoned these fashions. Upper class persons abandon fashions adopted by "everyone" because they no longer reflect their exclusivity. To "restore" their exclusivity, members of the upper class adopt new fashions, which are subsequently copied by the lower classes, and the cycle is repeated. The trickle-down concept is also congruent with the model of adopter categories (see Chapter 9). Invariably, as more people adopt a fashion or product, its price declines because more providers emerge. For instance, plastic surgery was once affordable only for movie stars and other very wealthy consumers. Today, even members of lower social classes can easily find a plastic surgeon whose services they can afford.

Affluent Consumers

Affluent households have large disposable incomes and are a lucrative target market for luxury cruises, foreign sports cars, ski resorts, second homes, fine jewelry, and art, among many other goods. Overall, the affluent are healthier, have higher life expectancies, and are more likely to become marketers' "customers for life" than the less wealthy.[40] However, some studies indicate that children of the affluent often have problems with substance abuse, anxiety, and depression, which are caused by excessive pressures to achieve and isolation from parents (both physically and emotionally).[41]

Americans' wealth grew dramatically during the 1990s, partially due to the longest bull stock market in U.S. history. From 2002 to 2004, the number of *high net worth individuals* (HNWIs) in North America, defined as individuals with a minimum net worth of $1 million, grew by 9.7% to 2.7 million. Between 2006 and 2007, this number grew from 2.9 million to more than 3 million, a gain of 3.7%.[42] Indeed, although North America has only 6% of the world adult population, it accounts for 34% of the world's household wealth.[43]

For more than 30 years, Ipsos Mendelsohn (a marketing research firm) has annually studied the **affluent market**, defined as households with annual incomes of $100,000 or more. The survey divided the affluent market into three segments:

1. *Least affluent:* Households with annual incomes of $100,000 to $149,000 (12% of American households, $1.7 trillion combined income).

2. *Middle affluent:* Households with annual incomes from $150,000 to $249,000 (6% of all households, $1.3 trillion combined income).

3. *Most affluent:* Household with annual incomes of $250,000 or more (2% of all households, $1.6 trillion estimated household income).

Although affluent households represent only 20% of total U.S. households, they account for more than half of the combined income of all the households in the United States. The average household income for the affluent is $195,600, with average household liquid assets of $500,900.[44] By some estimates, 9 million American households have a net worth of at least $1 million. The IPSOS/Mendelsohn Affluent Survey distinguishes between *affluence* and *wealth*; it defines wealthy household as having liquid assets of at least $1 million (e.g., cash or cash equivalents, such as CDs, mutual funds, stocks, bonds). According to this definition, out of the 23.3 million affluent households, about 3 million households are considered wealthy. In addition, more than 1 million households have both more than $1 million in wealth and annual household incomes of at least $250,000.[45]

The media habits of the affluent differ from those of the nonaffluent.[46] The members of households earning more than $100,000 a year watch less TV, read more newspapers and magazines, and listen to the radio more than less affluent persons. Table 10.9 lists magazines that cater to affluent consumers.[47]

Affluent consumers are not uniform; they can be divided according to their consumption habits and lifestyles. The "upper deck" consumers are the top 10% of the United States population in terms of annual income, and consist of several segments (see Table 10.10). Marketers can employ this segmentation in many ways. For instance, consumers belonging to the "no strings attached" segment are more interested in going to live theater performances; members of the "nanny's in charge" segment would rather attend a country music performance; and members of the "good life" segment are particularly interested in bird-watching.[48]

Middle-Class Consumers

There is no standard definition of "middle class" and business people and sociologists often define it somewhat differently. Many sociologists divide the middle class into two strata: The "upper or professional middle class", which includes highly educated, salaried professionals and managers (about

TABLE 10.9 Magazines That Cater to Households with Annual Incomes of $100,000 or More

MAGAZINE	READERSHIP (000)	MEDIAN AGE	MEDIAN HOUSEHOLD INCOME (00)	MEDIAN NET WORTH (00)
Allure	1,267	39.7	142.7	641.7
Architectural Digest	1,389	52.4	152.5	869.0
Barron's	414	53.7	163.3	1,015.0
Bicycling	685	44.0	148.6	636.4
Cigar Aficionado	276	48.8	168.5	613.0
Cosmopolitan	3,179	32.6	142.0	565.8
Essence	1,087	44.9	135.5	470.9
Men's Health	3,179	41.8	152.0	483.4
National Geographic	6,281	50.5	146.1	680.8
People	8,328	46.7	144.7	574.8
Robb Report	175	50.7	187.4	1,077.5
Rolling Stone	1,557	39.5	150.5	543.8
Scientific American	1,002	48.8	158.4	697.9
Time Magazine	4,904	51.5	149.3	850.1
Vanity Fair	1,602	48.0	155.8	768.8
Vogue	2,211	42.7	147.7	690.4

Source: Based on 2011 Survey Ipsos Mendelsolm.

TABLE 10.10 The Upper Deck Market Segments

NAME	SIZE	DESCRIPTION
Well-feathered nests	37.3% of Upper Deck	Households that have at least one high-income earner and children present
No strings attached	35.1% of Upper Deck	Households that have at least one high-income earner and no children
Nanny's in charge	8.3% of Upper Deck	Households that have two or more earners, none earning high incomes, and children present
Two careers	9.4% of Upper Deck	Households that have two or more earners, neither earning high incomes, and no children present
The good life	10.0% of Upper Deck	Households that have a high degree of affluence with no person employed or with the head of household not employed

15 to 20% of all Americans); and the "lower middle class", consisting mostly of semi-professionals, skilled craftspersons, and lower-level management (about one-third of the population). Sociologists describe middle-class persons as having comfortable living standards, economic security, and the expertise they need to maintain their lifestyles. To many, college education is a key indicator of middle-class status. Others focus on the nature of the occupations that are most commonly found among members of the middle class, which enable members to be independent, intrinsically motivated, non-conformist, and innovative.

Some define the middle class as 50% of the combined incomes of all American households, which amounts to about 57 million households earning between $25,000 and $85,000.[49] In contrast, some polls suggest that 90% or more of Americans consider themselves to be "middle class," "upper-middle class," or "working class."[50] Marketers generally consider middle class as households ranging from lower-middle to middle-middle class. Many researchers maintain that America's middle social class has been shrinking. They argue that some members of the middle class are moving upstream to the ranks of the upper-middle class, whereas others are losing ground and slipping backward to the working class.[51]

Procter and Gamble—the maker of virtually all brands of personal care and home maintenance products (globally)—defined middle class as the core of its business and as households with annual incomes between $50,000 and $140,000 (amounting to 40% of American households). As the stagnant economy, initiated by the financial crisis in fall 2008, has dragged on, the purchasing power of these households has steadily declined, and P & G discovered that its core customers were no longer willing to pay more for iconic, premium-priced brands (e.g., Pampers and Tide). In response, the company introduced lower-priced alternatives, such as Gain dish soap that goes for about half of what its Dawn Hand Renewal dish soap costs.[52]

Downscale Consumers

Working-class or blue-collar people—typically defined as households earning less than $40,000 annually—control somewhere near 30% of the total income in the United States and are an important market segment. Some studies have pointed out that these consumers are often more brand loyal than other groups because they cannot afford mistakes caused by switching to unfamiliar brands. Downscale consumers often spend higher percentages of their incomes on food than do middle-class shoppers.

Marketing to the working class can be tricky. For example, a study conducted in the UK showed that brands catering to blue-collar households often introduced "upmarket" makeovers, because research indicated that "working class" represents something to escape from, and to some is even a pejorative term. The study also showed that Pizza Express was among the most popular brands among the working class, presumably because its members are less likely to go to table-service restaurants.[53] To many working-class consumers, food represents an area of "indulgence," which may have undesirable outcomes. One British writer, reflecting on the growth of super-sized fast-food offerings in the United Kingdom, noted that "[i]t isn't the wealthy middle classes . . . that are generally obese—it's the under-class . . . with little budget [or] knowledge of diet . . . that is suffering."[54] Indeed, studies in the UK (and in the United States) confirmed that obesity among children from lower classes is significantly more common than among wealthier kids.[55]

Clothing, Fashion, and Shopping

A Greek philosopher once said, "Know, first, who you are; and then adorn yourself accordingly."[56] What is considered fashionable, tasteful, or elegant varies across social strata. For example, some working-class consumers often wear T-shirts, caps, and clothing that carry logos, trademarks, or names of celebrities or music group. In contrast, upscale consumers prefer clothing without conspicuous labels and in subtle colors and practical styles (e.g., L. L. Bean or Brooks Brothers).

America's upper social class has often been identified with the "preppy look" and often emulated by lower classes. Preppies (both males and females) prefer practical, comfortable, and timeless rather than trendy clothing. There are few designer labels and even fewer trends. Machine-washable khaki shorts and unisex dressing are very popular because khaki is to preppies what denim is to the lower classes: An everyday staple. Visors are a favorite for women—they keep the sun out of your eyes without messing up your hair, and they're excellent for tennis. Clothing embroidered with animals or sea creatures are always popular, like bathing trunks embroidered with crabs, as are shirts embroidered with club logos. Any excuse to wear themed clothing is embraced, and wearing red, white, and blue on the Fourth of July is expected at the holiday's parties. Polo shirts are an exception to the no-obvious-designer-labels rule; in fact, preps were wearing Polo long before it became a designer label. The preppy style originated among members of the upper class also known as WASPs (White Anglo-Saxon Protestant). WASPs are often irritated by shopping guides urging people—men in particular—to buy expensive designer clothes in order to "look like a WASP," such as ads for expensive, designer-label white buck shoes. Most preps have a pair of such shoes that, most likely, they purchased from Johnston & Murphy (for $130) years ago. Most importantly, preppies wear white bucks only for special occasions like weddings or cocktail parties, but not for running errands on a Saturday afternoon.[57]

A brand's social-class symbolism is a tricky issue. Although never publicly confirmed, some journalists have periodically reported that companies such as Timberland and L. L. Bean—perceived as the archetypal choices of upper-class Caucasians—were irritated after their products (particularly men's shoes) became popular among young members of minority groups residing in inner cities. Apparently, these marketers felt that such "undesirable" customers might blemish the images of their products. Ironically, some fashions originated among adolescents and teens residing in low-income neighborhoods. For example, several years ago, after observing lower-class kids, several designers began marketing pairs of men's shorts—one longer than the other—to be worn simultaneously, with one on top of the other; this new fashion was very successful. When shopping, consumers avoid stores that appeal to social classes significantly different from their own, but savvy marketers can cater to multiple social classes. For example, The Gap stores offer quality clothing to middle-class consumers. The Gap also introduced Old Navy clothing stores to sell good-value clothing to working-class families who usually purchased their casual and active wear clothing from general merchandise retailers such as Kmart, Walmart, or Target. The Gap also owns Banana Republic, originally a small retailer of safari-themed clothing that is now positioned as an upscale store.

Saving, Spending, and Credit Card Usage

The management of financial resources is closely related to social-class standing. Upper-class consumers are "future oriented" and confident of their financial acumen; they invest in insurance, stocks, and real estate. In comparison, lower-class consumers are generally concerned with "immediate gratification;" when they do save, they are primarily interested in safety and security. When it comes to bank credit card usage, members of the lower social classes use their bank credit cards for installment purchases, whereas members of the upper social classes pay their credit card bills in full each month. That is, lower-class purchasers use their credit cards to "buy now and pay later" for things they might not otherwise be able to afford, whereas upper-class purchasers use their credit cards as a convenient substitute for cash.

An Australian study focused on the differences in financial management and a "sense of empowerment" between working-class and young professionals (25–30 years of age). The study discovered that young professionals perceived themselves to be empowered in the sense that they could achieve whatever they set their minds to, and they were disciplined and results oriented. In contrast, working-class participants perceived themselves as being average and expressed frustration (e.g., "I can never finish things") and uncertainty about the future.[58]

Communications

When it comes to describing daily life, members of the lower class often portray it in personal and concrete terms, whereas members of the middle-class use different language, and upper-class members use their own lexicon. For instance, in the U.S. the following responses to the question *"Where do you usually purchase gas?"* illustrate such differences:

Upper-middle-class answer: *"At Exxon or Sunoco."*

Lower-middle-class answer: *"At the station on Seventh Street and Post Avenue."*

Lower-class answer: *"At Charlie's."*

Sociologically, linguistics indicates that middle-class consumers have a broader or more general view of the world, whereas lower-class consumers have a narrow and personal perspective and see the world only through their immediate experiences. There are also regional differences in terminology. For instance, the children's game of hopscotch (where players toss a small object into the numbered spaces of a pattern of rectangles outlined on the ground and then hop or jump through the spaces to retrieve it) is called "potsy" in Manhattan, but "sky blue" in Chicago.

Exposure to mass media differs by social class. In watching TV, the members of higher social classes prefer current events and drama, whereas lower-class individuals prefer soap operas, quiz shows, and situation comedies. Higher-class consumers read more magazines and newspapers than do their lower-class counterparts. Lower-class consumers have greater exposure to publications that dramatize romance and the lifestyles of movie and television celebrities. For example, magazines such as True Story appeal heavily to blue-collar or working-class women, who enjoy reading about the problems, fame, and fortunes of others. Middle-class consumers read fact-based and informative magazines and newspapers, and watch more movies and late-night programs, than lower-class persons.[59]

Downward Mobility

Commonly, in America, each generation lived better than its predecessor. However, there are now signs that some **downward mobility**, defined as moving down, rather than up the social ladder, is taking place. In fact, many predict that today's youngest generation—the Eco Boomers—will experience lower living standards than their parents.

Specifically, researchers have found that the odds that young men's incomes will reach middle-class levels by the time they reach their thirtieth birthday have been slowly declining, regardless of ethnicity, education, or parents' income.[60] For example, while household income grew by $1,869 from 1969–1979, by $2,855 from 1979–1989, and by $3,888 from 1989–2000, from 2000–2007 the change in household income was a *negative* $324.[61]

Additionally, income inequality has been rising to levels not seen since the 1880s—known as the "Gilded Age"—and the gap between the rich and the poor has widened considerably since 1970. Although the income of households in the top fifth grew 70% between 1979 and 2000, the real income of households in the bottom fifth rose only 6.4%. Although most Americans find little wrong with income inequality as long as plenty of social mobility still exists, there are signs that social mobility is also failing. Some data show that 42% of the individuals born into the poorest fifth remained at the bottom and that another 24% moved from the bottom only slightly, to the next-to-bottom group. Only 10% of adult men born into the bottom quarter ever made it to the top quarter.[62]

Geo-Demography and Social Class

Learning Objective

8 To understand how to employ geo-demographics to locate target markets.

Marketers use geo-demography to identify the geographic locations of consumers belonging to various social classes. The rationale for using geo-demographics is that "birds of a feather flock together"; that is, families with similar socioeconomic status reside in the same neighborhoods or communities. **Geo-demographic segments** are groups of households that have been identified, classified, and described according to Zip Codes and data from the U.S. Census and state and local governments.

The most sophisticated geo-demographic segmentation is Nielsen's **PRIZM**® (www.MyBest-Segments.com), which combines socioeconomic and demographic factors—education, income, occupation, family life cycle, ethnicity, housing, and urbanization—with consumer buying and media exposure data, and which marketers use to locate concentrations of consumers with similar lifestyles and buying behaviors. This framework designates every household in the United States as belonging to one of 66 segments (see Table 2.3). Figure 10.19A depicts how some of the 66 segments are classified according to urban density and wealth. PRIZM® also classifies all U.S. households into eleven "life stages," which are featured in Figure 10.19B.

Many marketers have studied the product usage, media exposure, and other consumption factors of the PRIZM® segments that are likely to purchase their products and services. For example, investment services should identify the financial websites that "Affluentials" visit frequently and observe what kind of investment opportunities these consumers find attractive. Marketers of very expensive vacations and conspicuous luxury goods should study the spending habits of "Young Accumulators." However, these marketers should not target the "Accumulated Wealth" segment, because its members have "old money" and shy away from buying conspicuous luxury goods, which they regard as being "in poor taste" "and showing off" one's money.

FIGURE 10.19A

PRIZM Fourteen Wealth Groups

Source: Copyrighted information of The Nielsen Company, licensed for use herein.

FIGURE 10.19B

PRIZM Eleven Life Stages

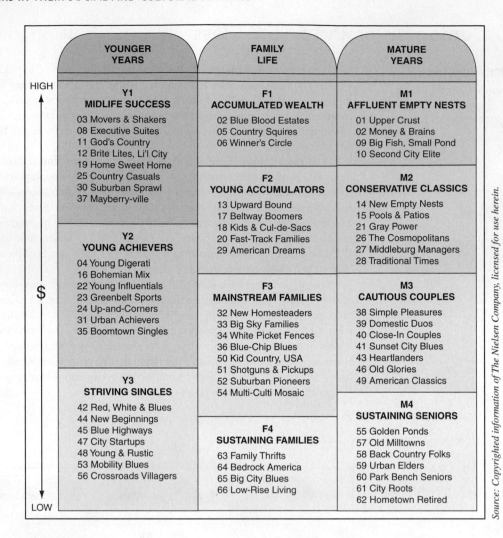

Source: Copyrighted information of The Nielsen Company, licensed for use herein.

Summary

Learning Objective 1: To understand the family as a consumer socialization agent.

The family is the primary reference group for many attitudes and behaviors. The family is also the prime target market for most products and product categories. As the most basic membership group, a family is defined as two or more persons related by blood, marriage, or adoption who reside together. Socialization is the process of making people behave in a way that is acceptable to their society. In the context of marketing, the most important role of the family is the socialization of family members, ranging from young children to adults. This process includes imparting to young children the basic values and modes of behavior consistent with their culture, including moral principles, interpersonal skills, acceptable dress and grooming standards, appropriate manners and speech, and the selection of suitable educational and occupational or career goals.

Learning Objective 2: To understand family decision-making and its members' consumption-related roles.

Marketers recognize that families operate as units in terms of consumption behavior, and many researchers have studied the dynamics of family decision-making. Specifically, marketers focus on husband–wife decision-making; the relative influence each

family member has regarding consumption; children's role in family decision-making; and the multiple roles family members can assume in buying, using, and maintaining their possessions. Most consumer studies classify family consumption decisions as husband-dominated, wife-dominated, joint, or autonomic decisions. The relative influence of a husband and wife on a particular consumer decision depends mainly on the product or service category. Over the past several decades, there has been a trend toward children playing a more active role in what the family buys, as well as in the family decision-making process. Measuring family decision-making is complex, because marketing research questionnaires are designed to be administered to only one respondent at a time. Also, family members may not all agree with each other's perspective regarding the degree of relative influence during a purchase decision, which precludes interviewing all members together.

Learning Objective 3: To understand the role of the family life cycle in market segmentation and targeting.

The family life cycle represents the life stages of a typical family. It is a composite variable that combines marital status, size of family, age of family members (focusing on the age of the oldest or youngest child), and employment status of the head of household, and then classifies the family into a "typical" stage. The ages of the parents and the relative amount of disposable income are inferred from the family's stage in the cycle. The family life cycle starts with bachelorhood and then moves on to marriage (and creation of the family unit). Marriage usually leads to a growing family (with the birth of children) and later to family contraction (as grown children leave the household). The cycle ends with the dissolution of the family unit (due to the death of one spouse).

Learning Objective 4: To understand the consumption patterns of nontraditional families and non-family households.

There are living arrangements that are not "typical." Families that do not readily fit into the family life cycle include childless couples, people who marry late in life, young people who continue to live with their parents or return after having moved out, and divorced couples. Living situations that are not legally defined as families (e.g., couples who live together but are not married) include unmarried couples, single parents, and gay spouses. The number of non-family households has been on a rather steep rise, which represents a marketing dilemma: Marketers of many products must now acknowledge the existence of nontraditional household segments, but must do so without offending members of traditional families who might react negatively to portrayals of nontraditional households, because of religion and beliefs as to what is or is not "right."

Learning Objective 5: To understand the impact of social stratification on consumer behavior.

Social stratification (or social class) is the division of members of a society into a hierarchy of distinct status classes, so that members of each class have relatively the same status and members of all other classes have either more or less status. Some form of class structure (or social stratification) has existed in all societies throughout history. In contemporary societies, people who are better educated or have prestigious occupations have more status relative to other members of the same society. Belonging to a given social class is also reflected in differences in the values, attitudes, and behaviors (including consumer behavior) among members of different social classes. Social class is a continuum along which society's members—usually as households—are placed into one stratum; that is, "assigned" to a social class according to their relative prestige within that society.

Learning Objective 6: To understand how to measure social class and segment consumers accordingly.

The measurement of social class is concerned with classifying individuals into social-class groupings. These groupings are of particular value to marketers, who use social classification as an effective way to identify and segment target markets. There are two basic methods for measuring social class: Subjective measurement

and objective measurement. Subjective measures rely on an individual's self-perception, whereas objective measures use specific socioeconomic measures, either alone (as a single-variable index) or in combination with others (as a composite-variable index). Composite-variable indexes, such as the Index of Status Characteristics and the Socioeconomic Status Score, combine a number of socioeconomic factors to form one overall measure of social-class standing.

Learning Objective 7: To understand the demographics, lifestyles, and consumption patterns of America's social classes.

Lifestyles, consumption patterns, leisure activities, hobbies, media exposure, and scores of other factors are homogeneous within and heterogeneous among social classes. There is no uniform definition or even general agreement as to how many distinct classes depict the class structure of the U.S. population accurately. Most early studies divided Americans into five or six social-class groups; other researchers have found nine-, four-, three-, and even two-class schemas suitable. The choice of how many separate classes there are depends on the amount of detail that the researcher believes is necessary to adequately explain the attitudes or behavior under study. We identified seven social classes:

1. Upper-Upper class—inherited wealth and privilege;
2. Nouveau Rich—new money;
3. Upper-Middle class—high educational attainment and prestige;
4. Lower-Middle class—semi-professional, non-managerial employees and skilled crafts people, whose lifestyle is considered average;
5. Upper-Lower class—solidly blue collar, with highly routinized jobs and steady incomes;
6. Working Poor—low on the social ladder and economically insecure); and
7. Underclass—mostly unemployed and dependent on the government).

Learning Objective 8: To understand how to employ geo-demographics to locate target markets.

Marketers use geo-demography to identify the geographic locations of consumers belonging to different social classes. The rationale for using geo-demographics is that families with similar socioeconomic status reside in the same neighborhoods or communities, as illustrated by the saying that "birds of a feather flock together." Geo-demographic segments are groups of households that have been identified, classified, and described according to Zip Codes and data from the U.S. Census and state and local governments. The most sophisticated geo-demographic segmentation is Nielsen's PRIZM®.

Review and Discussion Questions

10.1. As individuals reach the age of retirement, they become more dependent on services. These services can be provided by both private and public sectors. Identify which services are required, and how involved the government should be in providing these services.

10.2. For many years, the key subjective measurement of social class has been particular items of value, such as the type of car, brand of clothing, and technology that an individual has access to. Looking at recent advancements in technology and consumer buying power, is this still one of the measures used today?

10.3. Which of the five stages of the family life cycle constitutes the *most* lucrative segment for each of the following products and services: (a) TV cable subscriptions, (b) Club Med vacation, (c) Domino's Pizza, (d) iPods, (e) mutual funds, and (f) the fastest Internet access available in one's location? Explain your answers.

10.4. Why do marketing researchers use objective, rather than subjective, measures of social class?

10.5. A composite-variable index is used to better understand social class. Please explain and evaluate each element of the index. The three key elements are:

a. Occupation

b. Education

c. Income

10.6. Which status-related variable—occupation, education, or income—is the *most* appropriate segmentation base for: (a) family vacations, (b) opera subscriptions, (c) subscribing to online.wsj.com, (d) shopping at Whole Foods supermarkets, (e) buying from freshdirect.com, (f) purchasing new models of the iPhone, and (g) becoming a member of a 24-hour fitness center?

10.7. To what extent is technology an aspect of social class? Does it require its own social group?

10.8. You are the owner of two furniture stores, one catering to upper-middle-class consumers and the other to lower-class consumers. How do social-class differences influence each store's: (a) product lines and styles, (b) advertising media selection, (c) copy and communications style used in the ads, and (d) payment policies?

Hands-on Assignments

10.9. In this chapter, we have considered how parents and siblings play a role in the consumer socialization of their children and young brothers and sisters, and how adults continue to be socialized throughout their lives. However, we have not considered how children (especially teens and young adults) influence the socialization of their parents. Make a list of ten ways in which you have contributed to or influenced the ongoing socialization of your parents.

10.10. Discuss and evaluate the social changes in the last 100 years. Consider global events such as the two world wars, the global recessions of the 1930s and 2008, technology advancements, and changes in work-life balance. What has influenced changes in society over time, and how has family as a social institution influenced this change? Please provide examples.

10.11. Discuss what is meant by the term "social status," and explore the features you can identify in an individual's social group. Do you feel you belong to a social group?

Key Terms

- affluent market *284*
- authoritarian parents *262*
- authoritative parents *262*
- autonomic decisions *265*
- bachelorhood *269*
- consumer socialization *260*
- dissolution *272*
- downward mobility *288*
- extended family *258*
- family *258*
- family life cycle *258*
- geo-demographic segments *289*
- honeymooners *269*
- husband-dominated decisions *265*

- index of status characteristics (Warner's ISC) *281*
- indulgent parents *262*
- joint decisions *265*
- least affluent *284*
- middle affluent *284*
- most affluent *284*
- multivariable index *281*
- neglecting parents *262*
- non-family households *273*
- nontraditional families *273*
- nuclear family *258*
- objective measures *277*
- occupational prestige ranking *277*
- parenthood *271*

- post-parenthood *272*
- PRIZM *289*
- reference group *258*
- social class *259*
- social status *276*
- social-class consciousness *277*
- socialization *260*
- socialization agent *260*
- socioeconomic status score (SES) *281*
- subjective measures *276*
- trickle-down effect *284*
- upward mobility *282*
- wife-dominated decisions *265*

Culture's Influence on Consumer Behavior

Learning Objectives

1   To understand culture's role, dynamics, evolution, and impact on consumers' priorities and behaviors.

2   To understand language, symbols, and rituals as expressions of a learned culture.

3   To understand how to measure the influence of culture on consumer behavior.

4   To understand Americans' core values and how to apply them to persuasive communications.

5   To understand green marketing and ecologically responsible consumption.

CULTURE is the collective values, customs, norms, arts, social institutions, and intellectual achievements of a particular society. Cultural values express the collective principles, standards, and priorities of a community. Most of the promotional messages across the world reflect, to some degree, the target audiences' cultural values. For instance, Americans value personal achievement and success and like to demonstrate their accomplishments by showing off prosperity and material possessions. The Dodge ad in Figure 11.1 recognizes this desire. By telling consumers that they will make a "bold statement" to other drivers by driving a Dodge, the ad reflects and reinforces the eagerness to show off one's wealth. Americans also greatly value efficiency and progress, especially when it comes to technological innovations. Dell's ad in Figure 11.2 promotes an Ultrabook, which is small and thin, yet strong, powerful, and durable. The ad's tagline—"Everything. And More."—appeals to Americans' beliefs that technological advances provide them with more productive ways to work and manage their lives. As illustrated later in this chapter, achievement, success, efficiency, and progress are Americans' enduring, pervasive, and consumption-related priorities and are core values, which often determine what we buy and also explain why.

This chapter describes the societal role and dynamics of culture, explains how cultural values satisfy needs, and investigates how they are learned, expressed, and measured. Lastly, we discuss ten American core values, which we illustrate with ads and promotional themes, and conclude with a discussion of green marketing.

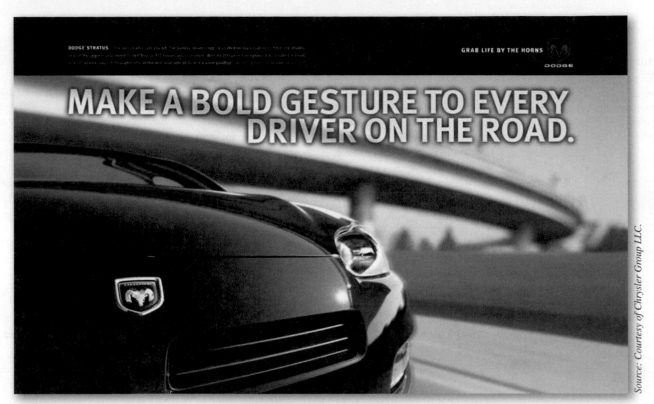

FIGURE 11.1 An Appeal Based on Personal Achievement and Prestige

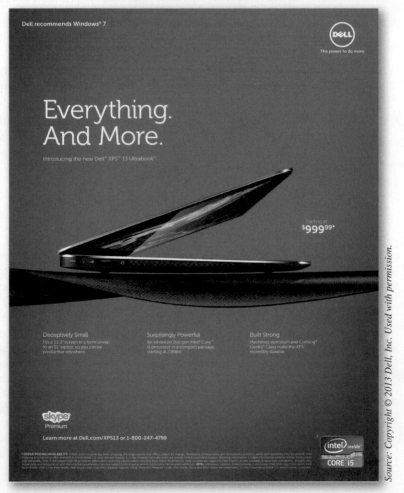

FIGURE 11.2 An Appeal Based on Progress, Efficiency, and Practicality

Culture's Role and Dynamics

Learning Objective

1   To understand culture's role, dynamics, evolution, and impact on consumers' priorities and behaviors.

We often refer to culture as an "invisible hand" that guides the actions of people of a particular society. When consumer researchers ask people why they do certain things, they frequently answer, "Because it's the right thing to do"—a response reflecting the ingrained influence of culture on our behavior. We can truly understand and appreciate the influence of our culture only after visiting other countries and observing the local values and behaviors. For instance, after visiting restaurants in France or Italy, many Americans may realize that they eat too much food and snack too often. Furthermore, if we travel within the United States, we will also observe differences in the norms and preferences of subcultures. For instance, whereas consumers living in the Northeastern section of the United States have historically preferred ketchup on their hamburgers, consumers living in other sections have liked mustard, or a mixture of mustard and ketchup (see Chapter 12).

Some researchers conceptualized different "levels" of cultural norms:

1. **The supranational** level reflects the underlying dimensions of culture that affect multiple societies (i.e., subcultural cross-national or cross-cultural boundaries). For instance, it might reflect regional character (e.g., people living in several nations in a particular region of South America), or racial and religious similarities or differences, or shared or different languages.

2. **The national** level reflects shared core values, customs, and personalities that represent the core of the "national character" of a particular country.

3. **The group** level reflects the subdivisions of a country or society, such as subcultures, and the influences of various reference groups.[1]

On the supranational level of culture, which crosses national boundaries, researchers have developed a lifestyle matrix for four segments of global youth aged 14 to 24:

1. **In-crowd:** It's all about privilege and reinforcement; members of this group seek approval from others and prefer classic brands like Nike and Abercrombie & Fitch to uphold tradition.

2. **Pop Mavericks:** Word-of-mouth spreads rapidly, and passion, individuality, and instant gratification are important; members prefer brands that they can personalize—brands like Diesel and Adidas.

3. **Networked Intelligentsia:** They are the hub of online social networks, and it's all about revolution, creativity, and deconstruction; members prefer cult brands, like Vespa (in America) and Vans, which add to their sense of obscurity.

4. **Thrill Renegades:** It's all about infamy, adrenaline, and anarchy (and pretending that law and order do not exist).[2]

Culture's Continuous Evolution

Marketers must always monitor cultural changes to discover new opportunities and abandon markets that have "dried up" because of cultural changes. To this end, marketers should periodically reconsider *why* consumers are doing what they do, *who* are the purchasers and the users of their offerings, *when* they do their shopping, *how* and *where* they can be reached by the media, and *what* new product and service needs are emerging. For example, cultural changes in America have increasingly recognized the expanded career options open to women. Today, most women work outside the home, and frequently in careers that were once exclusively male oriented. Later in this chapter, we explain why achievement and personal success are two of America's core values and how marketers can use them in advertising. Although traditionally associated with men, especially male business executives, achievement has become important for women as well, as they increasingly enroll in undergraduate and graduate business (and other college) programs and often attain top-level business positions. Also, many women are now in professions previously dominated by males (e.g., medicine, engineering, science). Therefore, many ads that target women now depict appeals that emphasize achievement and success, whereas some years ago the same kinds of promotions appealed to women's roles as mothers and housewives.

A longitudinal study examined how women have been depicted in advertising over the years, and discovered that changing gender roles were manifested in promotional messages. Specifically, there has been a fourfold increase in the number of women as the "figure" (i.e., the focal point of the print advertisement) compared to men, and a substantial increase in the number of ads portraying women as business professionals.[3]

Cultural Beliefs Reflect Consumers' Needs

Culture expresses and satisfies the needs of societies. It offers order, direction, and guidance for problem solving by providing "tried-and-true" methods of satisfying physiological, personal, and social needs. For example, culture provides standards about when to eat ("not between meals"); where to eat ("most likely, the restaurant is busy because the food is good"); what is appropriate to eat for breakfast (pancakes), lunch (a sandwich), dinner ("something hot and good and healthy"), and snacks ("something with quick energy, but not too many calories"); and what to serve to guests at a dinner party ("a formal sit-down meal"), at a picnic (barbecued "franks and burgers"), or at a wedding (champagne). Culture also determines whether a product is a necessity or discretionary luxury. For example, whereas mobile phones (initially introduced as car phones) were once expensive and uncommon, today they are a necessity because fewer and fewer people have landlines and payphones are largely extinct.

Culture also dictates which clothes are suitable for different occasions (such as what to wear around the house, and what to wear to school, to work, to church, at a fast-food restaurant, or to a movie theater). In recent years, dress codes have changed drastically and Americans have been dressing casually for occasions that once required more formal attire. For example, in large cities, only a handful of restaurants and clubs still require men to wear jackets and ties. With the relaxed dress code in the corporate work environment, fewer men are wearing dress shirts, ties, and business suits, and fewer women are wearing dresses, suits, and pantyhose. Instead, employees wear casual slacks, sports shirts and blouses, and even neat jeans and polo shirts.

Some customs, however, are unlikely to change. For example, soft-drink companies would prefer that consumers receive their morning "jolts" of caffeine from one of their products, instead of coffee. Because most Americans do not consider soda a suitable breakfast beverage, soft-drink companies have faced a dual challenge: "overcoming" culture, as well as the competition among breakfast drinks. Teas, soft drinks, and even caffeinated water have challenged coffee as the traditional source of morning caffeine—mostly unsuccessfully. Indeed, coffee is entrenched in our culture not only as a breakfast beverage, but also as the core of the "coffee break." Wisely, coffee marketers have not relied on their cultural advantage, but have been preempting their competitors by introducing assortments of gourmet and flavored coffees and also by aggressively targeting young adults with such exotics as espresso, cappuccino, and café mocha.

When a specific standard no longer satisfies the members of a society or reflects its needs, it is modified or replaced. For example, once it was unheard of for restaurant servers to pose questions of a personal nature. Now, we commonly answer servers' questions about our food allergies and other medical, food-related limitations. At times, society's collective interest contradicts an emerging custom. For instance, because most young Americans are now electronically connected all the time and at almost any place, distracted driving because of texting or calling on mobile phones is causing more car accidents. The two ads shown in Figure 11.3 are part of a government initiative to discourage distracted driving.

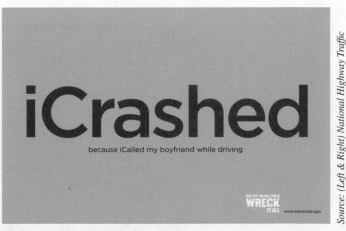

Source: (Left & Right) National Highway Traffic Safety Administration

FIGURE 11.3 Discouraging Distracted Driving

Learning Cultural Values

Learning Objective

2   To understand language, symbols, and rituals as expressions of a learned culture.

To be considered a cultural value, a belief or custom must be shared by a significant portion of the society, because culture is essentially a series of norms that guide personal and group conduct and link individuals into a largely cohesive group. Generally, members of a society share their values and customs through a common language, although some cultures include more than one language.

Forms of Learning

We learn cultural norms and customs mostly from family and peers, and begin to understand at a very young age that some behaviors are appropriate and others are not. Anthropologists have identified three forms of cultural learning. **Formal learning** takes place when parents, older siblings, and other family members teach younger members "how to behave." **Informal learning** takes place when children imitate the behaviors of selected others, such as family, friends, or TV and movie heroes and characters. **Technical learning** happens when teachers instruct children, in educational environments, about what should be done, how it should be done, and why it should be done, in social as well as personal settings. Our ethical values (e.g., the importance of kindness, honesty, and responsibility) are also formed during childhood as we learn them from parents, teachers, and other significant adults.[4]

Enculturation and Acculturation

Anthropologists distinguish between the learning of one's own (or native) culture and the learning of new cultures. **Enculturation** is learning one's own culture. **Acculturation** is learning new or foreign cultures. In Chapter 13, we demonstrate that acculturation is important for marketers that sell products in multinational markets. When selling products overseas, marketers must study the culture(s) of their potential customers so as to determine whether their products will be acceptable and how to communicate the characteristics of their products effectively and persuade consumers to buy them.

Sometimes, consumers can be "foreigners" in their own countries. For example, one study traced a group of provincial women in Thailand as they enrolled at a university in Bangkok (Thailand's capital city). As their first semester began, the women quickly formed their own group; they kept to themselves and did not mix with students from Bangkok or participate in the city's social scene. Ironically, the longer the provincial women lived in Bangkok, the more they resisted adopting Bangkok's culture and strongly expressed their provincial values.[5]

Key components of one's enculturation are the family and the process of **consumer socialization** (see Chapter 10). This process consists of teaching children and young adults consumption-related values and skills, such as the meaning of money and value, how to judge product quality, styles and preferences, product usage, and the meaning and objectives of promotional messages.[6] In addition to the family unit, educational and religious institutions also convey cultural values to younger members. Educational institutions impart the knowledge of arts, sciences, civics, and professional and specialized skills. Religious institutions provide spiritual and moral guidance and values, which often have a substantial impact on behavior.

Marketing Influences on Cultural Learning

The contents of media, advertising, and marketing reflect cultural values and convey them to all members of society very effectively. Given Americans' extensive exposure to print, broadcast, and online media, promotional messages are powerful vehicles for imparting cultural values. Every day, at almost any time, we are exposed to hundreds of promotional cues and messages, many of which we hear and see more than once. The repetition of marketing messages both conveys and reinforces cultural beliefs and values. For example, in the highly competitive environment of cellular communications, providers have aggressively promoted such features as low rates of dropped calls, high extent of coverage, and flexible pricing plans. After years of seeing such ads, wireless phone users learned to expect extensive benefits from cellular gadgets, and their expectation levels have been going up steadily—further reinforced by the frequent introductions of more sophisticated mobile communications.

In advertisements, cultural values are not only depicted in the advertising copy, but are also coded in the visual imagery, colors, movements, music, and other nonverbal elements of an advertisement.[7]

Many products became American icons and tangible expressions of the nation's cultural values. For example, the ever-popular baseball cap provides wearers with a cultural identity. Baseball caps function as trophies (as proof of participation in sports or travel to particular destinations), and many brands serve as self-proclaimed labels of belonging to a cultural category (e.g., Harley-Davidson owner) or even means of self-expression (e.g., highly customized Harley Davidson motorcycles). The statuses of Coca-Cola and Disney as the most recognized commercial American icons are illustrated by the millions of people wearing their logos (and their counterfeits) in virtually every location on our planet.

Marketers also transmit a lot of information that enables consumers to express shared cultural values. For example, advertising in sophisticated magazines such as Vogue, Bon Appetit, and Architectural Digest instructs readers how to dress, how to decorate their homes, and what foods and wines to serve guests. Online, people form virtual communities that are focused on products and enable consumers to exchange and learn product-related customs. Social media is rapidly becoming a key factor in conveying and sharing cultural values. People follow tweets of influential people and peers and write in blogs that are focused on their activities, interests, and opinions. As a result, for example, more people may get involved in civic groups and humanitarian causes. Their actions, respectively, express the importance of personal achievement and success and humanitarianism, which are two of our core values (discussed later in this chapter).

Language and Symbols

Cultural values are reflected in the languages, symbols, communications, and artifacts of a society. A **symbol** is anything that represents something else, and symbols can be either verbal or nonverbal. Words are verbal symbols, so the text of any ad is a composition of symbols. Nonverbal symbols, such as figures, colors, shapes, and even textures, are cultural cues that appear within advertisements, trademarks, packaging, and product designs. Many symbols have linguistic as well as psychological meanings. For example, the word "hurricane" is defined as a particular type of severe weather condition, but often stirs feelings of danger and thoughts of finding protection and safety. Similarly, the word "Cadillac" has symbolic meaning: To some it suggests a fine luxury automobile; to others it implies wealth and status (e.g., the phrase "the Cadillac of refrigerators" indicates that a refrigerator is the best in its product category).

Symbols can have contradictory meanings. For example, the advertiser that uses a trademark depicting an old craftsman to symbolize careful workmanship may instead be communicating an image of outmoded methods and lack of style. Marketers who use slang in advertisements directed at teenagers must do so with great care; slang that is misused or outdated will symbolically date the marketer's firm and product, and may also be offensive to some.

Prices and channels of distribution are symbols and reflect cultural meanings of products. For instance, the stores where clothes are sold (and also the prices of the items) symbolize their quality. In fact, all the elements of the marketing mix—the product, its promotion, price, and the stores at which it is available—are symbols that communicate the item's quality, value, and image.

Rituals

In addition to language and symbols, cultures include ritualized behaviors. A **ritual** is a type of symbolic activity consisting of a series of steps occurring in a fixed sequence and repeated periodically.[8] Rituals can be public, elaborate, or ceremonial (e.g., weddings), or mundane routines (e.g., daily grooming). Typically, ritualized behavior is formal and often scripted (e.g., a religious service or proper conduct in a court of law), and occurs repeatedly (e.g., singing the national anthem before the start of a sports event).

Many rituals include artifacts, and some products are marketed specifically for certain rituals. For instance, turkey, stuffing, and cranberries are part of the ritual of Thanksgiving Day. Rituals such as graduations, weekly card games, or visits to beauty salons include artifacts. Table 11.1 lists culturally appropriate artifacts for various occasions.

Ritualistic behavior is an action or series of steps that have become a ritual. For example, golfers who take a few practice swings before actually hitting the ball display a ritualistic behavior. Personal-care activities are often ritualized; Table 11.2 describes the daily ritual of a woman's facial care.

TABLE 11.1	Selected Rituals and Associated Artifacts
RITUAL	**ARTIFACTS**
Wedding	White gown (something old, something new, something borrowed, something blue)
Birth of child	U.S. savings bond, silver baby spoon
Birthday	Card, present, cake with candles
Fiftieth wedding anniversary	Catered party, card and gift, display of photos of the couple's life together
Graduation	Pen, U.S. savings bond, card, wristwatch
Valentine's Day	Candy, card, flowers
New Year's Eve	Champagne, party, elegant formal dress
Thanksgiving	A turkey dinner served to family and friends
Going to the gym	Towel, exercise clothes, water, iPod
Sunday football	Beer, potato chips, pretzels
Super Bowl party	Same as Sunday football (but more)
Starting a new job	Get a haircut and buy new clothes
Getting a job promotion	Taken out to lunch by coworkers and receive token gift
Retirement	Company party, a watch, and a plaque
Death	Send a card, send flowers, donate money to charity in honor of the deceased

TABLE 11.2	Facial Beauty Ritual of a Young Advertising Executive

1. I pull my hair back with a headband.
2. I take off my makeup with L'Oréal makeup remover.
3. Next, I gently rub a Qtip with some moisturizer around my eyes to make sure all of my eye makeup is removed.
4. I wash my face with Noxzema facial wash.
5. I apply Clinique Dramatically Different Lotion to my face and neck.
6. If I have a blemish, I dry it out with Clearasil Treatment.
7. Once a week, using a wet and warm cloth, I apply Clinique Clarifying Lotion 2 to my face and neck to remove dead skin cells.
8. Every three months, I get a professional salon facial to clean my pores deeply.

Measuring Cultural Values

Learning Objective

3 To understand how to measure the influence of culture on consumer behavior.

Culture reflects a society's values, customs, and rituals, which in turn reflect how we live and communicate. The most widely used measurements of cultural values are content analysis, consumer field observation, and value measurement instruments.

Content Analysis

Content analysis, as the name implies, focuses on the content of societies' verbal, written, and pictorial communications, including promotional messages. Content analysis can be applied to marketing, gender and age issues, sociology and political science, psychological studies, and many other fields. Among other concepts, content analysis can:

1. Identify the intentions, focus, or communication trends of an individual, group, or institutions.
2. Describe attitudinal and behavioral responses to communications.
3. Determine psychological or emotional state of persons or groups.[9]

Content analysis can determine what social and cultural changes have occurred in a specific society or compare different cultures. Content analysis of more than 250 ads appearing in 8 issues of Seventeen Magazine—4 Japanese issues and 4 American issues—found that teenage girls are portrayed quite differently. Portrayals of American teen girls often reflected images of independence and determination, whereas those of Japanese teen girls portrayed happy, playful, childlike girlish images.[10] Another content analysis study compared American and Chinese television commercials targeted to children and revealed that 82% of the Chinese ads aimed at children were for food products, whereas 56% of the ads directed at American children were for toys.[11]

Field Observation

When examining a specific society, anthropologists frequently study cultures through **field observation**, which consists of observing the daily behavior of selected members of a society. Based on their observations, researchers draw conclusions about the values, beliefs, and customs of the society under investigation. For example, if researchers were interested in how women select jeans, they might position trained observers in department and clothing stores and note how many and which types of jeans buyers pick up, look at, and try on.

Field observation:

1. Takes place within a natural environment.
2. Generally, the subjects are not aware that they are being watched.
3. Focuses on observation of behavior.

Because the emphasis is on a natural environment and observable behavior, field observation of buying and consumption activities occurs in stores, and, less frequently, during in-home product usage.

In some cases, researchers become **participant-observers**; that is, they become active members of the environment that they are studying and engage in the same behaviors, rituals, and customs that they study. For example, if researchers were interested in examining how consumers select a washing machine, they might take a sales position in an appliance store and observe and interact with the customers. Researchers who specialize in field observation often videotape subjects at work, at home, in their cars, and in public places. For instance, if researchers ask teenagers directly why they are buying certain T-shirts, teenagers might give answers that they believe will make them look sensible to the researchers. Instead, watching teenagers as they shop and listening to their conversations with other shoppers or salespersons might reveal more about the kids' motivations for buying. As a classic example, when Nissan was designing its Infiniti automobiles in the 1990s, two individuals, posing as students, rented rooms in the suburban homes of two families in the Los Angeles area and observed the car-related behaviors and preferences of "typical" Americans, without the families' awareness. Among other findings, they discovered that the Japanese notion of luxury was very different from the American notion; whereas the Japanese crave simplicity, Americans crave visible opulence.[12]

In addition to fieldwork, marketers have used **depth interviews** and **focus groups** (see Chapter 16) to study social and cultural changes. In focus group discussions, consumers are apt to reveal attitudes and behaviors that signal shifts in values that may affect, for example, the acceptance of new products and services. Focus groups have been used to generate ideas for persuasive strategies designed to reinforce customer loyalty and retention. Studies showed that established customers, especially for services (such as investment and banking), expected marketers to acknowledge their loyalty by providing them with more personalized services. Subsequently, several companies instituted loyalty (or frequency) programs tailored to customers' specific needs.

Researchers exploring the symbolic meanings of foods conducted 30 in-depth interviews (lasting 1.5 to 2.5 hours) of females and males within the (very wide) age range of 22 to 71 years old. They found that, in the context of cultural settings, there are seven types of foods: *Symbolic* foods (e.g., homemade and comfort foods); *individual* foods (e.g., healthy foods); *social* foods (e.g., foods typically shared with family and others); *cultural* foods (e.g., foods eaten during sexual encounters and believed to enhance libido); *ritualistic* foods (e.g., foods associated with nostalgic events); *context* foods (e.g., date and coffee-break foods); and *experience* foods (e.g., unfamiliar foods from other cultures).[13]

Value Measurements

Anthropologists have traditionally observed the behavior of members of a specific society and inferred the underlying values of the society from the behaviors observed. However, there are also structured, self-administered questionnaires that measure individuals' cultural values, such as the Rokeach Value Survey, the Values and Lifestyles **VALS** (discussed in Chapter 2) measure, and Gordon's survey of personal and interpersonal values.

Rokeach Values Survey

The **Rokeach Value Survey** is a self-administered, two-part values inventory:

1. Eighteen **terminal values** that reflect goals and desirable states of existence and are defined as *ends* (e.g., happiness, pleasure, freedom, self-respect).

2. Eighteen **instrumental values,** defined as the *means* to achieve the ends (e.g., ambitious, honest, polite, responsible).

Respondents are asked how important each value is to them as "a guiding principle" in their lives.

Within each set of values, there are also two subsets: Some terminal values focus on *personal* aspects (e.g., a comfortable or exciting life, happiness, inner harmony) and the others on *interpersonal* ones (e.g., a world of peace and beauty, national security). The instrumental values are composed of *competence* (e.g., ambitious, intellectual, responsible) and *moral* values (e.g., forgiving, helpful, polite).

According to the Rokeach typology, in terms of cultural orientation, individuals can belong to one of four types. Table 11.3 describes the characteristics of each type and also lists applicable, illustrative promotional themes.

As an example, let's assume that a study employed the Rokeach Value Survey to categorize a given population. The members of one segment uncovered were mostly concerned with "world peace," followed by "inner harmony" and "true friendship." Members of this segment were involved in domestic-oriented activities (such as gardening, reading, and going out with the family to visit relatives); they were less materialistic, nonhedonistic, and reluctant to try new products. In contrast, the members of another segment were self-centered and concerned with values such as "self-respect," "a comfortable life," "pleasure," "exciting life," "accomplishment," and "social recognition." They were least concerned with values related to the family and other people, such as friendship, love, and equality. Because they were self-centered, achievement-oriented, and pleasure seekers, they preferred provocative and highly fashionable clothes, enjoyed adventurous lifestyles, and were willing to try new products.

Gordon's Surveys of Personal and Interpersonal Values

Gordon's Survey of Personal and Interpersonal Values measures values that determine how people cope with their daily lives.[14] There are two surveys—one for **personal values** and one for **interpersonal values**—that are partially described in Table 11.4, together with the illustrative characteritics that exemplify each value. As expected, Gordon's values are strongly reflected in Americans' core values, which are discussed next.

TABLE 11.3	The Rokeach Typology and Illustrative Promotional Themes		
		TERMINAL VALUES: Goals and desired states of existence	
		PERSONAL VALUES: Personal focus	SOCIAL VALUES: Interpersonal focus
INSTRUMENTAL VALUES: Preferable behaviors and means for achieving terminal values.	COMPETENCE VALUES: Being ambitious, capable, and responsible. When violated, the person feels ashamed and inadequate.	Promotional messages should reflect consumers' sense of accomplishment, self-respect, and striving for a comfortable life and independence.	Rather than depicting merely concern, messages should show helping others and the role of one's skills in doing so.
	MORAL VALUES: Being cheerful, helpful, and honest. When violated, the person feels guilty.	Promotions should stress concern for societal issues and intense conviction to advance such causes.	The majority of Americans. Promotions should stress conformity, caring for others, and social consciousness.

TABLE 11.4	Marketing-Applicable Values from Gordon's Inventory	

PERSONAL VALUES	INTERPERSONAL VALUES
ACHIEVEMENT Enjoying challenge, growth, and accomplishment. Knowing what one wants to accomplish and doing so in an outstanding manner.	**LEADERSHIP** Being in charge and having authority and power. Not having to follow orders. Leading groups. Having others work under one's direction.
GOAL ORIENTATION Prefer having well-defined objectives and completing tasks. Knowing exactly what one is aiming for.	**RECOGNITION** Being looked up to, considered important, and admired. Having people make favorable remarks. Being noticed.
VARIETY Disliking routines and preferring new experiences. Visiting new places. Trying new and different things. Being able to have a variety of experiences and travel a lot.	**CONFORMITY** Doing the correct thing and following regulation. Doing what's accepted and proper. Conforming strictly to rules and moral standards.

American Core Cultural Values

Learning Objective

4 To understand Americans' core values and how to apply them to persuasive communications.

In this section, we identify several **American core values** that both affect and reflect the character of American society. Designating American core values is difficult. First, the United States is a diverse country, consisting of many subcultures whose members interpret and respond differently to the same set of values and beliefs (see Chapter 12). Second, America is a dynamic society that has undergone rapid changes throughout its relatively short history, as illustrated by the technological developments that have altered every aspect of our lives during the past twenty years. Finally, there are some contradictory values in American society. For instance, as a society, Americans embrace the freedom of choice, but among peers, many Americans tend to conform (in dress, in furnishings, and in fads) to the rest of society. In the context of consumer behavior, Americans like to have a wide choice of products and prefer those that uniquely express their personal lifestyles, but also often conform to peer pressures in their consumption behavior.

We used the following criteria to select and designate core values:

1. The value must be pervasive. That is, a significant portion of the American people must have accepted the value and used it to guide their attitudes and actions.

2. The value must be enduring. That is, it must have influenced Americans' actions over an extended period (as distinguished from fads and short-lived fashions).

3. The value must be related to consumption behavior. That is, it must provide insights that help us understand Americans' consumption habits.

The core values identified include achievement and success, time and activity, efficiency and practicality, progress, materialism (comfort and pleasure), individualism and conformity, freedom of choice, humanitarianism, youthfulness, and fitness and health.

Achievement and Success

Americans maintain that challenges and competition drive people to excel. For example, young children are encouraged to excel in their studies and sports and surpass others. Free enterprise is the core of the U.S. economic system, and has made Americans more productive and allowed them to enjoy better lifestyles than most other nations. Personal achievement is a fundamental American value, with historical roots in the Protestant work ethic, which considers hard work as wholesome, spiritually rewarding, and an appropriate end in itself. Historically, our society's focus on achievement has significantly affected American society's technical development and economic growth.[15] Individuals who consider a "sense of accomplishment" an important personal value are high achievers and strive for success. The Everlast ad in Figure 11.4 depicts striving for achievement. It encourages bike riders to train harder and states that Everlast's power packs enable them to recover faster from strenuous training. The ad shows a silhouette of a single biker riding vigorously against a dramatic sunset. The entire image is focused on the individual rider and his quest for achievement and fulfillment.

Source: Everlast Worldwide, Inc.

FIGURE 11.4 Portrayal of Achievement

Research has discovered that individuals who scored higher on "sense of accomplishment" use the Internet widely for learning or gathering information, making reservations or researching travel, doing work/business tasks, buying goods or services, looking up stock quotes, and participating in online auctions by buying or selling products. Conversely, Internet activities not associated with a high "sense of accomplishment" included surfing the Web, communicating with others in chat rooms, and gathering product or retail store information.[16]

Success is closely related to achievement, but the two are not identical. Specifically, achievement is its own direct reward (it implicitly satisfies the individual achiever), whereas success includes an extrinsic reward (such as luxury possessions, financial compensation, and high status). A study that examined the choices of majors among incoming students discovered that, for men, the most important factor was the field's potential for advancement and high salaries, whereas for women the most influential factor was aptitude and interest in the subject.[17]

Both achievement and success influence consumption and often provide justification for the acquisition of goods and services. For example, "You owe it to yourself," "You worked for it," and "You deserve it" are popular themes used by advertisers to coax consumers into purchasing their products, because marketers know that achievement-oriented people often enjoy conspicuous consumption, which enables them to display symbols of their personal accomplishments (e.g., a Rolex wristwatch).

Time and Activity

Americans consider time valuable (i.e., "time is money" and "time waits for no one") and many visitors from other countries often comment on how many times Americans look at their watches and how concerned they are about deadlines and promptness. We hold time in high regard because we can accomplish more and be more productive if we use time wisely, keep busy, and do not waste time. Americans dislike "wasting time" and are discouraged from "sitting around doing nothing," but like to plan and follow schedules and, at times, seem to be controlled by timetables. We often speak about *being* on time, *saving* time, *using* time wisely, and *not wasting* time.

Americans value being active and involved in society, and keeping busy in one's daily life is considered necessary. "Don't just stand there, do something" is an expression that we commonly use and clearly shows the American preference for action over inaction. Leisure activities occupy a relatively small portion of Americans' lives, and their number of nonwork days—holidays, time off, and vacations—is at least one-third less than Europeans'. Because we value leisure time less than, say, the Italians and French, but value time spent at work more, we often define ourselves by our professions, as evident in the question "What do you do for a living?" that we generally ask almost immediately after meeting strangers.

The premium placed on time has had both positive and negative effects on American society. For example, the quest for saving time has driven the development and growth of fast foods, the widespread and often too enthusiastic consumption of which has resulted in poorer health for many Americans and increased medical costs for all. Because Americans are preoccupied with time, they believe it is in short supply and want things to happen quickly (they hate waiting in line or for deliveries to arrive). Many ads portray products that assist consumers in managing their rushed lives. The ad for Campbell's Chunky Soup in Figure 11.5 emphasizes saving time and tells consumers that they can prepare the soup quickly and simultaneously receive value for their money.

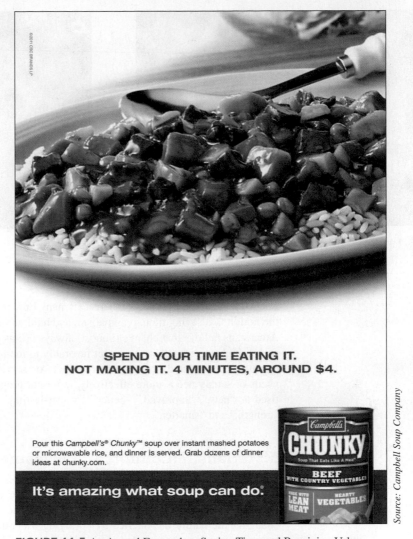

FIGURE 11.5 An Appeal Focused on Saving Time and Receiving Value

Efficiency and Practicality

Americans consider themselves highly efficient and pragmatic. Many business executives pay little attention to theoretical scenarios; instead, they often employ trial-and-error, a pragmatic approach that consists of trying several potential solutions to a given problem individually and selecting the most effective one. This pragmatic orientation has led Americans to develop more inventions than any other nations. In addition, Americans hold "practical" disciplines—such as management, economics, law, and medicine—in higher regard than philosophy, anthropology, the arts, and teaching, among many others.

Americans' practical orientation is reflected in their language: "Will the venture be profitable?" "Will it pay its own way?" "What's in it for me?" Rather than being emotional and thinking in subjective terms, Americans pride themselves on judging things on their own merits. Americans readily adopt practical products that enable them to be more efficient. For example, many manufacturers, in different product categories, offer arrays of interchangeable components, so consumers can design customized wall units (e.g., IKEA), computers, sunglasses, and many other items at reasonable prices. The ads for 3-In–One Oil in Figure 11.6 portray an efficient product that consumers can use in several ways.

Progress

Americans view change as desirable because it symbolizes development (personal as well as societal), improvement, and growth. Traditional cultures often consider change disruptive, try to avoid it, and value stability and continuity. For example, in the United States, one's wealth is generally more

Source: (Left & Right) 3 - IN - ONE ® is a registered trademark of WD-40 Company

FIGURE 11.6 An Appeal Focused on the Product's Efficiency

important than one's heritage, whereas in many European societies the opposite is true. Together with the notion that saving time, pragmatism, and hard work lead to achievement, innovation, and growth, Americans believe that change (almost) always brings about a better future. Because they hold progress in high regard, Americans react favorably to messages that mention or promise progress. In our consumption-oriented society, new products or services designed to fulfill previously unsatisfied needs or satisfy needs more effectively, represent progress. Therefore, we often buy products advertised as "new," "improved," "better," "longer-lasting," "quicker," "smoother and closer," "increased strength," and "smarter."

Materialism (Comfort and Pleasure)

Americans' desire for material goods goes back a long way. In an Atlantic Monthly essay in 1924, entitled "Things Are in the Saddle," Samuel Strauss coined the term "consumptionism," which he defined as "the science of compelling men to use more and more things."* Strauss felt that this was changing the nature of America by "bringing it about that the American citizen's first importance to his country is no longer that of citizen, but that of consumer."[18] For most Americans, from a very young age, material comfort and possessions signify attainment of "the good life"—a life that may include a new car, a dishwasher, an air conditioner, a hot tub, and an almost infinite variety of other convenience-oriented and pleasure-providing goods and services. Americans often compare themselves to others in terms of the value of their possessions and tend to believe that they are happier than those who have less. Nevertheless, as many popular songs point out, the ownership of material goods does not always lead to happiness. For instance, many very affluent people have failed marriages and dysfunctional children as a direct result of being extraordinarily wealthy. Still, the expression "He who dies with the most toys wins" is widely used, and not always ironically.

Stereotypically, people from other nations view Americans as too materialistic, a notion that most Americans shrug off based on their belief that material objects are desirable and just rewards for their hard work, as well as symbols of their achievement. However, most of us do accumulate more possessions than the members of other societies, and, to some extent, obtaining, maintaining, and protecting our possessions comes before developing and enjoying relationships. Our **materialism** is often expressed in preferring "bigger quantities of things" or "more of something." Recently, however, there has been a noticeable shift away from the "more is better" viewpoint to a "better is better" vision—one that stresses better quality and better design. Some refer to this trend as "the design economy"; that is, an economy based on the interaction of four elements: Sustained prosperity, ongoing technology, a culture open to change, and marketing expertise.[19] The activity of shopping has played an increasingly important role in our lives and many now refer to our "shopping culture" and "consumer culture." A widely quoted essay even suggested that: "Shopping is what we do to create value in our lives."[20] Still further, because online shopping is always available (as opposed to physical stores that are not always open), we now spend more time than ever before on viewing and comparing products, and, presumably, buy more objects that we do not *truly* need.

---

* Samuel Strauss "Things Are in the Saddle," Atlantic Monthly 1924

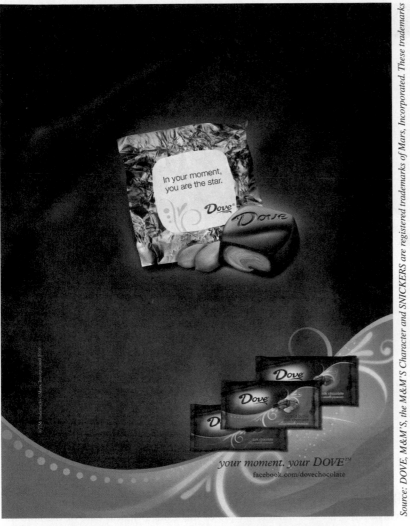

Source: DOVE, M&M'S, the M&M'S Character and SNICKERS are registered trademarks of Mars, Incorporated. These trademarks and advertisements are used with permission. Mars, Incorporated is not associated with Pearson Education, Inc.

FIGURE 11.7 An Appeal Focused on Comfort and Pleasure

Chocolate is one of the world's oldest and most exotic products. It is associated with love, luxury, and—because of its scientifically documented impact on brain activity—feeling happy and satisfied. The ad for DOVE® Chocolate in Figure 11.7 encourages consumers to feel pleased, enjoy a special moment, and even "be a star."

Individualism and Conformity

Americans value "being themselves." Self-reliance, self-interest, self-confidence, self-esteem, and self-fulfillment are popular expressions of individualism in our language. Striving for individualism is the rejection of dependency; that is, it is better to rely on oneself than on others. Indeed, the opposite of individualism is "collectivism," which implies that "being in a group" is a basic human endeavor, so that humans' self-concept involves group membership*; collectivism is also strongly associated with communism—a failed and largely distinct economic system.[21]American "rugged individualism" stems from the belief in self-reliance and competition, which consists of outperforming others in order to meet one's individual needs and fulfill one's goals. Rugged individuals consider solo performance superior to teamwork, and maintain that tasks should be accomplished alone and victory should be earned alone.[22] The objective of advertising appeals to individualism is to persuade consumers to buy products and services that reflect and emphasize their individual identities. For example, advertisements for high-style clothing and cosmetics promise consumers that these products will enhance their exclusive and distinctive characteristics and set them apart from others.

Conceptually, the marketing concept is congruent with individualism. The essence of the marketing concept lies in understanding consumers' needs and making only those products that customers truly believe will satisfy their needs. For instance, writing is an individualistic pursuit that often requires encouragement. The ads in Figure 11.8 imply that writing with the Cross Morph pen inspires and explores one's imagination.

Individualism and conformity exist side by side. Although Americans deeply embrace freedom of choice and individualism, they nevertheless accept the reality of conformity. The individualism-conformity paradox is also manifested in our product choices. On the one hand, standardized products, which have been made possible by mass production, reflect uniformity. On the other hand, online shopping increasingly enables people to purchase customized personal items (e.g., sneakers, sunglasses, clothing) easily (and often inexpensively) and readily express their individualism.

The acceptance of casual dressing in the workplace is an interesting example of the "ping-pong" relationship between seeking individualism and accepting conformity. Male and female executives alike are abandoning decades-old workplace dress codes and wearing casual slacks, sport shirts, and blazers to work rather than traditional business attire. Increasingly, businesspeople (including some lawyers and even accountants) have sought more comfortable work clothes and became more confident in their ability to choose casual yet appropriate clothing. As time went by, in many companies, blue blazers and gray slacks for men, and similar-style clothing for females, became the new "business uniform" and a norm to conform to.

Freedom of Choice

Freedom as an American core value stems from the nation's fundamental principles: Freedom of speech, press, assembly, and religion. Americans prefer and even expect to be able to choose from a wide range of alternatives in all aspects of their lives, as illustrated by the large number of competitive

* Source: N. Schwartz "Individualism and Collectivism" *Journal of Consumer Psychology* 14:4 (2006) 324.

FIGURE 11.8 Appeals Focused on Imagination and Inspiration

brands and product variations on the shelves of supermarkets, specialty stores, drugstores, and other outlets. Apparently, such varieties are uncommon outside of the United States. One of the authors, who resides in midtown Manhattan—an area where tourists are always present—has seen, on numerous occasions, tourists pointing excitedly at (and even taking pictures of) the scores of shampoos, soaps, shaving creams, and other personal-care products displayed in drugstores. For many products, American consumers can select from a wide variety of sizes, colors, flavors, features, styles, and even special ingredients. The HP ad in Figure 11.9 illustrates Americans' quest for choices when buying a PC.

Humanitarianism

Americans are often generous and willing (and even eager) to help those in need. They support many humane and charitable causes, and often sympathize with the underdog who must overcome adversity to get ahead. They also tend to be charitable and willing to aid people who are less fortunate than they are. Illustrations of attitudes about charitable giving appear in Table 11.5.[23]

Another study investigated the motivations of alumni who donated money to intercollegiate athletic programs and identified four distinct benefits that donors received from their monetary pledges:

1. *Belongingness*—being associated with and loyal to the institution, helping to build a successful athletic program and continue tradition
2. *Trusting*—confidence in the institution's leadership and vision
3. *Social-practical motivation*—exploring social and professional contacts, receiving priority seating at sports events and tax deductions
4. *Prestige*—pride in supporting a prestigious institution and sports teams.[24]

Based on knowledge of these motivations, universities and colleges can segment potential donors according to the benefits they seek and create persuasive messages directed at the different motivations for donating money.

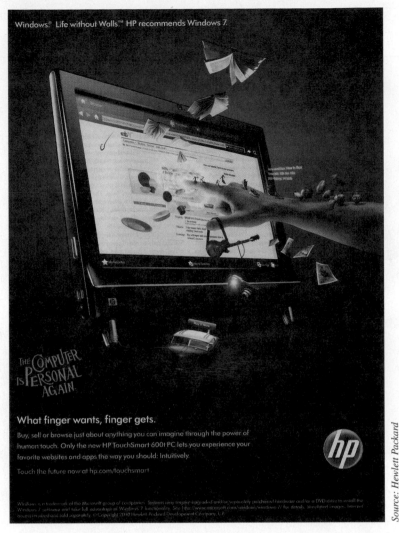

Windows.® Life without Walls.™ HP recommends Windows 7.

What finger wants, finger gets.

Buy, sell or browse just about anything you can imagine through the power of human touch. Only the new HP TouchSmart 600t PC lets you experience your favorite websites and apps the way you should: Intuitively.

Touch the future now at hp.com/touchsmart

Source: Hewlett Packard

FIGURE 11.9 Freedom of Choice: "Whatever finger wants, finger gets"

Americans' humanitarianism has also affected their consumption and investments. For example, some refuse to invest in companies that use child labor (in foreign countries), harm the environment, or make weapons, and investments in socially conscious mutual funds are now commonplace. One study showed that, during Christmas shopping, the number of consumers indicating that they intend to purchase from retailers "that support a cause" has been steadily increasing.[25] Another form of humanitarianism is American's notion of collective responsibility and respect, which involves stepping forward when confronted with actions that hurt others. The ad in Figure 11.10 encourages abused women—the underdog (i.e., the person who has little chance of winning)—to take action and report the abuse immediately.

Youthfulness

Americans are preoccupied with youthfulness. The emphasis on youthfulness contrasts sharply with traditional European and Asian societies, where older people are looked up to for their wisdom and the experience that comes with age. Nevertheless, youthfulness should not be confused with youth: Youth designates an age cohort. Americans are preoccupied with looking and acting young, regardless of their chronological age. For Americans, youthfulness is a state of mind and a state of being, sometimes expressed as being "young at heart," "young in spirit," or "young in appearance."

Many advertising messages create a sense of urgency about retaining one's youth and avoiding aging. Hand-cream ads talk about "young hands"; skin-treatment ads state, "I dreaded turning 30"; fragrance and makeup ads stress looking "sexy and young" or "denying your age"; detergent ads ask readers, "Can you match their hands with their ages?" Countless advertising themes promise consumers youthfulness and reflect the high premium Americans place on appearing and acting young.

Fitness and Health

Being fit and healthy is an important core value and very evident in many aspects of American life. Witness the large number of health clubs and chains of fitness-related services, including yoga and similar forms of body-and-mind conditioning; a seemingly endless array of innovative fitness equipment (often featured in long TV infomercials); fitness centers and activities in some companies; biking and running lanes in many cities; the increasing availability of organic, low-fat, and no-fat foods and foods with less sodium and sugar; the large number of fitness magazines; the large array of vitamins and other supplements, backed by aggressive advertising; the variety of diet programs and "gurus" and exercise equipment designed specifically for reducing weight; portable

TABLE 11.5 Attitudes Toward Donating Money to Charities
1. Willing to help others who are in need and less fortunate.
2. Those who are not in need should be charitable toward those who are.
3. People in need should receive support from others.
4. Money donated to charities goes to good uses and helps those in need.
5. Charitable organizations have been effective in assisting those who are needy.
6. Charitable organizations perform a useful function.

Source: Inspired by Deborah J. Webb, et.al. "Development of and Validation of Scales to Measure Attitudes Influencing Monetary Donations to Charitable Organizations," *Journal of the Academy of Marketing Science*, 28 (Spring 2000): 299–309.

Source: photo copyright Curtis Johnsona

FIGURE 11.10 An Appeal Focused on Humanitarianism: Helping the Underdog

monitors of heart rate, body fat, and the number of calories used during physical activities; the increasing popularity of "active" and "adventure" vacations (e.g., backroads.com); and reductions in health insurance costs to nonsmokers and people who enroll in wellness programs. These are only an exemplary few of the products and services available because of Americans' preoccupation with fitness and health.

Health and fitness are now reflected in our jargon, with such phrases as: "You are what you eat," "Fitness is a way of life," "well-balanced diet," "fitness culture," "wellness programs," and "No pain, no gain." Other, less popular slogans include: "Move it or lose it," "Why put off feeling good?" "Too fit to quit," "Commit to be fit," "Don't be a brat, burn that fat," and "Rest a while then run a mile."

Many studies have investigated the reasons behind the growing importance of fitness and health in America. One study suggested that Americans believe they have lost the ability to control their environment and, as a result, feel anxious and insecure and also experience self-doubt. People who feel that they lack external self-control turn inward; they feel that if they can't control the world, they can at least control and change their own bodies through exercise.[26]

Many Americans have adopted healthier lifestyles and buy healthier foods at least some of the time.[27] Virtually all food companies have modified at least some of their products to cater to health-conscious consumers. Frozen dinners have become more nutritious and some "junk foods" have become less unhealthy. Makers of high-calorie and low-nutrition snack foods have introduced "light," "fat-free," "low-sodium," "no-cholesterol," "no-preservatives," and "no trans fat" versions of their offerings. One study sponsored by Progressive Grocer, a leading food retailing publication, suggested that "the most lucrative consumer trend in the next five to ten years" is going to be "health and wellness," and that consumers who currently make their grocery shopping decisions based on price, taste, and convenience will upgrade "health benefits to a No. 1 or No. 2 priority."[28] Consumers have also become concerned with more hygienic home maintenance products, such as antimicrobial home-cleaning solutions.[29]

Websites are the most popular sources of health and fitness information. There are countless websites devoted to fitness and health, offering workout tips, nutritional information, and fitness-related products and services, among many others. In addition, most of the websites set up by companies that market consumer goods provide health and fitness information associated with their products (e.g., sellers of cleaning products offering advice on more sanitary housekeeping and marketers of sunglasses advising consumers how to protect their eyes from the sun even when not wearing glasses). A website that monitors online surfing reported that, in a given period, most Internet users have looked online for information on health topics, with increased interest in diet, fitness, drugs, health insurance, experimental treatments, and particular doctors and hospitals.[30]

In spite of the explosive growth of the fitness and wellness industry and the scores of healthier foods introduced, about two-thirds of Americans are overweight, and, as reported by the Centers for Disease Control and Prevention (CDC), 36% of American adults are obese (as defined clinically), as are 17% of children ages 2 to 19. At this rate, 44% of all American will be obese within the next 15 years or so; obesity-related medical costs, which presently amount to $150 billion, will double or even triple.[31] (A discussion of marketers' impact on obesity rates appears in Chapter 15.) As expected, losing weight and eating healthier have been at the top of Americans' New Year's resolutions for decades (usually followed by getting out of debt and saving more money).[32] Campbell's Healthy Request soup—featured in Figure 11.11—is one of the thousands of products introduced in response to Americans' health concerns.

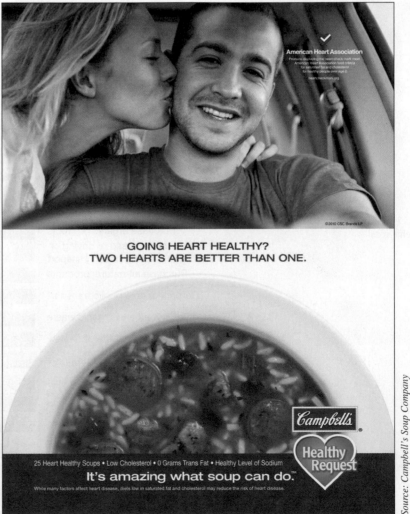

FIGURE 11.11 An Appeal Focused on Fitness and Health

Green Marketing

Learning Objective

5 To understand green marketing and ecologically responsible consumption.

Green marketing is producing and promoting reusable and eco-friendly products. Over the past twenty years or so, virtually all companies have adopted at least some environmentally friendly practices in response to the global awareness of climate change and its potentially dire consequences for our planet and its inhabitants. For instance, because emissions from cars are a prominent contributor to environmental deterioration, automobile makers now produce more environmentally sound cars. Most advertisers inform consumers that they use renewable, clean, and sustainable energy and recycled and nonpolluting materials.

Ecologically Responsible Consumption

Many Americans consider buying environmentally sound products to be part of their duties as consumers and a societal and cultural priority. Although many consumers claim to be "green" and support ecological causes, studies indicate that such attitudes do not always result in pro-environmental behavior. That is, there is a discrepancy between what people say and what they do.[33] Furthermore, consumers' eco-consciousness is fickle, and the sales of such products as recycled toilet paper, organic foods, and hybrid cars sharply decline during economic recessions.[34] Somewhat surprisingly, a Harris Poll indicated that "green" attitudes and behaviors declined over a three-year period. The poll's key findings are featured in Figures 11.12 and 11.13.[35]

FIGURE 11.12 Americans' "Green" Attitudes

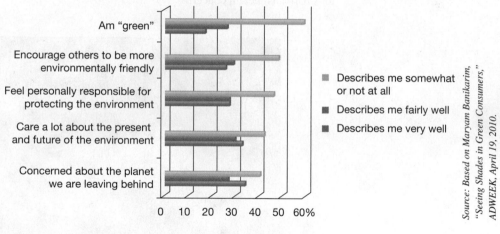

Source: Based on Maryam Banikarim, "Seeing Shades in Green Consumers," ADWEEK, April 19, 2010.

FIGURE 11.13 Americans' "Green" Behaviors

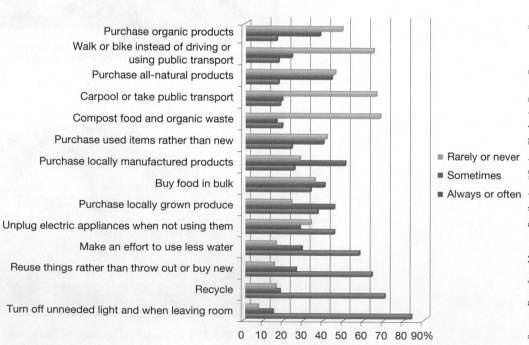

Source: Data from Maryam Banikarim, "Seeing Shades in Green Consumers," ADWEEK, April 19, 2010.

Several studies have focused on consumers' likelihood to buy environmentally safe products. One study examined consumers' willingness to purchase such goods in the context of their desires to buy quality products at reasonable prices, and developed a scale measuring consumers' attitudes toward green products and the firms making them (see Table 11.6).[36] Another study found that most consumers did not know which lifestyle changes were the best means to reduce global warming.[37] Research has also discovered that consumers find environmental labels difficult to understand and that this issue increases their price sensitivity regarding green ecologically sound products.[38] Yet another study indicated that even consumers with pro-environmental beliefs have difficulty correctly identifying green products (other than cleaning items) and do not find green marketing engaging.[39] Together, these studies indicate that marketers must improve their promotion of green products. Segmenting green consumers is covered in Chapter 2.

Table 11.7 summarizes Americans' core value and illustrates them with promotional themes.

TABLE 11.6	**A Scale Measuring Consumers' Attitudes Toward Green Products**

I believe there are a lot of exaggerations about companies taking environmental risks nowadays.

I believe the government is doing all that is possible to safeguard the environment.

I believe that we should not slow down industry progress because of concern for the environment.

I believe environmental safety is the responsibility of the government, not individual citizens.

I believe that government legislation adequately regulates environmental protection.

I believe a well-known brand is always a safe product to buy.

I believe that the quality of environmentally safe products is not as good as other products.

I believe that the price of environmentally safe products is usually more expensive than other products.

I believe Australian companies are generally doing a good job in helping to protect the environment.

I believe companies should place higher priority on reducing pollution than on increasing their own profitability.

I believe companies should place higher priority on reducing pollution than on increasing profitability even if jobs are at risk.

Source: Maryam Banikarim, "Seeing Shades in Green Consumers," ADWEEK, April 19, 2010.

TABLE 11.7	**Americans' Core Cultural Values and Illustrative Promotional Themes**	
CORE VALUE	**DEFINITION**	**ILLUSTRATIVE PROMOTIONAL THEMES**
Achievement and Success	Hard work and excelling in other aspects of life lead to success.	"Fact: Our car members experience more" "You're worth it" "For people who are in the best shape they've ever been in, but still aren't satisfied"
Time and Activity	Being active and busy in one's job and life and expanding one's horizons.	"A new challenge daily—Wow, I'm so fortunate" "Prepare today, to lead for a lifetime"
Efficiency and Practicality	Saving time and effort and finding pragmatic products and solutions. Less theory, more practice.	"The taste you want, the energy you need" "So easy, even an adult can open our container"
Progress	Seeking and adopting new processes that replace less advanced ones.	"One-step process to a better complexion" "Only 4 minutes to a great family meal"
Materialism (Comfort and Pleasure)	Accumulating possessions that enable a more comfortable and pleasurable life.	"Bring the family together: Create a great backyard" "Not rich? Start saving tomorrow"
Individualism and Conformity	*Individualism*: Be yourself and marching to the "beat of your own drum," as opposed to adhering to group norms and being the same as others. *Conformity*: Desire to fit in.	*Individualism*: "You answered to your own drum in college, now how about a challenging position for your career?" *Conformity*: "Drive carefully" "Respect others" "Be included: Vote this November"

(continued)

TABLE 11.7   Americans' Core Cultural Values and Illustrative Promotional Themes (continued)

CORE VALUE	DEFINITION	ILLUSTRATIVE PROMOTIONAL THEMES
Freedom of Choice	Having freedom of choice and expression.	"Almost more colors than hairs on your head" "America is about choice"
Humanitarianism	Helping the less fortunate and people in need.	"No kid should go hungry" "We combat natural disasters with human kindness"
Youthfulness	Looking youthful and remaining "young at heart" despite aging chronologically.	"Never look your age again" "Be Young. It's a state of open-mindedness"
Fitness and Health	Caring about one's health and ability to be physically active.	"Relax—It's the good fat" "Create your perfect body"
Ecological Responsibility	Caring about the environment and buying "green" products.	Toyota Prius hybrid car; Clorox Green Works cleaner; scores of products from Arm & Hammer, Palmolive, and most other firms

Summary

Learning Objective 1: To understand culture's role, dynamics, evolution, and impact on consumers' priorities and behaviors.

Culture is the collective values, customs, norms, arts, social institutions, and intellectual achievements of a particular society. Cultural values express the collective principles, standards, and priorities of a community. Most of the promotional messages across the world reflect, to some degree, the cultural values of the target audiences. Cultures always evolve, so marketers must monitor the sociocultural environment so as to market existing products more effectively and develop new products that are congruent with changing cultural trends. Understanding cultural changes is not an easy task, because many factors produce cultural changes within a given society, including new technologies, population shifts, resource shortages, and customs from other cultures.

Learning Objective 2: To understand language, symbols, and rituals as expressions of a learned culture.

To be considered a cultural value, a belief or custom must be shared by a significant portion of the society, because culture is essentially a series of norms that guide personal and group conduct and link together individuals into a largely cohesive group. Generally, society's members share their values and customs through a common language, although some cultures include more than one language. We learn cultural norms and customs mostly from family and peers, and begin at a very young age to understand that some behaviors are appropriate and others are not. Anthropologists have identified three forms of cultural learning: Formal learning, informal learning, and technical learning. Our ethical values are also formed during childhood, as we learn them from parents, teachers, and other significant adults. Anthropologists distinguish between enculturation (learning one's own culture) and acculturation (learning a new or foreign cultures). The contents of media,

advertising, and marketing reflect cultural values and convey them to all members of society very effectively. Given Americans' extensive exposure to print, broadcast, and online media, as well as the easily ingested and entertaining presentation formats of their contents, media and advertising are powerful vehicles for imparting cultural values.

Cultural values are reflected in societies' languages, symbols, communications, and artifacts. A symbol is anything that represents something else; symbols can be either verbal or nonverbal. Words are verbal symbols and the text of any ad is a composition of symbols. In addition to language and symbols, cultures include ritualized behaviors. A ritual is a type of symbolic activity consisting of a series of steps (multiple behaviors) occurring in a fixed sequence and repeated periodically.

Learning Objective 3: To understand how to measure the influence of culture on consumer behavior.

The most widely used measurements of cultural values are content analysis, consumer field observation, and value measurement instruments. Content analysis focuses on the content of societies' verbal, written, and pictorial communications, including promotional messages. When examining a specific society, anthropologists frequently study cultures through field observation, which consists of observing the daily behavior of selected members of a society. Based on their observations, researchers draw conclusions about the values, beliefs, and customs of the society under investigation. There are also structured, self-administered questionnaires that measure individuals' cultural values, such as the Rokeach Value Survey, the Values and Lifestyles instrument, and Gordon's Survey of Personal and Interpersonal Values.

Learning Objective 4: To understand Americans' core values and how to apply them to persuasive communications.

We identified eleven American core values that both affect and reflect the character of American society, using the criteria of pervasiveness, endurance, and consumption relatedness. The core values identified include achievement and success, time and activity, efficiency and practicality, progress, materialism (comfort and pleasure), individualism and conformity, freedom of choice, humanitarianism, youthfulness, fitness and health, and ecological responsibility. These values are often reflected in advertisements and are applicable to developing marketing strategies.

Learning Objective 5: To understand green marketing and ecologically responsible consumption.

Green marketing is producing and promoting reusable and eco-friendly products. Virtually all companies have adopted at least some environmentally friendly practices in response to the global awareness of climate change and its potentially dire consequences for our planet and its inhabitants. Many Americans now consider buying environmentally sound products to be part of their duties as consumers and a societal and cultural priority. Studies focused on consumers have found that favorable attitudes toward environmentally safe products do not always lead to purchase of such items. Researchers also discovered that consumers cannot easily understand many eco-labels and do not know which lifestyle changes can help the environment.

Review and Discussion Questions

11.1. In what ways do the three forms of cultural learning differ from one another? How can each be used effectively in marketing and advertisements?

11.2. Distinguish between terminal and instrumental values and their subsets. What does this classification identify? According to the Rokeach typology, in terms of cultural orientation, individuals can belong to one of four types. Make a list of them, with a section for the subsets, and analyze their characteristics.

11.3. The Citrus Growers of America is designing an advertising campaign aimed at getting consumers to switch to orange and grapefruit juices instead of soft drinks, as a "sugar jolt" in the late afternoon. Describe how the organization can use the Rokeach and the Gordon measures in planning its campaign.

11.4. For each of the following products and activities:

a. List two relevant core values and explain your choices.

b. Describe how each value either encourages or discourages buying the product or engaging in the activity.

The products and activities are:

1. Donating blood
2. Visiting tanning salons
3. Buying an e-reader
4. Buying a GPS device
5. Drinking diet beverages
6. Travelling overseas
7. Using sun protection products regularly
8. Buying a convection oven
9. Buying a pair of sneakers online
10. Following the latest fashions

11.5. Why is the Internet a relevant source of health and fitness information for people, and how can it be used for marketing purposes in this area?

11.6. Do the intended consumers react differently to green products depending on their countries of origin? If so, why?

Hands-on Assignments

11.7. Identify a singer or singing group whose music you like and discuss the symbolic function of the clothes that person (or group) wears.

11.8. Rituals and routines are highly subjective and culture-specific. For example, an Asian breakfast can be different from a Western one in terms of food selection, time of day, and favored locations. With the help of online research, try to identify the major differences in the two by preparing a list of the respective features and offer a suitable explanation. What values do the features transmit?

11.9. a. Summarize an episode of a TV or online series that you watch regularly. Describe how the episode transmitted cultural beliefs, values, and customs.

b. Select three commercials that were broadcast during the episode and describe how each reflects a cultural value(s).

11.10. An advertisement has to be quite specific in order to adequately target the interests of a populace. In many Asian countries language is the first variable of choice, and the specific language used in an ad can help to identify its intended customers. Select and study five different audio-visual advertisements of cars in South-East Asia. Try to identify the core values portrayed, and note how the ads are similar to or different from those of another country.

11.11. Find five ads promoting green products or activities and explain whether you believe each one is effective or not.

Key Terms

- acculturation *298*
- American core values *303*
- consumer socialization *298*
- content analysis *300*
- culture *294*
- depth interview *301*
- enculturation *298*
- field observation *301*
- focus group *301*

- formal learning *298*
- Gordon Survey of Personal and Interpersonal Values *302*
- green marketing *312*
- informal learning *298*
- instrumental values *302*
- interpersonal values *302*
- materialism *306*
- participant-observers *301*

- personal values *302*
- ritual *299*
- ritualistic behavior *299*
- Rokeach Value Survey *302*
- symbol *299*
- technical learning *298*
- terminal values *302*
- VALS *302*

Subcultures and Consumer Behavior

A SUBCULTURE is a group that shares certain beliefs, values, and customs and exists within a larger society. A subculture can stem from a person's ethnicity, religion, geographic location, age, or gender. Older consumers—who represent a subculture based on age—are a lucrative market segment because the American population is aging faster than the birth rate and life expectancy has been rising. Savvy companies have been adapting their products to the specific needs of older persons. For example, Kohler—a marketer of bathroom and kitchen products—introduced Elevance, a line of products designed to provide greater safety and independence (Figure 12.1). The Elevance Rising Wall Bath features an extra-wide opening, chair-height seat, integrated grab bar, and easy-to-lift rising wall. To enter the bathtub, the person sits on a comfortable seat, turns on the water, slides legs into the tub, and easily raises the wall until it latches (the wall has a double seal to ensure that no water spills out).

Diana Schrage—a senior interior designer at Kohler—said: "Physical and mental differences vary greatly from the moment of birth and are not just a factor of age. It is important to recognize that imperfect vision, hearing impairment, and limited mobility are a part of *all* life. A lever faucet handle is easy to operate with arthritis but equally easy to operate as a child. Grab bars stabilize an older person with less muscle tone but also stabilize the child who may slip and fall in a wet environment. Intent with products that serve the older consumer is the same as intent with market in general—what is the best experience a person can have with our product? How can the product be a joy to use? How can the consumer have their bathing needs met with the best designed, best functioning product possible?"[1]

Kohler's online video states that "Elevance helps you achieve the independence you desire," and features "added accessibility," "a stylish alternative to a traditional walk-in bath," and "a natural bathing experience." The description mentions no specific bathing problems—such as safely—but focuses on the solutions. Repeatedly, it stresses the benefits

FIGURE 12.1 Kohler's Elevance®

of the product and its advantages over traditional bath-tubs. The product's unique features benefit all consumers, regardless of age. Although people become more frail and prone to falling while bathing as they age, younger individuals also benefit from products that provide a safer wet environment.

Culture and Subcultures

Learning Objective

1 To understand the subcultures within the United States and their relationships to American culture.

This chapter explores the marketing opportunities created by subgroups that share certain beliefs, values, and customs and exist within the larger U.S. society. Subcultures are based on sociocultural and demographic variables, such as nationality, religion, geographic locality, ethnicity, age, and gender. When marketers single out a subculture, they must often modify the product to better meet the needs of the targeted consumers and also change the marketing message to suit the subculture's values and tastes. For instance, when targeting the Hispanic subculture, companies often supplement their English-language advertising with ads in Spanish, which are more effective than the English ads when targeting this rapidly growing market segment.

A society's cultural profile includes two elements: (1) The unique beliefs, values, and customs of specific subcultures; and (2) the core cultural values and customs that are shared by most of the population, regardless of specific subcultural memberships. Figure 12.2 presents a model of the relationship between two subcultural groups (Hispanic Americans and Asian Americans) and the larger or "more general" culture. As the figure shows, each subculture has its own unique traits, yet both groups share the dominant traits of the overall American culture.

Most Americans belong to more than one cultural group. For example, a 10-year-old girl might be African American, Baptist, a preteen, and a Texan. Membership in each different subculture provides its set of specific beliefs, values, attitudes, and customs. Subcultural analysis enables marketers to identify the sizeable and subcultural segments. Subcultures are dynamic—for example, the ethnic groups that comprise the U.S. population have been changing in size and economic power. The Caucasian white population of the United States, which made up 72% of Americans in the year 2011, is projected to decline to about 46% of the U.S. population by the year 2050.[2] The U.S. Census Bureau has estimated that by 2042, "Americans who identify themselves as Hispanic, black, Asian, American Indian, Native Hawaiian and Pacific Islander will together

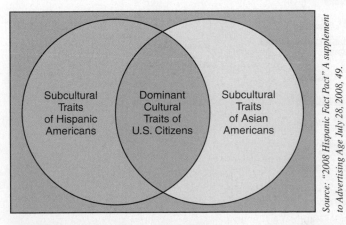

Source: "2008 Hispanic Fact Pact" A supplement to Advertising Age July 28, 2008, 49.

FIGURE 12.2 Culture and Subcultures

outnumber non-Hispanic whites.[3] Frequently, California is called a "window on America's future," and its multicultural or combined minority is now the state's majority population.

The following sections examine several subcultures stemming from nationality, ethnicity, religion, geographic regions, age, and gender.

Nationality and Ethnicity Subcultures

Learning Objective

2 To understand the influence of nationality and ethnicity subcultures on consumer behavior.

America's immigrants brought with them cultural values and lifestyles that blended into the American culture (i.e., the "melting pot" concept). Each cultural ancestry has blended, to some extent, into America's diversity, which many believe to be the country's key strength. The 2010 U.S. Census reveals that between 2000 and 2010, nearly 13% of the American population was foreign born (5.6% are naturalized citizens and 7.3% are currently noncitizens).[4] Still further, Queens County (one of the five boroughs that make up the City of New York) is one of the most multicultural counties in America, and 46% of its residents were born outside of the United States.[5] When it comes to consumer behavior, "ancestral pride" is manifested in the consumption of ethnic foods, travel to the "homeland," and the purchase of cultural artifacts (ethnic clothing, art, music, foreign-language newspapers). The three primary ethnic subcultures in America are Latinos or Hispanics, African Americans, and Asian Americans.

Savvy companies recognize subcultures in targeting consumers. For example, in one campaign, Kmart included spots that featured African American, Asian American, Hispanic, Anglo-American, and multi-ethnic families.[6] Figure 12.3 depicts the ethnic composition of the largest cities in the United States. Marketers must take into account ethnicities' media usage patterns. One study showed discovered pronounced differences in TV viewing, as shown in Figure 12.4.

Latino (Hispanic) Consumers

The 2010 U.S. Census found that 53% of all foreign-born U.S. citizens were from Latin America; these persons represent 15% of the U.S. population, and their number is estimated to become 30% of the U.S. population by the year 2050 (i.e., about 133 million).[7] In 2011, Latino Americans had an estimated purchasing power approaching $1.2 trillion, and 4 million Hispanic Americans had annual incomes of $75,000 or more.[8] In contrast to other American population segments, Hispanic Americans are younger: In 2006, when almost 34% of Hispanics were under 18 years of age, only 25% of the U.S. population was under 18. The median age for Hispanics is 27 years of age, whereas the median age for all of America is 36 years.[9] Hispanic Americans have larger families, and many live in extended family households consisting of several generations of family members. Hispanic households have more children than black or non-Hispanic American white families with children, and spend more time caring for their children.[10]

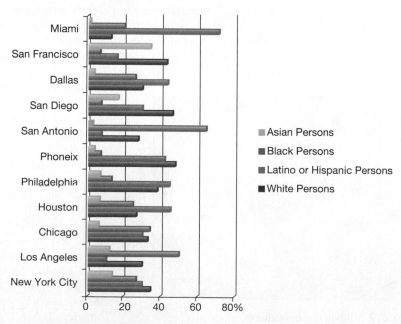

FIGURE 12.3 The Ethnic Composition (Percentages) of the Largest Cities in the United States

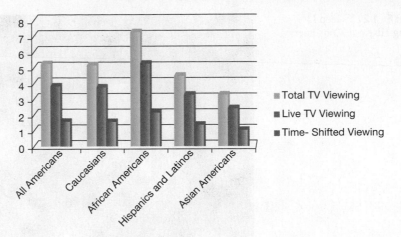

FIGURE 12.4 Ethnicity and Daily TV Viewing (Hours)

It is estimated that by 2020, only 34% of Hispanics living here will be foreign-born first generation; 36% will be U.S.-born second-generation children of immigrants, and 30% will be third-generation children of U.S.-born Hispanics.[11] In terms of acculturation, only 20% of the Hispanic/Latino market has recently migrated to the United States and speak only Spanish. Of the remaining 80%, some 20% speak only English and 60% speak both Spanish and English. Of the more than 44 million Latino Americans, 77% live in the 7 states that have a Hispanic population of 1 million or more (California, Texas, New York, Florida, Illinois, Arizona, and New Jersey). Still further, while Hispanics represented 42% of New Mexico's total population, the highest percentage of any state, some counties in North Carolina, Georgia, Iowa, Arkansas, Minnesota, and Nebraska are between 6 and 25% Hispanic.[12]

Some consider all Latinos as one subculture because of the common language. However, there are twelve distinct Hispanic subgroups in the United States. The three largest Hispanic subcultural groups are Mexican Americans (about 67% of America's Latinos), Puerto Ricans (8%), and Cubans (4%). These subcultures are heavily concentrated geographically, with more than 70% of their members residing in California, Texas, New York, and Florida; Los Angeles alone is home to one-fifth of the Hispanic population of the United States. Whereas more than 60% of all Mexican Americans (the largest Hispanic group) were born in the United States, 72% of Cuban Americans were born in Cuba.

Hispanic consumers have a strong preference for well-established brands, and traditionally prefer to shop at smaller stores. However, as Hispanics acculturate, they become less brand loyal and shop differently than they used to.[13] In New York City, many Hispanic consumers preferred to buy food in bodegas—small food specialty stores located in Spanish neighborhoods —despite lower food prices in supermarkets. However, as they adopt American customs, most Latinos in the United States begin buying food in supermarkets rather than small stores. Young Latinos are fashion conscious, loyal to well-known brands, and like the same brands as other young Americans. A study reported that female Hispanic high school students had a higher "need for uniqueness" than non-Hispanic females. Thus, marketers might appeal to some young Hispanics with advertising focused on nonconformity and independence.[14] The number of Hispanic households with Internet access has been increasing annually.[15] In fact, 78% of English-dominant Hispanics and 76% of bilingual Hispanics are Internet users.[16] Some evidence indicates that many Hispanics prefer Web content that reflects the culture of their country of origin. Older Latinos are not impulse shoppers, and many are suspicious of marketers.

Marketers targeting Latinos must be aware that identifying Hispanic consumers is complex. Some identify themselves as Latino because of their surnames or the fact that Spanish is their first language. From a marketing viewpoint, the best way to target a Hispanic market is on the basis of the group's degree of personal ethnic identification. Some marketers use Spanish to cater to Latinos. For example, Ford started promoting its Flex, a crossover vehicle, with product placement that had the car "starring" in Telemundo's 22-episode mini-novella Amores de Luna. Ford's message was aimed at a new type of Hispanic consumer known as the Nuevo Latino, a 30- to 39-year-old bicultural consumer who strongly identifies with the Hispanic ethnicity but increasingly embraces American customs and norms.[17] In recent years, Miller Lite has made soccer a priority in order to attract Hispanic beer drinkers, including striking a sponsorship deal with the Chivas de Guadalajara team of the Primera Division soccer league in Mexico.[18]

Jeep, a company with a strong American identity and rich history, uses the concept of lineage to target Hispanic consumers. The ad in Figure 12.5 appeals to the unique identity and ancestry of Hispanics and creates a bond between the legacy of Jeep and the Hispanic subculture.

FIGURE 12.5 Jeep Is Targeting Hispanic Consumers

Courtesy of Chrysler Group LLC

African American Consumers

According to the latest U.S. Census, the African American population of the United States consists of 42 million persons, and is estimated grow to 70 million African Americans by 2050.[19] This represents approximately 13.6% of the overall U.S. population. African Americans currently constitute the second largest minority in the United States (after Latinos), and have a purchasing power estimated to have reached $1 trillion. It is also important to note that more than half of African American consumers are less than 35 years of age.[20] Generally, the consumption of African Americans consumers is a function of their social standing rather than ethnicity. Nevertheless, compared with all American consumers, African Americans consumers prefer leading brands, are brand loyal, and are unlikely to purchase private-label and generic products. One study found that almost two-thirds of African Americans were willing to pay more to get "the best," even for brands that were relatively unknown. The study also reported that successful African Americans often bought high fashions and name brands to demonstrate their success and social advancement.[21] African Americans account for more than 30% of spending in the $4 billion hair care market, and they spend more on telephone services than any other consumer segment. Still further, they spend an average of $1,427 annually on clothing for themselves, which is $458 more than all U.S. consumers.[22] Similarly, African American teens spend more on clothing and video games than all U.S. teens and were more brand loyal.[23]

Radio One's study ("Black America Today") found that 64% favor businesses that give back to the black community, 49% prefer buying brands that are respectful of the black culture, and 33% favor brands that are popular with their culture.[24] One of Radio One's research report—"Black America Today"—identified some eleven segments for characterizing the African American market.[25] For example, there is the "Black Is Better" segment who shops in drugstores, convenience stores, and price clubs monthly; whereas the "New Middle Class" segment spends more than the other African American segments in terms of shopping on the Internet.

Approximately $400 million of the $1.7 billion spent annually on ads reaching out to African Americans is spent on magazine advertising, which includes such publications as Black Enterprise, Ebony, Essence, Jet, and Vibe. Because of the importance of "black media" to African American consumers, many marketers supplement their general advertising expenditures with ads placed in magazines, newspapers, and other media directed specifically to African Americans. Still further, Internet usage among African Americans is the same as among all Americans (68% of African Americans are online versus 71% of all Americans), and two-thirds of African Americans shop online.[26] The madd ad in Figure 12.6 targets African Americans and also portrays changes in the traditional gender roles.

Table 12.1 indicates that there are significant differences among Anglo-white, African American, and Hispanic American consumers in the purchase, ownership, and use of several product categories.[27] These findings support using nationality and ethnicity as segmentation bases.

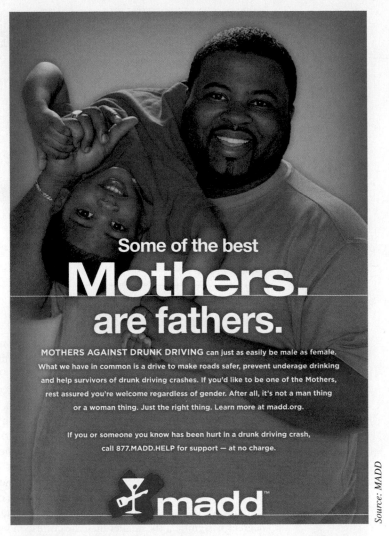

Source: MADD

FIGURE 12.6 Targeting African Americans and Portraying Changes in Gender Roles

TABLE 12.1	Comparison of Purchase Patterns of Anglo-White, African American, and Hispanic American Households (100 represents the average for the U.S. population)		
PRODUCT/ACTIVITY	ANGLO-WHITE	AFRICAN AMERICAN	HISPANIC AMERICAN
Breath fresheners	95	128	105
Body powder	93	157	99
Massage/last 6 months	105	70	80
Chewing gum	96	117	113
Ready-to-drink iced tea	90	149	121
Car rental—business use	96	127	78
Own luggage	108	74	67
Frozen main course	108	87	72
Play bingo	102	111	91
Raise tropical fish	103	107	72
Religious club member	105	107	65
Attend a movie 2–3 times a month	93	118	132

(Continued)

TABLE 12.1	Comparison of Purchase Patterns of Anglo-White, African American, and Hispanic American Households (Continued)		
PRODUCT/ACTIVITY	ANGLO-WHITE	AFRICAN AMERICAN	HISPANIC AMERICAN
Basketball, participate	89	165	102
Bicycling—mountain, participate	113	36	80
Fishing—freshwater, participate	115	50	52
Martial arts, participate	90	138	105
Bowling, attend	102	116	74
Own a handgun	119	31	52
Foreign travel for personal reasons	90	74	137
Foreign travel for vacation or honeymoon	104	55	99

Source: Based on Mediamark Research and Intelligence. Doublebase 2007 Report. All rights reserved. Reprinted by permission.

Asian American Consumers

There are approximately 17 million Asian Americans, representing 5.6% of the U.S. population, and they are the fastest-growing American minority, with some estimates showing that their numbers will reach 35 million by 2050. In 1990, there were 6.9 million Asian Americans; in 2000, there were 11.9 million. According to the 2010 Census, the largest nationalities within America's Asian population were Chinese (3.79 million), Filipino (3.41 million), Indian (3.18 million), Vietnamese (1.73 million), Korean (1.7 million), and Japanese (1.3 million). Thus, unlike Latinos, Asian Americans do not share a common language and are a highly diverse market segment. The Asian American population is greatly urbanized, with nearly three-quarters of them living in metropolitan areas with population greater than 2.5 million. The three metropolitan areas with the highest Asian American populations are the Greater Los Angeles Area, the New York metropolitan area, and the San Francisco Bay Area (see Figure 12.3). The most striking characteristics of Asian Americans is a high level of educational attainment. As shown in Figure 12.7A, the percentages of all Americans with college and advanced degrees is significantly smaller than the corresponding percentages for Asians (Figure 12.7B).

Asian Americans are largely family oriented, highly industrious, and strongly driven to achieve a middle-class lifestyle. They are an attractive market for an increasing numbers of marketers. During a recent year, Asian American households had the highest median income in the United States, at $65,637. Two years later, the median household income of Asian Americans had increased to $67,022. As with educational achievement, economic prosperity is not uniform among all Asian American groups. Census figures also show that an average white male with a college diploma earns around $66,000 a year, whereas similarly educated Asian men earn around $52,000 a year.

Asian Americans, on a per capita basis, more often own their own businesses than non-Asian American minorities. Those who do not own their own businesses are largely in professional, technical, or managerial occupations. Additionally, many Asian Americans are young and live a good part of their lives in multi-income households. Asian Americans also are likely to be more computer literate than the general population.

- Graduated High School
- Some college but no degree
- Associate's Degree: Occupational
- Associate's Degree: Academic
- Bachelor's Degree
- Master's Degree
- Advanced Professional Degree
- Doctorate

FIGURE 12.7A Educational Attainment of All Americans

- Graduated High School
- Some college but no degree
- Associate's Degree: Occupational
- Associate's Degree: Academic
- Bachelor's Degree
- Master's Degree
- Advanced Professional Degree
- Doctorate

FIGURE 12.7B Educational Attainment of Asian Americans

English-speaking Asian Americans are more likely than other Americans to get their news and information online. In addition, Asian American households are more likely than Hispanic and African American households to have Internet access.[28] During the decade of the 1990s, the buying power of Asian Americans increased about 125%, to more than $250 billion, and some believe it has reached $530 billion.[29] Asian Americans value quality (and associate quality with well-known, upscale brands). They tend to be loyal customers, are frequently more male oriented when it comes to consumption decisions, and welcome the American retailers who target them.

Asian Americans are really drawn from diverse cultural backgrounds. Therefore, although Asian Americans have many similarities, marketers should avoid treating Asian Americans as a single market, because they are so far from being homogeneous. For example, Vietnamese Americans are more likely to follow the traditional model in which the man makes the decisions concerning large purchases; however, Chinese American husbands and wives are more likely to share in the decision-making process. Vietnamese Americans also frown on credit, because in their culture owing money is viewed negatively. In contrast, Korean Americans and Chinese Americans, especially those who have been in the United States for years, accept using credit because the see it as "the American way."

The use of Asian American models in advertising is effective in reaching this market segment. Research reveals that responses to an ad for stereo speakers featuring an Asian model were significantly more positive than responses to the same ad using a Caucasian model. Additionally, the percentage of Asian Americans who prefer advertisements that are not in English varies among different Asian American groups. For instance, 93% of Vietnamese consumers prefer ad messages in the Vietnamese language, whereas only 42% of Japanese Americans prefer ad messages in Japanese.[30] Aware of the increasing importance of the Asian American market, Procter & Gamble has named its first Asian American advertising agency, and Walmart has begun running TV commercials in Mandarin, Cantonese, and Vietnamese, as well as Filipino print ads.[31] In contrast, though, it is important to note that according to the most recent Census, almost 80% of Asian Americans speak English "very well," with 20% indicating that they speak only English.

Religious Subcultures

Learning Objective

3 To understand the impact of religious affiliations on consumer behavior.

The United States reportedly has more than 200 different organized religious affiliations (or subcultures). Of this number, Protestant denominations, Roman Catholicism, Islam, and Judaism are the principal organized religious faiths. The members of all these religious groups at times are make purchase decisions that are influenced by their religious identity. Commonly, consumer behavior is directly affected by religion in terms of products that are symbolically and ritualistically associated with the celebration of various religious holidays. For example, Christmas has become the major gift-purchasing season of the year.

Several studies examined the impact of consumers' religion on their consumer behavior. Born-again Christians are the fastest-growing religious affiliation in America (they make up about 72 million of the 235 million Christians in the United States). Moreover, born-again Christians are generally defined as individuals "who follow literal interpretations of the Bible and acknowledge being born again through religious conversion." From a marketer's perspective, born-again Christians are fiercely loyal to a brand that supports their causes and viewpoint.[32]

A study of Jewish consumers found no significant differences with respect to brand loyalty and word-of-mouth between American Jews and non-Jews.[33] Religious requirements or practices do, however, sometimes take on an expanded meaning. For instance, dietary laws for an observant Jewish family represent an obligation, so there are toothpastes and artificial sweeteners that are kosher for Passover. The *U* and *K* marks on food packaging are symbols that the food meets Jewish dietary laws. For nonobservant Jews and an increasing number of non-Jews, however, these marks often signify that the food is pure and wholesome—a kind of "Jewish Good Housekeeping Seal of Approval." Packaging and print ads for food items that are kosher display a *K* or a *U* inside a circle and sometimes the word "*parve.*" This word tells shoppers that the product is kosher and that it can be eaten with either meat or dairy products (but not both).

In response to the broader meaning given to kosher-certified products, a number of national brands, such as Coors beer and Pepperidge Farm cookies, have secured kosher certification for their products. A kosher Manhattan steak house, the Prime Grill, claims that about half of its clientele are non-Jews, but offers a menu that "just happens to be kosher."[34]

Targeting specific religious groups with specially designed marketing programs can be profitable. For instance, the Shaklee Corporation, a multilevel marketer of the Shaklee Performance drink mix, recruits salespeople from a variety of different religious groups (e.g., Hasidic Jews, Amish, and Mennonites) to sell its products to members of their communities.[35]

Regional Subcultures

Learning Objective

4 To understand the influence of regional characteristics on consumer behavior.

The United States is a large country, one that includes a wide range of climatic and geographic conditions. Given the country's size and physical diversity, it is only natural that many Americans have a sense of "regional identification" when comparing and describing themselves to others (e.g., "he is a true Southerner"). Anyone who has traveled across the United States has probably noted many regional differences in consumption behavior, especially when it comes to food and drink. For example, a "mug" of black coffee typifies the West, whereas a "cup" of coffee with milk and sugar is preferred in the East. There also are geographic differences in the consumption of staple foods, such as bread. Specifically, in the South and Midwest, soft white bread is preferred, whereas on the East and West coasts, firmer breads (rye, whole wheat, and French and Italian breads) are favored. Regional differences also include brand preferences. Why do you suppose Skippy is the best-selling brand of peanut butter on both the East and West coasts, while Peter Pan sells best in the South and Jif sells best in the Midwest?

One study illustrated the differences in product purchase, ownership, and usage levels that occur among major metropolitan areas, which marketers can use in targeting urban consumers:[36]

1. New York:
   - Lowest purchase/usage of energy drinks
   - Highest purchase/usage of frozen yogurt
   - New York metropolitan area ranked first in ordering anything from catalog, mail order, phone, and use of Internet for shopping
2. Boston:
   - Lowest purchase/usage of massage past six months
   - Attend movie
   - Highest purchase/usage of frozen pizza
   - Attend adult educational courses, baseball games, watch TV
   - Boston metropolitan area ranked seventh terms of ordering anything from catalog, mail order, phone, and Internet
3. Chicago:
   - Not the lowest in any of the categories examined
   - Highest purchase/usage of energy drinks and board games
   - Chicago metropolitan area ranked fourth in terms of ordering anything from catalog, mail order, phone, and Internet
4. Atlanta:
   - Lowest purchase/usage of adult education courses
   - Highest purchase/usage of mouthwash
   - Atlanta metropolitan area ranked sixth in terms of ordering anything from catalog, mail order, phone, and Internet

5. San Francisco:
   - Lowest purchase/usage of board games and video games
   - Highest purchase/usage of massage in past six months; recycle products
   - San Francisco metropolitan area ranked seventh in terms of ordering anything from catalog, mail order, phone, and Internet

6. Los Angeles:
   - Lowest purchase/usage of energy drinks
   - Highest purchase/usage of frozen yogurt
   - Los Angeles metropolitan area ranked ninth in terms of ordering anything from catalog, mail order, phone, and Internet

A **national brand** is a brand that is available in all fifty states, although the market shares of most brands vary among geographic regions. A beer company's website states that "The U.S. beer market operates as a series of smaller, very different markets, and the company uses a marketing strategy tailored to the different conditions of each market."[37] These differences in market share across geographic markets may be the result of such factors as the common marketing practice of putting more merchandising dollars in markets that sell more.[38] Also, the availability of scanner data has allowed marketers to reallocate resources (e.g., moving inventory around the country and shifting ad expenditures) geographically and increase profitability.[39]

While geographic differences in sales and market share are common for many brands of consumer packaged goods in the United States, brands in nations, many smaller nations do not exhibit similar regional differences.[40] However, larger and more diversified countries, such as large Asian nations, are highly diverse geographically. A study conducted in mainland China found that urban children were more skeptical toward advertising than rural children.[41] Another study found that rural consumers' favorite product category was food, whereas urban consumers considered their computers their favorite possessions.[42] A study of Indian consumers found that regional differences stemming from various geographic, topological, and cultural factors—including values, motives, and lifestyle—were important determinants of both consumption and nonconsumption behaviors.[43]

Generational (Age) Subcultures

Learning Objective

5 To understand age and generational influences on consumer behavior.

According to the U.S. Census, there are 317 million Americans. Figure 12.8 shows the generational classification of the U.S. population and the proportion of each generation. Each generation is a distinct subculture and market segment, because its members have unique priorities and purchase patterns. For instance, don't you listen to different music than your parents and grandparents, dress differently, read different magazines, enjoy different TV shows, and visit different websites? Important shifts occur in an individual's demand for products and services as he or she goes from being a dependent child to a retired senior citizen. In this section we describe the consumption patterns and impact of technology on the following age (or generational) subcultures: Generation Z, Generation Y, Generation X, Baby Boomers, and older Americans.

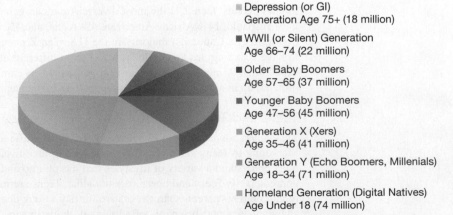

- Depression (or GI)
  Generation Age 75+ (18 million)
- WWII (or Silent) Generation
  Age 66–74 (22 million)
- Older Baby Boomers
  Age 57–65 (37 million)
- Younger Baby Boomers
  Age 47–56 (45 million)
- Generation X (Xers)
  Age 35–46 (41 million)
- Generation Y (Echo Boomers, Millenials)
  Age 18–34 (71 million)
- Homeland Generation (Digital Natives)
  Age Under 18 (74 million)

FIGURE 12.8 The Generation within the United States (millions)

FIGURE 12.9 Age and Sources of News Information (percentages)

FIGURE 12.10 Using Smartphones: Age and Household Income (percentages)

Technology is now the primary force driving consumer behavior. As shown in Figures 12.9 and 12.10, Americans of all generations have incorporated technologies into their lives. Generational differences in use of technology are discussed throughout this chapter.

Generation Z: Persons Born from 1997 to the Present

Generation Z (Homeland Generation, Digital Natives) is the cohort of people born from 2000 to the present day. Members of Gen Z are highly "connected," having had lifelong exposure to and use of communication and media technology like the Internet, instant messaging, text messaging, and mobile phones. Gen Z is the most diverse American generation ever, consisting of 54% Caucasian, 24% Hispanic, 14% African American, 4% Asian, and 4% mixed race/other. It is also the last generation to have a Caucasian majority in the U.S. Gen Z persons are more likely than older generations to have social circles that include people from different ethnic groups, races, and religions. Experts expect Gen Z members to be the first generation to earn less than their parents, because they are growing up in a period of fundamental changes in the wealth distribution in the U.S.

Teens and Tweens

This generation consists of two markets: **Teens** are those aged 13 to 17 and **tweens** are aged 8 to 12. Marketing to teens and tweens means targeting lucrative, elusive, and fickle customers. Marketers must understand a variety of lifestyles that morph into and out of each other and change quickly and unpredictably. Teens and tweens are not alike. Teens are more independent in their behavior and less reliant on their parents than tweens are for day-to-day decisions. Teens are beginning to develop the characteristics and behaviors of adulthood, while tweens still share many traits with their younger siblings. Families are more important to tweens in terms of their social lives as well.

In the past, teens and tweens were often lumped together with younger children, such as those age 6 to 11 or 5 to 12. Therefore, some marketers have alienated them, most often by talking down to them. Teens and tweens like companies whose messages are tailored directly to them. Marketers who effectively tailor products and brands to the needs and desires of this target market will succeed in making them customers. Tweens tend to be more brand-loyal and teens more brand skeptical. Technology is the center of both groups' lives and they fully accept technological innovation and obsolescence. Among teens and young adults, surfing the Internet is the primary leisure activity. Most teens and tweens create content on the Internet and use social networking sites. They go to the mall to socialize and buy things. The average teen or tween earns close to $30 per week from all sources, and 30% of teens and tweens are involved in family purchase decisions on items such as cable providers and cell phone service. All told, teens spend about $160 billion annually, whereas tweens have buying power at about one-quarter of that.[44]

Among 13- to 17-year-olds, YouTube was the most popular way to listen to music, with 64% using it. Radio was next, with 56%, followed by iTunes (53%), CDs (50%), and Pandora (35%). Among adults, the most popular ways to listen to music were radio (67%), CDs (61%), YouTube (44%), Pandora's custom radio service (32%), and Apple iTunes (29%).[45]

One study identified the psycho-demographic variables related to *connectedness* with reality television among preteens and teens. The results showed that young people who greatly valued popularity and physical attractiveness were more likely to feel connected to reality-television programs. In contrast, teens who were more interested in excitement were less likely to be connected to reality programming. The value of excitement was unrelated to connectedness among preteens. These results are important to marketers because viewers with a high level of connectedness to a program are more likely not only to view the program, but also to watch it in real time and without time shifting. Marketers can develop more effective strategies by understanding connectedness, rather than relying only on demographics.[46]

Generation Y: Born Between 1980 and 1996

Generation Y (Echo Boomers, Millennials) are people born between 1980 and 1996. However, some include people born in the late 1970s and late 1990s in this cohort. Gen Y members grew up with technology and embraced it. They are attracted to higher levels of stimulation and are bored easily. They are more confident than other generations were at their age, because of growing up in child-centric households, a youth-oriented society, and the American emphasis on self-esteem. As consumers, they want faster product turnover, personally relevant promotions, and interactive marketing platforms. Many want to design their own products, build and manage their own networks, and rate products.

Millennials are the largest users of cell phone and text messaging. Research found that 63% of Gen Y use text messaging, compared with only 31% of members of Gen X. In today's cell phone market, 76% of 15- to 19-year-olds and 90% of consumers in their early 20s regularly use text messaging, ringtones, and games. In contrast, only 18% of cell phone users in their 40s, and 13% in their 50s use such features regularly.[47] Gen Y adults do not respond to marketing the same way their parents did, and the most effective way to reach them are messages online and cable TV.[48] Through the use of instant messaging, blogs, chat rooms, social networking, and so on. For Gen Y, a "community" is an entity located in virtual space.[49] Figure 12.11 shows the primary online activities of Gen Y.[50]

Generation Y, like all generations, is not a uniformed group in terms of values and priorities. One researcher identified six segments of Millennials:

1. Hip-ennials: They believe that they can have an impact on the world and make it better. They are aware of what's going on globally, give to charity, and search for information regularly. Although they read social media content, they do not produce it.

2. Millennial Moms: They enjoy traveling, getting in shape, and treating their "children" as they were treated (pampered). They are confident, very family oriented, and proficient in technology. They participate in social networks online and are very attached to their peer groups.

3. Anti-Millennials: They care mostly about their businesses and their families, and avoid the Millennial "norms." They do not buy green products like most Millennials do. They seek comfort instead of change, whereas most Millennials embrace different activities to make life more interesting.

4. Gadget Gurus: They are always looking for the next big gadgets, usually from Apple, and will stand in line to get them first. They are highly egotistical, wired, free spirited, and laid back.

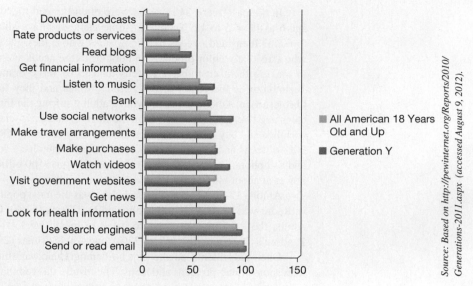

Source: Based on http://pewinternet.org/Reports/2010/ Generations-2011.aspx (accessed August 9, 2012).

FIGURE 12.11 Generation Y Online (percentages)

They often create content online and tweet continuously. Gadget Gurus are male dominated and single because they live in their own world.

5. Clean and Green Millennials: They take care of themselves and support others. They are driven by social causes, ecological issues, philanthropy, and positive outlooks on life.

6. Old-School Millennials: They did not adopt many of the typical Millennial rituals, like updating their Facebook pages during meals. They would rather meet people in person than online or through text, and read books instead of blogs. They are independent and self-directed, whereas most Millennials wants mentors and constant feedback.

Generation X: Born Between 1965 and 1979

Generation X (Xers) consists of about 50 million individuals born between 1965 and 1979. As consumers, they represent a market with a spending power in excess of $1 trillion. They do not like labels, are cynical, and generally do not want to be singled out and marketed to. Unlike their parents, the Baby Boomers, they are in no rush to marry, start a family, or work excessive hours to earn high salaries. For Generation X consumers, job satisfaction is typically more important than salary. It has been said, for example, that "Baby Boomers live to work, Xers work to live!" Xers reject the values of older coworkers who quite often neglect their families while striving to secure higher salaries and career advancement, and many have observed their parents getting laid off after many years of loyalty to their employers. Therefore, they are not particularly interested in long-term employment with a single company, but instead prefer to work for a company that can offer some work–life flexibility and can bring some fun aspects into the environment. Xers understand the necessity of money but do not view salary as a sufficient reason for staying with a company—the quality of the work itself and the relationships built while on the job are much more important. For Generation X, it is more important to enjoy life and have a lifestyle that provides freedom and flexibility.

The following is a list of some additional traits and/or lifestyle factors that can help us better understand the nature and make-up of Xers:[51]

• 62% are married

• 29.7 million are parents

• 51% of children under 18 living at home are in households headed by an Xer

• 31% of Xers have earned a college degree

• 81% of Xers are employed full-time or part-time

• 37% of Gen Xers' mothers worked outside the home when the kids were growing up

Members of Generation X are sophisticated consumers. Although many claim that they are not materialistic, they do purchase prestigious and pricey brands, but not necessarily designer labels. They want to be recognized by marketers as a group in their own right and not as mini–baby boomers.

Therefore, advertisements targeted to this audience must focus on their style in music, fashions, and language. One key for marketers appears to be sincerity. Xers are not against advertising, but strongly oppose insincerity.

The media exposure patterns of Baby Boomers and Xers are different. Specifically, while 65% of those aged 50 to 64, and 55% of 30- to 49-year-olds read a newspaper regularly, only 39% of younger Xers regularly read a newspaper.[52] Xers are the MTV generation and therefore use the Internet more than any other age cohort. For example, 60% of Xers have tried online banking, whereas only 38% of Generation Y members have tried online banking.[53]

Hotel chains are also making changes in their offerings to better attract the Gen X travelers, the fastest-growing group of hotel patrons. Marriott, for example, is remodeling rooms to include flat-panel LCD TVs, high-speed Internet access, ergonomic desk chairs, and high thread-count sheets.[54] Additionally, Xers are generally dissatisfied with most current shopping malls—they want to do more than just shop. For instance, Xers seek to be able to eat a proper sit-down meal at the mall, rather than "grab something quick" at the food court.

Being online comes easy to Xers. They grew-up with the advantages of computer technology, and spending time online and searching for information is an essential part of their daily lives. They see computers and cell phones and technology as "friendly" tools for managing their time, and feel that the Internet has had a great and positive impact on society. Figure 12.12 describes the online activities of members of Generation X.

Baby Boomers: Born Between 1946 and 1964

The term **Baby Boomers** refers to the age segment of the population that was born between 1946 and 1964. These 78 million or so baby boomers represent more than 40% of the U.S. adult population, which makes them a much sought-after market segment. In comparison, during the 19 years that followed the 19 years of the baby boom, only 66 million Americans were born (many refer to the "baby bust" of the 1970s).

In addition to their generation's size, baby boomers are marketers' most desirable target market because of several reasons:

1. They constitute about 50% of all those in professional and managerial occupations and more than one-half of those have at least one college degree.

2. They are a large and distinctive age category (the term "Baby Boomers" was probably the first distinct and universally recognized name of an American generation).

3. They frequently make similar purchase decisions that influence entire categories of consumer goods.

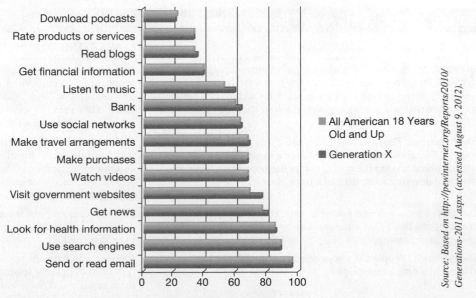

FIGURE 12.12 Generation X Online (percentages)

4. They include trendsetting, upwardly mobile professionals who have influenced the consumer tastes of all age segments.

5. They account for nearly half of consumer packaged goods spending and control between 65% and 75% of the disposable income in the United States.[55]

6. In the year 2010, fully one-third of all Americans, 97.1 million of them, were over 50 years old, and the American Association of Retired Persons (AARP) estimated that U.S. consumers in this age bracket own 80% of U.S. financial assets.[56]

The large increases in health club memberships and a boom in the sales of vitamin and health supplements are evidence that baby boomers are trying hard to look and feel "young"; they do not want to age gracefully but will fight and kick and pay whatever is necessary to look young. In advertisements, they want to be portrayed as they see themselves—lively and attractive.[57] Most important to marketers who understand them, they have money and they want to spend it on what they feel advances the quality of their lives.

Baby boomers enjoy buying for themselves, for their residences, and for others. They are consumption oriented. As baby boomers age, the nature of the products and services they need or desire changes. For example, because of the aging of this market segment, sales of "relaxed fit" jeans and "lineless" bifocal glasses are up substantially, as are the sales of walking shoes. Moreover, bank marketers and other financial institutions are also paying more attention to assisting boomers who are starting to think about retirement. Even St. Joseph's Aspirin has switched its target from "babies to boomers." Boomers are open-minded and as willing as younger consumers to try new products and services. "Yuppies" – the younger segment among the baby boomers that includes urban, upwardly mobile persons – are the most sought-after subgroup of baby boomers. They are well off financially, well educated, and in professional or managerial careers. Many buy status brand names, such as BMWs or Lexus hybrid cars, Prada shoes and clothing, Rolex watches, expensive adventurous vacations, and scores of pricey gadgets.

Today, though, as many yuppies are maturing, they are shifting their attention away from expensive status-type possessions to travel, physical fitness, planning for second careers, or some other form of new life directions. Indeed, there has been a move away from wanting possessions toward wanting experiences: "boomers today are more interested in doing things than having things." Still further, boomers are computer literate, with 70% of U.S. 55- to 64-year-olds using the Internet (compared, for example, to 11% for the same age cohort in Spain).[58]

Life after Retirement

While some baby boomers do not look forward to retirement, others do. People's outlooks about retiring are related to their levels of fulfillment during their professional careers, their accumulated financial resources, and their health status. Some researchers examine the relationship between baby boomers' job satisfaction and attitudes toward retirement. Table 12.2 details one study that identified

TABLE 12.2 Postretirement Segments and Marketing Opportunities

POSTRETIREMENT SEGMENTS	MARKETING OPPORTUNITIES
Unrewarded: People electing to retire "after unrewarding careers" often look forward to retiring. They view it as a fresh start and are inspired by the opportunity to pursue activities and interests that they could not pursue while working. Nevertheless, they may need some help in deciding to what to pursue.	Retirees are receptive to professional postretirement counseling services (e.g., local YMCA or colleges/universities) offering programs for "adjusting to" and "making discoveries" as to postretirement living. They respond positively to advice and training associated with selecting hobbies, travel, and nondegree coursework.
Mixed Feelings: People retiring after satisfying careers have strong mixed feeling about retirement. On the one hand, they are not euphoric about leaving their jobs, but, at the same time, they look forward to devoting more time to leisure pursuits.	Retirees seek and respond to advice as to how they can deal with lifestyle issues: travel, nondegree, or degree coursework in educational institutions. They travel, and attend seminars designed to provide guidance in selecting appropriate hobbies and enriching adult education courses.
Resentful: People who are forced to retire (e.g., mandatory retirement at a fixed age) often see leaving their careers as losing their self-esteem or identity.	Retirees would benefit from counseling as to the pros and cons of various retirement options, including many of the ones mentioned earlier.
Slowing Down: People for whom retirement signals the beginning of old age and a time to slow down.	Retirees who have already arranged life after retirement. Would benefit from training sessions for retiring employees designed to help them adjust and replace work with leisure activities.

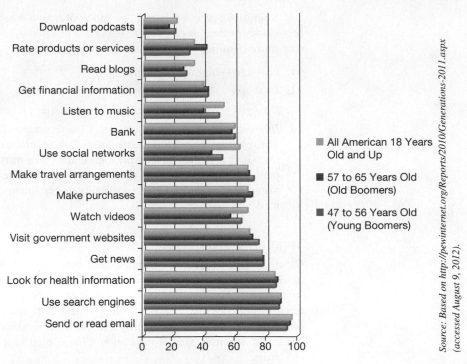

FIGURE 12.13 Baby Boomers Online (percentages)

Source: Based on http://pewinternet.org/Reports/2010/Generations-2011.aspx (accessed August 9, 2012).

four senior segments regarding adjustment to retirement. It then adds our thinking as to corresponding "marketing opportunities."[59] Marketers often divide baby boomers into two groups: Old and young. The online activities of both segments are shown in Figure 12.13.[60]

Older Consumers

America is aging. A large proportion of the baby boomers have already turned 60, with plenty more to come in the next decade. There 43 million Americans age 65 and over and it is anticipated that, by 2050, more than 88 million Americans (20% of the total population) will be 65 years of age or older.[61] In addition, from the start to the end of the twentieth century, life expectancy in the United States rose from about 47 years to 77 years; whereas a 65-year-old in 1900 could expect, on average, to live about 12 more years, a 65-year-old in 2002 can expect about 18 more years of life.[62]

It should also be kept in mind that "later adulthood" (i.e., those who are 50 years of age or older) is the longest adult life stage for most consumers (i.e., often 29 or more years in duration). This is in contrast to "early adulthood" (i.e., those who are 18 to 34 years of age), a stage lasting 16 years; and "middle adulthood" (i.e., those who are 35 to 49 years of age), a stage lasting 14 years. Remember that people over the age of 50 constitute about one-third of the adult U.S. market.

Some incorrectly view older consumers as people without substantial financial resources, in generally poor health, and with plenty of free time on their hands. In fact, more than 30% of men and more than 20% of women aged 65 to 69 are employed, as are 19% of men and 12% of women aged 70 to 74. Additionally, millions of seniors are involved in the daily care of a grandchild, and many do volunteer work. The annual discretionary income of this group amounts to 50% of the discretionary income of the United States, and these older consumers spend $200 billion a year on major purchases such as luxury cars, alcohol, vacations, and financial products. Americans over the age of 65 now control about 70% of the net worth of American households.[63]

Cognitive versus Chronological Age

Driving the growth of the elderly population are three factors: The declining birthrate, the aging of the huge baby boomer segment, and improved medical diagnoses and treatment. In the United States, "old age" is officially assumed to begin with a person's sixty-fifth birthday (or when the individual qualifies for full Social Security and Medicare). However, people over age 60 view themselves as being 15 years younger than their chronological age.

Cognitive age is a person's perception of how old he or she is. Marketers realize that people's perceptions of their ages are more important in determining behavior than their chronological ages. One study identified several dimensions of cognitive age:

1. *Feel Age* —how old one feels.

2. *Look Age* —how old one looks.

3. *Do Age* —how involved a person is in activities favored by his or her age group cohort.

4. *Interest Age* —how similar a person's interests are to those of others in his or her age group. The results indicated that the majority of older consumers perceived themselves as younger (cognitive age) than their chronological age.[64] For marketers, these findings underscore the importance of looking beyond chronological age to perceived or cognitive age when appealing to mature consumers and to the possibility that cognitive age might be used to segment the mature market.[65]

Segmenting Older Consumers

Older consumers are not a homogeneous subcultural group. Gerontologists have determined that older persons are more diverse in interests, opinions, and actions than other segments of the adult population.[66] Although this view runs counter to the popular myth that the elderly are uniform in terms of attitudes and lifestyles, both gerontologists and market researchers have repeatedly demonstrated that age is not necessarily a major factor in determining how older consumers respond to marketing activities. One segmentation scheme partitions the elderly into three chronological age categories:

1. *The young-old* – age 65 to 74.

2. *The old* – age 75 to 84.

3. *The old-old* – age 85 and older.

A study of elderly consumers' "quality-of-life orientation" identified a distinct group of older persons, which the researchers named the "new-age elderly."[67] The new-age elderly are individuals who feel, think, and do according to a cognitive age that is younger than their chronological age. They retire later than other elderly and feel more in control of their lives. They are self-confident in making consumer decisions and view themselves as more knowledgeable and alert consumers. Many are "selectively innovative" and only adopt innovations that truly enhance their lives. They seek new experiences and challenges over new possessions or things. They are satisfied and feel financially secure. To marketers, these findings indicate the significance of using cognitive rather than chronological ages when targeting older consumers.

Older Consumers and Technology

Although some people might think of older Americans as individuals who still use rotary phones and are generally resistant to change, this stereotype is far from the truth. Few older consumers are fearful of new technology, and there are more Internet users over the age of 50 than under the age of 20. Research studies have found that those over 55 are more likely than the average adult to use the Internet to purchase books, stocks, and computer equipment and that 92% of surfing seniors have shopped online.[68] In fact, older Internet users (aged 65 and older) are the fastest-growing demographic group with respect to the U.S. Internet market. Fifty-eight percent of Americans 66 to 74 years old and 30% of those 75 years old and up go online regularly. Figure 12.14 shows older Americans' online activities.[69]

Older persons have discovered that the Internet is a great way to communicate with friends and family members living in other states, including grandchildren in college. They also found out that it is an excellent source of information about stock prices, health and medication-related information, entertainment, and a sense of community. There is a relationship between the amount of time an older adult spends on the Internet and his or her level of out-of-home mobility (using the Internet may serve as a substitute for going out of the house). Having a computer and modem "empowers" older consumers, allowing them to regain some of the control that was lost due to the physical and/or social deterioration in their lives. For example, a consumer can pay bills, shop, and email friends. This may be part of the reason why the AARP claims that 2 million of its members are computer users.[70]

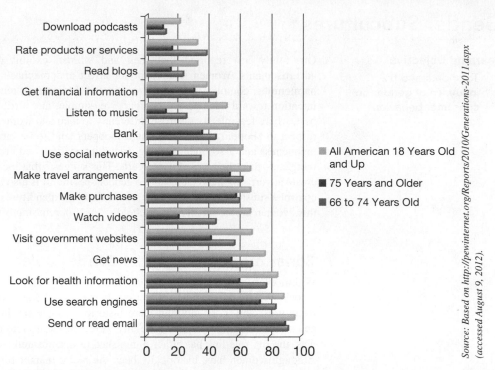

Source: Based on http://pewinternet.org/Reports/2010/Generations-2011.aspx (accessed August 9, 2012).

FIGURE 12.14 Older Americans Online

Promotional Appeals Targeting Older Consumers

Older consumers are open to being marketed to, but only for the "right" kinds of products and services and using the "right" advertising presentation. For example, older models are underrepresented in advertisements and, when they do appear, are often shown as being infirm or feeble. Part of the problem, according to some writers on the subject, is that the advertising professionals who create the ads are often in their twenties and thirties, and have little understanding of or empathy for older consumers. Seniors often want to be identified not for what they did in the past but by what they would personally like to accomplish in the future. Retirement or moving to a sunbelt community is viewed as the opening of a new chapter in life, not a quiet withdrawal from life. In the same vein, the increase in the number of older adults taking vacation cruises and joining health clubs signifies a strong commitment to remaining functionally young. Research has also found that when considering how to advertise to seniors, older adults have a higher liking for and better recall of emotional appeals (younger consumers have a higher liking for and recall of rational appeals).[71]

For some products and services, seniors do exhibit different shopping habits than younger consumers. For example, when shopping for a car, older consumers consider fewer brands, fewer models, and fewer dealers. They also are more likely to choose a long-established brand of automobile.[72] Older shoppers tend to be more store loyal than younger age groups, especially with respect to supermarkets. In addition, the importance of factors like store location (e.g., distance from home) is often a function of the senior's health status. The aging process can be difficult for consumers. Many elderly consumers do not hear as well as they did when they were younger, and many do not see as well. Jars and bottles that are easy for a 30-year-old to open often present problems when an 80-year-old tries to open them. Although some marketers have redesigned their products to make them easier for the elderly to cope with, many more product redesigns are needed. To provide an example, consider the following:

> When 80-year-old Martha Smith wants to boil a cup of water in her microwave, she turns the dial to the popcorn setting and hits "start." Unable to easily adjust the digital timer on the device, she repeats this three times before it is warm enough for a cup of tea. Martha has become a master of various microwave recipes, all measured in terms of how many "popcorns" it takes to cook the food.[73]

> Diana Schrage, a senior interior designer at Kohler, suggested that product designers try out what it is like to be older: "Experience what it is like to have limited vision—put Vaseline on Dollar Store glasses. Put duct tape on your knuckles and try to manipulate various controls. Use crutches/walkers and try to carry things. Visit a nursing home."[74]

Gender Subcultures

Learning Objective
6 To understand the influence of gender on consumer behavior.

One study has reported that men and women exhibit different reactions to identical print advertisements. Women show superior affect and purchase intention toward ads that are verbal, harmonious, complex, and category oriented. In contrast, men exhibit superior affect and purchase intention toward ads that are comparative, simple, and attribute oriented. Consequently, it may be best, where feasible, to advertise differently to men and women. Gender plays an important role with respect to shopping motives. Female shoppers tend to be more prone to such shopping motives as uniqueness and assortment seeking, social interaction, and browsing. Women are more loyal to local merchants than their male counterparts. This suggests that local merchants could use such insights to create advertising messages that are gender specific. It is also important to note that women generally control a substantial portion of the a household's expenditures and the family's spending. Because of this, women are frequently a household's "chief purchasing officer" or "chief financial officer."

Consumer Products and Gender Roles

Within every society, it is quite common to find products that are either exclusively or strongly associated with the members of one sex. In the United States, for example, shaving equipment, cigars, pants, ties, and work clothing were historically male products; bracelets, hair spray, hair dryers, and sweet-smelling colognes generally were considered feminine products. For most of these products, the sex role link has either diminished or disappeared (see Figures 9.1 and 12.6). For instance, although women have historically been the major market for vitamins, men are increasingly being targeted for vitamins exclusively formulated for men. Furthermore, in the past few years men have exhibited more of an interest in personal health and wellness, closing the gap with women in regard to these areas of personal concern. Marketers have realized that over the past decades the number of men who are the primary grocery shoppers for their households has grown steadily. One study showed that men under the age of 60 considered grocery shopping as gender neutral more frequently than older men, whereas many men 40 believed that the purchase of technical products (e.g., computers, cell phones, digital cameras) was gender neutral.[75]

Depictions of Women in Media and Advertising

Many women feel that the media and advertising create an expectation of beauty that most women can never achieve. Consequently, they want the "definition" of beauty to change. Dove has responded to this concern in its ongoing advertising campaign that has been challenging the "traditional portrayal of beauty" and offering a realistic portrayal of women. Indeed, women have voiced a very positive reaction to the ad messages that focus on "real women"—with gray hair, wrinkles, and flawed skin. Importantly, the campaign lets women know that beauty comes in many sizes, shapes, and ages. Moreover, it avoids the unrealistic conclusion that by using Dove's product a woman will start looking like the beautiful (and heavily Photoshopped) models appearing in most other beauty and make-up firms' advertising.

Working Women

Many marketers are interested in women who work outside of the home, especially married working women. They recognize that married working women are a large and growing market segment—one whose needs differ from those of women who do not work outside the home (frequently self-labeled "stay-at-home moms"). It is the size of the working woman market that makes it so attractive: Nearly 60% of American women (16 years of age and older) are in the labor force; more than half of all women with children under the age of one are working; and more than three-quarters of these women are mothers with children at home. When the time spent on everything that a working woman has to accomplish in a day is added together (e.g., work, child care, shopping, cooking), it constitutes a very long day!

To provide a richer framework for segmentation, marketers have identified segmentation categories that differentiate the motivations of working and nonworking women. For instance, a number of studies have divided the female population into four segments:[76]

1. Stay-at-home housewives.
2. Plan-to-work housewives.

3. Just-a-job working women.

4. Career-oriented working women.

There is an important distinction between "just-a-job" and "career-oriented" working women. "Just-a-job" women" work because the family requires the additional income, whereas "career-oriented" women are driven more by a need to achieve and succeed in their chosen careers.

With more female than ever before graduating college and joining the workforce, the number of competitive, career focused women has risen quickly. Forecasts indicate that more and more women would become the chief executives of mid-size or major corporations.

From the preceding discussion, we can identify the major some forces that have played a part in motivating more women to increasingly seek managerial positions, including positions as a firm's CEO:

1. As women have increasingly sought to become CEOs of major companies, their attainment of such positions is now occurring at an even faster pace and is now a more popular option.

2. Nearly 40% of working wives are currently out-earn their husbands (past success of female executives has increasingly demonstrated that more and more of them have skill sets that would make them good CEOs).

3. It has also been proposed that increased use of birth control (starting with the advent of "the Pill" in the 1960s) set off a trend that still encourages women to seek a career, and to delay marriage and child rearing.

4. Today, women commonly account for up to as much as 60% of the enrollment in U.S. colleges, and earn more masters and doctoral degrees than men.[77]

Table 12.3 summarizes a study that idendtified three segments of working women.[78]

TABLE 12.3 Segmenting Working Women

THE INDIE (INDEPENDENT) WOMAN

- Single, 28 to 34 years old, with a median income of $33,200 and college degree.
- Busy building her career and loves it. Puts off marriage and having kinds because she does not want to have obligations to others.
- Does not believe in being settled by the time she's 25.
- Likes to work late, go out late, and come and go as she pleases.
- Views weddings more as parties than as an obligatory step toward building a family, and may even have a child before marriage.
- Fashion is an indication of her success. She aspires to buy luxury brands across categories like travel, clothes, jewelry, and automobiles (e.g., Chanel, Prada, Ritz-Carlton and BMW). Yet, she loves to shop for bargains.
- Considers her virtual image as important as her real-world one. Heavy social media user, mostly via mobile devices.

THE MOM ACHIEVER

- Working mother, 35 to 45 years old, with a median income of $75,000.
- Highly driven, has advanced degrees, and earned executive jobs.
- Applies her professional knowledge and ethics to being a mom.
- Has a hard time leaving her job behind (can't wait to get back to work on Monday).
- Would choose a 50% pay raise over 50% more time with her kids.
- Spends a lot of money on herself, mostly on prestige beauty products and services. Most influenced by online reviews in deciding what to buy.
- Spends little time on research before buying high-end products, but is also thrifty and looks for discount websites.

THE ALPHA GODDESS

- Working mother, 55-to-64-year-old, with a median income of $69,000.
- "With age comes wisdom." Knows what she wants and has the resources to get it.
- Loves to lavish gifts on her family, but her top purchases are for herself (e.g., luxury cars, travel, prescription drugs).
- Buys expensive fragrances and is influenced by celebrity endorsements.
- Confident in her relationships. Whether married, widowed, divorced, or never married, she does not view a single life as a stigma.
- Very receptive to new technologies, especially smartphones. Some use online sources to find dates and new relationships.
- Watches more TV than other age groups, but is not a captive audience. While watching TV, she shops online, texts or reads books and magazines.
- Unlikely to compromise on either love or sexual attractiveness in order to have a committed relationship.

Summary

Learning Objective 1: To understand the subcultures within the United States and their relationships to American culture.

Subcultural analysis enables marketers to segment their markets to meet the specific needs, motivations, perceptions, and attitudes shared by members of a specific subcultural group. A subculture is a distinct cultural group that exists as an identifiable segment within a larger, more complex society. Its members possess beliefs, values, and customs that set them apart from other members of the same society; at the same time, they hold to the dominant beliefs of the overall society. Major subcultural categories in the United States include nationality and ethnicity, religion, geographic location, age, and gender. Each of these can be broken down into smaller segments that can be reached through special copy appeals and selective media choices. In some cases (such as the elderly consumer), product characteristics should be tailored to the specialized needs of the market segment. Because all consumers simultaneously are members of several subcultural groups, the marketer must determine how specific subcultural memberships interact to influence the consumer's purchases of specific products and services.

Learning Objective 2: To understand the influence of nationality and ethnicity subcultures on consumer behavior.

The three ethic subcultures in the United States that consistute unique market segments are Hispanics (or Latinos), African Americans, and Asian American consumers.

Latinos represent he 15% of the U.S. population, and their number is estimated to become 30% of the U.S. population by the year 2050. They have an estimated purchasing power approaching $1.2 trillion, larger families, and many live in extended family households consisting of several generations of family members.

African American population of the United States consists of 42 million persons, and is estimated grow to 70 million African Americans by 2050. African Americans have a purchasing power estimated to have reached $1 trillion. It is also important to note that more than half of African American consumers are less than 35 years of age. Generally, the consumption of African Americans consumers is a function of their social standing rather than ethnicity.

There are approximately 17 million Asian Americans, representing 5.6% of the U.S. population, and they are the fastest-growing American minority, with some estimates showing that their numbers will reach 35 million by 2050. The largest nationalities within America's Asian population are Chinese, Filipino, Indian, Vietnamese, Korean, and Japanese. Asian Americans do not share a common language and are a highly diverse market segment. The Asian American population is greatly urbanized, and the three metropolitan areas with the highest Asian American populations are the Greater Los Angeles Area, the New York metropolitan area, and the San Francisco Bay Area. The most striking characteristics of Asian Americans is a high level of educational attainment.

Learning Objective 3: To understand the impact of religious affiliations on consumer behavior.

The United States reportedly has more than 200 different organized religious subcultures. Of this number, Protestant denominations, Roman Catholicism, Islam, and Judaism are the principal organized religious faiths. The members of all these religious groups at times make purchase decisions that are influenced by their religious identity. Commonly, consumer behavior is directly affected by religion in terms of products that are symbolically and ritualistically associated with the celebration of various religious holidays.

Learning Objective 4: To understand the influence of regional characteristics on consumer behavior.

The United States is a large country that includes a wide range of climatic and geographic conditions, and Americans have a sense of regional identification and use it as a way of describing themselves and others. These labels often assist us in developing a mental picture and supporting a "stereotype" of the person in question. There are geographic differences in the consumption of staple foods, and brand preferences. National brands are products that are available in all fifty states, although the market shares of most brands vary among geographic regions.

While geographic differences in sales and market share are common for many brands of consumer packaged goods in the United States, brands in nations that are smaller in geographic area do not exhibit similar regional differences. However, the consumer behavior in more diversified countries, such as large Asian nations, varies significantly among regions.

Learning Objective 5: To understand age and generational influences on consumer behavior.

According to the latest U.S. Census, there are 317 million Americans. Each generation constitutes a distinct subculture and market segment, because its members have unique priorities and purchase patterns. Important shifts occur in an individual's demand for products and services as he or she goes from being a dependent child to a retired senior citizen. The primary age groups applicable to market segmentation are Generations X, Y, and Z, Baby Boomers, and older Americans.

Generation Z is the cohort of people born from 1997 to the present day. Members of Gen Z are highly "connected," having had lifelong exposure to and use of communication and media technology. Gen Z is the most diverse American generation ever, and is the last generation to have a Caucasian majority in the U.S. Gen Z persons have social circles that are much more diverse than older generations' and include people from different ethnic groups, races, and religions. Marketers expect Gen Z members to be the first generation to earn less than their parents, because they are growing up in a period of economic uncertainty.

Generation Y are people born between 1980 and 1996. Gen Y members grew up with technology and embraced it. They are attracted to higher levels of stimulation and are bored easily. They are more confident than other generations were at their age, because of growing up in child-centric households, a youth-oriented society, and the American emphasis on self-esteem. As consumers, they want faster product turnover, personally relevant promotions, and interactive marketing platforms. Many want to design their own products, get involved with messaging through their own networks and rate products. The most effective way to reach Gen Y persons is by messages appearing online and cable TV. Gen Y persons are the heaviest users of text messaging and smartphones.

Generation X consists of about 50 million individuals born between 1965 and 1979. As consumers, they represent a market with a spending power in excess of $1 trillion. They do not like labels, are cynical, and generally do not want to be singled out and marketed to. Unlike their parents, the baby boomers, they are in no rush to marry, start a family, or work excessive hours to earn high salaries. For Generation X consumers, job satisfaction is typically more important than salary. Therefore, they are not particularly interested in long-term employment with a single company, but instead prefer to work for a company that can offer some work–life flexibility and can bring some fun aspects into the environment. They want to be recognized by marketers as a group in their own right and not as mini–baby boomers.

Baby Boomers were born between 1946 and 1964. These 78 million or so baby boomers represent more than 40% of the U.S. adult population, which makes them a much sought-after market segment. They constitute about 50% of all those in professional and managerial occupations and more than one-half of those have at least one college degree. They are a large and distinctive age category (the term "baby boomers" was probably the first distinct and universally recognized name of an American generation). They frequently make similar purchase decisions that influence entire categories of consumer goods. They include trendsetting, upwardly mobile professionals who have influenced the consumer tastes of all age segments. They account for nearly half of consumer packaged goods spending and control between 65% and 75% of the disposable income in the United States. In the year 2010, fully one-third of Americans, 97.1 million of them, were over 50 years old, and the American Association of Retired Persons (AARP) estimated that U.S. consumers in this age bracket own 80% of U.S. financial assets.

America is aging. A large proportion of the baby boomers have already turned 60, with plenty more to come in the next decade. In 2006, there were more than 37 million people in this country who are 65 years of age or older (almost 12.5% of the population). Projecting ahead to the year 2050, it is anticipated that more than 88 million Americans (20% of the total population) will be 65 years of age or older. In addition, from the start to the end of the twentieth century, life expectancy in the United States rose from about 47 years to 77 years. Older consumers are not a uniformed group because people age differently in terms of physical mobility, heath, financial resources, and attitudes about retiring and getting older. Cognitive age is a person's perception of how old he or she is. Marketers realize that people's perceptions of their ages are more important in determining behavior than their chronological ages.

Learning Objective 6: To understand the influence of gender on consumer behavior.

Because gender roles have an important cultural component, it is quite fitting to examine gender as a subcultural category. All societies tend to assign certain traits and roles to males and others to females. In terms of role differences, women have historically been cast as homemakers with responsibility for child care, and men as the providers or breadwinners. Because such traits and roles are no longer relevant for many individuals, marketers are appealing to consumers' broader vision of gender-related role options. Also, the "gender gap" is narrowing for many areas, products, and behaviors that used to be strongly gender-linked. Marketers are paying particularly close attention to the working-woman segment of society, and investigating the various subgroups in this segment.

Review and Discussion Questions

12.1. Why is subcultural analysis especially significant in a country such as the United States?

12.2. Discuss the importance of subcultural segmentation to marketers of food products. Identify a food product for which the marketing mix should be regionalized. Explain why and how the marketing mix should be varied across geographic areas of the United States.

12.3. How can marketers of the following products use the material presented in this chapter to develop promotional campaigns designed to increase market share among African American, Hispanic, and Asian American consumers? The products are: (a) iPods, (b) ready-to-eat cereals, and (c) designer jeans.

12.4. Asian Americans are a small proportion of the total U.S. population. Why are they an important market segment? How can a marketer of tablet computers effectively target Asian Americans?

12.5. In view of the anticipated growth of the over-50 market, a leading cosmetics company is reevaluating its marketing strategy for its best-selling moisturizing face cream for women. Should the company market the product to younger (under 50) as well as older women? Would it be wiser to develop a new brand and formula for consumers over age 50 rather than trying to target both age groups with one product? Explain your answer.

12.6. Marketers realize that people of the same age often exhibit very different lifestyles. Using the evidence presented in this chapter, discuss how developers of retirement housing can use older Americans' lifestyles to segment their markets.

12.7. a. How should marketers promote products and services to working women? What appeals should they use? Explain.

    b. As the owner of a BMW automobile dealership, what kind of marketing and service strategies would you use to target working women?

Hands-on Assignments

12.8. Identify a group that can be regarded as a subculture within your university or college.

    a. Describe the norms, values, and behaviors of the subculture's members.

    b. Interview five members of that subculture regarding attitudes toward the use of credit cards.

    c. What are the implications of your findings for marketing credit cards to the group you selected?

12.9. Interview one baby boomer and one adult Generation Y consumer regarding the purchase of a car. Prepare a report on the differences in attitudes between the two individuals. Do your findings support the text's discussion of the differences between boomers and Gen Y buyers? Explain.

12.10. Many of your perceptions regarding price versus value are likely to be different from those of your parents or grandparents. Researchers attribute such differences to *cohort effects,* which are based on the premise that consumption patterns are determined early in life. Therefore, individuals who experienced different economic, political, and cultural environments during their youth are likely to be different types of consumers as adults. Describe instances in which your parents or grandparents disagreed with or criticized purchases you made. Describe the cohort effects that explain each party's position during these disagreements.

12.11. Find two good and two bad examples of advertising directed toward elderly consumers. To what degree are these ads stereotypical? Do they depict the concept of perceived age? How could these ads be improved by applying some of this chapter's guidelines for advertising to elderly consumers?

Key Terms

- Baby Boomers *331*
- cognitive age *334*
- Generation X (Xers) *330*
- Generation Y (Echo Boomers, Millennials) *329*
- Generation Z (Homeland Generation, Digital Natives) *328*
- national brand *327*
- subculture *318*
- teens *328*
- tweens *328*

Cross-Cultural Consumer Behavior: An International Perspective

PATEK PHILIPPE is one of the world's best Swiss timepiece makers. Its prices range from $15,000 to more than $1 million, and one of its 1928 models sold for $3.6 million. Patek Philippe is a **world brand** because its watches are manufactured, packaged, and positioned in exactly the same way regardless of the country in which they are sold. As the ads in Figure 13.1 illustrate, Patek Philippe created a global campaign, where the advertising copy is in different languages, but the message the ads communicate is the same: Patek Philippe is not only a unique watch, but also an heirloom. It is a timeless artifact passed on from one generation to the next. It is exclusive, indispensible, and represents parents' deep and forever lasting bonds with their children, which are universal and cross-cultural truths. Like all of Patek Philippe's ad campaigns, the tagline "Begin your own tradition" originates from the brand's foundation: "You never really own a Patek Philippe. You merely look after it for the next generation."

Not all products, or services, or firms lend themselves to a global marketing strategy. Indeed, Table 13.1 identifies four marketing strategies that are available to firms that sell consumer products across nations and cultures. A **global marketing strategy** consists of selling the same product using the same positioning approach and communications globally. A **local marketing strategy** consists of customizing both the product and the communications program for each unique market. Within this continuum are two **hybrid marketing strategies**, which consist of standardizing either the product or advertising message, while customizing the other one.

The four cells in Table 13.1 represent market growth opportunities. Marketers must conduct cross-cultural consumer analysis to obtain consumer reactions to alternative product and promotional themes, in order to choose the best strategy. For example, Frito-Lay, the U.S. snack-food giant, has been standardizing the promotional messages for its potato

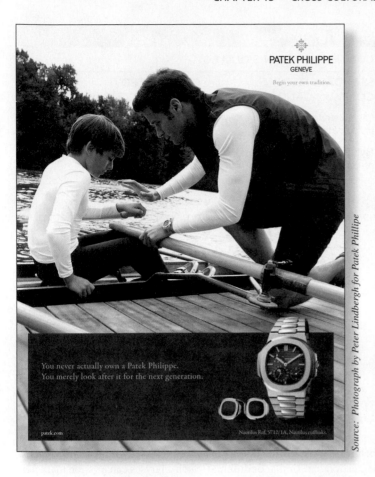

Source: Photograph by Peter Lindbergh for Patek Phillipe

Source: Photograph by Peter Lindbergh for Patek Phillipe

Source: Photograph by Peter Lindbergh for Patek Phillipe

FIGURE 13.1 Patek Philippe Globally

TABLE 13.1	Global Marketing Strategies	
PRODUCT STRATEGY	COMMUNICATION STRATEGY	
	STANDARDIZED COMMUNICATIONS	CUSTOMIZED COMMUNICATIONS
STANDARDIZED PRODUCT	Global strategy: Uniform product/uniform message	Hybrid strategy: Uniform product/customized message
CUSTOMIZED PRODUCT	Hybrid strategy: Customized product/uniform message	Local strategy: Customized product/customized message

This chapter explores consumer behavior across cultures and effective strategies for appealing to consumers around the globe.

chips across the world, but created different flavors for various markets. Thus, across nations and cultures, the top flavors of potato chips are:

1. Lay's Sour Cream & Onion (popular across the world)
2. Dill Pickle (Canada and North America)
3. Mushroom (UK), Garden Tomato & Basil (children across the world)

4. Pepper Relish (Mexico, Central America, Germany, and Western Europe)
5. Classic Potato Chips, Hot and Sour (Asian nations)
6. India's Mint Mischief, Limón (sprinkled with lemon juice and liked by kids)
7. Ruffles Mayonnaise Chips

Cross-Cultural Analysis and Acculturation

Learning Objective

1 To understand how to study the values and customs of different cultures in order to develop effective marketing strategies.

Within the scope of consumer behavior, **cross-cultural analysis** is defined as determining to what extent the consumers of two or more nations are similar or different. Such analyses can provide marketers with an understanding of the psychological, social, and cultural characteristics of the non-Americans they wish to target, so that they can design effective marketing strategies for the specific markets. Table 13.2 lists the research issues that should be considered in cross-cultural analysis. Cross-cultural consumer analysis might also include a comparison of subcultural groups (see Chapter 12) within a single country (such as English and French Canadians, Cuban Americans and Mexican Americans in the United States, or Protestants and Catholics in Northern Ireland).

The objective of cross-cultural consumer analysis is to determine how consumers in two or more societies are similar and how they are different. For instance, Table 13.3 presents the differences between Chinese and American cultural traits.[1] Countries like China and Mexico are "collectivistic" ("we") cultures, whereas the United States and the United Kingdom are "individualistic" ("I") cultures. A study of "I" versus "we" consumers in Montreal, Canada, found that collectivists rely more on word-of-mouth, preferring information from trusted, familiar sources when forming their expectations regarding airline travel. Individualists, in contrast, rely on unambiguous verbal or written communication, and attach more importance to explicit and implicit promises and third parties.[2] A study of consumers in Australia (an individualist nation) and Singapore (a collectivist country), found that Singaporean consumers were more responsive to social influence in a hypothetical buying situation than Australian consumers.

TABLE 13.2	Cross-Cultural Analysis
FACTORS	EXAMPLES
Differences in language and meaning	Words or concepts (e.g., "personal checking account") may not mean the same in two different countries.
Differences in market segmentation opportunities	The income, social class, age, and sex of target customers may differ dramatically between two different countries.
Differences in consumption patterns	Two countries may differ substantially in the level of consumption or use of products or services (e.g., mail-order catalogs).
Differences in the perceived benefits of products and services	Two nations may use or consume the same product (e.g., yogurt) in very different ways.

(Continued)

TABLE 13.2	Cross-Cultural Analysis (Continued)
FACTORS	**EXAMPLES**
Differences in the criteria for evaluating products and services	The benefits sought from a service (e.g., bank cards) may differ from country to country.
Differences in economic and social conditions and family structure	The "style" of family decision making may vary significantly from country to country.
Differences in marketing research and conditions	The types and quality of retail outlets and direct-mail lists may vary greatly among countries.
Differences in marketing research possibilities	The availability of professional consumer researchers may vary considerably from country to country.

TABLE 13.3	A Comparison of Chinese and American Cultures
CHINESE CULTURAL TRAITS	**AMERICAN CULTURAL TRAITS**
• Centered on a set of relationships defined by Confucian doctrine	• Centered on the individual
• Submissive to authority	• Greater emphasis on self-reliance
• Ancestor worship	• Resents class-based distinctions
• Passive acceptance of fate by seeking harmony with nature	• Active mastery in the person–nature relationship
• Emphasizes inner experiences of meaning and feeling	• Concerned with external experiences and the world of things
• A closed worldview, prizing stability and harmony	• An open view of the world, emphasizing change and movement
• Culture rests on kinship ties and tradition with a historical orientation	• Places primary faith in rationalism and is oriented toward the future
• Places weight on vertical interpersonal relationships	• Places weight on horizontal dimensions of interpersonal relationships
• Values a person's duties to family, clan, and state	• Values the individual personality

Source: Alexander Josiassen, "Consumer Disidentification and Its Effects on Domestic Product Purchases: An Empirical Investigation in the Netherlands," Journal of Marketing, Vol. 75 (March 2011): 124–140.

Moreover, Australian subjects were more internally oriented, whereas Singaporean subjects were more externally oriented. This resulted in Australians attributing more responsibility to themselves for good or bad outcomes of their buying decisions.[3]

An understanding of the similarities and differences that exist between nations is critical to the multinational marketer who must devise appropriate strategies to reach consumers in specific foreign markets. The greater the similarity between nations, the more feasible it is to use relatively similar marketing strategies in each nation. However, when the cultural beliefs, values, and customs of specific target countries are found to differ widely, then a highly individualized marketing strategy is indicated for each country. As another illustration, in addition to the IKEA furniture company's generic global website that uses English, the firm also offers a series of localized websites (in selected languages) and other mini-sites (in more languages) that only provide contact information.

A study in four Central European nations (Croatia, the Czech Republic, Hungary, and Poland) found that although these nations are in the same geographic region, national differences would make it unwise to employ the same advertising content and imagery in all four countries.[4] However, in contrast to these results, other consumer research examining the notion of an Asian regional brand has found that some marketers have been able to create a "multicultural mosaic" for their brand that can "appeal across national boundaries". They have done this by creating the image of an Asian consumer that is "urban, modern, and multicultural."[5]

A firm's success in marketing a product or service in a number of foreign countries is likely to be influenced by how similar the beliefs, values, and customs are that govern the use of the product in the various countries. For example, the worldwide TV commercials and magazine ads of major international airlines (American Airlines, British Airways, Continental Airlines, Air France, Lufthansa, Qantas, Swissair, United Airlines) all depict the luxury and pampering offered to their business-class and first-class international travelers. The reason for their general cross-cultural appeal is that these commercials speak to the same types of individual worldwide—upscale international business travelers—who have much in common.

A study in four countries (United States, United Kingdom, France, and Germany) examined whether there were differences in terms of "consumer style" (i.e., how a consumer approaches the purchase and consumption experience, including attitudes, beliefs, and decision rules about price, value, etc.) in the four nations.[6] Table 13.4 presents some of the differences among subject participants from the four countries. Based on consumer style, the researchers were able to segment these consumers

TABLE 13.4	"Consumer Styles" in Four Nations

GERMAN CONSUMERS:
- Less brand loyal
- More price-sensitive
- Least likely to seek variety in products
- Most likely to consider themselves impulsive shoppers
- Least likely to say they dislike shopping

U.S. CONSUMERS:
- More likely to seek new and different products than French and German consumers
- See advertising as more informative than do French and German consumers

UNITED KINGDOM CONSUMERS:
- More likely to seek new and different products than French and German consumers
- See advertising as more informative than do French and German consumers
- See advertising as insulting

FRENCH CONSUMERS:
- Believe shopping is no fun
- Claim to engage in comparison shopping, but are not the most likely to purchase products on sale

TABLE 13.5	Consumer Clusters (Segments) in Four Nations

CLUSTER	FRANCE	GERMANY	UNITED KINGDOM	UNITED STATES
Price-Sensitive Consumers	27.5	38.7	19.3	21.0
Variety-Seeking Consumers	22.0	19.4	22.4	23.3
Brand-Loyal Consumers	30.4	20.0	36.2	22.2
Information-Seeking Consumers	20.1	21.9	22.1	33.5

into four clusters: (1) Price-sensitive consumers, (2) variety-seeking consumers, (3) brand-loyal consumers, and (4) information-seeking consumers, which are described in Table 13.5. Because German consumers, for example, tend to be less brand loyal and more price sensitive than their counterparts from the other three nations in the study, it is not surprising that German participants are underrepresented in the brand-loyal consumer cluster and overrepresented in the price-sensitive cluster.[7]

Measures of Cross-Cultural Aspects

There are several frameworks for assessing consumption-related cultural differences. One study identified the dimensions that cross-cultural studies should address:[8]

1. Judgments regarding the quality of a country's products.
2. Willingness to buy a country's products.
3. Ethnocentrism—willingness to buy foreign-made products (see Chapter 3).
4. Perceptions of a country's consumption culture.
5. Acculturation—identification with a country's culture.
6. Ethnic self-identification.
7. National self-identification.

Another study investigated the interrelationship between consumers' attitudes toward local and global products and identified the following relevant dimensions for measuring such attitudes (sample statements for "agree"/"disagree" scales are shown for each item):[9]

1. *Entertainment:* "I enjoy entertainment that is popular in many countries around the world more than traditional entertainment that is popular in my own country."
   "I enjoy traditional entertainment that is popular in my own country as well as entertainment that is popular in many countries around the world."

2. *Furnishings:* "I prefer to have home furnishings that are traditional in my country rather than furnishings that are popular in many countries around the world."

   "I don't really like my own country's traditional home furnishings or furnishings that are popular in many countries around the world."

3. *Food:* "I enjoy foods that are popular in many countries around the world more than my own country's traditional foods."

   "I enjoy my own country's traditional foods as well as foods that are popular in many countries around the world."

4. *Lifestyles:* "I prefer to have a lifestyle that is traditional in my own country rather than one that is similar to the lifestyle of consumers in many countries around the world."

   "To be honest, I don't find the traditional lifestyle in my own country or the consumer lifestyle that is similar in many countries around the world very interesting."

5. *Brands:* "I prefer to buy brands that are bought by consumers in many countries around the world rather than local brands that are sold only in my country."

   "I prefer to buy both local brands that are sold only in my country and brands that are bought by consumers in many countries around the world."

Another study identified personal cultural orientations that can be used in cross-cultural measurement (a key statement for an "agree"/"disagree" scale is shown for each dimension):[10]

1. *Independence:* "I would rather depend on myself than others."
   "My personal identity, independent of others, is important to me."

2. *Interdependence:* "The well-being of my group members is important for me."
   "I feel good when I cooperate with my group members."

3. *Power:* "I easily conform to the wishes of someone in a higher position than mine."
   "It is difficult for me to refuse a request if someone senior asks me."

4. *Social Inequality:* "A person's social status reflects his or her place in the society."
   "It is important for everyone to know their rightful place in the society."

5. *Risk Aversion:* "I tend to avoid talking to strangers."
   "I prefer a routine way of life to an unpredictable one full of change."

6. *Ambiguity Tolerance:* "I find it difficult to function without clear directions and instructions."
   "I prefer specific instructions to broad guidelines."

7. *Masculinity:* "Women are generally more caring than men."
   "Men are generally physically stronger than women."

8. *Gender Equality:* "It is OK for men to be emotional sometimes."
   "Men do not have to be the sole breadwinner in a family."

9. *Tradition:* "I am proud of my culture."
   "Respect for tradition is important for me."

10. *Prudence:* "I believe in planning for the long term."
    "I work hard for success in the future."

11. *Consumer Ethnocentrism:* "We should not buy foreign products, because it hurts our economy."
    "Only products that are unavailable in our country should be imported."

12. *Consumer Innovativeness:* "I am more interested in buying new than known products."
    "I like to buy new and different products."

Acculturation

Acculturation is the process by which marketers learn—via cross-cultural analysis—about the values, beliefs, and customs of other cultures and then apply this knowledge to marketing products internationally. In fact, acculturation is a dual learning process: First, marketers must learn everything that is relevant to the product and product category in the society in which they plan to market; then they must persuade, or "teach," the members of that society to break with their traditional ways of doing things and adopt the new product. To gain acceptance for a culturally new product in a foreign society, marketers must develop a strategy that encourages members of that society to modify or even break with their own traditions (to change their attitudes and possibly alter their behavior). To illustrate the point, a social marketing effort designed to encourage consumers in developing nations to secure polio vaccinations for their children would require a two-step acculturation process. First, the marketer must obtain an in-depth picture of a society's present attitudes and customs with regard to preventive medicine and related concepts. Then the marketer must devise promotional strategies that will convince the members of a target market to have their children vaccinated, even if doing so requires a change in current attitudes.

Too many marketers contemplating international expansion believe that if their products are successful domestically, they will also succeed overseas. This biased viewpoint increases the likelihood of marketing failures abroad. It reflects a lack of appreciation of the unique psychological, social, cultural, and environmental characteristics of distinctly different cultures. To overcome such a narrow and culturally myopic view, marketers must learn everything that is relevant about the usage or potential usage of their products and product categories in the foreign countries in which they plan to operate. Take the Chinese culture, for example. For Western marketers to succeed in China, it is important for them to take into consideration *guo qing* (pronounced "gwor ching"), which means "to consider the special situation or character of China." An example of *guo qing* for Western marketers is the Chinese policy of limiting families to one child. An appreciation of this policy means that foreign businesses will understand that Chinese families are open to particularly high-quality baby products for their single child ("the little emperor").

Consumer Research Difficulties

Conducting consumer research studies in other foreign countries is often difficult. For instance, it is hard to conduct Western-style market research in the Islamic countries of the Middle East. In Saudi Arabia, for instance, it is illegal to stop people on the streets, and focus groups are impractical because most gatherings of four or more people (with the exception of family and religious gatherings) are outlawed. American firms desiring to do business in Russia have found a limited amount of information regarding consumer and market statistics. Similarly, marketing research information on China is generally inadequate, and surveys that ask personal questions arouse suspicion. Marketers have tried other ways to elicit the data they need. For example, Grey Advertising has given cameras to Chinese children so they can take pictures of what they like and do not like, rather than asking them to explain their preferences to a stranger. Moreover, ACNielsen conducts focus groups in pubs and children's playrooms rather than in conference rooms; and Leo Burnett has sent researchers to China to "hang out" with consumers.

Another issue in international marketing research concerns scales of measurement. In the United States, a 5- or 7-point scale may be adequate, but in other countries, a 10- or even 20-point scale may be needed. Still further, research facilities, such as telephone interviewing services, may or may not be available in particular countries or areas of the world. To avoid such problems, consumer researchers must familiarize themselves with the availability of research services in the countries they are evaluating as potential markets, and must learn how to design marketing research studies that will yield useful data. Researchers must also keep in mind that cultural differences may make "standard" research methodologies inappropriate.

Localization versus Standardization

Learning Objective

2 To understand how to decide whether to customize products for global markets or to sell standardized ones.

As illustrated in the chapter opener, American companies marketing overseas can adapt their offerings in other nations or market them the same way they do at home. For example, McDonald's is an example of a firm that tries to localize its advertising and other marketing communications to consumers in each of the cultural markets in which it operates.

Product and Service Customization for Local Cultures

The Ronald McDonald that we all know has been renamed Donald McDonald in Japan, because the Japanese language does not contain the *R* sound. Additionally, the McDonald's menu in Japan has been localized to include corn soup and green tea milkshakes.[11] In Sweden, McDonald's developed a new package using woodcut illustrations and a softer design to appeal to the consumers' interest in food value and the outdoors. Each French person eats about 150 grams of bread a day, or roughly 55 kilograms a year. The French eat some form of bread with all meals, viewing bread as an extension of the knife and fork for pushing food around on the plate. In France, McDonald's introduced McBaguette, a traditional French bread with a burger made from France's famed Charolais beef and topped with French-made Emmental cheese and mustard.[12] Filipinos like their dried chicken with either rice or spaghetti, and both KFC and McDonald's are serving them such dishes.

In contrast, when rival Pizza Hut ventured into China, parent company Yum Brands Inc. opted to introduce Pizza Hut Casual Dining, a chain that more closely resembles a Cheesecake Factory in terms of menu and motif, with a vast selection of American fare, including ribs, spaghetti, and steak, as well as café latte. However, Domino's was not interested in offering table service, even if that was what locals were used to. The company entered the new market with a tried-and-true business model of delivery and carryout pizza that it deploys around the world. In contrast, the chain's U.S. competitor, Pizza Hut, has reinvented itself for China, India, and other emerging markets, in order to mesh with the strikingly different consumer trends there.[13]

Starbucks adjusted its offering in several European countries. For instance, the British like to drink takeaway coffee, so Starbucks is planning hundreds of drive-through locations in Britain. Many Britons consider the Starbucks version too watery, so baristas in Britain recently began adding a free extra shot of espresso. Sixty percent of French people like espresso, but many complained that Starbucks' espresso tasted charred. In response, Starbucks introduced a lighter "blonde" espresso roast in Paris. In London, the company experimented with taking customers' names with their orders and then addressing them by name when filling it. Participating patrons got a free coffee, but, using Twitter, many others had complaints about bogus, American-style "chumminess". In Amsterdam, the company opened a striking space with local woods and avant-garde architecture, including a stage for poetry readings, designed to make Starbucks feel more like a trendy neighborhood shop.[14]

The maker of sunglasses bearing such brands as Ray-Ban, Ralph Lauren, and Prada has started making glasses in China specifically tailored for the Chinese. Part of their strategy included making technical tweaks to better suit Asian facial characteristics, such as a lower nose saddle, where glasses rest on the face, and prominent cheekbones. Ray-Ban, Oakley, and Vogue have also rolled out special Asian collections.[15] In contrast, Mattel shut its Barbie stores in China after learning that Chinese parents wanted their girls to model themselves after studious children, not flirts. Consequently, Mattel decided to market mostly educational toys in China. Home Depot Inc. closed about half its stores in China, finding scant interest among Chinese for do-it-yourself renovation, and decided to come up with a new strategy for the Chinese market.[16]

Linguistic Barriers

Many American brand names and slogans must be revised or changed altogether in non-English-speaking countries. Linguistic differences are probably the most challenging factor facing companies that are expanding globally, as illustrated by the following examples:

1. The slogan "Chevy Runs Deep" did not translate well in some languages. The company replaced it with the slogan "Find New Roads" because the car represents different things to different people, and the new theme resonates with consumers around the world.[17]

2. When General Motors introduced the Chevy Nova in South America, it was apparently unaware that "no va" means "it won't go." After the company figured out why it was not selling any cars, it renamed the car in its Spanish markets and called it Caribe.

3. When Parker Pen marketed a ballpoint pen in Mexico, its ads were supposed to say "It won't leak in your pocket and embarrass you." However, the company mistakenly thought the Spanish word "embarazar" meant "embarrass." Instead the ads said that "It won't leak in your pocket and make you pregnant."

4. When Vicks first introduced its cough drops on the German market, it was chagrined to learn that the German pronunciation of "v" is f—making its name in German the guttural equivalent of "sexual penetration."

5. In Taiwan, the translation of the Pepsi slogan "Come alive with the Pepsi Generation" came out as "Pepsi will bring your ancestors back from the dead."

The rapidly growing Chinese market represents an enormously difficult cultural and linguistic challenge. The name *Coca-Cola* in China was first rendered as *Ke-kou-ke-la*. Unfortunately, the Coke company did not discover until after thousands of signs had been printed that the phrase means "bite the wax tadpole" or "female horse stuffed with wax" (depending on the dialect). Coke then researched 40,000 Chinese characters and found a close phonetic equivalent, *ko-kou-ko-le*, which can be loosely translated as "happiness in the mouth." Some brands, like Cadillac (*Ka di la ke*), or Hilton (*Xi er dun*), are phonetic translations that mean nothing in Chinese. Nevertheless, a genuine Chinese name can say a lot about the product's characteristics and result in consumer attachment to the brand. For example:[18]

1. Snickers' Chinese name is *Shi Li Jia*, which literally means "honorary powerful support."

2. Tide detergent is called *Tai Zi*, which, in addition to resembling the name *Tide* phonetically, also means "gets rid of dirt."

3. Colgate is *Gao Lu Jie*, meaning "revealing superior cleanliness."

4. Mr. Muscle is *Wei Meng Xian Sheng*, which literally means "Mr. Powerful."

5. Citibank is *Hua Qi Yinhang*, which literally means "star-spangled banner bank."

6. Lay's is called *Le Shi*, meaning "happy things."

Promotional Appeals

Promotional appeals must reflect the local culture's values and priorities. For example, after surveys indicated that, globally, Coke was regarded as more "daring" and "energetic" than Pepsi, the Pepsi company came up with a new ad push with the tagline: "Live for Now," and then changed it to "People Who Define the Now" and its ads featured well-known disc jockeys, celebrities, and artists. Pepsi has a long history of using groundbreaking pop culture artists in its ads (e.g., Madonna, Michael Jackson).[19] A study revealed that there are significant differences between UK and Greek humorous advertising. Compared with the U.S., in the UK, riskier, more aggressive, and affective humorous advertisements are used. In contrast, Greeks preferred neutral humorous advertisements whose appeal was not perceived as very offensive. Additionally, in Greece, there was a lower percentage of print ads using humor, compared with the UK.[20] Another study showed that many fragrance ads shown in Western countries featured overt sexual appeals. However, in Asian countries, particularly those that are predominately Muslim or Buddhist, advertisers should not portray women in sexual poses.[21]

Regarding South Asian cultures, one study discovered that Australian, Chinese, and U.S. consumers form significantly different attitudes regarding the same ad. However, buying intentions toward the advertised brand are not significantly different. Despite the general assumption that Chinese consumers might react least favorably to sex-appeal ads, the study found that they hold similar attitudes toward such ads as U.S. consumers and even more favorable attitudes than Australian consumers.[22] A study of Chinese Generation X consumers, aged 18 to 35, with high incomes and education, found that they were equally persuaded by individualistic and collectivistic ad appeals, whereas their older counterparts were more persuaded by collectivistic rather than individualistic ad appeals.[23] A study focused on Chinese wine consumers discovered that some mixed red wine with lemonade and preferred corked (rather than twist-off or screw-cap) wine bottles. The study also uncovered a link between wine consumption and beliefs in traditional Chinese medicine. Interestingly, some Western medicine maintains that red wine consumption reduces cholesterol.[24]

Comparative advertising has been used more in the United States than in other countries. However, one study of American and Thai consumers discovered that the persuasive ability of comparative ads among both groups was related to the two personality traits: **Self-construal**, which refers to how individuals perceive, comprehend, and interpret the world around them, particularly the behavior or action of others towards themselves, and **need for cognition** (Chapter 3).[25] Another study compared American and Korean consumers and demonstrated that cultural values were more important in influencing reactions to comparative ads than reactions to noncomparative ads, and that need for cognition had an impact on the persuasiveness of comparative ads among consumers in both nations.[26] These studies and many others support the view that, if used properly and in the right context, comparative marketing is a highly effective positioning strategy.

Legal Barriers

At times, local laws force American marketers to alter their offerings. Here are a few examples:

1. Australia's parliament passed a law restricting logos, branding, colors, and promotional text on tobacco packets. Brand names have to appear in standard colors and positions in a plain font and size on packets colored a dark olive-brown, which government research has found holds the lowest appeal to smokers. Health warnings with graphic images of the harmful effects of smoking make up 75% of the front of the packaging.[27]

2. Singapore tightened its rules on casino advertising as part of efforts to limit the social impact of resort hotels on urbanites. Casinos must obtain government approval for all casino advertising and promotions, media-related activities, and sponsorships.[28]

3. The UK's Advertising Standards Authority said that it has referred Groupon Inc.—the Internet daily-deals company—to the Office of Fair Trading for breaches of the nation's advertising code. Apparently, Groupon failed to conduct promotions fairly, by not making significant terms and conditions clear, failing to provide evidence that offers are available, and exaggerating savings claims.[29]

4. China's regulators banned advertising during television dramas, dealing a blow to marketers who had ramped up ad spending to reach the nation's growing consumer class. The new rules restrict commercials from interrupting the plots of TV dramas, allowing showing ads only back-to back between programs.[30]

5. Chinese trademark laws are very "fluid." For instance, Michael Jordan sued Qiaodan Sports because, phonetically, the company's name resembles "Jordan." However, the company said that it had the exclusive right to the Qiaodan trademark and was operating "in accordance with Chinese laws."[31]

World Brands versus Local Brands

Marketers of products with a wide or almost mass-market appeal have also embraced a world branding strategy. For instance, multinational companies and their brands, such as General Motors, Gillette, Estée Lauder, Unilever, and Fiat, have each moved from a local strategy of nation-by-nation advertising to a global advertising strategy. Researchers examining more than 2,500 Taiwanese advertisements, in terms of the use of Western models and English brand names, found that less than half of ads were "global-looking."[32] The Lauder Company—marketer of popular brands like Estée Lauder, Clinique, and Bobbi Brown—introduced a hybrid East-Meets-West beauty line called Osiao (pronounced O-Shao). Osiao's specialized formulas contain Chinese plants like ginseng. To communicate the brand's imported status to consumers, the product names on the bottles appeared in English.[33]

A 12-nation consumer research project found that global brands tend to be viewed differently than local brands, and that consumers worldwide associate global brands with three characteristics:

1. *Quality Signal:* Consumers believe that the more people who purchase a brand, the higher the brand's quality (which often results in a global brand being able to command a premium price). Furthermore, consumers worldwide believe that global brands develop new products and breakthrough technologies at a faster pace than local brands.

2. *Global Myth:* Consumers view global brands as a kind of "cultural ideal"; their purchase and use make consumers feel like citizens of the world, and give them an identity (i.e., "Local brands show what we are; global brands show what we want to be").

3. *Social Responsibility:* Global companies are held to a higher level of corporate social responsibility than local brands, and are expected to respond to social problems associated with what they sell.

In this 12-nation study, the importance of these three dimensions was consistent, and the insights revealed by the research accounted for more than 60% of the variation in the overall brand preferences. The study also identified intracountry segments with respect to how a country's citizens view global brands:[34]

1. *Global Citizens* (55% of the total respondents) use a company's global success as an indication of product quality and innovativeness, and are concerned that the firm acts in a socially responsible manner.

2. *Global Dreamers* (23%) view global brands as quality products, and are not particularly concerned about social responsibility issues.

3. *Antiglobals* (13%) feel that global brands are higher quality than local brands, but dislike brands that preach U.S. values and do not trust global companies to act responsibly. Generally, they try to avoid purchasing global brands.

4. *Global Agnostics* (8%) evaluate global brands in the same way they evaluate local brands.[35]

A study of consumers from eight countries discovered that the following two means of presenting brands were perceived most favorably. First, *self-enhancement* advertisement stressing that the brand conveys one's status and exquisite taste. Second was advertising that stressed *openness* in terms of allowing people to pursue their goals in exciting ways.[36] A study comparing U.S. and South Korean adolescents found that Americans considered the availability of well-known brands significantly more important than the South Koreans did, and the Americans were more willing to pay high prices for clothes with a well-known brand name than their counterparts. However, one of the reasons may have been that well-known brands are very expensive in South Korea, and most adolescents there cannot afford them. Interestingly, American adolescents were motivated primarily by social approval and recognition, whereas their counterparts' main motive was self-expressions through the fashions they adopted.[37]

Distribution of consumer goods in other nations can sometimes seem nearly impossible. For example, a Nestlé sales agent in South Africa ventured into one of Johannesburg's high-crime neighborhoods—where most sales agents would not go—with just taxi money, two cell phones, and a briefcase with order forms. His objective was to distribute Nestlé products, such as baby food and nondairy creamers, in tiny shops and single-serving packages. Apparently, many South African customers are very price-sensitive and buy food items in smaller packages and in small stores, instead of supermarkets.[38]

Figure 13.2 shows four ads for the Patek Philippe watch illustrating a global brand. The ads express the same theme, but in different languages. Table 13.6 lists the most prominent global brands and Table 13.7 describes the global appeals of several brands.[39]

Source: Patek Philippe

Source: Patek Philippe

Source: Patek Philippe

Source: Patek Philippe

FIGURE 13.2 Patek Philippe Is a Global Brand

TABLE 13.6	The 20 Most Valuable Global Brands	
RANK	BRAND	2012 BRAND VALUE ($BILLIONS)
1	Coca-Cola	77.8
2	Apple	76.6
3	IBM	75.5
4	Google	69.8
5	Microsoft	57.9
6	GE	43.7
7	McDonald's	40.1
8	Intel	39.4
9	Samsung	32.9
10	Toyota	30.3
11	Mercedes-Benz	30.1
12	BMW	29.1
13	Disney	27.4
14	Cisco	27.1
15	Hewlett-Packard	26.1
16	Gillette	24.9
17	Louis Vuitton	23.6
18	Oracle	22.1
19	Nokia	21.0
20	Amazon	18.6

Source: Both tables are based on: "Best Global Brands 2012," Interbrand Report, http://www.Interbrand.com/en/news-room/press-releases/2012-10-02-7543da7.aspx

TABLE 13.7	Profiles of Several Global Brands
BRAND	PROFILE AND GLOBAL APPEAL
Coca-Cola	Universally recognized more than any other in the world because it makes people experience fun, freedom, and refreshment. The brand maintains a powerful sense of nostalgia that unites generations of Coke lovers and reinforces consumers' deep connections to the brand. Its edgy campaigns continue to push boundaries, and Coca-Cola reinforced its values through celebratory promotions relating to its 125th-year anniversary ("Sharing Happiness") and the London Olympics ("Move to the beat").
McDonald's	McDonald's stands out because of its exceptional brand management, significant global presence, and delivery of consistent quality and affordability. The company is also working to respond to critics by increasing the number of healthful menu options and effectively communicating its sustainability efforts to both customers and employees, building energy saving and waste reduction into staff incentives.
Louis Vuitton	Louis Vuitton's continued success can be attributed to consistently upholding its core values and remaining loyal to its travel-centric heritage. Louis Vuitton has also improved its digital presence—from charting its history on Facebook to launching an app that enables customers to share travel experiences. The brand expanded to new markets and became a top gift brand in China.
Amazon	Amazon aims to be a place where consumers can find anything they want to buy—online. It delivers by regularly expanding its products and services and, in doing so, has remained a leader in customer service. Amazon sustained the success of its Kindle brand, stretching it beyond its e-reader origins into a legitimate iPad alternative, introducing both the Kindle Touch and Kindle Fire in 175 countries.
H&M	With an ever-increasing number of competitors gaining traction globally and more big retailers stepping into low-cost fast fashion, H&M has been finding new ways to maintain industry leadership. It continues to partner with big-name designers, celebrities, and high-profile supermodels, and this strategy clearly resonates with the aspirations of its fashion-savvy, pop-culture-following target customers.

(Continued)

TABLE 13.7	Profiles of Several Global Brands (Continued)
BRAND	**PROFILE AND GLOBAL APPEAL**
Disney	It is heritage rich, meaningful, and worthwhile to millions of people of all ages and backgrounds around the world. The world of entertainment has been steadily transforming as audience behaviors evolve, content consumption habits change, and the old gives way to the new. Disney has demonstrated an ability to remain resilient over the years in the face of change.
Apple	While many assume it's the products that define Apple, it's really a certain kind of thinking, a certain set of values, and an unmistakable human touch that pervades everything Apple does—which is why our connections to the brand transcend commerce.
Google	With minimal room for growth in search engine market share, Google continues to transform itself into a broader IT company. New products and services include the Project Glass augmented-reality head-mounted display, Google TV, and Google Drive—a cloud computing service.
Microsoft	Microsoft also pushed into the hardware market with its own Surface tablets and into the competitive fray—the global market for converged software/hardware ecosystems. This move will likely define the brand's future.
Toyota	In addition to showing solid numbers with repeat customers, Toyota is strengthening its appeal with younger consumers. The brand has intensified its incentives push and reduced its fleet sales. This helps customers find a good deal while also holding the line on the resale value of their vehicles. Toyota's Prius customers continue to deepen their connection to the Toyota portfolio and the Prius lineup is creating an influx of new customers.
eBay	Most of eBay's growth has come from mobile retailing and PayPal, not its core e-commerce business. More than 90 million users have downloaded eBay's mobile app, and the brand is on track to double volume over both mobile and PayPal. However, eBay is not alone in its mobile e-commerce prowess. Amazon's customers have also embraced its mobile app, and the competition in this sector continues to intensify.
Nike	Nike continually increases the power of its brand through innovation. Slyly, as an "ambush marketer" rather than an official Olympic sponsor in London, the brand attracted publicity, spotlighted new products, and managed, as always, to link world-renowned athletes to its latest offerings. As part of its long-term growth strategy, Nike announced its intention to divest its Cole Haan and Umbro businesses, which will allow it to focus its resources on driving growth in the Nike, Jordan, Converse, and Hurley brands. Nike is also using social media skillfully to generate awareness and buzz, while continuing to engage the public through events and contests.

Source: Both tables are based on: "Best Global Brands 2012," Interbrand Report, http://www.Interbrand.com/en/news-room/press-releases/2012-10-02-7543da7.aspx

Brand Shares and Extensions

All companies continuously monitor their brand shares in domestic and foreign markets. Euromonitor International is the most prominent database of brand shares in virtually all product categories around the world. For example, Table 13.8 illustrates that Procter & Gamble and Unilever have successfully penetrated four important shampoo markets. In both the United States and China—the world's largest markets—Head & Shoulders dominates the shampoo sector, and other Procter & Gamble brands have significant presence. In contrast, in Germany, a local brand has the largest market share and Procter and Gamble's shampoo has had limited success. Interestingly, in each of the four countries, a large portion of the market represents lesser-known brands.

Local brands can sometime overtake well-established American offerings. China is P&G's second-largest market, with $6 billion in sales. However, while P&G's market share in diapers, laundry care, and hair care has risen in China, its share of oral care, bath and shower, and skin care has been slipping. Although Chinese herbal toothpaste for sensitive gums sells for double the price of a similar product by Procter & Gamble, Chinese consumers apparently prefer their local product. Although local Chinese brands are closing the perceived quality gap with foreign products, for some items consumers no longer readily distinguish between the two. A study of Chinese consumers in the country's smaller cities, where shoppers are sharply increasing their spending on home and personal care goods, indicated that 70% of consumers thought P&G's Ariel laundry detergent was a local brand.[40]

Just because a brand may be global in character does not mean that consumers around the world will necessarily respond similarly to a brand extension. One study examined reactions to brand extensions among Western culture (U.S.) and Eastern culture (India) consumers. It hypothesized that the Eastern holistic way of thinking (which focuses on the relationships between objects), rather than the Western analytic style of thinking (which focuses on the attributes or parts of objects), would affect the manner in which consumers judged the "fit" of a brand extension. The research results confirmed this hypothesis: Low-fit extensions (McDonald's chocolate bar and Coke popcorn)

TABLE 13.8	The Top Ten Shampoo Brands in Four Global Markets							
RANK	UNITED STATES		CHINA		GERMANY		BRAZIL	
	MARKETER	BRAND	MARKETER	BRAND	MARKETER	BRAND	MARKETER	BRAND
1	Procter & Gamble	Head & Shoulders (14.8%)	Procter & Gamble	Head & Shoulders (18.5%)	Henkel AG & Co KGaA	Schwarzkopf (17.9%)	Unilever	Sunsilk (19.9%)
2	P&G	Pantene (12.2%)	P&G	Rejoice (13.5%)	P&G	Pantene (9.6%)	Unilever	Clear (10.2%)
3	Unilever	Suave (12%)	P&G	Pantene (9%)	L'Oréal	L'Oréal Paris (7.4%)	L'Oréal	L'Oréal Paris (8%)
4	L'Oréal	Garnier (7.6%)	Unilever	Clear (6.6%)	Unilever	Dove (6.7%)	L'Oréal	Garnier (8%)
5	P&G	Clairol (6.7%)	Unilever	Lux (5.6%)	Beiersdorf AG	Nivea (6.5%)	Colgate-Palmolive Co.	Palmolive (7.4%)
6	Unilever	TRESemmé	Beiersdorf AG	Slek	Kao Corp	Guhl	P&G	Pantene
7	Unilever	Dove	Jiangsu Longliqi	Longliqi	P&G	Head & Shoulders	Unilever	TRESemmé
8	Johnson & Johnson	Neutrogena	Unilever	Dove	L'Oréal	Garnier	Unilever	Dove
9	Vogue	Organix	La Fang International	La Fang	Johnson & Johnson	Terzolin	Niely do Brasil	Niely Gold
10	L'Oréal	L'Oréal Paris	Henkel AG & Co KGaA	Syoss	P&G	Clairol	Natura Cosméticos SA	Natura

Note: Brands' market shares (in percentages) from Euromonitor International are available for the top five brands (to lower-tier subsciptions to the service).

received positive evaluations from the Eastern culture subjects. In contrast, moderate-fit extensions (Kodak greeting cards and Mercedes-Benz watches) received equal responses from both cultural groups. For the Eastern culture participants, liking Coke products, and the fact that Coke and popcorn are complementary products, in that they can be consumed together, were enough to make the brand extension acceptable. The American subjects, in contrast, saw little product-class similarity between Coke and popcorn.[41] As a follow-up, these same researchers replicated their earlier study, and went on to determine that American Indians were significantly more holistic in their thinking than Caucasian Americans; they reported that certain factors, such as corporate reputation, may be used more frequently by Easterners than by Westerners as a basis for judging the "fit" of a brand extension.[42]

Perhaps because of the dominance of English-language pages on the Internet, non-English-speaking European nations wish to distinguish themselves and their cultures by designing websites that reflect their countries and specific cultures. Thus, German websites might employ bright colors and a geometrical layout to give them a "German feel"; a French website might have a black "chic" background; and a Scandinavian website might provide a variety of images of nature. A study of global American brands examined how they standardize their websites in Europe (United Kingdom, France, Germany, and Spain). The study found that although the manufacturers' websites did have a minimal level of uniformity with respect to color, logo, and layout, the textual information and visual images were dissimilar from one market to the next. Still further, as with traditional advertising media, standardization for durable goods was higher than for nondurables.[43]

An interesting example of brand extension is DreamWorks Animation's China film project: Tibet Code, an Indiana Jones–type adventure story based on a wildly popular series of recent Chinese novels set in ninth-century Tibet. Although China's policies on Tibet are a persistent target of Western human-rights critics, and a constant challenge to its international image, the company dismissed suggestions that Tibet Code served any political purpose.[44]

Global Marketing Opportunities

Firms are increasingly selling their products worldwide, for a variety of reasons. First, there has been an ongoing buildup of "multinational fever," and the general attractiveness of multinational markets, products, or services originating in one country means that they are increasingly being sought out by consumers in countries in other parts of the world. Second, many American firms have realized that overseas markets represent an important opportunity for their future growth when their home markets reach maturity. This realization is propelling them to expand their horizons and seek consumers in markets all over the world. Moreover, consumers around the globe are eager to try "foreign" products that are popular in different and far-off places.

Global markets are dynamic, and new marketing opportunities emerge continuously. For example, Chinese shoppers have been shying away from conspicuous luxury goods, such as fancy watches and designer handbags, because luxury goods have become symbols of corruption and of the country's widening wealth gap.[45] As the country's disposable income has risen, Russia has become a lucrative market for American fast-food chains. McDonald's opened its first restaurant on Pushkin Square in 1990 and now operates 279 restaurants in Russia. Burger King has opened 22 restaurants, mostly in mall food courts, in 2 years. Carl's Jr. has 17 restaurants in St. Petersburg and Novosibirsk. Wendy's has opened 2 restaurants and plans 180 throughout Russia by 2020. The Subway sandwich chain has opened about 200 shops in Russia. Yum Brands, which owns KFC, Pizza Hut, and Taco Bell, operates a co-branded chicken restaurant chain in Russia, called Rostik's-KFC, and Il Patio in the Italian food segment, and has about 350 restaurants in Russia.[46]

Young Europeans are now embracing American fashions. After watching such U.S. television series as Gossip Girl, Glee, and Vampire Diaries, European teenagers are replacing Chanel jackets and knotted scarves with American casual tailored sweatpants and frayed oxfords. Abercrombie & Fitch now has a store on the Champs Élysées in Paris and other American fashions are following the trend.[47] Although formerly unthinkable within Japan's strong national culture, because of declining incomes, as well as fears about radiation from a nuclear disaster in Fukushima, a growing number of Japanese consumers have been abandoning their loyalty to expensive, premium-grade homegrown rice. Instead, they have been seeking out cheaper alternatives from China, Australia, and the United States.[48] During Christmas, Printemps, a high-end Paris department store whose stylish Christmas window displays are eagerly awaited every year, showed figures of Asian male and female dancers because a large portion of the store's shoppers are now Asians. Molson Coors, an originally American beer company, introduced more new products in Canada in 18 months than it did in the United States for the previous 15 years. Apparently, Canadians have been increasingly receptive to niche products and shunning mass-marketed goods. The company introduced Molson Canadian 67 Sublime, a lemon- and lime-infused version of the low-calorie beer. This and other products have been positioned as sophisticated and easy to drink. The company also discovered that the new products lured wine and spirits drinkers to the beer market.[49]

Spending Power and Consumption Patterns

The most important criterion for identifying global marketing opportunities is a country's consumer spending and its growth prospects. Figure 13.3 shows consumer gross income, disposable income, and consumer expenditures in numerous countries. Although Norway had the highest gross income, Norwegians' disposable income is not that much higher than that of Americans, because Norway's tax rates are much higher than those in the United States. The small gap between disposable income and consumer expenditures in the United States reflects the nation's modest savings rate. In Greece, consumer expenditures are slightly higher than disposable income, which indicates that Greeks have been "living beyond their means," which is probably a function of uncertainty regarding the future of the euro in Greece. Figure 13.4 shows the percentages of anticipated growth in consumer expenditures through the end of the decade. Clearly, the most growth is expected in Asia and South America, with only modest growth rates in Europe.

The five charts in Figure 13.5 depict the percentages of their disposable incomes that consumers in prominent nations spend on necessities. Figure 13.5A illustrates that clothing is a major expenditure for Russians and Hong Kong's Chinese. The Swiss and Norwegians—citizens of the world's two most affluent nations—spend a great deal on personal care products, which are expensive in these countries because of import taxes (the two nations are not members of the EU, where most import and export barriers have been greatly reduced or eliminated). The Russians and Polish are heavy consumers of meat, whereas Japan and Chinese in Hong Kong like seafood and fish (Figure 13.5B).

FIGURE 13.3
Spending Power and
Consumer Expenditures

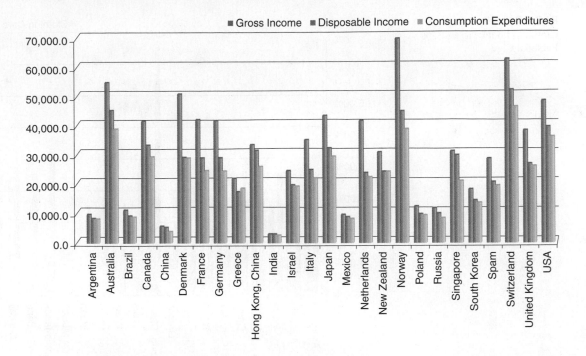

FIGURE 13.4
Forecasted Growth in Consumer
Expenditures Between 2012 and
2020 (percentages)

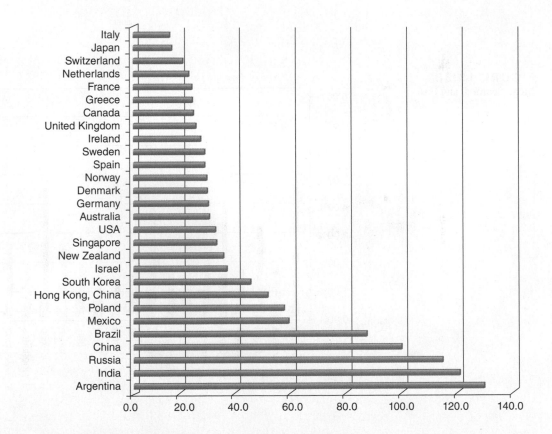

Very few nations, such as people in New Zealand, France, and Germany, consume more fruit than vegetables, because these countries are known for their fresh produce. On the other hand, people in Brazil, Mexico, India an Israel eat mostly vegetables. The data in Figure 13.5D—showing that India is the world's top consumer of breads and cereals—deserve further explanation. Consumers in India start the day with daily breads called chapatti, parantas, and dosas. The Indian breakfast is heavy and there is a feeling of fullness at the end. Kellogg introduced its cereals in India in the 1990s and positioned them as an alternative to the regularly consumed breakfast, but a Kellogg's Corn Flakes breakfast does not give that feeling of fullness. Additionally, the Indian breakfast is known for its

FIGURE 13.5A
Clothing, Footwear, and
Personal Care

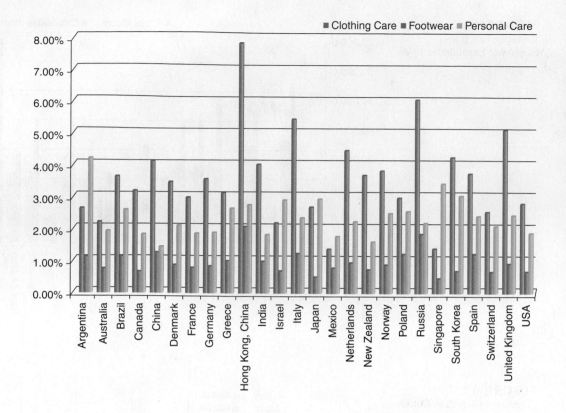

FIGURE 13.5B
Meat, Seafood, and Fish

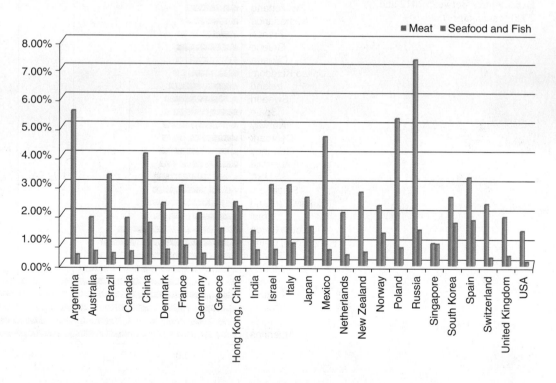

variety (e.g., depending on the region, there can be 30 types of dosas), and often an item that is eaten one day will not be consumed during the following two or three weeks. Offering Indians the same type of corn-flake-based breakfast each day contradicts their culture. Indians have spicy and hot food for breakfast and find corn flakes in cold milk too sweet. Indians have been taught from childhood that milk has to be consumed every day and that milk should always be consumed hot. Therefore, the data in Figure 13.5D reflect Indians' love of various breads, but not cereals. Figure 13.5E shows that Mexico, India, and Brazil are the world's heaviest buyers of bottled water, because clean, fresh water is scarce in these countries.

FIGURE 13.5C
Fruit and Vegetables

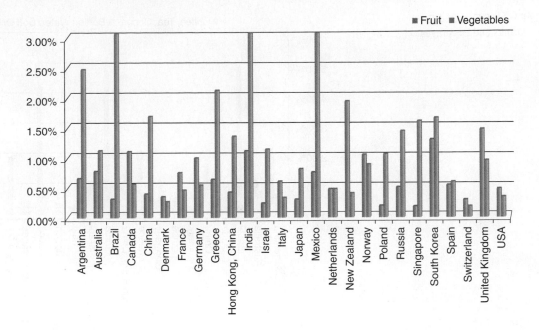

FIGURE 13.5D
Bread, Cereals, Cheese, and Eggs

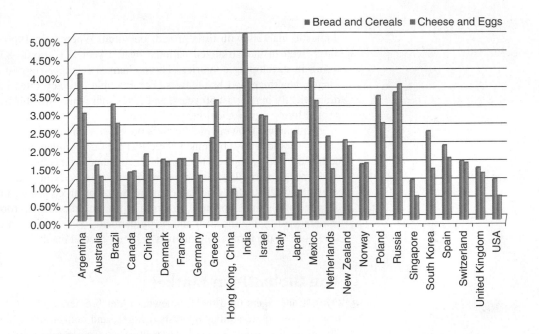

The Growing Global Middle Class

Recent projections state that the middle class will increase by 1.8 billion people over the next decade, of which 600 million will be in China. Within a decade, the middle class will grow from 30% to 52% of the world's population. By 2025, China will have the world's largest middle class, and India's middle class will be 10 times larger than it currently is.[50] The growing middle class in developing countries is a very attractive target to global marketers, who are always eager to identify more customers for their products. The news media have given considerable coverage to the idea that the rapid expansion of the middle class is based on the reality that, although per capita income may be low, there is nevertheless considerable buying power in a country such as China, where most income is largely discretionary (because of government subsidies of basic necessities). Indeed, this same general pattern of a growing middle class is taking place in many parts of South America, Asia, and Eastern Europe.

The rather rapid growth in the number of middle-class overseas has attracted the attention of many well-established marketing powerhouses, who have been facing mature and saturated

FIGURE 13.5E
Drinks and Beverages

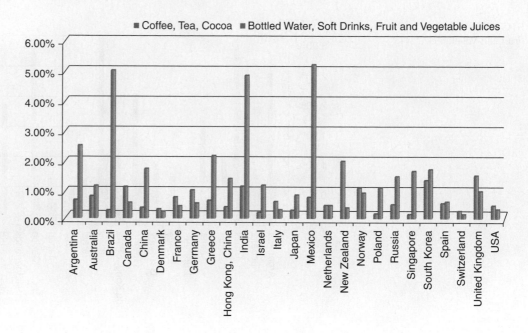

domestic markets with little growth potential. Whereas in 1960 two-thirds of the world's middle class lived in industrialized nations, by the year 2000 some 83% of middle-class citizens were living in developing countries. These changes strongly suggest that more people are now living longer, healthier, and better lives. For example, literacy rates in developing countries have risen dramatically in the past 50 years, and today more than two-thirds, rather than only one-third, of the people living in these nations are literate.[51]

Although a growing middle class provides a market opportunity for products like Big Macs and fries, it should always be remembered that the same product may have different meanings in different countries. For example, whereas a U.S. consumer wants his or her "fast food" to be fast, a Korean consumer is more likely to view a meal as a social or family-related experience. Consequently, convenient store hours may be valued more by a Korean consumer than shorter service time. In China, despite a traditional emphasis on "fresh" (just picked or killed) food, the emerging middle-class consumers, with rising incomes and rising demands on their time, are often willing to spend money to save time, in the form of alternatives to home-cooked meals.[52]

The Global Teen Market

Overall, teenagers (and their somewhat older brothers and sisters, the "young adult" segment) appear to have quite similar interests, desires, and consumption behavior no matter where they live. Therefore, in response to this perspective, consumer researchers have explored the makeup, composition, and behavior of this segment. One study considered the fashion consciousness of teenagers in the United States, Japan, and China.[53] The research revealed that American and Japanese teens were highly similar, differing only in that the Japanese teens were more likely than American teens to choose style over comfort (most likely because of the importance, in the Japanese Confucian society, of meeting the expectations of group members). In contrast, Chinese teens were less fashion conscious than either the American or the Japanese teens, which supports the idea that differences exist between highly developed and less highly developed nations with respect to teen fashion consciousness.[54]

A famous advertising agency conducted a World Global Teen Study that reported changing trends among the world's teenagers.[55] During the 1990s, according to the BBDO research, the "coolest" teens were found in the United States. Currently, though, the "coolest" teens, the Creatives, can be found in all of the 13 countries examined. The Creatives represent about 30% of all teenagers, and are especially numerous in Western Europe (some 23% of U.S. teens are Creatives). Table 13.9 presents the top values and bottom values of both Creatives and all teenagers. Notice, for example, that while 13% of all teens value traditional gender roles, only 1% of Creatives do.[56]

TABLE 13.9	Teenage Creatives' Values				
CREATIVES' TOP VALUES			**CREATIVES' BOTTOM VALUES**		
	ALL TEENS	**CREATIVES**		**ALL TEENS**	**CREATIVES**
Freedom	55%	66%	Public image	30%	17%
Honesty	49%	61%	Status	22%	12%
Equality	39%	50%	Wealth	23%	11%
Learning	37%	47%	Looking good	25%	9%
Preserving the environment	31%	45%	Traditional gender roles	13%	1%
Curiosity	34%	40%	Faith	19%	2%
Creativity	29%	36%			

Cross-Cultural Segmentation

Learning Objective

4 To understand how to apply psychographics to segmenting multinational markets.

As the world became more integrated—largely because of shared communication media—a global marketplace has emerged. For example, as you read this you may be sitting on an IKEA chair or sofa (made in Sweden), drinking Earl Grey tea (England), wearing a Swatch watch (Switzerland), Nike sneakers (China), a Polo golf shirt (Mexico), and Dockers pants (Dominican Republic). Some global market segments, such as teenagers, appear to want the same types of products, regardless of which nation they call home: They desire products that are trendy, entertaining, and image oriented. This global "sameness" allows, for example, a sneaker marketer to launch styles appealing to segments in different countries using the same global advertising campaign. However, cross-cultural differences also force marketers to adapt products for overseas markets. As an illustration, the core benefit that McDonald's provides is consistency and value by having a standardized, almost identical menu in each of its U.S. outlets. McDonald's had to adapt its uniform offerings to the needs and cultures of global consumers. Thus, in India, McDonald's does not serve beef products, and in Saudi Arabia, McDonald's outlets include separate dining sections for men and women.

In Chapter 2, we discussed the VALS framework, which is the most prominent lifestyle segmentation system in the United States (see Figure 2.5 and Table 2.7). Several other countries created their own VALS. For example, in Japan, businesses use the Japan-VALS framework to monitor Japan's consumer environment; generate new product ideas; segment Japanese consumers into potential target markets; differentiate brands; and develop effective pricing, distribution, and promotional strategies. The Japan-VALS segments stem from consumers' *primary motivations* and *degree of innovativeness*, where innovativeness is measured as attitudes toward social change. Primary motivations include tradition, achievement, and self-expression. As illustrated in Figure 13.6, Japanese consumers are classified according to their degree of innovativeness, where Integrators are the most innovative and Sustainers the least.

Research studies have identified many cross-cultural differences that enable marketers to segment overseas markets. For example, although more than 50% of Japanese and American women work outside the home (which enhances the need for many convenience and time-saving products), Japanese women have been slower to embrace the liberated attitudes of working women in the United States. Seen in this light, the determination of whether or not to market a time-saving cleaning device as a world brand is a critical strategic decision. Some firms might attempt to establish a global branding strategy, whereas others would design an individual or local marketing strategy—one that treats Japanese and American working women differently.

Global psychographic research often reveals cultural differences of great importance to marketers. For example, Roper Starch Worldwide, a major multinational marketing research company, interviewed 35,000 consumers in 35 countries in order to identify shared values, irrespective of national borders. The research sought to uncover the bedrock values in peoples' lives so as to understand the motivations that drive both attitudes and behavior. After completing the interviews in North and South America, Asia, and Europe, six global value groups were uncovered:

1. *Strivers*—ambitious and materialistic.
2. *Devouts*—responsible, respectful, and conservative.

FIGURE 13.6
Japan's VALS

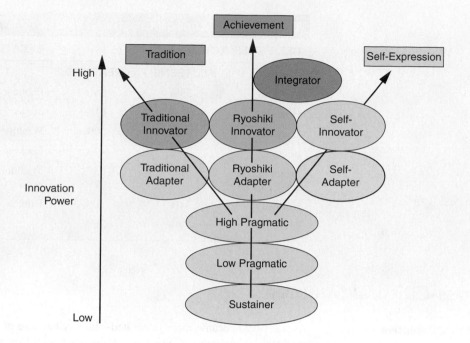

3. *Altruists*—unselfish in their concern for others, society, and the future.
4. *Intimates*—focus on social relationships and family.
5. *Fun Seekers*—young in age and outlook, value adventure and good times.
6. *Creatives*—seek knowledge and insight, and have a keen interest in books and new media.

Summary

Learning Objective 1: To understand how to study the values and customs of different cultures in order to develop effective marketing strategies.

Within the scope of consumer behavior, cross-cultural analysis is defined as determining to what extent the consumers of two or more nations are similar or different. Such analyses provides marketers with an understanding of the psychological, social, and cultural characteristics of the foreign consumers they wish to target, so that they can design effective marketing strategies for the specific national markets involved. An understanding of the similarities and differences that exist between nations is critical to the multinational marketer who must devise appropriate strategies to reach consumers in specific foreign markets. Some of the problems involved in cross-cultural analysis include differences in language, consumption patterns, needs, product usage, economic and social conditions, marketing conditions, and market research opportunities. Acculturation is the process by which marketers learn—via cross-cultural analysis—about the values, beliefs, and customs of other cultures and apply this knowledge to marketing products internationally.

Learning Objective 2: To understand how to decide whether to customize products for global markets or to sell standardized ones.

The greater the similarity between nations, the more feasible it is to use relatively similar marketing strategies in each nation. When the cultural beliefs, values, and customs of specific target countries are found to differ widely, then a highly individualized marketing strategy is indicated for each country. In deciding whether or not

to customize products to local cultures, marketers must consider local values, linguistic barriers, and legal issues.

Learning Objective 3: To understand how to identify global marketing opportunities.

Firms are increasingly selling their products worldwide, for a variety of reasons. Many firms have learned that overseas markets represent an important opportunity for their future growth when their home markets reach maturity. This realization is propelling them to expand their horizons and seek consumers in markets all over the world. Moreover, consumers around the globe are eager to try "foreign" products that are popular in different and far-off places. As increasing numbers of consumers come in contact with the material goods and lifestyles of people living in other countries, and as the number of middle-class consumers grows in developing countries, marketers are eager to locate these new customers and offer them the products.

Learning Objective 4: To understand how to apply psychographics to segmenting multinational markets.

Global psychographic research often reveals cultural differences of great importance to marketers. Psychographics identifies shared values, irrespective of national borders. Much of this research has sought to uncover the bedrock values in peoples' lives, in order to understand the motivations that drive both attitudes and behavior. The VALS research methodology has been used to identify psychographic segments in other countries.

Review and Discussion Questions

13.1. With all the problems facing companies that go global, why are so many companies choosing to expand internationally? What are the advantages of expanding beyond the domestic market?

13.2. In terms of consumer behavior, are the world's countries and their cultures becoming more similar or more different? Discuss.

13.3. What is cross-cultural consumer analysis? How can a multinational company use cross-cultural research to design each factor in its marketing mix for a non-domestic market? Illustrate your answer with examples.

13.4. What are the advantages and disadvantages of global promotional strategies?

13.5. What are the advantages and disadvantages of localized promotional strategies?

13.6. Give three examples of linguistic problems that companies have faced during marketing in global markets and describe how these problems could have been avoided.

13.7. Give three examples of product problems that companies have faced during marketing in global markets and describe how these problems could have been avoided.

13.8. An American company is considering introducing yogurt in Japan. What cultural aspects should the company study before deciding whether or not to do so?

13.9. Coca-Cola is considering introducing very small bottles of its product in Brazil. These would cost *less* than bottled water. Discuss whether or not the company should do so.

13.10. As shown earlier, Hong Kong's Chinese spend more on clothing than any other nation. Research Hong Kong's culture and geographic location and explain why they do so.

13.11. Looking at the charts presented earlier in this chapter, select a product that members of a particular nation consume heavily. Research the country's culture and geographic location and describe why they are heavy consumers of the product selected.

13.12. Looking at the charts presented earlier in this chapter, select a product that members of a particular nation consume very lightly. Research the country's culture and geographic location and describe why they are light users of the product selected.

Hands-on Assignments

13.13. Have you ever traveled outside the United States? If you have, identify some of the differences in values, behavior, and consumption patterns that you noted between people in a country you visited and Americans.

13.14. Interview a student from another culture about his or her use of: (a) credit cards, (b) fast-food restaurants, (c) shampoo, and (d) sneakers. Compare your consumption behavior to that of the person you interviewed and discuss the similarities and differences you discovered.

13.15. Select one of the following countries: Mexico, Brazil, Germany, Italy, Israel, Kuwait, Japan, or Australia. Assume that a significant number of people in the country you chose would like to visit the United States and have

the financial means to do so. Now, imagine that you are a consultant for your state's tourism agency and that you have been charged with developing a promotional strategy to attract tourists from the country you chose. Conduct a computerized literature search of the databases in your school's library and select and read several articles about the lifestyles, customs, and consumption behavior of the people in the country you chose. Prepare an analysis of the articles and, on the basis of what you read, develop a promotional strategy designed to persuade tourists from that country to visit the U.S.

Key Terms

- acculturation *347*
- cross-cultural analysis *344*
- global marketing strategy *342*
- hybrid marketing strategy *342*
- local marketing strategy *342*
- need for cognition *350*
- self-construal *350*
- world brand *342*

Case Five:

LG Mobile/LG Electronics MobileComm USA
"Before you text, give it a ponder"

Primary Agency: **Young & Rubicam/VML**
Contributing Agencies: **TRU, MindShare, Smith & Jones**

Strategic Challenge

Mobile textual harassment is no joke

For teens, texting is like talking; it's intertwined with the way they communicate and socialize. LG's research revealed that what adults and the media think of as "mobile bullying" is a behavior so ingrained in everyday teenage life that it is seen as a normal and expected part of communicating. But mobile textual harassment is in truth an enormous problem affecting millions of tweens and teens. Forty-one% admit they have sent, received or forwarded a text with rumors about someone that were untrue. Four million say they've received a threatening text, while more than 10 million teens also report having sent a "SEXT" message. Five million confess they have been pressured by a boyfriend or girlfriend to send a text with a naked photo. And an alarming 60% of kids who say they have been bullied electronically have never told their parents about the incident.

An opportunity to deliver the LG brand promise by shifting teens' attitudes

Cell phone misuse is expected to escalate as more kids get phones with web access and data plans become more affordable. While today the issue has garnered a lot of media attention, at the time of this effort no cell phone carrier, manufacturer or other commercial voice in the U.S. had become an advocate against the behavior.

At the heart of the LG brand essence "Life's Good" is an overt commitment to make a positive impact on the world. Encouraging teens to text responsibly was an ideal opportunity to continue delivering this promise, and most important, the right thing for LG to do as a technology leader. Although LG had a noble goal to help reduce mobile bullying, the advertising agency realized that it could never expect to stop the behavior, given its prevalence among youth. But, an effective campaign could change kids' attitudes about the seriousness and importance of the issue. The campaign's objective became to raise consciousness about a behavior that was unconscious.

The Adverising Agency—team agreed that if the campaign successfully changed attitudes, attitudes, it would have a positive impact on LG's business.

Strategic challenge: How could LG Mobile help change teens' attitudes about mean texting?

Objectives

The goal was to create a campaign whose positive impact on teens' attitudes about mobile bullying would also drive LG Mobile's brand perceptions, relevance and consideration among the target audience.

Taking into account that LG had never developed this type of campaign before, it was difficult to set benchmarks, benchmarks, but LG agreed that success would be changing attitudes by 15% and brand relevance and consideration by 10%. LG also aimed to increase brand equity and engagement and generate earned media.

The campaign had two types of objectives:

I. **Benchmark-Based**
   - **Attitudinal Shift**—Change teens' attitudes and perceptions about mean texting. Grow +15% based on pre-campaign in-market survey benchmark.
   - **Brand Relevance and consideration**—Increase by 10% based on pre-campaign in-market survey benchmark.

[1]TRU/LG Texting Education Survey, 2010

[2]LG Family Texting Study, 2009

[3]TRU/LG Texting Education Survey, 2010

[4]LG Family Texting Study, 2009

[5]I-Safe America Cyber Bullying Survey 2003–2004

II. **Other performance indicators**
- **Brand Value (equity)**—Increase equity of LG Mobile among teens as a socially responsible company.
- **Brand Engagement**—Motivate teens to interact with the LG brand.
- **Earned Media (and press coverage)**—Given that the effort would have minimal media investment ($1.7MM), LG wanted to generate unpaid media to achieve greater awareness of the issue and momentum around LG Mobile.

The Big Idea

Motivate teens to think about the personal consequences of sending a mean text.

Teens won't stop texting

LG's research . . . research (July 2009) revealed teens felt it was "ok" to share gossip because when they took a photo of a popular kid in a compromised position they were simply reporting on a truth, just like journalists. They were not able to consider the victim's feelings but all could describe a situation where they had sent a text they wished they hadn't. A time when sharing a text had personal consequences for them. Maybe it backfired. A girl wants to please her boyfriend and sends him a topless picture of herself but the guy then decides to pass it around to his friends when they break up. This they understood and wanted to avoid.

For the campaign . . . campaign to be successful, successful, it had to raise . . . to raise awareness about the personal consequences of mobile misuse. misuse. The big idea was to . . . to motivate teens to think of the personal consequences of sending a mean text, which text, which the advertising agency articulated . . . articulated strategically as "think before you text."

Consumer Decision-Making and Diffusion of Innovations

Learning Objectives

1   To understand the consumer's decision-making process.

2   To understand the dynamics of buying gifts.

3   To understand how innovative offerings gain acceptance within market segments and how individual consumers adopt or reject new products and services.

THIS CHAPTER integrates the concepts discussed so far into a framework that illustrates how consumers make buying decisions. Consumption decisions vary. For example, the ad featured in Figure 14.1 is by the Gemological Institute of America (GIA), a nonprofit educational institute of the jewelry industry. The tag line "Understand what you're buying" is directed at consumers seeking to buy diamonds. In consumer decision-making terms, purchasing a diamond represents **extensive problem solving** because consumers buy diamonds infrequently and have no established criteria for evaluating them. The GIA ad tells buyers what to look for in a diamond: Carat weight, clarity, color, cutting style, and other features. In contrast, the Advil ad in Figure 14.2 represents **routinized response behavior**, because consumers have experience with over-the-counter pain relievers and do not need to establish the criteria for evaluating them. More importantly, diamonds are not branded, whereas the Advil brand has a quality reputation and is instantly recognized by millions of consumers around the world. In stores, consumers reach for Advil without much thought. The ad also shows that Advil's reputation enables the brand to use **family branding**, which is marketing different versions of a product under the same brand (see Chapter 5).

When consumers have already have established the basic criteria for evaluating a product or service but still need additional information to understand the differences among brands, they engage in **limited problem solving**. This type of decision occurs when consumers purchase updated versions of products they have bought before, which often have additional features: For example, buying a new laptop computer with multiple input devices, some of which did not exist previously (e.g., a mini disk slot or a faster USB port).

FIGURE 14.1
Purchase Decision: Extensive
Problem Solving

Source: Gemological Institute of America

FIGURE 14.2
Purchase Decision: Routinized
Response Behavior

Source: Pfizer, Inc.

Consumer Decision-Making Model

Learning Objective

1 To understand the consumer's decision-making process.

Figure 14.3 presents a model of consumer decision-making that ties together the ideas on consumer decision-making and consumption behavior discussed throughout this book. It does not presume to provide an exhaustive picture of the complexities of consumer decision-making. Rather, it is designed to synthesize and coordinate relevant concepts into a significant whole. The model includes three components: input, process, and output.

Decision-Making: Input

The input component of the consumer decision-making model includes three types of external influences:

1. The marketing mix consists of strategies designed to reach, inform, and persuade consumers to buy the marketer's products repeatedly. They include the product, advertising and other promotional efforts, pricing policy, and the distribution channels that move the product from the manufacturer to the consumer.

2. The sociocultural influences include the consumer's family, peers, social class, reference groups, culture, and, if applicable, subculture, which are discussed in Chapter 9 and Part Four.

3. The input also includes communications, which are the mechanisms that deliver the marketing mix and sociocultural influences to consumers and are described in Part Three.

FIGURE 14.3
Consumer Decision-Making Model

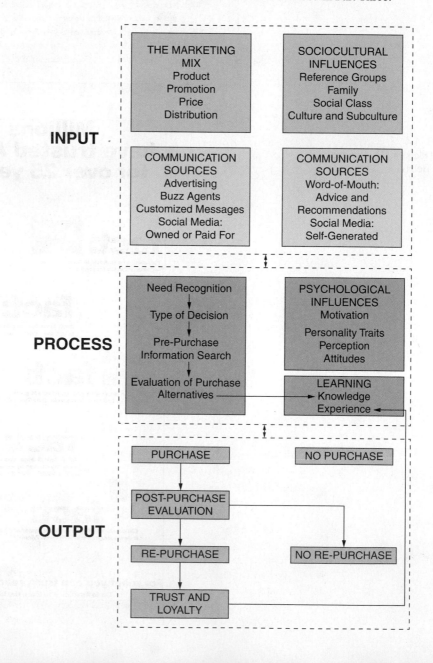

The impact of the marketing mix and sociocultural influences is the input that determines what consumers purchase and how they use what they buy. Because these influences may be directed to the individual or actively sought by the individual, a two-headed arrow is therefore used to link the *input* and *process* segments of the model (see Figure 14.3).

Decision-Making: Process

The process component of the model is concerned with how consumers make decisions. To understand this process, we must consider the influence of the psychological concepts examined in Part Two of this book. The model's *psychological field* consists of the internal influences (motivation, perception, learning, personality, and attitudes) that affect consumers' decision-making processes (what they need or want, their awareness of various product choices, their information-gathering activities, and their evaluation of alternatives).

Need Recognition

Need recognition occurs when a consumer is faced with a "problem." For instance, take a young executive who decides to purchase a new cell phone with a high-quality digital camera. He imagines that he would benefit from having a high-quality digital camera built into his phone because it would make it easier and more convenient to take more vivid and realistic photos, without having to lug around a separate digital camera. This executive has recognized a need and identified a suitable response.

There are two types of need recognition. Some consumers are *actual state* types, who perceive that they have a problem when a product fails to perform satisfactorily (e.g., a cordless telephone that develops constant static). In contrast, other consumers are *desired state* types, for whom the desire for something new may trigger the decision process.[1]

Pre-Purchase Search

Pre-purchase search begins when a consumer perceives a need that might be satisfied by the purchase and consumption of a product. Sometimes, recalling past purchases provides the consumer with adequate information to make the present choice. However, when the consumer has had no prior experience, he or she may have to engage in an extensive search for useful information on which to base a choice.

The consumer usually searches his or her memory (the *psychological field*) before seeking *external* sources of information regarding a given consumption-related need. Past experience is considered an *internal* source of information. The greater the relevant past experience, the less external information the consumer is likely to need to reach a decision. Many consumer decisions are based on a combination of previous experience (internal sources) and marketing and noncommercial information (external sources). The degree of perceived risk can also influence this stage of the decision process (see Chapter 4). In high-risk situations, consumers are likely to engage in complex and extensive information search and evaluation; in low-risk situations, they are likely to use very simple or limited search and evaluation.

The act of shopping is an important form of external information. According to consumer research, there is a big difference between men and women in terms of their response to shopping. Whereas most men do not like to shop, most women claim to like the experience of shopping; and although the majority of women found shopping to be relaxing and enjoyable, the majority of men did not feel that way.[2]

An examination of the external search effort associated with the purchase of different product categories found that, as the amount of total search effort increased, consumer attitudes toward shopping became more positive, and more time was made available for shopping. Not surprisingly, the external search effort was greatest for consumers who had the least amount of product category knowledge.[3] It follows that the less consumers know about a product category and the more important the purchase is to them, the more extensive their pre-purchase search is likely to be. Conversely, consumers high in subjective knowledge (a self-assessment of how much they feel that they know about the product category) will rely more on their own evaluations rather than on others' recommendations.

It is also important to point out that the Internet has had a great impact on pre-purchase search. Rather than visiting a store to find out about a product, or calling the manufacturer and asking for a brochure, consumers can go to manufacturers' websites to find much of the information they need about the products and services they are considering. For example, many automobile websites provide product specifications, prices, and dealer cost information; reviews; and even comparisons with competing vehicles. Volvo's website, for example, lets you "build" your own car, and see how it would look, for example, in different colors. Some auto company websites will even list a particular auto dealer's new and used car inventory. There are also websites that allow women to customize a large number of cosmetic products.

With respect to surfing the Internet for information, consider one consumer's comments drawn from a research study: "I like to use the Web because it's so easy to find information, and it's really easy to use. The information is at my finger-tips and I don't have to search books in libraries."[4] However, a Roper Starch Survey found that an individual searching the Internet gets frustrated in about 12 minutes, on average; other research suggested that although the Internet may reduce physical effort, there is nevertheless a "cognitive challenge" that limits consumers' online information searches.[5]

What happens if a search is a failure? According to a study of "search regret," consumers' post-purchase dissonance results from an unsuccessful pre-purchase search.[6] Furthermore, the same research revealed that failure can also have a damaging effect on retailers. However, retailers can help eliminate or reduce search regret by providing ample information, trying to reduce out-of-stock situations, and giving salespeople proper training.[7]

How much information a consumer will gather also depends on various situational factors. Table 14.1 lists several factors that increase consumers' pre-purchase information search. For some products and services, the consumer may have ongoing experience on which to draw (such as a golfer purchasing a "better" set of golf clubs), or the purchase may essentially be discretionary in nature (rather than a necessity), so there is no rush to make a decision.

Online versus Traditional Information Search

For a while now, researchers have been examining how the Internet has affected the way consumers make decisions. It is often thought that because consumers have limited information-processing capacity, they must develop a strategy for searching for information online. The strategy is based on both individual (e.g., knowledge, personality traits, demographics) and contextual factors (characteristics of the decision tasks). The three major contextual factors that have been researched are:[8]

1. *Task Complexity* – the number of alternatives and amount of information available for each alternative.
2. *Information Organization* – the presentation, format, and content.
3. *Time Constraint* – the amount of time the consumer has to decide.

Brand-Sets and Attributes Considered During Evaluation

Within the context of consumer decision-making, the **evoked set (consideration set)** refers to the specific brands (or models) a consumer considers in making a purchase within a particular product category. An **inept set** consists of brands (or models) that the consumer excludes from purchase

TABLE 14.1	Factors That Increase Pre-Purchase Information Search

PRODUCT FACTORS

Long periods of time between successive purchases
Frequent changes in product styling
Frequent price changes
Volume purchasing (large number of units)
High price
Many alternative brands
Much variation in features

SITUATIONAL FACTORS

Experience: First-time purchase; No past experience because the product is new; Unsatisfactory past experience within the product category.
Social Acceptability: The purchase is for a gift; The product is socially visible.
Value-Related Considerations: The purchase is discretionary rather than necessary; All alternatives have both desirable and undesirable consequences; Family members disagree on product requirements or evaluation of alternatives; Product usage deviates from important reference groups; The purchase involves ecological considerations; Many sources of conflicting information.

CONSUMER FACTORS

Demographics: Education, income, occupation, age, wealth, and marital status.
Personality Traits: One's degree of dogmatism, willingness to accept risk, product involvement, and novelty seeking.

FIGURE 14.4
Brand-Sets Considered During
Evaluation

consideration because they are unacceptable or seen as inferior. An **inert set** consists of brands (or models) the consumer is indifferent toward because they are perceived as not having any particular advantages. Regardless of the total number of brands (or models) in a product category, a consumer's evoked set tends to be quite small on average, often consisting of only three to five brands or models.

The evoked set consists of the small number of brands the consumer is familiar with, remembers, and finds acceptable. Figure 14.4 shows the evoked set as a subset of all available brands in a product category. Marketers must ensure that their products become a part of a consumer's evoked set if they are to be considered at all. Excluded products include:

1. Unknown brands or models because of the consumer's selective exposure to advertising media and selective perception of advertising stimuli.

2. Unacceptable brands of poor quality or not having specific features or attributes or inappropriate positioning in either advertising or product characteristics.

3. Brands that are perceived as not having any special benefits.

4. Overlooked brands that have not been clearly positioned.

5. Brands that are not selected because they do not satisfy perceived needs.

In each of these instances, the implication for marketers is that promotional techniques should be designed to impart a more favorable and relevant, product image to the target consumer. This may also require a change in product features or attributes (more or better features). An alternative strategy is to get consumers in a particular target segment to consider a specific offering and possibly put it in their evoked set.

Research also suggests that the use of white space and choice of typeface in advertisements may influence the consumer's image of the product. For example, quality, prestige, trust, attitude toward the brand, and purchase intention have been shown to be positively conveyed by white space, and typefaces were perceived as being attractive, warm, and liked when they were simple, more natural, and included serifs.[9] It has also been suggested that consumers may not, all at once, incorporate the entire number of possible choices into their evoked set, but instead may make several decisions within a single decision process. Consumers screen their options and eliminate unsuitable alternatives before they start the information search process, which makes reaching a final decision more manageable.[10]

In reality, the criteria consumers use to evaluate the products within their evoked sets are in the form of important product attributes. In addition to price, examples of product attributes that consumers have used while evaluating product are:

1. *E-Book readers*: Size, weight, touch screen, battery life, memory size, and the compatibility with a cell phone signal.

2. *Orange juice*: Amount of pulp, degree of sweetness, weakness or strength of flavor, color, and packaging.

3. *Wristwatches*: Alarm features, water resistance, quartz movement, and size of dial.

When a company knows that consumers will be evaluating alternatives, it sometimes advertises in a way that recommends the criteria consumers should use in assessing product or service options. We have probably all had the experience of comparing or evaluating different brands or models of a product and finding the one that just feels, looks, and/or performs "just right." Interestingly, research shows that when consumers discuss such "right" products, there is little or no mention of price; items often reflect personality characteristics or childhood experiences; and it is often "love at first sight." In one study, the products claimed to "just feel right" included Big Bertha golf clubs, old leather briefcases, Post-it notes, and the Honda Accord.[11]

Research has explored the influence of brand credibility (which consists of trustworthiness and expertise) on brand choice, and has found that it improves the chances that a brand will be included in the consumer's evoked set. Three factors that affect a brand's credibility are: The perceived quality of the brand, the perceived risk associated with the brand, and the information costs saved by deciding to buy the brand and end the search for information.[12] Furthermore, the study indicated that trustworthiness is more important than expertise when it comes to making a choice.

Consumer Decision Rules

Decision rules are procedures that consumers use to facilitate brands and other consumption-related choices. These rules reduce the burden of making complex decisions by providing guidelines or routines that make the process less taxing. There are two types of consumer decision rules. **Compensatory decision rules** come into play when a consumer evaluates brand or model options in terms of each relevant attribute and computes a weighted or summated score for each brand. The computed score reflects the brand's relative merit as a potential purchase choice. The assumption is that the consumer will select the brand that scores highest among the alternatives evaluated. In contrast, **noncompensatory decision rules** do not allow consumers to balance positive evaluations of a brand on one attribute against a negative evaluation on some other attribute.

There are three types of noncompensatory rules. In following a **conjunctive decision rule**, the consumer establishes a separate, minimally acceptable level as a cutoff point for each attribute. If any particular brand or model falls below the cutoff point on any one attribute, that option is eliminated from further consideration. Because the conjunctive rule can result in several acceptable alternatives, it becomes necessary in such cases for the consumer to apply an additional decision rule to arrive at a final selection (for example, accepting the first satisfactory brand). The conjunctive rule is particularly useful in quickly reducing the number of alternatives to be considered. The consumer can then apply another, more refined decision rule to arrive at a final choice.

In following a **lexicographic decision rule**, the consumer first ranks the attributes in terms of perceived relevance or importance. The consumer then compares the various alternatives in terms of the single attribute that is considered most important. If one option scores sufficiently high on this top-ranked attribute (regardless of the score on any of other attributes), it is selected and the process ends. When there are two or more surviving alternatives, the process is repeated with the second highest-ranked attribute (and so on), until the consumer reaches the point that one of the options is selected because it exceeds the others on a particular attribute.

With the lexicographic rule, the highest-ranked attribute (the one applied first) may reveal something about the individual's basic consumer (or shopping) orientation. For instance, a "buy the best" rule might indicate that the consumer is *quality oriented*; a "buy the most prestigious brand" rule might indicate that the consumer is *status oriented*; a "buy the least expensive" rule might reveal that the consumer is *economy minded*.

A variety of decision rules appear quite commonplace. According to a consumer survey, nine out of ten shoppers who go to the store for frequently purchased items possess a specific shopping strategy for saving money:[13]

1. *Practical Loyalists*—those who look for ways to save on the brands and products they would buy anyway.

2. *Bottom-Line Price Shoppers*—those who buy the lowest-priced item with little or no regard for brand.

3. *Opportunistic Switchers*—those who use coupons or sales to decide among brands and products that fall within their evoked set.

4. *Deal Hunters*—those who look for the best bargain and are not brand loyal.

TABLE 14.2	Applying the Decision Rules to Purchasing an E-Book Reader
DECISION RULE	**RATIONALE**
Compensatory	"I selected the e-book reader that came out as the best when I balanced the good ratings against the bad ratings."
Conjunctive	"I selected the e-book reader netbook that had no bad features."
Disjunctive	"I picked the e-book reader that excelled in at least one attribute."
Lexicographic	"I chose the e-book reader that scored the best on the attribute that I consider to be the most important."
Affect referral	"I bought the brand with the highest overall rating."

We have considered only the basic consumer decision rules. Most of the decision rules described here can be combined to form new variations, such as conjunctive-compensatory, conjunctive-disjunctive, and disjunctive-conjunctive rules. It is likely that, for many purchase decisions, consumers maintain in long-term memory overall evaluations of the brands in their evoked sets. This would make assessment by individual attributes unnecessary. Instead, using the **affect referral decision rule**, the consumer selects the brand with the highest perceived overall rating. This type of synthesized decision rule represents the simplest of all rules.

Table 14.2 applies the decision rules to purchasing an e-book reader.

Decision Rules and Marketing Strategy

An understanding of which decision rules consumers apply in selecting a particular product or service is useful for marketers in developing promotional programs. A marketer who is familiar with the prevailing decision rule can prepare a promotional message in a format that will facilitate consumer information processing. The promotional message might even suggest how potential consumers should make a decision. For instance, an advertisement for the latest cell phone might tell potential consumers "what to look for in a new feature-rich cell phone." The ad might advise consumers to consider the attributes of long battery life, high-resolution screen, high-resolution video recording, and a particularly high-quality digital camera.

Incomplete Information and Noncomparable Alternatives

In many decision-related situations, consumers have incomplete information on which to base decisions and must use alternative strategies to compensate for the missing elements. Missing information may result from advertisements or packaging that mention only certain attributes, the consumer's own imperfect memory of attributes for no present alternatives, or because some attributes are experiential and can only be evaluated after product use. There are four ways in which consumers can cope with missing information:

1. Consumers may delay the decision until the missing information is obtained.

2. Consumers may ignore missing information and decide to continue with the decision process using only the available information.

3. Consumers may change the decision strategy to one that better accommodates missing information.

4. Consumers may infer ("construct") the missing information.

In discussing consumer decision rules, we have assumed that a choice is made from among the brands (or models) evaluated. Of course, a consumer may also conclude that none of the alternatives offers sufficient benefits to warrant purchase. If this were to occur with a necessity, such as a home water heater, the consumer would probably either lower his or her expectations and settle for the best of the available alternatives or seek information about additional brands, hoping to find one that more closely met predetermined criteria. In contrast, if the purchase is more discretionary (e.g., a new pair of shoes), the consumer probably would postpone the purchase. In this case, information gained from the search up to that point would be transferred to long-term storage and retrieved and reintroduced as input when the consumer regained interest in making such a purchase (see Chapter 5).

Decision-Making: Output

The output portion of the consumer decision-making model consists of purchase behaviors and post-purchase evaluation of the purchases. Consumers make three types of purchases. When a consumer purchases a product (or brand) for the first time and buys a smaller quantity than usual, the purchase is a trial. Thus, a trial is the exploratory phase of purchase behavior in which consumers attempt to evaluate a product through direct use. For instance, when consumers purchase a new brand of laundry detergent about which they may be uncertain, they are likely to purchase a smaller quantity than if it were a familiar brand. Consumers can also be encouraged to try a new product through such promotional tactics as free samples, coupons, and/or sale prices.

When a new brand in an established product category (cookies, cold cereal, yogurt) is found by trial to be more satisfactory or better than other brands, consumers are likely to repeat the purchase. Repeat purchase behavior represents **brand loyalty**. Unlike a trial, in which the consumer uses the product on a small scale and without any commitment, a repeat purchase usually signifies that the product meets with the consumer's approval and that he or she is willing to use it again and in larger quantities.

Trial purchases are not always feasible. For example, with most durable goods (e.g., refrigerators, washing machines, electric ranges), a consumer usually moves directly from evaluation to a purchase and long-term commitment without an actual trial. While purchasers of a new Volkswagen Beetle were awaiting delivery of their just-purchased cars, they were kept "warm" by receiving a mailing that included a psychographic tool called "Total Visual Imagery" that was personalized to the point that it showed them the precise model and color they had ordered.[14]

Still further, post-purchase evaluation occurs after consumers have used the product, and in the context of their expectations. When a product's performance matches expectations, consumers feel neutral. **Positive disconfirmation of expectations** occurs when the product's performance exceeds expectations and the consumer is satisfied. **Negative disconfirmation of expectations** occurs when performance is below expectations and the consumer is dissatisfied.

Cognitive dissonance (see Chapter 6) occurs when consumers try to reassure themselves that they made wise choices. In doing so, they may rationalize the decision as being wise; seek advertisements that support their choice and avoid those of competitive brands; attempt to persuade friends or neighbors to buy the same brand (and thereby confirm their own choice); or turn to other satisfied purchasers for reassurance.

The degree of post-purchase analysis that consumers undertake depends on the importance of the product decision and the experience acquired in using the product. When the product lives up to expectations, the consumers probably will buy it again. When the product performance is disappointing or does not meet expectations, they will search for better alternatives. Thus, the consumer's post-purchase evaluation "feeds back" to the consumer's psychological field and influences similar decisions in the future. Studies show that customer retention is often an outcome of the brand's reputation—especially for products that consumers find difficult to evaluate.[15] Research also found that younger customers have more involvement and higher expectations of service offerings and often experience cognitive dissonance after purchasing services.[16]

Satisfied customers feel that they receive "value for their money." As an outcome of an evaluative judgment (i.e., the consumer purchases one of the brands or models in his or her evoked set), value implies the notion of a trade-off of benefits—the features of the purchased item—versus the sacrifice necessary to purchase it (the price of the product).[17] As early as 1911, researchers suggested that one should view consumption as "voting." Just as a consumer influences a political election by the act of voting, that same consumer influences the environment and society by his or her purchases.[18]

Consumer Gifting Behavior

Learning Objective

2   To understand the dynamics of buying gifts.

Gifts are a particularly interesting part of consumer decision-making. Gifts represent more than ordinary, "everyday" purchases, because they are symbolic, and mostly associated with important events (e.g., Mother's Day, births and birthdays, engagements, weddings, graduations, and many other accomplishments and milestones). **Gifting behavior** is a gift exchange that takes place between a giver and a recipient. The definition is broad in nature and embraces gifts given voluntarily ("Just to let you know I'm thinking of you"), as well as gifts that are an obligation ("I had to get him a gift").[19] It includes gifts given to (and received from) others and gifts to oneself ("self-gifts"). Moreover, the majority of products that we refer to as "gifts" are in fact items that we purchase for ourselves.

Gifting represents symbolic communication, with meanings ranging from congratulations, love, and regret to obligation and dominance. The nature of the relationship between gift giver and gift receiver determines the gift chosen, but can also have an impact on the subsequent relationship between the giver and the recipient.[20] There are several types of gifts:[21]

1. *Intergroup Gifting* occurs whenever one group exchanges gifts with another group (such as one family with another). Similarly, gifts given to families will be different than those given to individual family members. For example, a "common sense" wedding gift may include products for setting up a household rather than a gift that would be used personally by either the bride or the groom.

2. *Intercategory Gifting* takes place when either an individual is giving a gift to a group (a single friend is giving a couple an anniversary gift) or a group is giving an individual a gift (friends chip in and give another friend a joint birthday gift). The gift selection strategies "buy for joint recipients" or "buy with someone" are especially useful when it comes to a difficult recipient situation (when "nothing seems to satisfy her"). These strategies can also be applied to reduce some of the time pressure associated with shopping for the great number of gifts exchanged during the American Christmas-season gift-giving ritual. For example, a consumer may choose to purchase five intercategory gifts for five aunt-and-uncle pairs (intercategory gifting), instead of buying ten personal gifts for five aunts and five uncles (interpersonal gifting). In this way, less time, money, and effort may be expended.[22]

3. *Intragroup Gifting* is characterized by the sentiment "we gave this to ourselves"; that is, a group gives a gift to itself or its members. For example, a dual-income couple may find that their demanding work schedules limit leisure time spent together as husband and wife. Therefore, an anniversary gift ("to us") of a long weekend in Las Vegas would be an example of an intragroup gift. It would also remedy the couple's problem of not spending enough time together. In contrast, interpersonal gifting occurs between just two individuals: the gift giver and the gift receiver. By their very nature, interpersonal gifts are intimate because they provide an opportunity for a gift giver to reveal what he or she thinks of the gift receiver. Successful gifts communicate that the giver knows and understands the receiver and their relationship. For example, a pair of "just the right" cufflinks given to a friend is viewed by the receiver as "she really knows me." In contrast, an electric can opener given as a Valentine's Day gift, when the recipient is expecting a more intimate gift, can mean the deterioration of a relationship.

Researchers have discovered that both male and female gift givers feel more comfortable in giving gifts to the same sex. However, they also experienced more intense feeling with respect to gifts given to members of the opposite sex.[23] Additionally, although females get more pleasure than males from giving gifts, and generally play the dominant role in gift exchanges, both sexes are strongly motivated by feelings of obligation. Still further, everyone knows that selecting and giving a gift often causes "gifting anxiety" on the part of the givers, the recipients, and the gifting situations. Knowledge of gender differences is therefore useful for marketers, because it implies that additional support might be appreciated at the point of purchase (while in a store) when a consumer is considering a gift for an opposite-sex recipient.

One study of gifts purchased online found that **variety-seeking** (see Chapter 5) extends to gifting, as subjects with this trait considered a wider range of product categories when buying gifts for others.[24] A Hong Kong study identified a continuum of gift receivers: "romantic other," "close friend," and "just friends." For example, a gift given to a "romantic other" involves a high emotional expectation, but one given to a friend has a low emotional expectation.[25]

Intrapersonal gifting, or a self-gift, occurs when the giver and the receiver are the same individual.[26] A self-gift is a state of mind. If a consumer sees a purchase as the "buying of something I need," then it is simply a purchase. In contrast, if the same consumer sees the same purchase as a "self-gift," then it is something special, with special meaning. Consumers may treat themselves to self-gifts that are products (clothing, compact disks, or jewelry), services (hairstyling, restaurant meals, spa membership), or experiences (socializing with friends). For example, while purchasing holiday gifts for others, some consumers find themselves in stores that they might not otherwise visit or find themselves looking at merchandise (such as a scarf) that they want but would not ordinarily buy.

The gifting process starts with the question: "Should I give a gift to X?" The answer can be yes or no depending on a variety of factors (e.g., relationship, occasion). If the answer is yes, the gift giver continues by asking: "What shall I give X as a gift?" This leads to the next question: "Do I want to give X something that X desires (i.e., do I want to put in some real effort researching the gift)?" If the answer is yes, the gift giver is then faced with the question: "How do I learn what X desires as a gift?" Here there are two choices: predicting the preferences of the recipient or asking the recipient what he or she desires. If the consumer answers no to the question, "Do I want to give X something that X desires?" then the gift giver has two choices (according to the model): (1) to give a gift that he or she would like (i.e., "To you for me"), or (2) to give a gift that attempts to alter or improve the gift receiver to the gift giver's liking (i.e., "Identify imposition"). The symbolic messages associated with these gifts tend to be less valued by the recipient. If preference prediction rather than direct questioning of the recipient for a gift idea is chosen, then there will be an element of surprise. In addition, if the giver does not bother to learn the recipient's preferences, then the outcome can also be a surprise—but maybe not a good surprise.[27]

Diffusion and Adoption of Innovations

Learning Objective

3 To understand how innovative offerings gain acceptance within market segments and how individual consumers adopt or reject new products and services.

Diffusion of innovations is the macro process by which the acceptance of an innovation (i.e., a new product, new service, new idea, or new practice) takes place among members of a social system (or market segments), over time. This process includes four elements:

1. *The Innovation*: new product, model, or service.
2. *The Channels of Communication*: informal or formal, impersonal or personal groups.
3. *The social system*: a market segment.
4. *Time*.

In contrast, the **innovation adoption process** is a micro process that focuses on the stages through which an individual consumer passes when deciding to accept or reject a new product.

Types of Innovations

The definition of what is a "new product" varies among product developers and marketing strategists. From a consumer perspective, an **innovation** represents any item that the consumer perceives as new. Many marketers maintain that new products should be classified into three categories reflecting the extent to which they require consumers to change existing consumption behavior or buying patterns.

1. A **continuous innovation** has the least disruptive influence on established behavior. It involves the introduction of a modified product rather than a totally new product. Examples include the newly redesigned Apple MacBook, the latest version of Microsoft Office, reduced-fat Oreo cookies, Hershey Cacao (i.e., a form of dark) chocolate bars, American Express gift cards, Band-Aid Tough-Strips, and the Oral-B® Advantage Glide. Figure 14.2 is an example of continuous innovation.

2. A **dynamically continuous innovation** is somewhat more disruptive than a continuous innovation but still does not alter established behavior. It may involve the creation of a new product or the modification of an existing product. Examples include digital cameras, digital video recorders, MP3 players, DVRs, USB flash drives, and disposable diapers.

3. A **discontinuous innovation** requires consumers to adopt new behavior. Examples include airplanes, radios, TVs, automobiles, fax machines, PCs, videocassette recorders, medical self-test kits, and the Internet.

Product Features That Affect Adoption

Not all new products are equally likely to be adopted by consumers. Some products catch on very quickly (e.g., affordable cell phones), whereas others take a very long time to gain acceptance or never seem to achieve widespread consumer acceptance (e.g., electric cars). Diffusion researchers have identified five product characteristics that influence consumer acceptance of new products, which are detailed next.[28]

Relative advantage is the degree to which potential customers perceive a new product as superior to existing substitutes. For example, cellular telephones enable users to be in communication with the world and allows users to both receive and place calls and text messages. The fax machine offers users a significant relative advantage in terms of ability to communicate. A document can be transmitted in as little as 15 to 18 seconds at perhaps one-tenth the cost of an overnight express service, which will not deliver the document until the following day. (Of course, sending the document as an attachment to an email entails no cost and, like a fax, gets delivered in seconds.)

Compatibility is the degree to which potential consumers feel a new product is consistent with their present needs, values, and practices. For instance, an advantage of 3M's Scotch Pop-up Tape Strips is that they are easier to use than roll tape for certain tasks (such as wrapping gifts), yet they represent no new learning for the user. Similarly, in the realm of shaving products, it is not too difficult to imagine that a few years ago, when Gillette introduced the Fusion razor, some men made the transition from inexpensive disposable razors and other men shifted from competitive nondisposable razors (including Gillette's own MACH3 razors) to using the new product. This newer product is fully compatible with the established wet-shaving rituals of many men. However, it is difficult to imagine male shavers shifting to a new depilatory cream designed to remove facial hair. Although potentially simpler to use, such a cream is incompatible with most men's current values regarding daily shaving practices.

Compatibility varies across cultures. For example, although shelf-stable milk (milk that does not require refrigeration unless it has been opened) has been successfully sold for years in Europe, Americans thus far have generally resisted the aseptic milk package.

Complexity—the degree to which a new product is difficult to understand or use—affects product acceptance. Clearly, the easier it is to understand and use a product, the more likely that product is to be accepted. For example, the acceptance of such convenience foods as frozen french fries, instant puddings, and microwave dinners is generally due to their ease of preparation and use. Interestingly, although DVD players can be found in most American homes, many adults require the help of their children to use the devices to record particular television programs. The introduction of cable boxes with built-in DVRs has helped to reduce the ongoing challenge involved in easily recording a TV program. A study of the adoption of mobile commerce transactions conducted via a mobile device or wireless telecommunication found that "perceived ease of use" had a positive effect on the intention to adopt.[29]

The issue of complexity is especially important when attempting to gain market acceptance for high-tech consumer products. Four predominant types of "technological fear" act as barriers to new-product acceptance: (1) Fear of technical complexity, (2) fear of rapid obsolescence, (3) fear of social rejection, and (4) fear of physical harm. Of the four, technological complexity was the most widespread concern of consumer innovators.[30]

Trialability refers to the degree to which a new product can be tried on a limited basis. The greater the opportunity to try a new product, the easier it is for consumers to evaluate the product and ultimately adopt it. In general, frequently purchased household products tend to have qualities that make trial relatively easy, such as the ability to purchase a small or "trial" size. Because a computer program cannot be packaged in a smaller size, many computer software companies offer free working models (demo versions) of their latest software to encourage computer users to try the program and subsequently buy the program.

Aware of the importance of trial, marketers of new supermarket products commonly use substantial cents-off coupons or free samples to provide consumers with direct product experience. In contrast, durable items, such as refrigerators or ovens, are difficult to try without making a major commitment. This may explain why publications such as Consumer Reports are so widely consulted for their ratings of infrequently purchased durable goods.

Observability (communicability) is the ease with which a product's benefits or attributes can be observed, imagined, or described to potential consumers. Products that have a high degree of social visibility, such as fashion items, are more easily diffused than products that are used in private, such as a new type of deodorant. Similarly, a tangible product is promoted more easily than an intangible product (such as a service).

The Adoption Process

The innovation adoption process consists of five stages through which potential consumers pass in attempting to arrive at a decision to try or not to try a new or innovative product. The five stages are:

1. **Awareness**: The consumer becomes aware that an innovation exists.
2. **Interest**: The consumer becomes interested in the innovative product or service.
3. **Evaluation**: The consumer undertakes a "mental trial" of the innovation.
4. **Trial**: The consumer tries the innovation.
5. **Adoption**: If satisfied, the consumer decides to use the innovation repeatedly.

Although the traditional adoption process model is insightful in its simplicity, it does not adequately reflect the full complexity of the consumer adoption process. For one thing, it does not adequately acknowledge that quite often, consumers face a need or problem-recognition stage before acquiring an awareness of potential options or solutions (a need recognition preceding the awareness stage). Moreover, the adoption process model does not adequately provide for the possibility of evaluation and rejection of a new product or service after each stage, especially after trial (i.e., a consumer may reject the product after trial or never use the product on a continuous basis). Finally, it does not include post-adoption or post-purchase evaluation, which can lead to a strengthened commitment or to discontinued use.

Summary

Learning Objective 1: To understand the consumer's decision-making process.

Not all consumer decision-making situations require the same degree of information research. Extensive problem solving occurs when consumers have no established criteria for evaluating an item within a product category. Limited problem solving occurs when consumers have established the basic criteria for evaluating the product category, but need more information to decide among the brands and product models available. Routinized response behavior occurs when consumers have experience with the product category and the brands offered and buy items often and almost instinctively. A model of consumer decision-making ties together the consumption behavior discussed throughout this book. It includes three components: Input, process, and output.

Learning Objective 2: To understand the dynamics of buying gifts.

Gifts represent more than ordinary, everyday purchases, because they are symbolic, and mostly associated with important events. Gifting behavior is a gift exchange that takes place between a giver and a recipient. The definition is broad in nature and embraces gifts given voluntarily, as well as gifts that are an obligation. It includes gifts given to (and received from) others and gifts to oneself (self-gifts). Moreover, the majority of products that we refer to as "gifts" are in fact items that we purchase for ourselves.

Learning Objective 3: To understand how innovative offerings gain acceptance within market segments and how individual consumers adopt or reject new products and services.

Diffusion of innovations is the macro process by which the acceptance of an innovation (i.e., a new product, service, idea, or practice) takes place among members of a social system (or market segments), over time. This process includes four elements: (1) The innovation (new product, model, service); (2) the channels of communication (informal or formal, impersonal or personal groups); (3) the social system (a market segment); and (4) time.

In contrast, the innovation adoption process is a micro process that focuses on the stages through which an individual consumer passes when deciding to accept or reject a new product.

Review and Discussion Questions

14.1. To what extent does the channel of communication affect the level of success of a new innovative product? Think of examples that have been successful and unsuccessful due to channels of communication.

14.2. What are the differences among the three problem-solving decision-making approaches? What type of decision process would you expect most consumers to follow in their first purchase of a new product or brand in each of the following areas: (a) Chewing gum, (b) Sugar, (c) Men's aftershave lotion, (d) Carpeting, (e) Paper towels, (f) Smartphone, and (g) Luxury car? Explain your answers.

14.3. Consumers purchase products to satisfy their needs; these could be luxury items or products that are necessary. Many large consumer purchases require in-depth comparisons in terms of price, quality, and brand. Imagine you are looking to purchase a product that involves research and comparison. What influences your decision to purchase one particular product over another?

14.4. How can Apple use its knowledge of customers' expectations in designing a marketing strategy for a new iPad?

14.5. How do consumers reduce post-purchase dissonance? How can marketers provide positive reinforcement to consumers after the purchase to reduce dissonance?

14.6. The mobile telephone has vastly improved over the last few decades. It had its humble beginnings in the 1970s when Motorola saw the need for better communication. In today's society, users not only use mobile phones for phone calls and text messages, but many have their emails and social networks synced on their devices, staying connected at all times. Identify and explore who the first consumers of the mobile telephone were. Were they consumer innovators or non-innovators?

14.7. Think of the last time you purchased a gift for someone special. How did you know what that person would like, and what did you consider when purchasing the gift?

Hands-on Assignments

14.8. Identify a product, service, or style that was recently adopted by you and/or some of your friends. Identify what type of innovation it is and describe its diffusion process up to this point in time. What are the characteristics of the people who adopted it first? What types of people did not adopt it? What features of the product, service, or style are likely to determine its eventual success or failure?

14.9. It is difficult to find a global definition for the term "innovation," as it takes many forms. Organizations such as Google and the Virgin Group have succeeded in highly competitive industries due to their ability to provide some form of innovation – this could be obvious innovations of products or services, such as the move from black-and-white televisions to today's flat screens; innovation could also be in improved customer service and manufacturing. Toyota led the way in improving its production of automobiles, an innovation that has been adapted by many manufacturing organizations globally.

It has been argued that there are four key approaches to defining a new product innovation. Discuss the importance of each of the approaches identified below, and provide examples.

a. Firm-oriented

b. Product-oriented

c. Market-oriented

d. Consumer-oriented

14.10 Describe the need recognition process that took place before you purchased your last can of soft drink. How did it differ from the process that preceded the purchase of a new pair of sneakers? What role, if any, did advertising play in your need recognition?

14.11. List three colleges that you considered when choosing which college or university to attend and the criteria that you used to evaluate them. Describe how you acquired information on the different colleges along the different attributes that were important to you and how you made your decision. Be sure to specify whether you used compensatory or noncompensatory decision rules.

14.12. The key characteristics that influence buyer behavior toward new products are perceived risk, media influence, social characteristics, and demographic characteristics. Imagine that you are planning to purchase a brand new luxury motor vehicle, and explain how each of these factors would affect your purchase decision. Please use examples to support your responses.

Key Terms

- adoption *377*
- affect referral decision rule *373*
- awareness *377*
- cognitive dissonance *374*
- compatibility *377*
- compensatory decision rules *372*
- complexity *377*
- conjunctive decision rule *372*
- continuous innovation *376*
- diffusion of innovations *376*
- discontinuous innovation *376*
- dynamically continuous innovation *376*
- evaluation *377*
- evoked set *370*
- extensive problem solving *366*
- family branding *366*
- gifting behavior *374*
- inept set *370*
- inert set *371*
- innovation adoption process *376*
- innovation *376*
- interest *377*
- lexicographic decision rule *372*
- limited problem solving *366*
- need recognition *369*
- negative disconfirmation of expectations *374*
- noncompensatory decision rules *372*
- observability *377*
- positive disconfirmation of expectations *374*
- pre-purchase search *369*
- relative advantage *376*
- routinized response behavior *366*
- trial *377*
- trial ability *377*
- variety-seeking *375*

Marketing Ethics and Social Responsibility

Learning Objectives

1 To understand the meaning and importance of marketing ethics and social responsibility.

2 To understand how marketers can exploit consumers by targeting children and encouraging overeating and other forms of irresponsible buying.

3 To understand ethically questionable practices such as covert marketing, manipulative exposure to advertising, and truth-in-advertising issues.

4 To understand the nature and consequences of provocative advertisements.

5 To understand how marketers abuse consumers' privacy and the measures that can stop such practices.

6 To understand how marketers can advance society's interests by advocating socially beneficial conduct and discouraging adverse behavior.

MARKETING ETHICS are moral principles that govern marketers' behavior. On the personal level, these principles express the differences between right and wrong behavior and the goodness or badness of human character. The objective of most not-for-profit organizations and consumer advocacy groups is to promote good and socially beneficial behaviors such as contributing to charity, using energy responsibly, and reducing bad behaviors such as using drugs, discrimination, and driving while texting or drunk. For example, for decades, PETA (People for the Ethical Treatment of Animals) has campaigned against furriers and fashion designers that use fur and leather, discouraged consumers from using cosmetics manufactured with animal testing, and asked people to choose humane, solutions when they find mice, squirrels, raccoons, and other wild animals in their yards and homes. Figure 15.1 portrays two PETA ads promoting humans' loving coexistence with animals.

Why should marketers, whose objective is to make money, be concerned about ethics? After all, there are many federal consumer protection laws and scores of laws and regulations established by states and local governments. These laws dictate what marketers can and cannot do, and often regulate the manner in which they advertise, price and distribute their products and services. For example, some town and cities forbid placing vending machines for cigarettes and junk foods in public areas and near schools. As another example, New York City's government has been considering laws that will force all restaurants to post caloric information next to each item served and banning the sales of super-size sodas in restaurants. Furthermore, some cities no longer allow cigarette machines in bars (or anywhere else) and require retailers to ask for proof of age from young adults who try to buy cigarettes. Speaking of exploiting

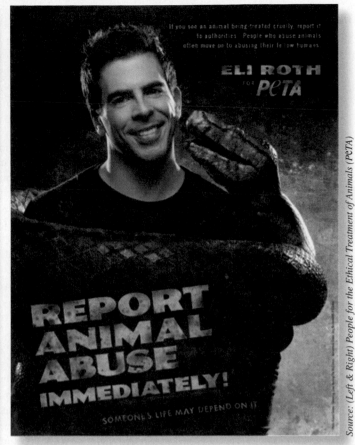

Source: (Left & Right) People for the Ethical Treatment of Animals (PETA)

FIGURE 15.1 P*e*TA Advocates Animals' Rights

children, there are laws that limit the amount of advertisements that can be shown during children's TV programs. In all of these examples, marketers' actions are regulated. Thus, why should marketers worry about what is morally right? After all, doesn't a widely quoted legal standard for engaging in a given practice state: "All that is not forbidden is allowed?"

Marketers must be concerned with ethics because not all that is allowed is in the best interest of society or, for that matter, marketers' goals. Marketing practices that overtly contradict societal interests end up with embarrassment,

loss of consumers, and, more often than not, increased regulation. In short, such practices lead to lost customers, decreased profits, and diminished consumer confidence in promotional messages and products. In this chapter, we will be straightforward and critical of amoral marketing strategies. We are proud of and enthusiastic about our field and experts in marketing and consumer behavior, and in no way antimarketing. In the following discussions, we follow the saying of Spencer Johnson, a famous contemporary writer: "Integrity is telling myself the truth. And honesty is telling the truth to other people."

The Societal Marketing Concept: Utopia or Reality?

Learning Objective

1 To understand the meaning and importance of marketing ethics and social responsibility.

As stated at the very beginning of this book, the essence of marketing is fulfilling the needs of consumers more effectively than competitors. Nevertheless, sometimes this concept is at odds with society's best interests. For example, products such as tobacco and alcohol "satisfy" consumer "needs" but are harmful, and many products that are convenient to use (and thus "satisfy needs") significantly contribute to environmental deterioration and climate change (e.g., products packaged in convenient but not reusable packaging, such as single-usage protective coverings used by dry cleaners). We must also consider the cumulative persuasive impact of advertising on consumer behavior. For example, depicting perfectly tanned people is likely to result in excessive sun bathing or tanning via ultraviolet light, despite undeniable documentation that such practices significantly increase the chances of developing cancer. Many studies have shown that repeated exposure to very thin "ideal" figures in promotional messages leads to negative self-perceptions (particularly in women) and is largely responsible for the increase in eating-related disorders. More Americans with eating disorders and cancer means higher public health expenditures, which lead to a decline in our living standards. Marketers know that ads focused on beauty and attractiveness, especially if they stress the importance of these attributes over other personal characteristics, are likely to be scrutinized by the media, consumer advocacy groups. Therefore, many advertisements now portray more realistic-looking models and beauty product ads stress that although a person's physical appearance is important, one's self-worth or "true beauty" comes from "within." A study of the sexual objectification of women in advertising showed that although the number of ads containing such portrayals has been increasing, females became less offended by these images, and that such ads had little impact on women's purchase intentions.[1]

Given the fact that all companies prosper when society prospers, companies should integrate social responsibility into every marketing decision. Thus, a more appropriate conceptualization of the traditional marketing concept is the **societal marketing concept**, which advocates balancing society's interests with the needs of consumers and marketers. This concept calls upon marketers to satisfy the needs and wants of their target markets in ways that preserve and enhance the well-being of consumers and society as a whole, while also fulfilling the profit objectives of their organizations. According to the societal marketing concept, fast-food restaurants should serve foods that contain less fat and sugar, but more nutrients. In addition, marketers should not advertise foods to young people in ways that encourage overeating. Furthermore, companies should not use professional athletes in liquor or tobacco advertisements, because celebrities often serve as role models for the young and using them in ads may result in underage youngsters' use of these products.

A serious deterrent to implementation of the societal marketing concept is the short-term orientation of many business executives, which stems from the fact that managerial performance is evaluated on the basis of short-term results. Thus, a young and ambitious advertising executive may create a striking advertising campaign, using unreasonably slim females with pale faces and withdrawn expressions, in order to increase the sales of the advertised product, without considering the negative impact of the campaign, such as an increase in eating disorders among young women. The societal marketing concept maintains that companies would be better off in a stronger, healthier society, and that companies that incorporate ethical behavior and social responsibility in their business dealings attract and maintain loyal consumer support over the long term.

The purpose of studying consumer behavior is to understand why and how consumers make their purchase decisions. These insights enable marketers to design more effective marketing strategies, especially when advanced technologies allow them to collect more data about consumers and target customers more precisely. Some maintain that an in-depth understanding of consumer behavior makes it possible for unethical marketers to exploit human vulnerabilities in the marketplace and engage in other unethical marketing practices to achieve corporate business objectives.

In response to public criticisms and concerns, many trade associations representing marketers of consumer goods have developed industry-wide codes of ethics. They recognize that industry-wide self-regulation is in marketers' best interests, in that it deters government from imposing its own regulations on industries. A number of companies have incorporated specific social goals into their mission statements, and include programs in support of these goals as integral components of their strategic planning. Most companies also recognize that socially responsible activities improve their image among consumers, stockholders, the financial community, and other relevant publics. They have found that ethical and socially responsible practices are simply good business, resulting not only in a favorable image, but also ultimately in increased sales. The converse is also true: Perceptions of a company's lack of social responsibility or unethical marketing strategies negatively affect consumer purchase decisions. Figure 15.2 contains a letter from a consumer advocacy group to McDonald's. The letter accuses McDonald's of failing to keep a promise it made to eliminate trans fats from its cooking oil, and clearly illustrates the damage that socially irresponsible actions can inflict on a company's image.

Although some companies have taken steps toward more responsible marketing, others have not. For example, Coca-Cola broadened the distribution of its low-calorie drinks and said it would put calorie counts on the front of its packaging around the world as part of its global efforts to counter accusations that its sugary drinks are fueling obesity. The company also promised to sponsor physical activity and committed to not marketing its drinks to children under 12 years of age—but it did not specify exactly how it plans to do so.[2] Other companies engage in practices that are, intuitively, against society's interests. For example, the FDA discovered that food makers have been adding caffeine to candy, potato chips, waffles, and a range of other items. For instance, A pack of Wrigley's Alert Energy Caffeine Gum can deliver the equivalent of four cups of coffee, or about 320 milligrams of caffeine. Although the package contain a warning that it is "not recommended for children or persons sensitive to caffeine," the FDA would like food companies to agree to voluntary limits for caffeine.[3]

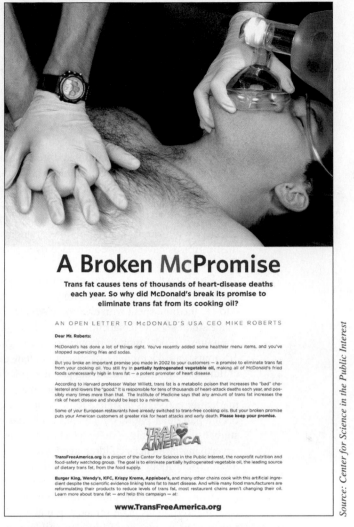

Source: Center for Science in the Public Interest

FIGURE 15.2 Irresponsible Marketing Can Damage a
Company's Image

In this chapter, we describe several unethical forms of marketing and suggest what can be done to prevent them. The topics covered here are exploitive marketing, crafty (i.e., less than honest) marketing communications, provocative marketing, and abuses of consumers' privacy. On the positive side, we discuss forms of marketing focused on social responsibility.

Exploitive Marketing

Learning Objective

2 To understand how marketers can exploit consumers by targeting children and encouraging overeating and other forms of irresponsible buying.

There are many targetable segments that can be easily exploited because they are more vulnerable than most other consumers, because of less education, old age, low income, and no political power. Next, we examine two particular forms of exploitive marketing: Targeting children and encouraging overeating and irresponsible buying.

Marketing to Children

Consumer socialization is the processes by which young people acquire skills, knowledge, and attitudes relevant to their functioning as consumers in the marketplace. A comprehensive review of twenty-five years of research on consumer socialization identified three stages:

1. *Perceptual* (3–7 years old), during which children begin to distinguish ads from programs, associate brand names with product categories, and understand the basic script of consumption.

2. *Analytical* (7–11 years), during which children capture the persuasive intent of ads, begin to process functional cues regarding products, and develop purchase influence and negotiation strategies.

3. *Reflective* (11–16 years), when children understand advertising tactics and appeals, become skeptical about ads, understand complex shopping scripts, and become capable at influencing purchases.[4]

Children become brand aware as they age and begin to prefer brands more than nonbranded items.[5] Brand knowledge starts with child-oriented product categories such as toys and food, and by age 8 children can name multiple products in categories targeted to them. Children's consumption requests start with food-related items and grow to include toys, clothing, sporting goods, and video games as children age. Children have the most influence over child-related items and children from higher socioeconomic classes influence parents more than those of lower socioeconomic status.[6] Overall, the older the child, the more influence he or she has on a parent's purchase behavior. Older children are better negotiators and learn strategies such as bargaining and persuasion that are more effective with parents than emotional strategies such as begging and crying.[7] Some children perceive themselves as having more influence over purchases, particularly with regard to food items, than do their parents.[8]

The growth of the Internet and electronic technology resulted in a significant increase in the amount of time children spend with various forms of media. A study reported that, among children aged 8 to 18, the time spent with electronic devices increased by 1 hour and 17 minutes from 2004 to 2010. Some studies showed that children spend a total of 7 hours and 38 minutes a day in front of televisions, computers, iPods, mobile phones, or video games. Including multitasking, children are exposed to 10 hours and 45 minutes of media content during that time. Furthermore, fewer than half of the children studied reported having parental rules regarding media viewing.[9]

More media consumption provides marketers with increased opportunities to target children with marketing messages designed to influence their purchase behavior. Food and beverage marketing has been a particular public policy concern because of its influence on the diets and health of children. A study by the Committee on Food Marketing and the Diets of Children and Youth found that television advertising influences children aged 2 to 11, and that a lot of these promotions were for high-calorie, low-nutrient foods associated with adiposity.[10] Research sponsored by the Center for Science in the Public Interest discovered that marketing of high-calorie, low-nutrition foods to children has been increasing dramatically and becoming more aggressive and sophisticated.[11] The report concluded that such marketing has undermined parental authority regarding food consumption and called for restrictions on the marketing of foods to children. In the absence of regulation, parents play a mediational role in children's consumption and media exposure and may welcome intervention by public policy makers.

Self-Regulation versus Laws

Advertising to children is subject to self-regulation, according to guidelines developed by the Children's Advertising Review Unit (CARU) of the Council of Better Business Bureaus. Among others, the CARU guidelines state that product presentations or claims must not mislead children about the product's performance or benefits, that presentations must not exploit the child's imagination or create unrealistic expectations, that products must be shown in safe situations, and that ads must refrain from encouraging behavior that is inappropriate for children. Because, according to stimulus–response theory, children can easily form associations between stimuli and outcomes, the guidelines also direct marketers to avoid ads that: (1) Encourage children to pressure their parents to buy the products advertised, and (2) make children feel that ownership of a given product will make them more accepted by peers. Regarding loyalty-building measures such as kid's clubs, premiums, and sweepstakes, the CARU guidelines acknowledge that children do not always understand the true purpose of such measures, and direct marketers to ensure that loyalty programs do not exploit children.[12]

CARU's news releases illustrate many possible misuses in advertising to children. For example, in response to CARU's routine monitoring of children's advertising and its subsequent request, a marketer of cotton candy machines agreed to modify a TV commercial that featured children operating an electrical candy machine without parental supervision and while dancing or talking on the phone. In another case, after viewing a commercial showing Oreo cookies going into a toaster and popping out as KoolStuf pastries, a 4-year-old child inserted Oreos into a toaster and, when they did not pop out, tried to retrieve them with a pair of scissors. The child's mother complained to CARU, which brought the incident to the attention of Oreo's marketer, who subsequently agreed to modify the commercial. Procter & Gamble agreed to modify a TV spot for Pringles that CARU believed encouraged excessive consumption of the snack food.[13]

A major concern is that food marketers "teach" children to eat more than they should and thereby cause the surging obesity and health problems among young consumers. Marketers spend at least $10 billion annually on promoting foods and beverages to America's children. At the same time, the number of obese or overweight children has at least doubled over the past 15 years and keeps going up steadily and alarmingly. Over the past few years, lawmakers have called for legislation regulating food advertising to children; presumably to avoid such regulation, several companies have voluntarily modified their marketing practices. For example, Kraft Foods stopped TV advertising of certain products to children, and increased its advertising of sugar-free drinks and smaller packages of cookies. McDonald's, a company frequently accused of selling junk foods with too much fat and poor nutritional quality, eliminated some of its "super-sized" offerings and began selling more salads. It even offers apples as a dessert alternative to calorie-laden pies. More recently, McDonald's had a program that awarded food prizes to small kids who got good grades on their report cards; the program was advertised on book jackets and discontinued after McDonald's was criticized by parents and consumer advocacy groups and even ridiculed by some media.[14]

Rules proposed by the Obama administration, which would take effect in 2016, would only allow foods that contain no trans fat, have and not more than 1 gram of saturated fat and 13 grams of added sugar per "eating occasion" to be marketed to children. Also, the foods could not contain more than 210 milligrams of sodium per serving. The sodium restrictions would tighten by 2021. Additionally, the foods must provide a "meaningful contribution to a healthful diet," including ingredient from at least one major healthy food group such as fruit, vegetables, whole grain, fish, eggs, and beans. The proposed guidelines also expand the traditional definition of "children" from kids under the age of 12 to children aged 2 through 17, although the final rules for teenagers will likely be "narrower in scope and possibly limited to in-school marketing activities and social media." While some experts say that the guidelines do not go far enough, advertisers have been fighting them aggressively and it is unlikely that all will be mandated legally.[15]

Nevertheless, the rate of self-regulation has accelerated. In an effort to stop the spread of anti-soda measures in city halls after New York City moved to limit portion sizes and other cities levied taxes on sugary beverages, soda makers will start displaying the calorie contents of their drinks on vending machines and point consumers toward less sugary versions.[16] McDonald's began posting calorie counts on all its menus—a move that could put pressure on other fast-food restaurants to do the same. The company also unveiled several menu additions aimed at making its offerings more healthful. They include an egg-white McMuffin, a grilled chicken option for the Happy Meal, and seasonal fruits and vegetables like blueberries and cucumbers. The Walt Disney Company announced that all products advertised on its child-focused television channels, radio stations, and websites must comply with a strict new set of nutritional standards. Several years earlier, Disney sharply curtailed the use of its name and characters with foods high in sugar, salt, and fat. Mickey Mouse stopped appearing on boxes of Pop-Tarts, and Buzz Lightyear and his Toy Story pals disappeared from McDonald's Happy Meals. Nickelodeon and Discovery Kids instituted similar restrictions shortly thereafter.[17]

Trying to be more socially responsible is not always possible or easy. General Mills reduced the sugar in most of its kids' cereals to 10 grams per serving from levels as high as 15 grams. However, surveys showed that to get kids to like the cereals, not only do the cereal's frosted oats need to taste sweet enough, but they also have to float in milk for at least 3 minutes. The company knew that 9 grams of sugar per serving was the point where the sweetness is not enough for a kid to eat regularly. The company has been reducing the sugar amounts in its cereals gradually, so that consumers get used to a lower sweetness level a little at a time (see discussion of the **JND** in Chapter 4).[18]

California passed a state law that banned the sale or rental of violent video games to minors. However, the Supreme Court overturned this law because it is unconstitutional, even if it is designed to protect children.[19] Side by side with overeating, children's lack of physical activity greatly contributes to children's high rates of overweight and obesity.

Clearly, there are merits to the argument that, ultimately, any consumption behavior, including excessive eating, is the responsibility of the adults who consume overly rich foods or allow their children to consume them and not of the marketers who produced the foods. However, children are a vulnerable population. In addressing this issue and fearing that "McDonald's-made-me-fat" lawsuits will gain momentum, the food companies have pursued legislation that will not allow obese persons to sue them for personal damages.[20]

Regarding advertising to children, there is a consensus that even if children understand the purpose of promotional messages, marketers must take special care in advertising to them because of the amount of time kids spend viewing TV and online. Generally, advertising to children in the United States is less regulated than in European countries. Regulating marketing to children does not always work. Table 15.1 indicates that numerous practices generally forbidden in marketing to children online are widely employed by websites targeting children.[21] As yet another example of abusing children's privacy, a study of 40 popular and free child-friendly apps, conducted by The Wall Street Journal, discovered that nearly half transmitted a device ID number, which is a major tracking tool. Some 70% passed along information about how the apps were used, and, in some cases, specified which buttons were clicked and in which order. Although the FTC regulations do not allow gathering information from apps and online services "directed to children" under 13 without parental knowledge, the FTC has no strict definition of this regulation.[22]

Inspiring Overeating and Irresponsible Spending

Marketing is a form of persuasion. In order to learn how to convince consumers to adopt a product or induce consumption, marketers have carefully studied the situational factors surrounding the buying decision. For example, people become hungrier in cold environments, so it is always cold in supermarkets (some nutritionists advise consumers to go food shopping directly after a filling meal). Marketers know that the longer consumers stay in the store and wander around, the more they buy. Therefore, in supermarkets and other stores, the displays are moved around systematically; that's why you often discover that the cereal aisle has been moved since you last visited the supermarket. Men are much more likely than women to deviate from shopping lists and prior consumption plans. That's why supermarket personnel are instructed to approach any men they see just standing around and offer help. Fairly recently, many Web retailers noticed that their online sales peak between 6:30 and 10:30 p.m., across time zones. Apparently, consumers who are drinking alcohol have fewer inhibitions and are likely to spend more freely. Thus, many online retailers started offering special sales and sending promotional emails during this time period.[23]

TABLE 15.1	Regulating Online Marketing to Children

PART A: COMMON PRACTICES IN MARKETING FOODS TO CHILDREN ONLINE THAT ARE GENERALLY FORBIDDEN UNDER FEDERAL OR SELF-REGULATION

1. Promoting foods of low nutritional quality; not providing enough nutritional labeling; misleading nutritional claims.
2. Embedding food ads in games and facilitating children's learning to consume the foods advertised.
3. Creating "buzz" about the products and encouraging children to send ads to their friends (i.e., viral marketing).
4. Offering children brand-related items that they can use after leaving the Web sites and tying the online advertising with other exposures to the brands.
5. Not including "ad breaks" and reminders that the content watched is advertising.
6. Offering children that may be too young opportunities and prizes if they register at the Web site.
7. Offering direct inducements to purchase (e.g., access to a secret site).

PART B: AN ILLUSTRATION OF THE LIMITED SUCCESS OF SELF AND FEDERAL REGULATION REGARDING WEB SITES TARGETING CHILDREN

CONTENT ANALYSIS FINDINGS	CURRENT GUIDE AND REGULATORY EFFORTS
64% of Web sites encouraged children to send email greetings or invitations to visit the Web site to their friends.	Advertising should not urge children to ask parents or others to buy products. (CARU)
53% of Web sites offered unlimited viewing of television advertisements.	Advertisements are limited to 10.5–12 minutes per hour. (Children's Television Act of 1990 [47 U.S.C. § 303])
CONTENT ANALYSIS FINDINGS	CURRENT GUIDE AND REGULATORY EFFORTS
76% of Web sites offered at least one brand "extra," and 52% offered two or more: 43% offered sweepstakes: and 31% offered premiums to stimulate sales.	Advertisers should take special care in using these kinds of promotions to guard against exploiting children's immaturity. (CARU)

(Continued)

TABLE 15.1 Regulating Online Marketing to Children (Continued)	
CONTENT ANALYSIS FINDINGS	**CURRENT GUIDE AND REGULATORY EFFORTS**
39% of Web sites offered specific purchase incentives, such as game rewards.	Advertisers should avoid using sales pressures in advertising to children. (CARU)
18% of the Web sites provided ad break reminders that the content was advertising.	The Federal Communications Commission requires ad breaks for children's television programming.
47% of the Web sites offered a tie-in to movie or television shows and characters.	Television advertising should not use program personalities (live or animated) adjacent to their shows. (CARU and Federal Communications Commission)

Source: Part A. Journal of Public Policy and Marketing. Elizabeth S. Moore, American Marketing Association, 2007. Part B: Journal of Public Policy and Marketing. Kathryn Seiders, American Marketing Association, 2007.

Designing foods that encourage overeating is a scientific process. For example, marketers know that some processed foods actually make people feel hungrier after eating them. Research has identified the "bliss point" at which consumers like, say, sweetness, the most; at lower and higher levels of sweetnes, consumers dislike the product's taste. Marketers have been using their knowledge of humans' responses to taste to design foods that produce the highest levels of craving. The cardinal rule in processed foods is "when in doubt, add sugar." Oscar Mayer introduced a desert Lunchable in the form of Fun Pack, which, in addition to bologna and white bread, includes a Snickers bar, a package of M&M's (or a Reese's Butter Cup), and a sugary drink.[24]

A report based on data from the Center for Disease Control and Prevention (CDC) projected that obesity rates, across states, would reach at least 44% by 2030, and in 13 states that number would exceed 60%. Obesity raises the risk of numerous diseases, from type 2 diabetes to endometrial cancer, meaning more sick people and higher medical costs in the future. The increasing burden of illness will add $66 billion in annual obesity-related medical costs over and above today's $147 billion to $210 billion. Another study found that by 2030, 42% of U.S. adults could be obese, adding $550 billion to healthcare costs over that period.[25]

Marketers are directly responsible for Americans' decreasing physical activity and their consumption of unreasonably large quantities of unhealthy and non-nutritious foods. One study demonstrated that consumers believe that foods that are *less* healthy taste *better*, are enjoyed *more*, and are preferred when a hedonic meal takes place.[26] In the course of getting us to eat more, marketers have studied our eating habits in detail and used the results in packaging and determination of portion sizes. Marketers have also used their knowledge of perception to increase the quantities of foods consumers eat by the way these items are packaged or presented. For example, studies showed that:[27]

1. Both children and adults consume more juice when the product is presented in short, wide glasses than in tall slender glasses.
2. Candies placed in clear jars were eaten much quicker than those presented in opaque jars.
3. Sandwiches in transparent wrap generated more consumption than those in opaque wraps.
4. The visibility and aroma of tempting foods generated greater consumption.
5. Presenting foods in an organized manner, such as mixed assortments in bowls (or "grab bags"), buffets, potlucks, or dinner-table settings leads to more eating.
6. Assortment size or duplication, in forms such as multiple product tastings, multiple offerings of party snacks, duplicate buffet lines, and family dinners with multiple dishes, stimulate eating.
7. Minimal variations in the size of serving bowls whenever multiple options and sizes are present lead to eating more.
8. People generally do not keep track of how much food they consume. When told, they are often surprised at how much they have consumed.
9. Large inventories of foods at home increase the quantity believed to be appropriate for a given meal.
10. Small packages do not necessarily decrease consumption and can sometimes actually increase it. Responsible companies should sell small packages individually, rather than bundling them together in a larger container, because the availability of multiple small packages leads to overconsumption.

Another form of encouraging irresponsible consumption is banks' targeting of teenagers and college students and providing them with too much easy credit, which puts them into financial difficulties for years. For example, because of very aggressive marketing of credit cards to college students, college loan debt has been rising: The average graduate leaves college with more than $18,000 in credit card debt, often coupled with a low credit rating.[28] One study showed that, on average, students received their first credit card at age 18 (some did so when they were as young as 15). More than 10% owned more than 5 cards. Most of these young people did not keep credit card receipts, did not check their monthly statements against their purchases, and were unaware of the interest rates they were charged; about 10% paid only the minimum required payment every month.[29] Recognizing that the marketing of credit cards to college students has become far too aggressive and against society's best interests, many states have passed, or are in the process of passing, strict rules limiting the marketing that banks and credit card companies can do on college campuses. In response to criticism, several banks began limiting the promotion of credit cards directed at students.[30]

One study identified several personality traits that contribute to students' misuse of credit cards and outlined promotional appeals that marketers can use in encouraging more responsible credit card usage among students.[31] Interestingly, two important personality traits were impulsiveness and materialism, which have also been linked to compulsive buying and addictive tendencies.[32] The study proposed that both marketers and public policymakers must educate younger customers about avoiding the trap of credit card misuse.

Manipulative or Uninformative Nutritional Labeling

Nutritional labels are placed on all packaged food items sold in the United States. Nevertheless, many critiques have pointed out that the current format of such labels is unclear and somewhat manipulative. For example, the labels list information on a "per-serving" basis. However, the Food and Drug Administration regulations allow manufacturers some discretion in setting serving sizes. For example, Kellogg's Frosted Flakes uses a serving size of 3/4 cup. Healthy Choice Chicken Tortilla Soup (microwaveable bowl) has a serving size of one cup, and Ritz Crackers have a serving size of five crackers. According to its label, a pint of Häagen-Dazs ice cream contains four servings. However, do most consumers eat only a fourth of a container of Cookies & Cream, then put the rest away for another day? A large package of Cool Ranch Doritos lists a single serving as one ounce, or roughly 12 chips, but consumers are highly unlikely to keep a chip count as they dig into bags. Although 160 calories and 2 grams of saturated fat sounds like a small price to pay for enjoying a serving of Oreo cookies, technically speaking, a serving is only 3 cookies.[33] Listing smaller serving sizes enables marketers to reduce the reported calories, fat, sugar, and carbohydrates in a product serving, and encourage consumers to consume more calories than they think they do. A study indicated that consumer attention to nutrition information focuses on calorie information but not serving size. In addition, manipulating service sizes reduces consumers' consumption-related "guilt."[34]

Under mounting criticism, the Food and Drug Administration has been under pressure to force marketers to list realistic serving sizes on packaged food labels. According to the Center for Science in the Public Interest (CSPI), a consumer advocacy group, the worst manipulators of the serving sizes ratios are labels for canned soups, ice cream, coffee creamers, and nonstick cooking sprays—all of which grossly understate the calories, sodium, and saturated fat the average person typically consumes when eating these foods. For instance, on its label, a single serving of Campbell's Chunky Classic Chicken Noodle soup is one cup—just under half a can—and contains about 790 milligrams of sodium. In a national survey of 1,000 consumers, only 10% of people said they would eat a one-cup portion. About 64% said they would eat an entire can at one time, taking in 1,840 milligrams of sodium in a sitting. That is roughly 80% of the 2,300 milligrams recommended as the upper limit for daily salt intake, and well above the 1,500 milligrams that health officials have said may cause hypertension. Sixty-one percent said they would also eat the entire can of a condensed soup, like Campbell's Chicken Noodle, which lists 2.5 servings per can. A single serving contains 890 milligrams of sodium, and the full can has 2,390 milligrams. About 27% of respondents said they would eat just half a can in one sitting. The Healthy Request line that Campbell's has introduced consists of soups that contain less than 480 milligrams of sodium per serving. Nevertheless, the amount of sodium that people actually end up consuming when they eat an entire can is enormous, according to the CSPI.[35]

A project at the University of California, Berkeley, School of Journalism conducted a competition to redesign food packages, and two of the best designs are shown in Figures 15.3 and 15.4. The design in Figures 15.3A and B uses colorful boxes to depict the relative proportion of ingredients in a product. It is visually dramatic and its use of colors is clever. However, it may not work with

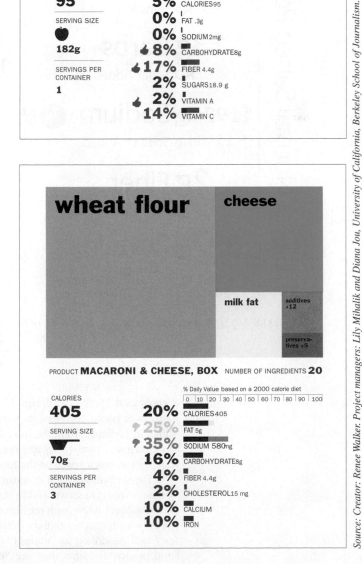

FIGURE 15.3A Colorful Boxes Designate Ingredients

Source: Creator: Renee Walker. Project managers: Lily Mihalik and Diana Jou, University of California, Berkeley School of Journalism.

FIGURE 15.3B Food Groups Key

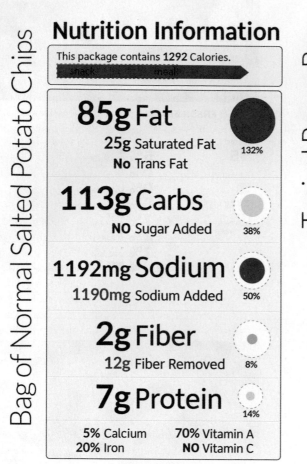

FIGURE 15.4 Total Instead of Serving Size Calories

Source: Creator: Joe Brunelle. Project managers: Lily Mihalik and Diana Jou, University of California, Berkeley School of Journalism.

complicated foods. The design in Figure 15.4 replaces serving size calories with total calories per package or bottle. It represents food ingredients using bold, colorful rectangles showing how much of which ingredients are in the food. A green, yellow, and red color-coding system denotes reasonable, questionable, or unhealthy amounts of carbohydrates or fat. The label is very attractive, but probably requires too much space on the food package.[36]

The definitions used in nutritional labeling are not always logical. For example, food labeled "organic" must meet verifiable standards set by the federal government, while that labeled "natural" is subject to no such requirements. Ironically, although sales of both "organic" and "natural" foods, which cost more than other foods, have been growing, surveys found that consumers prefer foods described as "natural" to those labeled "organic." In one case, a line of Nature Valley food products claims they are "natural," although the items include high fructose corn syrup, high maltose corn syrup, and maltodextrin (a thickener than can also impart a slight sweetness to food). These ingredients are highly processed, do not exist in nature, and cannot be considered natural even under a very lenient definition. According to some studies, these ingredients cause hyperactivity and attention deficit among young children. Realizing the negative connotation associated with "high fructose corn syrup," the Corn Refiners Association asked the FDA to allow it to change the ingredient name to "corn sugar" on nutrition labels, but the FDA denied permission.[37]

Another interesting labeling battle revolves around bioengineering companies like Monsanto and DuPont, which have spent millions of dollars to fight a California ballot initiative aimed at requiring the labeling of genetically modified foods. Strangely, marketers of the biggest organic brands in the country—Kashi, Cascadian Farm, Horizon Organic—also have joined the antilabeling effort and contributed a lot of money to the effort to defeat the initiative. In contrast, the smaller, independent businesses and farms that most shoppers envision when they buy an organic peach or shampoo—companies like Nature's Path, one of Kashi's largest competitors—have been strongly supporting the labeling initiative.[38]

Direct-to-Consumer Pharmaceutical Advertising

The promotion of pharmaceutical products directly to consumers has been permitted since 1997—and has increased the consumption of numerous categories of medications. In studies, consumers confirmed that they obtained most of the information about these medications from TV commercials rather than from their physicians.[39] Recognizing that direct-to-consumer advertising has become too aggressive, the pharmaceutical industry has developed voluntary restrictions regarding this marketing method. The Senate has called for a temporary moratorium on advertising new drugs to consumers, and a major pharmaceutical company has volunteered not to advertise new drugs to consumers during their first year on the market.[40] Online search engines further complicate the direct selling of medications to consumers. The FDA urged pharmaceutical companies to include risk information about drugs in the companies' search advertisements in the form of a short text that appears besides the results of one's Google search. But, since Google limits such ads to 95 characters, it is unclear how this can be done.[41] Because they can market products directly to consumers, pharmaceutical companies are more eager than ever to "extend the life" of products that have become consumer favorites, as the dates for patent expiration and the availability of generic versions of these products near. For example, Pfizer began selling a chewable form of Viagra; other companies are testing erectile dysfunction drugs that melt under the tongue and act more quickly than pills that are swallowed.[42]

Crafty Promotional Messages and Techniques

Learning Objective

3 To understand ethically questionable practices such as covert marketing, manipulative exposure to advertising, and truth-in-advertising issues.

Marketers can also manipulate consumers' interpretations of marketing stimuli through the context in which those stimuli are featured. For example, in QVC's Extreme Shopping, during which rare and expensive products are offered, consumers perceived $200 art prints as reasonably priced when the prints were shown immediately after much more expensive items.[43] Inadvertently, marketers can also affect the content and duration of news and other information-focused broadcasts. For example, many marketers carefully screen the context in which their messages are shown, because they recognize that advertisements are perceived more positively when placed within more positive programs. Thus, they may choose not to place ads in news broadcasts or programs that cover serious issues, such as wars and world hunger, where some of the content is bound to be unpleasant. Because broadcasts are driven by advertising revenue, media companies may choose to shorten the coverage of serious and disagreeable topics.

A crafty marketing strategy, which is perfectly legal, occurs when marketers reduce the amount of products in packaging, but leave the prices unchanged. They do so because their margins are going down (e.g., because of higher raw-materials prices) and they are reluctant to raise prices. Marketers recognize that consumers are much more likely to notice price increases than small and below the JND (see Chapter 4) reductions in the packages' quantities of food, drink, and household products. Although legal, such reductions can be viewed as misleading and manipulative. For example, many cereal boxes and bags of chips became lighter over the years, which companies refer to as "weight outs." A Snickers bar was reduced from 2.07 ounces to 1.86 ounces (Mars said this was done to reduce calories to 250 per bar), and the bottle size of Tropicana Pure Premium orange juice declined from 64 to 59 ounces. Kimberly-Clark introduced a box of Kleenex that has 13% fewer sheets, a measure referred to as "desheeting." The company said that the new Kleenex tissues are 15% "bulkier" and fewer tissues are needed to get the job done. Similarly, the number of sheets in various Cottonelle toilet paper roles declined from 176 to 230 sheets to between 166 and 216 sheets per role.[44]

Covert Marketing

Covert marketing (masked or stealth marketing) consists of marketing messages and promotional materials that appear to come from independent parties when, in fact, they are sent by marketers. Some maintain that covert marketing strategies often violate the FTC's definition of deceptive advertising, endorsement guidelines, and other regulations pertaining to marketing, and believe that the FTC should establish clearer rules to reduce the use of masked advertising.[45] Others argue that the widespread use of covert advertising abuses consumers' efforts to avoid advertising and will result in increased consumer distrust of product information; of particular concern here is the increased number of communications that are created by marketers but made to resemble genuine word-of-mouth.[46]

Popular methods of covert marketing include:

1. Actors posing as customers telling people the product benefits and giving them a chance to examine or try the product.

2. Paying bartenders for praising brands of alcoholic beverages and recommending them to customers.

3. Employees posing as customers online—in chat-rooms, blogs, etc.—and spreading positive word-of-mouth about the product and even providing samples. They also encourage people to tell others about the samples they have received.

4. Emails disguised as "urgent" messages or personal thank-you notes.

5. As discussed in Chapter 4 (on consumer perception), inserting advertising messages into the content of programs and disguising advertising messages as entertainment.

Product Placement: Advertising Embedded within Entertainment

Marketers increasingly use techniques that blur the distinctions between **figure and ground** and make it difficult for consumers to clearly distinguish advertising from entertainment content (see Chapter 4). For example, to combat fast-forwarding by consumers who wish to avoid TV commercials, marketers are increasingly turning to **product placements**, where the line between television shows and ads is virtually nonexistent. Six-packs of Mountain Dew were given to the winners of personal challenge contests on Survivor, and the judges of American Idol always have a Coca-Cola within easy reach. A new product developed by Burger King went on sale the day after it was featured on The Apprentice, and another show of this series focused on developing an ad for Dove Cool Moisture Body Wash. In addition, some news programs contain embedded ads, and promotional messages were also inserted into the dialogue of entertainment programs. While forecasts indicate that companies are going to steadily increase expenditures on branded entertainment, a newly formed consumer advocacy group, Commercial Alert, is lobbying for legislation that will require advertisers to disclose upfront ads that are designed as product placements.

Marketers also blend promotion and program content by positioning a TV commercial so close to the storyline of a program that viewers are unaware they are watching an advertisement until they are well into it. Because this was an important factor in advertising to children, the Federal Trade Commission has strictly limited the use of this technique. TV stars or cartoon characters are now prohibited from promoting products during the children's shows in which they appear. An **advertorial** is another potential misuse of figure-and-ground and occurs in print ads that closely resemble editorial matter. In broadcast media, **infomercials**, are 30-minute (or even longer) commercials that appear to the average viewer to be documentaries, and thus command more attentive viewing than obvious commercials would receive.

Many surveys have examined the impact of product placements in films on brand awareness, attitudes, and purchase intent. However, there is no evidence that firms' investments in film product placements are worthwhile.[47] Some studies showed that prominent placements, though more memorable, do not have much influence on consumption, whereas subtle placements, though less memorable, nonetheless have a greater impact on consumption. Thus, if they intend to continue using this tactic, marketers must design placements that have strong effect on memory as well as behavior.[48]

False or Misleading Advertising

The ethical issues related to advertising focus on the accuracy of the information provided and the potential misuse of promotional messages' persuasive abilities. Regarding accuracy, a toothpaste ad stating that "brand A is the best" is considered an acceptable form of advertising "puffery" because consumers generally understand that there is no credible way to determine what "best" means. A toothpaste ad stating that the brand is "endorsed by the American Dental Association" is an objective statement of fact that includes easily verifiable information. However, is an ad stating that the brand "provides more cavity protection than any other toothpaste" permissible advertising puffery, or is it false or misleading? The answer depends on how most reasonable consumers are likely to interpret the ad. Do they believe that there is a scientific way to measure the degree of cavity protection and that the maker of the brand has conducted a scientific study of all brands of toothpaste on the market and that the study proved the ad's claim? It is clear that determining how most reasonable consumers are likely to interpret an ad is a complex undertaking, and therefore there is no definitive answer to the question: At what point does puffery become deceptive? As discussed in Chapter 7, humor is the most popular advertising appeal. Regrettably, one study discovered that deceptive claims were found in about three-quarters of humorous ads, and that humor was often used to mask deceptive claims.[49]

Truth-in-advertising laws protect consumers from false advertisements. Over time, the FTC has developed guidelines as to what constitutes **deceptive advertising**, and it holds marketers responsible for determining their ads' potential to mislead consumers. However, although the FTC is responsible for stopping false or misleading ads, it is apparent that such ads continue to exist. For example, the FTC's website featured a "Red Flag" button alerting consumers that "misleading weight loss advertising is everywhere" and warning them against weight-loss claims that are too good to be true. Sample claims include that the product causes "substantial weight loss no matter how much you eat" or promises of "a weight loss of two pounds or more a week for a month or more without dieting or exercise."[50] The FTC encourages and investigates complaints by consumers and companies regarding false or misleading ads, but its public advice for consumers regarding weight-loss products illustrates that it cannot stop all misleading ads. The FTC can also require companies that have misled consumers to run **corrective advertising**. For example, years ago Listerine's maker was forced to correct the claim that the product prevents colds. A study indicated that corrective advertising sometimes resulted in consumer distrust toward other products sold by the company, and also toward similar products sold by unrelated marketers; this result suggested that corrective promotional messages may often not achieve their desired objectives.[51]

In addition to the FTC, there is the National Advertising Review Council (NARC), a self-regulatory group that monitors complaints from companies and consumers regarding truth in advertising and often determines what ads can or cannot state. For example, NARC determined that Colgate-Palmolive provided supportive evidence for the claim that its Oxy-Plus product "blasts away grease faster" than P&G's Ultra Dawn, but decided that there was no evidence supporting GlaxoSmithKline's claim that Super PoliGrip provides the "strongest hold ever"—a claim that the company subsequently withdrew. NARC also supported a challenge to promotions for cancer treatment which claimed that "Chemotherapy doesn't work for everyone."[52] In some cases, powerful companies can persuade media to stop running ads they deem deceptive. For example, Anheuser-Busch persuaded ABC, CBS, and NBC to stop running Miller Beer ads depicting consumers comparing beers and saying that the Miller beers have more flavor.[53] Table 15.2 gives examples of false or deceptive promotions.[54]

Apparently, a large number of promotional violations occur in the marketing of medications. One study identified the three major categories of violations:[55]

1. Unsubstantiated effectiveness claims: Representing the drug as more effective than the evidence available suggests; representing the drug as useful in a broader scope than the research evidence indicates.

2. Omitted risk information: Failure to reveal risks resulting from using the drug correctly; failure to present information on side effects; stating the risks in unclear language.

3. Unsubstantiated superiority claims: Presenting the drug as more effective or safer than others in spite of the fact that there is no evidence supporting such a claim.

TABLE 15.2	Deceptive or False Promotional Claims	
PRODUCT	**ISSUE**	**DESCRIPTION**
Dannon Yogurt	Claimed health benefit	In response to consumer demand for products containing certain strains of live bacteria, Dannon's promotions for its probiotic dairy drinks—Activia and DanActive—claimed that bacterial cultures will help prevent colds or alleviate digestive problems. The FTC forced Dannon to drop the ad because it could not claim that the product will relieve digestive issues unless it also mentioned that a person has to eat at least three servings daily to get this benefit. The FTC allowed Dannon to state that Activia helps regulate the digestive system and DanActive helps to support the immune system.
Nestlé	Claimed health benefit	The FTC stopped Nestlé's advertising claiming that its Boost Kids Essential beverages help kids avoid colds and reduce school absences.
Pom Wonderful	Claimed health benefit	The marketer of this pricy pomegranate juice advertised that the product reduces the risk of heart disease, prostate cancer, and impotence. The FTC charged the marketer with making false and unsubstantiated claims.
Procter & Gamble Nyquil	Forbidden product attributes	Procter and Gamble wanted to add Vitamin C to its Vicks cold formulas. The FDA does not allow the addition of dietary supplements to drugs, because that may give consumers the impression that these drugs were evaluated and approved by the FDA.
Skechers Toning Shoes	False claim	The company claimed that its shoes help consumers tone muscles and lose weight. One of the taglines said: "Get in shape without setting a foot in the gym." The FTC fined the company $50 million.
Ab Circle Pro	False claim	Ads for the Ab Circle Pro, a circular disk on which people swing back and forth, said that a 3-minute daily workout was equivalent to 100 sit-ups and would allow consumers to lose 10 pounds in 2 weeks. The FTC forced the company to give customers refunds.
Lancôme	Questionable claim	L'Oréal's Lancôme claimed that one of its products "boosts the activity of genes and stimulates the production of youth proteins." This implies that the product affects the way the human body works, which is a standard used to classify new drugs, not cosmetics. The FDA rebuked the company.
Twitter	Full disclosure	The FTC said that Twitter ads should include full disclosure, just like TV and print ads. For example, ads should include the average effectiveness of a weight-loss shake or note that a celebrity was paid to push a product. Making room for this kind of text in a 140-character tweet on Twitter is unrealistic, but other ways to include full disclosure are being considered.

Source: Amy Schatz and Ilan Brat, "Dannon Settles Complaints Over Yogurt Ads," December 16, 2010 online.wsj.com; Edward Eyatt, "Regulators Call Health Claims in Pom Juice Ads Deceptive," nytimes.com September 27, 2010; Associated Press, "FDA Warns P&G for Adding Vitamin C to Nyquil," nytimes.com October 14, 2009; Brent Kendall, "Sketvhers Settles With FTC Over Deceptive-Advertising of Toning Shoes," online.wsj.com May 16, 2012; Anemona Hartocollis, "Dispute Over City's Ads Against Sodas," nytimes.com October 28, 2010.

What Is "Deceptive"?

It is often difficult to determine what constitutes "misleading" or "deceptive" advertising. For example, Sterling, a jewelry marketer, took legal action to stop Zale, its competitor, from advertising its product line as the "most brilliant diamonds in the world." Advertising can include *subjective* claims, such as "our wine has the most unique taste among red wines." However, Sterling claimed that the brilliance of a diamond *can* be systematically, reliably, and scientifically measured, and therefore the claim "most brilliant diamonds" is not a subjective claim. The court sided with Zale because there are no objective standards by which to measure a diamond's "cut" or "brilliance." Other subjective claims in the jewelry sector—that are perfectly legal ads—include "the first diamond ever to be certified visibly brighter" and "the world's most perfectly cut diamond."[56] The New York City Health Department put together a media campaign about how drinking a can of soda a day "can make you 10 pounds fatter a year." Although few would argue that soda is nutritious, and there is a body of evidence showing a high correlation between rising obesity and the consumption of sugary drinks, some health experts question the scientific validity of directly linking sugar consumption to gaining weight, because the reasons behind weight gain vary widely.[57] Organix is a manufacturer of hair-care products. Although the company has never claimed that its products are organic, critics maintain that the name in misleading. Furthermore, when Vogue—the company owning Organix—became available for sale, potential buyers expressed concerns regarding its Organix brand.[58]

Provocative Marketing

Learning Objective

4 To understand the nature and consequences of provocative advertisements.

Regrettably, too many marketing messages convey socially undesirable stereotypes and images. Some years ago, the makers of an American icon—G.I. Joe—introduced a substantially more muscular version of the doll and were subsequently accused of sanctioning the use of muscle-building drugs by teenagers. Similarly, the makers of Barbie—a doll that has gradually become thinner and bustier— were accused of conveying an unrealistic body image to young girls. Some objectionable ads can be the result of good intentions. For example, a not-for-profit organization in New York City ran an ad campaign aimed at raising public awareness of such children's disorders as autism, depression, and eating-related illnesses. The ads featured "Ransom Notes" depicting how the diseases held the families of the sick children captive by taking over their lives. Although many agreed that this advertising approach was effective in the context of the campaign's objectives, some parents of children afflicted with the illnesses featured found the ads too emotional and personal, and the campaign was discontinued. With social media outlets such as Twitter and Facebook making it even easier for complaints about provocative ads to go viral, many marketers began testing their Super Bowl commercials on audiences in advance of the big game. A research firm that specializes in **neuromarketing**, the study of advertising's effect on brain activity, worked with several Super Bowl advertisers. The firm strapped electrodes to focus group participants to see how different parts of their brains reacted to the commercials. While some experts question the validity of this research, marketers have been increasingly using the techniques.[59]

In trying to illustrate that some ads may bring about undesirable, although unintended, behavior, a New Jersey professor showed his students a magazine ad featuring a fit, smiling young man on a sidewalk in New York City with yellow cabs, pedestrians, and buildings in the background. The bright-red headline read, "Just once a day!" All other copy elements of the ad were concealed to disguise the actual product advertised. When the professor asked his students to guess what kind of product the ad was promoting, the consensus of the guesses was that the ad was for some kind of a pill, probably a vitamin. In fact, the ad was for a medication that is used as part of an HIV therapy regimen by persons who are HIV positive. Because visual images are very persuasive, is it possible that the fit young man and the bright-red "Just once a day!" caption could convey to young adults that being HIV positive is an easily manageable condition, and that one can therefore engage in unsafe sex with impunity? However, marketers have limited options, even if some misperceive the ads. Clearly, featuring an individual who looks unhealthy in an ad for a pharmaceutical designed to control a serious medical condition will not be effective. The Food and Drug Administration has alerted marketers of HIV medications to the fact that some of their ads, which often show healthy-looking persons involved in rigorous physical activity, may be conveying the notion that because the drugs can restore or maintain one's health, they implicitly encourage unsafe sex.

Many studies have focused on the use of objectionable themes in advertising. For example, one study of TV commercials directed at children discovered that diverse ethnicities were underrepresented compared to Caucasians and pointed out the need for more diverse ethnic representation in children's TV advertising. This is an important recommendation because children are generally deeply engaged in TV viewing and advertising's portrayals influence their views of social ethnicity.[60] A study of promotional elements found that images and words unsuitable for children produced the most consumer complaints, followed by bad language. The study also discovered that consumers felt more insulted by offensive themes than by the products, services, or ideas featured in the ads, and that consumers viewed ads delivered via intrusive media as more offensive than those delivered via other media.[61] Table 15.3 includes examples of provocative marketing.[62]

Although marketers continuously sponsor ads portraying values or behaviors that some (or many) consumers find distasteful or wrong, the importance of public scrutiny must not be underestimated. For example, one broadcast of the Super Bowl included many ads portraying crude humor and gags that were later criticized by many (and also amplified by the coincidental "wardrobe malfunction" of a female entertainer during the half-time show). As a result, advertisers during the following year's Super Bowl broadcast took special care to develop ads that were more mainstream and traditional—not an easy task, as Super Bowl ads (expected to be creative and unique) —are the most analyzed group of ads in American broadcasting.[63] In recent years, marketers have been testing Super Bowl commercials well in advance, with different publics, and changing any elements that appeared controversial.

TABLE 15.3	Examples of Provocative Marketing	
PRODUCT	**PROVOCATION**	**DESCRIPTION**
Blast by Colt 45	Appealing to underage drinkers	Blast by Colt 45—a fruit-flavored beverage—was endorsed by the rapper Snoop Dogg, who also mentioned the brand in one of his songs. Sweetened alcoholic beverages are sometimes called "cocktails on training wheels" and young drinkers call them "alcopops."
Four Loko	Deadly combination masked as "an energy drink"	A company marketing a fruit-flavored malt beverage with 12% alcohol content and caffeine targeted college students. Some drinkers ended up in hospitals. While under FDA investigation, the company took the caffeine out of the product.
Adidas	Selling the same product for different prices in two countries	The shirts of New Zealand's premier rugby team—marketed by Adidas—were being sold online in the United States for approximately 50% less that their New Zealand price.
Nivea skincare	Despicable advertising	An ad for the product featured a black man holding a decapitated head with an afro and beard. The ad's tagline was: "Re-civilize yourself."
Groupon	Insensitive humor	One ad made fun of the people of Tibet, who are abused under Chinese rule; another ad made fun of endangered species.
A vodka named Wodka	Tasteless and negative stereotypical portrayals in advertising	An ad for Wodka—a very cheap vodka brand sold in Brooklyn, N.Y.—read: "Christmas quality, Hanukah pricing," and also featured one dog wearing a yarmulke and another one wearing a Santa hat. Another ad read: "Escort quality, hooker prices."
Benetton	Creative but objectionable	Benetton—made famous by creative but highly explicit advertising—came up with an "UNHATE" campaign featuring world leaders kissing other leaders whom they oppose, such as President Obama kissing Venezuela's leader and the prime minister of Israel kissing the Palestinian leader.

Sources: WSJ Staff, "Oh, Benetton. You and Your Controversial Ad Campaigns," online.wsj.com November 16, 2011; Jonathan Hutchinson, "The Price of a Jersey Sets Rugby Fans Against Adidas," NYTIMES.com August 24, 2011; Andrew Newman, "A Line of Brews Draws a Star Endorser," nytimes.com April 17, 2011; Abby Goodnough, "Caffeine and Alcohol Drink Is Potent Mix for Young," nytimes.com October 26, 2010; Sarah Nir, "Nivea Pulls Ads After Online Outcry," nytimes.com August 12, 2011.

Abusing Consumers' Privacy

Learning Objective

5 To understand how marketers abuse consumers' privacy and the measures that can stop such practices.

Consumers' loss of privacy is an increasingly problematic ethical issue, as marketers identify and reach out to increasingly smaller audiences through innovative media and more sophisticated tracking. The collection and dissemination of this information raises many privacy issues and various governmental bodies have proposed measures to ensure consumers' privacy. For example, some senators proposed a Commercial Privacy Bill of Rights, but the proposal fails to require businesses to provide consumers with data about themselves, which they can do very easily.[64]

Some retailers started testing new technology that allowed them to track customers' movements by following the Wi-Fi signals from customers' smartphones. The retailers gather data about in-store shoppers' behavior, using video surveillance and signals from their cellphones and apps to identify customers' genders, how many minutes they spend in the candy aisle and how long they look at merchandise before buying it. Retailers can also identify returning shoppers, because mobile devices send unique identification codes when they search for networks. Thus, stores can tell how repeat customers behave and the average time between visits. When customers found out about being tracked, many complained and said that they felt "stalked" and "creepy" while shopping under surveillance.[65]

The **e-score** is a digital calculation that evaluates people's buying power and value as consumers. However, these scores are largely invisible to the public. Fueled by Google Analytics, this digital ranking of American society is unlike anything that came before it. Nevertheless, unlike personal credit reports, consumers cannot find out what their e-scores are.[66]

The Federal Trade Commission recommended a "do not track" mechanism that is similar to the national "do not call" registry. It also proposed legislation regulating so-called data brokers, which compile and trade a wide range of personal and financial data about millions of consumers from online and offline sources. The suggested legislation would give consumers access to information collected about them and allow them to correct and update such data. Another proposal is to let consumers choose whether they want their Internet browsing and buying habits monitored.[67] The Digital Advertising Alliance—a group of digital advertising trade organizations—designed a turquoise triangle in the upper right-hand corner of banner ads. The AdChoices icon allows users who click on the turquoise triangle to opt out of having their behavior tracked online. The group's website has received about 100,000 inquiries about the icon. Facing several bills introduced in Congress calling for tighter regulation of mobile and digital privacy, as well as more control over online advertising to children, the group launched a campaign educating consumers about the turquoise triangle.[68]

Online marketers monitor and track consumers more closely and accurately than most people realize or would probably allow. For example, Facebook had a program called "beacon," which traced where users were going and sent their friends alerts about the goods that the users who were monitored bought or viewed online. After a public outcry, Facebook incorporated into the program a feature allowing users to opt out of it easily.[69] More recently, Facebook—which has 500 million users globally—unveiled a set of controls that it said would help people understand what they were sharing online, and with whom, and would simplify its opt out system.[70] Radically, newer versions of several browsers come with the don't-track-me option automatically enabled. During installation, a notice appears in a customization menu giving users the choice to keep that preselected don't-track-me preference as is, or switch it off.[71] Adlock is the name of software that, presumably, allows consumers to surf online and block some ads, but without ever missing the advertising that they were meant to see.[72] A survey presented at the Amsterdam Privacy Conference indicated that most Americans surveyed did not want any information at all collected about which websites they visit, and that they did not find online advertisements useful. Nearly 90% said they had never heard of a proposal by the Federal Trade Commission, known as a "do not track" mechanism, that would let users opt out of having their personal data collected for serving tailored advertisements.[73]

We must also note that the popularity of "do not track" threatens the barter system wherein consumers allow sites and third-party ad networks to collect information about their online activities in exchange for open access to maps, email, games, music, social networks, and much more. Marketers have been fighting to preserve this arrangement, saying that collecting consumer data powers effective advertising tailored to a user's tastes. In turn, according to this argument, those tailored ads enable smaller sites to thrive and provide rich content. A general council for the Interactive Advertising Bureau—an industry group—said that eliminating relevant advertising would make the Internet less diverse, less economically successful, and significantly less interesting.[74] Furthermore, although consumers lose a lot of privacy online, such is not always the case. In websites using "first party" behavioral advertising, the site collects consumer information to deliver targeted advertising at its site, but does not share any of that information with third parties. Additionally, **contextual advertising**, which targets advertisements based on the Web page a consumer is viewing or a search query the consumer has made, involves little or no data storage.

Finding and reading websites' privacy policies is difficult. Buried deep within the legalese used in privacy policies is information on how Web publishers collect and handle the data they use to show ads to their visitors. PrivacyChoice—a company that has analyzed and indexed the data in hundreds of privacy policies across the Web—has developed a scale ranking websites from 0 to 100, based on how a site collects and uses personal data. Websites and their users can easily compare privacy practices across the Internet and make smarter decisions about their own data. This tool would also result in more protective privacy practices by sites and tracking companies.[75]

Little-known software installed on millions of smartphones is raising even more questions about what data are being collected from mobile devices, where the data are going, and what they are being used for. The package—from a company named Carrier IQ Inc.—collected information on one carrier's smartphone with Google Inc.'s Android operating system. The software, which was not transparently visible to consumers, tracks actions such as when buttons are pressed and collects personal data such as the content of text messages. Google said that it is not affiliated with Carrier IQ.[76]

Even without special software, cell phones undermine privacy. Marketers can learn not only *who* you are (e.g., your personal characteristics) and *what* specific purchases you make, but can also learn *where* you are at any given moment because your cell phone, mobile email device, and the GPS integrated into your car or sports watch are "electronic bracelets" that monitor your movements. If you travel abroad with a roaming cell phone, upon landing at your destination, you may quickly receive a text welcoming you to that destination and offering you additional services designed for travelers. Clearly, in the not-too-distant future, when you drive a car equipped with a GPS with the radio on, the commercial that you will hear may alert you to, say, a McDonald's two exits down the highway. Another driver in a different location and listening to the same radio station would hear a different ad. In several large cities, advertisers use cabs equipped with GPS and advertising billboards on their roofs to create ever-changing advertising messages; the changing ad displays corresponded to the businesses the cabs pass as they travel (in some cabs, screens inside the cabs also display ads).

In one futuristic movie thriller set in 2054, the hero passes a billboard featuring the American Express card, which, after scanning his retina, becomes a hologram (presumably visible only to him) portraying his picture and personal data and urging him to use the card. He then enters a Gap store, where he is met by voices greeting him by name, asking how he liked his previous purchases, and suggesting items that he may like based on his past purchases. New types of coupons, printed from the Internet or sent to mobile phones, are packed with information about the customers who use them, and follow the customers to malls. The coupons look standard, but their bar codes often include identification information about the customer, his or her Internet address, Facebook page information, and even the search terms the customer used to find the coupon in the first place. In the mall, if a man walks into a Filene's Basement to buy a suit for his wedding and shows a coupon he retrieved online, the company's marketing agency can figure out whether he used the search terms "Hugo Boss suit" or "discount wedding clothes" before his purchase. The coupons can, in some cases, be tracked not just to an anonymous shopper but to an identifiable person: A retailer could know that Amy Smith printed a 15%-off coupon after searching for appliance discounts at Ebates.com on Friday at 1:30 p.m. and redeemed it later that afternoon at the store.[77]

In summary, experts point out that given the vast flow of information that consumers entrust to the Internet every day, it is hard to believe there is no general law to protect people's privacy online. Companies harvest data about people as they surf the Net, assemble it into detailed profiles, and sell it to advertisers or others without ever asking permission. Because there are no uniform international laws to deal with violations of online privacy, and because no one specifically monitors for potential violations of consumers' rights to privacy online, there is no consensus as to whether government regulation or voluntary measures could alleviate this concern.[78]

Promoting Social Causes

Learning Objective

6 To understand how marketers can advance society's interests by advocating socially beneficial conduct and discouraging adverse behavior.

Many not-for-profit organizations, including consumer advocacy groups, exist primarily to promote socially beneficial behaviors such as contributing to charity or using energy responsibly, and reducing such negative behaviors as abusing drugs, discriminating on the basis of race or sexual orientation, and driving while texting or drunk. Many companies try to increase their credibility by being "good corporate citizens" and integrating socially desirable practices into their operations. For example, Disney agreed not to feature any smoking in Disney-branded films.[79] One study indicated that a societal marketing program had a powerful impact on creating positive consumer attitudes toward the sponsoring company.[80] Another study found that a solid perceptual fit between the sponsoring organization and the cause(s) promoted enhances both consumers' involvement in the causes and their purchase intentions.[81]

Advocating Beneficial and Discouraging Detrimental Conduct

The primary objective of many not-for-profit organizations is to promote socially desirable behaviors and discourage ones that produce negative outcomes. For example, The Advertising Council—a group founded during World War II and dedicated to the advancement of socially worthy causes through advertising—ran a campaign that discouraged the use of derogatory phrases regarding a person's sexual orientation. The campaign's title was "Think Before You Speak," and its objective was to reduce the harassment and bullying of teenagers who are gay, lesbian, bisexual, or transgender (see Figure 15.5).[82] With the alarming increase of "digital harassment" among teenagers, The Advertising Council initiated a campaign entitled "That's Not Cool," alerting young adults that excessive and unwelcome sending of text messages can quickly become illegal stalking.[83] The Christopher

FIGURE 15.5
Using Derogatory Terms: "Think Before You Speak"

Source: Courtesy of GLSEN, the Gay, Lesbian & Straight Network and the Ad Council's "Think Before You Speak" campaign

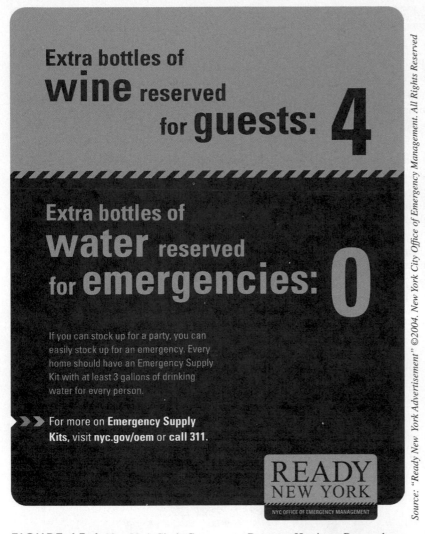

FIGURE 15.6 New York City's Government Promotes Hurricane Preparedness

Reeve Foundation is a not-for-profit group dedicated to raising money for treating people who live with spinal impairment and finding a cure for spinal injury; the group ran an ad campaign under its new slogan: "Today's Care. Tomorrow's Cure."[84]

Sometimes, even government organizations try to induce public behavior that they see fit. For example, because many TV series and films are shot on the streets of New York City, some hurried New Yorkers have grown increasingly annoyed at the delays and inconveniences caused by film crews, who must often close and obstruct city blocks and sidewalks during filming. The New York City mayor's office ran a campaign asking New Yorkers to play host to film crews even if they are reluctant to do so; the ads featured New Yorkers who work in the film industry and stressed the economic benefits of the industry's strong presence in the city.[85] The ad by New York City's Office of Emergency Management (shown in Figure 15.6) encourages the city's residents to become more aware of the city's vulnerability to hurricanes and be prepared for such weather.

One of the most heavily discouraged detrimental behaviors in the past few years has been texting or using mobile phones while driving. Cellular carriers have even been working on technologies that would automatically disable mobile phones in moving cars.[86] Scores of not-for-profit organizations, companies, and local governments have been campaigning against this highly dangerous and often fatal practice using such ads as the one featured in Figure 15..

The list of worthy social causes has been increasing steadily. Table 15.4 includes a list of recent promotions of lesser-known socially beneficial causes.

Cause-Related Marketing

Some firms engage in **cause-related marketing**, where they contribute a portion of the revenues they receive from selling certain products to causes that are socially desirable and supported by the American public. The Hertz ad in Figure 15.8 is an excellent example of such marketing. The ad welcomes

FIGURE 15.7
Discouraging Texting While
Driving

TABLE 15.4 Promoting Socially Worthy Causes

ORGANIZATION	CAUSE	CAMPAIGN'S DESCRIPTION
Soprano's actor Joe Pantoliano	Mental illness awareness	Established a foundation and raised money by selling a DVD of a documentary he directed and fees from personal appearances.
Blood Center of Central Texas	Donating blood	Humorously suggest that the good deed of donating blood could offset everyday bad behavior.
United Methodist Church in Nashville	Eliminating Malaria	"A world of people united in the fight against a needless killer."
Keep California (not-for-profit group)	Keeping California's beaches clean	Using humor and filmed on the same beach where "beach blanket" movies were shot in the 1960s, the commercial satirizes the teenagers who appeared in those films.
The Advertising Council	Encouraging parents to read with their children	"Read to your child today and inspire a lifelong love of reading." The campaign features Curious George—an iconic monkey character—featured in a series of children's books.
American Heart Association	Using hands-only CPR	A "hands symphony" theme in TV spots. The campaign's website lets users create their own hand symphonies and an instructional application of the CPR is offered to users of smartphones.
Advertising Council	Greater involvement of fathers in their children's lives	Targeting American-Indian, Asian-American, and Hispanic fathers, the tagline is "Take time to be a dad today." Studies have shown that children of "absent fathers" do poorly in school and have lower levels of self-esteem.

FIGURE 15.8
Hertz's Cause-Related Marketing

Source: The Hertz Corporation

soldiers returning home from combat overseas and asks consumers to rent Hertz cars so that the company can offer free rentals to returning troops. Fashion designers such as Armani and Ralph Lauren have donated selected portions of their sales to AIDS research and other charities. To acknowledge National Breast Cancer Awareness Month in October, many beauty and cosmetics companies earmarked a portion of the price of their "pink-ribbon" products to breast cancer charities. A few years ago, following a tsunami in Southeast Asia, several designers sold tsunami-relief T-shirts; many others encouraged consumers to make donations to a fund that was set up to help the storm's victims, and even included links to this fund on their websites. Other kinds of corporate-sponsored special events include marching bands, fireworks displays, parades, laser shows, and traveling art exhibits.

These sponsorships convey a subtle message to consumers: "We're a great (kind, good-natured, socially responsible) company; we deserve your business." One study demonstrated the importance of the fit between the sponsored cause and the company's positioning strategy, and showed that a low fit can harm the company's image.[87] In another study, an ad with a cause-related message elicited more favorable consumer attitudes than a similar ad without a cause-related message.[88] Yet another study showed that cause-related advertising is more effective among consumers who are more involved.[89]

Consumer Ethics

Marketers implement ethical strategies in order "to do the right thing," to improve their image in the eyes of their constituencies, to reduce scrutiny, and as an alternative to government legislation. A study focused on measuring consumers' views and perceptions of companies that have been accused of such practices as exploitation of the Third World, animal testing, damage to the environment, and recycling. The researchers developed a scale that measures consumers' views regarding ethical business issues and companies that adopt morally "right" strategies. It includes questions about the personal, social, and money aspects of adopting ethical views, as well as potential positive and negative outcomes (see Table 15.5).[90]

TABLE 15.5	A Scale Measuring Ethical Awareness and Concerns towards Marketing-Related Issues

Respondents used a 7-point scale ranging from "strongly agree" to "strongly disagree."

PERSONAL POSITIVES

My friends are concerned with this issue.

People who matter to me would respect me for being concerned about this issue.

This is an issue that I like to be associated with.

I feel better about myself if I take some form of action against firms that violate this issue.

SOCIAL POSITIVES

It would be better for everyone in the long run if people favoured products that address this issue.

It would help if people bought from firms that address this issue.

Society would benefit from the removal of products that violate this issue.

People could make fairer choices if they were aware of which companies had high ethical principles regarding this issue.

PERSONAL NEGATIVES

It would be too much hassle to buy only from businesses that do not violate this issue.

It is not my responsibility to punish firms that ignore this issue.

It would take the pleasure out of shopping if I had to choose only from products that support this issue.

It would make shopping less convenient if I had to choose only from products that support this issue.

SOCIAL NEGATIVES

People would be annoyed if they were pressured into being concerned with this issue.

People are too busy today to be concerned with this issue.

People might think it was a waste of time to try to influence big business over this issue.

Having to take account of this issue would make shopping less convenient for people.

MONEY ISSUES

It does not cost me any more money to take this issue into account when shopping (*item reversed for these analyses*).

It costs more to take account of this issue when shopping.

Source: With kind permission from Springer Science+Business Media: "Motivations of the Ethical Consumer", *Journal of Business Ethics*, 79 (2008):, Oliver M. Freedstone and Peter J. McGoldrick.

Another facet of consumer ethics is *buyers'* dishonest behavior in the marketplace. For example, many stores started charging restocking fees, limiting return policies, and tracking abnormal return patterns because of buyers who bought items, used them, and then returned them for a refund (some stores encountered shoplifters who tried to return stolen merchandise). Also, in the digital world, software piracy is a major problem. One study that focused on ways to reduce consumers' software theft discovered that increasing the risk of getting caught is unlikely to reduce this practice and may actually increase piracy levels. The study also found that consumers were less likely to pirate and more willing to pay for software if the websites involved offered them extra value, such as downloadable ringtones and videos.[91]

Airlines enable and inadvertently encourage many forms of "creative"—possibly unethical—customer behavior. For instance, to avoid checked luggage fees, some passengers use vacuum-seal bags inside carry-on bags. The bags, which shrink down to a compact package when air is pulled out by a vacuum cleaner, allow them to fit considerably more items in a carry-on than would normally be possible. Others buy special trench coats, vests, and other garments made with large built-in pockets that allow people to carry everything from folded shirts to an iPad. When flights are cancelled because of weather, some passengers stay with friends and then present the airlines with bills from expensive hotels. Some passengers whose bags were lost claimed that their bags were filled with furs, computers, and lots of couture clothing. Some fliers who travel with wheelchairs or motorized scooters claim that their devices were damaged in the cargo hold during the flight.[92]

Summary

Learning Objective 1: To understand the meaning and importance of marketing ethics and social responsibility.

The marketing concept is sometimes incompatible with society's best interests. The societal marketing concept requires that all marketers adhere to principles of social responsibility in the marketing of their goods and services. Since all companies prosper when society prospers, companies must integrate social responsibility into all marketing decisions, and many have adopted the societal marketing concept. A serious deterrent to more widespread implementation of the societal marketing concept is the short-term orientation of most business executives and corporate boards in their drive to quickly increase market share and profits.

Learning Objective 2: To understand how marketers can exploit consumers by targeting children and encouraging overeating and other forms of irresponsible buying.

The study of consumer behavior allows marketers to understand why and how consumers make their purchase decisions, but it also enables unethical marketers to exploit human vulnerabilities in the marketplace and engage in other unethical marketing practices. Such practices include targeting vulnerable consumers such as children, teenagers, the elderly, and less-educated consumers, who may not have the knowledge or experience to evaluate the products or services being promoted and the potential negative consequences of using them.

Learning Objective 3: To understand ethically questionable practices such as covert marketing, manipulative exposure to advertising, and truth-in-advertising issues.

Marketers can manipulate consumers' interpretations of marketing stimuli through the context in which those stimuli are featured. Covert marketing consists of marketing messages and promotional materials that appear to come from independent parties but are, in fact, sent by marketers. Some maintain that covert marketing strategies often violate the FTC's definition of deceptive advertising, endorsement

guidelines, and other regulations of marketing, and believe that the FTC should establish clearer rules to reduce the use of masked advertising. The FTC has developed guidelines as to what constitutes deceptive advertising, and it holds marketers responsible for determining their ads' potential to mislead consumers. Although the FTC is responsible for stopping false or misleading ads, and the agency encourages and investigates complaints by consumers and companies regarding false or misleading ads, it cannot locate and stop all misleading ads. The FTC can also require companies that have misled consumers through their advertising to run corrective advertising.

Learning Objective 4: To understand the nature and consequences of provocative advertisements.

Too many marketing messages convey socially undesirable stereotypes and images, some of which tend to encourage risky or illegal behavior or create unrealistic perceptions. Many studies have focused on the use of objectionable themes in advertising and discovered that negative portrayals of certain people or objects affect consumers' perceptions.

Learning Objective 5: To understand how marketers abuse consumers' privacy and the measures that can stop such practices.

Consumers' loss of privacy is an increasingly problematic ethical issue as marketers identify and reach out to increasingly smaller audiences through innovative media and more sophisticated tracking. The collection and dissemination of this information raises many privacy issues and various governmental bodies have proposed measures to ensure consumers' privacy. "Do not track" and opt-out mechanisms, regulation of data brokers and harvesters, and increased consumer access to the information collected about them are options for combatting the invisible tracking that is being done via Internet, cell phone, and coupon use.

Learning Objective 6: To understand how marketers can advance society's interests by advocating socially beneficial conduct and discouraging adverse behavior.

Many not-for-profit organizations, including consumer advocacy groups, exist primarily to promote socially beneficial behaviors. Many companies try to increase their credibility by being "good corporate citizens" and integrating socially desirable practices into their operations. Some firms engage in cause-related marketing, where they contribute a portion of the revenues they receive from selling certain products to causes which are socially desirable and supported by the American public. A good fit between the company and the cause appears to be crucial to the effectiveness of these campaigns.

Review and Discussion Questions

15.1. Some say that targeting *any* group of consumers who are willing and able to purchase a product is simply good marketing. For example, advertising sweet and fatty foods to young children is perfectly okay because children like sweets, and when parents buy these products at their children's request, the needs of both the kids and their parents are met and satisfied. What is your reaction to this view?

15.2. A soft-drink company distributed cell phones to preadolescents in low-income areas. The phones routinely received advertising messages for the drink. Following criticism, the company said that the benefits to the disadvantaged children from having the cell phones (e.g., safety) outweighed any "exploitive targeting" considerations. Do you agree or disagree with the company's position? Explain your answer.

15.3. At a time when many consumers can avoid advertising messages via time shifting devices, marketers increasingly use product placements (also known as branded entertainment). In your view, is this a wise strategy or not? Explain your answer.

15.4. Is it right to advertise prescription medications *directly* to consumers? Why or why not?

15.5. Why is it important to study consumer ethics?

15.6. What are the privacy implications of companies' increasingly widespread monitoring of online consumers?

Hands-on Assignments

15.7. Find, and discuss ads that depict each of the following:

a. Exploitive targeting of children

b. Overaggressive advertising

c. Direct-to-consumer advertising of pharmaceuticals

d. Cause-related marketing

e. Societal marketing by a not-for-profit group

f. Societal marketing by a for-profit company

g. Socially undesirable representation

15.8. Online, find three examples of advertising embedded within entertainment content and discuss them.

15.9. Compile a list of consumption behaviors that *you* consider unethical. For each behavior listed, explain why you view it as wrong. Also, for each behavior listed, discuss the possible reasons a person engaging in that practice may use to justify it.

15.10. Visit the news section at www.caru.org. Select three of the press releases featured there (other than those discussed in this chapter) and illustrate how they depict the unethical applications of learning or perception (see Chapters 4 and 5) in targeting children.

Key Terms

- advertorials *392*
- cause-related marketing *399*
- consumer socialization *369*
- contextual advertising *397*
- corrective advertising *393*
- covert marketing (masked or stealth marketing) *392*
- deceptive advertising *393*
- e-score *396*
- figure and ground *392*
- infomercials *392*
- JND *385*
- marketing ethics *380*
- neuromarketing *395*
- product placements *392*
- societal marketing concept *382*
- truth-in-advertising laws *393*

Consumer Research

DISNEY'S CINDERELLA is one of the best-known characters in the world. Like any company, Disney needs to come up with new ideas and offerings to expand its markets, especially when the company is rapidly transmitting its contents to children via many forms of media, and not only through movies and theme parks, as was the case when Cinderella was first introduced. Besides, the elements of the Cinderella story originated in ancient Greece and the character no longer reflects modern role models. Therefore, for five years, a team of child psychologists, sociologists, and storytelling experts worked to create a new royal girl: Sofia the First.

Sofia is the product of years of research involving interviews and observations of children playing with toys, discussing role models with parents, and testing storylines as the new princess was coming to life. This effort represents **consumer research**, which is the process and tools used to study consumer behavior (see Figure 16.1). As the research progressed, Disney uncovered the traits that today's children aged 2 to 5 expect in a modern princess, which, in many ways, is an "anti-Cinderella." Sophia could not be a young woman looking for a man, in order to avoid the stereotype of girls needing a prince to save them. Evil stepmothers too could not be present. Sophia is the daughter of Miranda, an unmarried shoe-cobbler, living in a village in the kingdom of Enchancia. Miranda meets and marries Enchancia's King Roland. Sophia has to adjust to a royal way of life, new school, and two stepsiblings.

The development team tested the plotlines on preschoolers before writing the scripts. While testing one storyline, the researchers found out that kids did not understand the phrase "slumber party," and renamed the episode "The Big Sleepover." As the children listened to the story, the researchers filmed them and took notes, which they later on used in developing the plots. The show's producers made Sofia the child of a single mother because doing so offered an easy way to explore themes of kids adapting to new living arrangements, which many young children can identify with. In addition, the writers introduced multicultural

FIGURE 16.1

The Consumer Research Process

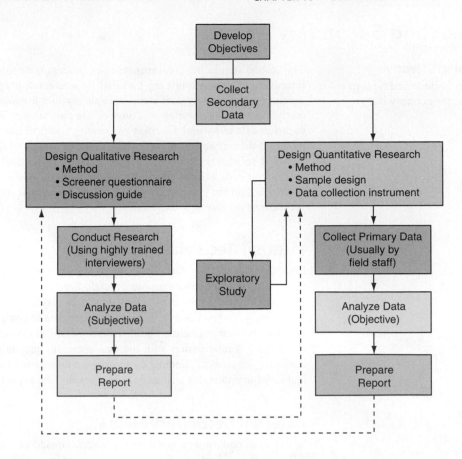

family dynamics: Although Miranda was not born in En-chancia, she married its king. Nevertheless, Sophia is still a Disney princess. She's pretty, lives in a castle, wears gowns, and even got advice from Cinderella, who visited her in the first episode.[1]

This chapter begins with an examination of exploratory research and secondary data. Then, we describe **primary research**, defined as new research especially designed and collected for purposes of a current research problem. The two categories of primary consumer research are: **Qualitative research**, which consists primarily of focus groups and depth interviews, and projective methods; and **quantitative research**, which includes observational research, experimentation, and survey research.

Developing Research Objectives

Learning Objective

1 To understand how to develop research objectives

The first and most difficult step in the consumer research process is to accurately define the objectives of the research. Is it to segment the market for electronic readers? Is it to examine consumer attitudes about the experience of online shopping? What percentage of households shop for food online? Whatever the key research question, it is important for the marketing manager and the research manager to agree at the outset as to the specific purposes and objectives of the proposed consumer study. A clearly written statement of research objectives ensures that the information needed is indeed collected and costly errors are avoided.

If the purpose of a study is to come up with new ideas for products or promotional themes, the researchers use qualitative research. Qualitative studies consist of focus groups and/or one-on-one depth interviews, in which sampled consumers are individually interviewed by professionally trained interviewers. Alternatively, for example, if the purpose of the study is to find out how many consumers match the demographics or psychographics of the target market, or the characteristics of consumers who buy given brands and whether or not they are brand loyal, marketers conduct quantitative research.

Commonly, marketers use qualitative research before conducting large quantitative studies, because their results enable marketers to define the research objectives the large and expensive studies more precisely.

Collecting Secondary Data

Learning Objective

2 To understand how to collect secondary data.

The second step in the consumer research process is to search **secondary data**, defined as existing information that was originally gathered for a research purpose other than the present research. The rationale for secondary data searches is simply that it makes good sense to investigate whether currently available information will answer—in part or even in full—the research question at hand. It seems unwise to expend the effort and money, and rush into collecting new information before determining if there is any available information that would provide at least a good starting point. In other words, if secondary data can in part or full answer the question, new primary research can either be cut back or even avoided altogether. Secondary consumer-related data can be secured from internal sources within the company or organization, or external sources for free or at a cost. The following subsections explore secondary data.

Internal Secondary Data

Internal information or data could consist of previously collected in-house information that was originally used for some other purpose. It might have originally been gathered as part of a sales audit, or from past customer service calls, or letters of inquiry from customers, or collected via warranty cards. Increasingly, companies use internal secondary data to compute **customer lifetime value profiles** for various customer segments. These profiles include customer acquisition costs (the resources needed to establish a relationship with the customer), the profits generated from individual sales to each customer, the costs of handling customers and their orders (some customers may place more complex and variable orders that cost more to handle), and the expected duration of the relationship.

External Secondary Data

External secondary data come from sources outside of the firm or organization. They take many different forms. Some are free and can be found in a public library, other information is available for only a nominal fee, and still other data or information are quite expensive to secure. The following sections discusses some of the specific types of consumer behavior secondary information available from outside of the firm.

Government Secondary Data

Much data are collected by government bodies or their agencies, and are generally made available for a very nominal cost. For instance, within the United States, a major source of these data is the federal government, which publishes information collected by scores of government agencies about the economy, business, and virtually all demographics of the U.S. population. The best depositories of marketing-applicable information are FedStats, the U.S. Census Bureau, and the CIA's World Factbook. State and local governments, as well as studies prepared by the United Nations and various foreign governments, are also very useful for examining selective consumer behavior topics.

Periodicals and Articles Available from Online Search Services

Business-relevant secondary data from periodicals, newspapers, and books are readily accessible via online search engines. Two quite popular examples are ProQuest and LexisNexis. These two engines provide access to major newspapers such as The Wall Street Journal and The New York Times; business magazines such as Business Week, Forbes, Fortune, and Harvard Business Review; and marketing journals and applied publications focused specifically on marketing, such as Advertising Age, Brandweek, Marketing News, Journal of Marketing, Journal of Marketing Research, Journal of Consumer Research, and European Journal of Marketing. These materials are available in public and private libraries, especially business specialty libraries.

Syndicated Commercial Marketing and Media Research Services

Commercially available information about consumers is collected by syndicated research services that sell it to subscribing marketers. For example, Nielsen's MyBestSegment provides demographic and lifestyle profiles of the consumers residing in each U.S. Zip Code, Ipsos Mendelsohn offers its Affluent Media Survey to advertisers and their ad agencies, and Mediamark collects information on magazine audience profiles. Future research into consumers' exposure to media will consist of monitoring consumers via digital cable set-top boxes. Presently, digital cable boxes are primarily used to send signals to consumers' TVs to enable them to watch movies on demand and expanded channel lineups. However, the boxes can easily record all the programs that consumers tune into, channel surfing, avoiding commercial breaks, and recordings for later viewing, using digital video recorders that cable companies increasingly offer to subscribers. So far, cable companies have been reluctant to monitor consumers' viewing closely due to privacy concerns. However, some companies are exploring methods that will transform data from digital cable boxes into information that can be used for precise targeting of consumers while still protecting their privacy.[2]

Consumer Panels

For decades, marketers have purchased information from secondary data providers who collected consumer behavior data from household or family **consumer panels**. The members of these panels were paid for recording their purchases and media viewing habits in diaries. The diaries' data were then combined with additional information about households collected by, say, the U.S. Census. Marketers and advertising agencies paid the panel providers a subscription fee for their findings. Often the information not only told marketers about the families, purchases of the marketers' products, but also included the same information about competitors' brands.

Today, online technology enables panel research companies to collect increasingly sophisticated data from respondents. For example, a manufacturer of customized snowboards discovered that 10,000 snowboarding fans used its site's discussion forum to chat about their hobbies and buying habits, and also to rate different designs of snowboards. The snowboard marketer then started selling the data it collected from this online panel to other marketers interested in targeting the young, mostly male, respondents who so enthusiastically revealed so much about themselves while discussing snowboards online. Similarly, automobile manufacturers purchase consumer behavior panel data about recent car purchases from independent panel companies. Again, information about a marketer's own brands and competitors' brands, as well as information about the demographic differences among households that purchase various brands, gives the data buyers' insights for creating an effective marketing campaigns.

Obtaining secondary data before engaging in primary research offers several advantages. First, secondary data may provide a solution to the research problem and eliminate the need for primary research altogether. Even if this is not the case, secondary data used in exploratory research may help to clarify and refine the objectives of the primary study and provide ideas about selecting research tools and the difficulties that may occur during the full-scale study.

Although secondary information can be obtained more cheaply and quickly than primary data, it has some limitations. First, information may be categorized in units that are different from those that the researcher seeks (e.g., clustering consumers into the 15–20 and 21–25 age groups is useless to a researcher interested in consumers 17–24 years old). Some secondary data may not be accurate because of errors in gathering or analyzing it, or because the data were collected in a biased fashion to support a particular point of view. Also, secondary data may be outdated.

Designing Primary Research

Learning Objective

3 To understand qualitative and quantitative research methods.

Figure 16.1 shows that after considering the collection of secondary research, the diagram splits into two paths, with the left-side route taking a path of qualitative research, and the right-side route taking a path of quantitative research. The split reflects the purpose of the research objectives. If the purpose is to get new ideas (e.g., for positioning or repositioning a product), a qualitative study is often undertaken; alternatively, if descriptive and quantitative information is sought, some form of a quantitative study should be undertaken. The merits of using the different measurement instruments of qualitative and quantitative research are described in the two following subsections.

Qualitative Research

Contemporary qualitative consumer research is the result of understanding that consumers are not rational decision makers who objectively evaluate the goods and services available to them and select those that give them the highest utility (satisfaction) at the lowest cost. Qualitative consumer researchers are also known as **motivational researchers**. The central tenet of their orientation was that consumers were not always consciously aware of why they made the decisions they did. Even when they were aware of their basic motivations, consumers were not always willing to reveal those reasons to others, or even to themselves.

The leader of the motivational research movement was the Viennese psychoanalyst Dr. Ernest Dichter, who, after arriving in New York in the late 1930s, began to apply qualitative Freudian psychoanalytic techniques to uncover the hidden or unconscious motivations of consumers.[3] By the late 1950s and early 1960s, this research orientation became quite popular, and focus groups and depth interviews were used by many advertising agencies and consumer products companies in order to better understand consumer needs and motivations. Today, focus groups and depth interviews are very well-established research tools that are regularly used not only to secure insights about consumers' underlying needs and motivations, but also to gain consumer input for new product development efforts (including the creation of new products and even future advertising messages).[4] Because sample sizes are necessarily often small, findings cannot be generalized to larger populations. Nevertheless, qualitative research contributes extensively to the initial identification and development of new promotional campaigns and new product development that can eventually be further refined through a variety of quantitative research methods.

In designing and implementing an appropriate research strategy for conducting a qualitative study, the researcher must consider the purpose of the study, the type of interviews that are likely to be most appropriate given the purpose of the research, and the types of data instruments most suitable for securing the information needed. Although the specific research methods used may differ in composition, most forms of qualitative research questioning have their roots in psychoanalytic and clinical aspects of psychology. Specifically, they feature open-ended and free-response types of questioning and use of visual materials to stimulate respondents to reveal their innermost thoughts and beliefs.

The key methods used in qualitative studies are depth interviews and/or focus group sessions.

Depth Interviews

A **depth interview**, also frequently referred to as a "one-on-one" interview, is a lengthy, nonstructured interview (often 20 to 60 minutes in duration) between a single respondent and a highly trained researcher (often the same person who moderates focus group sessions). Commonly, the interviewer's strategy is to minimize his or her own talking time and provide as much time as possible for the consumer being interviewed to express his or her thoughts and behaviors, and respond to specific verbal and visual materials (e.g., mock-up of a potential print ad campaign). The researcher also must establish an atmosphere that encourages the consumer respondent to relax and open up in order to provide valuable insights. In many cases, the researcher's role is to probe the respondent by encouraging the person to talk freely about the product category and/or brand under study.

Generally, a series of the depth interviews takes place in a professionally set up interviewing room. These rooms are designed to provide audio and video recording equipment, and a one-way mirror for clients to view the interview without disrupting it (the researcher tells the participants that they are being observed).

Depth interview studies provide marketers with valuable ideas about product design or redesign, as well as insights for positioning or repositioning products. As already suggested, as part of a depth interview research project, a variety of stimulus materials is developed to enhance the discussion between the researcher and the respondent. They may take the form of written concept statements (describing a new product idea), drawings, or photos of new products, actual product samples, or rough renditions or videotapes of print ads or TV commercials. The purpose of such "stimulus materials," is to assist the respondent in expressing his or her inner thoughts and to encourage a more precise or accurate response to what is being investigated. Over the course of a day of conducting depth interviews, a researcher is likely to be able to complete about five to eight hours of interviews, depending on the length of each interview. Examples of probing questions for depth interviews are listed in Figure 16.2.

Focus Groups

A "discussion group" or **focus group** often consists of 8 to 10 participants who meet with a moderator-researcher-analyst to "focus on" or "explore" a particular product or product category (or any other

FIGURE 16.2

Examples of Probing Questions for Focus Groups and Depth Interviews

Source: Naomi R. Henderson, "The Power of Probing," Marketing Research (Winter 2007): 39.

> **Request for elaboration:** "Tell me more about that." "Give me an example of. . . ."
>
> **Request for definition:** "What do you mean by . . . ?" "What does the term _____ mean to you?"
>
> **Request for word associations:** "What other word(s) do you link with _____?" "Give me some synonyms that also describe _____."
>
> **Request for clarification:** "How does that differ from . . . ?" "In what circumstances do you . . . ?"
>
> **Request for comparison:** "How is _____ similar to _____?" "Which costs more, X or Y?"
>
> **Request for classification:** "Where does _____ fit?" "What else is in the category of _____?"
>
> **"Silent" probe:** This is a non-verbal probe and is characterized by such actions as raised eyebrows or hand gestures such as moving the right hand in a rolling motion that signifies "Tell me more."

topic or subject of research interest). During a focus group session (often two hours in duration), participants are encouraged to discuss their reactions to product and service concepts, or new advertising or marketing communications campaigns.

Because a focus group generally takes about two hours to complete (sometimes they can last for three or more hours), a researcher can generally conduct two or three focus groups (with a total of about thirty respondents) in one day; in contrast, it might take that same researcher five or six days to conduct 30 individual depth interviews. Analysis of responses from both depth interviews and focus groups requires a great deal of skill on the part of the researcher. Like depth interviews, focus group sessions are invariably audiotaped and videotaped, to assist in the analysis and to provide the client with a record of the sessions. Like depth interviews, focus groups are usually held in specially designed conference rooms with one-way mirrors that enable marketers and advertising agency staff to observe the sessions without disrupting or inhibiting the respondents.

For focus groups (and also depth interviews), respondents are recruited on the basis of a carefully drawn consumer profile that is detailed in a form called a **screener questionnaire**. The purpose of the "screener" is to ensure that the appropriate individuals are invited to participate in the research study, and that those who are not in the target market are not invited. An appropriate respondent is often paid $100 or more for his or her participation in the research process. In organizing focus group sessions, sometimes users of the company's brands are clustered in one or more groups, and their responses are compared to those of nonusers interviewed in separate sessions. Figure 16.3 presents a screener questionnaire that was used to recruit participants for focus groups for a study that dealt with introducing a premium line of canned vegetable soups. The screener questionnaire is designed to identify target consumers to be invited to participate in either an all-male or all-female focus group session. Individuals who are "screened out" (called "terminated" in research terminology) are those who do not meet the specifications for participation.

Some marketers prefer focus groups because they feel that the dynamic interaction between participants that takes place in focus groups tends to yield a greater number of new ideas and insights than depth interviews. Also, timing is sometimes very critical. In such cases, again, focus groups might be selected because it generally takes less time to complete a series of focus groups than a project of individual depth interviews. Other marketers (and in particular advertising agency professionals) prefer individual or depth interviews because they believe that individually interviewed respondents are free of group pressures and are less likely to give socially acceptable (and not necessarily truthful) responses. Moreover, the single participant is more likely to remain attentive during the entire interview, and—because of the greater personal attention received—is more likely to reveal private thoughts.

Discussion Guides

A **discussion guide** is a step-by-step outline that sets out the line of questioning the researcher needs to cover with the respondent in a depth interview, or a group of respondents during a focus group session.

FOOD PREFERENCE STUDY SCREENER

ASK TO SPEAK WITH A FEMALE OR MALE HOUSEHOLD MEMBER WHO IS BETWEEN 18 AND 35 YEARS OF AGE. WHEN THE CORRECT PERSON IS LOCATED INTRODUCE YOURSELF.

Hello, I'm _____, from _____. We are involved in a research project that is interested in knowing more about people's feeling and preferences with regard to food products. I want to assure you that this is research and <u>not</u> a "sales pitch." May I ask you a few questions?

1. CHECK ONE:
Female . . . . [ ]-POTENTIAL FOR GROUP 1
Male . . . . [ ]-POTENTIAL FOR GROUP 2

RECRUITER: Q1. RECRUIT 12 FEMALES AND 12 MALES.

2. In which of the following age groups are you? (READ CHOICES)
Under 18 years of age . . . . [ ]-TERMINATE
18 to 24 years of age . . . . [ ]
25 to 29 years of age . . . . [ ]
30 to 35 years of age . . . . [ ]
Over 35 years of age . . . . [ ]-TERMINATE

RECRUITER: Q2. SECURE A GOOD MIX ACROSS THE AGE SPAN INDICATED.

3. Do you or anyone else in your household work for any of the following types of businesses? (READ CHOICES)

	No	Yes
A market research firm or agency	[ ]	[ ]-TERMINATE
An advertising or public relations firm or agency	[ ]	[ ]-TERMINATE
A company that sells, manufactures, or distributes any type of food products	[ ]	[ ]-TERMINATE

4. a. Have you ever participated in a depth interview, focus group, or discussion group?
Yes . . . . [ ]-ASK Q4b.
No . . . . [ ]-SKIP TO Q5.
b. When was the last time you participated in a depth interview, focus group, or discussion group?
Within the past 6 months . . . . [ ]-TERMINATE
More than 6 months ago . . . . [ ]-CONTINUE

5. For classification purposes, please tell me how much formal education you have completed. (DO <u>NOT</u> READ CHOICES)
Less than a college graduate . . . . [ ]-TERMINATE
At least a college graduate . . . . [ ]

RECRUITER: Q5 ALL RESPONDENTS ARE TO BE COLLEGE GRADUATES.

6. Also, for classification purposes, please tell me into which of the following categories your <u>total</u> family's or personal income falls. (READ CHOICES)
Under $25,000 . . . . [ ]-TERMINATE
$25,000 to $49,999 . . . . [ ]
$50,000 or more . . . . [ ]

RECRUITER: Q6 ALL PARTICIPANTS MUST HAVE INCOMES OF AT LEAST $25,000.

7. Which of the following food products have you eaten within the past 5 days? READ FULL LIST.

	Yes	No
Frozen pizzas	[ ]	[ ]
Prepackaged cold cuts	[ ]	[ ]
Pre-sliced packaged cheeses	[ ]	[ ]
Canned soup	[ ]	[ ]
Potato chips	[ ]	[ ]
Canned fruit	[ ]	[ ]
Peanut butter	[ ]	[ ]
Frozen vegetables	[ ]	[ ]

RECRUITER: Q7. RESPONDENT MUST SAY "YES" TO <u>CANNED SOUP</u>; OTHERWISE TERMINATE.

FIGURE 16.3 Screener Questionnaire for Recruiting Respondents for a Consumer Study

8. **FOR SOUP AND ANY ONE OTHER FOOD ITEMS ANSWERED "YES" ("EATEN") IN Q7, ASK:**
   a. During the course of one week how often do you eat _____?
      Number of time_____
   b. During the course of one week how often do you have soup____?
      Number of time_____

RECRUITER: Q8b. MUST SAY "AT LEAST TWO TIMES," OTHERWISE TERMINATE.

9. Now, I would like you to use your imagination. If you could serve dinner to a famous person from the past, who would it be? What would you serve for dinner?

RECRUITER: Q9 IS AN ARTICULATION QUESTION. THE RESPONDENTS SHOULD SHOW "CREATIVITY/GOOD IMAGINATION," AND BE ABLE TO ADD TO THE GROUP DISCUSSION.

10. As part of our current research we are conducting a discussion with 8 to 10 individuals. The discussion is called a "focus group." During the interview, you will have an opportunity to express your views and interact with the other participants on a variety of lifestyle and food consumption topics.

    The focus group will last for a full **2 hours.** You will receive $100.00 to help defray the cost of your time and travel.

    We would like to invite you to participate in the focus group session. It should prove to be an interesting and enjoyable session. The focus group will be held at (NAME OF FACILITY), which is located at (GIVE ADDRESS). It will take place on (DATE) at (GIVE CHOICE OF TIME). Can we count on having you attend?

    Yes . . . .[ ]-RECORD PARTICIPANT INFORMATION.
    REPEAT DAY, DATE, TIME, AND GIVE
    DIRECTIONS TO LOCATION.

    No . . . .[ ]-TERMINATE

THANK YOU FOR AGREEING TO PARTICIPATE, WE WILL CALL YOU THE DAY BEFORE THE RESEARCH TO REMIND YOU.

Record: A **female** participant, recruited for the 6:00 PM focus group   _____
          A **male** participant, recruited for the 8:00 PM focus group   _____

FIGURE 16.3 *(Continued)*

Some moderator-researchers prefer to closely follow (question by question) the order set out in a discussion guide; other moderator-researchers "go with the flow" and allow the single respondent or focus group participants to go in the direction of what turns out to be particularly important to them. Surprisingly, a good researcher, following either the "question-by-question" or "go-with-the-flow" approach, will tend to finish with more information than was originally anticipated by the client. Indeed, it is common for qualitative research to produce strategically important insights that were not anticipated or even sought before the actual qualitative research was conducted. Such "extra" insights are a special benefit of both depth interviews and focus groups: namely, that they can provide extremely valuable and unanticipated information. Figure 16.4 shows a discussion guide created for a focus group used in a study of creating the new line of premium vegetable soups. Whereas the screener questionnaire was designed to recruit a sample of the target consumer participants for the focus group sessions on the proposed premium line of vegetable soups, the discussion guide was created to help the moderator lead the discussion and manage the flow of the key themes or "lines of questioning."

It is extremely rare for a moderator-researcher to conduct depth interviews or focus group sessions without the aid of a discussion guide. A discussion guide is a kind of "agenda" of topics and issues to be covered over the course of each depth interview or focus group session. However, qualitative research is much like jazz music: The expertise lies in the ability to improvise depending on the circumstance of the interview or the makeup of the group session.

Projective Techniques

When it comes to tapping into the underlying motives of individuals, **projective techniques** are a useful tool, borrowed from psychoanalytic theory and practice and adapted for studying the unconscious associations of consumers who may be concealing or suppressing some of their thoughts or reactions. Thus, projective exercises consist of a variety of disguised "tests" that contain ambiguous stimuli, such as incomplete sentences, untitled pictures or cartoons, word-association tests, and other-person characterizations. They are all designed to make it easier for consumers to express themselves and reveal their inner motivations. Projective techniques are sometimes administered as part of focus group research, but more often are used during depth interviews. Some of the most commonly used projective methods are featured in Table 16.1.

FOCUS GROUP:
CREATING A SUPERIOR LINE OF VEGETABLE SOUPS
Discussion Guide

I. INTRODUCTION

A. Introduce myself and my role
B. Tell participants about their roles
C. Identify session video-sound recording system and one-way mirror
D. Have each participant introduce him/herself—briefly talking about work, about household composition and interests/hobbies
E. Describe the "basic" purpose of the focus group discussion—TO CREATE A LINE OF SUPERIOR VEGETABLE SOUPS

II. SOUP BACKGROUND: *EARLIEST MEMORIES*

A. As you were growing up, what were your early memories of eating soup? Anything else?
B. In particular, what do you think of vegetable soup? In the "world of soup," where does "vegetable soup" fit in comparison to other soups? What do you think?
C. When you think of a "line of vegetable soups," what comes to mind? Are there six or more different vegetable soups?
D. Right now, what is your favorite vegetable soup?
E. Over the years, has your favorite vegetable soup been changing? In what ways?
F. How has your favorite vegetable changed from childhood to adulthood? Any other changes?
G. How would you characterize the difference between a really good restaurant vegetable soup, and a "homemade" vegetable soup? Which do you prefer? Why?

III. SOUP CONSUMPTION CIRCUMSTANCES

A. For you, is vegetable soup "a meal" or is it "a part of a meal"? Why is it this way for you?
B. What is the difference between vegetable soup as a "meal" and as "part of meal"? Anything else?
C. Is there such a person as a "soup person"? Describe such a person. Give me a profile of a "soup person." How do "soup people" tend to differ from non-soup people? Any other thoughts?

IV. SOUP SELECTION AND DECISION MAKING

A. In your household, how is the decision made as to which brand of soup is purchased and eaten? (Probe for various aspects of family choice and influence.)
B. Is there a single brand of soup that your family all agrees on? Which brand? Why?
C. How do you approach the selection of soup? Would you consider yourself to be: A specialist? An experimenter? A habitual purchaser?
D. What is your idea of a "soup connoisseur"? Describe such a person. Tell me more.
E. When it comes to food store soups, which is your favorite? Why?
F. In your mind's eye, what is a perfect vegetable soup?

V. SOUP TASTING EXERCISE
INTRODUCTION: "WE HAVE FIVE DIFFERENT VEGETABLE SOUPS FOR EACH OF YOU TO TRY, TONIGHT."

AFTER TRYING EACH ONE, I WANT YOU TO WRITE ON YOUR PADS YOUR THOUGHTS ABOUT THE PARTICULAR VEGETABLE SOUP.

A. What is your reaction to the *first* (repeat for each) vegetable soup that I gave you to try? Any other thoughts or feelings?
B. How would you describe it to a person who has not tasted it?
C. If this soup was available in a retail store, would you buy it? Why/Why not?
D. Any ideas as to how to make the soup taste even better?
E. **REPEAT FOR THE NEXT VEGETABLE SOUP, UNTIL EACH OF THE FIVE ARE SAMPLED.**
F. **[WRITE ON YOUR PAD]** Which of the five soups did you like the best? Which soup did you like the least? Again, write your answers down on your pad.
G. **[AROUND THE ROOM]** So, which one was the best?
H. Let's reflect on your reactions to the five soups.
I. **[WRITE ON YOUR PAD]** Considering the five vegetable soups, are there any other distinctive vegetables that need to be featured to make the overall selection better?

VI. ANY FINAL FEELINGS/THOUGHTS

A. Any final ideals or thoughts about the line of premium vegetable soups?
B. What would make it better? Anything else?
C. Where would you expect to purchase such a line of vegetable soups?

FIGURE 16.4 Focus Group Discussion Guide

Online Focus Groups

Over the past 5 to 10 years, there has been a substantial amount of interest in, trial of, and acceptance of online focus groups and depth interviews. However, what is being called an "online focus group" can vary greatly. On the one hand, they can be very similar in nature and quality to a traditional focus group (i.e., sessions held in a local focus group facility, with moderator and participants interacting

TABLE 16.1	Projective Techniques	
	DESCRIPTION	APPLICATIONS
Word Associations	The researcher has a list of words, some of them to be studied and some just as "filler." The researcher asks the respondent(s) to react, one-at-a-time, to each word by stating or (in a focus group setting) writing on a pad the first word that comes to mind, and to explain the link.	The word association exercise tends to be used when marketers seek to know what certain words (or a phrase) mean to consumers. The exercise is used to determine if a word or words have a sufficiently positive meaning or relevance to a product, or even a proposed product's name or description.
Sentence Completions	The researcher has a series of incomplete sentences that the respondent(s) needs to complete with a word or phrase.	The sentence completion exercise is an alternative to the word association exercise (it is used for the same purpose). In reality, it is easier to use and generally provides for more useable consumer insights than the word association exercise.
Photo/Visual for Storytelling	The researcher creates/selects a series of photos of consumers, different brands or products, range of print ads, etc., to serve as stimuli. The respondents are asked to discuss or tell a story based on their response to a photo or some other visual stimulus.	The product or consumer ideas secured from responding to the photos/visuals, in the form of "free association" or "storytelling" reveals how the participants feel about a topic, brands, or consumer within the context of the photos or other visual forms (e.g., cartoons). Ideas for new products or communication themes are possible outcomes.
Role-Playing	Is quite similar to storytelling; however, instead of telling a story, the participant(s) will be given a situation and asked to "act out" the role(s), often with regard to a product or brand, or particular selling situation.	Role-playing is appropriate in a focus group environment where different participants can be asked to role play and to act out different interacting roles.

together). In such cases, they are often real focus group sessions that are "broadcasted" to individual client's laptops, or to a "sister" research facility in the client's hometown, and viewed by a gathering of clients. On the other hand, there is the option to select an online specialty research company, such as Harris Interactive, that provides focus group recruiting services from its very large panel of online consumers ready to participate. In addition, Harris Interactive has the capability of offering clients access to a "virtual version" of traditional focus groups. Specifically, it can provide a "virtual focus group room" environment: one where consumer participants and a moderator can log on to participate in an online focus group session. In certain ways, it can be similar to a regular offline focus group session.

The Scope of Quantitative Research

Marketers use quantitative research to understand the acceptance of various products or specific brands, as well as the impact of promotional messages on consumers. In other cases, the objectives are to assist marketers in pinpointing consumers' level of satisfaction with a product, service, distributor, or retailer, or possibly to attempt to identify areas in which the consumer has unmet needs, or even to attempt to better "predict" future consumer needs or behavior. The broad category of quantitative research includes experimentation, survey techniques, and observation. The findings are descriptive and empirical, and, if collected using appropriate sampling, can be generalized to larger populations. Because the data collected are quantitative, they lend themselves to sophisticated statistical analysis. Next, we consider three basic research designs: observational research, experimentation (in a laboratory or in the field, such as in a retail store), and surveys.

Observational Research

Watching or carefully observing consumers' actions of purchasing and consuming, especially in realistic surroundings (e.g., in stores, in malls, watching TV, and even in their home environments), is an extremely insightful way to learn what is valuable or meaningful to consumers. Indeed, **observational research** is an important research tool because marketers recognize that often the best way to gain an in-depth understanding of the relationship between people and products is by watching them in the process of buying and/or using the products.[5] Observing consumers in action enables researchers to comprehend what the product symbolizes to a consumer and provides greater insight into the bond between people and products that is the essence of brand loyalty. It is also important in uncovering issues or problems with a product. Many large corporations and advertising agencies use trained researchers/observers to watch, note, and sometimes videotape consumers in stores, malls, or even (with permission) in their own homes. For example, in studying responses to a new mint-flavored Listerine, the marketers hired a research firm that paid 37 New York City families to let it install cameras in their bathrooms to videotape mouthwash usage. The study found that consumers who used Scope gave the product a swish and spit it out. In contrast, users of the new Listerine kept the mouthwash in their mouths for much longer (one subject even held the mouthwash in his mouth as he left home and got into the car, and only spit it out after driving a couple of blocks).[6] Procter & Gamble (P&G) sent video crews to scores of households around the world, which enabled P&G executives in Cincinnati to watch a mother in Thailand feed her baby. They discovered that the mother was multitasking while feeding her baby and even glanced at her TV from time to time. Understanding such behavior can lead to the development of products and packages that will give P&G a strong competitive advantage in the marketplace.[7]

As an alternative to having trained observers view consumers, some firms prefer to use mechanical or electronic devices, such as counting or video-recording devices to capture customers' behaviors or responses to a particular marketing stimulus. For example, when Duane Reade—a large chain of drugstores in and around New York City—considers a location for a new store, the company uses electronic beams or hand counters to count the numbers of passersby at different times and under different weather conditions.[8] Government planners use data collected from electronic E-ZPass devices in passenger cars to decide which roads should be expanded, and banks use security cameras to observe problems customers may have in using ATMs.

Increasingly, consumers use automated systems in their purchases because these instruments make purchases easier and often provide rewards for using them. For example, consumers who use supermarket frequent shopper cards often receive special offers for promotional discounts tailored for them at checkout counters. Moviegoers who order tickets online can pick them up at ATM-like devices at movie theaters and avoid waiting in line at the box office. As consumers use more and more highly convenient technologies, such as credit and ATM cards, EZ-Passes, frequent shopper cards, cellular phones, and most of all online shopping, there are more and more electronic records of their consumption patterns. Consequently, observation of consumer behavior via electronic means has grown significantly and, as illustrated in the earlier discussion of portable people meters and two-way digital cable boxes, electronic observation of consumption behavior will become increasingly sophisticated.

Gambling casinos have been in the forefront of developing systems that track individual customer data collected during the various stages of a customer's visit, and cross-matching them with data collected during previous visits by that customer (including spending usage). They use this data to classify visitors into categories based on their "loyalty levels," and implement corresponding rewards that are delivered almost immediately. For example, normally about 50,000 people a day visit the Foxwoods Resort Casino in Connecticut. Most of them use magnetic cards called "frequent player cards." Sophisticated electronic network systems monitor the gaming patterns, eating habits, and room preferences of all visitors. Within seconds of a player taking a seat at a table, the casino's manager can read the guest's history on the screen, including alcoholic beverages preferred and gaming habits. Because there are electronic tags in the chips issued to each player, when a player leaves the table, his or her record is updated instantly and made available at any contact point for that customer throughout the entire casino complex. Thus, the casino can instantly reward customers who are good for business by giving free meals and room upgrades and inviting them to gamble in designated VIP lounges. The customers love the frequent player cards because the cards enable them to keep track of their spending, and the casinos benefit from each swipe of the card because it provides more information about each customer. The casino has two identical computer systems and, if needed, can switch to a backup immediately and thus avoid the loss of many thousands of dollars incurred during an even brief period of operating without computers.[9] More casinos are employing increasingly sophisticated software to create real-time and personal rewards to day-trippers who bet relatively small amounts of money—$50 to $100 per visit—but visit the casinos frequently. Casinos have recognized that although these consumers wager little money per trip, they view gaming as their primary entertainment, and observing their behavior and immediately using the data to encourage them to spend more money is likely to increase profits greatly over time.[10]

Another form of mechanical observation that entails monitoring the sales of products. A key component of Walmart's competitive advantage is the retailing giant's use of technology in its product audits. At any given moment, the company knows what is selling, how fast, and how much of the product remains in its inventory. Maintaining small inventories and moving products quickly enable the company to lower its prices and attract more customers. Walmart's record profits are derived from low per-item profits multiplied by selling billions of products quickly, and also moving products rapidly to where consumers are likely to buy them. For example, after observing that the sales of strawberry Pop-Tarts increased dramatically before a hurricane and that the top preseller before a hurricane was beer, the company quickly transports large quantities of these items to the locations a storm is set to hit.[11]

Marketers also use **physiological observation** devices that monitor respondents' patterns of information processing. For example, an electronic eye camera may be used to monitor the eye movements of subjects looking at a series of advertisements for various products, and electronic sensors placed on the subjects' heads can monitor their brain activity and attentiveness levels involved in viewing each advertisement. Neuroscientists monitoring cognitive functions in 12 different regions of the brain while consumers watched commercials for different products claimed that the data collected show the respondents' levels of attention and the decoding and recall of the promotional messages.[12]

Experimentation

Experiments (causal research) identify cause-and-effect relationships among factors. For instance, it is possible to test the relative sales appeal of many types of variables, such as package designs, alternative price points, or different promotional offers, by experiments designed to identify cause and effect. In the simplest form of such experiments, only one variable is manipulated (called the *independent variable*), while all other elements are kept constant. A **controlled experiment** ensures that any difference in the outcome (the *dependent variable*, which is most often sales) is due to different treatments of the variable under study and not to extraneous factors. For example, one study tested the effectiveness of using an attractive versus unattractive endorser in promoting two types of products: products that are used to enhance one's attractiveness (e.g., a men's cologne) and products that are not (e.g., a pen). The endorser used was a fictitious character named Phil Johnson who was described as a member of the U.S. Olympic water polo team. The photograph depicting the attractive endorser was a scanned image of an attractive athletic man, whereas the picture depicting the unattractive endorser was the same image graphically modified to reduce attractiveness. The subjects viewed each endorser-product combination for 15 seconds (simulating the viewing of an actual print ad) and then filled out a questionnaire that measured their attitudes and purchase intentions toward the products advertised. In this study, the combinations of the product (i.e., used/not used to enhance one's attractiveness) and the endorser's attractiveness (i.e., attractive or not attractive endorser) were the "manipulated treatments" (i.e., the independent variables), and the combination of the attitudes and purchase intentions toward the product was the dependent variable. The study discovered that the attractive endorser was more effective in promoting both types of products.[13]

A major application of causal research is **test marketing**. Sometimes, even after conducting depth interviews, focus groups, and survey research, the marketing firm realizes that it still needs to secure additional real-world feedback for a new product, service, or marketing communications program that it is considering, before it commits itself to a full-scale marketing rollout. In such situations, test marketing is a logical next step. Test marketing typically includes the selection of a representative single market area and then the conduct of a market introduction (only in that market) to test actual consumer response to the marketing effort under actual marketing conditions. From the test-marketing effort, the marketing firm hopes to be able to project how the entire market may respond to its marketing effort, without the full risks associated with skipping a test-marketing stage. Still further, some research firms carry out small-scale experiments that test consumer responses to alternative marketing strategies. This can be done prior to selecting a new product, redesigning a package, changing the price of a product, or trying out a new marketing campaign—all of these are marketing actions that can benefit from small-scale experimentation that manipulates variables in a controlled setting in order to predict sales or gauge the possible responses to the product.

Unlike a test market, which is usually in the real world, many experiments are conducted in a lab environment. Today some researchers employ "virtual reality methods." For example, in a market test, respondents can view, on a computer screen, supermarket shelves that are stocked with many products, including different versions of the same product; they can "pick up" an item by touching the image, examine it by rotating the image with a track ball, and place it in a shopping cart if they decide to buy it. The researchers observe how long the respondents spend in looking at the product, the time spent in examining each side of the package, the products purchased, and the order of the purchases. In general terms, it is quite important for marketers to continuously experiment and test-market their products and services.[14]

Survey Research

If researchers wish to ask consumers about their purchase preferences and consumption experiences, they can do so in person, by mail, by telephone, or online. Each of these survey methods has certain advantages and certain disadvantages that the researcher must weigh when selecting the method of contact.

Personal interview surveys (that are face-to-face) most often take place in a public space or a retail shopping area, such as within the public area of a mall, or a rented space within an office located in a mall. The latter, referred to as "mall intercepts," are used more frequently, as a replacement for

TABLE 16.2	The Advantages and Disadvantages of Mail, Telephone, Personal Interview, and Online Surveys			
	MAIL	TELEPHONE	PERSONAL INTERVIEW	ONLINE
Cost	Low	Moderate	High	Low
Speed	Slow	Immediate	Slow	Fast
Response Rate	Low	Moderate	High	Self-selected
Geographic Flexibility	Excellent	Good	Difficult	Excellent
Interviewer Bias	N/A	Moderate	Problematic	N/A
Interviewer Supervision	N/A	Easy	Difficult	N/A

the in-home interviews that used to be commonplace, because of the high incidence of not-at-home working women and the reluctance of many people today to allow a stranger into their homes.

Telephone interview surveys are also used to collect consumer data; however, evenings and weekends are often the only times to reach telephone respondents, who tend to be less responsive—if not actively hostile—to calls that interrupt dinner, television viewing, or general relaxation. Other problems arise, however, from the increased use of answering machines, telephone company voice-mail systems, and caller ID to screen calls. Some market research companies have tried to automate telephone surveys, but many respondents are even less willing to interact with an electronic voice than with a live interviewer. Table 16.2 compares the survey contact methods.

Mail surveys are conducted by sending questionnaires directly to individuals at their homes. One of the major problems of mail questionnaires is a low response rate, but researchers have developed a number of techniques to increase returns, such as enclosing a stamped, self-addressed envelope, using a provocative questionnaire, and sending notifications in advance as well as follow-up letters. Also, to deal with the ongoing problems of low response rates to unsolicited mail surveys, some consumer marketing companies are establishing their own ongoing consumer panels and periodically mail or email a questionnaire to consumer panel participants to fill out. As a motivation to complete the task, and ensure a satisfactory response rate, it is commonplace to pay respondents a prearranged participation fee for each round of completed surveys. Sometimes panel members are also asked to keep diaries of their purchases.[15]

Email surveys are an increasingly popular alternative to using the postal service as a means of distributing questionnaires to target consumers. One of the key attractions of using email is that it is as easy and quick to distribute a survey around the world as it is to distribute it down the block. Moreover, with an accurate list of email addresses, it is very inexpensive to distribute even a large number of questionnaires. We can expect that as the world increasingly turns to the Web for many types of social communications, we will see continued growth of emailing as a way to distribute surveys.[16]

Furthermore, there has been a rapid increase in the number of consumers who are interested in participating in **Internet surveys**. Potential respondents are directed to the marketer's (or researcher company's) website by online ads or targeted email invitations. Often, responses to online surveys are from consumer respondents who are self-selected, and therefore the results cannot be projected to the larger population. Most computer polls ask respondents to complete a profile consisting of demographic questions that enable the researchers to classify the responses to the substantive product or service questions.

Quantitative Research Data Collection Instruments

Data collection instruments are developed as part of a study's total research design to systematize the collection of data and to ensure that all respondents are asked the same questions in the same order. Data collection instruments include questionnaires, personal inventories, and attitude scales. These instruments are usually pretested and "debugged" to assure the validity and reliability of the research study. A study is said to have **validity** if it does, in fact, collect appropriate data needed to answer the questions or objectives stated in the first (objectives) stage of the research process. A study is said to have **reliability** if the same questions, asked of a similar sample, produce the same findings. Often a sample is systematically divided in two, and each half is given the same questionnaire to complete. If the results from each half are similar, the questionnaire is said to be reliable.

TABLE 16.3   Guidelines for Wording Questions

1. *Avoid leading questions.* For example, questions such as "Do you often shop at such cost-saving stores as Staples?" or "Weren't you satisfied with the service you received at Staples today?" introduce bias into the survey.

2. *Avoid two questions in one.* For example, "In your view, did you save money and receive good service when you last visited Staples?" is really two questions combined; they should be stated separately.

3. *Questions must be clear.* For example, "Where do you usually shop for your home office supplies?" is unclear because the term usually is vague.

4. *Use words that consumers routinely use.* For example, do not use the verb to rectify; use the verb to correct.

5. *Ensure that respondents are able to answer the question.* For example, it is unlikely that any respondent can accurately answer a question such as "How many newspaper or TV ads for Staples did you read or see during the past month?"

6. *Make sure that respondents are willing to answer the question.* Questions about money, health issues, personal hygiene, or sexual preferences can embarrass respondents and cause them not to answer. Sometimes asking the question in a less personal fashion can help generate more responses. For example, rather than asking older consumers whether they experience incontinence, the researcher should ask, "Millions of Americans experience some level of incontinence. Do you or anyone you know experience this difficulty?"

Questionnaires

For quantitative research, the primary data collection instrument is the questionnaire, which can be sent through the mail or online to selected respondents for self-administration or can be administered by field interviewers in person or by telephone. To motivate respondents to take the time to respond to surveys, researchers have found that questionnaires must be interesting, objective, unambiguous, easy to complete, and generally not burdensome. To enhance the analysis and facilitate the classification of responses into meaningful categories, questionnaires include both substantive questions that are relevant to the purposes of the study and pertinent demographic questions. Questionnaires consist of two types of questions:

1. **Open-ended questions** require answers in the respondent's own words (e.g., essay type questions).
2. **Closed-ended questions** require respondents to check the appropriate answer from a list of options (e.g., multiple-choice and true or false questions).

Open-ended questions yield more insightful information but are more difficult to code and to analyze; closed-ended questions are relatively simple to tabulate and analyze, but the answers are limited to the alternative responses provided (i.e., to the existing insights of the questionnaire designer).

Wording of the questions represents the biggest challenge in constructing questionnaires; Table 16.3 includes guidelines for writing clear and effective questions. The sequence of questions is also important: The opening questions must be interesting enough to "draw" the respondent into participating; the questions must proceed in a logical order; and demographic (classification) questions should be placed at the end, where they are more likely to be answered. The format of the questionnaire and the wording and sequence of the questions affect the validity of the responses and, in the case of mail questionnaires, the number (rate) of responses received.

There are many types of questionnaires that are commonly used in carrying out consumer research studies. In the real world of consumer research, one form of consumer survey is a **magazine readership survey**, like the one for *EARTH* (a fictitious magazine) that is presented in Figure 16.5. Such surveys are conducted to provide the publisher, editors, and circulation directors with reader feedback, as well as to provide the marketing and sales staff with information that would enable them to create a more convincing marketing package for selling adverting pages to potential advertisers and their advertising agencies. In particular, a standard use of the data secured from magazine readership surveys is preparation of a profile of a publication's readers so that potential advertisers can determine whether the publication delivers the audience that is most likely to respond positively to their advertising.

Attitude Scales

Researchers often present respondents with a list of products or product attributes, toward which they are asked to indicate their relative feelings or evaluations. The instruments most frequently used to capture this evaluative data are called **attitude scales**. The most frequently used attitude scales are Likert scales, semantic differential scales, behavior intention scales, and rank-order scales.

The **Likert scale** is the most popular form of attitude scale because it is easy for researchers to prepare and to interpret, and simple for consumers to answer. They check or write the number corresponding to their level of "agreement" or "disagreement" with a series of statements, each referring

EARTH Magazine: IPSOS MENDELSOHN READERSHIP SURVEY

ABOUT YOU AND *EARTH MAGAZINE*

1. Where did you purchase this issue of *EARTH Magazine?*
   Local newsstand ....☐1
   Airport terminal newsstand ....☐2
   Bookstore (e.g., Borders, Barnes & Noble) ....☐3
   Other ....☐4

2. Why did you buy this issue of *EARTH Magazine? (Please 'X' all that apply.)*
   Intrigued by headlines on cover wrap ....☐1
   Attracted by the cover art ....☐2
   Curious about a specific article ....☐3

   Heard about issue through:
   Word-of-mouth ....☐4
   Print medium ....☐5
   Broadcast medium ....☐6
   Internet ....☐7

   For a regular feature:
   Index ....☐1
   Notebook ....☐2
   Readings ....☐3
   Puzzle ....☐4
   Findings..........☐5
   Annotation ....☐6
   Reviews ....☐7
   Forum ....☐8

   For a regular feature (Cont'd):
   Photo essay ....☐1
   Fiction ....☐2
   Political reporting.........☐3
   Overseas reporting ....☐4
   Narrative non-fiction ......☐5
   Personal essays ....☐6

3. How many issues of *EARTH Magazine* did you buy on the newsstand/bookstore in the last 12 months?
   1 issue ....☐1
   2–3 issues ....☐2
   4–5 issues ....☐3
   6–7 issues ....☐4
   8–9 issues ....☐5
   10–11 issues ....☐6
   12 issues ....☐7
   None ....☐8

4. How long have you been a reader of *EARTH Magazine?*
   Less than 6 months ....☐1
   7–12 months ....☐2
   1 to under 2 years ....☐3
   2 years or more ....☐4

5. How many of the last 4 issues of *EARTH Magazine* have you read or looked into?
   4 out of the last 4 ....☐1
   3 out of the last 4 ....☐2
   2 out of the last 4 ....☐3
   1 out of the last 4 ....☐4
   None out of the last 4 ....☐5

6. On average, how much time do you spend reading or looking into a typical issue of *EARTH Magazine?*
   Less than 1 hour ....☐1
   1 hour to less than 2 hours ....☐2
   2 hours to less than 3 hours ....☐3
   3 hours to less than 4 hours ....☐4
   4 hours or more ....☐5

7. Have you ever made a purchase as a result of advertising you saw in *EARTH Magazine?*
   Yes ....☐1
   No ....☐2

8. How do you rate *EARTH Magazine* overall compared to other publications you read?
   One of my favorites ....☐1
   Very good ....☐2
   Good ....☐3
   Average ....☐4
   Poor ....☐5

EARTH MAGAZINE WEBSITE

1. Have you visited the *EARTH Magazine* website in the past 12 months?
   Yes ....☐1
   No ....☐2 → *Please go to Question 4*

2. How often do you visit the *EARTH Magazine* website?
   Once a month ....☐1
   Less than once a week ....☐2
   Once a week ....☐3
   2–3 times a week ....☐4
   4–5 times a week....................☐5
   More than 5 times a week ....☐6

3. On average, how much time do you spend on the *EARTH Magazine* website per visit?
   Less than 5 minutes ....☐1
   5–9 minutes ....☐2
   10–19 minutes ....☐3
   20–29 minutes ....☐4
   30–59 minutes.....................☐5
   One hour or more...................☐6

4. Would you be willing to pay for archived issues of *EARTH Magazine* going back to 1950 if they were available on the *EARTH Magazine* website?
   Yes. ....☐1
   No ....☐2→*Please go to "About You" section below*

5. *(If yes)* How much would you be willing to pay per year for archived issues of *EARTH Magazine?*
   $1–$9 ....☐1
   $10–$19 ....☐2
   $20–$29 ....☐3
   $30–$39 ....☐4
   $40–$49 ....☐5
   $50 or more....................☐6

FIGURE 16.5 Magazine Readership Survey

Source: EARTH Magazine Readership Survey (New York, Ipsos Mendelsohn, 2008).

ABOUT YOU

1. Are you: a man ...... □1   a woman ...... □2
2. Please 'X' your age group.
   Under 21 .... □1   35 to 44 .... □3   55 to 64 .... □5
   21 to 34 .... □2   45 to 54 .... □4   65 or older .... □6

3. Are you . . .
   Married .... □1   Single .... □3   Separated .... □5
   Partnered .... □2   Widowed .... □4   Divorced .... □6

4. Please 'X' the highest level of education you have attained.
   Some high school or less .... □1   Some college .... □3   Postgraduate study .... □5
   High school graduate .... □2   College degree .... □4   Postgraduate degree .... □6

5. Please indicate your employment status.
   Employed full time (35 hrs or more per week) .... □1   Not currently employed .... □3   ⎤ Please skip
   Employed part time (less than 35 hrs per week) ...... □2   Retired .... □4   ⎦ to Question 6
   What is your job title, position, or rank?
   (Please be specific: e.g., partner, CEO, president, vice president, etc.) _____

   What do you do for a living? (Please be specific: e.g., accountant, bookkeeper, lawyer, architect, etc.) _____

6. What was your total estimated household income, before taxes, for last year? (Please include income for all household members and from all sources, including salaries or wages, profits, capital gains, rentals, social security, etc.)

Less than $50,000 .... □1	$500,000 to $749,999 ...... □1	$2,500,000 to $2,999,999 .... □1
$50,000 to $99,999 .... □2	$750,000 to $999,999 ...... □2	$3,000,000 to $3,999,999 .... □2
$100,000 to $199,999 .... □3	$1,000,000 to $1,499,999 .... □3	$4,000,000 to $4,999,999 .... □3
$200,000 to $299,999 .... □4	$1,500,000 to $1,999,999 .... □4	$5,000,000 or more .... □4
$300,000 to $499,999 .... □5	$2,000,000 to $2,499,999 .... □5	

Please join us! The *EARTH Magazine* **Reader Advisory Panel** is an exclusive panel made up of *EARTH Magazine* readers. Through future surveys, your perspective on consumer trends — from tech innovations, culture, and travel — will have a direct impact on what you see and read in the pages of *EARTH Magazine*. If you would like to join our Reader Advisory Panel, please <u>print</u> your e-mail address below:

Your e-mail address:_____@_____

THANK YOU VERY MUCH

Please mail the completed survey in the reply envelope *(no postage necessary).*

FIGURE 16.5 *(Continued)*

to the object under investigation. The scale consists of an equal number of agreement/disagreement choices on either side of a neutral choice. A principal benefit of the Likert scale is that it gives the researcher the option of considering the responses to each statement separately or of combining the responses to produce an overall score.

The **semantic differential scale**, like the Likert scale, is relatively easy to construct and administer. The scale typically consists of a series of bipolar adjectives (such as "good/bad," "hot/cold," "like/dislike," or "expensive/inexpensive") anchored at the ends of an odd-numbered (e.g., five- or seven-point) continuum. Respondents are asked to evaluate a concept (or a product or company) on the basis of each attribute by checking the point on the continuum that best reflects their feelings or beliefs. Care must be taken to vary the location of positive and negative terms from the left side of the continuum to the right side to avoid consumer response bias. Sometimes an even-numbered scale is used to eliminate the option of a neutral answer. An important feature of the semantic differential scale is that it can be used to develop graphic consumer profiles of the concept under study. Semantic differential profiles are also used to compare consumer perceptions of competitive products and to indicate areas for product improvement when perceptions of the existing product are measured against perceptions of the "ideal" product.

The **behavior intention scale** measures the likelihood that consumers will act in a certain way in the future, such as buying the product again or recommending it to a friend. These scales are easy to construct, and consumers are asked to make subjective judgments regarding their future behavior.

With **rank-order scales**, subjects are asked to rank items such as products (or retail stores or websites) in order of preference in terms of some criterion, such as overall quality or value for the money. Rank-order scaling procedures provide important competitive information and enable marketers to identify areas where improvement is needed in product design and product positioning. Figure 16.6 provides examples of the attitude scales described.

Customer Satisfaction Measurement

Gauging the level of customer satisfaction and its determinants is critical for every company. Marketers can use such data to retain customers, sell more products and services, improve the quality and value

---

LIKERT SCALE

Next to each of the following statements, please record the number that best describes the extent to which you agree or disagree with each statement.

1. Strongly Agree	2. Somewhat Agree	3. Neither Agree nor Disagree	4. Somewhat Disagree	5. Strongly Disagree

_____ It's fun to shop online.
_____ I am afraid to give my credit card number online.

CUSTOMER SATISFACTION GUIDE

Overall, how satisfied are you with Bank X's online banking? _____

1. Very Satisfied	2. Somewhat Satisfied	3. Neither Satisfied nor Dissatisfied	4. Somewhat Dissatisfied	5. Very Dissatisfied

IMPORTANCE SCALE

The following list of features is associated with shopping on the Internet. Next to each feature, please record the number that best expresses how important or unimportant that feature is to you.

1. Extremely Important	2. Somewhat Important	3. Neither Important nor Unimportant	4. Somewhat Unimportant	5. Not at all Important

_____ Speed of downloading the order form
_____ Being able to register with the site

SEMANTIC DIFFERENTIAL SCALE

For each of the following features, please check one alternative that best expresses your impression of how that feature applies to online banking:

Competitive rates ├──┼──┼──┼──┼──┤ Noncompetitive rates
Reliable ├──┼──┼──┼──┼──┤ Unreliable

Note: The same semantic differential scale can be applied to two competitive offerings, such as online banking and regular banking, and a graphic representation of the profiles of the two alternatives, along with the bipolar adjectives included in the scale, can be easily constructed.

BEHAVIOR INTENTION SCALES

How likely are you to continue using Bank X's online banking for the next six months? _____

1. Definitely Will Continue	2. Probably Will Continue	3. Might or Might Not Continue	4. Probably Will Not Continue	5. Definitely Will Not Continue

How likely are you to recommend Bank X's online banking to a friend? _____

1. Definitely Will Recommend	2. Probably Will Recommend	3. Might or Might Not Recommend	4. Probably Will Not Recommend	5. Definitely Will Not Recommend

RANK-ORDER SCALE

We would like to find out about your preferences regarding banking methods. Please rank the following banking methods by placing a "1" in front of the method that you prefer most, a "2" next to your second preference, and continuing until you have ranked all of the methods.

_____ Inside the bank   _____ Online banking   _____ Banking by telephone
_____ ATM   _____ Banking by mail

FIGURE 16.6 Attitude Scales

of their offerings, and operate more effectively and efficiently. **Customer satisfaction measurement** includes quantitative and qualitative measures, as well as a variety of contact methods with customers.

Customer satisfaction surveys measure how satisfied the customers are with relevant attributes of the product or service, and the relative importance of these attributes (using an importance scale). Generally, these surveys use five-point semantic differential scales, ranging from "very dissatisfied" to "very satisfied." Research shows that customers who indicate they are "very satisfied" (typically a score of 5 on the satisfaction scale) are much more profitable and loyal than customers who indicate that they are "satisfied" (a score of 4). Therefore, companies that merely strive to have "satisfied" customers are making a crucial error.[17] Some marketers maintain that customers' satisfaction or dissatisfaction is a function of the difference between what they had *expected* to get from the product or service purchased and their perceptions of what they *received*. A group of researchers developed a scale that measures the performance of the service received against two expectation levels: *adequate* service and *desired* service, and also measures the customers' future intentions regarding purchase of the service.[18] This approach is more sophisticated than standard customer satisfaction surveys and more likely to yield results that can be used to develop corrective measures for products and services that fall short of customers' expectations.

Mystery shoppers are professional observers who pose as customers and interact with and provide unbiased evaluations of the company's service personnel in order to identify opportunities for improving productivity and efficiency. For example, one bank used mystery shoppers who, while dealing with a bank employee on another matter, dropped hints about buying a house or seeking to borrow college funds. Employees were scored on how quickly and effectively they provided information about the bank's pertinent products or services. A company that requires sales clerks to check youthful customers' IDs when they seek to buy video games with violent content may employ mystery shoppers to see whether their employees are actually doing so.

Analyzing customer complaints is crucial for improving products and customer service. Research indicates that only a few unsatisfied customers actually complain. Most unsatisfied customers say nothing but switch to competitors. A good **complaint analysis** system should encourage customers to:

1. Complain about an unsatisfactory product or service.

2. Provide suggestions for improvements by completing forms asking specific questions beyond the routine "how was everything?"

3. Establish "listening posts" such as hotlines where specially designated employees either listen to customers' comments or actively solicit input from them (e.g., in a hotel lobby or on checkout lines).

Because each complaint, by itself, provides little information, the company must have a system in which complaints are categorized and analyzed so that the results may be used to improve its operations.

Analyzing customer defections consists of finding out why customers leave the company. Customer loyalty rates are important because it is generally much cheaper to retain customers than to get new ones. Therefore, finding out why customers defect, and intervening when customers' behaviors show that they may be considering leaving, is crucial. For example, one bank that was losing about 20% of its customers every year compared 500 transaction records of loyal customers with 500 transaction records of defectors, using such dimensions as number of transactions, frequency of transactions, and fluctuations in average balances. The bank then identified transaction patterns that tended to indicate future defection and started targeting potential defectors and encouraging them to stay.[19]

Sampling and Data Collection

Because it is almost always impossible to obtain information from *every* member of the population or universe being studied, researchers use samples. A **sample** is a subset of the population that is used to estimate the characteristics of the entire population. Therefore, the sample must be representative of the universe under study. As the well-established Nielsen Media Research company recently found out, suspicions that a sample may not be representative of its universe endanger the credibility of all the data collected, and therefore must be addressed promptly. Although Nielsen's TV ratings have been used to estimate TV audiences and calculate advertising rates for many decades, its clients recently charged that the Nielsen sample was no longer representative of the U.S. population, because it did not reflect accurately America's changing demographics and the large numbers of consumers who use devices such as TiVo to "time shift" and to avoid commercials during both live and recorded programs. In response to these criticisms, Nielsen redesigned its sample to include significantly more ethnic groupings and to reflect the changes in TV viewing habits.[20]

An integral component of a research design is the **sampling plan**. Specifically, the sampling plan addresses three questions: whom to survey (the sampling unit), how many to survey (the sample size), and how to select them (the sampling procedure). Deciding whom to survey requires explicit definition of the universe or boundaries of the market from which data are sought, so that an appropriate

TABLE 16.4	Types of Samples
PROBABILITY SAMPLE	
Simple Random Sample	Every member of the population has a known and equal chance of being selected.
Systematic Random Sample	A member of the population is selected at random and then every *n*th person is selected.
Stratified Random Sample	The population is divided into mutually exclusive groups (such as age groups), and random samples are drawn from each group.
Cluster (Area) Sample	The population is divided into mutually exclusive groups (such as blocks), and the researcher draws a sample of the groups to interview.
NONPROBABILITY SAMPLE	
Convenience Sample	The researcher selects the most accessible population members from whom to obtain information (e.g., students in a classroom).
Judgment Sample	The researcher uses his or her judgment to select population members who are good sources of accurate information (e.g., experts in the relevant field of study).
Quota Sample	The researcher interviews a prescribed number of people in each of several categories (e.g., 50 men and 50 women).

sample can be selected (such as working mothers). The size of the sample is dependent on both the size of the budget and the degree of confidence that the marketer wants to place in the findings. The larger the sample, the more likely the responses will reflect the total universe under study. It is interesting to note, however, that a small sample can often provide highly reliable findings, depending on the sampling procedure adopted.

There are two types of samples. In a **probability sample**, respondents are selected in such a way that every member of the population studied has a known, nonzero chance of being selected. In a **nonprobability sample**, the population under study has been predetermined in a nonrandom fashion on the basis of the researcher's judgment or decision to select a given number of respondents from a particular group. Table 16.4 summarizes the features of various types of probability and nonprobability designs.

Data Collection

The step following sample selection is data collection. As indicated earlier, qualitative studies usually require highly trained social scientists to collect data. A quantitative study generally uses a field staff that is either recruited and trained directly by the researcher or contracted from a company that specializes in conducting field interviews. Completed questionnaires are reviewed on a regular basis as the research study progresses to ensure that the recorded responses are clear, complete, and legible.

Combining Qualitative and Quantitative Research

Learning Objective

4 To understand how to combine qualitative and quantitative research.

Researchers adapt the research processes to the special needs of the study. For example, if a researcher is told that the purpose of the study is to develop a segmentation strategy for a new online dating service, he or she would first collect secondary data, such as population statistics (e.g., the number of men and women online in selected metropolitan areas within a certain age range, their marital status, and occupations). Then, together with the marketing manager, the researcher would specify the parameters (i.e., define the sampling unit) of the population to be studied (e.g., single, college-educated men and women between the ages of 18 and 45 who live or work within the Boston metropolitan area). A qualitative study (e.g., focus groups) might be undertaken first to gather information about the target population's attitudes and concerns about meeting people online, their special interests, and the specific services and precautions they would like an online dating service to provide. This phase of the research should result in tentative generalizations about the specific age group(s) to target and the services to offer.

The marketing manager then might instruct the researcher to conduct a quantitative study to confirm and attach "hard" numbers (percentages) to the findings that emerged from the focus groups. The first-phase study should have provided sufficient insights to develop a research design and to launch directly into a large-scale survey. If, however, there is still doubt about any element of the research design, such as question wording or format, the marketing manager and the researcher might decide first to do a small-scale exploratory study. Then, after refining the questionnaire and any other needed elements of the research design, they would launch a full-scale quantitative survey, using a probability sample that would allow them to project the findings to the total population of singles (as originally defined). The analysis should cluster prospective consumers of the online dating service into segments based on relevant sociocultural or lifestyle characteristics and on media habits, attitudes, perceptions, and geodemographic characteristics.

Marketers frequently conduct research projects that include qualitative and a quantitative components. For example, they use qualitative research findings to discover new ideas and develop promotional strategies, and quantitative research findings to estimate the extent or amount of consumers who react in a particular way (i.e., positive or negative) to various promotional inputs. Frequently, ideas stemming from qualitative research are tested empirically through quantitative studies. The predictions made possible by quantitative research and the understanding provided by qualitative research together produce a richer and more robust profile of consumer behavior than either research approach used alone.

In reality, many consumer research studies carry out—concurrently or in sequence—a series of interrelated qualitative and quantitative studies, or move back and forth between one or more rounds of qualitative research and one or more rounds of quantitative research. In the many studies that the lead author of this book conducted for AT&T, it was quite common for him to undertake a number of focus groups or depth interview research studies that were followed by a quantitative stage using a very large internal consumer database, or the services of survey research companies that specialized in mail or telephone questionnaire surveys. The main point to keep in mind is that among marketing-oriented firms, consumer research is not commonly composed of a single study, but rather consists of a series of studies, often composed of a mix of qualitative research (most commonly focus groups and/or depth interviews) and quantitative research (most commonly some form of survey research, consumer panel data, or possibly an experiment). Commonly, the insights secured from a particular round of research are evaluated to determine whether more research is required, and if so, what should be the purpose and type of additional research. The combined findings enable marketers to design more meaningful and effective marketing strategies. Table 16.5 compares the quantitative and qualitative research designs.

TABLE 16.5	A Comparison of the Elements of Quantitative and Qualitative Research Designs	
	QUALITATIVE RESEARCH	**QUANTITATIVE RESEARCH (QUAN)**
Study purpose	Studies are designed to provide insights about new product ideas and identify positioning strategies aimed at a target market. Ideas uncovered should be tested via quantitative studies. QUAL studies are also often used to refine the objectives and wording of QUAN studies.	QUAN studies are aimed at describing a target market—its characteristics and possible reactions of various segments to the elements of the marketing mix. Results are used for making strategic marketing decisions.
Types of questions and data collection methods	Open-ended, unstructured questions, stressing probing by the moderator or highly skilled interviewer. QUAL research also uses projective techniques, including disguised questions and response to pictures or prototypes.	QUAN research often consists of closed-ended questions with predefined response choices and limited numbers of open-ended questions that have to be coded.
Main methods	Focus groups and depth interviews.	Survey questionnaires, including attitude scales and questions that are not disguised. QUAN questioning often consists of surveys that are self-administered, or conducted in person, by phone or mail, or online. Observation of consumers, experimentation, and consumer panels are other QUAN data collection methods.
Sampling methods	Small, nonprobability samples; findings are generally not representative of the universe under study.	Large probability samples. If the data collection instruments are valid and reliable, the results can be viewed as representative of the universe.
Data analysis	Data consist of transcripts or tapes of the verbal responses. The analysis is performed by skilled behavioral science researchers. Researchers seek to identify reoccurring "themes" of responses coming from participants.	After data are collected, they are coded and entered in the database. The researcher analyzes the data, using a variety of statistical methods of analysis, and estimates the extent to which the results represent the universe.

Data Analysis and Reporting Research Findings

Learning Objective

5 To understand how to analyze data and report research findings

In qualitative research, the moderator-researcher usually analyzes the responses received. In quantitative research, the researcher supervises the analysis: Open-ended responses are first coded and quantified (i.e., converted into numerical scores); then all the responses are tabulated and analyzed using sophisticated analytical programs that correlate the data by selected variables and cluster the data by selected demographic characteristics.

In both qualitative and quantitative research, the research report includes a brief executive summary of the findings and recommendations for marketing action. The body of the report includes a full description of the methodology used and, for quantitative research, also includes tables and graphics to support the findings.

Summary

Learning Objective 1: To understand how to develop research objectives

The first and most difficult step in the consumer research process is to accurately define the objectives of the research. Is it to segment the market for electronic readers? Is it to examine consumer attitudes about the experience of online shopping? What percentage of households shop for food online? Whatever the key research question, it is important for the marketing manager and the research manager to agree at the outset as to the specific purposes and objectives of the proposed consumer study. A clearly written statement of research objectives ensures that the information needed is indeed collected and costly errors are avoided.

Learning Objective 2: To understand how to collect secondary data

Secondary data is existing information that was originally gathered for a research purpose other than the present research. The rationale for secondary data searches is simply that it makes good sense to investigate whether currently available information will answer—in part or even in full—the research question at hand. It seems unwise to expend the effort and money, and rush into collecting new information before determining if there is any available information that would provide at least a good starting point.

The first source of secondary data is previously collected in-house information that was originally used for some other purpose. It might have originally been gathered as part of a sales audit, or from past customer service calls, or letters of inquiry from customers, or collected via warranty cards.

The second source of secondary data is information from sources outside of the firm or organization. They take many different forms. Some are free and can be found in a public library, other information is available for only a nominal fee, and still other data or information are quite expensive to secure. The major sources of external secondary data are: the government, articles from popular, professional, and academic publications, and syndicated commercial sources.

Learning Objective 3: To understand qualitative and quantitative research methods

If the purpose of a study is to come up with new ideas for products or promotional themes, the researchers use qualitative research. Qualitative studies consist of focus groups, depth interviews, and projective techniques.

If the purpose of the study is to find out how many consumers match the demographics or psychographics of the target market, or the characteristics of consumers who buy given brands and whether or not they are brand loyal, marketers conduct quantitative research. Quantitative research includes observation, experiments, and surveys.

Learning Objective 4: To understand how to combine qualitative and quantitative research

Marketers frequently conduct research projects that combine both a qualitative component (often composed of focus groups and/or depth interviews) and a quantitative component (often consisting of a survey research). For example, they use qualitative research findings to discover new ideas and develop promotional strategies, and quantitative research findings to estimate the extent or amount of consumers who react in a particular way (i.e., positive or negative) to various promotional inputs. Frequently, ideas stemming from qualitative research are tested empirically through quantitative studies. The predictions made possible by quantitative research and the understanding provided by qualitative research together produce a richer and more robust profile of consumer behavior than either research approach used alone.

Learning Objective 5: To understand how to analyze data and report research findings

In qualitative research, the moderator-researcher usually analyzes the responses received. In quantitative research, the responses are coded and analyzed statistically.

In both qualitative and quantitative research, the research report includes an executive summary of the findings, description of the methodology used, and recommendations for marketing actions.

Review and Discussion Questions

16.1. Have you ever been selected as a respondent in a marketing research survey? If yes, how were you contacted and where were you interviewed? Why do you think you, in particular, were selected? Did you know or could you guess the purpose of the survey? Do you know the name of the company or brand involved in the survey?

16.2. What is the difference between primary and secondary research? Under what circumstances might the availability of secondary data make primary research unnecessary? What are some major sources of secondary data?

16.3. Explain the distinction between primary and secondary data, and note the characteristics of each.

16.4. A manufacturer of a new product for whitening teeth would like to investigate the effects of package design and label

information on consumers' perceptions of the product and their intentions to buy it. Would you advise the manufacturer to use observational research, experimentation, or a survey? Explain your choice.

16.5. Quantitative research methods are often the preferred method of choice for many analyses. Explain why.

16.6. There are a few sampling methods in use. Which of the preferred ones feature a randomized component?

16.7. Illustrate with examples the advantages and disadvantages of different methods of conducting surveys, such as mail, telephone, personal interview, and online surveys. How would you decide which is the most appropriate?

Hands-on Assignments

16.8. Neutrogena is a manufacturer of personal care products for young adults. The company would like to extend its facial cleansers product line. Design (1) a qualitative and (2) a quantitative research design for the company focused on this objective.

16.9. Based on the discussion of focus groups and depth interviews (including Figures 16.2 and 16.3), develop a discussion guide for studying college students' reactions to their brand and model of cell phone.

16.10. Which methods of survey would you adopt to investigate the attitudes of a group regarding the shopping experience

in Japanese department stores, such as Isetan, Sogo, and Mitsukoshi?

16.11. Nestlé conducted extensive and accurate market research before deciding to put Nespresso in production. Using web sources, press articles, and the corporate website, outline your background research and provide the reasons for the success of the famous espresso brand, which featured George Clooney and Matt Damon in a testimonial and has become a veritable case of successful marketing.

Key Terms

- attitude scales *417*
- behavior intention scale *419*
- closed-ended questions *417*
- cluster (area) sample *422*
- complaint analysis *421*
- consumer panels *407*
- consumer research *404*
- controlled experiment *415*
- convenience sample *422*
- customer lifetime value profiles *406*
- customer satisfaction measurement *421*
- customer satisfaction surveys *421*
- depth interview *408*
- discussion guide *409*
- email surveys *416*
- experiments (causal research) *415*
- exploratory study *423*

- focus group *408*
- Internet surveys *416*
- judgment sample *422*
- Likert scale *417*
- magazine readership survey *417*
- mail surveys *416*
- motivational researchers *408*
- mystery shoppers *421*
- nonprobability sample *422*
- observational research *413*
- open-ended questions *417*
- personal interview surveys *415*
- physiological observation *415*
- primary research *405*
- probability sample *422*
- projective techniques *411*
- qualitative research *405*

- quantitative research *405*
- quota sample *422*
- rank-order scales *419*
- reliability *416*
- sample *421*
- sampling plan *421*
- screener questionnaire *409*
- secondary data *406*
- semantic differential scale *419*
- simple random sample *422*
- stratified random sample *422*
- systematic random sample *422*
- telephone interview surveys *416*
- test marketing *415*
- validity *416*

Case Six:

Pima Air and Space Museum
"The Great Paper Airplane Project"

Lead Agency: BBDO San Francisco
Contributing Agency: Hunter Public Relations

Strategic Challenges

Hidden in the vast Arizona desert near Tucson, the Pima Air and Space Museum showcases over 300 aircraft and 125,000 artifacts. The purpose of the museum is to showcase and explain aerospace history. In July 2011, more than 50% of the museum's visitors were over 60 years of age and passionate fans of aerospace history. The museum recognized that it had to attract a new generation in order to give the museum a robust future. Management knew that because of the nature of the content, they would naturally capture parents and their children.

Objectives

1. To put Pima "on the map." Pima is a world-class destination literally hidden in a desert. In order to increase attendance, the museum had to get media exposure beyond Tucson.

2. To shift audience demographics by attracting younger visitors. Ideally, young parents between 25 and 50 years old.

Insights

Interviews with moms of young kids revealed that many moms saw Pima not as a showcase of heroic feats, but rather a sad reminder of "over-militarization." Many of Pima's airplanes were icons of military history, but a lot of the items demonstrated that aviation originates in applied mathematics, physics, engineering, design, and environmental science.

Pima's greatest attraction is a Lockheed SR-71 "Blackbird." The plane is an advanced, long-range, Mach 3+ strategic reconnaissance aircraft built in the 1960s. During reconnaissance missions, the SR-71 operated at high speeds and altitudes to allow it to outrace threats. If the pilot detected a surface-to-air missile, he accelerated and outflew it. The SR-71 served with the U.S. Air Force from 1964 to 1998. Thirty-two aircraft were built; 12 were lost in accidents, but none lost to enemy action.

The Big Idea

Pima wanted to create a new generation of aviation fans by giving them a hands-on lesson in designing, building and flying the world's largest paper airplane

Bringing the Idea to Life

The museum engaged local schools—teachers and their students—in a paper-airplane competition. It sent out invitations to 390 local teachers, along with a custom-built lesson plan that showed how to fold a paper airplane and how to teach lessons about airspeed, lift, and force. Two hundred local school kids participated in the competition and the winner's plane flew a distance of 90 feet.

Working with a team of experts, the winner's plane was transformed into the world's largest paper airplane. Then, the 45 foot long plane was hoisted by helicopter 3,000 feet over the Arizona desert, and released for its first—and only—flight. After a short free fall, the plane leveled off for a flight of almost (0.93) a mile at a top speed of 98 mph. Following a less than graceful landing, the world's largest paper airplane was then put on display for all to see in the museum, along with a documentary of the contest and building it.

Questions

1. What are the psychological, socio-cultural and communication factors that played a role in designing the paper airplane competition?

2. Discuss the issue that the museum was facing from a positioning standpoint.

3. The building and launch of the world's largest airplane was a one-time event. How can it be the basis for further and more extensive media exposure for the museum?

4. How would you measures whether or not the museum has achieved its objectives?

5. Assuming that the museum attracted new visitors, how can it retain them and make them visit repeatedly?

Source: Effie Worldwide, Effie Showcase Winners. Reprinted by permission. Pima Air and Space Museum is a 2013 Gold Effie Winner. For information on Effie's programs for students, visit the Collegiate Effies at www.effie.org

Endnotes

Chapter 1

1. American Marketing Association, 2007.
2. Davis Hounshell, *From the American System to Mass Production 1800–1932* (Baltimore/London: John Hopkins University Press, 1984), 224.
3. www.gm.com/company/corp_info/history
4. Mike Esterl, "Monster Beverage Under Fire," online.wsj.com, May 6, 2013.
5. Julie Jason, "New Ad Targets McDonald's," online.wsj.com, September 14, 2010.
6. Erica Phillips, "Music Fan Sites to Pay Privacy Fine," online.wsj.com, October 3, 2012.
7. David Streitfeld, "Google Is Faulted for Impeding U.S. Inquiry on Data Collection," nytimes.com, April 14, 2012.
8. Leslie Kaufman and Tanzina Vega, "Media Giants Chase Online Ads with Original Shows," nytimes.com, May 5, 2013.
9. Graphs composed by the authors based on portions of the data from Julia Angwin and Jeremy Singer-Vine, "Selling You on Facebook," online.wsj.com, April 8, 2012.
10. A general ad space buy costs around $1 to $2 for a thousand impressions. If many competitors bid, that may rise to $4 to $15 for a thousand impressions. However, these figures very widely and do not represent the millions of bids that are submitted daily.
11. Suzanne Vranica, "Ads Let Viewers Be Mad Men," online.wsj.com, February 2, 2013; Suzanne Vranica, "Tweets Spawn Ad Campaigns," online.wsj.com, October 21, 2012.
12. William Launder, "Retailers Become Judges on NBC's 'Fashion Star,'" nytimes.com, March 13, 2012.
13. Spencer E. Ante, "Online Ads Can Now Follow You Home," online.wsj.com, April 29, 2013.
14. Suzanne Vranica, "MTV Aims for Multitasker," online.wsj.com, September 5, 2012.
15. Nikolaus Franke, Peter Keinz, and Christoph J. Steger, "Testing the Value of Customization: When Do Customers Really Prefer Products Tailored to Their Preferences?" *Journal of Marketing*, Vol. 73 (September 2009): 103–121.
16. Ann Zimmerman and Elizabeth Holmes, "Target to Match Online Prices, Following Best Buy," online.wsj.com, October 16, 2012.
17. Stephanie Clifford," "Retailers Add Gadgets for Shoppers at Ease with Technology," nytimes.com, November 23, 2012.
18. Jessica Vascellaro and Shara Tibken, "Apple Jumps into Textbooks," online.wsj.com, January 20, 2012.
19. Ellen Byron, "In-Store Sales Begin at Home," online.wsj.com, April 25, 2011.
20. Greg Bensinger, "Amazon's New Secret Weapon: Delivery Lockers," online.wsj.com, August 7, 2012.
21. Robin Sidel, "Retailers Join Payment Chase," online.wsj.com, March 2, 2012.
22. Christine Haughney, "Guided by *Lucky* Magazine, Shopping Will Soon Require Less Clicking," nytimes.com, August 5, 2012.
23. Daniella Zalcman, "Online Ingredients for Success," online.wsj.com, May 24, 2011.
24. Stephanie Clifford, "Shopper Alert: Price May Drop for You Alone," nytimes.com, August 9, 2012.
25. Frederick F. Reichheld and W. Earl Sasser, Jr., "Zero Defections: Quality Comes to Services," *Harvard Business Review* (September–October 1990): 105–111; Michael Treacy and Fred Wiersema, "Customer Intimacy and Other Value Disciplines," *Harvard Business Review* (January–February 1993): 84–93.
26. Andrew Adam Newman, "Marketers Promoting a Granola Bar Hit the Trails in National Parks," nytimes.com, March 7, 2012.
27. Suzanne Vranica, "Ads Let Viewers Be Mad Men," online.wsj.com, February 2, 2013; Suzanne Vranica, "Tweets Spawn Ad Campaigns," online.wsj.com, October 21, 2012.
28. Stephanie Clifford, "Social Media Are Giving a Voice to Taste Buds," nytimes.com, July 30, 2012.
29. Rolph E. Anderson and Srinivasan Swaminathan, "Customer Satisfaction and Loyalty in E-Markets: A PLS Path Modeling Approach," *Journal of Marketing Theory & Practice,* Vol. 19 (2) (Spring 2011): 221–234.
30. C. M. Sashi, "Customer Engagement, Buyer-Seller Relationships, and Social Media," *Management Decision,* Vol. 50 (2) (2012): 253–272.
31. Based on Thomas O. Jones and W. Earl Sasser, Jr., "Why Satisfied Customers Defect," *Harvard Business Review,* (November–December 1995): 88–99.
32. Zeithami, Valerie A. et. al. "The Customer Pyramid: Creating and Serving Profitable Customers," *in California Management Review,* vol. 43, no. 4, Summer 2001. © 2001 by the Regents of the University of California. Published by the University of California Press.
33. Valerie A. Zeithaml, Roland T. Rust, and Katherine N. Lemon, "The Customer Pyramid: Creating and Serving Profitable Customers," *California Management Review* (Summer 2001): 118–142.
34. Susanne Craig, "What Restaurants Know (About You)," nytimes.com, September 4, 2012.
35. Shalini Ramachandran, "Pay-TV Providers Get Picky about Their Customers," online.wsj.com, May 9, 2013.
36. Tillmann Wagner, Thorsten Hennig-Thurau, and Thomas Rudolph, "Does Customer Demotion Jeopardize Loyalty?" *Journal of Marketing,* Vol. 73 (May 2009): 69–85.

Chapter 2

1. Information from the publications' websites (June 2012).
2. Based on selected data from MyBestSegments at claritas.com (May 2012).
3. Colgate's website (May 2012).
4. Brian Stelter, "MTV Is Looking Beyond 'Jersey Shore' to Build a Wider Audience," nytimes.com, October 24, 2010; Tanzina Vega, "A Campaign to Introduce Keds to a New Generation," nytimes.com, February 22, 2011.

5. Michelle Kung, "Movie Studios Smell Out Teen Spirits," online.wsj.com, April 25, 2011.

6. Based on selected portions of a report issued by Pew Internet (accessed May 2012).

7. Stuart Elliott, "Vodka Brand Goes Edgy as It Reaches Out to Women," nytimes.com, August 9, 2010.

8. Stephanie Clifford, "Frito-Lay Tries to Enter the Minds (and Lunch Bags) of Women," nytimes.com, February 25, 2009.

9. Lauren A. E. Schuker, "VH1 Cultivates Its Female Side," online.wsj.com, April 17, 2011.

10. Elizabeth Holmes, "Dude, Pass the Exfoliator," online. wsj.com, April 26, 2012.

11. Ellen Byron, "Dove Men + Care," online.wsj.com, February 13, 2013.

12. Anil Mathur, Lee Euehun, and George P. Moschis, "Life-Changing Events and Marketing Opportunities," *Journal of Targeting, Measurement & Analysis for Marketing,* Vol. 14 (2) (January 2006): 115–128.

13. Ellen Byron, "As Middle Class Shrinks, P&G Aims High and Low," online.wsj.com, September 12, 2011.

14. Stephanie Clifford, "Even Marked Up, Luxury Goods Fly Off Shelves," nytimes.com, August 3, 2011.

15. Tanzina Vega, "Marketers, and Media Companies, Set Their Sights on Latin Women," nytimes.com, December 8, 2011.

16. Stuart Elliott, "Pretty as (Census) Picture," nytimes.com, March 28, 2011.

17. Stowe Shoemaker and Dina Marie V. Zemke, "The 'Locals' Market: An Emerging Gaming Segment," *Journal of Gambling Studies,* Vol. 21 (4) (Winter 2005): 379–407.

18. Allen Salkin, "Before It Disappears," nytimes.com, December 16, 2007.

19. Stuart Elliott, "Loved the Ads? Now Pour the Drink," nytimes.com, August 27, 2008.

20. Stuart Elliott, "Campaign Says 'Cheers' to Expanding a Regional Favorite," nytimes.com, April 25, 2011.

21. Stuart Elliott, "In New Ads, Some (Drinkers) Like It Hot," nytimes.com, November 28, 2011.

22. Steve brooks, "The Green Consumers," *Restaurant Business* (September 2009): 20–22.

23. Tara McBride Mintz, "Profiling Green Consumers: A Descriptive Study," MBA Thesis, Appalachian State University, North Carolina, May 2011.

24. Maryam Banikarim, "Seeing Shades in Green Consumers," *ADWEEK,* April 19, 2010.

25. Based on Stuart J. Barnes, "Segmenting Cyberspace: A Customer Typology for the Internet," *European Journal of Marketing,* Vol. 41 (1/2) (2007): 71–93.

26. Based on VALS at strategicinsights.com (May 2012).

27. Colgate's website (May 2012).

28. Paul G. Patterson, "Demographic Correlates of Loyalty in a Service Context," *Journal of Services Marketing,* Vol. 21 (2) (2007): 112–125.

29. David Martin-Consuegra, Arturo Molina, and Agueda Esteban, "The Customers' Perspective on Relational Benefits in Banking Activities," *Journal of Financial Services Marketing,* Vol. 10 (4) (2006): 98–108.

30. Carlos Flavian and Raquel Gurrea, "The Role of Readers' Motivations in the Choice of Digital versus Traditional Newspapers," *Journal of Targeting, Measurement & Analysis for Marketing,* Vol. 14 (4) (2006): 325–335.

31. Brian T. Ratchford, Debabrata Talukdar, and Myung-Soo Lee, "The Impact of the Internet on Consumers' Use of Information Sources for Automobiles: A Re-Inquiry," *Journal of Consumer Research,* Vol. 34 (June 2007): 111–119.

32. Gillian Sullivan Mort and Judy Drennan, "Marketing M-Services: Establishing a Usage Benefit Typology Related to Mobile User Characteristics," *Database Marketing & Consumer Strategy Management,* Vol. 12 (4) (2005): 327–341.

33. Muhammad Alijukhadar and Sylvain Senecal, "Segmenting the Online Consumer Market," *Marketing Intelligence & Planning,* Vol. 29 (4) (2011): 421–435.

34. Jaime R. S. Fonseca and Margarida G. M. S. Cardoso, "Supermarket Customers Segments Stability," *Journal of Targeting, Measurement and Analysis for Marketing,* Vol. 15 (4) (2007): 210–221.

35. Carmen Rodriguez Santos, Miguel Cervantes Blanco, and Ana Gonzalez Fernandez, "Segmenting Wine Consumers According to Their Involvement with Appellations of Origin," *Brand Management,* Vol. 13 (4/5) (April–June 2006): 300–312.

36. Stuart Elliott, "A Push to Promote Familiar Brands Online," nytimes.com, November 17, 2011.

37. Dana Mattioli and Miguel Bustillo, "Can Texting Save Stores?" online.wsj.com, May 8, 2012.

38. Charles Duhigg, "How Companies Learn Your Secrets," nytimes.com, February 16, 2012.

39. Stuart Elliott, "Bounty Now Promises a Competent Clean," June 28, 2010 nytimes.com

40. Christina Passariello and Max Colchester, "L'Oreal Slogan Must Be Proved Anew," online.wsj.com, November 15, 2011.

41. Stuart Elliott, "Bounty Now Promises a Competent Clean," nytimes.com, June 28, 2010.

42. www.crest.com

43. Visine's website (June 2012).

44. Crest's website (October 2012).

45. Sources: Stuart Elliott, "Choosing Between a Hard Rock and a Place," nytimes.com, November 22, 2010; Stuart Elliott, "It Only Takes an Instant, Lottery Ads Declare," nytimes.com, May 9, 2011; Stuart Elliott, "A Wine Brand Creates a New Theme to Help Spur Growth," nytimes. com, August 29, 2011; Vivian S. Toy, "Goodbye, Glitzy Condo Pitches," nytimes.com, August 20, 2010; Louise Story, "In Ads, Banks Try the Warm, Cozy Approach," nytimes.com, June 9, 2009; Andrew Newman, "Bold Commercials and Flavors Aim to Spice Up Chili's Brand," nytimes.com, September 29, 2011.

46. Louise Story, "Home Equity Frenzy Was a Bank Ad Come True," nytimes.com, August 15, 2008.

Chapter 3

1. Chung-Yao Huang, Yong-Zheng Shen, Hong-Xiang Lin, and Shin-Shin Chang, "Bloggers' Motivations and Behavior: A Model," *Journal of Advertising Research,* 47 (4) (December 2007): 472–483.

2. Adapted from Kanghui Baek, Avery Holton, Dustin Harp, and Carolyn Yaschur, "The Links That Bind: Uncovering Novel Motivations for Linking on Facebook," *Computers in Human Behavior,* 27 (2011): 2245–2267.

3. Craig Martin, "Consumption Motivation and Perceptions of Malls: A Comparison of Mothers and Daughters," *Journal of Marketing Theory & Practice*, 17 (Winter 2009): 49–61.

4. See Tillmann Wagner and Thomas Rudolph, "Toward a Hierarchy of Shopping Motivations," *Journal of Retailing & Consumer Services*, 17 (2010): 415–429.

5. See Abraham H. Maslow, "A Theory of Human Motivation," *Psychological Review*, 50 (1943): 370–396; Abraham H. Maslow, *Motivation and Personality* (New York: Harper & Row, 1954); Abraham H. Maslow, *Toward a Psychology of Being* (New York: Van Nostrand Reinhold, 1968): 189–215.

6. Maslow 1954, 1968.

7. Abraham H. Maslow, Motivation and Personality (New York: Harper & Row, 1954); and Abraham H. Maslow, Toward a Psychology of Being(New York: Van Nostrand Reinhold, 1968): 189–215.

8. Matthew Jelavic and Kristie Oglilvie, "Maslow and Management: Universally Applicable or Idiosyncratic?" *Canadian Manager* (Winter 2010): 16–17.

9. Sylvia Miller, M. Clinton, and John Camey, "The Relationship of Motivation, Needs, and Involvement Factors to Preferences for Military Recruitment Slogans," *Journal of Advertising Research*, 47 (1) (March 2007): 66–78.

10. Wann-Yih Wu and Badri Munir Sukoco, "Why Should I Share? Examining Consumers' Motives and Trust on Knowledge Sharing," *Journal of Computer Information Systems* (Summer 2010): 11–19.

11. *Sources:* Emily Eakin, "Penetrating the Mind by Metaphor," *New York Times*, February 23, 2002, B9, Bl-1; Ronald B. Leiber, "Storytelling: A New Way to Get Close to Your Customer," *Fortune*, February 3, 1997; Bernice Kramer, "Mind Games," *New York*, May 8, 1989, 33–40.

12. Neale Martin and Kyle Morich, "Consumer Choice: Toward a New Model of Consumer Behavior," *Journal of Brand Management*, 18 (March 2011): 483–505.

13. For example, see Karen Horney, *The Neurotic Personality of Our Time* (New York: Norton, 1937).

14. Joel B. Cohen, "An Interpersonal Orientation to the Study of Consumer Behavior," *Journal of Marketing Research*, 6 (August 1967): 270–278; Arch G. Woodside and Ruth Andress, "CAD Eight Years Later," *Journal of the Academy of Marketing Science* 3 (Summer–Fall 1975): 309–313; see also Jon P. Noerager, "An Assessment of CAD: A Personality Instrument Developed Specifically for Marketing Research," *Journal of Marketing Research*, 16 (February 1979): 53–59.

15. Stefan Soyez and Kat Soyez, "A Cognitive Model to Predict Domain-Specific Consumer Innovativeness," *Journal of Business Research*, 63 (2010): 778–785.

16. Bert Vandecasteele and Maggie Geuens, "Motivated Consumer Innovativeness: Concept, Measurement, and Validation," *International Journal of Research in Marketing*, 27 (2010): 308–318.

17. Tanawat Hirunyawipada and Audhesh K. Paswan, "Consumer Innovativeness and Perceived Risk: Implications for High Technology Product Adoption," *Journal of Consumer Marketing*, 23 (7) (2006): 197; Ji Eun Park, Jun Yu, and Joyce Xin Zhou, "Consumer Innovativeness and Shopping Styles," *Journal of Consumer Marketing*, 27 (5) (2010): 437–446.

18. Gilles Roehrich, "Consumer Innovativeness," and Angela D'Auria Stanton and Wilbur W. Stanton, "To Click or Not to Click: Personality Characteristics of Internet versus Non-Internet Purchasers," in *2001 AMA Winter Educators' Conference*, 12, edited by Ram Krishnan and Madhu Viswanathan (Chicago: American Marketing Association, 2001): 161–162.

19. Walfried M. Lassar, Chris Manolis, and Sharon S. Lassar, "The Relationship Between Consumer Innovativeness, Personal Characteristics, and Online Banking Adoption," *International Journal of Bank Marketing*, 23 (2) (2005): 190–201.

20. Isita Lahiri and Amitava Gupta, "Brand Extensions in Consumer Non-durables, Durables and Services: A Comparative Study," *South Asian Journal of Management*, 12 (4) (October–December 2005): 34–42.

21. Byoungho Jin and Yong Gu Suh, "Integrating Effect of Consumer Perception Factors in Predicting Private Brand Purchase in a Korean Discount Store Context," *Journal of Consumer Marketing*, 22 (2) (2005): 62–77.

22. Milton Rokeach, *The Open and Closed Mind* (New York: Basic Books, 1960).

23. Kurt Matzler, Sonja Bidmon, and Sonja Grabner-Kräuter, "Individual Determinants of Brand Affect: The Role of Personality Traits of Extraversion and Openness to Experience," *Journal of Product & Brand Management*, 15 (7) (2006): 434–451.

24. Ann Marie Fiore, Hyun-Jeong Jin, and Jihyun Kim, "For Fun and Profit: Hedonic Value from Image Interactivity and Responses Toward an Online Store," *Psychology & Marketing*, 22 (8) (2005): 675–686.

25. Ann Marie Fiore, Leung-Eun Lee, and Grace Kunz, "Individual Differences, Motivations, and Willingness to Use a Mass Customization Option for Fashion Products," *European Journal of Marketing*, 38 (7) (2004): 835–849.

26. Walter Wymer. Donald Self, and Carolyn Sara Findley, "Sensation Seekers as a Target Market for Volunteer Tourism," *Service Marketing Quarterly*, 31 (2010): 348–362.

27. Elizabeth C. Hirschman, "Innovativeness, Novelty Seeking and Consumer Creativity," *Journal of Consumer Research*, 7 (1980): 283–295; Piyush Sharma, Bharadhwaj Sivakumaran, and Roger Marshall, "Impulse Buying and Variety Seeking: A Trait-Correlates Perspective," *Journal of Business Research*, 63 (2010): 276–283.

28. Chingching Chang, "Diagnostic Advertising Content and Individual Differences," *Journal of Advertising*, 36 (3) (Fall 2007): 79–87.

29. Chien-Huang Lin and Pei-Hsun Wu, "The Effect of Variety on Consumer Preferences: The Role of Need for Cognition and Recommended Alternatives," *Social Behavior & Personality*, 34 (7) (2006): 874–889.

30. Tracy L. Tuten and Michael Bosnjak, "Understanding Differences in Web Usage: The Role of Need for Cognition and the Five Factor Model of Personality," *Social Behavior & Personality*, 29 (4) (2001): 391–398.

31. Dahui Li and Glenn J. Browne, "The Role of Need for Cognition and Mood in Online Flow Experience," *Journal of Computer Information Systems*, 46 (3) (Spring 2006): 15–28; Maria Sicilia, Salvador Ruiz, and Jose L. Munuera, "Effects of Interactivity in a Web Site," *Journal of Advertising*, 34 (3) (Fall 2005): 40–53.

32. Maria Kozhevnikov, Stephen Kosslyn, and Jeffifer Shepard, "Spatial versus Object Visualizers: A New Characterization of Visual Cognitive Style," *Memory & Cognition*, 33 (4) (2005): 710–722.

33. Elaine Sherman, Leon Schiffman, and Yong Zhang, "A Cross-Cultural Investigation of Consumer Frugality: The Case of the United States and China," *Global Business & Technology Conference Proceedings*, Istanbul, Turkey (July 2011); Jeffrey Podoshen, Lu Li, and Junfeng Zhang, "Materialism and Conspicuous Consumption in China: A Cross-Cultural Examination," *International Journal of Consumer Studies*, 35 (2011): 17–25; Srinivas Durvasula and Steven Lysonski, "Money, Money, Money—How Do Attitudes Toward Money Impact Young Chinese Consumers?" *Journal of Consumer Marketing*, 27 (2) (2010): 169–179.

34. Marsha L. Richins and Scott Dawson, "A Consumer Values Orientation for Materialism and Its Measurement: Scale Development and Validation," *Journal of Consumer Research*, 19 (December 1992): 303–316; Jeff Tanner and Jim Roberts, "Materialism Cometh," *Baylor Business Review* (Fall 2000): 8–9.

35. Scott I. Rick, Cynthia E. Cryder, and George Loewenstein, "Tightwads and Spendthrifts," *Journal of Consumer Research*, 34 (April 2008): 767–782.

36. Alain d'Astous and Jonathan Deschenes, "Consuming in One's Mind: An Exploration," *Psychology & Marketing*, 22 (1) (January 2005): 1–30.

37. Helga Dittmar, "A New Look at 'Compulsive Buying': Self-Discrepancies and Materialistic Values as Predictors of Compulsive Buying Tendency," *Journal of Social & Clinical Psychology*, 24 (6) (September 2005): 832–859. Also see Laurence Claes et al., "Emotional Reactivity and Self-Regulation in Relation to Compulsive Buying," *Personality & Individual Differences*, 49 (2010): 526–530.

38. Hui-Yi Lo and Nigel Harvey, "Shopping Without Pain: Compulsive Buying and the Effects of Credit Card Availability in Europe and the Far East," *Journal of Economic Psychology*, 32 (2011): 79–92; Kay Palan, Paula Morrow, Allan Trapp, and Virginia Blackburn, "Compulsive Buying Behavior in College Students: The Mediating Role of Credit Card Misuse," *Journal of Marketing Theory & Practice*, 19 (1) (2011): 81–96.

39. Olaf Werder and Marilyn S. Roberts, "Generation Y's Consumer Ethnocentrism: Implications for Advertisers in a Post September 11th World," *American Academy of Advertising Conference Proceedings* (2005): 185; Gregory S. Black and Leon F. Dube, "Implications of Collective Trauma on Consumer Purchase Attitudes," *Atlantic Economic Journal* (published online), December 20, 2006.

40. Osman Mohamad, Zafar U. Ahmed, Earl D. Honeycutt, Jr., and Taizoon Hyder Tyebkhan, "Does 'Made In . . .' Matter to Consumers? A Malaysian Study of Country of Origin Effect," *Multinational Business Review* (Fall 2000): 69–73; Irvin Clarke, Mahesh N. Shankarmahesh, and John B. Ford, "Consumer Ethnocentrism, Materialism and Values: A Four Country Study," in *2000 AMA Winter Educators' Conference*, 11, edited by John P. Workman and William D. Perreault (Chicago: American Marketing Association, 2000): 102–103.

41. Subhash Sharma, Terence A. Shimp, and Jeongshin Shin, "Consumer Ethnocentrism: A Test of Antecedents and Moderators," *Journal of the Academy of Marketing Science*, 23 (1995): 27.

42. Hamin Elliott and Greg Elliott, "A Less-Developed Country Perspective of Consumer Ethnocentrism and 'Country of Origin' Effects: Indonesian Evidence," *Asia Pacific Journal of Marketing & Logistics,* 18 (2) (2006): 79–92.

43. George Balabanis and Adamantios Diamantopoulos, "Domestic Country Bias, Country-of-Origin Effects, and Consumer Ethnocentrism: A Multidimensional Unfolding Approach," *Journal of the Academy of Marketing Science,* 32 (Winter 2004): 80–95.

44. Byeong-Joon Moon, "Effects of Consumer Ethnocentrism and Product Knowledge on Consumers' Utilization of Country-of-Origin Information," *Advances in Consumer Research,* 31 (2004): 667–673.

45. Fang Liu, Jamie Murphy, Jianyao Li, and Xiangping Liu, "English and Chinese? The Role of Consumer Ethnocentrism and Country of Origin in Chinese Attitudes Towards Store Signs," *Australasian Marketing Journal,* 14 (2) (2006): 5–16.

46. Jufei Kao, "Is It a Foreign Product? A Scale to Classify Products in an Era of Globalization," *Advances in Consumer Research,* 31 (2004): 674–682.

47. Shintaro Okazaki, "Excitement or Sophistication? A Preliminary Exploration of Online Brand Personality," *International Marketing Review*, 23 (3) (2006): 279–303.

48. Pankaj Aggarwal and Ann L. McGill, "Is That Car Smiling at Me? Schema Congruity as a Basis for Evaluating Anthropomorphized Products," *Journal of Consumer Research*, 34 (December 2007): 468–479.

49. Vanitha Swaminathan, Karen M. Stilley, and Rohini Ahluwalia, "When Brand Personality Matters: The Moderating Role of Attachment Styles," *Journal of Consumer Research*, 35 (April 2009): 567–579.

50. Didier Louis and Cindy Lombart, "Impact of Brand Personality on Three Major Relational Consequences (Trust, Attachment, and Commitment to the Brand)," *Journal of Product & Brand Management*, 19 (2) (2010): 114–130.

51. Scarlett C. Wesley, Deborah C. Fowler, and Maria Elena Vazquez, "Retail Personality and the Hispanic Consumer: An Exploration of American Retailers," *Managing Service Quality,* 16 (2) (2006): 177–180.

52. Qimei Chen and Shelly Rodgers, "Development of an Instrument to Measure Web Site Personality," *Journal of Interactive Advertising*, 7 (1) (Fall 2006). Retrieved from http://jiad.org/article86.

53. Tara Parker-Pope, "Are Most People in Denial about Their Weight?" nytimes.com, April 18, 2012.

54. Russell W. Belk, "Possessions and the Extended Self," *Journal of Consumer Research*, 15 (September 1988): 139–168; Amy J. Morgan, "The Evolving Self in Consumer Behavior: Exploring Possible Selves," in *Advances in Consumer Research*, 20, edited by Leigh McAlister and Michael L. Rothschild (Provo, UT: Association for Consumer Research, 1992): 429–432.

55. Richard G. Netemeyer, Scot Burton, and Donald R. Lichtenstein, "Trait Aspects of Vanity: Measurement and Relevance to Consumer Behavior," *Journal of Consumer Research*, 21 (March 1995): 613–627.

Chapter 4

1. Interviews with Helen Priestley, McCain Foods Marketing Director, and Nir Wegrzyn, CEO, BrandOpus, London, May 25, 2013. Interviewer: Joseph Wisenblit.
2. Serena Ng, "Pet-Food Brand's Image Bites Back at Colgate," online.wsj.com, February 5, 2013.
3. Jeff Bennett, "Chevrolet Ads Take 'New Road,'" online.wsj.com, January 8, 2013.
4. Daniel Milotic, "The Impact of Fragrance on Consumer Choice," *Journal of Consumer Behaviour,* (December 2003): 179; Lawrence K. Altman, "Unraveling Enigma of Smell Wins Nobel for 2 Americans," *New York Times*, December 5, 2004, A18.
5. Aradhna Krishna, May O. Lwin, and Maureen Morrin, "Product Scent and Memory," *Journal of Consumer Research,* Vol. 37 (June 2010): 57–67.
6. For example, Joann Peck and Jennifer Wiggins, "It Just Feels Good: Customers' Affective Response to Touch and Its Influence on Persuasion," *Journal of Marketing*, Vol. 70 (October 2006): 59–69.
7. Stephanie Clifford, "Stuff Piled in the Aisle? It's There to Get You to Spend More," nytimes.com, April 7, 2011.
8. WSJ Video, "When a Sound Is Worth a Thousand Words," online.wsj.com, October 23, 2012.
9. Amy Schatz, "FCC Turns Down Volume of TV Commercials," online.wsj.com, December 13, 2011.
10. Catherine Saint Louis, "Fragrance Spritzers Hold Their Fire," nytimes.com, April 15, 2011.
11. Sources: Louise Story, "Times Sq. Ads Spread via Tourists' Cameras," nytimes.com, December 11, 2006; Stuart Elliott, "Show and Tell Moves into Living Room," nytimes.com, April 4, 2008; Stuart Elliott, "Joint Promotion Adds Stickers to Sweet Smell of Marketing," nytimes.com, April 2, 2007; Louise Story, "Anywhere the Eye Can See, It's Likely to See an Ad," nytimes.com, January 15, 2007; Stuart Elliott, "Brainy Brand Names Where They're Least Expected," nytimes.com, October 3, 2008; Stuart Elliott, "You Are Here (and Probably Seeing an Ad)," nytimes.com, August 14, 2008; Elizabeth Olson, "Practicing the Subtle Sell of Placing Products on Webisodes," nytimes.com, January 3, 2008; Stephanie Clifford, "More Bells, Whistles and Packets of All Sorts," nytimes.com, April 22, 2008.
12. Stephanie Clifford and Catherine Rampell, "Food Inflation Kept Hidden in Tinier Bags," nytimes.com, March 28, 2011.
13. Sheri J. Broyles, "Subliminal Advertising and the Perpetual Popularity of Playing to People's Paranoia," *Journal of Consumer Affairs*, Vol. 40 (2) (Winter 2006): 392–406.
14. Rob Walker, "Subconscious Warm-Up: Can a Brand Make You Perform Better?" *New York Times Magazine*, October 5, 2008, 22; Grainne M. Fitzsimons, Tanya L. Chartrand, and Gavan J. Fitzsimons, "Automatic Effects of Brand Exposure on Motivated Behavior: How Apple Makes You 'Think Different,'" *Journal of Consumer Research,* Vol. 35 (1) (June 2008): 21–35.
15. Jane Levere, "3 Ads about Budget Cuts for Children's Programs," nytimes.com, August 6, 2012.
16. Sigurd Villads Troye and Magne Supphellen, "Consumer Participation in Coproduction: 'I Made It Myself' Effects on Consumers' Sensory Perceptions and Evaluations of Outcome and Input Product," *Journal of Marketing,* Vol. 76 (33) (March 2012): 33–46.
17. Stephanie Clifford, "Product Placements Acquire a Life of Their Own on Shows," nytimes.com, July 14, 2008.
18. Elizabeth Cowley and Chris Barron, "When Product Placement Goes Wrong: The Effects of Program Liking and Placement Prominence," *Journal of Advertising,* Vol. 37 (1) (Spring 2008): 89–99.
19. William Lauder, "Retailers Become Judges on NBC's 'Fashion Star,'" online.wsj.com, March 13, 2012; Sam Schechner and Lauren A. E. Schuker, "Lights, Camera, Advertisements," online.wsj.com, September 14, 2011; Mike Esterl, "Bud Angles for Buzz with Reality Show," online.wsj.com, December 12, 2011.
20. Andrew Adam Newman, "Taking Pickles Out of the Afterthought Aisle," nytimes.com, April 25, 2011.
21. Joandrea Hoegg and Joseph W. Alba, "Taste Perception: More Than Meets the Tongue," *Journal of Consumer Research*, Vol. 33 (March 2007): 490–498.
22. Linda M. Scott and Patrick Vargas, "Writing with Pictures: Toward a Unifying Theory of Consumer Response to Images," *Journal of Consumer Research,* Vol. 34 (October 2007): 341–356.
23. Leonard L. Berry, Edwin F. Lefkowith, and Terry Clark, "In Services, What's in a Name?" *Harvard Business Review* (September–October 1988): 28–30.
24. Aysen Bakir, Jeffrey G. Blodgett, and Gregory M. Rose, "Children's Response to Gender-Role Stereotyped Advertisements," *Journal of Advertising Research,* Vol. 48 (2) (June 2008): 255–266.
25. Karl Kunkel, "Making Mattresses Tick: Manufacturers Rely on Distinctive Colors and Textures to Create Products That Entice Consumers with a Great First Impression," *HFN: The Weekly Newspaper for the Home Furnishings Network* (December 12, 2005): 33.
26. Joe Sharkey, "Hotels Learn the Importance of Expectations Built into a Brand Name," *New York Times*, June 18, 2002, C12.
27. Phred Dvorak, Suzanne Vranica, and Spencer E. Ante, "BlackBerry Maker's Issue: Gadgets for Work or Play?" online.wsj.com, September 30, 2011.
28. Based on the descriptions in the brands' respective websites (accessed June 16, 2012).
29. Mark Hachman, "Dell's 'More You' Ads Mean a Renewed Consumer Push," online.wsj.com, July 5, 2011; Stuart Elliott, "Google Remixes Old Campaigns, Adding a Dash of Digital Tools," nytimes.com, March 8, 2012; Stuart Elliott, "In New Ads, Stirring Memories of Commercials Past," nytimes.com, January 12, 2012; Stuart Elliott, "Sit Under the Apple Tree With Me, Juice Brand Asks," nytimes.com, June 7, 2010; Stuart Elliott, "Promoting a Potato Chip Using Many Farmers, and Less Salt," nytimes.com, May 25, 2010; Stuart Elliott, "So, Virginia, What's the Story," nytimes.com, February 1, 2010.
30. Ulrich R. Orth and Keven Malkewitz, "Holistic Package Designs and Consumer Brand Impressions," *Journal of Marketing,* Vol. 72 (May 2008): 64–81.
31. Jochen Wirtz, Anna S. Mattila, and Rachel L. P. Tan, "The Role of Arousal Congruency in Influencing Consumers' Satisfaction Evaluations and In-Store Behaviors," *International Journal of Service Industry Management*, Vol. 18 (1) (2007): 6–24.

32. Andreas Herrmann, Lan Xia, Kent B. Monroe, and Frank Huber, "The Influence of Price Fairness on Customer Satisfaction: An Empirical Test in the Context of Automobile Purchases," *Journal of Product & Brand Management,* Vol. 16 (1) (2007): 49–58.

33. Ben Lowe and Frank Alpert, "Measuring Reference Price Perceptions for New Product Categories: Which Measure Is Best?" *Journal of Product & Brand Management,* Vol. 16 (2) (2007): 132–141.

34. Daniel J. Howard and Roger A. Kerin, "Broadening the Scope of Reference Price Advertising Research: A Field Study of Consumer Shopping Involvement," *Journal of Marketing,* Vol. 70 (October 2006): 185–204.

35. Keith S. Coulter and Robin A. Coulter, "Distortion of Price Discount Perceptions: The Right Digit Effect," *Journal of Consumer Research,* Vol. 34 (August 2007): 162–173.

36. Sara Campo and Maria J. Yague, "Effects of Price Promotions on the Perceived Price," *International Journal of Service Industry Management,* Vol. 18 (3) (2007): 269–286.

37. Ritesh Saini, Raghunath Singh Rao, and Ashwani Monga, "Is That Deal Worth My Time? The Interactive Effect of Relative and Referent Thinking on Willingness to Seek a Bargain," *Journal of Marketing,* Vol. 74 (January 2010): 34–48.

38. Joan Lindsey-Mullikin, "Beyond Reference Price: Understanding Consumers' Encounters with Unexpected Prices," *Journal of Product & Brand Management,* Vol. 12 (2/3) (2003): 140–154.

39. Sarah Nassauer, "Marketing Decoder: Sandwich Meat," online.wsj.com, March 19, 2013.

40. Brian Wansink and SeaBum Park, "At the Movies: How External Cues and Perceived Taste Impact Consumption Volume," *Food Quality & Preference,* 12 (2001): 69–74.

41. Celina Gonzalez Mieres, Ana Maria Diaz Martin, and J. A. T. Gutierrez, "Antecedents of the Difference in Perceived Risk Between Store Brands and National Brands," *European Journal of Marketing,* Vol. 40 (1/2) (2006): 61–82.

42. Torben Hansen, "Understanding Consumer Perception of Food Quality: The Cases of Shrimp and Cheeses," *British Food Journal,* Vol. 107 (7) (2005): 500–525.

43. Ray Johnson and Johan Bruwer, "Regional Brand Image and Perceived Wine Quality: The Consumer Perspective," *International Journal of Wine Business Research,* Vol. 19 (4) (2007): 276–297.

44. Frank Vigneron and Lester W. Johnson, "Measuring Perceptions of Brand Luxury," *Journal of Brand Management,* Vol. 11 (6) (July 2004): 484.

45. Jeana H. Frost, Zoe Chance, Michael I. Norton, and Dan Ariely, "People Are Experience Goods: Improving Online Dating with Virtual Dates," *Journal of Interactive Marketing,* Vol. 22 (1) (Winter 2008): 51–61.

46. The research on expected versus perceived service quality and SERVQUAL appears in Valarie A. Zeithaml, A. Parasuraman, and Leonard L. Berry, *Delivering Quality Service: Balancing Customer Perceptions and Expectations* (New York: The Free Press, 1990); Valarie A. Zeithaml, Leonard L. Berry, and A. Parasuraman, "The Nature and Determinants of Customer Expectation of Service," *Journal of the Academy of Marketing Science* (Winter 1993): 1–12; A. Parasuraman, Leonard L. Berry, and Valerie A. Zeithaml, "Refinement and Reassessment of the SERVQUAL Scale," *Journal of Retailing,* Vol. 67 (4) (Winter 1991): 420–450; A. Parasuraman, Leonard L. Berry, and Valerie A. Zeithaml, "Understanding Customer Expectations of Service," *Sloan Management Review* (Spring 1991): 39–48.

47. Ibid.

48. By shirt number: (1) sold at Bloomingdale's, designed by Donatella; (2) sold at Macy's, designed by Polonimo; (3) sold at Camicia (a store in NYC's Soho district), designed by Bertoliani; (4) sold by street vendors in NYC, made in China; (5) sold at Barney's under the store's name; (6) sold at H&M, designed by Xaas.

49. After looking at the shirt photos and the names of the stores and designers, the most expensive shirt is the one you believe to be so. The photos in Figure 4.1 are generic, and the information regarding the stores and designers is fictitious, used here only as illustration.

50. Benedict Carey, "$2.50 Placebo Gives More Relief Than a 10 Cents One," nytimes.com, March 5, 2008.

51. Shibin Sheng, Andrew M. Parker, and Kent Nakamoto, "The Effects of Price Discounts and Product Complimentarity on Consumer Evaluations of Bundle Components," *Journal of Marketing Theory & Practice,* Vol. 15 (1) (Winter 2007): 53–64.

52. John Tierney, "Calculating Consumer Happiness at Any Price," nytimes.com, June 30, 2009.

53. Thomas E. DeCarlo, Russell N. Laczniak, Carol M. Motley, and Sridhar Ramaswamy, "Influence of Image and Familiarity on Consumer Response to Negative Word-of-Mouth Communications about Retail Entities," *Journal of Marketing Theory & Practice,* Vol. 15 (1) (Winter 2007): 41–51.

54. Annie Gasparro, "Whole Foods Aims to Alter 'Price Perception' as It Expands," online.wsj.com, February 15, 2012.

55. Nat Ives, "Wal-Mart Turns to Ads to Address Its Critics," nytimes.com, January 14, 2005; Stuart Elliott, "Wal-Mart's New Realm: Reality TV," nytimes.com, June 3, 2005.

56. Kevin Coupe, "The Halo Effect, Revisited," *Chain Store Age* (February 2006): 36–37.

57. Louise Story, "In Ads, Banks Try the Warm, Cozy Approach," nytimes.com, June 9, 2009.

58. Erik Holm, "Progressive's # Fails in Social Media May Be Warning to Insurers," online.wsj.com, August 21, 2012.

59. Anthony D. Cox, Dena Cox, and Susan Powell Mantel, "Consumer Response to Drug Risk Information: The Role of Positive Affect," *Journal of Marketing,* Vol. 31 (74) (July 2010): 31–44.

60. Fang He and Peter P. Mykytyn, "Decision Factors for the Adoption of an Online Payment System by Customers," *International Journal of E-Business Research,* Vol. 3 (4) (October–December 2007): 1–32.

61. Tibert Verhagen, Sellmar Meents, and Yao-Hua Tan, "Perceived Risk and Trust Associated with Purchasing at Electronic Marketplaces," *European Journal of Information Systems* (2006): 542–555; Sally Harridge-March, "Can Building of Trust Overcome Consumer Perceived Risk?" *Marketing Intelligence & Planning,* Vol. 24 (7) (2006): 747–761.

62. Jung-Hwan Kim and Sharron J. Lennon, "Information Available on a Web Site: Effects on Consumers' Shopping Outcomes," *Journal of Fashion Marketing & Management,* Vol. 14 (2) (2010): 247–262; Man-Ling Chang and Wann-Yih Wu, "Revisiting Perceived Risk in the Context of Online Shopping: An Alternative Perspective of Decision-Making Styles," *Psychology & Marketing,* Vol. 29 (5) (May 2012): 378–400.

Chapter 5

1. Charles Duhigg, "How Companies Learn Your Secrets," nytimes.com, February 16, 2012.
2. Verolien Cauberghe and Patrick De Pelsmacher, "The Impact of Brand Prominence and Game Repetition on Brand Responses," *Journal of Advertising,* Vol. 39 (1) (Spring 2010): 5–18; Andrea L. Micheaux, "Managing E-Mail Advertising Frequency from the Consumer Perspective," *Journal of Advertising,* Vol. 40 (4) (Winter 2011): 45–65.
3. Marciej Szymanowski and Els Gijsbrechts, "Consumption-Based Cross-Brand Learning: Are Private Labels Really Private?" *Journal of Marketing Research,* (April 2012): 231–246; Zain-ul-Abideen and Abdul Latif, "Do Brand Extensions Affect Consumer Attitude: An Empirical Experience with Reference to Pakistani Consumers," *The Clute Institute,* Vol. 27 (2) (March/April 2011): 19–36.
4. Shobha G. Iyer, Bibek Banerjee, and Lawrence L. Garber, "Determinants of Consumer Attitudes Toward Brand Extensions: An Experimental Study," *International Journal of Management,* Vol. 28 (3) (September 2011): 809–821.
5. Tsan-Ming Choi, "Fast Brand Extensions: An Empirical Study of Consumer Preferences," *Brand Management,* Vol. 17 (7) (2010): 472–487.
6. Tom Meyvis and Chris Janiszewski, "When Are Broader Brands Stronger Brands? An Accessibility Perspective on the Success of Brand Extensions," *Journal of Consumer Research,* (September 2004): 346–358; Eva Martinez and Jose M. Pina, "Consumer Responses to Brand Extensions: A Comprehensive Model," *European Journal of Marketing,* Vol. 44 (7) (2010): 1182–1206.
7. Uri Gneezy and Aldo Rustichini, "A Fine Is a Price," *Journal of Legal Studies,* Vol. 29 (1, part 1) (2000): 1–18.
8. Gangseog Ryu and Lawrence Feick, "A Penny for Your Thoughts: Referral Reward Programs and Referral Likelihood," *Journal of Marketing,* Vol. 71 (January 2007): 84–94.
9. Anne Martensen, "Tweens' Satisfaction and Brand Loyalty in the Mobile Phone Market," *Young Consumers,* Vol. 8 (2) (2007): 108–116.
10. Jolie M. Martin and Michael I. Norton, "Shaping Online Consumer Choice by Partitioning the Web," *Psychology & Marketing,* Vol. 26 (10) (2009): 908–926.
11. John Tierney, "How Many Memories Fit in Your Brain?" nytimes.com, June 22, 2007.
12. Kathryn A. Braun-LaTour, Michael S. LaTour, and George M. Zinkhan, "Using Childhood Memories to Gain Insight into Brand Meaning," *Journal of Marketing,* Vol. 71 (April 2007): 45–60.
13. Rik Pieters and Michel Wedel, "Goal Control of Attention to Advertising: The Yarbus Implication," *Journal of Consumer Research,* Vol. 34 (August 2007): 224–233.
14. Hyun Seung Jin, Jaebeom Suh, and Todd Donovan, "Salient Effects of Publicity in Advertised Brand Recall and Recognition: The List-Stretch Paradigm," *Journal of Advertising,* Vol. 37 (1) (Spring 2008): 45–58.
15. William E. Baker, "Does Brand Imprinting in Memory Increase Brand Information Retention?" *Psychology & Marketing* (December 2003): 1119+.
16. Tina M. Lowery, L. J. Shrum, and Tony M. Dubitsky, "The Relation Between Brand-Name Linguistic Characteristics and Brand-Name Memory," *Journal of Advertising* (Fall 2003): 7–18; Eric Yorkston and Geeta Menon, "A Sound Idea: Phonetic Effects of Brand Names on Consumer Judgments," *Journal of Consumer Research* (June 2004): 43–52.
17. Sandra Blakeslee, "If Your Brain Has a 'Buy Button,' What Pushes It," nytimes.com, October 19, 2004.
18. Yuval Rottenstreich, Sanjay Sood, and Lyle Brenner, "Feeling and Thinking in Memory Versus Stimulus-Based Choices," *Journal of Consumer Research,* Vol. 33 (March 2007): 461–469.
19. For example, Jan Meller Jensen and Torben Hansen, "An Empirical Examination of Brand Loyalty," *Journal of Product & Brand Management,* Vol. 15 (7) (2006): 442–449.
20. Ivonne M. Torres and Elten Briggs, "Identification Effects on Advertising Response," *Journal of Advertising,* Vol. 36 (3) (Fall 2007): 97–109.
21. Marjolein Moorman, Peter C. Neijens, and Edith G. Smit, "The Effects of Program Involvement on Commercial Exposure and Recall in a Naturalistic Setting," *Journal of Advertising,* Vol. 36 (1) (Spring 2007): 121–138.
22. Mira Lee and Ronald J. Faber, "Effects of Product Placement in On-Line Games on Brand Memory," *Journal of Advertising,* Vol. 36 (4) (Winter 2007): 75–91.
23. Martin Holzwarth, Chris Janiszewski, and Marcus M. Neumann, "The Influence of Avatars on Online Consumer Shopping Behavior," *Journal of Marketing,* Vol. 70 (October 2006): 19–36.
24. Janet Rae-Dupree, "Let Computers Compute. It's the Age of the Right Brain," nytimes.com, April 6, 2008.
25. Herbert E. Krugman, "The Impact of Television Advertising: Learning Without Involvement," *Public Opinion Quarterly,* Vol. 29 (Fall 1965): 349–356; "Brain Wave Measures of Media Involvement," *Journal of Advertising Research,* Vol. 11 (February 1971): 3–10; "Memory Without Recall, Exposure Without Perception," *Journal of Advertising Research,* Vol. 1 (September 1982): 80–85.
26. George R. Franke, Bruce A. Huhmann, and David L. Mothersbaugh, "Information Content and Consumer Readership of Print Ads: A Comparison of Search and Experience Products," *Academy of Marketing Science Journal* (Winter 2004): 20+.
27. Source: Rebekah Bennett and Sharyn Rundle-Thiele, "A Comparison of Attitudinal Loyalty Measurement Approaches," *Journal of Brand Management* (January 2002): 193–209.
28. Spiros Gounaris and Vlasis Stathakopoulos, "Antecedents and Consequences of Brand Loyalty: An Empirical Study," *Journal of Brand Management,* (April 2004): 283–307.
29. 2013 Harris Poll EquiTrend® Rankings harrisinteractive .com/insights/equitrendrankings.aspx#Sports (accessed April 13, 2013).

Chapter 6

1. Geoffrey L. Cohen, Joshua Aronson, and Claude M. Steele, "When Beliefs Yield to Evidence: Reducing Biased Evaluation by Affirming the Self," *Personality & Social Psychology Bulletin*, 26 (9) (September 2000): 1151–1164.

2. Stuart Elliott, "As Technology Evolves, AT&T Adjusts a Theme," nytimes.com, April 8, 2012.

3. Martin Fishbein, "An Investigation of the Relationships Between Beliefs about an Object and the Attitude Toward the Object," *Human Relations*, 16 (1963): 233–240; Martin Fishbein, "A Behavioral Theory Approach to the Relations Between Beliefs about an Object and the Attitude Toward the Object," in *Readings in Attitude Theory and Measurement*, ed. Martin Fishbein, pp. 389–400 (New York: John Wiley & Sons, 1967).

4. Shwu-Ing Wu, "The Relationship Between Consumer Characteristics and Attitude Toward Online Shopping," *Marketing Intelligence & Planning*, 21 (1) (2003): 37–44.

5. Terence A. Shimp and Alican Kavas, "The Theory of Reasoned Action Applied to Coupon Usage," *Journal of Consumer Research*, 11 (December 1984): 795–809; Blair H. Sheppard, Jon Hartwick, and Paul R. Warshaw, "The Theory of Reasoned Action: A Meta-Analysis of Past Research with Recommendations for Modifications and Future Research," *Journal of Consumer Research*, 15 (September 1986): 325–343; Sharon E. Beatly and Lynn R. Kahle, "Alternative Hierarchies of the Attitude-Behavior Relationship: The Impact of Brand Commitment and Habit," *Journal of the Academy of Marketing Science*, 16 (Summer 1988): 1–10; Richard P. Bagozzi, Hans Baumgartner, and Youjae Yi, "Coupon Usage and the Theory of Reasoned Action," in *Advances in Consumer Research*, 18, eds. Rebecca H. Holman and Michael R. Solomon, pp. 24–27 (Provo, UT: Association for Consumer Research, 1991); Hee Sun Park, "Relationships Among Attitudes and Subjective Norms: Testing the Theory of Reasoned Action Across Cultures," *Communication Studies*, 51 (2) (Summer 2000): 162–175; Hung-Pin Shih, "An Empirical Study on Predicting User Acceptance of e-Shopping on the Web," *Information & Management* (Amsterdam), 41 (January 2004): 351.

6. Richard P. Bagozzi and Paul R. Warshaw, "Trying to Consume," *Journal of Consumer Research*, 17 (September 1990): 127–140; Richard P. Bagozzi, Fred D. Davis, and Paul R. Warshaw, "Development and Test of a Theory of Technological Learning and Usage," *Human Relations*, 45 (7) (July 1992): 659–686; Anil Mathur, "From Intentions to Behavior: The Role of Trying and Control," in *1995 AMA Educators' Proceedings*, eds. Barbara B. Stern and George M. Zinkan, pp. 374–375 (Chicago: American Marketing Association, 1995).

7. Stephen J. Gould, Franklin S. Houston, and Jonel Mundt, "Failing to Try to Consume: A Reversal of the Usual Consumer Research Perspective," in *Advances in Consumer Research*, eds. Merrie Brucks and Deborah J. MacInnis, pp. 211–216 (Provo, UT: Association for Consumer Research, 1997).

8. Durriya Z. Khairullah and Zahid Y. Khairullah, "Relationships Between Acculturation, Attitude Toward the Advertisement, and Purchase Intention of Asian-Indian Immigrants," *International Journal of Commerce & Management*, 9 (3/4) (1999): 46–65.

9. Dan Petrovici and Marin Marinov, "Determinants and Antecedents of General Attitudes Towards Advertising: A Study of Two EU Accession Countries," *European Journal of Marketing*, 3 (4) (2007): 307–326.

10. Stuart Elliott, "Time to Eat Tuna? 'Wonder' No More," nytimes.com, March 7, 2011.

11. Daniel Katz, "The Functional Approach to the Study of Attitudes," *Public Opinion Quarterly*, 24 (Summer 1960): 163–191; Sharon Shavitt, "Products, Personality and Situations in Attitude Functions: Implications for Consumer Behavior," in *Advances in Consumer Research*, 16, ed. Thomas K. Srull, pp. 300–305 (Provo, UT: Association for Consumer Research, 1989); Richard Ennis and Mark P. Zanna, "Attitudes, Advertising, and Automobiles: A Functional Approach," in *Advances in Consumer Research*, 20, eds. Leigh McAlister and Michael L. Rothschild, pp. 662–666 (Provo, UT: Association for Consumer Research, 1992).

12. Barbara A. Lafferty and Ronald E. Goldsmith, "Cause-Brand Alliances: Does the Cause Help the Brand or Does the Brand Help the Cause?" *Journal of Business Research*, 58 (April 2005): 423–429.

13. Nora J. Rifon, Sejung Marina Choi, Carrie S. Tripble, and Hairong Li, "Congruence Effects in Sponsorship," *Journal of Advertising*, 33 (Spring 2004): 29–42.

14. Chan-Wook Park and Byeong-Joon Moon, "The Relationship Between Product Involvement and Product Knowledge: Moderating Roles of Product Type and Product Knowledge Type," *Psychology & Marketing* (November 2003): 977.

15. Richard E. Petty et al., "Theories of Attitude Change," in *Handbook of Consumer Theory and Research*, eds. Harold Kassarjian and Thomas Robertson (Upper Saddle River, NJ: Prentice Hall, 1991); Richard E. Petty, John T. Cacioppo, and David Schumann, "Central and Peripheral Routes to Advertising Effectiveness: The Moderating Role of Involvement," *Journal of Consumer Research*, 10 (September 1983): 135–146. Also see Curtis P. Haugtvedt and Alan J. Strathman, "Situational Product Relevance and Attitude Persistence," in *Advances in Consumer Research*, 17, eds. Marvin E. Goldberg, Gerald Gorn, and Richard W. Pollay, pp. 766–769 (Provo, UT: Association for Consumer Research, 1990); Scott B. Mackenzie and Richard A. Spreng, "How Does Motivation Moderate the Impact of Central and Peripheral Processing on Brand Attitudes and Intentions?" *Journal of Consumer Research*, 18 (March 1992): 519–529.

16. Jon D. Morris, ChongMoo Woo, and A. J. Singh, "Elaboration Likelihood Model: A Missing Intrinsic Emotional Implication," *Journal of Targeting, Measurement & Analysis for Marketing*, 14 (1) (December 2005): 79–98.

17. Shin-Chieh Chuang and Chia-Ching Tsai, "The Impact of Consumer Product Knowledge on the Effect of Terminology in Advertising," *Journal of the American Academy of Business*, 6 (March 2005): 154–158; Jaideep Sgupta, Ronald C. Goldstein, and David S. Boninger, "All Cues Are Not Created Equal: Obtaining Attitude Persistence under Low-Involvement Conditions," *Journal of Consumer Research*, 23 (March 1997): 351–361.

18. Young "Sally" Kim, "Applications of the Cognitive Dissonance Theory to the Service Industry," *Services Marketing Quarterly*, 32 (2011): 96–112.

19. For example, David C. Matz and Wendy Wood, "Cognitive Dissonance in Groups," *Journal of Personality & Social Psychology*, 88 (January 2005): 22–37; Jillian C. Sweeney and Tanya Mukhopadhyay, "Cognitive Dissonance after Purchase: A Comparison of Bricks and Mortar and Online Retail Purchase Situations," *American Marketing Association Conference Proceedings: 2004 AMA Winter Educators' Conference*, 15, pp. 190–191 (Chicago: American Marketing Association, 2004); Martin O'Neill and Adrian Palmer, "Cognitive Dissonance and the Stability of Service Quality Perceptions," *Journal of Services Marketing*, 18 (6/7) (2004): 433–449; Robert A Wicklund and Jack W. Brehm, "Internalization of Multiple Perspectives or Dissonance Reduction?" *Theory & Psychology* (London), 14 (June 2004): 355–371; Alex R. Zablah, Danny N. Bellenger, and Westley J. Johnson, "Customer Relationship Management Implementation Gaps," *Journal of Personal Selling & Sales Management*, 24 (Fall 2004): 279–295.
20. Geoffrey N. Soutar and Jillian C. Sweeney, "Are There Cognitive Dissonance Segments?" *Australian Journal of Management*, 28 (December 2003): 227–239.
21. Phil Lampert, "Cognitive Dissonance," *Progressive Grocer*, 83 (May 15, 2004): 16.
22. Mohammed M. Nadeem, "Post-Purchase Dissonance: The Wisdom of the 'Repeat' Purchases," *Journal of Global Business Issues*, 1 (2) (Summer 2007): 183–193.
23. Edward E. Jones et al., *Attribution: Perceiving the Causes of Behavior* (Morristown, NJ: General Learning Press, 1972); Bernard Weiner, "Attributional Thoughts about Consumer Behavior," *Journal of Consumer Research*, 27 (3) (December 2000): 382–387.
24. Rifon et al., "Congruence Effects in Sponsorship," 29; Andrea C. Morales, "Giving Firms an 'E' for Effort: Consumer Responses to High-Effort Firms," *Journal of Consumer Research*, 3 (March 2005): 806–812.
25. S. Christian Wheeler, Richard E. Petty, and George Y. Bizer, "Self-Schema Matching and Attitude Change: Situational and Dispositional Determinants of Message Elaboration," *Journal of Consumer Research*, 31 (March 2005): 787–797.
26. For example, Leslie Lazar Kanuk, *Mail Questionnaire Response Behavior as a Function of Motivational Treatment* (New York: CUNY, 1974).
27. Angelos Rodafinos, Arso Vucevic, and Georgios D. Sideridis, "The Effectiveness of Compliance Techniques: Foot in the Door Versus Door in the Face," *Journal of Social Psychology*, 145 (April 2005): 237–239.
28. Harold H. Kelley, "Attribution Theory in Social Psychology," in *Nebraska Symposium on Motivation*, 15, ed. David Levine, p. 197 (Lincoln: University of Nebraska Press, 1967). Based on Andrea M. Sjovall and Andrew C. Talk, "From Actions to Impressions: Cognitive Attribution Theory and the Formation of Corporate Reputation," *Corporate Reputation Review*, 7 (Fall 2004): 277–289.

Chapter 7

1. Louise Story, "It's an Ad, Ad, Ad, Ad World," nytimes.com, August 6, 2007.
2. Ji Hee Song and George M. Zinkhan, "Determinants of Perceived Web Site Interactivity," *Journal of Marketing*, Vol. 72 (March 2008): 99–113.
3. Laura M. Holson, "In CBS Test, Mobile Ads Find Users," nytimes.com, February 6, 2008.
4. Edward Wyatt, "Publisher Aims at Cellphones," nytimes.com, February 18, 2008.
5. Louise Story, "Madison Avenue Calling," nytimes.com, January 20, 2007.
6. Shira Ovide, "Twitter to Target Ads Based on Interests," online.wsj.com, August 30, 2012.
7. Louise Story, "A TV Show's Content Calls the Commercial Plays," nytimes.com, December 21, 206.
8. Tim Arango, "Cable Firms Join Forces to Attract Focused Ads," nytimes.com, Match 10, 2008; Stephanie Clifford, "Cable Companies Target Commercials to Audience," nytimes.com, March 4, 2009.
9. Rik Pieters, Michel Wedel, and Rajeev Batra, "The Stopping Power of Advertising: Measures and Effects of Visual Complexity," *Journal of Marketing*, Vol. 74 (September 2010): 48–60.
10. Stuart Elliott, "Paring Down Marketing to a Few Simple Basics," nytimes.com, July 26, 2012.
11. Richard Buda and Bruce H. Chamov, "Message Processing in Realistic Recruitment Practices," *Journal of Managerial Issues* (Fall 2003): 302+.
12. Jennifer L. Aaker and Angela Y. Lee, "'I' Seek Pleasure and 'We' Avoid Pains: The Role of Self-Regulatory Goals in Information Processing and Persuasion," *Journal of Consumer Research* (June 2001): 33–49.
13. Dena Cox and Anthony D. Cox, "Communicating the Consequences of Early Detection: The Role of Evidence and Framing," *Journal of Marketing* (July 2001): 91–103.
14. Baba Shiv, Julie A. Edell Britton, and John W. Payne, "Does Elaboration Increase or Decrease the Effectiveness of Negatively Versus Positively Framed Messages?" *Journal of Consumer Research* (June 2004): 199–209.
15. William E. Baker, Heather Honea, and Cristel Antonia Russell, "Do Not Wait to Reveal the Brand Name: The Effect of Brand-Name Placement on Television Advertising Effectiveness," *Journal of Advertising* (Fall 2004): 77–86.
16. Nathalie Dens and Patrick De Pelsmacker, "Consumer Response to Different Advertising Appeals for New Products: The Moderating Influence of Branding Strategy and Product Category Involvement," *Journal of Brand Management*, Vol. 18 (1) (2010): 50–65.
17. Marc Reinhard and Matthias Messner, "The Effects of Likeability and Need for Cognition on Advertising Effectiveness Under Explicit Persuasion," *Journal of Consumer Behavior*, Vol. 8 (2009): 179–191.
18. Kenneth C. Manning, Paul W. Miniard, Michael J. Barone, and Randall L. Rose, "Understanding the Mental Representations Created by Comparative Advertising," *Journal of Advertising*, (Summer 2001): 27–39.
19. Chingching Chang, The Relative Effectiveness of Comparative Advertising: Evidence for Gender Differences in Information-Processing Strategies," *Journal of Advertising*, Vol. 36 (1) (Spring 2007): 21–36.
20. Shailendra Pratap Jain, Charles Lindsey, Nidhi Agrawal, and Durairaj Maheswaran, "For Better or For Worse? Valenced Comparative Frames and Regulatory Focus," *Journal of Consumer Research*, Vol. 34 (June 2007): 57–65.
21. "Tesco pay damages to Aldi over inaccurate price comparisons," bbc.co.uk, December 12, 2012.

22. James Davey, "Sainsbury's takes price comparison spat with Tesco to high court," ukreuters.com, October 30, 2013.

23. Beth Brooks, "Sainsbury's ads take aim at Tesco Price Promise," thegrocer.co.uk, November 1, 2013.

24. Ron Lennon, Randall Rentfro and Bay O'Leary, "Social Marketing and Distracted Driving Behaviors Among Young Adults: The Effectiveness of Fear Appeals," *Academy of Marketing Studies Journal*, Vol. 14 (2), (2010): 95–113.

25. Patrick De Pelsmacker, Verolien Cauberghe, and Nathalie Dens, "Fear Appeal Effectiveness for Familiar and Unfamiliar Issues," *Journal of Social Marketing*, Vol. 1 (3) (2011): 171–191.

26. Karen H. Smith and Mary Ann Stutts, "Effects of Short-Term Cosmetic Versus Long-Term Health Fear Appeals in Anti-Smoking Advertisements on the Smoking Behavior of Adolescents," *Journal of Consumer Behavior* (December 2003): 157+.

27. Andrea Morales, Eugenia Wu and Gavan Fitzsimons, "How Disgust Enhances the Effectiveness of Fear Appeals," *Journal of Consumer Research*, Vol. XLIX (June 2012): 383–393.

28. Martin Eisend, "How Humor in Advertising Works: A Meta-Analytic Test of Alternative Models," *Springer Science [plus] Business Media* (May 2010): 115–132.

29. Graeme Galloway, "Humor and Ad Liking: Evidence That Sensation Seeking Moderates the Effects of Incongruity-Resolution Humor," *Psychology and Marketing*, Vol. 26 (9) (September 2009): 779–792.

30. Thomas W. Cline, Moses B. Altsech, and James J. Kellaris, "When Does Humor Enhance or Inhibit Ad Responses? The Moderating Role of the Need for Humor," *Journal of Advertising* (Fall 2003): 31–46.

31. James J. Kellaris and Thomas W. Cline, "Humor and Ad Memorability: On the Contributions of Humor Expectancy, Relevancy, and Need for Humor," *Psychology and Marketing,* Vol. 24 (6) (June 2007): 497–509.

32. Thomas W. Cline and James J. Kellaris, "The Influence of Humor Strength and Humor-Message Relatedness on Ad Memorability: A Dual Process Model," *Journal of Advertising,* Vol. 36 (1) (Spring 2007): 55–68.

33. ChangHyun Jin and Jorge Villegas, "The Effect of the Placement of the Product in Film: Consumers' Emotional Responses to Humorous Stimuli and Prior Brand Evaluation," *Journal of Targeting, Measurement and Analysis for Marketing,* Vol. 15 (4) (2007): 244–255.

34. Elizabeth Olson, "Not Every Bad Day Needs to End With Ice Cream," nytimes.com, August 14, 2012.

35. Stuart Elliott, "The 'Moore' the Merrier, Paint Marketer Proclaims," nytimes.com, April 26, 2010.

36. Edward F. McQuarrie and David Glen Mick, "Visual and Verbal Rhetorical Figures Under Directed Processing Versus Incidental Exposure to Advertising," *Journal of Consumer Research* (March 2003): 579–588.

37. Stuart Elliott, "Is This a New 'Era' for Detergent Advertising?" nytimes.com, June 13, 2011.

38. Andrew Newman, "Small Carrier Gets Big Tailwind From Social Media," nytimes.com, April 6, 2011; Tanzina Vega, "From Zappos, an Unadorned Approach," nytimes.com, July 10, 2011.

39. Tom Reichert, Michael LaTour, and John Ford, "The Naked Truth: Revealing the Affinity for Graphic Sexual Appeals in Advertising," *Journal of Advertising Research* (June 2011): 436–448.

40. Iain Black, George Organ, and Peta Morton, "The Effect of Personality on Response to Sexual Appeals", *European Journal of Marketing*, Vol. 44 (9/10) (2010): 1453–1477.

41. Stuart Elliott, "Striving for Balance Between Losses and Laughs," nytimes.com, October 15, 2008.

42. Stephanie Clifford and Stuart Elliott, "Goodbye Seduction, Hello Coupons," nytimes.com, November 10, 2008.

43. Stuart Elliott, "Business District Tries Soft Selling for Holidays," nytimes.com, December 8, 2008.

44. Stuart Elliott, "Capitalizing on Consumer Anxiety, One Halloween Deal at a Time," nytimes.com, October 14, 2008.

45. Stuart Elliott, "Ads That Soothe When Banks Are Failing," nytimes.com, October 7, 2008; Stuart Elliott, "Down Economic Times Elicit Upbeat Consumers," nytimes.com, March 10, 2009; Vivian Toy, "Goodbye, Glitzy Condo Pitches," nytimes.com, August 20, 2010; Patricia Cohen, "Marketing Broadway: Selling Hope for a Song," nytimes.com, December 10, 2008; Andrew Newman, "Using Appeals to Emotions to Sell Paint," nytimes.com, June 7, 2010; Stuart Elliott, "In New Ads, Stirring Memories of Commercials Past," nytimes.com, January 12, 2012.

Chapter 8

1. "Companies That 'Like' Facebook Ads," online.wsj.com, November 2, 2011.

2. S. Ramachandran, "Dish's Ads to End All Ads," online.wsj.com, May 16, 2012.

3. J. Jurgensen, "Binge Viewing: TV's Lost Weekends," online.wsj.com, July 12, 2012.

4. Miguel Helft and Tanzina Vega, "Retargeting Ads Follow Surfers to Other Sites," nytimes.com, August 29, 2010.

5. A. Efrati, "Google to Require Retailers to Pay," online.wsj.com, June 1, 2012.

6. Wikipedia.

7. J. Dohnert, "Consumers Most Annoyed by Ads on Social Networking Sites," *Incisive Interactive Marketing*, December 13, 2012.

8. J. Angwin and J. Singer-Vine, "Selling You on Facebook," online.wsj.com, April 8, 2012.

9. Ibid.

10. "McDonald's Social Media Director Explains Twitter Fiasco," paidContent.org, January 23, 2012.

11. E. Holmes, "Twitting Without Fear," online.wsj.com, December 11, 2011.

12. S. Elliott, "Selling New Wine in Millennial Bottles," nytimes.com, October 25, 2010.

13. J. Levere, "Cosmo Campaign Puts Viewers in the Photo Shoot," nytimes.com, September 29, 2010.

14. S. Kolesnikov-Jessop, "Selling a Watch via Social Media," nytimes.com, November 22, 2012.

15. E. Rusli and S. Banjo, "Facebook's Wal-Mart Gambit," online.wsj.com, December 16, 2012.

16. A. A. Newman, "Brands Now Direct Their Followers to Social Media," nytimes.com, August 3, 2011.

17. J. L. Levere, "A Mexican Beer Rides a Social Media Wave," nytimes.com, August 13, 2012; G. Schimdt, "A Product with Devotees Tries to Widen Its Niche," nytimes.com, August 15, 2012.

18. S. Elliott, "Early Kickoff for Marketers at Super Bowl," nytimes.com, December 11, 2012.

19. R. Rivera, "Social Media Strategy Was Crucial as Transit Agencies Coped with Hurricanes," nytimes.com, December 14, 2012.

20. T. Wayne, "Age Gap Narrows on Social Networking," nytimes.com, December 26, 2010.

21. G. A. Fowler, "Are You Talking to Me?" online.wsj.com, April 25, 2011; J. L. Levere, "Choosing a Marketing Plan: Traditional or Social Media?," nytimes.com, February 25, 2010.

22. L. Kwoh and M. Korn, "140 Characters of Risk: Some CEOs Fear Twitter," online.wsj.com, September 25, 2012.

23. Interactive Advertising Bureau (IAB), "Social Media Buyer's Guide," February 2010.

24. Ibid.

25. K. M. Heussner, "U.S. to Top the World in Mobile Ad Spending for the First Time," gigaom.com/2012/08/01/us-to-top-the-world-in-mobile-ad-spending-for-the-first-time, August 1, 2012.

26. E. Rusli and S. Banjo, "Facebook's Wal-Mart Gambit," online.wsj.com, December 16, 2012.

27. M. Pihlstrom and G. J. Brush, "Comparing the Perceived Value of Information and Entertainment Mobile Services," *Psychology & Marketing*, Vol. 25 (8) (August 2008): 732–755.

28. C. Taylor and D. H. Lee, "Introduction: New Media: Mobile Advertising and Marketing," *Psychology & Marketing*, Vol. 25 (8) (August 2008): 711–713.

29. J. Mantel and Y. Sekhavat, "The Impact of SMS Advertising on Members of a Virtual Community," *Journal of Advertising Research* (September 2008): 363–373.

30. S. Ovide and G. Bensinger, "Mobile Ads: Here's What Works and What Doesn't," online.wsj.com, September 27, 2012.

31. C. C. Miller and S. Sengupta, "In Mobile World, Tech Giants Scramble to Get Up to Speed," online.wsj.com, October 22, 2012.

32. R. Stross, "Smartphones Ads and Their Drawbacks," nytimes.com, September 15, 2012.

33. B. Stone, "Amazon.com Invades the Apple App Store," nytimes.com, December 3, 2008.

34. Tim Arango, "Digital Sales Surpass CDs at Atlantic," nytimes.com, November 26, 2008.

35. Michael Grynbaum, "Taxi TV Screens Gain Ad Business in New York," nytimes.com, December 10, 2010.

36. Louise Story, "Madison Avenue Calling," nytimes.com, January 20, 2007.

37. Emily Steel and Jessica Vascellaro, "A Rare Apple Compromise," online.wsj.com, December 13, 2011.

38. Elizabeth Olson, "Bar Codes Add Detail on Items in TV Ads," nytimes.com, September 26, 2010.

39. S. Clifford and C. Miller, "Retailers Retool Sites to Ease Mobile Shopping," nytimes.com, April 17, 2011.

40. T. Vega, "Google Search That Leads to Brand Marketing," nytimes.com, November 15, 2010.

41. D. Mattioli, "Grocers Are Testing Smartphones," nytimes.com, October 11, 2011.

42. K. Belson, "With This App, a Souvenir Without the Stand," nytimes.com, August 26, 2011.

43. S. Elliott, "If You Can't Stand the Web Camera, Get Out of the Kitchen," nytimes.com, December 7, 2009.

44. D. Armano, "Six Social-Digital Trends for 2013," *Harvard Business Review*, (December 12, 2012): 34–47.

45. Ibid.

46. Shayndi Raice, "Inside Facebook's Push to Woo Big Advertisers," online.wsj.com, August 14, 2012.

47. "Social Media Ad Metrics Definitions," Interactive Advertising Bureau (IAB), May 2009.

48. www.comscore.com/Products_Services/Web_Analytics/Audience_Demographics (accessed August 1, 2012).

49. Louise Story, "How Many Site Hits? Depends Who's Counting," nytimes.com, October 22, 2007.

50. William Launder and Suzanne Vranica, "Nielsen to Branch Out with Arbitron," online.wsj.com, December 18, 2012.

51. Stu Woo and Geoffrey Fowler, "Daily Deals Rescue Local-Ad Market," online.wsj.com, June 14, 2011.

52. Stu Woo and Geoffrey Fowler, "Banner Ads and Other 'Local' Flops," online.wsj.com, June 14, 2011.

53. Compiled from data listed in Stuart Elliott, "Magazine Ad Pages Fell 3.1% in 2011, with a Weak End to the Year," nytimes.com, January 10, 2012.

54. http://www.nytimes.com/interactive/2009/01/30/business/20090201_metrics.html (accessed January 14, 2013).

55. Keach Hagey, "Magazines Cross the Digital Divide," online.wsj.com, January 18, 2013.

56. Shannon Terlep and Suzanne Vranica, "GM to Forgo Pricey Super Bowl Ads," online.wsj.com, May 18, 2012.

57. Sam Schechner, "TV Networks See Key Audience Erode," online.wsj.com, May 27, 2011.

58. Shalini Ramachadram, "Evidence Grows on TV Cord-Cutting," online.wsj.com, August 7, 2012.

59. Miriam Gottfried, "Online Streaming Gives Cable Networks a Sporting Chance," online.wsj.com, August 15, 2012.

60. www.ensequence.com

61. Stephen Richard Dix, Steven Bellman, Hanadi Haddad, and Duane Varan, "Using Interactive Program-Loyalty Banners to Reduce TV Ad Avoidance: Is It Possible to Give Viewers a Reason to Stay Tuned during Commercial Breaks?" *Journal of Advertising Research* (June 2010): 154–161.

62. Barbara Chai, "'Person of Interest' Takes to Streets to Give People a Taste of the Show," online.wsj.com, September 12, 2011.

63. Stuart Elliott, "Hot Food, and Air, at Bus Stops," nytimes.com, December 2, 2008.

64. pqmedia, *Global Digital Out-of-Home Media Forecast 2012–2016*, "Executive Summary" (2011).

65. Doreen Carvajal, "Placing the Product in the Dialogue, Too," nytimes.com, January 17, 2006; Louise Story, "So That's Why They Drink Coke on TV," nytimes.com, December 9, 2007; Stuart Elliott, "Up Next, a Show from Our Sponsor," nytimes.com, June 12, 2008; Stephanie Clifford, "A Product's Place Is on the Set," nytimes.com, July 22, 2008.

66. Verolien Cauberghe and Patrick de Pelsmacker, "Advergames: The Impact of Brand Prominence and Game Repetition on Brand Responses," *Journal of Advertising*, Vol. 39 (1) (Spring 2010): 5–18.

Chapter 9

1. Marina Krakovsky, "Less Wash, More Dry," *Scientific American* (November 2008): 28–29.
2. Andrew Adam Newman, "A Lucky Few, This Band of Brothers, and the Less Blood Shed the Better," nytimes.com, November 17, 2010.
3. Peeter W. J. Verleigh, Ad Th. H. Pruyn, and Kim A. Peters, "Turning Shoppers into Sellers: Two Experiments on Member-Get-Member Campaigns," *Advances in Consumer Research*, 30 (2003): 346.
4. Charles Passy, "Waiting in Line: Good for the Ego, Bad for the Wallet," online.wsj.com, October 9, 2012.
5. Gary Kritz, Héctor R. Lozada, and Mary M. Long, "When Can Online Group Behavior Be an Aid: Can the Foodies Help Marketers Learn about Consumption?" *Journal of Business & Behavioral Sciences*, Vol. 24 (1) (Spring 2012): 58–71.
6. Feng Zhu & Xiaoquan (Michael) Zhang, "Impact of Online Consumer Reviews on Sales: The Moderating Role of Product and Consumer Characteristics," *Journal of Marketing*, Vol. 74 (March 2010): 133–148.
7. Robert Madrigal, "The Influence of Social Alliances with Sports Teams on Intentions to Purchase Corporate Sponsors' Products," *Journal of Advertising*, 29 (Winter 2000): 13–24.
8. Katherine Rosman, "Books Women Read When No One Can See the Cover," online.wsj.com, March 14, 2012.
9. George D. Deitz, Susan W. Myers, and Marla R. Stafford, "Understanding Consumer Response to Sponsorship Information: A Resource-Matching Approach," *Psychology & Marketing*, Vol. 29 (4) (April 2012): 226–239.
10. Jennifer Lemanski and Lee Hyung-Seok, "Attitude Certainty and Resistance to Persuasion: Investigating the Impact of Source Trustworthiness in Advertising," *International Journal of Business & Social Sciences*, Vol. 3 (1) (January 2012): 6675.
11. Zafer Erdogan, Michael J. Baker, and Stephen Tagg, "Selecting Celebrity Endorsers: The Practitioner's Perspective," *Journal of Advertising Research* (May/June 2001): 39–48.
12. Roobina Ohanian, "The Impact of Celebrity Spokes-persons: Perceived Image on Consumers' Intention to Purchase," *Journal of Advertising Research* (February–March 1991): 46–54.
13. Carolyn Tripp, Thomas D. Jensen, and Les Carlson, "The Effects of Multiple Product Endorsements by Celebrities on Consumers' Attitudes and Intentions," *Journal of Consumer Research*, Vol. 20 (March 1994): 535–547; David C. Bojanic, Patricia K. Voli, and James B. Hunt, "Can Consumers Match Celebrity Endorsers with Products?" in *Developments in Marketing Science*, ed. Robert L. King (Richmond, VA: Academy of Marketing Science, 1991): 303–307.
14. Alan J. Bush, Craig A. Martin, and Victoria D. Bush, "Sports Celebrity Influence on the Behavioral Intentions of Generation Y," *Journal of Advertising Research* (March 2004): 108–118.
15. Ben Sisario, "In Beyoncé Deal, Pepsi Focuses on Collaboration," nytimes.com, December 9, 2012.
16. Suzanne Vranica, "Bringing Sexy Back to Golf?" online.wsj.com, January 24, 2012.
17. Brian Stelter, "After Apology, National Advertisers Are Still Shunning Limbaugh," nytimes.com, March 13, 2012.
18. Stuart Elliott, "A Noisy Casting Call as Thousands Quack for Aflac," nytimes.com, April 5, 2011.
19. Associated Press, "Nike Makes No Plans for Pistorius in Future Ads," online.wsj.com, February 18, 2013.
20. Kenneth E. Clow, Karen E. James, Sarah E. Sisk, and Henry S. Cole, "Source Credibility, Visual Strategy and the Model in Print Advertisements," *Journal of Marketing Development & Competitiveness*, Vol. 5 (3) (2011): 24–31.
21. Andria Cheng, "Marketers Seek Out Geeks," online.wsj.com, October 15, 2012.
22. Mathew Ingram, "Should You Care How High Your Klout Score Is?" GIGAOM, October 27, 2011; Meredith Popolo, "How to Boost Your Klout Score," online.wsj.com, November 2, 2011.
23. Jo Brown, Amanda J. Broderick, and Nick Lee, "Word of Mouth Communication within Online Communities: Conceptualizing the Online Social Network," *Journal of Interactive Marketing*, Vol. 21 (3) (Summer 2007): 2–20.
24. Shahana Sen and Dawn Lerman, "Why Are You Telling Me This? An Examination into Negative Consumer Reviews on the Web," *Journal of Interactive Marketing*, Vol. 21 (4) (Autumn 2007): 76–94.
25. Wu Paul and Wang Yun Chen, "The Influence of Electronic Word-of-Mouth Message Appeal and Message Source Credibility on Brand Attitude," *Asia Pacific Journal of Marketing & Logistics*, Vol. 23 (4) (2011): 448–472.
26. Ted Smith, James R. Coyle, Elizabeth Lightfoot, and Amy Scott, "Reconsidering Models of Influence: The Relationship Between Consumer Social Networks and Word-of-Mouth Effectiveness," *Journal of Advertising Research*, Vol. 47 (4) (December 2007): 387–397.
27. David Kirkpatrick and Daniel Roth, "Why There's No Escaping the BLOG," *Fortune*, January 10, 2005, 44–50.
28. John Jannarone, "When Twitter Fans Steer TV," online.wsj.com, September 16, 2012.
29. Stephanie Clifford, "Spreading the Word (and the Lotion) in Small-Town Alaska," nytimes.com, October 9, 2008.
30. Robert V. Kozinets, Kristine de Valck, Andrea C. Wojnicki, and Sarah J. S. Wilner, "Networked Narratives: Understanding Word-of-Mouth Marketing in Online Communities," *Journal of Marketing*, Vol. 74 (March 2010): 71–89.
31. Stuart Elliott, "Laugh at the Web Clips, Then Buy the Gel," nytimes.com, December 19, 2007.
32. Louise Story, "Facebook Is Marketing Your Brand Preferences (with Your Permission)," nytimes.com, November 7, 2007.
33. Keach Hagey, "The Advertorial's Best Friend," online.wsj.com, October 7, 2012.
34. Joseph E. Phelps, Regina Lewis, Lynne Mobilio, David Perry, and Niranjan Raman, "Viral Marketing or Electronic Word-of-Mouth Advertising: Examining Consumer Responses and Motivations to Pass Along Email," *Journal of Advertising Research* (December 2004): 333–348.
35. Kirthi Kalyanam, Shelby McIntyre, and Todd Masonis, "Adaptive Experimentation in Interactive Marketing: The Case of Viral Marketing at Plaxo," *Journal of Interactive Marketing*, Vol. 21 (3) (Summer 2007): 72–85.

36. Yang Hongwei, Liu Hui, and Zhou Liuning, "Predicting Young Chinese Consumers' Mobile Viral Attitudes, Intents and Behavior," *Asia Pacific Journal of Marketing & Logistics,* Vol. 24 (1) (2012): 59–77.

37. Rob Walker, "The Hidden (in Plain Sight) Persuaders," www.nytimes.com, December 5, 2004.

38. Katherine Rosman, "Big Marketers on Campus," nytimes.com, April 3, 2012.

39. Natasha Singer, "You've Won a Badge (and Now We Know All About You)," nytimes.com, February 4, 2012.

40. Eric Pfanner, "Taxi Drivers in London Take a Turn as Pitchmen," nytimes.com, January 21, 2008.

41. Thorsten Hennig-Thurau, Kevin P. Gwinner, Gianfranco Walsh, and Dwayne D. Gremler, "Electronic Word-of-Mouth Via Consumer-Opinion Platforms: What Motivates Consumers to Articulate Themselves on the Internet?" *Journal of Interactive Marketing* (Winter 2004): 38–52.

42. Eun-Ju Lee, Kyoung-Nan Kwon, and David W. Schumann, "Segmenting the Non-adopter Category in the Diffusion of Internet Banking," *International Journal of Bank Marketing,* Vol. 23 (5) (2005): 414–437.

Chapter 10

1. Pamela Kruger, "Why Johnny Can't Play," *Fast Company* (August 2000): 271–272. See also Daniel Thomas Cook, *The Commodification of Childhood: The Children's Clothing Industry and the Rise of the Child Consumer* (Durham, NC: Duke University Press, 2004).

2. Rafael Bravo, Elena Fraj, and Eva Martinez, "Intergenerational Influences on the Dimensions of Young Customer-Based Brand Equity," *Young Consumers,* Vol. 8 (1) (2007): 63.

3. Amy Rummel, John Howard, Jennifer M. Swinton, and D. Bradley Seymour, "You Can't Have That! A Study of Reactance Effects and Children's Consumer Behavior," *Journal of Marketing Theory & Practice* (Winter 2000): 38–45.

4. Jason E. Lueg and R. Zachary Finney, "Interpersonal Communication in the Consumer Socialization Process: Scale Development and Validation," *Journal of Marketing Theory & Practice,* Vol. 15 (Winter 2007): 25–39.

5. Based on Sabrina M. Neeley and Tim Coffey, "Understanding the 'Four-Eyed, Four-Legged' Consumer: A Segmentation Analysis of U.S. Moms," *Journal of Marketing Theory & Practice,* Vol. 15 (3) (Summer 2007): 251–261.

6. Lan Nguyen Chaplin and Deborah Roedder John, "Growing Up in a Material World: Age Differences in Materialism in Children and Adolescents," *Journal of Consumer Research,* Vol. 34 (December 2007): 480–493.

7. David B. Wooten, "From Labeling Possessions to Possessing Labels: Ridicule and Socialization among Adolescents," *Journal of Consumer Research,* Vol. 33 (September 2006): 188–198.

8. Marie J. Lachance and Frederic Legault, "College Students' Consumer Competence: Identifying the Socialization Sources," *Journal of Research for Consumers,* no. 13 (2007): 1–5.

9. Deborah Moscardelli and Catherine Liston-Heyes, "Consumer Socialization in a Wired World: The Effects of Internet Use and Parental Communication on the Development of Skepticism to Advertising," *Journal of Marketing,* Vol. 13 (3) (Summer 2005): 62–75; Maria Eugenia Perez, Dan Padgett, and Willem Burgers, "Intergenerational Influence on Brand Preferences," *Journal of Product & Brand Management,* Vol. 20 (1) (2011): 5–13.

10. John Fetto, "'Woof Woof' Means, 'I Love You,'" *American Demographics* (February 2002): 11; Sharon L. Peters, "Are American Crazy for Treating Our Pets Like Kids?" *USA Today,* December 18, 2011; available at http://yourlife.usatoday.com/parenting-family/pets/story/2011-12-18/Are Americans crazy . . .

11. See, for example, Carter A. Mandrik, Edward F. Fern, and Yeqing Bao, "Intergenerational Influence in Mothers and Young Adult Daughters," *Advances in Consumer Research,* Vol. 31 (2004): 697–699.

12. U.S. Census Bureau, "Average Annual Expenditures of All Consumer Units by Selected Major Types of Expenditures: 1990 to 2009," *Statistical Abstract of the United States: 2012,* Table 684. Available at http://www.census.gov/comendia/statab/2012/1250684.pdt.

13. Sheryll Alexander, "What Women Want . . . in a Car," CNN.com, March 14, 2008.

14. Ibid.

15. Sam Marsden, "Women Now in Charge of Major Financial Decisions," telegraph.co.uk, September 28, 2012.

16. John B. Ford, Michael S. LaTour, and Tony L. Henthorne, "Perception of Marital Roles in Purchase Decision Processes: A Cross-Cultural Study," *Journal of the Academy of Marketing Science,* Vol. 23 (2) (1995): 120–131; Tony L. Henthorne, Michael S. LaTour, and Robert Matthews, "Perception of Marital Roles in Purchase Decision Making: A Study of Japanese Couples," in *Proceedings of the AMA,* 321–322 (Chicago: American Marketing Association, 1995).

17. Yang Xia, Zafar U. Ahmed, Ng Kuan Hwa, Tan Wan Li, and Wendy Teo Chai Ying, "Spousal Influence in Singaporean Family Purchase Decision-Making Process: A Cross-Cultural Comparison," *Asia Pacific Journal of Marketing,* Vol. 18 (3) (2006): 201–222.

18. Michael J. Dotson and Eva M. Hyatt, "Major Influence Factors in Children's Consumer Socialization," *Journal of Consumer Marketing,* Vol. 22 (1) (2005): 35–42; Aviv Shoham, "He Said, She Said They Said: Parents' and Children's Assessment of Children's Influence on Family Consumption Decisions," *Journal of Consumer Marketing,* Vol. 22 (3) (2005): 152–160; L. A. Flurry and Alvin C. Burns, "Children's Influence in Purchase Decisions: A Social Power Theory Approach," *Journal of Business Research,* Vol. 58 (May 2005): 593–601.

19. Malene Gram, "Children as Co-decision Makers in the Family? The Case of Family Holidays," *Young Consumers,* Vol. 8 (1) (2007): 19–28.

20. Joyantha S. Wimalasiri, "A Cross-National Study on Children's Purchasing Behavior and Parental Response," *Journal of Consumer Marketing,* Vol. 21 (4) (2004): 274–284.

21. Michael A. Belch, Kathleen A. Krentler, and Laura A. Willis-Flurry, "Teen Internet Mavens: Influence in Family Decision Making," *Journal of Business Research,* Vol. 58 (May 2005): 569–575.

22. Stephanie Thompson, "Million-Dollar Baby," *Advertising Age,* May 30, 2005, 1, 50.

23. Bodil Stilling Blichfeldt, "A Nice Vacation: Variations in Experience Aspirations and Travel Careers," *Journal of Vacation Marketing,* Vol. 13 (2) (2007): 149–164.

24. U.S. Census Bureau, *Statistical Abstract of the United States, 2008*; available at http://www.census.gov/ compendia/; U.S. Census Bureau, "American's Families and Living Arrangements, 2004, available at http://www .census.gov/prod/census2010/briefs/c2012br-14.

25. U.S. Census Bureau, "Households, Families, Subfamilies, and Married Couples: 1980 to 2006," and "Households by Age of Householder and Size of Household: 1990 to 2006," *Statistical Abstract of the United States: 2008,* Tables 58 and 61, accessed at www.census.gov/ compendia/statab; U.S. Census Bureau, "Marital Status of People 15 Years and Over, by Age, Sex, Personal Earnings, Race, and Hispanic Origin, 2006," *Current Population Survey 2006, Annual Social and Economic Supplement,* March 27, 2007, Table A1.

26. Compiled from data at: U.S. Census Bureau, *Census 2010 Summary File 1 counts shown in American Fact Finder.* Available at http://www.comsus.gov/prod/ cen2010/briefs/c2010br-14/.

27. Nabil Razzouk, Victoria Seitz, and Karen Prodigalidad Capo, "A Comparison of Consumer Decision-Making Behavior of Married and Cohabiting Couples," *Journal of Consumer Marketing,* Vol. 24 (5) (2007): 264–274.

28. Julie Tinson, Clive Nancarrow, and Ian Brace, "Purchase Decision Making and the Increasing Significance of Family Types," *Journal of Consumer Marketing,* Vol. 25 (1) (2008): 45–56.

29. Charles M. Schaninger and Sanjay Putrevu, "Dual Spousal Work Involvement: An Alternative Method to Classify Households/Families," *Academy of Marketing Science Review,* Vol. 10 (8) (2006): 1–21; Charles Schaninger and Sanjay Putrevu, "Dual Spousal Work Involvement," *European Advances in Consumer Research*, Vol. 8, ed. Stefania Borghinl, Mary Ann McGrath, and Cele Otnes (Duluth, MN: Association for Consumer Research, 2007): 80–86.

30. "Brand Stats: Market Focus—Instant Coffee," *Brand Strategy (London),* May 10, 2005, 50.

31. Takashina Shuji, "The New Inequality," *Japan Echo,* August 2000, 38–39.

32. *Source:* U.S. Census Bureau, *Statistical Abstract of the United States*, 2012, available at census.gov/ prod/2011pubs/12statab/income.

33. Tamar Lewin, "A Marriage of Unequals," *New York Times,* May 19, 2005, A1, 14–15.

34. David Leonhardt, "The College Dropout Boom," *New York Times,* May 24, 2005, A1, 18–19.

35. Michael D. Yates, "A Statistical Portrait of the U.S. Working Class," *Monthly Review,* Vol. 56 (April 2005): 12–31.

36. *Source:* MRI Spring 2012, www.fwmedia.com, accessed July 16, 2012.

37. Robert B. Settle, Pamela L. Alreck, and Denny E. McCorkle, "Consumer Perceptions of Mail Phone Order Shopping Media," *Journal of Direct Marketing,* Vol. 8 (Summer 1994): 30–45.

38. W. Lloyd Warner, Marchia Meeker, and Kenneth Eells, *Social Class in America: Manual of Procedure for the Measurement of Social Status* (New York: Harper & Brothers, 1960).

39. *Methodology and Scores of Socioeconomic Status,* Working Paper No. 15 (Washington, DC: U.S. Bureau of the Census, 1963).

40. Janny Scott, "In America, Living Better and Living Longer Is a Major Factor in Health Care and the Gaps Are Widening," *International Herald Tribune,* May 17, 2005, 2.

41. Suniya S. Luthar and Shawn J. Latendresse, "Children of the Affluent; Challenges to Well-Being," *Current Directions in Psychological Science,* Vol. 14 (February 2005): 49.

42. Merrill Lynch and Capgemini, *World Wealth Report, 2008,* available at www.capgemini.com/resources/ thought_leadership/world_wealth_report_2008; Merrill Lynch and Capgemini, *World Wealth Report, 2005,* available at www.capgemini.com/resources/thought_ leadership/world_wealth_report_200.

43. James Davies, Susanna Sandstrom, Anthony Shorrocks, and Edward Wolff, "The World Distribution of Household Wealth," *World Institute for Development Economies Research of the United Nations University,* 2006, available at www.mindfully.org/WTO/2006/ Household-Wealth-Gap5dec06.htm.

44. *The 2008 Mendelsohn Affluent Survey*, Ipsos Mendelsohn, 2008.

45. Ibid.

46. *The 2008 Mendelsohn Affluent Survey,* 2008.

47. *2011 Ipsos Mendelsohn Survey.*

48. Ibid.

49. *Statistical Abstract of the United States 2008,* Table 671.

50. www.factcheck.org/askfactcheck/is_there_a_standard_ accepted_definition_of.html, accessed October 2008.

51. Gregory L. White and Shirley Leung, "Stepping Up," *Wall Street Journal,* March 29, 2002, A1.

52. Ellen Byron, "As Middle Class Shrinks, P&G Aims High and Low," online.wsj.com, September 12, 2011.

53. Gemma Charles, "The New Working-Class Brands: PizzaExpress, Tesco and BBC One," brandrepublic.com, July 7, 2011.

54. George Pitcher, "Being Super-Sized Boils Down to Personal Choice," *Marketing Week (London),* October 7, 2004, 33.

55. Owain Thomas, "Working Class Children Suffer Greater Risk of Obesity," covermagazine.co.uk, December 15, 2009.

56. Epictetus, "Discourses" (second century) in *The Enchiridion,* 2, trans. Thomas Higginson (Indianapolis: Bobbs-Merrill, 1955).

57. David Colman, "One Step Forward, Three Steps Back," nytimes.com, July 8, 2009.

58. Paul C. Henry, "Social Class, Market Situation, and Consumers' Metaphors of (Dis)Empowerment," *Journal of Consumersearch,* Vol. 31 (March 2005): 766–778.

59. Youn-Kyung Kim and Seunghae Han, "Perceived Images of Retail Stores and Brands: Comparison among Three Ethnic Consumer Groups," *Journal of Family & Consumer Sciences,* Vol. 92 (3) (2000): 58–61.

60. Randy Kennedy, "For Middle Class, New York Shrinks as Home Prices Soar," *New York Times,* April 1, 1998, A1, B6; "Two Tier Marketing," *Business Week,* March 17, 1997, 82–90; Keith Bradsher, "America's Opportunity Gap," *New York Times,* June 4, 1995, 4.

61. Jared Bernstein, "Income Picture: Median Income Rose as Did Poverty in 2007," *Economic Policy Institute* (August 26, 2008), available at www.epi.org/content.cfm/webfeatures_economindictors_iancome_20080826

62. Ibid.

Chapter 11

1. Elena Karahanna, J. Roberto Evaristo, and Mark Strite, "Levels of Culture and Individual Behavior: An Integrative Perspective," *Journal of Global Information Management,* Vol. 13 (April–June 2005): 1–20.

2. Tim Stock and Marie Lena Tupot, "Common Denominators: What Unites Global Youth?" *Young Consumers* (Quarter 1) (2006): 36–43.

3. Jeff Strieter and Jerald Weaver, "A Longitudinal Study of the Depiction of Women in a United States Business Publication," *Journal of the American Academy of Business,* Vol. 7 (September 2005): 229–235.

4. Virginia Richards, "Perpetuating Core Consumer Sciences," *Journal of Family & Consumer Sciences,* Vol. 97 (3) (September 2005): 8–10.

5. Kritsadarat Wattanasuwan, "Balancing the Hybrid Self in the Competing Landscapes of Consumption," *Journal of the American Academy of Business, Cambridge,* Vol. 11 (1) (March 2007): 9–17.

6. For a discussion of socialization, see Jason E. Lueg and R. Zachary Finney, "Interpersonal Communication in the Consumer Socialization Process: Scale Development and Validation," *Journal of Marketing Theory & Practice,* Vol. 15 (1) (Winter 2007): 25–39.

7. Elizabeth C. Hirschman, "Men, Dogs, Guns, and Cars: The Semiotics of Rugged Individualism," *Journal of Advertising,* Vol. 32 (Spring 2003): 9–22.

8. Dennis W. Rook, "The Ritual Dimension of Consumer Behavior," *Journal of Consumer Research,* Vol. 12 (December 1985): 251–264.

9. Bernard Berelson, *Content Analysis in Communication Research* (New York: Free Press, 1952).

10. Michael L. Maynard and Charles R. Taylor, "Girlish Images across Cultures: Analyzing Japanese versus U.S. *Seventeen* Magazine Ads," *Journal of Advertising,* Vol. 28 (1) (Spring 1999): 39–45.

11. Mindy F. Ji and James U. McNeal, "How Chinese Children's Commercials Differ from Those of the United States: A Content Analysis," *Journal of Advertising,* Vol. 30 (3) (Fall 2001): 79–92.

12. Lawrence Osborne, "Consuming Rituals of the Suburban Tribe," *New York Times Magazine,* January 13, 2002, 28–31; Margaret Littman, "Science Shopping," *Crain's Chicago Business,* January 11, 1999, 3; Marvin Matises, "Top of Mind: Send Ethnographers into New-SKU Jungle," *Brandweek,* September 25, 2000, 32–33.

13. Maria Kniazeva and Alladi Venkatesh, "Food for Thought: A Study of Food Consumption in Postmodern US Culture," *Journal of Consumer Behavior,* Vol. 6 (November–December 2007): 419–435.

14. Leonard V. Gordon, *Survey of Personal and Interpersonal Values* (Science Research Associates, 1976).

15. David C. McClelland, *The Achieving Society* (New York: Free Press, 1961): 150–151.

16. Leon G. Schiffman, Elaine Sherman, and Mary M. Long, "Toward a Better Understanding of the Interplay of Personal Values and the Internet," *Psychology & Marketing,* Vol. 20 (February 2003): 169–186.

17. Charles A. Malgwi, Martha A. Howe, and Priscilla A. Burnaby, "Influences on Students' Choice of College Major," *Journal of Education for Business,* Vol. 80 (May/June 2005): 275–282.

18. Joe Renouard, "The Predicaments of Plenty: Interwar Intellectuals and American Consumerism," *Journal of American Culture,* Vol. 30 (1) (March 2007): 59.

19. Frank Gibney, Jr., and Belinda Luscombe, "The Redesigning of America," *Time Magazine,* June 26, 2000, unnumbered insert section.

20. Juliet Schor, "Point of Purchase: How Shopping Changed American Culture," *Contemporary Sociology,* A. Turock "Health Consciousness Tipping Point" Progressive Grocer 87:6 (May 2008) p. 38. (January 2005): 43–44.

21. Daphna Oyserman, "High Power, Low Power, and Equality: Culture Beyond Individualism and Collectivism," *Journal of Consumer Psychology,* Vol. 16 (2006): 354; Norbert Schwarz, "Individualism and Collectivism," *Journal of Consumer Psychology,* Vol. 16 (4) (2006): 324.

22. Hirschman, "Men, Dogs, Guns, and Cars."

23. Inspired by Deborah J. Webb, et al., "Development of and Validation of Scales to Measure Attitudes Influencing Monetary Donations to Charitable Organizations," *Journal of the Academy of Marketing Science,* Vol. 28 (Spring 2000): 299–309.

24. Rodoula Tsiotsou, "An Empirically Based Typology of Intercollegiate Athletic Donors: High and Low Motivation Scenarios," *Journal of Targeting, Measurement & Analysis for Marketing,* Vol. 15 (2) (2007): 79–87.

25. Becky Ebenkamp, "Out of the Box: Gifts That Keep on Giving," *Brandweek,* December 11–25, 2006, 12.

26. Barbara J. Phillips, "Working Out: Consumers and the Culture of Exercise," *Journal of Popular Culture,* Vol. 38 (February 2005): 525–551.

27. D. Gail Fleenor, "Beyond Burgers," *Frozen Food Age,* Vol. 55 (6) (January 2007): 22.

28. A. Turock "Health Consciousness Tipping Point" Progressive Grocer 87:6 (May 2008) p. 38.

29. Mike Duff, "Marketers Making Most of Healthy Home," *Retailing Today,* Vol. 45 (5) (April 9, 2007): 17.

30. pewinternet.org/PPF/r/156/report_display.asp (accessed November 2008).

31. in.reuters.com/article/2012/09/18/health-obesity-us-idINL1E8KIA8D20120918 (accessed September 19, 2012).

32. "Bike Retailers Can Tap into Consumers' Fitness Resolutions," *Bicycle Retailer & Industry News,* Vol. 17 (January 1, 2008): 38.

33. Mark Cleveland, Maria Kalamas, and Michel Laroche, "'It's Not Easy Being Green': Exploring Green Creeds, Green Deeds, and Internal Environmental Locus of Control," *Psychology & Marketing,* Vol. 29 (5) (May 2012): 293–305.

34. Stephanie Storm, "Rethinking Recycling," nytimes.com, March 23, 2012.

35. Selected findings from Kathy Steinberg, "Fewer Americans 'Thinking Green': New Poll Reveals

Continued Decrease on 'Green' Attitudes and Behaviors since 2009," *The Harris Poll* (41) (April 22, 2012).

36. Claire D'Souza, Mehdi Taghian, and Rajiv Khosla, "Examination of Environmental Beliefs and Its Impact on the Influence of Price, Quality and Demographic Characteristics with Respect to Green Purchase Intentions," *Journal of Targeting, Measurement * Analysis for Marketing,* Vol. 15 (2) (2007): 69–78.

37. Sheila Bonini and Jeremy Oppenheim, "Cultivating the Green Consumer," *Stanford Social Innovation Review* (Fall 2008): 56–61.

38. Claire D'Souza, Mehdi Taghian, and Peter Lamb, "An Empirical Study on the Influence of Environmental Labels on Consumers," *Corporate Communications: An International Journal,* Vol. 11 (2) (2006): 162–173.

39. Josephine Pickett-Baker and Ritsuko Ozaki, "Pro-environmental Products: Marketing Influence on Consumer Choice Decision," *Journal of Consumer Marketing,* Vol. 25 (5) (2008): 281–286.

Chapter 12

1. Diana Schrage—a Senior Interior Designer at Kohler

2. U.S. Census Bureau, *National Population Projections,* "Table 4. Projections of the Population by Sex, Race, and Hispanic Origin for the United States: 2010 to 2050" (2008), available at www.census.gov/population/www/projections/summarytables.html.

3. Sam Roberts, "In a Generation, Minorities May Be the U.S. Majority," New York Times, August 14, 2008 nytimes.com

4. United States Census Bureau, "The Foreign-Born Population in the United States: 2010," *American Community Survey Report* (May 2012), available at http://www.census.gov/prod/2012pubs/acs-19.pdf.

5. M. Monks, "Report Shows Nearly Half of Queens Is Foreign Born," *Jackson Heights Times,* January 27, 2005, accessed November 2008 at http://gothamgazette.com/community/21/news/1184.

6. Natalie Zmuda, "Kmart's Holiday Spots to Showcase Shift in Approach to Ethnic Markets," *Advertising Age,* November 1, 2010.

7. U.S. Census Bureau, *Statistical Abstract of the United States 2008,* Table 8, "Largest Minority Group: Hispanics," *New York Times,* January 22, 2003, A17; Hispanic.com: Hispanic Spending, available at http://hispanic.com/topics/hispanicspending.aspx.

8. Deborah L. Vence, "Pick Up the Pieces: Companies Target Lifestyle Segments of Hispanics," *Marketing News,* March 15, 2005, 13–15; Richardo Villarreal and Robert A. Peterson, "Hispanic Ethnicity and Media Behavior," *Journal of Advertising Research,* (June 2008): 179.

9. U.S. Census Bureau, *Statistical Abstract of the United States 2008,* Table 8.

10. U.S. Census Bureau, *America's Families and Living Arrangements* (2006), available at www.census.gov/population/www/socdemo/hh-fam/cps2006.html.

11. Laurel Wentz, "Multicultural? No, Mainstream," *Advertising Age,* May 2, 2005, 3, 57.

12. U.S. Census Bureau, *Statistical Abstract of the United States 2008,* Table 18; U.S. Department of Commerce, "The Hispanic Population: Census 2000 Brief," available at www.census.gov; "2003 American Community Survey Data Profile Highlights," *U.S. Census Bureau—American FactFinder,* available at http://factfinder.census.gov.

13. "Hispanic Power," *Chain Store Age,* Vol. 83 (11) (November 2007): 26.

14. Michael Chattalas and Holly Harper, "Navigating a Hybrid Cultural Identity: Hispanic Teenagers' Fashion Consumption Influences," *Journal of Consumer Marketing,* Vol. 24 (6) (2007): 351–357.

15. http://www.marketingcharts.com/direct/laptops-desktops-grow-in-opposite-directions-14641/pew-computer-ownership-oct-2010jpg/.

16. "Multitaskers," *Brandweek,* April 23, 2007, 18.

17. Della de Lafuente, "Ford Flex Finds *Novela* Way to Reach Latino Consumers," *Brandweek,* June 30–July 7, 2008, 12.

18. E. J. Schultz, "Miller Lite Starts U.S. Hispanic-Agency Review," *Advertising Age,* March 15, 2013.

19. "Black (African-American) History Month," *U.S. Census Bureau News,* February 2012 (Washington, DC: U.S. Department of Commerce).

20. Mike Beirne, "Has This Group Been Left Behind?" *Brandweek,* March 14, 2005, 33–35.

21. Youn-Kyung Kim and Seunghae Han, "Perceived Images of Retail Stores and Brands: Comparison among Three Ethnic Consumer Groups," *Journal of Family & Consumer Sciences,* Vol. 92 (3) (2000): 58–61.

22. "African American Market Profile 2008," Magazine Publishers of America, 8, magazine.org/marketprofiles.

23. Ibid.

24. "Black America Today," *Radio One,* June 2008, available at http://blackamericastudy.com/fact-sheets/black_consumer_final2.pdf.

25. Ibid., 27.

26. Pepper Miller, "The Truth about Black America," *Advertising Age,* July 15, 2008.

27. Mediamark Research and Intelligence, 2011.

28. John Fetto, "Cyber Tigers," *American Demographics,* Vol. 24 (3) (March 2002): 9–10; Sheila Thorne, "Reaching the Minority Majority," *Pharmaceutical Executive,* Vol. 21 (4) (April 2001): 156–158.

29. "Asian-American Market Profile 2008," Magazine Publishers of America, 8, www.magazine.org/marketprofiles.

30. See www.ewowfacts.com/pdfs/chapter/61.pdf (page 609); *Orienting the U.S. Food and Beverage Market: Strategies Targeting Asian American to 2010* (Alexandria, VA: Promar International, June 2000): 87.

31. Laurel Wentz, "AZN TV Makes It Easier to Reach Asians," *Advertising Age,* April 18, 2005, 38.

32. Michael Fielding, "The Halo: Christian Consumers Are a Bloc That Matters to All Marketers," *Marketing News,* February 1, 2005, 18, 20.

33. Jeffrey Steven Podoshen, "Word of Mouth, Brand Loyalty, Acculturation and the American Jewish Consumer," *Journal of Consumer Marketing,* Vol. 23 (5) (2006): 266–282.

34. Victoria Rivkin, "Godly Gains," *Crain's New York Business,* October 13, 2003, 21, 27; see also the website http://theprimegrill.primehospitalityny.com/.

35. Heidi J. Shrager, "Closed-Circle Commerce," *Wall Street Journal*, November 19, 2001, B1, B11.

36. *Source:* Doublebase Mediamark Research, Inc. *2007 Doublebase Report*, All rights reserved by Mediamark.

37. Pierre Dube, "National Brand, Local Branding: Conclusions and Future Research Opportunities" *Journal of Marketing Research*, 44 (February 2007): 26–28.

38. Michael W. Kruger, "How Geographic Variation Persists: Comments on 'Consumer Packaged Goods in the United States: National Brands, Local Branding,'" *Journal of Marketing Research*, Vol. 44 (February 2007): 21–22.

39. Leonard M. Lodish, "Another Reason Academics and Practitioners Should Communicate More," *Journal of Marketing Research*, Vol. 44 (February 2007): 23–25.

40. M. Berk Ataman, Carl F. Mela, and Harald J. Van Heerde, "Consumer Packaged Goods in France: National Brands, Regional Chains, and Local Branding," *Journal of Marketing Research*, Vol. 44 (February 2007): 14–20.

41. Kara Chan, "Chinese Children's Perceptions of Advertising and Brands: An Urban Rural Comparison," *Journal of Consumer Marketing*, Vol. 25 (2) (2008): 74–84; John D. Nicholson and Philip J. Kitchen, "The Development of Regional Marketing—Have Marketers Been Myopic?" *International Journal of Business Studies*, Vol. 15 (1) (June 2007): 107–125.

42. Francis Piron, "China's Changing Culture: Rural and Urban Consumers' Favorite Things," *Journal of Consumer Marketing*, Vol. 23 (6) (2006): 327–334.

43. Himadri Roy Chaudhuri, Sr., and A. K. Haldar, "Understanding the Interrelationship Between Regional Differences and Material Aspiration in the Context of Indian Diversity: Results of an Exploratory Study," *Asia Pacific Journal of Marketing & Logistics*, Vol. 17 (4) (2005): 3.

44. Research and Markets (EPM Communications Inc.), "Marketing to Teens & Tweens," April 2010.

45. Ethan Smith, "Forget CDs. Teens Are Tuning into YouTube," online.wsj.com, August 13, 2012.

46. Anthony Patino, Velitchka Kaltcheva, and Michael Smith, "The Appeal of Reality Television for Teen and Pre-Teen Audiences," *Journal of Advertising Research* (March 2011): 288–297.

47. Rob McGann, "Generation Y Embraces SMS," *ClickZ Stats*, accessed November 2008 at www.clickz.com/stats/sectors/wireless/article.php/3489776; Jyoti Thottam, "How Kids Set the (Ring) Tone," *TIME*, April 4, 2005, 40–42, 45.

48. Marianne Wilson and Katherine Field, "Defining Gen Y," *Chain Store Age*, Vol. 83 (3) (March 2007): 36.

49. Mike Beirne, "Generation Gab," *Brandweek*, June 30–July 7, 2008, 16–20.

50. Available at http://pewinternet.org/Reports/2010/Generations-2011.aspx (accessed August 9, 2012).

51. "The Scoop on Gen X," *Work & Family Life*, Vol. 19 (January 2005): 1.

52. Paula M. Poindexter and Dominic L. Lasorsa, "Generation X: Is Its Meaning Understood?" *Newspaper Research Journal*, Vol. 20 (4) (Fall 1999): 28–36.

53. Rob McGann, "Only Banking Increased 47 Percent Since 2002," *ClickZ Stats*, accessed November 2008 at http://clickz.com/stats/sectors/finance/article.php.3481976.

54. "Marriott Revamp Targets Gen Xers," *Hotels*, Vol. 39 (May 2005): 14; Ed Watkins, "Meet Your New Guest: Generation X," *Lodging Hospitality*, Vol. 61 (March 15, 2005): 2.

55. http://www.vocus.com/blog/marketing-to-baby-boomers-online.5.27.13.

56. Linda Jane Coleman, Marie Hladikova, and Maria Savelyeva, "The Baby Boomer Market," *Journal of Targeting, Measurement & Analysis for* Marketing, Vol. 14 (3) (April 2006): 191–209.

57. "Boomer Facts," *American Demographics* (January 1996): 14. Also see Diane Crispell, "U.S. Population Forecasts Decline for 2000, but Rise Slightly for 2050," *Wall Street Journal*, March 25, 1996, B3; "Advertising to 50s and Over," *Brand Strategy (London)*, April 5, 2005, 57.

58. Coleman, Hladikova, and Savelyeva, "The Baby Boomer Market," *American Demographics* (January 2009): 21–32.

59. Christopher D. Hopkins, Catherine A. Roster, and Charles M. Wood, "Making the Transition to Retirement: Appraisals, Post-Transition Lifestyle, and Changes in Consumption Patterns," *Journal of Consumer Marketing*, Vol. 23 (2) (2006): 89–101.

60. http://pewinternet.org/Reports/2010/Generations-2011.aspx (accessed August 9, 2012).

61. "Table 2. Projections of the Population by Selected Age Groups and Sex for the United States: 2010 to 2050," available at www.census.gov/population/www/projections/summarytables.html; "Table 8. Resident Population by Race, Hispanic Origin, and Age: 2000 and 2006," *Statistical Abstract of the United States 2008*, available at www.census.gov/compendia/statab/cats/population.html (accessed November 2008).

62. Christine L. Himes, "Elderly Americans," *Population Bulletin*, Vol. 56 (4) (December 2001): 3–40; "Table 98. Expectations of Life at Birth, 1970 to 2004, and Projections, 2010 and 2015" and "Table 99. Average Number of Years of Life Remaining by Sex and Age: 1979 to 2003," *Statistical Abstract of the United States 2008*, available at www.census.gov/prod/2007pubs/08abstract/vitstat.pdf (accessed November 2008).

63. Tim Reisenwitz, Rajesh Iyer, David B. Kuhlmeier, and Jacqueline K. Eastman, "The Elderly's Internet Usage: An Updated Look," *Journal of Consumer Marketing*, Vol. 24 (7) (2007): 406–418.

64. Benny Barak and Leon G. Schiffman, "Cognitive Age: A Nonchronological Age Variable," in *Advances in Consumer Research*, 8, ed. Kent B. Monroe, pp. 602–606 (Ann Arbor, MI: Association for Consumer Research, 1981); Elaine Sherman, Leon G. Schiffman, and William R. Dillon, "Age/Gender Segments and Quality of Life Differences," in *1988 Winter Educators' Conference*, eds. Stanley Shapiro and A. H. Walle, pp. 319–320 (Chicago: American Marketing Association, 1988); *Marketing News*, August 28, 1995, 28–29.

65. Elaine Sherman, Leon G. Schiffman, and Anil Mathur, "The Influence of Gender on the New-Age Elderly's Consumption Orientation," *Psychology & Marketing*, Vol. 18 (10) (October 2001): 1073–1089.

66. Elaine Sherman, quoted in David B. Wolfe, "The Ageless Market," *American Demographics* (July 1987): 26–28, 55–56.

67. Leon G. Schiffman and Elaine Sherman, "The Value Orientation of New-Age Elderly: The Coming of an

Ageless Market," *Journal of Business Research,* Vol. 22 (2) (April 1991): 187–194.

68. Isabelle Szmigin and Marylyn Carrigan, "Leisure and Tourism Services and the Older Innovator," *The Service Industries Journal* (London), Vol. 21 (3) (July 2001): 113–129; I. Polyak, "The Center of Attention," *American Demographic,* Vol. 22 (2000) 32.

69. Available at http://pewinternet.org/Reports/2010/Generations-2011.aspx (accessed August 9, 2012).

70. Charles A. McMellon and Leon G. Schiffman, "Cyber-senior Empowerment: How Some Older Individuals Are Taking Control of Their Lives," *Journal of Applied Gerontology,* Vol. 21 (2) (June 2002): 157–175; Charles A. McMellon and Leon G. Schiffman, "Cybersenior Mobility: Why Some Older Consumers May Be Adopting the Internet," *Advances in Consumer Research,* Vol. 27 (2000): 138–144.

71. Patti Williams and Aimee Drolet, "Age-Related Differences in Responses to Emotional Advertisements," *Journal of Consumer Research,* Vol. 32 (December 2005): 343–354.

72. Raphaëlle Lambert-Pandraud, Gilles Laurent, and Eric Lapersoone, "Repeat Purchasing of New Automobiles by Older Consumers: Empirical Evidence and Interpretations," *Journal of Marketing,* Vol. 69 (April 2005): 97–113.

73. Cabrini Pak and Ajit Kambil, "Over 50 and Ready to Shop: Serving the Aging Consumer," *Journal of Business Strategy,* Vol. 27 (6) (2006): 18.

74. Phone interview with Diana Schrage—a senior interior designer at Kohler—on October 15, 2012. Interviewer: Joseph Wisenblit.

75. C. Jeanne Hill and Susan K. Harmon, "Male Gender Role Beliefs, Coupon Use and Bargain Hunting," *Academy of Marketing Studies Journal,* Vol. 11 (2) (2007): 107–121.

76. Thomas Barry, Mary Gilly, and Lindley Doran, "Advertising to Women with Different Career Orientations," *Journal of Advertising Research,* Vol. 25 (April–May 1985): 26–35.

77. Based on Patricia Sellers, Liza Mundy and Nancy Gibbs, "Why Women Are Out-Earning Men," http://postcards.blogs.fortune.cnn.com/2012/03/16/richer-sex-time-mundy, accessed July 12, 2012.

78. N. O'Leary, "How to Talk to Women," Adweek, February 27, 2012, 53–60.

Chapter 13

1. Carolyn A. Lin, "Cultural Values Reflected in Chinese and American Television Advertising," *Journal of Advertising,* Vol. 30 (3) (Winter 2001). Used with permission of M.E. Sharpe, Inc. All Rights Reserved. Not for reproduction.

2. Michel Laroche, Maria Kalamas, and Mark Cleveland, "'I' Versus 'We': How Individualists and Collectivists Use Information Sources to Formulate Their Service Expectations," *International Marketing Review,* Vol. 22 (3) (2005): 279–308.

3. Kritika Kongsompong, "Cultural Diversities Between Singapore and Australia: An Analysis of Consumption

Behavior," *Journal of the American Academy of Business,* Vol. 9 (2) (September 2006): 87–92.

4. Ultrich R. Orth, Harold F. Koenig, and Zuzana Firbasova, "Cross-National Differences in Consumer Response to the Framing of Advertising Messages," *European Journal of Marketing,* Vol. 41 (3/4) (2007): 327–348.

5. Julien Cayla and Giana M. Eckhardt, "Asian Brands and the Shaping of a Transnational Imagined Community," *Journal of Consumer Research,* Vol. 35 (August 2008): 216–230.

6. John A. McCarty, Martin I. Horn, Mary Kate Szenasy, and Jocelyn Feintuch, "An Exploratory Study of Consumer Style: Country Differences and International Segments," *Journal of Consumer Behaviour* (January–February 2007): 53–63.

7. *Source:* John A. McCarty, Martin I. Horn, Mary Kate Szenasy, and Jocelyn Feintuch, "An Exploratory Study of Consumer Style: Country Differences and International Segments," *Journal of Consumer Behaviour* (January–February 2007): 53–54. Copyright © 2007 John Wiley & Sons, Ltd.

8. Alexander Josiassen, "Consumer Disidentification and Its Effects on Domestic Product Purchases: An Empirical Investigation in the Netherlands," *Journal of Marketing,* Vol. 75 (March 2011): 124–140.

9. Jan-Benedict E. M. Steenkamp and Martijn G. de Jong, "A Global Investigation into the Constellation of Consumer Attitudes Toward Global and Local Products," *Journal of Marketing,* Vol. 74 (November 2010): 18–40.

10. Piyush Sharma, "Measuring Personal Cultural Orientations: Scale Development and Validation," *Journal of the Academy of Marketing Science,* Vol. 38 (2010): 787–806.

11. Drew Martin and Paul Herbig, "Marketing Implications of Japan's Social-Cultural Underpinnings," *Journal of Brand Management,* Vol. 9 (3) (January 2002): 171–179.

12. Marion Issard, "To Tailor Burgers for France, McDonald's Enlists Baguette," online.wsj.com, February 24, 2012.

13. Annie Gasparro, "Domino's Sticks to Its Ways Abroad," online.wsj.com, April 17, 2012.

14. Liz Alderman, "In Europe, Starbucks Adjusts to a Café Culture," nytimes.com, March 30, 2012.

15. Christina Passariello, "Fitting Shades for Chinese," online.wsj.com, April 21, 2011.

16. Laurie Burkitt and Bob Davis, "Chasing China's Shoppers," online.wsj.com, June 14, 2012.

17. Jeff Bennett, "Chevrolet Ads to Take 'New Road,'" online.wsj.com, January 8, 2013.

18. Michael Wines, "Picking Brand Names in China Is a Business Itself," nytimes.com, November 11, 2011.

19. Suzanne Vranica, "PepsiCo Adds Fizz to Its Cola," online.wsj.com, March 29, 2012.

20. Leonidas Hatzithomas, Yorgos Zotos, and Christina Boutsouki, "Humor and Cultural Values in Print Advertising: A Cross-Cultural Study," *International Marketing Review,* Vol. 28 (1) (2011): 57–80.

21. Sukanlaya Sawang, "Sex Appeal in Advertising: What Consumers Think," *Journal of Promotion Management,* Vol. 16 (2010): 167–187.

22. Fang Liu, Hong Cheng, and Jianyao Li, "Consumer Responses to Sex Appeal Advertising: A Cross-Cultural Study," *International Marketing Review,* Vol. 26 (4/5) (2009): 501–520.

23. Jing Zhang, "The Persuasiveness of Individualistic and Collectivistic Advertising Appeals among Chinese Generation-X Consumers," *Journal of Advertising,* Vol. 39 (3) (Fall 2010): 69–80.

24. Simon Somogyi, Elton Li, Trent Johnson, Johan Bruwer, and Susan Bastian, "The Underlying Motivations of Chinese Wine Consumer Behavior," *Asia Pacific Journal of Marketing & Logistics,* Vol. 23 (4) (2011): 473–485.

25. Kawpong Polyorat and Dana L Alden, "Self-Construal and Need-for-Cognition Effects on Brand Attitudes and Purchase Intentions in Response to Comparative Advertising in Thailand and the United States," *Journal of Advertising* (Spring 2005): 37–49.

26. Yung Kyun Choi and Gordon E. Miracle, "The Effectiveness of Comparative Advertising in Korea and the United States," *Journal of Advertising* (Winter 2004): 75–88.

27. Rebecca Thurlow, "Australia Cigarette-Packaging Curbs Prompt Suit," online.wsj.com, November 21, 2011.

28. Chun Han Wong, "Singapore Tightens Rules on Casino Advertising," online.wsj.com, November 25, 2011.

29. Lilly Vitorovich, "Groupon Ads Draw U.K. Scrutiny," online.wsj.com, December 2, 2011.

30. Laurie Burkitt, "China Bans Ads in TV Dramas," online. wsj.com, November 29, 2011.

31. Laurie Burkitt, "In China, Air Cheow-DAN Cries Foul," online.wsj.com, February 24, 2012.

32. Chingching Chang, "The Effectiveness of Using a Global Look in an Asian Market," *Journal of Advertising Research* (June 2008): 199–214.

33. Natasha Singer, "At Estée Lauder, a Brand Is Developed Just for China," nytimes.com, September 24, 2012.

34. Douglas B. Holt, John A. Quelch, and Earl L. Taylor, "How Global Brands Compete," *Harvard Business Review* (September 2004): 68–75.

35. Ibid.

36. Carlos J. Torelli, Ayşegül Özsomer, Sergio W. Carvalho, Hean Tat Keh, and Natalia Maehle, "Brand Concepts as Representations of Human Values: Do Cultural Congruity and Compatibility Between Values Matter?" *Journal of Marketing,* Vol. 76 (July 2012): 92–108.

37. Jessie H. Chen-Yu, Keum-Hee Hong, and Yoo-Kyoung Seock, "Adolescents' Clothing Motives and Store Selection Criteria: A Comparison between South Korea and the United States," *Journal of Fashion Marketing & Management,* Vol. 14 (1) (2010): 127–144.

38. Devon Maylie, "By Foot, by Bike, by Taxi, Nestlé Expands in Africa," online.wsj.com, December 1, 2011.

39. Both tables are based on: "Best Global Brands 2012," Interbrand Report, available at http://www.Interbrand. com/en/news-room/press-releases/2012-10-02-7543da7. aspx (accessed January 20, 2013).

40. Laurie Burkitt and Emily Glazer, "In China, Some Imports Get a Local Run for the Money," online.wsj.com, August 5, 2012.

41. Alokparna Basu Monga and Deborah Roedder John, "Consumer Response to Brand Extensions: Does Culture Matter?" *Advances in Consumer Research,* Vol. 31 (2004): 216–222.

42. Alokparna Basu Monga and Deborah Roedder John, "Cultural Differences in Brand Extension Evaluation: The Influence of Analytic versus Holistic Thinking," *Journal of Consumer Research,* Vol. 33 (March 2007): 529–536.

43. Shintaro Okazaki, "Searching the Web for Global Brands: How American Brands Standardize Their Web Sites in Europe," *European Journal of Marketing,* Vol. 39 (1/2) (2005): 87–109.

44. Andrew Browne, James T. Areddy, and Merissa Marr, "Katzenberg Unveils a China Film Project," online.wsj .com, April 19, 2013.

45. Laurie Burkitt, "Bling Toned Down in Beijing," online. wsj.com, August 6, 2012.

46. Andrew Kramer, "Russia Becomes a Magnet for U.S. Fast-Food Chains," nytimes.com, August 3, 2011.

47. Stephanie Clifford and Liz Alderman, "A New American Invasion," nytimes.com, June 16, 2011.

48. Hiroko Tabuchi, "Japanese Consumers Reconsidering Rice Loyalty," nytimes.com, July 19, 2012.

49. David Kesmodel, "Feeling Stale, Molson Reinvents Itself in Canada," online.wsj.com, April 13, 2011.

50. Moises Naim, "Can the World Afford a Middle Class?" *Foreign Policy,* Vol. 165 (March–April 2008): 95–96.

51. Peter Marber, "Globalization and Its Contents," *World Policy Journal* (Winter 2004–2005): 29–37.

52. Ann Veeck and Alvin C. Burns, "Changing Tastes: The Adoption of New Food Choices in Post-Reform China," *Journal of Business Research,* Vol. 58 (2005): 644–652.

53. R. Stephen Parker, Charles M. Hermans, and Allen D. Schaefer, "Fashion Consciousness of Chinese, Japanese and American Teenagers," *Journal of Fashion Marketing & Management,* Vol. 8 (2) (2004): 176–186.

54. Ibid., 182.

55. Energy BBDO, "The GenWorld Teen Study," available at www.businessfordiplomaticaction.com/learn/articles/ genworld_leave_behind.pdf (accessed November 2008).

56. Based on: Becky Ebenkamp, "Creative Consciousness," *Brandweek,* January 16, 2006, 14.

Chapter 14

1. Gordon C. Bruner, II, "The Effect of Problem-Recognition Style on Information Seeking," *Journal of the Academy of Marketing Science,* Vol. 15 (Winter 1987): 33–41.

2. Matthew Klein, "He Shops, She Shops," *American Demographics* (March 1998): 34–35.

3. Sharon E. Beatty and Scott M. Smith, "External Search Effort: An Investigation across Several Product Categories," *Journal of Consumer Research,* 14 (June 1987): 83–95.

4. Niranjan V. Raman, "A Qualitative Investigation of Web-Browsing Behavior," in *Advances in Consumer Research,* eds. J. Brucks and S. MacInnis (Provo, UT: Association for Consumer Research, 1997): 511–516.

5. "Just the Facts," *Journal of Business Strategy,* Vol. 22 (2) (March/April, 2001): 3–4; Kuan-Pin Chiang, Ruby Roy

Dholakia, and Stu Westin, "Needle in the Cyberstack: Consumer Search for Information in the Web-Based Marketspace," *Advances in Consumer Research,* Vol. 31 (2004): 88–89.

6. Kristy E. Reynolds, Judith Anne Garretson Folse, and Michael A. Jones, "Search Regret: Antecedents and Consequences," *Journal of Retailing,* 82, no. 4 (2006): 339

7. Reynolds, Folse, and Jones, "Search Regret."

8. Lan Xia, "Consumer Choice Strategies and Choice Confidence in the Electronic Environment," in *1999 AMA Educators Proceedings,* Vol. 10, eds. Stephen P. Brown and D. Sudharshan (Chicago: American Marketing Association, 1999): 270–277.

9. John W. Pracejus, G. Douglas Olsen, and Thomas C. O'Guinn, "Nothing Is Something: The Production and Reception of Advertising Meaning through the Use of White Space," *Advances in Consumer Research,* Vol. 30, eds. Punam Anand Keller and Dennis W. Rook (Valdosta, GA: Association for Consumer Research, 2003): 174; Pamela Henderson, Joan Giese, and Joseph A. Cote, "Typeface Design and Meaning: The Three Faces of Typefaces," *Advances in Consumer Research,* Vol. 30 (2003): 175.

10. Ashley Lye, Wei Shao, and Sharyn Rundle-Thiele, "Decision Waves: Consumer Decisions in Today's Complex World," *European Journal of Marketing,* Vol. 39 (1/2) (2005): 216–230; see also Lam-Ying Huang and Ying-Jiun Hsieh, "Consumer Electronics Based on Innovation Attributes and Switching Costs: The Case of e-Book Readers," *Electronic Commerce Research & Applications,* Vol. 11 (2012): 218–228.

11. Jeffrey F. Durgee, "Why Some Products 'Just Feel Right,' or, the Phenomenology of Product Rightness," in *Advances in Consumer Research,* Vol. 22, eds. Frank R. Kardes and Mita Sujan (Provo, UT: Association for Consumer Research, 1995): 650–652.

12. Tulin Erdem and Joffre Swait, "Brand Credibility, Brand Consideration, and Choice," *Journal of Consumer Research,* Vol. 31 (June 2004): 191–198.

13. Laurie Peterson, "The Strategic Shopper," *Adweek's Marketing Week*, March 30, 1992, 18–20.

14. Emily Booth, "Getting Inside a Shopper's Mind," *Marketing (U.K.),* June 3, 1999, 33.

15. Kare Sandvik, Kjell Gronhaug, and Frank Lindberg, "Routes to Customer Retention: The Importance of Customer Satisfaction, Performance Quality, Brand Reputation and Customer Knowledge," in *AMA Winter Conference,* eds. Debbie Thorne LeClair and Michael Hartline (Chicago: American Marketing Association, 1997): 211–217.

16. Mohammed M. Nadeem, "Post-Purchase Dissonance: The Wisdom of the 'Repeat' Purchases," *Journal of Global Business Issues,* Vol. 1 (2) (Summer 2007): 183–193.

17. Raquel Sanchez-Fernandez and M. Angeles Iniesta-Bonillo, "Consumer Perception of Value: Literature Review and a New Conceptual Framework," *Journal of Consumer Satisfaction, Dissatisfaction & Complaining Behavior,* Vol. 19 (2006): 40–58.

18. Deirdre Shaw, Terry Newholm, and Roger Dickinson, "Consumption as Voting: An Exploration of Consumer

Empowerment," *European Journal of Marketing,* Vol. 40 (9/10) (2006): 1049–1067.

19. Russell W. Belk and Gregory S. Coon, "Gift Giving as Agapic Love: An Alternative to the Exchange Paradigm Based on Dating Experiences," *Journal of Consumer Research,* Vol. 20 (December 1993): 393–417.

20. Julie A. Ruth, Cele C. Otnes, and Frédéric F. Brunel, "Gift Receipt and the Reformulation of Interpersonal Relationships," *Journal of Consumer Research,* Vol. 25 (March 1999): 385–402.

21. Adapted from Deborah Y. Cohn and Leon G. Schiffman, "Gifting: A Taxonomy of Private Realm Giver and Recipient Relationships" (Working Paper), City University of New York, Baruch College, 1996.

22. Deborah Y. Cohn and Leon G. Schiffman, "A Taxonomy of Consumer Gifting Relationships," in *Navigating Crisis and Opportunities in Global Markets: Leadership, Strategy and Governance, International Conference of the Global Business and Technology Association*, eds. Nejdet Delener and Chiang-nan Chaoin (June 8–12, 2004): 164–171.

23. Stephen J. Gould and Claudia E. Weil, "Gift-Giving and Gender Self-Concepts," *Gender Role,* Vol. 24 (1991): 617–637.

24. Tilottama G. Chowdhury, S. Ratneshwar, and Kalpesh K. Desai, "Do Unto Others as You Would Do Unto Yourself: Variety-Seeking Motives in Gift Giving," *Advances in Consumer Research,* Vol. 31, eds. Barbara E. Kahn and Mary Frances Luce (Valdosta, GA: Association for Consumer Research, 2004): 22–23.

25. Annamma Joy, "Gift Giving in Hong Kong and the Continuum of Social Ties," *Journal of Consumer Research,* Vol. 28 (2) (September 2001): 239–256.

26. Suri Weisfield-Spolter and Maneesh Thakkar, "A Framework for Examining the Role of Culture in Individuals' Likelihood to Engage in Self-Gift Behavior," *Academy of Marketing Studies Journal*, Vol. 16 (1) (2012): 39–52.

27. Leon G. Schiffman and Deborah Y. Cohn, "Are They Playing by the Same Rules? A Consumer Gifting Classification of Marital Dyads," *Journal of Business Research,* (forthcoming): 1054–1062.

28. Hsiang Chen and Kevin Crowston, "Comparative Diffusion of the Telephone and the World Wide Web: An Analysis of Rates of Adoption," in *Proceedings of WebNet '97—World Conference of the WWW, Internet and Intranet,* eds. Suave Lobodzinski and Ivan Tomek, (AACE: Toronto, Canada): 110–115; see also Edward D. Conrad, Michael D. Michalisin, and Steven J. Karu, "Measuring Pre-Adoptive Behavior Towards Individual Willingness to Use IT Innovations," *Journal of Strategic Innovation and Sustainability,* Vol. 8 (1) (2012): 81–93.

29. Tariq Bhatti, "Exploring Factors Influencing the Adoption of Mobile Commerce," *Journal of Internet Banking & Commerce,* Vol. 12 (3) (2007): 1–13.

30. Susan H. Higgins and William L. Shanklin, "Seeding Mass Market Acceptance for High Technology Consumer Products," *Journal of Consumer Marketing,* Vol. 9 (Winter 1992): 5–14.

Chapter 15

1. Amanda Zimmerman and John Dahlberg, "The Sexual Objectification of Women in Advertising: A Contemporary Cultural Perspective," *Journal of Advertising Research,* Vol. 48 (1) (March 2008): 21–38.

2. Mike Esterl and Paul Ziobro, "Coke to Curb Ads to Kids, Push Diet Drinks," online.wsj.com, May 8, 2013.

3. Bill Tomson, "Caffeinated Snacks Draw FDA Scrutiny," online.wsj.com, April 30, 2013.

4. Deborah Roedder John, "Consumer Socialization of Children: A Retrospective Look at Twenty-Five Years of Research," *Journal of Consumer Research*, Vol. 26 (2) (1999): 183–213.

5. D. Borzekowski and T. Robinson, "The 30-Second Effect: An Experiment Revealing the Impact of Television Commercials on Food Preferences of Preschoolers," *Journal of American Dietetic Association*, Vol. 10 (1) (2001): 42–46.

6. K. Corfman and B. Harlam, "Relative Influence of Parent and Child in the Purchase of Products for Children," *Journal of Marketing Theory & Practice*, Vol. 12 (2) (2001): 132–146.

7. K. Palan and R. Wilkes, "Adolescent-Parent Interaction in Family Decision Making," *Journal of Consumer Research*, Vol. 24 (2) (1997): 159–169.

8. D. Marshall, S. O'Donohoe, and S. Kline, "Families, Food, and Pester Power: Beyond the Blame Game?" *Journal of Consumer Behaviour*, Vol. 6 (1) (2007): 164–181.

9. Kaiser Family Foundation, "Daily Media Use among Children and Teens up Dramatically from Five Years Ago" (January 20, 2010). News Release: http://www.kff.org/entmedia/entmedia012010nr.cfm (accessed August 11, 2012).

10. Institute of Medicine of the National Academies, *Food Marketing to Children and Youth* (Washington, DC: National Academies Press, 2005).

11. Center for Science in the Public Interest, "Pestering Parents: How Food Companies Market Obesity to Children" (November 2003).

12. www.caru.com (accessed August 11, 2012).

13. CARU New Releases: "Roseart Supports CARU and Children's Safety . . .," (January 5, 2005); "Nabisco Puts Safety First in TV Ads," (October 4, 2000); "Procter and Gamble Works with CARU on Pringles Commercial," (April 15, 2004). All available at www.caru.org/news/index.asp (accessed August 11, 2012).

14. Stuart Elliott, "McDonald's Ending Promotion on Jackets of Children's Report Cards," nytimes.com, January 18, 2008.

15. E. J. Schultz, "Advertisers Rebuke Obama Administration's Proposed Rules on Marketing Food to Kids," *Ad Age* online, April 28, 2011.

16. Mike Esterl, "Soda Makers to Post Calories on Vending Machines," online.wsj.com, October 8, 2012.

17. Brooks Barnes, "Promoting Nutrition, Disney to Restrict Junk-Food Ads," nytimes.com, June 5, 2012; Stephanie Storm, "McDonald's Menu to Post Calorie Data," nytimes.com, September 12, 2012.

18. Julie Jargon, "Success Is Only So Sweet in Remaking Cereals," online.wsj.com, October 11, 2011.

19. Jess Bravin, "California Can't Curb Children's Access to Videogames," online.wsj.com, June 28, 2011.

20. Melanie Warner, "The Food Industry Empire Strikes Back," nytimes.com, July 5, 2005.

21. Elizabeth S. Moore and Victoria J. Rideout, "The Online Marketing of Food to Children: Is It Just Fun and Games?" *Journal of Public Policy & Marketing*, Vol. 26 (2) (Fall 2007): 202–220; Kathleen Seiders and Ross D. Petty, "Taming the Obesity Beast: Children, Marketing, and Public Policy Considerations," *Journal of Public Policy & Marketing*, Vol. 26 (2) (Fall 2007): 236–242.

22. Jeremy Singer-Vine and Anton Troianovski, "How Kids Apps Are Data Magnets," online.wsj.com, June 27, 2013.

23. Stephanie Clifford, "Online Merchants Home In on Imbibing Consumer," nytimes.com, December 27, 2011.

24. Michael Moss, "The Extraordinary Science of Addictive Junk Food," nytimes.com, February 20, 2013.

25. Reuters, "Fat and Getting Fatter: U.S. Obesity Rates to Soar by 2030," September 19, 2012.

26. Rajagopal Raghunathan, Rebecca Walker Naylor, and Wayne D. Hoyer, "The Unhealthy = Tasty Intuition and Its Effects on Taste Inferences, Enjoyment, and Choice of Food Products," *Journal of Marketing,* Vol. 70 (October 2006): 170–184.

27. Brian Wansink and Koert van Ittersum, "Bottoms Up! The Influence of Elongation on Pouring and Consumption Value," *Journal of Consumer Research* (December 2003): 455–463; Brian Wansink, "Environmental Factors That Increase the Food Intake and Consumption Volume of Unknowing Consumers," *Annual Reviews* 24 (Nutrition, 2004): 455–479; Barbara E. Kahn and Brian Wansink, "The Influence of Assortment Structure on Perceived Variety and Consumption Quantities," *Journal of Consumer Research* (March 2004): 519–534; Jennifer J. Argo and Katherine White, "When Do Consumers Eat More? The Role of Appearance Self-Esteem and Food Packaging Cues," *Journal of Marketing*, Vol. 76 (March 2012): 67–80.

28. "Credit Scores Plummet as Student Debt Rises," *Business Wire*, New York, April 8, 2005.

29. So-Hyun Joo, John E. Grable, and Dorothy C. Bagwell, "Credit Card Attitudes and Behaviors of College Students," *College Student Journal* (September 2003): 405–416.

30. "New York Law Targets Credit Card Ads at Universities," *Bank Marketing International* (December 2004): 1; Jonathan D. Glater, "Marketing Code for Student Lenders," nytimes.com, September 10, 2008.

31. Stephen F. Pirog III and James A. Roberts, "Personality and Credit Card Misuse among College Students: The Mediating Role of Impulsiveness," *Journal of Marketing Theory & Practice*, Vol. 15 (1) (Winter 2007): 65–77.

32. James A. Roberts and Stephen F. Pirog III, "A Preliminary Investigation of Materialism and Impulsiveness as Predictors of Technological Addictions among Young Adults," *Journal of Behavioral Addictions*, Vol. 2 (1) (March 2013): 56–62.

33. Anahad O'Connor, "The Problem with Serving Sizes," nytimes.com, August 2, 2011.

34. Gina S. Mohr, Donald R. Lichtenstein, & Chris Janiszewski, "The Effect of Marketer-Suggested Serving

Size on Consumer Responses: The Unintended Consequences of Consumer Attention to Calorie Information," *Journal of Marketing*, Vol. 76 (January 2012): 59–75.

35. O'Connor, "The Problem with Serving Sizes."

36. Tara Parker-Pope, "Designing a Better Food Label," nytimes.com, July 28, 2011.

37. Stephanie Storm, "Lawsuit Forces General Mills to Defend the Accuracy of Its 'Natural' Labeling," nytimes.com, July 26, 2012.

38. Stephanie Storm, "Uneasy Allies in the Grocery Aisle," nytimes.com, September 13, 2012.

39. R. Stephen Parker and Charles E. Pettijohn, "Ethical Considerations in the Use of Direct-to-Consumer Advertising and Pharmaceutical Promotions: The Impact on Pharmaceutical Sales and Physicians," *Journal of Business Ethics* (December 2003): 279–287; Nat Ives, "Consumers Are Looking Past Commercials to Study Prescription Drugs," nytimes.com, March 25, 2005.

40. Stephanie Saul, "A Self-Imposed Ban on Drug Ads," nytimes.com, June 15, 2005.

41. Stephanie Clifford, "FDA Rules on Drug Ads Sow Confusion as Applied to Web," nytimes.com, April 16, 2009.

42. Duff Wilson, "As Generics Near, Makers Tweak Erectile Drugs," nytimes.com, April 13, 2011.

43. Thomas F. Stafford, "Alert or Oblivious? Factors Underlying Consumer Responses to Marketing Stimuli," *Psychology & Marketing* (September 2000): 745–760.

44. Serena Ng, "Toilet-Tissue 'Desheeting' Shrinks Rolls," online.wsj.com, July 24, 20–13.

45. Ibid.Plumps Margins,"

46. Kelly D. Martin and Craig Smith, "Commercializing Social Interaction: The Ethics of Stealth Marketing," *Journal of Public Policy & Marketing*, Vol. 27 (1) (Spring 2008): 45–56.

47. Michael A. Wiles & Anna Danielova, "The Worth of Product Placement in Successful Films: An Event Study Analysis," *Journal of Marketing*, Vol. 73 (July 2009): 44–63.

48. Ignacio Redondo, "The Behavioral Effects of Negative Product Placements in Movies," *Psychology & Marketing*, Vol. 29 (8) (August 2012): 622–635.

49. Haseeb Shabbir and Des Thwaites, "The Use of Humor to Mask Deceptive Advertising: It's No Laughing Matter," *Journal of Advertising*, Vol. 36 (2) (Summer 2007): 75–86.

50. Federal Trade Commission

51. Peter R. Darke, Laurence Ashworth, and Robin J. B. Ritchie, "Damage from Corrective Advertising: Causes and Cures," *Journal of Marketing*, Vol. 72 (November 2008): 81–97.

52. Nat Ives, "Advertisers Have a Deep Concern for the Truth, Especially When It Comes to a Rival's Claim," *New York Times*, September 21, 2004, C4.

53. Ibid.

54. Amy Schatz and Ilan Brat, "Dannon Settles Complaints over Yogurt Ads," online.wsj.com, December 16, 2010; Edward Eyatt, "Regulators Call Health Claims in Pom Juice Ads Deceptive," nytimes.com, September 27, 2010; Associated Press, "FDA Warns P&G for Adding Vitamin

C to Nyquil," nytimes.com, October 14, 2009; Brent Kendall, "Skechers Settles with FTC over Deceptive Advertising of Toning Shoes," online.wsj.com, May 16, 2012; Anemona Hartocollis, "Dispute over City's Ads against Sodas," nytimes.com, October 28, 2010; Brent Kendall, "FTC Targets 'Ab Circle Pro' Ads," online. wsj.com, August 23, 2012; Jennifer Corbett Dooren and Emily Glazer, "FDA Rebukes Lancôme on Marketing," online.wsj.com, September 11, 2012; Danny Yadron and Shira Ovide, "FTC Says Tweet Ads Need Some Fine Print," online.wsj.com, March 12, 2013.

55. Martha Myslinski Tipton, Sundar Bharadwaj, and Diana Robertson, "Regulatory Exposure of Deceptive Marketing and Its Impact on Claimed Value," *Journal of Marketing* (November 2009): 230–243.

56. Ann Zimmerman, "Judge to Consider Zale's Brightest Diamond Claim," online.wsj.com, December 16, 2012.

57. Anemona Hartocollis, "E-Mails Reveal Dispute over City's Ad against Sodas," nytimes.com, October 28, 2010.

58. Dana Mattioli and Ryan Dezember, "Would-Be Buyers of Organix Naturally Hesitant on Name," online.wsj.com, April 30, 2013.

59. Suzanne Vranica, "Advertisers Practice for Super Bowl," online.wsj.com, February 3, 2012.

60. Jill K. Maher, Kenneth C. Herbst, Nancy M. Childs, and Seth Finn, "Racial Stereotypes in Children's Television Commercials," *Journal of Advertising*, Vol. 37 (1) (March 2008): 80–93.

61. Fred K. Beard, "How Product and Advertising Offend Consumers," *Journal of Advertising*, Vol. 37 (1) (March 2008): 13–21.

62. WSJ Staff, "Oh, Benetton. You and Your Controversial Ad Campaigns," online.wsj.com, November 16, 2011; Jonathan Hutchinson, "The Price of a Jersey Sets Rugby Fans against Adidas," nytimes.com, August 24, 2011; Andrew Newman, "A Line of Brews Draws a Star Endorser," nytimes.com, April 17, 2011; Abby Goodnough, "Caffeine and Alcohol Drink Is Potent Mix for Young," nytimes.com, October 26, 2010; Sarah Nir, "Nivea Pulls Ads after Online Outcry," nytimes.com, August 12, 2011.

63. Stuart Elliott, "Emphasizing Taste, and Not Just in Beer, at Super Bowl," *New York Times*, January 26, 2005, C1; Stuart Elliott, "Ad Reaction Claims Super Bowl Casualty," nytimes.com, February 3, 2005; Stuart Elliott, "Super Bowl Spot Provokes after Only One Broadcast," nytimes.com, February 8, 2005.

64. Richar Thaler, "Show Us the Data. (It's Ours, After All.)," nytimes.com, April 23, 2011.

65. Stephanie Clifford and Quentin Hardy, "Attention, Shoppers: Store Is Tracking Your Cell," nytimes.com, July 14, 2013.

66. Natasha Singer, "Secret E-Scores Chart Consumers' Buying Power," nytimes.com, August 18, 2012.

67. Edward Wyatt and Tanzina Vega, "F.T.C. Backs Plan to Honor Privacy of Online Users," nytimes.com, December 1, 2010; Edward Wyatt and Tanzina Vega, "U.S. Agency Seeks Tougher Consumer Privacy Rules," nytimes.com, March 26, 2012.

68. Tanzina Vega, "For Online Privacy, Click Here," nytimes.com, January 19, 2012.

69. Louise Story and Brad Stone, "Facebook Retreats on Online Tracking," nytimes.com, November 30, 2007.
70. Miguel Helft and Jenna Wortham, "Facebook Bows to Pressure over Privacy," nytimes.com, May 26, 2010.
71. Nathasha Singer, "When the Privacy Button Is Already Pressed," nytimes.com, September 15, 2012.
72. Noam Cohen, "An Ad Blocker Opens the Gate, Ever So Slightly," nytimes.com, January 1, 2012.
73. Somini Sengupta, "Study Finds Broad Wariness over Online Tracking," online.wsj.com, October 8, 2012.
74. Natasha Singer, "Do Not Track? Advertisers Say 'Don't Tread on Us,'" nytimes.com, October 13, 2012.
75. Tanzina Vega, "A New Tool in Protecting Online Privacy," nytimes.com, February 12, 2012.
76. Ian Sherr and Anton Troianovski, "Tracking-Software Maker Stirs Phone-Privacy Fears," online.wsj.com, December 2, 2011.
77. Stephanie Clifford, "Web Coupons Know Lots about You, and They Tell," nytimes.com, April 16, 2010.
78. Héctor R. Lozada, Gary H. Kritz, and Alma Mintu-Wimsatt, "The Challenge of Online Privacy to Global Marketers," *Journal of Marketing Development & Competitiveness* (2013; forthcoming).
79. Brooks Barnes, "Bowing to Pressure, Disney Bans Smoking in Its Branded Movies," nytimes.com, July 26, 2007.
80. Apisit Chattananon, Meredith Lawley, Jirasek Trimetsoontorn, Numachi Supparekchaisakul, and Lackana Leelayouthayothin, "Building Corporate Image through Societal Marketing Programs," *Society & Business Review,* Vol. 2 (3) (2007): 230–253.
81. Stefanie Rosen Robinson, Caglar Irmak, and Satish Jayachandran, "Choice of Cause in Cause-Related Marketing," *Journal of Marketing*, Vol. 76 (July 2012): 125–139.
82. Stuart Elliott, "A Push to Curb Casual Use of Ugly Phrases," nytimes.com, October 8, 2008.
83. Stephanie Clifford, "Teaching Teenagers about Harassment," nytimes.com, January 27, 2009.
84. Stuart Elliott, "Standing Up for Those Who Cannot," nytimes.com, September 29, 2008.
85. Stuart Elliott, "A New York Job Behind Every Light and Camera," nytimes.com, December 22, 2008.
86. Matt Richtel, "A Short-Circuit to Distracted Driving," nytimes.com, January 20, 2011.
87. Carolyn J. Simmons and Karen L. Becker-Olsen, "Achieving Marketing Objectives through Social Sponsorships," *Journal of Marketing,* Vol. 70 (October 2006): 154–169.
88. Xiaoli Nan and Kwangjun Heo, "Consumer Responses to Corporate Social Responsibility (CSR) Initiatives: Examining the Role of Brand-Cause Fit in Cause-Related Marketing," *Journal of Advertising,* Vol. 36 (2) (Summer 2007): 63–75.
89. Stacy Landreth Grau and Judith Anne Garreston Folse, "The Influence of Donation Proximity and Message-Framing Cues on the Less-Involved Consumer," *Journal of Advertising,* Vol. 36 (4) (Winter 2007): 19–34.
90. Oliver M. Freestone and Peter J. McGoldrick, "Motivations of the Ethical Consumer," *Journal of Business Ethics,* Vol. 79 (2008): 445–467.
91. Rajiv K. Sinha and Naomi Mandel, "Preventing Digital Music Piracy: The Carrot or the Stick?" *Journal of Marketing,* Vol. 72 (January 2008): 1–15.
92. David Segal, "Appalling Behavior, This Time by Customers," nytimes.com, July 10, 2010; Janet Morrissey, "Avoiding Luggage Fees," nytimes.com, February 6, 2012.

Chapter 16

1. Katherine Rosman, "Test-Marketing a Modern Princess," online.wsj.com, April 9, 2013.
2. Jon Gertner, "Our Rating, Ourselves," www.nytimes.com, April 10, 2005.
3. Ernest Dichter, "Whose Lifestyle Is It Anyway?" *Psychology & Marketing* (1986): 3; Ernest Dichter, *Handbook of Consumer Motivation* (New York: McGraw-Hill, 1964); Emanuel H. Demby, "A Remembrance of Ernest Dichter," *Marketing News,* Vol. 6 (January 6, 1992): 21. Also see Michelle R. Nelson, "The Hidden Persuaders: Then and Now," *Journal of Advertising*, Vol. 37 (Spring 2008): 113–126.
4. Stan Maklan, Simon Knox, and Lynette Ryals, "New Trends in Innovation and Customer Relationship Management: A Challenge for Market Researchers," *International Journal of Market Research*, Vol. 50 (2008): 221–238.
5. Nick Lee and Amanda J. Broderick, "The Past, Present and Future of Observational Research in Marketing," *Qualitative Market Research: An International Journal,* Vol. 10 (2007): 121–129.
6. Leslie Kaufman, "Enough Talk," *Newsweek*, August 19, 1997, 48–49.
7. Emily Nelson, "P&G Checks Out Real Life," *Wall Street Journal* (Eastern Edition), May 17, 2001, B1.
8. Ian Mount, "The Mystery of Duane Reade," *New York Magazine*, June 6, 2005, 28–31.
9. Kim S. Nash, "Casinos Hit Jackpot with Customer Data," *Computer World*, July 2, 2001, 16–17; *Modern Marvels: Casino Technology* [VHS videotape], 1999, A&E Television Networks.
10. Alex Salkever, "The Technology of Personalized Pitches," *Business Week Online*, June 22, 2004.
11. Constance L. Hays, "What Wal-Mart Knows about Customers' Habits," www.nytimes.com, November 14, 2004.
12. Melanie Wells, "In Search of the Buy Button," *Forbes*, September 1, 2003, 62.
13. Brian D. Till and Michael Busler, "The Match-Up Hypothesis: Physical Attractiveness, Expertise, and the Role of Fit on Brand Attitude, Purchase Intent and Brand Beliefs," *Journal of Advertising* (Fall 2000): 1–13.
14. Yoram Wind, "Marketing by Experiment," *Marketing Research* (Spring 2007): 10–16.
15. See the following for additional viewpoints: Jenny Clark, Clive Nancarrow, and Lee Higgins, "Using Consumer Panel Participants to Generate Creative New Product

Ideas," *Journal of American Academy of Business,* Vol. 12 (September 2007): 139–144.

16. Nina Michaelidou and Sally Dibb, "Using Email Questionnaires for Research: Good Practice in Tackling Non-Response," *Journal of Targeting, Measurement & Analysis for Marketing*, Vol. 14 (July 2006): 289–296.

17. Thomas O. Jones and W. Earl Sasser, Jr., "Why Satisfied Customers Defect," *Harvard Business Review* (November–December 1995): 88–99.

18. A. Parasuraman, Valarie A. Zeithaml, and Leonard L. Berry, *Moving Forward in Service Quality Research: Measuring Different Customer-Expectation Levels, Comparing Alternative Scales, and Examining the Performance-Behavioral Intentions Link* (Report No. 94–114) (Cambridge, MA: Marketing Science Institute, 1994).

19. Michael M. Pearson and Guy H. Gessner, "Transactional Segmentation to Slow Customer Defections," *Marketing Management* (Summer 1999): 16–23.

20. Stuart Elliott, "Nielsen Presents a Research Plan to Quell Concerns about Accuracy," www.nytimes.com, February 22, 2005; Stuart Elliott, "Nielsen Will Address Potential Undercounting of Minority TV Viewers," www.nytimes.com, March 24, 2005.

Glossary

Absolute Threshold. The lowest level at which an individual experiences a sensation. The point at which a person can detect a difference between "something" and "nothing." *See Differential Threshold.*

Acculturation. Learning a new culture. *See Enculturation.*

Achievement Need. Regarding personal accomplishment as an end by itself, being self-confident, and enjoying taking calculated risks.

Actual Self-Image. The way individuals perceive themselves. *See Social Self-Image and Ideal Self-Image.*

Addressable Advertising. Customized messages that are sent to individual consumers and are based on the messages' receivers' prior shopping and surfing online, which marketers have tracked.

Adopter Categories. A classification showing where consumers stand in relation to other consumers in terms of the first time they had purchased an innovation (e.g., a new product or model). *See the five adopters' categories: Innovators, Early Adopters, Early Majority, Late Majority, and Laggards.*

Adoption. The final stage of Innovation Adoption, which is a term designating the process leading to a person's decision of whether or not to adopt an innovation. After becoming aware of and interested in the innovation, and evaluating and trying it, the person adopts (purchases) the innovation. If satisfied, he (or she) would buy the innovative product again. If not, there will be no repeat purchase. *See Innovation Adoption.*

Advergames. Brands embedded in video games played at homes, arcades, or online.

Advertising Wear-Out. Overexposure to repetitive advertising that causes individuals to become satiated, pay less attention to advertising, and remember fewer ads.

Advertorials. Printed ads that closely resemble content and editorial material.

Affect Referral Decision Rule. A decision rule by which consumers make product choices based on the products' overall ratings rather than considering specific product attributes. *See Noncompensatory Decision Rules.*

Affective Component. The second component of the Tri-Component Model of attitudes. It represents the person's *emotions* and *feelings* regarding the attitude object, which are considered *evaluations* because they capture the person's overall assessment of the attitude object (i.e., the extent to which the individual rates the attitude object as "favorable" or "unfavorable," "good" or "bad"). *See Likert Scale, Sematic Differential Scale, and Tri-Component Model.*

Affiliation Need. A psychological need that is similar to social need and reflects one's desire for friendship, acceptance, and belonging.

Affluent Market. Upscale market segment that consists of households with incomes that are, according to most definitions, over $ 100,000. However, what is considered "affluent" varies among geographic locations. *See Social Class.*

Aggresion. Responding aggresively when encountering frustration. *See Defense Mechanisms.*

Aggressive Individuals. One of three groups identified by Karen Horney (a neo-Freudian researcher), it designates persons who move against others, excel, and desire to be admired. *See Compliant Individuals and Detached Individuals.*

AIDA. An acronym of a cognitive learning model favored by advertisers, which states that product-related learning occurs in four stages: awareness, interest, desire, and action. *See Cognitive Learning.*

Aided Recall. A recognition test, that measures the effectiveness of learning and communications, where consumers are shown ads and asked whether or not they remember seeing them and can recall any of their salient points. *See Unaided Recall.*

Ambient Advertising (Experiential Marketing). *See Experiential Marketing.*

Ambush Marketing. Placing ads in places where consumers do not expect to see them and cannot avoid them readily.

American Core Values. Priorities and codes of conduct that both affect and reflect the character of American society. These values are: pervasive (i.e., a significant portion of the American people have accepted them); enduring (i.e., unlike fads, they have influenced Americans' actions over an extended period); and related to consumption behavior (i.e., in the context of this textbook). *See Culture.*

Anthropology. The comparative study of human societies' cultures and developments. *See Content Analysis, Culture, and Field Observation.*

Anthropomorphism. Assigning human characteristics to an object. *See Brand Personification.*

Approach Objects. Positive outcomes that people seek. *See Avoidance Objects.*

Apps (Applications). Chunks of software—installed on one's computer, tablet, or smartphone—that are gateways to games, online resources, and social networking.

Attitude. A learned predisposition to behave in a consistently favorable or unfavorable way toward a given object. *See Attitude Measures.*

Attitude-Toward-Behavior Model. A model stating that a consumer's attitude toward a specific behavior is a function of how strongly he or she believes that the action will lead to a specific outcome (either favorable or unfavorable).

Attitude-Toward-Object Model. A model stating that a consumer's attitude toward a product or brand is a function of the presence of certain attributes and the consumer's evaluation of those attributes.

Attitude-Toward-the-Ad Model. A model maintaining that a consumer form various feelings (affects) and judgments (cognitions) as the result of exposure to an advertisement, which, in turn, affects the consumer's attitude toward the ad and beliefs and attitudes toward the brand advertised.

Attribution Theory. A theory focused on how people assign causality to events and form or alter their attitudes after assessing their own or other people's behavior.

Authoritarian Parents. Parents who are very restrictive and not nurturing during their children's consumer socialization. *See Authoritative Parents, Indulgent Parents, and Neglecting Parents.*

Authoritative Parents. Parents who are very nurturing but also very restrictive during their children's consumer socialization. *See Authoritarian Parents, Indulgent Parents, and Neglecting Parents.*

Autonomic Decisions. Purchase decisions where either the husband or wife is the primary or only decision maker. *See Husband-Dominated Decisions, Joint Decisions, and Wife-Dominated Decisions.*

Avoidance Objects. Negative outcomes that people want to prevent. *See Approach Objects.*

Awareness. The first stage of Innovation Adoption, which is a term designating the process leading to a person's decision of whether or not to adopt an innovation. In this stage, the person becomes aware that the innovation is available. *See Innovation Adoption.*

Baby Boomers. The age cohort representing people born between 1946 and 1964. *See Subculture.*

Bachelorhood. In the context of the Family Life Cycle, individuals who are not married and have no children. *See Family Life Cycle.*

Behavior Intention Scale. An instrument that measures the likelihood that consumers will act a certain way in the future, such as if they will buy a product again or recommend it to friends. *See Quantitative Research.*

Behavioral Data. Behavioral segmentation data assembled through direct questioning (or observation) of consumers, and categorized using objective and measurable criteria, such as demographics. This information includes: (a) consumer-intrinsic dimensions (e.g., a person's age, gender, marital status, income, and education); (b) consumption-based behaviors (e.g., quantity of product purchased, frequency of leisure activities or the frequency of buying a given product). *See Cognitive Factors.*

Behavioral Learning (Stimulus-Response Learning). The premise that observable responses to specific external stimuli signal that learning has taken place. *See Classical Conditioning.*

Behavioral Targeting. Sending consumers personalized offers and promotional messages designed to reach specific persons and deliver to them highly relevant messages at the right time and more accurately than when using conventional segmentation techniques.

Benefit Segmentation. A segmentation approach based on the benefits that consumers seek from products and services.

Blog (Weblog). A discussion or informational site published on the Internet and consisting of discrete entries ("posts").

Brand Community. An online community formed by consumers who share an attachment to a brand.

Brand Equity. The intrinsic value of a brand name, which stems from consumers' perception of the brand's superiority, the social esteem that using it provides, and the customers' trust and identification with the brand.

Brand Loyalty. A measure of how often consumers buy a given brand, whether or not they switch brands and, if they do, how often, and the extent of their commitment to buying the brand regularly. *See Covetous Brand Loyalty, Inertia Brand Loyalty, and Premium Brand Loyalty.*

Brand Personification. Communicating human features of a brand in advertising. *See Anthropomorphism.*

Branded Entertainment. Featuring products within entertainment content or building entertainment content around promoted brands. *See Product Placement.*

Broad Categorizers. Low-risk perceivers who prefer to choose from a wide range of alternatives because they would rather face the consequences of a wrong decision than limit the number of alternatives from which they choose. *See Narrow Categorizers, Perceived Risk, and Risk Aversion.*

Buzz Agent. A consumer, employed by a marketer who promotes products clandestinely in exchange for (mostly) free product samples. *See Word-of-Mouth.*

Captive Advertising Screens. Promotional messages placed in locations where consumers spend time (and generally do not expect to see advertisements), such as elevators, cinemas, retail stores, restaurants, bars, fitness clubs, college campuses, and transit. *See Ambush Marketing.*

Cause-Related Marketing. Process in which a firm contributes a portion of its revenues from selling certain products to supporting needy groups, such as helping people with incurable diseases or hurt by inclement weather.

Celebrity Actor. A celebrity who plays a part in a commercial for a product.

Celebrity Endorsement. An ad where a celebrity appears of behalf of a product, with which he may or may not have direct experience or familiarity.

Celebrity Spokesperson. A celebrity who endorses a brand, social cause, or company over an extended period.

Celebrity Testimonial. A promotional message where a celebrity attests to the product's quality based on his or her usage of the product.

Central Route to Persuasion. A promotional approach maintaining that that highly involved consumers are best reached and persuaded through ads focused on the product's attributes. *See Elaboration Likelihood Model and Peripheral Route to Persuasion.*

Chunking. The process during which consumers recode what they have already encoded, which often results in recalling additional relevant information. "Chunks" are groupings of information.

Classical Conditioning. A form of behavioral learning stating that animal and human alike, can be taught behaviors and associations among stimuli through repetition. Some describe it as a "knee jerk" (or automatic) response to a drive that builds up through repeated exposure to a stimulus. *See Behavioral Learning, Conditioned Stimulus, and Conditioned Response.*

Closure. The instinct to organize pieces of sensory input into a complete image or feeling. Individuals need closure, which means that if they perceive that a stimulus is incomplete, they are compelled to figure out its complete meaning.

Cluster (Area) Sample. A probability sample where the population is divided into mutually exclusive groups (such as blocks), and the researcher draws a sample of the groups to study. *See Probability Sample.*

Cognitive Age. An individual's perceived, not chronological, age.

Cognitive Associative Learning. A learning theory that views classical conditioning as learning of associations among events that enable consumers to expect and anticipate and events, rather than being a reflexive action.

Cognitive Component. The first component of the Tri-Component Model of attitudes. It represents the person's *knowledge* and *perceptions* of the features of the attitude object, which, collectively, are the *beliefs* that the object possesses or does not possess specific attributes. *See Likert Scale, Semantic Differential Scale, and Tri-Component Model.*

Cognitive Dissonance. The mental discomfort that people experience when facing conflicting information about an attitude object. *See Post-Purchase Dissonance.*

Cognitive Factors. Segmentation data assembled through measures of psychological factors. This data includes: (a) consumer-intrinsic dimensions, such as personality traits, cultural values, and attitudes towards consumption and social issues; and (b) consumption-specific attitudes, behaviors and preferences, the benefits sought in products, and attitudes regarding many aspects of consumption. *See Behavioral Data.*

Cognitive Learning. The premise that learning occurs in the form of sequential, mental processing of information when people face problems that they wish to resolve. *See Innovation Adoption and Tri-Component Model.*

Communication. The process of imparting or exchanging information. In the context of consumer behavior, it is the transmission of messages from senders (the sources) to receivers (the consumers) via media (the channels of transmission). *See Formal Source, Impersonal Communications, Informal Source, and Interpersonal Communications.*

Communication Feedback. The responses of the receivers to communication messages that indicate to the senders as to whether their intended messages were received. *See Recall Test and Recognition Test.*

Comparative Advertising. An advertising appeal where marketers proclaim that their products are better than competing brands named in the ads. *See Two-Sided Message.*

Comparative Influence. A process that takes place when people compare themselves to others, whom they respect and admire, and then adopt their values or imitate their behaviors. *See Normative Influence and Reference Groups.*

Compatibility. One of the five characteristics identified as a determinant of consumer acceptance of a new product representing the degree to which potential customers perceive a new product as consistent with their present needs, values, and practices. *See the other four characteristics: Complexity, Observability, Relative Advantage, and Trial-ability.*

Compensatory Decision Rules. A group of decisions rules in which a consumer evaluates each brand in terms of each relevant attribute, weighted by the importance of that attribute, and then selects the brand with the highest weighted score. *See Noncompensatory Decision Rules.*

Complaint Analysis. Gathering complaints from unsatisfied customers and analyzing them in order to identify defects and improve the delivery of the product or service.

Complexity. One of the five characteristics identified as a determinant of consumer acceptance of a new product representing the degree to which a new product is difficult to understand or use. *See the other four characteristics: Compatibility, Observability, Relative Advantage, and Trial-ability.*

Compliant Individuals. One of three groups identified by Karen Horney (a neo-Freudian researcher), it designates persons who move toward others and desire to be loved, wanted, and appreciated. *See Aggressive Individuals and Detached Individuals.*

Compulsive Consumption. Addictive and out of control buying, that often has damaging consequences to the compulsive shoppers and those around them.

Conative Component. The third component of the Tri-Component Model of attitudes. It represents he *likelihood* that an individual will *behave in a particular way* with regard to the attitude object. In consumer behavior, the conative component is treated as an expression of the consumer's *intention to buy. See Behavior Intention Scale and Tri-Component Model.*

Conditioned Response. A response to conditioned stimulus. *See Conditioned Stimulus.*

Conditioned Stimulus. A stimulus that became associated with a particular event or feeling as a result of repetition. *See Classical Conditioning, Conditioned Respone, and Unconditioned Stimulus.*

Conjunctive Decision Rule. A noncompensatory decision rule in which consumers establish a minimally acceptable cutoff point for each product attribute evaluated. Brands that fall below the cutoff point on any attribute are not considered further. *See Noncompensatory Decision Rules.*

Consumer Behavior. The study of consumers' actions during searching for, purchasing, using, evaluating, and disposing of products and services that they expect will satisfy their needs.

Consumer Imagery. A term referring to consumers' perceptions of all the components of products, services, and brands, and to how consumers evaluate the quality of marketers' offerings. *See Perception.*

Consumer Involvement. The degree of personal relevance that the product or purchase holds for the consumer. *See High-Involvement Purchases and Low-Involvement Purchases.*

Consumer Learning. The process through which consumers acquire knowledge from experiences with products and observations of others' consumption, and use that knowledge in subsequent buying. *See Learning.*

Consumer Panels. A research method where a group of people are paid to record their purchases and/or media viewing habits in diaries, which are then compiled and analyzed to determine trends. *See Consumer Research and Primary Research.*

Consumer Research. The process and tools used to study consumer behavior. *See Qualitative Research and Quantitative Research.*

Consumer Socialization. The process by which children acquire the skills, knowledge, attitudes, and experiences necessary to function as consumers. *See Socialization and Socialization Agent.*

Content Analysis. Analyzing the content of verbal and/or pictorial communications of a given society in order to uncover its members' values, this method is often used in anthropological and sociological studies. *See Anthropology, Sociology, and Culture.*

Contextual Advertising. Targeted ads that originate in the web page a consumer is viewing or a search query the consumer has made.

Continuous Innovation. A new product that is an improved or modified version of an existing product rather than a totally new product, which therefore has very little disruptive influence on established consumption patterns. *See Discontinuous Innovation and Dynamically Continuous Innovation.*

Continuous Reinforcement. A method used in instrumental conditioning where a desired behavior is reinforced after every time it occurs. *See Instrumental Conditioning and Reinforcement.*

Controlled Experiment. An experimental design aimed at ensuring that any differences in the outcome (e.g., sales, a dependent variable) are due to different treatments of the variable under study (e.g., price, an independent variable) and not to extraneous factors (e.g., respondents' incomes). *See Experiments.*

Convenience Sample. A nonprobability sample where the researcher selects the most accessible people as the study's sample (e.g., students in a classroom). *See Nonprobability Sample.*

Corrective Advertising. A retraction or clarification a company must issue after it has made a false or misleading advertising claim because it was mandated to do so by the federal or local government.

Covert Marketing (Masked or Stealth Marketing). Marketing messages and promotional materials that appear to come from independent parties although, in fact, they come from marketers. *See Ambush Marketing.*

Covetous Brand Loyalty. Purchase behavior where consumers do not purchase the same brand consistently, but still have strong attachment and favorable predisposition toward the brand. *See Brand Loyalty.*

Cross-Cultural Analysis. A research method that compares the consumption patterns of members of different societies.

Cross-Screen Marketing. A promotional strategy that consists of tracking and targeting users across their computers, mobile phones, and tablets, and sending them personalized ads based on their interests, as observed by marketers.

Cues. Stimuli that direct motivated behavior. *See Learning.*

Culture. The collective values, customs, norms, arts, social institutions, and intellectual achievements of a particular society which express its principles, standards, and priorities. *See American Core Values, Content Analysis, and Field Observation.*

Customer Lifetime Value Profile. A forecasted estimate of how much a customer will spend on a particular product or service over the customer's entire "stay" with the offering's seller.

Customer Retention. Turning individual consumer transactions into long-term customer relationships.

Customer Satisfaction. Customers' perceptions of the performance of the product or service in relation to their expectations.

Customer Satisfaction Measurement. Quantitative and qualitative measures that gauge the level of customer satisfaction and its determinants.

Customer Satisfaction Survey. *See Customer Satisfaction Measurement.*

Customer Value. The ratio between customers' perceived benefits (i.e., economic, functional, and psychological) and the resources they have used to obtain those benefits (i.e., monetary, time, effort, psychological).

Data Aggregators. Data aggregation is an "information mining" process where data is searched, gathered and sold to marketers who use it to target customers. Data aggregators are organizations that compile information about consumers from many databases (including cookies that track online surfing) and use very sophisticated analysis to construct profiles of individual consumers or households.

Day-After Recall Test. A measure of ads' attention-getting and persuasive power where viewers of TV shows or listeners to radio broadcasts are interviewed a day after watching or listening to a given program, and asked to describe the commercials they recall. *See Unaided Recall.*

Daydreaming. Responding to frustration by fantasizing and imaginary gratification of unfilled needs. *See Defense Mechanisms.*

Deceptive Advertising. Marketing advertising claims that mislead consumers.

Defense Mechanisms. Cognitive and behavioral ways of handling frustration in order to protect one's self esteem. *See Aggression, Daydreaming, Identification, Projection, Rationalization, Regression, Repression, and Withdrawal.*

Defensive Attribution. Behavior or thoughts that occur when people accept (or take) credit for success (internal attribution), but assign failure to others or outside events (external attribution). *See Self-Perception Attribution.*

Demographic Segmentation. Dividing consumers according to age, gender, ethnicity, income and wealth, occupation, marital status, household type and size, and geographical location. These variables are objective, empirical, and can easily be determined through questioning or observation.

Depth Interview. A lengthy and unstructured interview designed to uncover a consumer's underlying attitudes and/or motivations. *See Discussion Guide and Qualitative Research.*

Detached Individuals. One of three groups identified by Karen Horney (a neo-Freudian researcher), it designates persons who move toward others and desire to be loved, wanted, and appreciated. *See Aggressive Individuals and Compliant Individuals.*

Differential Decay. A cognitive phenomenon where the memory of a low-credibility source decays faster than the contents of the message received from the source. *See Sleeper Effect.*

Differential Threshold (Just Noticeable Difference or JND). The minimal difference that can be detected between two similar stimuli. *See Absolute Threshold and Weber's Law.*

Diffusion of Innovations. The framework for exploring the evolution of consumers' acceptance of new products throughout the social system. *See Adopter Categories, Diffusion Process, Innovation, and Innovation Adoption.*

Discontinuous Innovation. A dramatically new product entry that greatly disrupts existing consumption behavior and requires the establishment of new practices. *See Continuous Innovation and Dynamically Continuous Innovation.*

Discussion Guide. A step-by-step outline that sets out the line of questioning the researcher needs to cover with the respondent in a depth interview, or a group of respondents in a focus group session. *See Depth Interview and Focus Group.*

Dissolution. The last stage of the Family Life Cycle where only one spouse survives. *See Family Life Cycle.*

Distributed Learning. Learning designed to take place over a period of time. *See Massed Learning.*

Dogmatism. A personality trait representing one's degree of cognitive rigidity—the opposite of being open-minded—towards information and opinions contradictory to one's own.

Door-in-the-Face Technique. A strategy aimed at changing attitudes where a large and costly first request—that is likely refused to be refused—is followed by a second, more realistic, and less costly request. *See Foot-in-the-Door Technique.*

Downward Mobility. Represented by people who have a lower social class level than their parents in terms of the jobs they hold, their residences, level of disposable income, and savings. *See Social Class and Upward Mobility.*

Dynamically Continuous Innovation. A new product entry that is sufficiently innovative to have some disruptive effects on established practices. *See Continuous Innovation and Discontinuous Innovation.*

E-Score. A digital calculation of people's buying power.

E-WOM. Word-of-mouth taking place online and occurring in social networks, brand communities, blogs, chat rooms, and twits.

Early Adopters. An adopter category designating consumers who buy new products within relatively short periods following the products' introductions, but not as early as the innovators. *See Adopter Categories, Innovators, Early Majority, Late Majority, and Laggards.*

Early Majority. An adopter category designating consumers who buy innovations after the early adopters had done so. *See Adopter Categories, Innovators, Early Adopters, Late Majority, and Laggards.*

Earned Social Media. Independent online media channels that are neither owned nor controlled by marketers.

Ego-Defensive Function. A functional approach to understanding attitudes where researchers believe that people replace doubt with feelings of security and confidence. *See Functional Approach.*

Ego. A Freudian term referring to the individual's conscious control in the form of an internal monitor that balances the impulsive demands of the id and the sociocultural constraints of the superego. *See Freudian Theory, Id, and Superego.*

Egoistic Needs. Psychological needs manifested in self-acceptance, self-esteem, success, independence, prestige, status, and recognition from others.

Elaboration Likelihood Model (ELM). The proposition that attitudes can be changed by either one of two different routes to persuasion—a central route or a peripheral route—and that the cognitive elaboration related to the processing of information received via each route is different. *See Central Route to Persuasion and Peripheral Route to Persuasion.*

Email Survey. Consumer research surveys conducted via email.

Emotional Bonds. Customers' high levels of personal commitment and attachment to a company and its products that extend beyond individual transactions. *See Transactional Bonds.*

Encoding. Assigning a word or visual image in order to represent an object during communications.

Enculturation. Learning one's own culture. *See Acculturation.*

Ethnocentrism. A personality traits representing one's tendency towards buying or not buying foreign-made products.

Evaluation. The third stage of Innovation Adoption, which is a term designating the process leading to a person's decision of whether or not to adopt an innovation. In this stage, the person evaluates the innovation and decides whether he (or she) wants to try using it. *See Innovation Adoption.*

Evoked Set. The specific brands (or models) a consumer considers during deciding which item to purchase within a particular product category. *See Inept Set and Inert Set.*

Experiential Marketing. Advertising designed to simulate consumers' sensory experiences with products by enabling them to physically interact with the products or providing sensory input (e.g., smell) that is part of the product.

Experiments. A consumer research approach designed to identify cause-and-effect relationships among purchase-related factors. *See Controlled Experiments, Quantitative Research, and Test Marketing.*

Exploratory Study. Research conducted before undertaking a full-scale market study.

Extended Family. A nuclear family with at least one grandparent or other relation living within the same household. *See Nuclear Family.*

Extensive Problem Solving. Purchase situations that occur infrequently and where the consumer does not have prior criteria to evaluate the product considered. *See Limited Problem Solving and Routinized Response Behavior.*

Extinction. A phenomenon that occurs when a learned response is no longer reinforced and the link between the stimulus and the expected reward is eliminated. *See Forgetting.*

Extrinsic Cues. Characteristics that are not physically inherent in the product, such as packaging, price and promotions. *See Intrinsic Cues.*

Family. Two or more persons related by blood, marriage, or adoption residing together. *See Nuclear Family, and Extended Family.*

Family Branding. Marketing a whole line of products under the same brand name, which is a marketing application of stimulus generalization. *See Stimulus Generalization.*

Family Life Cycle. A composite variable that includes marital status, size of family, age of family members (focusing on the age of the oldest or youngest child), and employment status of the head of household classifies the family into a "typical" stage. *See Bachelorhood, Honeymooners, Parenthood, Post-Parenthood, and Dissolution.*

Field Observation. A research method, used in anthropological and sociocultural studies, that consists of observing the daily behavior of selected members of a society in order to learn about its beliefs, values, and customs. *See Anthropology, Culture, Participant-Observers, and Sociology.*

Figure and Ground. An element of perception that describes the interrelationship between the stimulus itself (i.e., figure) and the environment or context within which is appears (i.e., ground).

Fixated Consumption. A personality trait referring to one's tendency to persistently buy items that are related to his or her collection or hobby and proudly display them for friends and other collectors.

Fixed Ratio Reinforcement. A method used in instrumental conditioning consisting of reinforcing a desired behavior every *n*th time (e.g., after every third time the behavior occurs). *See Instrumental Conditioning and Reinforcement.*

Focus Group. A method of qualitative research consisting of eight to ten participants who meet with a moderator-researcher-analyst and "focus on" or "explore" a particular product or product category (or any other topic or subject of research interest). *See Discussion Guide and Qualitative Research.*

Foot-in-the-Door Technique. A strategy aimed at changing attitudes consisting of getting people to agree to a large request after convincing them to agree to a small and modest request first. *See Door-in-the-Face Technique.*

Forgetting. A point at which the link between the stimulus and the expected reward seizes to exist because of lack of engagement in the applicable purchase situation for a lengthy period. *See Extinction.*

Formal Learning. Learning that occurs when parents, older siblings and other family members teach younger members "how to behave." *See Informal Learning and Technical Learning.*

Formal Source. A communication source that speaks on behalf of a company, such as an endorser, salesperson, or advertiser. *See Communication, Informal Source, and Source Credibility.*

Freudian Theory. A theory maintaining that unconscious needs or drives, especially biological and sexual ones, are at the heart of human motivation and personality. *See Ego, Id, and Superego.*

Frustration. The feeling that results from failure to achieve a goal. *See Defense Mechanisms.*

Functional Approach. An approach to changing attitudes by appealing to the reasons (or motivations) behind people's attitudes. These reasons are called "functions." *See Ego-Defensive Function, Knowledge Function, Utlitarian Function, and Value-Expressive Function.*

Generation X (Xers). The age cohort representing people born between 1965 and 1979.

Generation Y (Echo Boomers, Millennials). The age cohort representing people born between 1980 and 1996. Some definitions also include people born in the late 1970s and 1990s in this cohort.

Generation Z (Homeland Generation, Digital Natives). The age cohort representing people born from 1997 till the present.

Generic Goals. Outcomes that consumers seek in order to satisfy physiological and psychological needs. *See Product-Specific Goals.*

Geo-Demographic Segments. Segments identified through geodemographics.

Geodemographics. A hybrid segmentation scheme based on the premise that people who live close to one another are likely to have similar financial means, tastes, preferences, lifestyles, and consumption habits (as an old adage states, "Birds of a feather flock together").

Geofencing. Promotional alerts sent to the smartphones of customers, who opted into this service, when the customers near or enter the store.

Gestalt Psychology. The principles underlying perceptual organization. "Gestalt" means "pattern" or "configuration" in German. *See Perception.*

Gifting Behavior. Consumer behavior involving giving gifts.

Global Marketing Strategy. Selling the same product using the same positioning and communication approach globally. *See Hybrid Marketing Strategy and Local Marketing Strategy.*

Goals. Sought after outcomes of motivated behavior. *See Motivation.*

Google Analytics. A service offered by Google that enables advertisers to evaluate the effectiveness of their websites and profiles their users.

Gordon Survey of Personal and Interpersonal Values. A research instrument measuring the values that represent how people cope with their daily lives. *See Interpersonal Values and Personal Values.*

Grouping. People's instinctive tendency to group stimuli together and unite them into one entity. *See Perception.*

Halo Effect. An evaluation of an object based on only one (or several) positive dimension. Linguistically, the definition of "halo" signifies light, honor, and glory. Thus, in marketing, the term refers to a prestigious image of a product "rubbing on" other products marketed under the same brand name.

Hemispheric Lateralization (Split-Brain Theory). A theory whose premise is that the human brain is divided into two distinct cerebral hemispheres that operate together, but "specialize" in the processing different types of cognitions. The left hemisphere is the center of human language; it is the linear side of the brain and primarily responsible for reading, speaking, and reasoning. The right hemisphere of the brain is the home of spatial perception and nonverbal concepts; it is nonlinear and the source of imagination and pleasure. *See Passive Learning.*

High-Involvement Purchases. Purchases that are very important to the consumer and provoke a lot of perceived risk, and extensive problem solving and information processing. *See Consumer Involvement, Extensive Problem Solving, Low-Involvement Purchases, and Perceived Risk.*

Honeymooners. In the context of the Family Life Cycle, young and newly married couples. *See Family Life Cycle.*

Husband-Dominated Decisions. Purchase decisions where the husband's influence is greater than the wife's. *See Autonomic Decisions, Joint Decisions, and Wife-Dominated Decisions.*

Hybrid Marketing Strategy. While selling overseas, standardizing either the product or advertising message and customizing the other one. *See Global Marketing Strategy and Local Marketing Strategy.*

Id. A Freudian term referring to the "warehouse" of primitive and impulsive drives—basic physiological needs such as thirst, hunger, and sex—for which the individual seeks immediate satisfaction without concern for the specific means of satisfaction. *See Ego, Freudian Theory, and Superego.*

Ideal Self-Image. The way people like to see themselves.

Ideal Social Self-Image. The way people like others to see them.

Identification. Resolving frustration identifying with other persons who have experienced the same or similar frustrating situation. *See Defense Mechanisms.*

Impersonal Communications. Messages that companies (formal sources) develop and transmit through their marketing departments, advertising or public relations agencies, and spokespersons. *See Communication, Formal Source, and Interpersonal Communications.*

Impression-Based Targeting. A technique where advertisers specify the criteria of the persons they wish to reach online and then bid in real time for the opportunities to reach such people. A person reached is termed an "eyeball" or "impression." Impression-based ads often "follow" consumers online and thus keep reminding them about the products they were interested in. *See Real Time Bidding and Segment-Based Targeting.*

Index of Status Characteristics (Warner's ISC). A measure of social class in the form of a weighted index of occupation, source (not amount) of income, house type, and the quality of the dwelling area. *See Multivariable Index.*

Indulgent Parents. Parents who are very nurturing and highly permissive during their children's consumer socialization. *See Authoritarion Parents, Authoritative Parents, and Neglecting Parents.*

Inept Set. Brands (or models) that the consumer excludes from purchase consideration because they are unacceptable and often considered inferior. *See Evoked Set and Inert Set.*

Inert Set. Brands (or models) the consumer is indifferent toward because they are perceived as not having any particular advantages. *See Evoked Set and Inept Set.*

Inertia Brand Loyalty. Purchasing the same brand consistently because of habit and convenience, but without any emotional attachment to it. *See Brand Loyalty.*

Infomercials. Long commercials that appear to be documentaries rather than advertisements.

Informal Learning. Learning that occurs when children imitate the behaviors of selected others, such as family members, friends, or TV and movie heroes or characters. *See Formal Learning and Technical Learning.*

Informal Source. A person whom the message receiver knows personally, such as a parent or friend, or an individual met online, who provides the receiver with product information and advice. *See Communication, Formal Source, and Source Credibility.*

Information Overload. A situation that occurs when consumers receive too much information and find it difficult to encode and store it.

Inner-Directed. Consumers who rely on their own inner values and standards in evaluating new products, and are also likely to be consumer innovators. *See Other-Directed.*

Innovation. *See Continuous Innovation, Diffusion of Innovation, Discontinuous Innovation, and Dynamically Continuous Innovation.*

Innovation Adoption. A form of cognitive learning, developed by researchers of Diffusion of Innovations, this term designates the process leading to a person's decision of whether or not to adopt an innovation. This process consists of five stages. *See Awareness, Interest, Evaluation, Trial, and Adoption.*

Innovation Adoption Process. *See Innovation Adoption.*

Innovation Decision-Making. A form of cognitive learning, developed by researchers of Diffusion of Innovations, stating that learning about new products and deciding whether or not to adopt them occurs in the following manner: knowledge, persuasion, decision, and confirmation. This process is very similar to Innovation Adoption.

Innovativeness. The degree of a consumer's willingness to adopt new products and services shortly after they are they have been introduced. *See Innovators.*

Innovators. Consumers who are open to new ideas and are among the first to try new products, services, or practices. *See Innovativeness, Adopter Categories, Early Adopters, Early Majority, Late Majority, and Laggards.*

Institutional Advertising. Advertising that promotes a company's overall image without referring to specific products.

Instrumental Conditioning (Operant Conditioning). A form of behavioral learning based on the notion that learning occurs through a trial-and-error process, with habits formed as a result of rewards received for certain responses or behaviors. *See Behavioral Learning and Reinforcement.*

Instrumental Values. Within the Rokeach Value Survey, values that are defined as the "means" to achieve end goals. *See Rokeach Value Survey and Terminal Values.*

Interactive TV (iTV). A medium that combines TV broadcasts and the interactivity of the Internet. iTV and can be delivered to one's TV, computer, or mobile device in the form of a two-way communication between subscribers and providers of cable or satellite TV.

Interest. The second stage of Innovation Adoption, which is a term designating the process leading to a person's decision of whether or not to adopt an innovation. In this stage, the person begins to be interested in the innovation. *See Innovation Adoption.*

Internal Marketing. Marketing the organization to its personnel and treating them like "internal customers" in order to get them to "go the extra mile" in handling and retaining "real" customers.

Internet Survey. A research study conducted online.

Interpersonal Communications. Messages sent by either formal sources (e.g., a salesperson in a physical or virtual retail location) or informal sources (e.g., peers with whom the consumer communicates face to face or via electronic means). *See Communication, Formal Source, Impersonal Communications, and Informal Source.*

Interpersonal Values. Within Gordon's Survey of Personal and Interpersonal Values, measures of one's achievement need, goal orientation, and seeking new experiences. *See Gordon's Survey and Personal Values.*

Intrinsic Cues. Physical characteristics of the product itself, such as size, color, flavor, or aroma. *See Extrinsic Cues.*

JND (Just Noticeable Difference). *See Differential Threshold.*

Joint Decisions. Purchase decisions where the husband and wife's influence are equal. *See Autonomic Decisions, Husband-Dominated Decisions, and Wife-Dominated Decisions.*

Judgment Sample. A nonprobability sample where researchers use their own judgments to select the respondents. *See Nonprobability Sample.*

Key Informant Method. A technique of measuring opinion leadership that consists of gathering information from a person who is keenly knowledgeable about the nature of social communications among members of a specific group. *See Opinion Leadership.*

Klout Score. A numerical value that measures persons' influence online based on their ability to generate engagement with and feedback to their online postings.

Knowledge Function. A functional approach to studying attitudes where researchers maintain that people form attitudes because they have a strong need to understand the characters of the people, events, and objects they encounter. *See Functional Approach.*

Laggards. The very last consumers to adopt innovations. *See Adopter Categories, Innovators, Early Adopters, Early Majority, and Late Majority.*

Late Majority. People who buy innovations only after most other consumers have adopted them. *See Adopter Categories, Innovators, Early Adopters, Early Majority, and Laggards.*

Learning. Applying one's past knowledge and experience to present circumstances and behavior. *See Motivation, Cues, Response, and Reinforcement.*

Lexicographic Decision Rule. A noncopensatory decision rule where the consumer first ranks the attributes in terms of perceived relevance or importance. The consumer then compares the various alternatives in terms of the single attribute that is considered most important. *See Noncompensatory Decision Rules.*

Licensing. An application of stimulus generalization that contractually allows affixing a brand name to the products of another manufacturer. *See Stimulus Generalization.*

Likert Scale. The most popular form of attitude scale, where consumers are asked to check numbers corresponding to their level of "agreement" or "disagreement" with a series of statements about the studied object. The scale consists of an equal number of agreement/disagreement choices on either side of a neutral choice. *See Quantitative Research.*

Limited Problem Solving. Purchase decisions where consumers buy updated versions of products they have bought before and have set criteria to evaluate these items. *See Extensive Problem Solving and Routinized Response Behavior.*

Local Marketing Strategy. Customizing both the product and communication approach for overseas market. *See Global Marketing Strategy and Hybried Marketing Strategy.*

Long-Term Store. A location in the brain where information is retained for extended periods of time. *See Sensation, Sensory Store, and Short-Term Store.*

Low-Involvement Purchases. Purchases are not very important to the consumer, hold little relevance, have little perceived risk, and, thus, provoke very limited information processing. *See Consumer Involvement, High-Involvement Purchases, Perceived Risk, and Routinized Response Behavior.*

Magazine Readership Survey. A form of consumer survey. *See Starch Readership Ad Study.*

Mail Survey. A research study consisting of sending questionnaire by mail.

Market Research. A process that links the consumer, customer, and public to the marketer through information in order to identify marketing opportunities and problems, evaluate marketing actions, and judge the performance of marketing strategies.

Market Segmentation. The process of dividing a market into subsets of consumers with common needs or characteristics. Each subset represemts a consumer group with shared needs that are different from those shared by other groups.

Marketing. The activity, set of institutions, and processes for creating, communicating, delivering, and exchanging offerings that have value for customers, clients, partners, and society.

Marketing Concept. The premise that marketing consists of satisfying consumers' needs, creating value, and retaining customers, and that companies must produce only those goods that they have already determined that consumers would buy.

Marketing Ethics. Moral principles designed to guide marketers' behavior.

Marketing Mix (Four Ps). A business plan that includes four elements: the product (or service), price, place (or distribution), and promotion.

Marketing Myopia. A focus on the product rather than on the needs it presumes to satisfy.

Maslow's Hierarchy of Needs. A theoretical framework consisting of five levels of human needs, which rank in order of importance from lower-level (biogenic) needs to higher-level (psychogenic) needs. The theory states that individuals seek to satisfy lower-level needs before higher-level needs.

Massed Learning. Bunched up learning designed to teach people all at once. *See Distributed Learning.*

Materialism. A personality traits that gauges the extent to which an individual is preoccupied with the purchase and display of non-essential and often conspicuous luxury goods.

Media. The channels for transmitting communications. *See Communication.*

Media Exposure Effects. A measure of how many consumers were exposed to the message and their characteristics.

Membership Group. A group to which a person either belongs or can join and whose values he or she adopt. *See Reference Groups and Symbolic Group.*

Message. A thought, idea, attitude, image, or other information that the sender wishes to convey to the intended audience, and it can be verbal (spoken or written), nonverbal (a photograph, an illustration, or a symbol), or a combination of the two.

Microblog. A site that has less content than the traditional blog and allow users to exchange small elements of content, such as short sentences, individual images, and video links, mostly via Twitter. *See Blog.*

Mobile Ads. *See Mobile Advertising.*

Mobile Advertising. Sending promotional messages to consumers' cell phones, iPads, electronic readers, and other devices that people carry while on the go.

Motivation. The driving force within individuals that impels them to act.

Motivational Research. A "term of art" that refers to qualitative studies conducted by Dr. Ernest Dichter in the 1950s and 1960, which were designed to uncover consumers' subconscious or hidden motivations in the context of buying and consumption. *See Projective Techniques and Qualitative Research.*

Multi-Attribute Attitude Models. Models that portray consumers' attitudes as functions of their assessments of the objects' prominent attributes.

Multivariable Index. A measure of social class that combines several demographics to determine social class standing. *See Index of Status Characteristics and Socioeconomic Status Score.*

Mystery Shoppers. Professional observers who pose as customers and interact with and provide unbiased evaluations of the company's service personnel in order to identify opportunities for improving productivity and efficiency. *See Consumer Research.*

Narrow Categorizers. High-risk perceivers who prefer to limit their choices to a few safe alternatives rather than face the consequences of a wrong decision. *See Broad Categorizers, Perceived Risk, and Risk Aversion.*

Narrowcasting. Communication channels that enable marketers to send addressable, customized, interactive, and more response-measurable messages, to narrowly defined market segments.

National Brand. A brand that is available in all fifty states.

Need for Cognition (NFC). A personality traits that reflects a person's craving for or enjoyment of thinking.

Need for Humor. A person's tendency to enjoy, engage in, or seek out amusement.

Need for Self-Actualization (or Self-Fulfillment). An individual's desire to fulfill his or her potential—to becoming everything he or she is capable of becoming. *See Maslow's Hierarchy of Needs.*

Need for Uniqueness. Individuals' attempts to differentiate themselves through the acquisition of consumer goods that enhance their personal and social identities.

Need Recognition. The first step in the consumer decision-making process occurring when the consumer identifies and faces a "problem" that can be solved by buying a product or service.

Needs. Circumstances or things that that are wanted or required, and therefore direct the motivational forces. *See Motivation.*

Negative Disconfirmation of Expectations. A situation that occurs when a product's performance is below expectations and the consumer is dissatisfied. *See Positive Disconfirmation of Expectations.*

Negative Message Framing. A promotional message that stresses the benefits to be lost by not using the product. *See Positive Message Framing.*

Negative Reinforcement. Removing an unpleasant stimulus. *See Positive Reinforcement.*

Neglecting Parents. Parents who are very permissive, but provide their children with little or no nurturing during their children's consumer socialization. *See Authoritarian Parents, Authoritative Parents, and Indulgent Parents.*

Neo-Freudian Personality Theory. A theory based on the premise that social relationships play a crucial role in the development of personality, in addition to the aspects outlined by Freud.

Neuromarketing. The study of advertising's effects on brain activity. *See Physiological Measures.*

New Media. Online channels, social networks, and mobile electronic devices. Unlike traditional media, these channels allow marketers to send personalized messages to individual consumers who can respond to the messages immediately.

Non-Family Households. Living situations that are not legally defined as families. *See Family.*

Noncompensatory Decision Rules. A group of decision rules that do not allow consumers to balance positive evaluations of a brand on one attribute against negative evaluations on other attributes. *See Compensatory Decision Rules.*

Nonprobability Sample. Selecting study respondents in a nonrandom fashion based on researchers' judgments. *See Cluster Sample, Convenience Sample, Judgment Sample, and Quota Sample.*

Nontraditional Families. Families that do not readily fit into the Family Life Cycle. *See Family Life Cycle.*

Normative Influence. Learning and adopting a group's norms, values, and behaviors. *See Comparative Influence and Reference Groups.*

Nuclear Family. A married couple with one or more children. *See Extended Family.*

Objective Measures. Measures of social class that include one or more of the following variables: occupation, amount of income and education, and other related factors (e.g., source of income). *See Multivariable Index and Subjective Measures.*

Observability (Communicability). One of the five characteristics identified as a determinant of consumer acceptance of a new product representing the ease with which a product's benefits or attributes can be observed, imagined, or described to potential consumers. *See the other four characteristics: Compatibility, Complexity, Relative Advantage, and Trial-ability.*

Observational Learning (Modeling). Learning that occurs when people observe and later imitate observed behaviors.

Observational Research. A research tool where marketers because marketers gain an in-depth understanding of the relationship between people and products is by watching them in the process of buying and/or using the products. *See Quantitative Research.*

Occupational Prestige Ranking. Rankings that represent society's collective beliefs regarding the occupation's social worth and desirability, as stemming from the knowledge required to attain it (i.e., educational level) and the material

rewards that occupants receive (i.e., income). *See Social Class and Social Status.*

One-Sided Message. A message that ignores competitors' products.

Online Display Ads. Fixed banners posted on websites.

Opinion Leadership. The process by which one person (the opinion leader) informally influences others, who might be either opinion seekers or recipients. This influence occurs between two or more people neither of whom represents a commercial seller nor would gain directly from providing advice or information. *See Buzz Agent and Word-of-Mouth.*

Optimum Stimulation Level (OSL). A personality traits that reflects the degree to which a person likes novel, complex and unusual experiences (i.e., high OSL), or prefers simple, uncluttered, and calm existence (i.e., low OSL).

Other-Directed. Consumers who look up to others for guidance as to what is appropriate or inappropriate and are unlikely to be consumer innovators. *See Inner-Directed.*

Out-of-Home Media. Communications vehicles that target consumers in captive and less cluttered environments outside of their homes.

Owned Social Media. Online communication channels that marketers control. *See Paid Social Media.*

Paid Social Media. Online communication channels that marketers pay for using. *See Owned Social Media.*

Parenthood. In the context of the Family Life Cycle, married couples with at least one child living at home. *See Family Life Cycle.*

Participant-Observers. Researchers who become active members of the society whose customs and values they are observing and studying. *See Field Observation.*

Passive Learning. *See Hemispheric Lateralization.*

Perceived Price. The customer's view of the value that he or she he receives from the purchase. *See Perception.*

Perceived Risk. The uncertainty that consumers face when they cannot foresee the consequences of their purchase decisions. The types of perceived risk include functional, physical, financial, psychological and time risks. *See Perception.*

Perception. The process by which individuals select, organize, and interpret stimuli into a meaningful and coherent picture of the world. It can be described as "how we see the world around us."

Perceptual Defense. A cognitive activity occurring when consumers subconsciously screen out stimuli that they find psychologically threatening, even though exposure has already taken place. *See Perception, Selective Attention, Selective Exposure, and Subliminal Perception.*

Perceptual Mapping. Constructing a maplike diagram representing consumers' perceptions of competing brands along relevant product attributes. Perceptual maps show marketers: (1) how consumers perceive their brand in relation to competition; (2) determine the direction for altering undesirable consumers' perception of their brands; and (3) find gaps, in the form of "un-owned" perceptual positions, that represent opportunities for developing new brands or products. *See Perception.*

Peripheral Route to Persuasion. A promotional approach maintaining that uninvolved consumers can be best persuaded by the ad's visual aspects rather than its informative copy (i.e., the product's attributes). *See Central Route to Persuasion and Elaboration Likelihood Model.*

Personal Interview Survey. A study where researchers interview respondents in person.

Personal Values. Within Gordon's Survey of Personal and Interpersonal Values, measures of one's leadership, desire to be recognized, and conformity. *See Gordon's Survey and Interpersonal Values.*

Personality. The inner psychological characteristics that both determine and reflect how we think and act.

Persuasion Effects. Measures that indicate whether the message was received, understood, and interpreted correctly.

Physiological Measures. Electronic instruments that track bodily responses to stimuli. *See Neuromarketing.*

Physiological Needs. Innate (biogenic, primary) motivational forces that sustains biological existence. They include the need for food, water, air, protecting the body from the outside environment (i.e., clothing and shelter), and sex. *See Psychological Needs.*

Physiological Observation. *See Physiological Measures.*

Portable People Meters (PPMs). Small devices, equipped with GPS, that consumers clip into their belts and wear all day (in exchange for monetary incentives). The devices monitor codes embedded in into the audio streams of media that consumers receive and can also capture visual images of the screens and written materials that consumers are exposed to.

Positioning. The process by which a company creates a distinct image and identity for its products, services and brands in consumers' minds. The image differentiates the company's offering from competition by communicating to the target audience that the product, service or brand fulfills the target consumers' needs better than alternatives. *See Repositioning.*

Positive Disconfirmation of Expectations. A situation that occurs when the product's performance exceeds expectations and the consumer is satisfied. *See Negative Disconfirmation of Expectations.*

Positive Message Framing. A promotional message that stresses the benefits to be gained by using a specific product. *See Negative Message Framing.*

Positive Reinforcement. Rewarding a particular behavior and strengthening the likelihood of a specific response during the same or similar situation in the future. *See Negative Reinforcement.*

Post-Parenthood. In the context of the Family Life Cycle, older couples with no children living at home. *See Family Life Cycle.*

Post-Purchase Dissonance. Cognitive dissonance that occurs after a purchase. *See Cognitive Dissonance.*

Power Need. A psychological force that is closely related to the egoistic need and reflects the individual's desire to control his or her environment, including controlling other persons and objects.

Pre-Purchase Search. A stage in the consumer decision-making process where the consumer tries to identify a product that will satisfy a recognized need better than other alternatives.

Predictive Analytics. Measures designed to predict consumers' future purchases on the bases of past buying information and other data, and also evaluate the impact of personalized promotions stemming from these predictions.

Premium Brand Loyalty. Solid attachment to the brand represented by continuous repeated purchases. *See Brand Loyalty.*

Price/Quality Relationship. A situation occurring when consumers rely on prices as indicators of product quality and view more expensive products as having higher quality and value. *See Perception.*

Primacy Effect. An indication that material presented first during communications is more noticeable and persuasive than subsequent materials. *See Recency Effect.*

Primary Research. New research especially designed and collected for purposes of a current research problem. *See Qualitative Research and Quantitative Research.*

PRIZM. A framework designed by Nielsen that is widely used in geodemographic segmentation. It consists of sixty-six segments classified according to ZIP codes and enables marketers to locate specific consumer groups readily.

Probability Sample. A method when studies' respondents are selected in such a way that every member of the population studied has a known, nonzero chance of being selected. *See Simple Random Sample, Stratified Random Sample, and Systematic Random Sample.*

Product Awareness Status. The degree of a consumer's awareness of the product and its features, and whether or not he or she intends to buy it reasonably soon.

Product Concept. A premise that consumers buy the product that offers them the highest quality, the best performance, and the most features.

Product Form Extensions. Offering the same product in a different form but under the same brand, which is a marketing application of stimulus generalization. *See Stimulus Generalization.*

Product Line Extensions. Additions of related items to an established brand because they are likely to be adopted, since they come under a known and trusted brand name, which is a marketing application of stimulus generalization. *See Stimulus Generalization.*

Product Placement. A form of promotion where marketers "disguise" promotional cues by integrating products (i.e., "figures") into TV shows, films or other entertainment content (i.e., "grounds"), or building entertainment content around products. *See Branded Entertainment and Figure and Ground.*

Product-Specific Goals. Sought outcomes to be achieved by using a given product or service. *See Generic Goals.*

Production Concept. A premise that consumers are mostly interested in product availability at low prices; its implicit marketing objectives are cheap, efficient production and intensive distribution of products.

Projection. Responding to frustration by projecting blame for failures and inabilities on other objects or persons. *See Defense Mechanisms.*

Projective Techniques. A research tool requiring respondents to interpret stimuli that do not have clear meanings, with the assumption that the subjects will "reveal" or "project" their subconscious, hidden motives into (or onto) the ambiguous stimuli. *See Qualitative Research.*

Psychographics (AIOs). Segmenting consumers according to their lifestyles, which consist of consumers' activities, interests, and opinions (i.e., AIOS).

Psychological Needs. Motivational forces that are learned from our parents, social environment, and interactions with others. *See Physiological Needs.*

Psychological Noise. Competing advertising messages or distracting thoughts that impact the reception of promotional messages.

Psychology. The study of the human mind and the mental factors that affect behavior (i.e., needs, personality traits, perception, learned experiences, and attitudes).

Qualitative Research. Studies that attempt to delve into the consumer's unconscious or hidden motivations. This research utilizes focus groups, depth interviews, motivational research, and projective techniques. *See Depth Interview, Focus Group, Motivational Research, and Projective Techniques.*

Quantitative Research. Gathering and analyzing statistical data, utilizing observational research, experimentation, and survey research. *See Behavior Intention Scale, Email Survey, Experiments, Internet Survey, Likert Scale, Mail Survey, Observational Research, Personal Interview Survey, Semantic Differential Scale, Rank Order Scale, and Telephone Interview Survey.*

Quota Sample. A nonprobability sample where the researcher interviews a prescribed number of people in each of several categories (e.g., 50 men and 50 women). *See Nonprobability Sample.*

Rank-Order Scale. A research instrument requiring participants in a study to rank items (e.g., products) in order of preference in terms of some criterion, such as overall quality or value for the money. *See Quantitative Research.*

Rationalization. Resolving frustration by inventing plausible reasons for being unable to attain goals or deciding that the goal is not really worth pursuing. *See Defense Mechanisms.*

Real Time Bidding. A technique that allows advertisers to reach the right user, in the right place, at the right time, and also sets the price that advertisers pay for each "eyeball" or "impression" (i.e., for each person reached). *See Impression-Based Targeting.*

Recall Test. *See Unaided Recall.*

Recency Effect. An indication that the material presented last during communications is more noticeable and persuasive than preceding materials. *See Primacy Effect.*

Recognition Test. *See Aided Recall.*

Reference Groups. Groups that serve as sources of comparison, influence, and norms for people's opinions, values, and behaviors. *See Comparative Influence, Membership Group, Normative Influence, and Symbolic Group.*

Regression. Reacting to a frustrating situation with childish or immature behavior. *See Defense Mechanisms.*

Rehearsal. The process that information in the short-term store undergoes, in the form of silent, mental repetition of information, after which the information is transferred to the long-term store.

Reinforcement. In learning, particularly in instrumental conditioning, it is a reward, in the form of pleasure, enjoyment, and other benefits, for a desired behavior. In consumer behavior, it is the benefits, enjoyment, and utilities that consumers receive from products purchased. *See Continuous Reinforcement, Fixed Ratio Reinforcement, Negative Reinforcement, Positive Reinforcement, and Variable Reinforcement.*

Relative Advantage. One of the five characteristics identified as a determinant of consumer acceptance of a new product representing the degree to which potential customers perceive a new product as superior to existing substitutes. *See* *the other four characteristics: Compatibility, Complexity, Observability, and Trial-ability.*

Reliability. A measure has reliability if the same questions, asked of a similar sample, produce the same findings. *See Validity.*

Repetition. In the context of consumer learning, the mechanism used continuously to establish and maintain associations between brands and unfulfilled needs. *See Classical Conditioning and Instrumental Conditioning.*

Repositioning. The process by which a company strategically changes the distinct image and identity of that its products, services, and brands. *See Positioning.*

Repression. Responding to frustration by "forcing" the failure to achieve a goal out of conscious awareness. *See Defense Mechanisms.*

Response. Reaction to a drive or cue. *See Learning.*

Retargeting. Ads for specific products that consumers have looked at online that "follow" these consumers repeatedly and show up whenever the consumers go online using the same computers.

Retrieval. The process by which people recover information from the long-term store, that is frequently triggered by external cues.

Risk Aversion. The reluctance to take risks and low tolerance of ambiguous situations.

Ritual. A symbolic activity consisting of a fixed sequence of steps that is repeated periodically.

Ritualistic Behavior. An action that has become a ritual.

Rokeach Value Survey. A self-administered, two-part values inventory. *See Instrumental Values and Terminal Values.*

Routinized Response Behavior. Purchase decisions that are "automatic" and made without much thought because the products involved are inexpensive and purchased frequently. *See Extensive Problem Solving and Limited Problem Solving.*

Safety and Security Needs. Psychological forces that are concerned not only with physical safety but also include order, stability, routine, familiarity, and control over one's life. *See Maslow's Hierarchy of Needs.*

Sales Effects. Measures that indicate whether the messages of a given campaign have generated the sales level defined in the campaign's objectives.

Sample. A presumably representative subset of the population under study that is used to estimate the entire population's characteristics. *See Nonprobability Sample and Probability Sample.*

Screener Questionnaire. A questionnaire designed to ensure that only individuals who fulfill a preset criteria are used as respondents in a research study. *See Consumer Research.*

Search Advertising. Placing online advertisements on Web pages that show results from search engine queries.

Secondary Data. Information that was gathered previously and not in the course of the study presently undertaken. *See Primary Research.*

Segment-Based Targeting. A atrategic method where advertisers pre-negotiate prices for advertising space in media (e.g., magazines or TV shows), whose audiences, presumably, largely (but never completely) match the profiles of the consumers the advertisers target. *See Impression-Based Targeting.*

Selective Attention. Consumers' heightened awareness of stimuli that meet their needs and interests and minimal awareness of stimuli irrelevant to their needs. *See Perception, Perceptual Defense, and Selective Exposure.*

Selective Exposure. Consumers seeking out sympathetic, pleasant messages and deliberately avoiding messages that they find painful or threatening. See *Perception, Perceptual Defense, and Selective Attention.*

Self–Construal. A trait that refers to how individuals perceive, comprehend, and interpret the world around them, particularly the behavior or action of others towards themselves.

Self-Designating Method. A technique of measuring opinion leadership that employs a self-administered questionnaire where respondents are asked to evaluate the extent to which they have provided others with information about a product or brand, or have otherwise influenced the purchase decisions of others. *See Opinion Leadership.*

Self-Image. *See Actual Self-Image.*

Self-Perception Attribution. A mental interpretation that reflects the way people see themselves when they form causalities about prior events, which consists of internal and external attributions. *See Defensive Attribution.*

Self-Reported Measures of Motives. Measures that consist of written statements, and where respondents are asked to indicate how relevant each statement is to them.

Selling Concept. A premise that marketers' primary focus should be selling the products that they have decided to produce through the "hard sell" approach.

Semantic Differential Scale. A measure consisting of a series of bipolar adjectives (such as "good/bad," "hot/cold," "like/dislike," or "expensive/inexpensive") anchored at the ends of an odd-numbered (e.g., five- or seven-point) continuum. *See Quantitative Research.*

Sensation. The immediate and direct response of the sensory organs to stimuli. *See Perception, Sensory Receptors, and Stimulus.*

Sensation Seeking. A personality traits that is closely related to OSL and reflects one's need for varied, novel, and complex sensations and experiences, and the willingness to take risks for the sake of such experiences.

Sensory Adaptation. Getting used to high levels of sensory input and therefore less able to notice a particular stimulus.

Sensory Receptors. The human organs (the eyes, ears, nose, mouth, and skin) that receive sensory inputs. Their sensory functions are to see, hear, smell, taste, and touch. *See Sensation and Stimulus.*

Sensory Store. A location in the brain where the sensory input lasts for just a second or two. If it is not processed immediately, it is lost. *See Long-Term Store and Short-Term Store.*

SERVQUAL Scale. Perceptual measure of the gap between customers' expectations of services and their perceptions of the actual service delivered, based on five dimensions: reliability, responsiveness, assurance, empathy, and tangibility. These dimensions are divided into two groups: the "outcome dimension," which focuses on the reliable delivery of the core service, and the "process dimension," which focuses on how the core service is delivered (i.e., the employees' responsiveness, assurance, and empathy in handling customers) and the service's tangible aspects.

Shaping. Reinforcement before the desired consumer behavior actually takes place, which increases the probability that the desired behavior will occur.

Short-Term Store (Working Memory). A location in brain where information is retained for a very short period. *See Long-Term Store, Sensation, and Sensory Store.*

Showrooming. Consumers using smartphones to scan the bar codes of products displayed in physical stores and then checking the items' prices online in order to purchase them at the lowest prices.

Simple Random Sample. A probability sample where every member of the population has a known and equal chance of being selected. *See Probability Sample.*

Sleeper Effect. A person's disassociation of the message from its source over time, which results in remembering only the message's content, but not its source. *See Differential Decay.*

Social Class. The division of members of a society into a hierarchy of distinct status classes, so that members of each class have relatively the same status and members of all other classes have either higher or lower status. *See Occupational Prestige Rankings, Social Class Consciousness, and Social Status.*

Social Media. Means of interactions among people in which they create, share, and exchange information and ideas in virtual communities and networks. Social media depend on mobile and Web-based technologies to create highly interactive platforms through which individuals and communities share, co-create, discuss, and modify user-generated content.

Social Needs. The psychogenic needs for love, affection, belonging, and acceptance. *See Maslow's Hierarchy of Needs.*

Social Network. Virtual community where people share information about themselves with others, generally with similar interests, with whom they had established relationships that, for the most part, exist only in cyberspace.

Social Self-Image. The image that reflects about how people believe others see them. *See Actual Self-Image.*

Social Status. The degree of prestige the members of one social class have in comparison with members of other social classes. Status is composed of several factors, including wealth (amount of economic assets), power (the degree of influence over others), and the amount of esteem one receives from others. *See Occupational Prestige Rankings and Social Class.*

Social-Class Consciousness. A person's level of identification with a given social class. *See Objective Measures.*

Socialization. The process by which people learn how to behave in ways that are acceptable to other members of their society. *See Socialization Agent.*

Socialization Agent. The person or organization involved in the socialization process because of frequency of contact with the individual being socialized and control over the rewards and punishments given to him or her. *See Consumer Socialization.*

Societal Marketing Concept. A premise that requires marketers to fulfill the needs of the target audience in ways that improve, preserve, and enhance society's well-being, while also meeting their business objectives.

Socioeconomic Status Score (SES). A measure of social class, developed by the U.S. Census Bureau, that combines occupation, family income, and educational attainment to determine social standing. *See Multivariable Index.*

Sociology. The study of the development, structure, functioning, and problems of human society. *See Content Analysis, Culture, and Field Observation.*

Sociometric Method. A technique of measuring opinion leadership that records person-to-person communications about a product or brand among members of a community where most people know each other by name. *See Opinion Leadership.*

Source Credibility. A source's persuasive impact, stemming from its perceived expertise, trustworthiness, and believability.

Starch Readership Ad Study. A research method that evaluates the effectiveness of magazine advertisements along three criteria: "Noticing" the ad, "associating" the ad with the brand advertised, and "involvement" with the ad (defined as having read most of the ad's text). *See Learning.*

Stereotypes. Biased notions that people carry in their minds about the meanings of various stimuli. When presented with these stimuli, people "add" these biases to what they see or hear and form mostly distorted impressions. *See Perception.*

Stimulus. Any input to any of the senses. *See Sensation and Sensory Receptors.*

Stimulus Discrimination. The strategy that is the opposite of stimulus generalization aimed at getting consumers to select a specific stimulus from among similar stimuli, whose objective is to position products and services in such a way that differentiates them effectively from competitive offerings. *See Positioning, Stimulus, and Stimulus Generalization.*

Stimulus Generalization. Responding the same way to slightly different stimuli. *See Stimulus and Stimulus Discrimination.*

Stratified Random Sample. A probability sample where the population is divided into mutually exclusive groups (such as age groups), and random samples are drawn from each group. *See Probability Sample.*

Subculture. A group that shares certain beliefs, values, and customes, stemming from ethnicity, religion, geographic location, age, or gender, while also being a part of a larger society.

Subjective Measures. Asking people to evaluate their own social class. *See Objective Measures and Social Class Consciousness.*

Subliminal Perception. A situation that occurs when the sensory receptors receive stimuli that are beneath the person's conscious awareness (i.e., the absolute threshold). *See Absolute Threshold, Perception, and Sensory Receptors.*

Superego. A Freudian term referring to the individual's internal expression of society's moral and ethical codes of "proper" or "correct" conduct. The superego's role is to see that individuals satisfy their needs in a socially acceptable fashion. Thus, the superego is a "brake" that restrains or inhibits the impulsive forces of the Id. *See Ego, Freudian Theory, and Id.*

Symbol. A verbal or non-verbal thing that represents or stands for something else.

Symbolic Group. A group to which an individual is unlikely to belong, but whose values and behaviors he or she adopts nevertheless. *See Membership Group and Reference Groups.*

Systematic Random Sample. A probability sample where members of the population are selected at random and then every nth person is selected. *See Probability Sample.*

Targeting. Selecting the segments that the company views as prospective customers and pursuing them.

Technical Learning. Learning that occurs when teachers instruct children about how to behave and "do things" in social and personal settings. *See Formal Learning and Informal Learning.*

Teens. The age cohort representing youngsters who are between 13 and 17 years old.

Telephone Interview Survey. A study conducted via the phone.

Terminal Values. Within the Rokeach Value Survey, values that reflect goals and desired states of existence (i.e., "ends). *See Instrumental Values and Rokeach Value Survey.*

Test Marketing. Selecting a geographic market, that it presumably representative of other markets, and then introducing a product (i.e., all the elements of the Marketing Mix) in order to examine consumers' responses to the offering under actual marketing conditions. *See Experiments.*

Thematic Apperception Test. Showing pictures to respondents and asking them to tell a story about each picture. *See Projective Techniques and Qualitative Research.*

Theory of Reasoned Action. An approach to studying attitudes that measures the "subjective norms" that influence a person's intention to act, which include his (or her) beliefs as to what relevant others (e.g., family, friends, roommates, co-workers) might think of the person's contemplated action.

Theory of Trying-to-Consume. An approach to studying attitudes referring to cases where positive attitudes lead to actions, although the personal and environmental impediments that the person faces may (or are even likely) to prevent the desired outcome.

Three-Hit Theory. A marketing assumption that just three exposures to an advertisement are needed in order for learning to take place: one to make consumers aware of the product, a second to show consumers the relevance of the product, and a third to remind them of its benefits.

Time Shifting. Electronic devices that enable consumers to skip commercials by pausing and resuming play during live broadcasts, or recording programs and viewing them later on.

Traditional Media. Impersonal, communication channels that are generally classified into print (newspapers, magazines, billboards) and broadcast (radio, television) media, where the communications' receivers get the same (one-way) message and cannot interact with the senders.

Trait Theory. A personality research approach focused on empirical measures of specific psychological characteristics (called traits) that distinguish people from one another.

Transactional Bonds. Convenience and transaction-related relationships between customers and companies. *See Emotional Bonds.*

Tri-Component Model. A model describing the structure of attitudes, it maintains that an attitude consists of three components. *See Affective Component, Cognitive Component, and Conative Component.*

Trial. The fourth stage of Innovation Adoption, which is a term designating the process leading to a person's decision of whether or not to adopt an innovation. After becoming aware and interested in the innovation, and undertaking a "mental trial" (or evaluation), the consumer tries the innovative product, either by buying it (while being able to return it) or receiving a free sample. *See Innovation Adoption.*

Trial ability. One of the five characteristics identified as a determinant of consumer acceptance of a new product representing the degree to which a new product can be tried on a limited basis. *See the other four characteristics: Compatibility, Complexity, Relative Advantage, and Observability.*

Trickle-Down Effect. Originally applied to fashion, the concept states that members of lower classes adopt the fashions of the upper class and maintain them even after the upper class has abandoned these fashions, presumably because they no longer reflect the exclusivity of the upper class. To "restore" their exclusivity, members of the upper class adopt new fashions, which are subsequently copied by the lower classes, and the cycle is repeated.

Truth-in-Advertising Laws. Laws designed to protect consumers against false advertising.

Tweens. The age cohort representing youngsters who are between 8 and 12 years old.

Twitter. An online social networking service and microblogging service that enables its users to send and read text-based messages of up to 140 characters, known as "tweets."

Two-Sided Message. A message that acknowledges competing products. *See Comparative Advertising and One-Sided Message.*

Umbrella Positioning. A statement or slogan that describes the universal benefit of a company's offerings. *See Positioning.*

Unaided Recall. A recall test, that measures the effectiveness of learning and communications, where consumers are asked whether or not they have read a particular magazine or have watched a particular TV show. Afterwards, they are asked whether they can recall any of the ads featured in these media and their salient points. *See Aided Recall.*

Unconditioned Stimulus. A stimulus that occurs naturally in response to given circumstances. *See Conditioned Stimulus.*

Upward Mobility. The opportunity to move from a lower social class to a higher one because of the availability of educational resources and free enterprise. *See Downward Mobility and Social Class.*

Usage Occasion Segmentation. A segmentation strategy based on the fact that many products are purchased and used in the context of specific occasions.

Usage Rate Segmentation. A segmentation strategy based on the differences among heavy, medium, and light users of a given product.

Utilitarian Function. A functional approach to understanding attitudes where researchers believe that that consumers' attitudes reflect the utilities that brands provide. *See Functional Approach.*

Validity. A measure has validity if it does, in fact, collects appropriate data needed to answer the questions or objectives stated in the first (objectives) stage of the research process. *See Reliability.*

VALS ™. An acronym for "values and lifestyles" representing a widely used segmentation method that classifies America's adult population into eight distinctive subgroups: innovators, thinkers, achievers, experiencers, believers, strivers, makers, and survivors.

Value-Expressive Function. A functional approach to studying attitudes where researchers believe that attitudes reflect people's values and beliefs. *See Functional Approach.*

Variable Ratio Reinforcement. A method used in instrumental conditioning consisting of reinforcing a desired behavior randomly. *See Instrumental Conditioning and Reinforcement.*

Variety and Novelty Seeking. Exploratory purchase behavior (e.g., switching brands to experience new, different, and possibly better alternatives), vicarious exploration (e.g., securing information about a new or different alternative and then contemplating buying it), and "use innovativeness" (using an already adopted product in a new or novel way).

Verbalizers. People who respond favorably to verbal messages and pay less attention to visual and pictorial messages. *See Visualizers.*

Viral Marketingv (Viral Advertising). A marketing techniques that uses social networks to increases brand awareness by encouraging individuals to pass along online email messages or other contents.

Visualizers. People who respond favorably to visual and pictorial messages and pay less attention to verbal messages. *See Verbalizers.*

Web-Search Ads. Ads generated by consumers' online searches.

Weber's Law. A principal stating that the stronger the initial stimulus, the greater the additional intensity needed for the second stimulus to be perceived as different. *See Differential Threshold and JND.*

Webisodes. Short videos featuring entertainment content centered around brands.

Wife-Dominated Decisions. Purchase decisions where the wife's influence is greater than the husband's. *See Autonomic Decisions, Husband-Dominated Decisions, and Joint Decisions.*

Withdrawal. Resolving frustration by withdrawing from the situation. *See Defense Mechanisms.*

Word Association Method. A projective research technique that consists of presenting respondents with words, one at a time, and asking them to say the first word that comes to mind. *See Projective Techniques and Qualitative Research.*

Word-of-Mouth. An oral or written communication in which satisfied customers tell others how much they like a business, product, service, or event. *See Buzz Agent and Opinion Leadership.*

World Brand. A brand that is sold and widely recognized globally.

Company Index

Name Index

A

Aaker, Jennifer L., 205
Aggarwal, Pankaj, 108
Agrawal, Nidhi, 207
Ahluwalia, Rohini, 108
Ahmed, Zafar U., 106, 266
Alba, Joseph W., 130
Alden, Dana L, 350
Alderman, Liz, 349, 356
Alexander, Sheryll, 266
Alijukhadar, Muhammad, 68
Alpert, Frank, 136
Alreck, Pamela L., 281
Altman, Lawrence K., 118
Altsech, Moses B., 209
Anderson, Rolph E., 42
Andress, Ruth, 97
Angwin, J., 220
Ante, Spencer E., 39, 133
Arango, Tim, 203, 225
Areddy, James T., 355
Argo, Jennifer J., 387
Ariely, Dan, 139
Armano, D., 226
Aronson, Joshua, 178
Ashworth, Laurence, 393
Ataman, M. Berk, 327

B

Baek, Kanghui, 85
Bagozzi, Richard P., 184
Bagwell, Dorothy C., 388
Baker, Michael J., 242
Baker, William E., 163, 206
Bakir, Aysen, 131
Balabanis, George, 106
Banerjee, Bibek, 154
Banikarim, Maryam, 64
Banjo, S., 219, 224
Bao, Yeqing, 264
Barak, Benny, 334
Barnes, Brooks, 385, 398
Barnes, Stuart J., 65
Barone, Michael J., 207
Barron, Chris, 126
Barry, Thomas, 336
Bastian, Susan, 350
Bates, Kenneth, 370
Batra, Rajeev, 204
Baumgartner, Hans, 184
Beard, Fred K., 395
Beatty, Sharon E., 184, 369
Becker-Olsen, Karen L., 401
Beirne, Mike, 322, 329
Belch, Michael A., 267
Belk, Russell W., 110, 374–375

Bellenger, Danny N., 189
Bellman, Steven, 230
Belson, K., 225
Bennett, Jeff, 116, 349
Bennett, Rebekah, 168
Bensinger, G., 225
Bensinger, Greg, 40
Berelson, Bernard, 300
Bernstein, Jared, 288
Berry, Leonard L., 130, 139, 140, 421
Bharadwaj, Sundar, 393
Bhatti, Tariq, 377
Bidmon, Sonja, 100
Bizer, George Y., 191
Black, Gregory S., 106
Black, Iain, 210
Blackburn, Virginia, 105–106
Blakeslee, Sandra, 163
Blanco, Miguel Cervantes, 70
Blichfeldt, Bodil Stilling, 272
Blodgett, Jeffrey G., 131
Bojanic, David C., 242
Boninger, David S., 189
Bonini, Sheila, 313
Booth, Emily, 374
Borzekowski, D., 384
Bosnjak, Michael, 103
Boutsouki, Christina, 350
Brace, Ian, 273
Bradsher, Keith, 288
Brat, Ilan, 393
Braun-LaTour, Kathryn A., 162
Bravin, Jess, 385
Bravo, Rafael, 260
Brehm, Jack W., 189
Brenner, Lyle, 158
Briggs, Elten, 166
Britton, Julie A. Edell, 205
Broderick, Amanda J., 248, 413
Bronnenberg, Bart J., 327
Brooks, Beth, 207
Brooks, Steve, 61
Brown, Jo, 248
Browne, Andrew, 355
Browne, Glenn J., 103
Broyles, Sheri J., 121
Brunel, Frédéric F., 375
Bruner, Gordon C. II, 369
Brush, G. J., 224
Bruwer, Johan, 139, 350
Buda, Richard, 205
Bui, Anjala My, 370
Burgers, Willem, 263
Burkitt, Laurie, 349, 350, 351, 354, 356
Burnaby, Priscilla A., 304
Burns, Alvin C., 266, 360
Burton, Scot, 110–111
Bush, Alan J., 242
Bush, Victoria D., 242

Busler, Michael, 415
Bustillo, Miguel, 70
Byron, Ellen, 40, 59, 60, 286

C

Cacioppo, John T., 189
Camey, John, 92
Campo, Sara, 137
Capo, Karen Prodigalidad, 273
Cardoso, Margarida G. M. S., 68
Carey, Benedict, 141
Carlson, Les, 242
Carrigan, Marylyn, 334
Carvajal, Doreen, 231
Carvalho, Sergio W., 351
Cauberghe, Verolien, 153, 208, 231
Cayla, Julien, 345
Chai, Barbara, 230
Chamov, Bruce H., 205
Chan, Kara, 327
Chance, Zoe, 136
Chang, Chingching, 103, 207, 351
Chang, Man-Ling, 144
Chang, Shin-Shin, 85
Chaplin, Lan Nguyen, 263
Charles, Gemma, 286
Chartrand, Tanya L., 121
Chattalas, Michael, 321
Chattananon, Apisit, 398
Chaudhuri, Himadri Roy Sr., 327
Chen, Hsiang, 376
Chen, Qimei, 109
Chen, Wang Yun, 248
Chen-Yu, Jessie H., 351
Cheng, Andria, 245
Cheng, Hong, 350
Chernev, Alexander, 75
Chiang, Kuan-Pin, 370
Childs, Nancy M., 395
Choi, Sejung Marina, 187
Choi, Tsan-Ming, 156
Choi, Yung Kyun, 350
Chowdhury, Tilottama G., 375
Chuang, Shin-Chieh, 189
Claes, Laurence, 105
Clark, Jenny, 416
Clark, Terry, 130
Clarke, Irvin, 106
Cleveland, Mark, 312, 344
Clifford, S., 225
Clifford, Stephanie, 40, 42, 58, 60, 118, 119, 126, 203, 211, 231, 250, 356, 386, 391, 396, 398
Cline, Thomas W., 209
Clinton, M., 92
Clow, Kenneth E., 244
Coffey, Tim, 260
Cohen, Geoffrey L., 178

Subject Index

Note: Italicized page numbers indicate figures, tables, and illustrations.